DISPENSATIONALISM, ISRAEL AND THE CHURCH

The Search for Definition

Craig A. Blaising and Darrell L. Bock, Editors

Darrell L. Bock	J. Lanier Burns
Bruce A. Ware	David K. Lowery
Carl B. Hoch, Jr.	John A. Martin
Robert L. Saucy	David L. Turner
W. Edward Glenny	Kenneth L. Barker

with responses by
Walter C. Kaiser, Willem VanGemeren, Bruce Waltke

Zondervan Publishing House
Academic and Professional Books
Grand Rapids, Michigan
A Division of HarperCollins*Publishers*

Dispensationalism, Israel and the Church
Copyright © 1992 by Craig A. Blaising and Darrell L. Bock

Requests for information should be addressed to:
Zondervan Publishing House
Academic and Professional Books
Grand Rapids, Michigan 49530

Library of Congress Cataloging-in-Publication Data

Dispensationalism, Israel and the church: the search for definition / edited by Craig A.
Blaising and Darrell L. Bock.
    p.   cm.
   Includes bibliographical references and index.
   ISBN 0-310-34611-8 (alk. paper)
   1. Dispensationalism.   2. Bible. N.T.—Relations to the Old Testament.   3. Israel
(Christian theology).   4. Church.   I. Blaising, Craig A.   II. Bock, Darrell L.
  BT157.D57   1992
  230'.046—dc20   92-17751
                                                  CIP

Edited by Leonard G. Goss and Craig Noll
Cover design by Jack Rogers

Printed in the United States of America

   93 94 95 96 97 / CH / 10 9 8 7 6 5 4 3 2

This edition is printed on acid-free paper and meets the American National Standards
Institute Z39.48 standard.

Contents

Abbreviations

AB	Anchor Bible
ANET	J. B. Pritchard, ed., *Ancient Near Eastern Texts*
ATJ	*Africa Theological Journal*
ATR	*Anglican Theological Review*
BAG	W. Bauer, W. F. Arndt, and F. W. Gingrich, *Greek-English Lexicon of the New Testament*, 4th rev. ed.
BAGD	W. Bauer, W. F. Arndt, F. W. Gingrich, and F. W. Danker, *Greek-English Lexicon of the New Testament*, 2d ed.
BCNT	Biblical Commentary on the New Testament
BCOT	Biblical Commentary on the Old Testament
BDB	F. Brown, S. R. Driver, and C. A. Briggs, *Hebrew and English Lexicon of the Old Testament*
BDF	F. Blass, A. Debrunner, and R. W. Funk, *A Greek Grammar of the New Testament*
BEB	*Baker Encyclopedia of the Bible*
BKCNT	*Bible Knowledge Commentary: New Testament*
BSac	*Bibliotheca Sacra*
BST	Bible Speaks Today
CBQ	*Catholic Biblical Quarterly*
CBQMS	Catholic Biblical Quarterly Monograph Series
CD II/2	*Church Dogmatics*, vol. 2, part 2 (Karl Barth)
COT	Commentary on the Old Testament
CTJ	*Calvin Theological Journal*
CTM	*Concordia Theological Monthly*
CTR	*Criswell Theological Review*
DNTT	*Dictionary of New Testament Theology*
EBC	Expositor's Bible Commentary
EGT	*Expositor's Greek New Testament*
EH	Europäische Hochschulschriften
Enc	*Encounter*
ERT	*Evangelical Review of Theology*
EvQ	*Evangelical Quarterly*
ExA	*Ex Auditu*

GJ	*Grace Journal*
GTJ	*Grace Theological Journal*
HBC	*Harper's Bible Commentary*
HNTC	Harper's New Testament Commentaries
HTR	*Harvard Theological Review*
IB	*Interpreter's Bible*
IBD	*Interpreter's Bible Dictionary*
ICBI	International Council of Biblical Inerrancy
ICC	International Critical Commentary
IDB	*Interpreter's Dictionary of the Bible*
Int	*Interpretation*
ISBE	*International Standard Bible Encyclopedia*, rev.
JAOS	*Journal of American Oriental Society*
JBC	*Jerome Biblical Commentary*
JBL	*Journal of Biblical Literature*
JES	*Journal of Ecumenical Studies*
JETS	*Journal of the Evangelical Theological Society*
JSJ	*Journal for the Study of Judaism in the Persian, Hellenistic, and Roman Period*
JSNT	*Journal for the Study of the New Testament*
JSNTSup	Journal for the Study of the New Testament Supplement Series
LW	*Lutheran World*
LXX-A	Septuagint—Alexandrinus
LXX-Theod	Septuagint—Theodotion
MNTC	Moffatt New Testament Commentary
MT	Masoretic Text
NBC	New Bible Commentary
NCBC	New Century Bible Commentary
NCCHS	*New Catholic Commenmtary on Holy Scripture*
NICNT	New International Commentary on the New Testament
NICOT	New International Commentary on the Old Testament
NIDNT	*New International Dictionary of the New Testament*
NIGTC	New International Greek Testament Commentary
NovT	*Novum Testamentum*
NTC	New Testament Commentary
NTS	*New Testament Studies*
OTL	Old Testament Library
RevExp	*Review and Expositor*
RTR	*Reformed Theological Review*
SEBT	*Scottish Bulletin of Evangelical Theology*
SBLMS	Society of Biblical Literature Monograph Series

SBT	Studies in Biblical Theology
SE	*Studia Evangelica*
SJT	*Scottish Journal of Theology*
ST	*Studia Theologica*
Str-B	H. Strack and P. Billerbeck, *Kommentar zum Neuen Testament*
TSB	Twin Brook Series
TC	Thornapple Commentaries
TD	*Theology Digest*
TDNT	*Theological Dictionary of the New Testament*
TDOT	*Theological Dictionary of the Old Testament*
TJ	*Trinity Journal*
TNTC	Tyndale New Testament Commentaries
TOTC	Tyndale Old Testament Commentaries
TSFB	*TSF Bulletin*
TToday	*Theology Today*
TWOT	*Theological Wordbook of the Old Testament*
TynBul	*Tyndale Bulletin*
UBS	United Bible Societies
UM	*Urban Mission*
VT	*Vetus Testamentum*
VTSup	Vetus Testamentum, Supplements
WBC	Word Biblical Commentary
WBE	*Wycliffe Bible Encyclopedia*
WEC	*Wycliffe Exegetical Commentary*
WPC	Westminster Pelican Commentary
WTJ	*Westminster Theological Journal*
ZAW	*Zeitschrift für die Alttestamentliche Wissenschaft*
ZPEB	*Zondervan Pictorial Encyclopedia of the Bible*

Foreword

It's odd what I, the son of a fundamentalist Baptist preacher, remember from my childhood. Or at least it strikes me as odd that a kid who was far more interested in model airplanes, bicycle chains, and a good rousing game of pingpong would remember many details about his father's dispensational understanding of the Bible. And it's even more odd that these recollections would have any bearing on the topic of this book, but in a strange sort of way I believe they do. Let me explain.

My father was not raised in a particularly religious home, and he became a Christian as a young man through the preaching of an itinerant evangelist who happened to be holding revival meetings in the remote mining community of Globe, Arizona. My father would often tell the story of how the motivating factor in his conversion was the fear that he would be left behind by the pretribulational rapture of the church, consigned to eternal hellfire. The preacher must have been a dispensationalist, because it wasn't long before my father made his way over the wooden plank road that snaked its way over the sand dunes west of the Colorado River and up through the Imperial Valley to Los Angeles to attend BIOLA, the Bible Institute of Los Angeles.

If my father did not already own a *Scofield Reference Bible* by that time, it surely would not have been long before he did. BIOLA was known as a center for the propagation of dispensational teaching. And what he was exposed to there took hold, for by the time I came along and was old enough to remember anything about my father's pastoral ministry, it was clear he wasn't anything if he wasn't a dispensationalist. I never knew him to use anything but a *Scofield Reference Bible*, and it was one of the first purchases he would recommend to a new believer. He took great pains to make sure his congregation, even the youth group that he personally taught on Friday evenings and Sunday mornings, was well-versed in the dispensational scheme of redemptive history. A huge canvas version of the famous Clarence Larkin chart of the seven dispensations frequently graced the otherwise empty expanse above and behind the pulpit.

To this day I clearly remember the Scofield definition of a dispensation and can still clearly walk you through his sevenfold division of biblical history, even though it has been years since I've picked up a *Scofield Reference Bible* to actually read and study it. And I still remember with what great pride as a kid of eight or nine I received my first *Scofield Reference Bible* from my father. Now I not only had a fine example of the printer's and binder's craft, but I had that same sure guide that my father so faithfully studied and that my older brother Bob was already well on the way to mastering. It wasn't long before I too was remembering particular passages more by their placement on the particular Scofield page layout than I was by chapter and verse.

Sounds pretty typical, doesn't it; almost stereotypical? Similar stories have often been told by others raised in such circumstances. Critics of dispensationalism have not hesitated to poke fun at what they've regarded as Scofield's simplistic analysis of Scripture and at the varieties of dispensational charts that were at one time so popular.

But that is only part of the story, for my father's dispensational teachers and the *Scofield Reference Bible* itself had taught him to be first of all a student of Scripture. In spite of the fact that he regarded Scofield's notes as a good guide for new believers seeking a basic understanding of Scripture, he carefully cautioned that they must always remember to make a distinction between the notes of Scofield and the text of the Bible itself. It was the latter that always judged the former. Indeed, even the seven dispensations were more of a mnemonic device than a rigid division of epochs of redemptive history. And my father warned his students that Scofield seemed to teach injudiciously that salvation in the Old Testament came by works of law and that this was patently an error. I remember with what alarm my father viewed the fact that the son of one of his former parishoners was going to attend Dallas Theological Seminary! He was concerned because he was fearful that Dallas might be too rigid in its dispensational orientation, perhaps even bordering on hyperdispensationalism.

It is really no great surprise, then, that when my brother and I left the immediate influences of home for college and seminary, we felt free to reevaluate our dispensational heritage in light of Scripture.

Now the point of these very personal reminiscences is simply this: At its best, within dispensationalism has always been a dynamic that drives it to be constantly correcting itself in the light of Scripture. The critics of dispensationalism have found it all too easy to find doctrinaire exponents for whom the dispensationist scheme has become a grid through which everything had to be sifted. But that has not been the historic mainstream or the overarching tendancy.

Dispensationalism has been in the process of change since its earliest origins within the Plymouth Bretheren movement of the nineteenth century. Even a cursory reading of dispensationalist writers through the nineteenth and twentieth centuries quickly shows that the process has continued.

It continued for me personally even as I studied in two dispensational institutions of higher learning. I found that teachers also questioned such typically dispensational teachings as a distinction between the kingdom of heaven and the kingdom of God; two entirely separate peoples of God, one his heavenly people and the other his earthly people; two new covenants, one for Israel and one for the church; etc. I was encouraged in my search for answers by writers like Eric Sauer and Alva J. McClain and teachers like Charles Feinberg and Robert Saucy.

Critics of dispensationalism have always found it easier to identify the simplistic approaches of Scofield, to criticize the excesses of Lewis Sperry Chafer, and to poke fun at the charts of Clarence Larkin than to understand and appreciate the self-critical and self-corrective drive that has characterized dispensationalism at a deeper level. But such critiques are superficial and generally at least fifty years out of date! They have failed to understand that dispensationalism and its proponents have been and continue to be in process.

That's what this book is all about. Some of the best minds in contemporary dispensational thinking explore the key issues that divide dispensationalists from nondispensationalists. In my career as a theologian and as a publisher I have been involved as both a participant in and a facilitator of the ongoing dispensationalist discussion. I feel honored that the two editors of this work quite unexpectedly asked me to write the foreword. But even more, I am pleased that as the publisher of this title, I can present a book to dispensationalists that will stimulate their search for an even better understanding of God's Word, and that I can present to nondispensationalists a book that will show them a side of contemporary dispensationalist thinking that perhaps they were not aware even existed.

And who knows?—if nondispensationalists would be as willing to be open to new understandings of biblical truth and to refinements of their own theological heritage as the forward-looking dispensationalist writers in this book, perhaps the two camps will eventually discover that they have far more in common than they ever believed possible.

Stanley N. Gundry

Dispensationalism: The Search for Definition

Craig A. Blaising

We believe that all the Scriptures from first to last center about our Lord Jesus Christ, in His person and work, in His first and second coming; and hence that no chapter even of the Old Testament is properly read or understood until it leads to Him . . . .

We believe that the Church is composed of all who are united by the Holy Spirit to the risen and ascended Son of God, that by the same Spirit we are all baptized into one body, whether we be Jews or Gentiles, and thus being members one of another, we are responsible to keep the unity of the Spirit in the bond of peace, rising above all sectarian prejudices and denominational bigotry, and loving one another with a pure heart fervently.

Doctrinal statement of *Niagara Bible Conference*[1]

There is no more primary problem in the whole matter of dispensationalism than that of definition.

Charles C. Ryrie in *Dispensationalism Today*[2]

WHAT'S IN A NAME?

Recently, one of my students wrote a paper on current issues in dispensationalism. At the beginning he quoted a prominent pastor who identified dispensationalism as that dangerous heresy of date-setting. The student, of course, dismissed this charge as simply uninformed. Dispensationalism is a futurist premillennialism. Its very reception in late nineteenth-century American Christianity was due in no small part to its distinction from the date-setting tendencies of historicist premillennialism.

A few days later, I was having lunch with a missionary who told me of

---

[1]"Declaration of Doctrinal Belief of [the] Niagara Bible Conference," *The Truth*, 20 (1894): 510–11.

[2]C. Ryrie, *Dispensationalism Today* (Chicago: Moody, 1965), 22.

various misperceptions about dispensationalism among missionaries and clergy he had encountered. These caricatures ranged from works salvation (or two ways of salvation) to cheap grace, from social pessimism (or hostility to social reform) to rejection of the local church! As I returned to my office, still shaking my head, I thought of the recent visit to our campus by a well-known evangelical theologian. In a discussion with some students he remarked that he disagreed with dispensationalism because it taught the gap theory interpretation of Genesis 1:1. The students were astonished, as he supported his creedal discovery solely by means of a note in the *Scofield Reference Bible*. Asked if he had ever read Charles Ryrie's *Dispensationalism Today* (published in 1965), a standard definitional treatment lacking this confessional point, he said no but affirmed that he would try to make time for it.

Such examples could be multiplied. Sometimes dispensationalists find these caricatures quite bizarre, and their frequent repetition has a surrealistic quality.[3]

---

[3]There is a significant gap between certain portrayals of dispensationalism in recent literature and the interests, concerns, and self-perceptions of dispensationalists who are writing on their own tradition. As noted later in this essay, the direction and orientation of topics in this book follow a definitional agenda set over twenty-five years ago, which dispensationalists feel is directly relevant to the developing identity of this tradition. The recent book by John Gerstner, *Wrongly Dividing the Word of Truth: A Critique of Dispensationalism* (Brentwood, Tenn.: Wolgemuth & Hyatt, 1991), not only ignores dispensational self-understanding but makes its claim over against the acknowledged objections of well-known dispensational theologians. In fact he even cites dispensationalists against the position which he feels is essential to dispensational thought (appealing to John MacArthur, for example, against Charles Ryrie and Zane Hodges). A similar fallacy is committed in Crenshaw and Gunn in *Dispensationalism Today, Yesterday, and Tomorrow* (Memphis, Tenn.: Footstool Publications, 1985) on the matter of hermeneutics, appealing to S. Lewis Johnson against Charles Ryrie (there are other problems with this book which I was only able to note briefly in the review published in *BSac* 145 [1988]: 104–5). Rather than proving their points, they show at best that diversity exists among dispensationalists on soteriological and hermeneutical matters (although I am not convinced by Gerstner that Antinomianism as traditionally understood is representative of dispensationalism). The widely parroted notion that dispensationalism is pessimistic regarding social action needs to be reexamined historically. Timothy Weber's *Living in the Shadow of the Second Coming: American Premillennialism 1875–1925* (New York: Oxford, 1979) is helpful but struggles with conflicting data. Many such studies also overlook the meaning of the terms *pessimism* and *optimism* as they were used in nineteenth-century polemics between premillennialism and postmillennialism, and they do not make allowance for important historical differences in the meaning of social ministry. Unfortunately, present-day dispensationalists have written very little in proposing a theology of social ministry (see, however, Emilio A. Núñez and William D. Taylor, *Crisis in Latin America, An Evangelical Perspective* [Chicago: Moody, 1989]). Hopefully more such works will be forthcoming. Finally, on the matter of sensational apocalypticism, many point to Hal Lindsey as if he typifies the meaning of dispensationalism. It might be said that Lindseyism is to dispensationalism as Reconstructionism is to Reformed Theology. In each case there are many in the latter who would not want to be identified as the former. Such extremes should not be taken as the defining types of the tradition to which they are related. But in the case of Lindseyism, besides many hermeneutical problems, there is the matter of

At the same time, however, many dispensationalists are ambivalent about the label *dispensationalism*. Some see it as having no distinct significance. They may in fact be more conscious of their own identity as evangelicals (or Baptists, etc.) than as dispensationalists, for many ideas and concerns associated with dispensationalism have become part and parcel of mainstream evangelicalism. For those who do see it as having some significance, most would use the label to refer to a tradition within evangelical theology. But many of them are still unclear about its distinctives. This uncertainty can be traced to varied senses given to the term *dispensationalism* in its polemical origin. But it is also fed by a growing awareness of diversity within the tradition, a diversity that reflects changes in the thinking of dispensationalists.

Today under the label *dispensationalism* one can find representatives of various stages of the tradition's history. In light of their close adherence to interpretations found in the notes of the *Scofield Reference Bible,* some might be classified as Scofieldian, although they themselves would probably not use that term. Others find their identity through the definitional approach of Charles Ryrie and would agree with the terminology and ideas of the dispensationalism of the 1960s. Many dispensationalists, however, are reexamining that terminology, seeking dispensational structures that are more accurate biblically. Their work constitutes a development of American dispensationalism that brings a different perspective to traditional themes while maintaining continuity with earlier dispensationalism, even invoking some principles obscured by intervening generations.

This book will be useful to readers interested in exegetical and hermeneutical studies on the relationship between Israel and the church in biblical theology. It will also be of interest to readers who want to understand modifications currently taking place in dispensational thought. But to understand the significance of these changes, one needs to see them in light of the history of American dispensationalism. Regrettably, however, most historical studies focus only on the early period of British and American dispensationalism, usually in relationship to rising fundamentalism.[4] This has left some with the impression

compromising the futurism that has always been central to dispensational eschatology (for the distinction between futurism and historicism, see Weber, *Living in the Shadow of the Second Coming,* 9–11, 16–17). It is not correct simply to identify the popular apocalypticism of Hal Lindsey with dispensationalism.

[4]For example, C. Bass, *Backgrounds to Dispensationalism: Its Historical Genesis and Ecclesiastical Implications* (Grand Rapids: Eerdmans, 1960); and C. Norman Kraus, *Dispensationalism in America: Its Rise and Development* (Richmond: John Knox, 1958). Helpful studies of early dispensationalism can be found in E. Sandeen, *The Roots of Fundamentalism, British and American Millenarianism, 1800–1930* (Chicago: University of Chicago Press, 1970); T. Weber, *Living in the Shadow of the Second Coming*; and G.

that dispensationalism is equivalent to Scofieldism, fundamentalism, and separatism.

The story of dispensationalism, however, includes its form before and especially after Scofieldism, as well as an inclusive view of the church, an intense preoccupation with hermeneutics (which has brought changes in the tradition), and an oftentimes ambiguous and reluctant relationship with a label that continues to have its own polemical history. It is the story of a theological tradition that is currently reexamining itself in a process of self-definition, a process to which this book contributes. The survey below notes briefly some historical factors that have led to this reexamination and that form the context for the biblical studies that follow.

SOME THINGS OLD AND SOME THINGS NEW

Debut at Niagara

The late nineteenth-century Niagara Bible Conference seemed to be a foretaste of the Millennium. Each summer believers from various Protestant denominations laid aside their differences and gathered to worship Jesus Christ and to be filled with the knowledge of God. In time, Niagara proved to be the training ground for many who assumed leadership roles in rising fundamentalism. It was also the forum for introducing and developing American dispensationalism.[5]

Two features of the conference especially lent themselves to the development of dispensationalism. One was a view of the church that went beyond local churches and denominations. The dispensational theology of British Brethrenism, especially in the work of John Nelson Darby, had criticized Established and Dissenting churches for failing to seek the unity of all who are in Christ by faith. Darby argued that communion with Christ and the unity of the Spirit as described in Scripture should be the integrating factors for true ecumenicity.[6] By the time of the Niagara conferences, however, Brethrenism not only had

Marsden, *Fundamentalism and American Culture: The Shaping of Twentieth-Century Evangelicalism, 1870–1925* (New York: Oxford, 1980).

[5]For a history of the Niagara Conference, see the works listed in the previous note. Before the conference settled permanently at Niagara (1883), it met in various locations as "The Believers' Meeting for Bible Study" (beginning in Chicago in 1875). Much information about Niagara can be gathered from *The Truth*, a journal published by James Brookes, one of the founders and president of the conference.

[6]See J. N. Darby, "Considerations on the Nature and Unity of the Church of Christ," in *The Collected Writings of J. N. Darby*, 34 vols., ed. Wm. Kelly, reprint ed. (Sunbury, Pa.: Believers Bookshelf, 1971), 1:20–35.

become one of the "sects" (as denominations were called) but had undergone many painful subdivisions as well.[7]

The Niagara Bible Conference has been called the American version of Darby's ecumenical vision.[8] Instead of trying to create a pure church to replace the impure models of their day (and so become a separatist movement), Niagara sought a visible experience of unity among those who belonged to and continued in different churches and denominations.[9] This it found in the neutral (and idyllic) setting of a vacation resort where clergy and laity from various denominations would study the Bible and worship together for one week each year. It was a "rising above," not a separation from or replacement of ongoing ecclesiastical ministries. It aimed for a higher, inclusive experience of ecclesia seeking unity in the Spirit and communion with Christ, even through mutual participation in the Lord's Table.[10]

The way for this mutual experience had been prepared on the American scene by evangelical cooperation in revivalist movements. Having experienced varying degrees of unity for the work of conversion (the unity of "one gospel"), some American evangelicals now began to experience unity in the nurture and expression of the faith (the unity of "one church," where *church* in this sense did not preempt the meaning of *churches*), a transition in American evangelical cooperation from evangelism to catechesis.[11]

The second feature of the Niagara Conference that lent itself to the development of dispensationalism was its emphasis on the Bible. Brethrenism viewed itself as a restorationist movement cast entirely on a successful appeal to Scripture (through the illumination of the Spirit). At Niagara, the Bible was affirmed as the inspired Word of God, and instruction was to be based upon it alone.[12] But the unique vision of the

---

[7]This state of affairs called forth a rebuke from James Brookes in an article entitled, "Plymouth Brethren," *Truth* 21 (1895): 249–52; note also a subsequent article in the same volume, "Brethren Fighting," 309–12.

[8]Sandeen, *Roots of Fundamentalism*, 136.

[9]"Nearly all evangelical denominations were represented, and it was delightful to see Episcopalians, Methodists, Congregationalists, Baptists, and Presbyterians, gathered by one Spirit unto the name of the Lord, to Worship in perfect sympathy and fellowship, and in utter forgetfulness of all differences, before one Father" ("Conference at Clifton Springs," *Truth* 5 [1879]: 410 [at this time the conference had not yet made Niagara its permanent location, hence the different location in the title of this article]).

[10]George Needham, "Believer's Meeting For Bible Study," *Truth* 8 (1882): 470.

[11]Some viewed the conference as a "Bible School"; ibid., 467. See also *Truth* 21 (1895): 271, where the conference is described as "one large Bible class." There was also talk about establishing a more formal school to institutionalize the conference experience. This appears in conference advertisements: *Truth* 8 (1882): 387; note also "Young Men at Niagara," *Truth* 16 (1890): 385–87.

[12]"But the Niagara Bible Conference is precisely what its name implies. It is a meeting for the study of the Bible, and for nothing but the study of the Bible. Every man who leads

conference was the perception that the Bible could serve as the matrix for evangelical unity.[13] The key to the vision's success lay in the promotion of a nonpartisan method of Bible study. Several principles composed this method, which left a lasting imprint on the hermeneutics of American dispensationalism.

The first principle was *Christocentricity*. All Scripture points to Christ and is interpreted correctly only with respect to Christ. Faith in Christ is a faith directed by the Scripture. Consequently, studying the Bible Christologically encourages true ecumenicity because it nurtures one faith in one Lord.

A second principle was *piety*. Piety contributed to the ecumenical hermeneutic by tying interpretation to the one Spirit. All believers are illumined by the Spirit as they read the Scripture. But piety also linked hermeneutics to the reality of the one church. True catholicity manifests itself in love (for God and for one another). Consequently, the conference was promoted as a time of believers' fellowship and study together in an atmosphere of worship. If a dispute broke out concerning the correct interpretation of a passage, the session might very well be dissolved into prayer.[14] Controversy was shunned as unscriptural, even to the point of solemnly proscribing it in conference advertisements.[15]

The third principle was a procedure of *"inductive" Bible study*, a "scientific" approach designed to free the Bible from sectarian interpretations. A characteristic feature was the practice of "Bible readings," a kind of concordance organization of biblical passages under doctrinal headings, keying in on thematic terms and phrases.[16] Following this

---

attempts at least to prove every point he makes by the authority of Scripture; and it is not uncommon to give in each study forty, fifty, or more texts and passages of Holy Writ, which are read by the students, or repeated by the leader. . . . It has been frequently said by ministers of the gospel that they hear more Scripture at these conferences in one week than they heard in three years in theological seminaries." "Niagara Bible Conference," *Truth* 16 (1890): 362.

[13] "All Evangelical Christians, therefore, are cordially invited to attend, with the assurance that the only object in view is the devout and diligent searching of the Bible, in order to obtain clearer and more consecrating views of Him who is the centre of God's counsels, and the sum of His revelation." "Believer's Meeting for Bible Study," *Truth* 5 (1879): 270.

[14] Mrs. George Needham wrote a description of the fifteenth annual Niagara Conference, in which she explains how the moderator of the session maintained order: "Under the Holy Spirit, the sweetness, reverence and unity which characterized every session of the Niagara meeting was largely due to Capt. Moreton's sanctified tact, who was ever ready when the slightest peril from levity or controversy menaced the congregations, to rise and say, "Brethren let us have a word of prayer." Thus he held us all so close to the mercy seat that carnal ways and words fell back abashed, and holy fear prevailed." "The Niagara Conference," *Truth* 17 (1891): 412.

[15] *Truth* 4 (1878): 403; 5 (1879): 271.

[16] Bible Readings of Niagara are often found in James Brooke's journal, *Truth*. Some examples are included in the conference report in *Truth* 8 (1882): 389–90.

adaptation of what we might call Baconianism, the Bible could be studied ecumenically, with clergy and laity from various denominations working side by side to understand the Bible naturally, plainly, and in accordance with its own internal structures, just as scientists of varying nationalities could study the same natural order and come to a common understanding of it.[17]

The naïveté of the founders' vision became apparent by the third year, and in 1878 the conference modified its inclusive ideal by adopting a doctrinal statement.[18] Still, the Articles of Belief outlined a general evangelical position that avoided denominational differences. Its primary intent was to exclude views advocated by newly established cults, views such as annihilation and soul sleep. But it also proscribed postmillennialism. Consequently, Niagara was known as a premillennial conference, although prophecy was not the only topic of study; there were expositions of Scripture (sometimes an entire book of the Bible) and presentations covering the range of doctrines in the articles.[19]

The supradenominational unity of the church and the inspiration of Scripture were affirmed in the Articles of Belief, as were also the principles of Christological hermeneutics and piety.[20] And although no article explicitly mentioned inductive Bible study, each article was presented as the summary of Bible readings with a list of references at the end.

The organizers and participants at Niagara were not conscious of developing something called dispensationalism, although the word *dispensations* did appear often in conference discussions and affiliated literature.[21] Outlines of biblical dispensations (usually seven) were

[17]For the influence of Baconian inductivism and common sense realism on nineteenth-century biblical interpretation see T. Bozeman, *Protestants in an Age of Science; The Baconian Ideal and Antebellum American Religious Thought* (Chapel Hill: University of North Carolina Press, 1977), esp. 132–59. See also Marsden, *Fundamentalism and American Culture,* 55–62; also M. Noll, "Common Sense Traditions and American Evangelical Thought," *American Quarterly* 37 (1985): 216–38. In "How to Study the Bible" (*Truth* 3 [1877]: 89–92), W. J. Erdman, the secretary of the Niagara Conference, explains the "inductive" and "scientific" method of Bible study which gathers words and phrases, classifies and arranges them in self-interpreting structures with mathematical symmetry.

[18]See "Believers' Meeting for Bible Study," *Truth* 4 (1878): 450–58; also, *Truth* 20 (1894): 509–11.

[19]The list of topics in conference advertisements and published conference papers in *Truth* bear this out. The 1894 advertisement noted: "Though this Conference has been known for nearly a score of years as a witness to the doctrine of the Premillennial Coming of the Lord Jesus Christ, yet this and kindred themes are not, as some supposed, the only subjects of study" (*Truth* 20 [1894]: 338).

[20]Note Articles 9 and 10, quoted in part at the beginning of this essay.

[21]One should not assume that everyone at Niagara was a "dispensationalist" in some later sense of that word. Tension over pretribulationalism, for example, led the 1894 conference announcement to say: "It is needless to say that all brethren holding the

occasionally presented and expounded.[22] But there was nothing particularly unique in this. What is important for later dispensationalism was Niagara's employment of the notion of dispensations to develop and support premillennialism.[23] From the perspective of those at Niagara, postmillennialism, the dominant eschatology of the day, had substituted ideas of church growth or cultural progress for the kingdom of God predicted in Scripture. It failed to account for the apocalyptic coming of the kingdom in many biblical texts. By asserting that the present dispensation was becoming or would become the kingdom by virtue of its own internal principles, postmillennialists confused the dispensations, inflating the significance of present history and devaluing the idea of the kingdom in Scripture. By placing Christ's coming at the end of a "millennium" of complete world-Christianization, they missed the significance of that coming as being the necessary judicial event that transforms and transitions the present dispensation into the kingdom. Consequently, Niagara saw in postmillennialism an eschatology that was Christologically deficient. On a practical level, this view subverted the church's hope in the visible, bodily return of Christ.

The contrast between the present and future dispensations was sharpened by the doctrine of the two peoples. Here the influence of Brethren theology was most direct. In the present dispensation, God is forming a heavenly people, the church, for a heavenly (spiritual) mode of life in a heavenly destiny. In the future dispensation, when the heavenly people will fill the heavens, God will resume his purpose for an earthly people, Israel and Gentiles, who have an earthly mode of life and an earthly destiny in the kingdom of Christ. To confuse these dispensations is to mix up heaven and earth, to misunderstand the purposes of God, to demean the calling of the church, and to fall prey to Gentile arrogance against the Jews. Along with this premillennial interest in dispensations, a host of expositions and interpretations of Scripture on various themes filled the annual conferences at Niagara. Many of these teachings along with the hermeneutic by which they were supported would later be identified as dispensationalism.

---

common evangelical faith, whatever may be their differences of opinion on certain questions pertaining to the Premillennial Advent, are heartily invited to attend" (*Truth* 20 [1894]: 338). This followed two conferences which specifically included among their topics studies on the divine purpose with respect to Jews, Gentiles, and the church (*Truth* 12 [1886]: 320; and 14 [1888]: 271). Niagara dispensationalism was inclusive; it had no distinct identity as "dispensationalism." But dispensations and dispensational ideas were present in the study of premillennialism.

[22]One such presentation, entitled "Dispensations," by H. M. Parsons of Toronto, is published in *Truth* 11 (1885): 460–66.

[23]Among the topics listed for the 1885 conference is "the Dispensations and the Second Coming of our Lord." These are listed together as one topic (*Truth* [1885]: 314).

Scofieldism

In 1909, C. I. Scofield, a participant in the latter years of the Niagara Conference, presented the world with a reference Bible. It contained extensive notes and annotations claiming to be the fruit of fifty years of Bible study.[24] By this Scofield meant Niagara as well as other conferences spawned by it and various publications associated with it.[25] It was fitting that a tribute came to Niagara in the form of a Bible. But this format also introduced a limitation. Certainly the scope was as wide as that in the conference—the whole Bible and associated doctrines. However, the plural participation and the repetitive nature of the conference allowed numerous presentations on the same topics. The Scofield Bible gave only one. And while a typical Niagara perspective can be seen in Scofield's notes, the singleness of the latter's presentation masks differences of nuance and reservation in the former.

The *Scofield Reference Bible* became the Bible of fundamentalism, and the theology of the notes approached confessional status in many Bible schools, institutes, and seminaries established in the early decades of this century. If Scofield had chosen a label for his system, it would most likely have been *premillennialism*. Some modernists, however, launched special attacks on this premillennialism, attempting to reverse fundamentalist charges by criticizing novelties in Scofieldian interpretation.[26] Tensions broke out in the ranks of fundamentalism. In Reformed circles, where the apologetic of traditional confession weighed heavily in the battle with modernism, some began to criticize Scofieldian peculiarities as "dispensationalism," and disputes flared up between *dispensationalists* and *covenantalists*.[27]

Dispensationalists were no more prepared to admit to theological novelty than any other fundamentalists. They expressed dismay that any issue should be made about dispensations, when in fact the recognition

---

[24]"Introduction," *The Scofield Reference Bible* (Oxford: Oxford University Press, 1909).

[25]C. Blaising, "Development of Dispensationalism by Contemporary Dispensationalists," *BSac* 145 (1988): 256, n. 4.

[26]Sandeen, *The Roots of Fundamentalism*, 235–36; Marsden, *Fundamentalism and American Culture*, 145–48; Weber, *Living in the Shadow of the Second Coming*, 118–20.

[27]Machen exemplifies the early non-Scofieldian fundamentalist response to the modernist attack on the new premillennialism. He noted his disagreement with "premillennialism" by saying it "causes us serious concern; it is coupled, we think, with a false method of interpreting Scripture which in the long run will be productive of harm." Then he advocated closing ranks in support of the authority of Scripture (J. G. Machen, *Christianity and Liberalism*, reprint ed. [Grand Rapids: Eerdmans, 1923], 49). In the 1930s, the rift widened, as exemplified by the interchange between Oswald T. Allis ("Modern Dispensationalism and the Doctrine of the Unity of Scripture," *EvQ* 8 [1936]: 22–35) and Lewis S. Chafer ("Dispensationalism," *BSac* 93 [1936]: 390–449; reprinted as *Dispensationalism* [Dallas: Dallas Seminary Press, 1936]). Sandeen sees 1936 as the pivotal year of controversy (*The Roots of Fundamentalism*, 255–60).

of biblical dispensations was quite traditional in Christian thought. The real point of tension was certain peculiar interpretations in the Scofield notes that asserted a fundamental contrast of God's relationship to the church in the present and future dispensations to his relationship to Jews and Gentiles in the past and future dispensations, views that arose relatively recently in the history of Christian thought. To the extent that aspects of the real issue were grasped, dispensationalists saw it as a tension between the Bible and human tradition, since in typical Niagara fashion, Scofieldian views were thought to be inductive summaries of Scripture, often presented in the typical Bible reading format. For their part, antidispensational fundamentalists, most often Reformed covenantalists, perceiving their own theological views in a Baconian manner, rejected the idea that their tradition was anything other than true biblical induction.

Aggravating the controversy was the failure of either side to recognize the deeper hermeneutical problem of the historicity of theological thought.[28] The apologetic need to deny and oppose novelty allied to a sincere belief in purely objective biblical interpretation made the failure certain. Consequently, neither side comprehended, much less appreciated, the phenomena of dispensationalism as a *developing* subtradition in American evangelicalism. The label *dispensationalism* was itself a victim of the hermeneutical problem and further masked the historical reality of the movement. Dispensationalists capitalized on the label's imprecision to define it as the common recognition of biblical dispensations.[29] Thus they obscured (even to themselves) the fact that they were engaged in theological reconstruction appropriating new perspectives on biblical apocalyptic, redemption history, and ecclesiastical ecumenicity. Covenantalists defined dispensationalism as Scofieldism, not only obscuring the fact that it was not always that, but also blinding themselves to forces that were more powerful than the occasional albeit quite influential phenomena of a published reference Bible. Dispensationalists could not comprehend why laborious apologetics focusing on the history of recognizing dispensations had little effect on their critics, and nondispensationalists were conceptually

---

[28]The problem is the failure to recognize that all theological thought, including one's own theological thought, is historically conditioned. In other words, theological and biblical interpretations are conditioned by the tradition to which that theologian belongs as well as personal and cultural factors such as education or experience. These factors condition an interpreter to think in a certain way. Awareness of them can be a step towards recognizing and rectifying misunderstanding. Studies on this aspect of hermeneutics can be found in note 60, below.

[29]See A. Ehlert, "A Bibliography of Dispensationalism," *BSac* 101–3 (1944–46); reprinted as *A Bibliographic History of Dispensationalism* (Grand Rapids: Baker, 1965).

unprepared (and in some cases still are) for a dispensationalism that would continue to develop beyond Scofieldism.

The Sine Qua Non of Dispensationalism

For many years, Scofieldism was the scholastic form of dispensationalism, being practically canonized in Bible schools, colleges, and seminaries. It even attained the form of a systematic theology in the work of Lewis S. Chafer.[30] However, modifications were becoming evident by the 1960s. And in 1967, the notes of the *Scofield Reference Bible* were revised by an editorial committee in response to various criticisms.

In 1965 Charles Ryrie wrote an irenic apologetic entitled *Dispensationalism Today*. The importance of this work for the self-understanding of late twentieth-century dispensationalism cannot be overstated. At the very beginning, Ryrie asserted that "dispensational teaching has undergone [both] systematization and development." He claimed that criticisms of dispensationalism (i.e., of Scofieldism) often misrepresented the views of "present-day dispensationalists." His purpose, he said, was to correct "misconceptions" and "false charges" and "to give a presentation of dispensationalism as it is being taught today."[31] In the conclusion of the book, the word "today" is replaced by the phrase "the *latter* [emphasis his] part of the twentieth century," and in the bibliography, an annotation identifies representatives of this newer, later, more developed dispensationalism.[32] Furthermore, Ryrie classified dispensationalists as "conservative, evangelical Christians," carefully avoiding the label *fundamentalist,* which was becoming increasingly uncomfortable for many.[33]

Most important, Ryrie provided a definition of dispensationalism that avoided earlier equivocations and appeared suitable to the phenomena of a developing tradition. In classical fashion, he sought to define its essence, which was both unique and remained unchanged through its history. This he set forth in three aspects in a section entitled "The *Sine Qua Non* of Dispensationalism." It can be summarized as follows: "The essence of dispensationalism, then, is the distinction between Israel and the Church. This grows out of the dispensationalist's consistent employment of normal or plain interpretation, and it reflects an understanding of the basic purpose of God in all His dealings with

---

[30]L. S. Chafer, *Systematic Theology*, 8 vols. (Dallas: Dallas Seminary Press, 1947).
[31]C. Ryrie, *Dispensationalism Today*, 9.
[32]Ibid., 206, 213.
[33]Ibid., 10, 209–12.

mankind as that of glorifying Himself through salvation and other purposes as well."[34]

By making the distinction between Israel and the church the central defining feature, Ryrie meant to identify the earlier dispensational teaching on the two peoples of God: the heavenly people and the earthly people. Others had spoken of God's distinct purposes for Jews, Gentiles, and the church of God as "dispensational truth." Ryrie considered all these as different ways of saying the same thing.[35] But they are not synonymous.

The heavenly-earthly division refers to distinct destinies in the plan of God as well as contrasting modes or rules of life. It is first of all a vision of eternity in which the completion of the divine purpose yields an anthropological dualism: one humanity fit and destined for heaven, and another fit and destined for the earth.[36] The meaning of life is then interpreted in light of one's intended destiny. Darby defined the heavenly people as all those who would be resurrected or directly translated into their immortal destiny. This included not only the church but also believers from earlier dispensations. The earthly people would be Jews and Gentiles of a future time who, under the preserving rule of Christ, would fulfill the political, social, and otherwise physical promises of the Old Testament not only in a millennium but forever.[37]

The doctrine of the two peoples, heavenly and earthly, was promoted in American dispensationalism down to the time of Lewis Chafer. The only difference was that American dispensationalists tended to focus on the uniqueness of the church vis-à-vis all groups, including other heavenly or resurrected people. Or they focused so exclusively upon the church that it dominated the concept of heavenly people. This was especially the case with Lewis Chafer, for whom the terms *church* and *heavenly people* were practically synonymous. "The dispensationalist believes that throughout the ages God is pursuing two distinct purposes: one related to the earth with earthly people and earthly objectives involved, which is Judaism; while the other is related to heaven with heavenly people and heavenly objectives involved, which is Christianity."[38] And again he writes: "Every covenant, promise, and provision for Israel is earthly, and they continue as a nation with the earth when it is created new. Every covenant or promise for the church is for a heavenly

[34]Ibid., 47.
[35]Ibid., 44–45.
[36]There is, of course, a humanity condemned to hell; they are not in view here.
[37]F. S. Elmore, "A Critical Examination of the Doctrine of the Two Peoples of God in John Nelson Darby" (Th.D. diss., Dallas Theological Seminary, 1990), esp. 201–311.
[38]Chafer, *Dispensationalism*, 107.

reality, and she continues in heavenly citizenship when the heavens are recreated."[39]

The new dispensationalists of the 1950s and 1960s, however, were uncomfortable with the notion of eternally separate heavenly and earthly destinies. They believed that after the Millennium, all the redeemed would be together for eternity, although they were not agreed as to where this would be. Some placed them all in "heaven"; others grouped them together on "the new earth."[40] Consequently, the distinguishing terminology of *heavenly* and *earthly* people is scarcely found in their writings. The doctrine of the two peoples was now to be understood precisely as *Israel and the church,* a distinction that Ryrie insisted must be eternally maintained, even if both were ultimately heavenly or ultimately (new) earthly people.

Certain features of the earlier dispensationalism's heavenly-earthly transcendental dualism were carried over to the distinction between Israel and the church, including, for example, the parenthetical nature of the present dispensation of the church within God's national and political purpose for Israel. A remnant of the doctrine of dual destinies was retained for the Millennium—the church inhabiting heaven, and Israel on the earth. But now a heavenly Israel, resurrected Old Testament saints, had to be clearly distinguished from the heavenly church, the latter being marked by an exclusive relationship to the Lord expressed in biblical metaphors such as its being the "body" and "bride" of Christ. At the same time, the new dispensationalism rejected Chafer's rigid distinction between God's covenant promises with Israel and his covenant promises with the church, even though many of them had themselves earlier supported that distinction. The relationship between Christ and the church should be seen precisely in terms of the Abrahamic and the new covenants.[41] There, however, the covenantal connection stopped. The Davidic covenant was thought to belong exclusively to Israel.

The qualification that this covenantal relationship brings to the distinction between Israel and the church as well as to the very structure of transcendental dispensationalism (one that contrasts heavenly and earthly peoples) was not explored by the new dispensationalists. The tendency, rather, was to invoke older hermeneutical categories, saying, for example, that the church participates "spiritually" in the Abrahamic and the new covenants. However, this creates a problem for the new

---

[39]Chafer, *Systematic Theology,* 4:47.

[40]Ryrie puts them in heaven (*Dispensationalism Today,* 147); J. D. Pentecost places them on the new earth (see his *Things to Come* [Grand Rapids: Zondervan, 1958], 561–62).

[41]See Blaising, "Development of Dispensationalism," 277–78. Also see J. Walvoord, *Major Bible Prophecies* (Grand Rapids: Zondervan, 1991), 188–89.

dispensationalism's exclusively literal hermeneutic, a problem that also was left unresolved.

Through all of the repositioning, continuity was maintained with the older dispensationalism's expectation of a future for national and political Israel, a hope that was not preempted by the present reality of the church. The tendency, however, was to limit the fulfillment of that expectation to the Millennium alone.[42]

Supporting the distinction between Israel and the church is the second aspect of the sine qua non of dispensationalism: the consistent practice of literal hermeneutics. *Literal* here is not opposed to *figurative* but rather to *allegorical* or *spiritual*. The terms *normal* or *plain* may be used in place of *literal,* since it is interpretation according to the normal use of language.[43] In explaining these terms, Ryrie refers to well-known evangelical works on hermeneutics, indicating that what he means by literal hermeneutics is an approach shared broadly in evangelicalism at that time.[44] He is quite insistent that the difference between a dispensational and a nondispensational hermeneutic is that the former is consistent in the employment of literal or normal interpretation. The presence of spiritual or allegorical interpretation to any extent "in a system of interpretation is indicative of a nondispensational approach."[45]

However, this was not the position of earlier dispensationalists. Both Darby and Scofield approved of spiritual or allegorical interpretation of the Old Testament, although Scofield excluded it from prophecy.[46] The point at which they agreed was that the literal interpretation of prophecy must always be taken into theological consideration; it should never be replaced by spiritual interpretation. Specifically their concern was for prophecies of the second coming of Christ and of Israel's national and political future. The new generation of dispensationalists shared this concern. But in their day, evangelicals generally devalued spiritual interpretation. The new dispensationalists went further by proscribing it altogether.

Finally, Ryrie asserted that the essence of dispensational thought

---

[42]Ryrie is quite clear that the Millennium is the goal of history. Pentecost, however, sees a continuance of history on the new earth (*Things to Come*, 561–62). Consequently, whereas both reject the eternal dualism of former dispensationalism, Pentecost envisions the eternal fulfillment of the national promises in the Old Testament, while Ryrie has (ironically) "spiritualized" them.

[43]Ryrie, *Dispensationalism Today*, 45–46, 86–87.

[44]He cites B. Ramm, *Protestant Biblical Interpretation* (Boston: W. A. Wilde, 1956), and A. B. Mickelsen, *Interpreting the Bible* (Grand Rapids: Eerdmans, 1963).

[45]Ryrie, *Dispensationalism Today*, 45–46.

[46]See C. I. Scofield, *Scofield Bible Correspondence Course* (Chicago: Moody Bible Institute, 1959–60), 142, 146; see also the discussion on Scofield's hermeneutics in V. Poythress, *Understanding Dispensationalists* (Grand Rapids: Zondervan, 1987), 22–27. For Darby, see Elmore, "A Critical Examination," 164–200.

included the view that all of God's works unite in one purpose, which is to bring glory to himself. Early in his book, Ryrie offers this goal as the dispensational philosophy of history, although he says it is also possible to see history eschatologically, that is, from the standpoint of the goal of history.[47] Later, Ryrie defends his choice of divine self-glorification on the basis of its usefulness in integrating suprahistorical works of God as well.[48]

It would be difficult to identify this perspective as a particularly distinctive feature of earlier dispensationalism. Most evangelicals, especially among the Reformed, would have agreed on the comprehensive doxological purpose of God.[49] Ryrie's insistence on this point can be seen as a calculated response to covenantalist criticisms that dispensationalism (Scofieldism) divides up the salvific unity of the Bible.[50] Ryrie distinguishes dispensationalism from covenantalism as the difference between a doxological versus a soteriological perspective. The fundamental issue was whether or not the divine purpose is broader than the salvation of individual souls and the spiritual communion of the church. The proposed doxological unity was supposed to embrace these broader purposes, which include Israel's national and political future. But in spite of its categorical breadth, divine self-glorification does not seem particularly useful for explaining changes within history. At Niagara, the unity of the dispensations was found in the person and history of Jesus Christ. Scofield saw history in terms of human failure, a notion that Ryrie dismisses as secondary and inappropriately anthropocentric.[51] Other dispensationalists used salvation and redemption as integrating themes but defined them to include national and political salvation and even the redemption of the entire creation.[52]

Dispensationalism Today was primarily directed to those who were neutral (or even hostile) toward dispensationalism. It was an attempt to take control of the label *dispensationalism,* which was being victimized in the polemical fires of a fundamentalism turned in on itself or an evangelicalism looking for a scapegoat for the debacle from which it had recently emerged. While not exactly an invitation for dialogue, the book did call for mutual acceptance and recognition in Christ and a more cordial and respectful acknowledgment of differing traditions among

---

[47]Ryrie, *Dispensationalism Today*, 18, 104.

[48]Ibid., 103.

[49]The first reply in the *Westminster Confession* says that the chief end of man is "to glorify God and enjoy him forever."

[50]See Blaising, "Development of Dispensationalism," 267–68.

[51]Ryrie, *Dispensationalism Today*, 36–39, 46 ("Scripture is not man-centered . . . but it is God-centered because His glory is the center").

[52]See E. Sauer, *From Eternity to Eternity, An Outline of the Divine Purposes,* trans. G. H. Lang (Grand Rapids: Eerdmans, 1954).

..s. Regrettably, such a call has not been fully heeded. Even ..uay one can find examples of the harsh tones of earlier polemics. Some persist in identifying dispensationalism as confessional Scofieldism, while elsewhere the label is given contradictory senses or has degenerated to being used merely as a term of reproach without real knowledge of its teachings.

In dispensationalist circles, Ryrie's sine qua non led the tradition to accept exclusive ownership of the label *dispensationalism,* while at the same time instilling it with a generic sense that could be distinguished from Scofieldism. This in turn served to legitimize the changes from Scofieldism that were actually taking place in the work of the new generation of dispensationalists, allowing them to claim continuity in the midst of change and establishing them as the heirs of the tradition. Many of the changes introduced at that time have now become commonplace in the dispensational tradition, although dispensationalists have not been in agreement in every detail. In dispensational schools, *Dispensational- ism Today* soon acquired textbook status, which led to widespread acceptance of many of the modifications promoted within its pages. These included a new definition of *dispensation* along with a new set of characteristics for distinguishing one from another.[53] Also generally accepted was a less problematic and more unified view of salvation across the dispensations.[54] Changes were introduced in the rationale for some traditional beliefs such as pretribulationism,[55] and various inter- pretations of Scripture were revised.[56] Dispensational views on the kingdom especially underwent modification at this time. Traditionally, dispensationalists had distinguished the terms *kingdom of God* and *kingdom of heaven.* That distinction was now dropped, and in its place were offered competing interpretive structures, such as those formulat- ed by McClain, Pentecost, and Sauer.[57] The first two of these have had widespread influence among the constituencies of their respective schools, while Sauer is receiving renewed interest today.[58]

While the notion of essential dispensationalism did lead dispensation-

[53]Ryrie, *Dispensationalism Today,* 22–43.

[54]Ibid., 110–31.

[55]Ibid., 159–60.

[56]Blaising, "Development of Dispensationalism," 256–63.

[57]A. J. McClain, *The Greatness of the Kingdom: An Inductive Study of the Kingdom of God* (Winona Lake, Ind.: BMH Books, 1959); Pentecost, *Things to Come*; Sauer, *From Eternity to Eternity.* See Ryrie's discussion in *Dispensationalism Today,* 174–76. A discussion of some of the differences is given by M. Bailey, "Dispensational Definitions of the Kingdom," unpublished paper presented to the Dispensational Study Group, Wheaton, Ill., Nov. 1988.

[58]R. Bowers, "Dispensational Motifs in the Writings of Erich Sauer," *BSac* 148 (1991): 259–73.

alists beyond confessional Scofieldism, they generally did not gain a historical understanding of the tradition or of the transition they had undergone. The problem lies in the way the sine qua non attempted to express continuity with earlier dispensationalism.

First, the essentialist view of dispensationalism sought for continuity in certain elements (expressed as the sine qua non) that remained unchanged through the history of the tradition. However, as already noted, while there is no question that the elements of the proposed sine qua non are *related* to traditional views and practice, nevertheless one must regard them as modifications and reformulations, whether small or great, that were part of the changes then taking place. They were in fact the central tenets of a *new* dispensationalism. But when that which is in fact new is presented and accepted as if it had always been the case, the result is not only historical confusion but a conceptual naïveté that resists both the idea and the fact of further development in the tradition.

Second, many important beliefs, emphases, and values that the new dispensationalism actually shared with earlier dispensationalism were obscured by the restrictive nature of the sine qua non. These included a high regard for the authority of the Bible, a sense of the divine purpose for history manifested in biblical dispensations, premillennialism, an emphasis on grace as especially manifested in the present dispensation, and the recognition of the present theological relevance of biblical prophecy and apocalyptic especially as it relates to the national and political future of Israel. Others could be mentioned. What is important here is that features such as these more accurately characterize the abiding identity of dispensationalists across the history of the tradition (including the present day, as seen, for example, in the dispensationalist chapters in this book). But they were ignored in a definitional process in search of beliefs that had always been unique to dispensationalists alone.

Third, the failure of the new dispensationalism to define itself in terms of historically unchanging central beliefs and hermeneutical practice can be traced to a methodological deficiency in the very hermeneutic that it proposed. Like most of fundamentalism and evangelicalism at the time, it possessed no methodological awareness of the historicity of interpretation, and consequently it was unable to account for how and why a transition from Scofieldism was taking place. Furthermore, this hermeneutical deficiency was structured into the very meaning of dispensational thought and practice in its advocacy of clear, plain, normal, or literal interpretation. Although the word *historical* is used once in *Dispensationalism Today* in conjunction with *grammatical* interpretation, it appears to be a relatively new expression whose implications have not yet been thought through. At any rate, it is quickly equated with clear, normal interpretation.[59] We have, then, a generation of theologians who find identity in a self-conscious hermeneutic that lacks methodological awareness of the historical nature of interpretation—a situation that under the pressures of apologetical exigencies seems particularly vulnerable to the danger of anachronism.

What is needed today is a new approach to defining dispensationalism. The issue is one not of excluding features shared by nondispensationalists, but of noting the emphases, values, and beliefs that together as a pattern form an abiding identity in the dispensational tradition. Furthermore, it must be an approach actually suited to a living tradition, one that may reformulate previous views or that may in fact adopt new features along the way and even bring them into the central pattern by which it identifies itself (as was the case with the dispensationalism of the 1950s and 1960s with respect to earlier dispensationalism), or one that may rehabilitate and revise features that were central to an earlier dispensationalism but may have been eclipsed by the concerns of an intervening generation (such as the factors of inclusivity and Christocentricity, which present-day dispensationalists share more closely with the Niagara dispensationalists than they do with their immediate predecessors).

Beyond the Sine Qua Non

Over the past three decades important developments have taken place in the evangelical perception and practice of historical and literary interpretation. Appreciation has grown for the historicity of both subject and object in the act of interpretation. This includes respect for the problem of historical distance resulting in horizontal differences between text and interpreter, the role of the interpreter's preunderstanding, and methodological applications of the hermeneutical spiral. Likewise, the role of community in interpretation is increasingly recognized. This leads to an awareness of the influence of tradition upon the interpreter's preunderstanding as well as the broader dialogic context of interpretive questions and possible answers.[60]

The crucial place of history in biblical revelation has been given special attention in the study of biblical theology, which in turn has

---

[59]Ryrie, *Dispensationalism Today*, 86–88.

[60]The literature on these matters is quite extensive. Two helpful surveys are Josef Bleicher, *Contemporary Hermeneutics: Hermeneutics as Method, Philosophy and Critique* (London: Routledge, 1980), and Georgia Warnke, *Gadamer: Hermeneutics, Tradition and Reason* (Stanford: Stanford University Press, 1987). Also see A. Thiselton, *The Two Horizons* (Exeter: Paternoster, 1980), esp. 3–139, 439–45. For an application to evangelical theological method, see A. McGrath, *The Genesis of Doctrine* (Oxford: Basil Blackwell, 1990).

distinguished that field from previous uses of the label *biblical theology* by earlier evangelicals.[61] Related to this is interest in the matter of tradition history, especially in the case of the New Testament use of the Old Testament.[62] This in turn is linked to the subject of authorial and editorial compositional techniques.[63] We should also mention advancing studies on literary genre as well as new studies in the field of semantics that evidence, among other things, a growing appreciation for the evocative nature of language in the literary craft.[64] This brings a new meaning to context (as well as contexts) and to the structures that unite them such as typology.[65]

Many dispensationalists have welcomed these developments as clarifying insights into the normal function of literary language and its interpretation. However, these hermeneutical advancements present a challenge to the Baconian perceptions of "clear" and "plain" hermeneutics as well as to the meaningfulness of the label *literal,* which dispensationalists had claimed uniquely to themselves, against all others who "spiritualize" (even if only a little bit). An interpretation claimed to reflect the simple meaning of the text may in fact be an impression that has not been tested against the literary features of the text. It may indicate a reading into the text (i.e., an eisegesis) of the teachings of

[61]Compare J. Lindsay, "Biblical Theology" (*ISBE*, 4 vols., ed. J. Orr [Grand Rapids: Eerdmans, 1956], 1:469–72), and G. Ladd, "Biblical Theology, Nature of" (*ISBE*, rev. ed., 4 vols., ed. G. Bromiley [Grand Rapids: Eerdmans, 1979], 1:505–9). Also see C. C. Scobie, "The Challenge of Biblical Theology" (Part 1), *TynBull* 42 (1991): 31–61.

[62]See, for example, E. Earle Ellis, *Paul's Use of the Old Testament* (Grand Rapids: Baker, 1957); D. Moo, *The Old Testament in the Gospel Passion Narratives* (Sheffield: Almond Press, 1983); R. Longenecker, *Biblical Exegesis in the Apostolic Period* (Grand Rapids: Eerdmans, 1985); and M. Silva, "The New Testament Use of the Old Testament: Text Form and Authority," in *Scripture and Truth*, ed. D. Carson and J. Woodbridge (Grand Rapids: Zondervan, 1983), 147–65. Note the survey given in Darrell L. Bock, "Evangelicals and the Use of the Old Testament in the New," *BSac* 142 (1985): 209–23, 306–19.

[63]See D. Bock, *Proclamation from Prophecy and Pattern: Lucan Old Testament Christology*, JSNT Supp. 12 (Sheffield: JSOT, 1987). See also D. Carson, "Redaction Criticism: On the Legitimacy and Illegitimacy of a Literary Tool," in *Scripture and Truth*, 119–42.

[64]For an overview, see D. Carson, "Recent Developments in the Doctrine of Scripture," in *Hermeneutics, Authority, and Canon*, ed. D. Carson and J. Woodbridge (Grand Rapids: Zondervan, 1986), 5–48. Also note papers on various themes in E. Radmacher and R. Preus, eds., *Hermeneutics, Inerrancy, and the Bible* (Grand Rapids: Zondervan, 1984). One cannot mention works on semantics without reference to J. Barr, *The Semantics of Biblical Language* (Oxford: Oxford University Press, 1961). Also, see J. Louw, *Semantics of New Testament Greek* (Philapelphia: Fortress, 1982); M. Silva, *Biblical Words and their Meaning* (Grand Rapids: Zondervan, 1983); and P. Cotterell and M. Turner, *Linguistics and Biblical Interpretation* (Downers Grove, Ill.: InterVarsity, 1989).

[65]See L. Goppelt, *Typos: The Typological Interpretation of the Old Testament in the New* (Grand Rapids: Eerdmans, 1982); F. Foulkes, *The Acts of God: A Study of the Basis of Typology in the Old Testament* (London: Tyndale, 1958); and R. Davidson, *Typology in Scripture* (Berrien Springs, Mich.: Andrews University Press, 1981).

one's tradition or other familiar patterns of thought that condition the interpreter's preunderstanding. Consequently, what is clear to one may be quite unclear to another with a different preunderstanding.

Evangelicals today, including dispensationalists, affirm historical-grammatical interpretation as the proper hermeneutical method. One of the advantages of this label is its adaptability to the literary and historical developments in hermeneutics mentioned above. As evangelicals have worked together exploring these developments, the old divisions of spiritual versus literal interpretation have been left behind. Dispensationalists who have simply identified "literal interpretation," their traditional label, with historical-grammatical interpretation have become aware of the present-day inapplicability of Ryrie's exclusive hermeneutic. Few evangelicals today claim to practice spiritual or allegorical interpretation. The issues are more complex, but the evangelical community is working inclusively on these matters.[66] It is a matter not of an exclusive hermeneutic but of a skillful application of a method we all profess.[67]

These hermeneutical developments have led to the search for a new definition of dispensationalism, since clear, plain, literal, normal hermeneutics had been identified as an element of the very essence of dispensational thought. Since the late 1970s, a number of articles and books written by dispensationalists have questioned the usefulness of Ryrie's sine qua non.[68] In 1985, an annual forum was established for discussing these matters.[69] Some have sought to preserve Ryrie's definitional method while adjusting the contents of the definition he proposed. This has led to the quest for an essence within the essence, usually a reduction of the sine qua non from three principles to one. *However, it is becoming increasingly clear that this approach will not be successful.*

---

[66]The distinction Poythress makes in *Understanding Dispensationalists* between dispensationalists who practice historical-grammatical interpretation and those who have not advanced beyond a "flat level" form of literal interpretation is helpful. His book testifies to the hermeneutical inclusiveness experienced by present-day evangelicals which, while not bringing theological uniformity, has brought about a more cordial and dialogical relationship in the community. Also see the following exchange of papers: E. Johnson, "What I Mean by Historical-Grammatical Interpretation and How That Differs from Spiritual Interpretation," and T. Longman, III, "What I Mean by Historical-Grammatical Interpretation and How that Differs from Literal Interpretation" (papers presented to the Dispensational Study Group, New Orleans, Nov. 15, 1990; to be published in a forthcoming issue of *Grace Theological Journal*).

[67]This is the point made by Ramm in the prologue to his *Protestant Biblical Interpretation*, ix.

[68]A number of these writings have been referenced in Blaising, "Development of Dispensationalism," 266–80.

[69]R. Clutter, "Dispensational Study Group: An Introduction," *GTJ* 10 (1989): 123–24.

There are three reasons for this. First, as already noted, the essentialist approach to defining dispensationalism is too narrow. It omits beliefs, perspectives, and emphases that form a more natural identity. Furthermore, it has failed to grasp the living, developing, historical character of dispensationalism. Consequently, it is unable to explain how identity features may themselves develop historically; it is in fact unable to explain itself, how and why it came to be and its relationship to those who came before and will follow after. A reduction of this approach only aggravates the problem.

Second, the essentialist approach has as the object of its quest beliefs or (hermeneutical) practice that belong *exclusively* to dispensationalists. Nowhere did Ryrie assert this more strongly than in the area of hermeneutics. But nowadays this is simply not the case. While hermeneutical self-consciousness does characterize present dispensationalism, it does not pretend to exclusivity. Rather, we find a hermeneutical inclusivity that is more akin to the atmosphere in which early American dispensationalism developed. Certainly, the goal is not difference for its own sake but spiritual growth in faith and hope informed by the Scriptures and manifesting itself in love. We all desire, whatever the tradition, to understand what God is saying; we should be able to discuss the options with one another openly, honestly, and methodologically.

Finally, the reduction of the essentialist approach ignores the relationship between hermeneutical principles and the other elements of the sine qua non. The study of biblical theology—especially with regard to the role of history in divine revelation and contextualized studies of New Testament views on the fulfillment of Old Testament prophecy, including studies of historical typology (not to mention studies in literary genre and semantics)—have led dispensationalists to reexamine biblically the distinction between Israel and the church. This does not lead in turn to a simple identification of Israel and the church, a position that dispensationalism has traditionally rejected. But it has led many dispensationalists to abandon the *transcendental distinction* of heavenly versus earthly peoples in favor of a *historical distinction* in the progressive revelation of the divine purpose.[70] The unity of divine revelation, of the various dispensations, is found in the goal of history, the kingdom of God. And since this kingdom is centered in the person and work of Jesus Christ, the dispensational unity of Scripture and of history is Christological as much as it is eschatological.

The present book of biblical studies finds its identity precisely at this

---

[70]Robert Saucy, "The Crucial Issue Between Dispensational and Nondispensational Systems" and "The Locus of the Church," *CTR* 1 (1986–87): 149–65, 387–99.

point: *the hermeneutical reexamination of the relationship between Israel and the church, which in turn contributes to the process of self-definition currently underway in dispensationalism.* The authors of the various chapters in the next part are all dispensationalists. They are experienced educators and respected scholars. Except for chapter 10, which is broader in scope, the topics examine aspects of the Israel-church relationship in New Testament theology. The approach is exegetical and biblical-theological, which reflects the traditional value dispensationalists have placed on Scripture as the basis and authority for all such theological formulations. However, there is no exclusive hermeneutic here. The context for these studies is the field of evangelical biblical scholarship (which in turn interfaces with the broader field of international biblical interpretation). The insights, views, and conclusions offered should be tested dialogically in this community of interpretation. All of our evangelical subtraditions need to be so engaged, if only to avoid the dogmatic illusions that arise from prolonged introversion. More than that, we are accountable to one another in a common profession of biblical authority. Consequently, in the interest of promoting such dialogue, we have invited three evangelical scholars to respond to these hermeneutical studies. Their essays appear in Part 2. Following them, my co-editor and I will return to the subject of definition and offer a concluding word on the implications of all of these essays for the present identity of dispensationalism.

Part 1

Biblical Studies

CHAPTER 1

The Reign of the Lord Christ

Darrell L. Bock

Terms are not the only key to biblical themes.[1] For example, more is required for a study of the kingdom than simply picking up a concordance and looking up βασιλεία (kingdom) and its related verbal forms. Likewise a study of the covenants requires more than an examination of passages containing the term διαθήκη (covenant), and a study of promise involves more than the texts where ἐπαγγελία (promise) occurs.[2] A thorough treatment of any theme requires a look at associated concepts as well as individual terms. If one wants to see how God accomplishes his kingdom program, one must see how that program and the promises tied to it are linked together through the Scripture's description of the career of Jesus Christ.

The theme of God's rule as expressed in covenant and promise is one of the scriptural concepts that ties the program of God together. A key writer on this theme is Luke, who focuses on the continuity between what God did and planned in the old era and what he is now doing and will be doing in Christ. This chapter examines a particularly crucial section of Luke's writing and the stages of Jesus' career. Its goal is to argue that any reconstruction of New Testament eschatology—indeed of messianic eschatology—must take into account the perspective of both Acts 2 and Acts 3.

In the space of these two key chapters in Acts, Luke discusses three major Old Testament covenants (the Abrahamic, the Davidic, and the new covenants). Reference is often made, not through the identification of a single term or by naming a specific covenant, but through clear allusions to features of the covenants in question. Through allusion,

---

[1] I would like to thank the Dispensationalism Study Group of the Evangelical Theological Society, which interacted with an early draft of this chapter. Their comments proved very helpful and their interaction stimulating.

[2] One could add Hebrew terms; our main concern, however, is Luke-Acts, so only Greek terms apply.

Luke indicates either fulfillment or anticipation of fulfillment. By this clever association of concepts, Luke presents Jesus as the fulfillment of promises and covenants made to Israel. Yet Luke still notes that some of what Jesus is to do is yet to come. As such, the continuity between Jesus' first and second comings and their relationship with Old Testament promise, with the Old Testament covenants, and with messianic hope is consistently maintained in the various stages of Jesus' career.

This study is comprised of four parts. First comes the background of the kingdom promise in Luke-Acts up to Acts 2, especially the issue of the present form of the kingdom in the gospel and the comments of Acts 1:6–11. The issue of the present form of the kingdom receives special attention because it is the nature of the current form of the kingdom that is most debated.[3] In most theological systems, references to a still-future, consummated kingdom are not really denied, only its exact form is debated. Next is an examination of the current fulfillment theme as expressed in Acts 2. Third, the note of fulfillment and yet future expectation in Acts 3 is considered. Fourth is a quick overview of passages from Revelation. Finally comes a concluding summary that expresses the implications of the results for eschatology.

THE KINGDOM CONCEPT IN LUKE'S GOSPEL

In his gospel, Luke consistently associates the kingdom with Jesus' life and ministry. In Luke 1:32–33, the angel tells Mary that God will give the throne of David to the child that will be born to her. The child will rule over the house of Jacob forever, and his kingdom will never end. Here is an outline of the career of Jesus. Though no details are supplied at this point, it is clear from the hymns of Mary and of Zechariah that they understand it to include national-political as well as spiritual aspects (vv. 51–55, 69–75, 78–79). Both hymns mention explicitly the Abrahamic promise that is being fulfilled in the career of Jesus (vv. 55, 72–73). In addition, Luke 1:69 alludes to the Davidic promise by mentioning the arrival of the Davidic horn as the central theme of praise. The aorist tense in this verse makes it clear that the Davidic ruler has arisen ($\H{\eta}\gamma\varepsilon\iota\rho\varepsilon\nu$). The fact that God has visited and made redemption for his people (v. 68) is grounded in the promise of a Davidite in the Old Testament prophets (v. 70). The passage also appeals to the language of Psalm 132:17, an allusion that links this

---

[3]The only exception to a belief in a still-future consummated kingdom is the variations of realized eschatology like that of C. H. Dodd, but such a view falls into trouble with passages like Acts 3.

passage to Acts 2:30–32, since Acts 2 refers to Psalm 132:11. Thus the Davidic connection of Acts 2 is tied to the hymn of Luke 1. These linked passages betray any attempt to argue that the Davidic rule, and thus at least some aspect of the covenant, is not tied to Jesus' first coming, since this hymn presents Jesus as fulfilling prophetic promise and goes on to discuss national deliverance *and* forgiveness of sins side by side. Such juxtaposition of themes does not mean that all the events of the hymn happen at the same time, but it does mean that both concepts are associated with Jesus' work as a Davidic king. Confirmation of this association comes later, since a similar juxtaposition occurs in Luke 2:25–38, where the consolation of Israel, messianic illumination of the Gentiles, and redemption for Jerusalem are placed side by side as the prophets Simeon and Anna predict Jesus' career. It is the promised Davidic horn who does all of these things. His activity is tied to that of John the Baptist, so that his first coming is clearly indicated. At the very start of his gospel, Luke signals that Jesus will fulfill Old Testament promise in terms of both the national hope of Israel and the spiritual needs of those who participate in God's covenant. The messianic deliverance promised to Abraham is realized in David's seed, a deliverance of both physical and spiritual dimensions.

Jesus himself describes his mission as that of preaching the kingdom in synagogues in various cities (Luke 4:43–44). Luke 4:16–30 is often regarded as a sample of such preaching. Luke 4 refers to the "today" fulfillment and cites Isaiah 61:1–2 and 58:6. This Luke 4 passage mentions mostly the spiritual dimensions of his mission and stops before mentioning the line in Isaiah that referred to the judgment of God. The omission may suggest some delay in the execution of God's judgment, although John the Baptist earlier suggested that the ax was laid at the root of the tree, a clear allusion to the nearness of judgment (Luke 3:7–9). The Lukan text implies stages in the execution of the career of Jesus or at least reveals an emphasis in the current availability of the kingdom. It is a time of grace. Jesus' ministry offers a present opportunity against the backdrop of an implied future judgment (Luke 19:41-44; 21:5–36).

Luke 7:28 is a very significant text. Here Jesus distinguishes between the period of John the Baptist and that of the kingdom. John as the prophet who goes before the Lord is the greatest person yet born; nevertheless, the least person in the kingdom of God is greater than he. The fundamental point here is that the kingdom period, one that followed the ministry of John, is so great that the least who share in it are greater than the greatest prophet of the older era. One gets the clear impression from this text that the period of the kingdom of God begins with Jesus' ministry and message, since the context of the remark is a discussion about whether Jesus is "the Coming One."

The proximity of the kingdom is also noted when the Seventy-two are sent to various locales in Palestine. In Luke 10:9, the messengers are to proclaim ἤγγικεν ἐφ᾽ ὑμᾶς ἡ βασιλεία τοῦ θεοῦ. There is currently a large debate about the meaning of the term ἤγγικεν. Does the perfect tense here of the verb "to draw near" mean "to approach," or does it mean "to arrive"? Lexically the term can carry either sense.[4] But the context is the key in making the decision. The decisive preposition ἐπί is a spatial term that means "upon." It is awkward to say one approaches upon a person, in the sense that one draws near upon a person but does not come upon them. However, to come upon people is to arrive where they are. Lukan usage of the verb often suggests the sense of arrival (Luke 12:33; 15:1; 18:40; 22:47; 24:15, 28; Acts 21:33). The point seems to be that with the coming of Jesus and the preaching of the message he commissions, the kingdom has arrived. Even if one prefers the sense of "approach," the kingdom is at least very near. When the verb "to come near" is present, ἐπί takes on a temporal force. The force is at least of proximate future.

However, any doubt about the force of ἤγγικεν being "arrival" in Luke 10 is removed when one looks at the conceptual parallel to Luke 11:20, which is treated below. In sum, the kingdom's presence, or at least its very close proximity, is tied to the first phase of Jesus' career. What Jesus is suggesting is not that the kingdom has arrived *in fullness* but that signs of its initial stages have come.

A note of continuity in the presentation of the kingdom comes in Luke 10:11. The disciples shake the dust from their feet when a town rejects their message. This action is repeated in Acts 13:51. The parallelism of these two texts is very significant. It ties the precross and postcross message together in that the two events share the same symbolism for rejection. Though the Acts message has more detail and focuses more clearly on Jesus, the message is essentially the same: *the reign of God is inaugurated.* In that inauguration the deliverance of God has come, and the future full rule of God has been guaranteed. Shaking off the dust shows that the rejecting city is separated from blessing. The same judgment applies to both settings.[5]

Luke 10:18 confirms the arrival of authority with the announcement of the kingdom. Here the ministry of the messengers is also discussed. Jesus notes that he saw the fall of Satan from heaven, a clear image of defeat for the archdemon in the exorcism ministry of the Seventy-two.

---

[4]J. A. Fitzmyer, *The Gospel According to Luke X–XXIV*, AB (Garden City, N.Y.: Doubleday, 1985), 848; N. Perrin, *The Kingdom of God in the Teaching of Jesus* (Philadelphia: Westminster, 1963), 64–66.
[5]Str-B 1:571.

In Judaism, the coming of Messiah and the demonstration of his authority were seen as marking the end for Satan (1 Enoch 55:1; Jub. 23:29; T. Sim. 6:6; T. Jud. 25:3; As. Moses 10:1–3).[6] Satan's defeat in the New Testament is often expressed in relation to the cross or the return of Jesus (John 12:31–32; Col. 2:14–15; Rev. 12:10–12; 20:1–3). In Luke 10:18, however, the stress is on current events in Jesus' earthly ministry that spell defeat for Satan. The image of Satan's defeat is important for it pictures his fall not just from heaven but from rule, as the next passage shows. The portrait of Luke 10 is of Jesus' authority *as expressed through his followers.* This anticipates their postcross activity as well. Although this is not Satan's ultimate fall (Rev. 20:7–10), his authority now stands challenged and defeated in a decisive way. The ministry of Jesus and the disciples is a turning point. The exorcisms by Jesus and the disciples are tied to the kingdom's presence, as the next key text, Luke 11:20, makes clear. Any attempt to limit the meaning of this fall of Satan to just the activity of Jesus or to see it as merely proleptic fails. An appeal only to the presence of God's kingly power in the person and message of Jesus misses the significance of this transfer of power to others and ignores the kingdom association Jesus makes in explaining these activities in Luke 11:20.

Luke 11:20 is part of Jesus' reply in defense of the source and significance of his exorcisms. Jesus says that if his work is by the finger of God, then the kingdom "has come upon you." Note the repetition of the key spatial-temporal preposition ἐπί (upon), which was also present in Luke 10:9. Does it speak of nearness or of arrival? The imagery as well as context favors the latter. Luke 11:21–23 presents the image of a stronger one overtaking Satan and dispensing spoils of victory. Such imagery is used elsewhere in the New Testament of the first coming of Jesus, specifically of Jesus' death and resurrection (Eph. 4:7–10; Col. 2:14–15). In addition, the normal meaning of the verb φθάνω, which here looks to the past with the aorist ἔφθασεν, is "arrival" (Rom. 9:31; Phil. 3:16; 1 Thess. 2:16).[7] Again, the kingdom's arrival is declared.

Little detail appears about the nature of the kingdom or the makeup of the spoils. But what is said is consistent with fuller discussions of the kingdom elsewhere in Luke and in Acts. The picture of Satan's fall and

---

[6]Ibid. 2:167–68.

[7]Interestingly, in 1 Thess. 2 there is the tension between the future work of God and his present wrath, showing that something present now has implications for the future. On the compound of φθάνω with ἐπί, meaning "overtake," see Dan. 4:24 LXX-Theod; W. Kümmel, *Promise and Fulfillment,* trans. Dorothea M. Barton, SBT 23 (Naperville, Ill.: Allenson, 1957), 105–9; *TDNT* 9:88–92; I. H. Marshall, *The Gospel of Luke,* NIGTC (Grand Rapids: Eerdmans, 1978), 476. There is no possibility that this term can be read proleptically, given the presence of the preposition.

of the disciples' authority to heal as a picture of deliverance is an indication confirming the call that the kingdom is near. The picture of healing recalls the kingdom message of Luke 4:16–18, which Jesus says is currently fulfilled (Luke 4:21).[8] The kingdom begins to arrive with Jesus' ministry. But this beginning is not complete until the bestowal of the Father's promise of the Spirit in Acts 2, an act that inaugurates the new covenant, which in turn finds its basis in the death of Christ (Luke 22:20).[9] So Luke 10–11 proclaims a sign of the arrival of the kingdom through the mission of the Seventy-two. Jesus' ministry and that of the disciples is a *transition* to the kingdom's arrival with its spiritual provision. It is a transition from anticipation to arrival. The extent of the authority already granted is expressed in Luke 10:22, when Jesus says that all authority is granted to him. There is nothing left to be received; what remains is to carry out the exercise of that authority.[10] The king is here; manifestations of his power are already present and are shared with his closest associates. It is time to respond and enter in.

The next key text is Luke 17:21. Here Jesus is debating with the Pharisees about the signs of the kingdom's arrival. He contends that they do not need to look here or there for it. The kingdom of God is ἐντὸς ὑμῶν. Again debate exists. Is he saying that the kingdom is "in you," depicting a spiritual kingdom located in the hearts of individuals; or is it "among them," depicting a kingdom located before them or in their midst? A third option is to take the term as future, in the sense of "will be in your midst."[11] A fourth possibility is "within your reach."[12] Again, the context is clear in deciding the matter. The term cannot mean "within" because contextually Jesus is addressing Pharisees. The last thing he would say to them in their conflict with him is that the kingdom of God is found in their hearts.[13] The idea must be that the kingdom is in their midst, or perhaps in their reach. In either case, the kingdom is presently available through Jesus' ministry.

Discussion also revolves around ἐστιν (is). Does the verb allude to

---

[8]Luke 4:16–30 sets forth Jesus' preaching, while Luke 4:43 says that Jesus' mission is the call to preach the kingdom, of which Luke 4:16–30 is an example.

[9]See Luke 24:47–52, which looks forward to the Acts 2 event.

[10]The aorist passive verb παρεδόθη (is given over) is a theological passive. Jesus receives this authority from God.

[11]A. Mattill, *Luke and the Last Things* (Dillsboro, N.C.: Western North Carolina Press, 1979), 198–201, argues for the force of a future tense.

[12]Marshall, *Luke,* 655–56, opts for this meaning, citing papyri support in C. H. Roberts, "The Kingdom of Heaven (Luke xvii.21)," *HTR* 41 (1948): 1–8, but goes on to note in his next paragraph that the force is "within your reach in the present" because of the present tense of the verb in the verse. He says it equals Luke 11:20 in meaning. The papyri evidence is not unchallenged; A. Wikgren, "ΕΝΤΟΣ," *Nuntius* 4 (1950): 27–28, argues that the papyri phrases mean "in your presence" or "in your domain."

[13]R. Maddox, *The Purpose of Luke-Acts* (Edinburgh: T. & T. Clark, 1982), 134.

the presence of the kingdom, or should it be read proleptically in reference to the future kingdom as possibly suggested by the following discourse? Context decides. There is an interchange of tenses in Luke 17:20–21. The term ἐροῦσιν (they will say) is future. Given this future tense, the subsequent choice of the present-tense ἐστιν is clearly temporally contrastive. It would certainly be awkward if what is really meant by ἐστιν is a future idea, especially since one does not normally express a futuristic present idea with εἰμί, but with ἔρχομαι.[14] Jesus' remark contrasts popular speculations about the future kingdom with its surprising present appearance. The passage goes on to discuss the future, but that is because the kingdom is a program in stages, initiated by Jesus and consummated in judgment, as the image of the gathering vultures in verse 37 suggests. The point of the remark is that the kingdom has come because the king stands before them. The kingdom is inaugurated with Jesus' first coming, but the program culminates in his return in full glory. Jesus consistently rebukes the Pharisees for failing to see what God is doing before their very eyes (Luke 7:31–35; 11:20 with 27–28, which calls on people to respond to what God is doing through Jesus; Luke 11:29–32, 12:54–56). If they really understood God's call, they would repent and share in the kingdom's presence.

Still another confirming clue to the kingdom's presence comes in the parable of the ten minas. In Luke 19:12, a nobleman "goes to receive a kingdom" and then returns. Now the nobleman clearly portrays Jesus in his resurrection. Verse 15 makes the point that he returns λαβόντα τὴν βασιλείαν (having received the kingdom). In other words, the reception of the kingdom precedes his return. Verse 14 notes that some did not want him to rule over them, a picture of the Jewish response to the present possibility of his rule, not to his future return.[15]

Covenantal imagery returns at the Last Supper, one of the more emotional times in Jesus' career. In Luke 22:20, as Jesus distributes the elements, he notes that the cup represents the new covenant in his blood, shed on behalf of his disciples. Here the new covenant is tied explicitly to Jesus' death. In the Old Testament the fulfillment of the new covenant is tied to the inauguration of the kingdom (Jer. 31–33; Ezek. 36–37). In this passage in Luke key aspects of inauguration are tied to his work on the cross and initiate the promise God made in Jeremiah 31. There is an intensification of inauguration in the death of Jesus, so that the kingdom program reaches a crucial phase with Jesus' death. The New Testament did not miss this connection, not only as

---

[14]BDF §323; R. Geiger, *Die lukanischen Endzeitreden,* EH 16 (Frankfurt: Peter Lang, 1973), 45.

[15]Luke 19:14 translated fairly literally is "We do not wish this man to rule over us."

Acts 2 makes clear, with its reference to the sending of the Spirit, but as 2 Corinthians 3 and Hebrews 8–10 show in using the association of new covenant with Jesus' work. In fact, 1 Corinthians 11:25 and its description of this meal looks back at this Lukan language as Paul portrays what happens in all the churches, including the largely Gentile congregation in Corinth. At the heart of the message brought to the church is the initiation of new-covenant promises made to Israel, which now have a much broader scope as Jesus' own teaching indicates. Again Luke does not tell us in his gospel exactly how this inauguration is intensified, since there is no mention of the promise of the Spirit here. He simply notes that the way for the inauguration of the new covenant is clear, so a major, even decisive phase of kingdom inauguration is present, having its basis in the death of Jesus. Inauguration is a process in Luke's gospel, but it is not really complete until Jesus dies and is raised.

The final text of Luke's gospel claims that the entirety of Jesus' career was promised in the Scripture. No specific Old Testament texts are given, but one can suggest that these specific passages are saved for the speeches in Acts, since Acts deals with these themes. The key to the end of Luke 24 is found in the three promises that are mentioned and in the reference to the promise of the Father in verse 49. The three promises are tied to three parallel infinitives. The Old Testament looked to the suffering of Christ (παθεῖν), his resurrection from the dead on the third day (ἀναστῆναι), and the preaching in Jesus' name of repentance for the forgiveness of sins to all the nations (κηρυχθῆναι). This third element is the most revealing. By referring to the message of repentance, continuity is established between the preaching of the apostles and that of John and of Jesus (Luke 3:10–14; 5:32; 24:47; Acts 2:38; 11:18; 17:30; 26:20). The key Christological point in this passage is the reference to Jesus as the promised Messiah (Christ) of the Old Testament, clearly a regal function, something that is his through his connection to David as David's seed. A king, indeed, shows his authority by ruling a kingdom. Jesus rules by saving and calling a new community made from all nations.

These three time frames—Baptist, Jesus, and apostles—are tied together in the call to repentance. With resurrection no racial distinction exists for the message, which goes to all. Preaching occurs "in his name," a key phrase that alludes here and in Acts to Jesus' authority with respect to salvation (Acts 3:6; 3:16 is especially clear; 4:10, 12, 18; 5:28; 8:12; 10:43 is also clear; 15:14; 16:18; 22:16). It should be remembered that Jesus characterized his message as the preaching of the kingdom and described his mission as calling sinners to repentance (see Luke 4:14–15; 5:31–32; the parables of Luke 15). Wrapped up in the message is a call. Wrapped up in the call is a person. Wrapped up in the person is the period. What allows the person and the period to come together is the realization of promise and the grant of authority to the Anointed One.

Continuity in the preaching of the kingdom is found in the promise of the Spirit as it is tied to repentance. John the Baptist had specifically noted that one of the distinctive features of Jesus' ministry versus his own was the baptism of the Spirit, which the "Coming One" would supply (Luke 3:15–18). Luke 24:49 refers to "the promise of the Father" that Jesus shall send and for which the disciples must wait. This must be an Old Testament promise, given the context of Old Testament fulfillment in Luke 24. Acts 1:4 alludes again to this promise, and its delivery in Acts 2 is the catalyst for one of the most crucial passages in the whole of Luke's two volumes. The Acts 2 event has covenantal and promise elements that help to tie together the Lukan picture of the career of the Lord Christ and show which Old Testament texts are seen as fulfillments. Nonetheless, certain tensions remain as Luke moves from the period of the earthly ministry of Jesus to the period of apostolic preaching. The kingdom, at least in some form, is present; the promise, at least in some way, is anticipated as imminent. And yet after lengthy teaching by Jesus about the kingdom, Acts 1 suggests that this kingdom is still expected by the disciples in a certain form that relates to Israel. How is this tension to be resolved? What is the reign of the Lord Christ to look like?

The tension between kingdom present and kingdom to come is raised immediately in Acts with the disciples' question of when the kingdom will be restored to Israel (1:6). The context has already made it clear that Jesus has been teaching the disciples about the kingdom (v. 4). That the kingdom is absent or that it has taken a different form for all time is not stated here. Rather it is the connection of the kingdom to Israel and to consummation that is at issue here. When will sacred promises made to Israel be consummated? Jesus replies in terms of the disciples' immediate task. It is not for them to know when God will work out what he has set to do. In the meantime, they are to await the coming of the Holy Spirit, in whose power they will preach as witnesses to Jesus.

Some have seen Jesus' remark as a repudiation and rejection of the question about Israel. But this is hardly clear. Jesus simply notes that the time is not theirs to know, not that the question is improper. In fact, the context supplies a clue to the answer of the question. The Ascension (v. 11) contains the promise of Jesus' return from heaven. The role of this verse in the total picture of Luke's eschatology has not been sufficiently stressed. It serves as a reply to the question. The time of the restoration of the kingdom to Israel is not for you to know, but be assured that Jesus will return as he has departed. At least this is how one could construe the argument of the unit. Is this the way to read Acts 1:6–11? In fact, how the disciples put this "exit only to return" package together is something the speeches of Acts 2–3 make clear. The return is specifically set forth in Peter's remarks in Acts 3. They learned not only from the exposition of Jesus in Luke 24 but from the record of this event in Acts 1.

What emerges is a picture of a career that comes in stages as different aspects of what the Old Testament promised are brought to fulfillment at different phases of Jesus' work. One might characterize these phases as the "already" and the "not yet" of Jesus' career, or by reference to the kingdom, as the invisible and the visible kingdom of God. One should not fear "already and not yet" terminology, since all Bible students accept its presence in soteriology: "I am saved (i.e., justified) already— but I am not yet saved (i.e., glorified)" is good theology. The same structure applies to Christology that is wedded to eschatology. But both the "already" and the "not yet" need careful defining, for covenant theologians of the past have tended to overemphasize the "already" in their critiques of dispensationalism, while underemphasizing the "not yet." Dispensationalists have tended to underemphasize the "already," minimizing what is presently fulfilled in God's program in an attempt to maintain distinctions. The rest of this chapter suggests a corrective to both approaches.

The descriptions *invisible* and *visible* do not characterize the kingdom as ineffective or secret now, versus powerful later. Rather, the terms are intended Christologically to describe the nature of Jesus' rule. In the current period, he is not visible, though he sits in heaven and reigns from the right hand of God through the work of the Spirit in his disciples. In the future period, he will reign visibly on the earth. The kingdom is present in both periods. The kingdom is a powerful manifestation of God's activity in the world, but the King's visibility differs between the two periods. Also, the primary focus of the current kingdom is in Jesus' authority to save, especially as shown in the work of transformation. The kingdom community in the present era is the church, where transformation should be manifest. The church serves in the world as a distinct institution and is to be a light to all, a light that is manifested through it by the Spirit (Acts 13:49). This present form of the kingdom of God is the church existing among the other kingdoms of earth. In New Testament language, believers are citizens of heaven and aliens and strangers in the world (Phil. 3:20; 1 Peter 2:11). In this present community, people are to get a glimpse, a "sneak preview," of what is to come, as Jesus' rule is evident in the lives of believers. In the future that rule will be manifested through a visibly present Jesus, who will reign with full justice and righteousness in a kingdom over all. In the era to come, the kingdom will swallow up the other kingdoms and complete the promises made to Israel.

ACTS 2: THE "ALREADY" REIGN

Throughout the survey of the kingdom concept in Luke's gospel, passages keep appearing that set forth the kingdom as present. But what is its nature? What relationship does it have to the ministry, death, and resurrection-ascension of Jesus? How does it fit in with what the Old Testament promised? Some of these questions find answers in Acts 2. Although the term *kingdom* never appears in the entire chapter, the imagery of rule and the features of God's covenants are present. In fact, the chapter is saturated with such images and allusions. In this way, Acts explains an aspect of God's program as it relates to his promises and Messiah's rule.

The essence of Peter's speech is found in three clear Old Testament citations and one crucial linking allusion between the second and third citations. The first citation is Joel 2:28–32 (3:1–5, LXX), which is offered as the explanation for what has just occurred in Acts 2.

Several features of the passage are important. First, the quotation is introduced in Acts 2:16 with as explicit a citation formula as could be used to denote fulfillment: $\tau o \hat{v} \tau \acute{o}\ \acute{\epsilon} \sigma \tau \iota \nu\ \tau \grave{o}\ \epsilon \acute{\iota} \rho \eta \mu \acute{\epsilon} \nu o \nu$ (this is that which is spoken). Such phrases were used at Qumran to indicate the presence of fulfillment.[16] Peter uses the formula to make an identification that answers the charge of drunkenness; it is not a comparison.[17]

Second, the one major change in the Joel citation concerns the time of fulfillment. Rather than saying "after these things" as Joel does, Peter says, "in the last days," a phrase that shows how Peter sees the period into which humankind has fallen as a result of recent events. The period of the "last days" is by its very nature a period of fulfillment. In saying this, it is not necessary, or correct, to go on and say that the period of ultimate consummation is present, for the New Testament can still speak of the "age to come" (see Luke 18:30; Acts 3:18–20; 1 Cor.

[16]R. Longenecker, *Biblical Exegesis in the Apostolic Period* (Grand Rapids: Eerdmans, 1975), 100, speaks of the "this is that" pesher formula. The variety of such pesher formulas in Aramaic is found in M. Horgan, *Pesharim: Qumran Interpretations of Biblical Books,* CBQMS 8 (Washington, D.C.: Catholic Biblical Association of America, 1979), 239–44.

[17]A. Gaebelein, *The Acts of the Apostles,* reprint ed. (Neptune, N.J.: Loizeaux Brothers, 1961), 54, argues for a comparison between these events and those of the last days, but this ignores the one major alteration in the New Testament text from the Old Testament text, the nature of the citation formula, and the allusion to the gift of the Holy Spirit as it relates to promise in vv. 38–39.

15:20–28; Rev. 1:19). What is present is an inauguration of events, not a total completion, as the nature of the fulfillment of Joel in Acts shows. The "last days" points to the presence of the eschaton, but not to the presence of all of it.

Third, the event that is singled out as that which fulfills Joel is the pouring out of the Spirit on all believers. In fact, the idea is mentioned twice in the space of the quotation (vv. 17b, 18b), with the second mention being an addition to the quotation for emphasis. This event must be the "promise of the Father" that was spoken of in Luke 24:49 and Acts 1:4. In fact, the promise is referred to directly in Acts 2:38–39, as it is in 2:33. Peter perceives this event as a messianic distribution of the promised Spirit. In fact, the Spirit's distribution is a major burden of the speech, as verses 32–36 also return to this concept. The term in verse 33 is ἐχέξεεν (he poured out), which is the same verb as appears in verses 17 and 18, where Peter cites Joel's promise of the Spirit's outpouring.

Now what kind of fulfillment is present? Is it total or partial? Against a total fulfillment is the reference to the approaching Day of the Lord in verse 20. Also against a total fulfillment is the absence of any cosmic signs in Luke-Acts like those described in Acts 2:19b–20b.[18] So the first of a series of events is present, a series that makes up a large period known as the last days. Peter is saying that a promised program is coming to pass and that a key element of what God promised has taken place. In other words, what begins with the Spirit's outpouring leads eventually into the rule and judgment that is tied to the Day of the Lord. The period is a package, and the program of fulfillment has begun. In other words, a careful study of the use of Joel in Acts 2 shows that "this is that" is not "this is *all* of that" or "this is *like* that"; the meaning, rather, is "this is the *beginning* of that," since the cosmic signs of Joel 2 are not fulfilled in the first coming of Jesus.[19]

One question remains for the Joel text. What is the promise that is suggested by the Spirit's coming? Again an association of concepts is in view here. The speech focuses on the Spirit's provision for all of God's people. In fact, "the promise of the Father" alludes not only to Joel but to a key promise of the new covenant in Jeremiah 31, an important eschatological text that promised a bestowal of the Spirit to God's people. Numerous New Testament passages allude to the coming of the new covenant or to the Spirit's coming. These references start with the Baptist's preaching, as was noted in the discussion of Luke 3:15–18 and

---

[18]D. Bock, *Proclamation from Prophecy and Pattern*, JSNTSup 12 (Sheffield: JSOT, 1987), 166–67.

[19]Ibid., 166, 346.

Luke 22:20. Peter's contention to his Jewish audience is that the Spirit's outpouring represents the first signs of the presence of new-covenant promise. The Spirit's coming is a sign that drives toward the Day of the Lord and its accompanying judgment. The eschaton has begun; the movement toward the culmination of the eschaton has started, as have the benefits associated with the coming of the Day of the Lord. Peter's listeners now need to call on the Lord for salvation, which comes through a confession to Lord Messiah Jesus, a confession that delivers one from the consequences of that day (Acts 2:36–40).

Having mentioned the need to call on the Lord, Peter turns to recent events. He recounts Jesus' ministry and death but notes that death is not able to hold him (vv. 22–24). Peter goes on to note that such impotency for death was predicted in Psalm 16, the second Old Testament citation in Acts 2 (vv. 25–28). This text is clearly presented as having been fulfilled in Jesus' resurrection. The Psalm 16 citation leads into the mention of David and a defense of the fact that a resurrection understanding of the text cannot refer to David, since he is buried (v. 29).

The crucial linking allusion appears at this point. Peter notes that David was a prophet.[20] Not only was David a prophet, he was the conscious beneficiary of an oath God had made to him that one "of the fruit of his [David's] loins" (KJV) would sit on his throne (Acts 2:30). The key term is καθίσαι (to sit), which is reintroduced in the citation of Psalm 110 (note κάθου, "sit," in v. 34). The allusion in verse 30 is to Psalm 132:11, a psalm which is strongly Israelitish and national in tone (see vv. 12–18). The psalm in turn is a reflection of the promise made to David in 2 Samuel 7, especially verse 12. This 2 Samuel passage is better known as the Davidic covenant. What is crucial is that David's awareness of this covenant promise is immediately linked to his understanding of the resurrection promise in Psalm 16, which in turn is immediately tied to the resurrection proof text of Psalm 110 (vv. 31–35). *Being seated on David's throne is linked to being seated at God's right hand.* In other words, Jesus' resurrection-ascension to God's right hand is put forward by Peter as a fulfillment of the Davidic covenant, just as the allusion to Joel fulfills the new covenant. To say that Peter is only interested to argue that Messiah must be raised misses the point of connection in these verses and ignores entirely the allusion to Psalm 132 and the Davidic covenant. This passage and Luke 1:68–79 also counter the claim that no New Testament text asserts the present work of Jesus as a reigning Davidite sitting on David's throne. The throne on which

---

[20]On the Palestinian character of this description, see J. Fitzmyer, "'David, Being Therefore a Prophet . . .' (Acts 2:30)," *CBQ* 34 (1972): 332–39.

Jesus is said to sit is the one promised to David's descendant through the Davidic promise of 2 Samuel, which was initially passed on through Solomon. Jesus sits here as David's promised Son on David's promised throne. This fits Old Testament imagery as well. The idea of sitting describes the idea of rule, as the parallelism of Jeremiah 22:30 shows. As the Davidic heir, Jesus sits in and rules from heaven.

Peter's treatment raises hermeneutical questions. The Davidic throne and the Davidic covenant were perceived largely in the Old Testament and in the infancy material as including an earthly, political position (2 Sam.–2 Chron.; Luke 1:46–55, 70–73).[21] Does this nonearthly connection in Acts constitute a denial of that older connection? Acts 3 supplies detailed answers to the question, but the reference in Acts 2 to the Day of the Lord suggests where things are headed. Peter is warning his audience that a program is in motion that concludes with the coming of the Day of the Lord (v. 20). Such a day was predicted in the Old Testament and involves the visible, earthly demonstration of God's authority on earth. As such, the earthly character of Jesus' rule is not eliminated by what is asserted here. Rather, that assertion reveals a development of the picture of Jesus' career much like the apostolic realization that the Messiah would accomplish all of his work in two comings, not one. As such, the Petrine association of Psalm 110 with the Davidic promise is not a hermeneutical leap that ignores Old Testament expectation but is part of the function of the progress of Christian understanding about what God was doing through Jesus. That revelation makes the stages of the program clear. What is asserted here does not exclude what had been promised in the Old Testament, nor should it be separated from what the Old Testament promised. Peter's use of Psalm 110 is an explanatory addition to the Davidic promise that initially fulfills that promise.

One may object that the throne at the right hand of God is not the Davidic throne, which is earthly. The objection might be raised by appealing to a text like Revelation 3:21, where Jesus distinguishes between "my throne," on which the overcomer will sit, and the Father's throne, on which Jesus currently sits. The argument is made that the throne on which Jesus sits in Acts is the Father's throne, not David's.

---

[21]However, also note that Luke 1 associated the raising up of the Davidic horn with spiritual elements through an appeal to imagery from Ps. 132:17. Luke 1 and Acts 2 are linked conceptually. In addition, Ps. 89 with its declaration that the promised Davidic son would bring justice and righteousness makes clear that a spiritual element is an essential part of this promise. This is reinforced by several prophecies in Isaiah (9, 11), Jeremiah (23, 33), and Ezekiel (37) that predict the righteousness of the future Davidic king. The last passage links his reign to the fulfillment of the spiritual characteristics of the new covenant.

It should first be pointed out that "throne" is a pictorial description for rule, and that the allusion to Jesus' sitting next to God is an allusion to the promise of Psalm 110, a Davidic promise. Hebrews makes the point that Jesus is already a priest according to the order of Melchizedek as a result of this seating through exaltation. Now how can one allow the fulfillment of Melchizedekian priesthood for the present age from Psalm 110 and then deny the present rule of Jesus, which is also tied to the language of the same psalm? Consistency demands that both texts be fulfilled in Jesus' first coming, especially when the rule that Peter specifically alludes to in Acts 2 is through the regal image, not the priesthood image. Peter establishes the Davidic connection by linking Psalm 110 to Psalm 132 and thus to 2 Samuel 7. Actually, the distinction of thrones in Revelation is not a distinction but an equation. The rule is extended from the Father to the disciple through the Son, the one who in Revelation 3:7 says he *has* "the key of David."[22] Further confirmation of a lack of distinction comes in the Old Testament, where Solomon, as Davidic king, sits on the Lord's throne (1 Chron. 29:23; 2 Chron. 9:8).

The handling of Psalm 16 and Psalm 110 confirms something about the approach taken with Joel 2. Both of these Old Testament texts from the Psalter are seen beyond any doubt as presently fulfilled in the Resurrection, with Psalm 110 fulfilled at least in terms of inauguration. Peter goes on to declare that this Lord (Jesus) sits by God's side until all enemies are a footstool for the Lord's feet, something that is yet to be fully realized. So inauguration is present, but consummation is not. As such, the fulfillment of Psalm 16 and Psalm 110 makes it inherently likely that Joel 2, with its reference to the gift of the Spirit, is also seen as fulfilled. All three Old Testament texts in this passage point to fulfillments in the death and resurrection of Jesus and to events that follow this decisive hour, even though two of these passages also possess unfulfilled elements.

There also is corroboration of the Davidic covenant connection in a later speech in Acts. In Acts 13:34 Paul alludes to promises made to David and given to the people. The citation is Isaiah 55:3, which alludes to the Davidic covenant. In the exposition that follows, resurrection and justification through faith are noted as part of the benefits associated with that Davidic promise. The book of Acts shows both Peter and Paul making allusion to Davidic promise as they declare the offer of salvation in Jesus Christ. Efforts by some to deny any Davidic covenant allusions tied to the first coming of Jesus fail because of the Acts 2:30 use of

---

[22]Revelation texts will be treated in detail later.

Psalm 132, the use of Isaiah 55 in Acts 13, and the summary of the career of the Davidite in Luke 1:68–79.

How are salvation benefits tied to Davidic promise? The continuing exposition of Acts 2 makes the connection clear. The climax of the Acts 2 speech is the citation of Psalm 110. Peter declares in verse 33 that the Resurrection has led to the seating of Jesus at God's right hand, where he also has received and has poured out the promise of the Holy Spirit. In fact, the audience is observing the results of that exaltation in the activity of his disciples. The Resurrection, promised in Psalm 16, has led to the fulfillment of Psalm 110 and its promise that a descendant of David would sit at the side of God. This seating shows Jesus to be not only Christ but Lord (κύριος, "Lord," is the key title and is in the emphatic position in v. 36). What is crucial here is that Psalm 110 is a regal psalm that depicts the Davidic king seated and ruling beside God. The heavenly seating of Jesus is presented as an initial yet certain fulfillment of the Davidic promise and is a presupposition to the right to bestow the Spirit in accordance with the new-covenant promise. Salvation benefits of the "last days" (v. 39) are present. Thus, Acts 2 shows the same linkage of the Davidic promise with salvation benefits as found in Acts 13. As he rules at the side of God, Jesus is the one placed in authority over salvation benefits, and as such he has the title *Lord*. There is no interlude period in view here, only the beginning of the realization of God's salvific promises through the ruling hand of Lord Messiah Jesus. Just as the fulfillment of Psalm 110 and Psalm 132 is the fulfillment of regal expectations, so the confession of Jesus as Messiah is a regal confession. Efforts to suggest that Psalm 110 is fulfilled but that this fulfillment points only to a priestly, Melchizedekian priesthood cannot be accepted for Acts 2, since all the imagery here is regal and therefore is presented in terms of Davidic promise. It is a connection that goes back in Luke-Acts to Luke 1:31–35 and is restated in the very name Jesus Christ—that is, Messiah, or Anointed One, Jesus. Psalm 110 is regal and messianic because that is exactly how Jesus introduces it in Luke 20:41–44, when he asks a question about David's Son, "the Christ," whose more appropriate title is "Lord," as the use of Psalm 110 imagery in Luke 22:69 and in Acts 2 shows. It is the Psalm 132 allusion, which clearly brings in the promise of 2 Samuel 7, that clarifies Peter's declaration as a Davidic inauguration. He sees the inaugural fulfillment of the Psalm 132 promise in the events interpreted in the language of Psalm 110 (vv. 30–36). In fact, the title *Messiah* makes the establishment of an inaugurated Davidic rule clear, for what else is the presence of the rule of the Anointed One but the inauguration of a promise to David (Pss. 2, 89, 132)?

The new title of Acts 2—Lord—is also at the heart of Lukan

Christological confession. In both volumes Luke demonstrates that Jesus is not only the promised Messiah, he is Lord with authority over salvation. Such authority allows salvation to be offered in his name (Luke 24:47), baptism to occur in his name (Acts 2:38), and apostolic healing to occur in his name (Acts 3:6). The claim of such authority is what caused him to be crucified (Luke 22:69). In fact, in Luke 22 Jesus told his accusers that "from now on" he would be seated, functioning as the exalted Lord at God's right hand. In the movement of Luke-Acts, Acts 2 represents the culmination, vindication, and demonstration of the truth of Jesus' claim.[23] The two images of salvific and judgment authority indicate the executive Davidic rule that Jesus exercises. They are regal, Davidic functions. The images show that elements of his current rule extend over all people.[24]

This authority and rule are at the heart of Jesus' career in the "already," or "sneak preview," kingdom. Jesus' rule is present in the salvation benefits he bestows as part of the initial phase of his rule. The kingdom is invisible in the sense that he does not rule over every person directly, but in those who share in the benefits he offers, especially in the provision of the Spirit. Those who share the Spirit show the influence of God in the world and reflect his work on earth, both in his powerful transformation of them and in their love toward those around them. They are a kingdom alongside other kingdoms, and the two realms are not to be confused. Jesus works in and through those who belong to his kingdom. Nevertheless, elements of Jesus' lordship are eventually made universal in this age in the remarks of Acts 10:34–43, as the blessings are clearly shown to include Gentiles. But Jesus rules from heaven, not earth, and thus the kingdom is invisible only in the sense that the rule does not originate visibly from earth. And yet this invisible kingdom, lacking a visible king, is a "sneak preview" kingdom in that this new community is to show God's active power in the transformation of sinners from sin to righteousness (1 Cor. 1:18–25; Rom. 1:16–17). The transformation previews what the consummate rule of righteousness and justice for all in the coming phase of the kingdom will be like. Thus there is continuity with the future kingdom in the present kingdom, though there is a distinction in the visibility of the King in the two phases of the reign and in the fact that the current kingdom lacks political, nationalistic elements. This "preview" is visible

---

[23]For more on Jesus as Lord in Acts, see D. Bock, "Jesus as Lord in Acts and the Current Gospel Message," *BSac* 143 (1986): 146–54; and idem, "A Review of *The Gospel According to Jesus*," ibid. 146 (1989): 33–34. On the Lukan treatment of Ps. 110, see Bock, *Proclamation from Prophecy and Pattern*, 128–32; 139–43; 181–86.

[24]Other Acts texts where the kingdom is seen as present are 8:12; 14:22; 19:8; 20:25; 28:23, 31.

only in the Spirit-indwelt community, whose mission it is to reflect that divine activity as light in the world (Matt. 5:14–16).

Jesus rules in the present kingdom over the whole earth, but it is not yet a full, direct rule over every person (Heb. 2:5–8), nor does it reflect its future political, sociological character. And yet as Acts 2 suggests and other passages make clear, Jesus does have authority over every person now, for those who do not join him will one day face him as Judge. Then Jesus will visibly demonstrate and assert the rule he now has (Acts 10:42–43; 17:30, an allusion to the Day of the Lord). Thus Jesus' ruling authority, though not fully visible to all, is demonstrated in the reality of his exaltation and in the message to repent. All will have to deal with the returning Jesus. In this limited sense, he rules all people now, but this rule really anticipates his later rule. When people respond, they enter into the new community, which is the realm where Jesus' active, current rule is most manifest in the mediation and powerful work of the Spirit. The idea of a realm that presently extends over all the earth, and alongside of it, makes this formulation of the "already, not yet" kingdom different from Ladd's view, which emphasized the dynamic character of the rule without discussing a realm.[25] The view of the kingdom defended here is not covenant premillennialism, for two reasons. First is the way this form of dispensationalism sees the kingdom's present realm. It still defers many aspects of Old Testament promises to the future kingdom. Second is the way it portrays the fulfillment of the Old Testament as described in Acts 3, a fulfillment that reintroduces Israel into the culmination of the divine plan. However, the kingdom's presence now makes it clear that God's kingdom exists in the midst of the kingdoms of earth.

On the basis of Jesus' current authority over all, Peter makes his emphatic call to the crowd to repent and be baptized in the name of Jesus Christ (Acts 2:38). Salvation's benefits are so totally in Jesus' hands that sacred rites are now carried out in his name. Those who would come to God must come through Jesus. The Lord on whom one must call to be saved (Joel 2 and Acts 2:21) is Jesus, the Lord at God's right hand (Ps. 110 and Acts 2:34–36). Jesus' ascension elevates him to the point where what was said of Yahweh in the Old Testament can now be said just as easily about Jesus! The vindication is complete, and the rule of the Lord Christ over salvation benefits is absolute. That is the character of the "already," invisible kingdom Peter describes in Acts 2, a rule that fulfills in an inaugural way both the Davidic and the new covenants. Thus, Acts 2 details in what sense the kingdom is present,

---

[25]G. Ladd, *The Presence of the Future* (Grand Rapids: Eerdmans, 1974).

and it explains how the claims of its presence in Luke's gospel are to be understood.

One more question about the current kingdom remains. When did it begin? The Gospels and Acts are not clear on this point. Certain passages such as Luke 11:20 declare its presence in the power that comes with the healings performed by Jesus and his disciples. Acts 2 ties it explicitly to resurrection-ascension. The key to the answer is that it is the presence of Jesus that brings the kingdom. The Gospels picture a *transition* period with its display of authority (Luke 11:20). These displays show Jesus' current authority and the presence of fulfillment. But the benefits that are really tied to the kingdom and to Old Testament promise do not come until the Spirit is bestowed after Jesus' ascension (Acts 2). In the Spirit comes the real inauguration of new-covenant blessings that display regal authority, benefits that required Jesus' death and resurrection to be realized. The kingdom's power and blessing are not given fully to manifest the transformation and deliverance of people until after the Resurrection. The ambiguity of Luke's gospel is the ambiguity of a program in transition, but it is a transition in continuity with God's promise.

But what of the rest of the program? How will the rule of the Lord Christ continue? What of the issue of restoration and Israel, which the disciples raised in Acts 1? Acts 3 answers these remaining questions and places the resolution in Jesus' future career, which will be visible to all the earth.

ACTS 3: THE "NOT YET" REIGN

Peter's speech in Acts 3 is largely a presentation of Jesus from the perspective of the Torah. After invoking the God of Abraham and the patriarchs (Acts 3:13), he reviews Jesus' career and declares Jesus' authority as the source of the healing that has just occurred (vv. 14–16). At the end of the speech, three Old Testament texts are cited: Deuteronomy 18:15; Leviticus 23:29; and Genesis 12:3 (Acts 3:22–26). For the sake of his Jewish audience, Peter focuses his remarks on what for Jews was the most fundamental portion of the ancient Scriptures: the Torah. He makes his case for Jesus from this central unit. But in the midst of the exposition, Peter excuses their past action (v. 17). He invites them to respond to Jesus, offering as a basis for their response what God has done and will do through Jesus. The prophets said that the Christ would suffer, and in fact this has been fulfilled (Acts 3:18). After calling the people to repentance (v. 19), Peter outlines Jesus' remaining career in three parts: the coming of periods of refreshing, the sending of the appointed Jesus, and the necessity of heaven receiving Jesus until the promised times of restitution come (vv. 19–21).

The key to unraveling the order of these events is found in the last phrase, ἀποκαταστάσεως (restoration), for it recalls a term present earlier in Luke-Acts. In Acts 1:6 the verbal form of this term, ἀποκαθιστάνεις, appears when the disciples ask if this is the time Jesus "will restore" the kingdom to Israel. In the LXX, this verb ἀποκαθίστημι is a technical term for God's political restoration of Israel (Ps. 16:5; Jer. 15:19; 16:15; 23:8; 24:6; Ezek. 16:55; 17:23; Hos. 11:11).[26] In fact, a second term appears in Acts 1 that also links it to Peter's remark here. The Acts 3:21 term, χρόνων (times), appears also in Acts 1:6. The term is in the singular in Acts 1 and looks at a specific point of time and the arrival of a specific event.[27] The disciples' question in Acts 1 concerned whether the present is the time for the kingdom's restoration to Israel. Peter states in Acts 3 that the "times" of "restoration" are associated with Jesus' return. In fact, heaven holds him until this time comes. Putting the two texts together, it appears that Peter learned from the ascension event of Acts 1 that Jesus would restore the kingdom to Israel at the time of his return. Thus, there is the reference in Acts 3:21 that with the return come the times of restoration in fulfillment of all that the prophets taught. The technical term ἀποκαταστάσεως along with the reference to all of Old Testament promise confirms this understanding.

Carroll's otherwise fine study errs here. He distinguishes between a restoration about which God had spoken and a restoration of things promised, so that the phrase refers to what is happening now in the church, which is the "restored Israel." In his view Acts 3:21 refers to a promise of restoration without including the actual things as described in the Old Testament. Yet this division of sense seems very unlikely. Why refer to Old Testament promise from the prophets and *exclude* the actual contents of what they said?[28] In other words, what the Old Testament promised for Israel still remains in God's plan and in the execution of the Lord Christ's kingdom program. The derivation of ἀποκαταστάσεως from the technical term ἀποκαθίστημι along with the tie between Acts 3:21 and Acts 1:6–11 form the basis for this interpretation.

Given this understanding, the earlier expression of Acts 3:19, "the periods of refreshing," could refer to the current period. Sins can be

---

[26]J. Carroll, *Response to the End of History: Eschatology and Situation in Luke-Acts* (Atlanta: Scholars Press, 1989), 146, n. 124.

[27]W. Kurz, "Acts 3:19–26 as a Test of the Role of Eschatology in Lukan Christology," in *SBL 1977 Seminar Papers,* ed. P. Achtemeier (Missoula, Mont.: Scholars Press, 1977), 309–11, discusses the singular and plural distinction in detail.

[28]Carroll, *Response to the End of History,* 145–47.

wiped away as "refreshing" takes place through repentance. In other words, the times of refreshing is a distinct time before the times of restoration. Again, there is confirmation of this distinction in Acts 1:6–7. While the disciples ask only if the time of restoration for Israel has come, Jesus replies in verse 7 that neither the periods nor the times are for them to know. In other words, Jesus speaks of two categories of time in place of the one in their inquiry. Not only does Jesus refer to χρόνους (times) but also to καιρούς (seasons) in verse 7. In Acts 3:20, the phrase chosen is καιροὶ ἀναψύξεως (seasons of refreshing). Again a term Jesus used earlier is repeated in Acts 3. In other words, the last days of fulfillment have two parts. There is the current period of refreshing, which is correlated to Jesus' reign in heaven and in which a person shares, if he or she repents. Then at the end of this period Jesus will come to bring the restoration of those things promised by the Old Testament. Peter does not predict when Jesus will come, but with his return will come the second period of fulfillment, the times of restoration. This is a time when promises made to Israel are completed, as the linkage between Acts 1 and 3 shows.

While the overall thesis of this chapter is not dependent on it, the observation that Luke has specific terminology fitting the twofold breakdown enhances the argument previously given. The terminology appears to be unique to Luke among New Testament authors.[29] Among the points in support of this distinction is that in the LXX translation by Symmachus, a reference to the descent of the Spirit in Isaiah 32:15 uses the term ἀνάψυξις (refreshment), a term related to the one in Acts 3:20.[30] We already noted Carroll's argument that both phrases in Acts refer to the present. As was also noted, this conclusion seems to go against his own findings about the terms of the Acts 3 passage. But as Carroll notes in commenting on Lane's analysis of Acts (which he rejects), "It would not substantially alter the lines of interpretation of Acts 3:19-21," since it is clear that two fulfillment stages are present in Luke's mind.[31]

Carroll's own reason for rejecting a future reference in either of these

---

[29]This breakdown of the Acts 3 phrases is supported by William Lane, "Times of Refreshment: A Study of Eschatological Periodization in Judaism and Christianity" (Ph.D. diss., Harvard University, 1962), 164–86. A variation of this view appears more recently with detailed defense by P. F. Feiler, "Jesus the Prophet: The Hidden Portrayal of Jesus as the Prophet Like Moses" (Ph.D. diss., Princeton University, 1985), 81–90. He sees "the times" as the period extending to the Parousia rather than referring to the period after the Parousia. He sees fulfillment coming before the Second Coming. I see it coming with the return.

[30]Lane studied these phrases in detail ("Times of Refreshment"). His view and others are discussed in detail in Carroll, *Response to the End of History*, 141–51.

[31]Carroll, *Response to the End of History*, 148.

phrases comes from his perception of the eschatological pattern of Luke-Acts. Carroll believes Luke regards the return as a clean break in the eschatological calendar, what Carroll calls an eschatological separation. It is a break because the return is set off by cosmic events and includes a total redemption of believers. Consequently for Carroll, the return is not an inauguration of an era of restoration but is the end of the eschaton. But is "eschatological separation" Luke's view, if the eschatological kingdom can be said to be coming with the Son of Man's return in texts like Luke 17:23–37, especially when such a text is placed next to a text that says the eschatological kingdom is present (Luke 17:20–22)? Or is this view correct, when Peter cites in Acts 2 the current outpouring of the Spirit as part of the "last days" in a passage that also refers to still-future cosmic signs of the yet-to-arrive Day of the Lord? It is clear that the kingdom comes in two distinct, *but related,* phases, which can be considered either together or separately, depending on the passage in question. The total separation of the "already" from the "not yet" is wrong, as is the attempt to mix them completely together, whether this error focuses exclusively on the present or exclusively on the future.

Regardless of how one views "times" and "seasons" and the correctness of a distinction between the phrases, the verbal linkage between Acts 1 and Acts 3 is important because it shows that the disciples learned the answer to their question about Israel's restoration when the promise of the return of Jesus was given in Acts 1:11. The nation will share both in the end and in the program of the Lord Christ. God will honor his promises to Israel, but for individual Israelites in the first stage of the program to share in the second stage as well as in the benefits of the first stage, they must repent. Acts 3:23 with its use of Leviticus 23:29 shows that the threat of individuals being cut off is real. Avoiding judgment depends on people's responding to the prophet to come, who is Jesus. They are to respond to his message as given through his witnesses, the apostles. Blessing in the total two-stage program of Jesus' rule depends on their turning to him (v. 26). The kingdom of God comes in two stages, and the second, visible stage will involve the restoration of the nation and the completion of God's promises to it.

This two-stage view and the possible distinction in the Acts 3 phrases may also explain why in Luke 21:24 Jesus calls the current period "the seasons of the Gentiles," using the terms καιροὶ ἐθνῶν to refer to the present era. The Luke 21 passage suggests that to regard χρόνους and καιρούς as synonyms in Acts 1 and 3 will not work.[32] Putting Luke

---

[32]This is the one error in Kurz's approach—that there is one period in view with various terms to refer to it; see Kurz, "Acts 3:19–26," 309–11.

21:24 with Acts 1:6 and with Acts 3:19, we see that καιρός, *when applied to eschatological periods,* is used consistently to refer to this first period. These texts represent the only eschatological uses of these terms in Luke-Acts, which is a key limitation in examining their use.

Even if this terminological argument of Acts 3 is not correct, there still is corroboration in Luke-Acts of the picture of Israel's continuation. In the context of the Last Supper we find a remark unique to Luke. Jesus says, in Luke 22:15–16, that he will not eat *the Passover meal* with the disciples until "it finds fulfillment in the kingdom of God." This reference to fulfillment (πληρωθῇ, "it is fulfilled") refers to the completion of the promise, the consummation. The kingdom in Jesus' remark is definitely future and consummative. And yet there is a reference to the Passover meal, an Israelite feast, at the eschatological banquet table, since the Passover is the only possible contextual referent for the pronoun αὐτό in Luke 22:16. Jesus' remark suggests some type of continuing memorial meal in the kingdom. An allusion to the "Lord's Table" is not meant here, for such an allusion is entirely lacking from the Lukan context, and the parallel remark about the fruit of the vine in Luke 22:18 also employs eschatological banquet imagery (Isa. 25:6–7; 64:3; 65:13–14; Ezek. 32:4; 39:17–20).

One other point about Acts 3 needs mention. In Acts 3:25–26, reference is made to the opportunity for sons of the covenant to share in the promise of blessing made to Abraham. In Acts 3:25, Peter cites the promise of Genesis 12:3 as expressed in its repeated form in Genesis 22:18. In Jesus comes the call of the Abrahamic covenant. Abrahamic blessing through Jesus is the argument of Acts 3:26 with the term εὐλογοῦντα (blessing) linking up with the term ἐνευλογηθήσονται (they will be blessed) from the citation in verse 25. Blessing comes to the audience, not through physical lineage, but through turning to the one who has authority to give blessing. With the allusion to the Abrahamic covenant, all three major covenants receive mention in either Acts 2 or Acts 3. Jesus' career represents the opportunity for individuals to share in the fulfillment of all of God's promises, a fulfillment set forth in clear distinct stages and yet a fulfillment that is presented as a package. God's promises and his kingdom program are both "already" and "not yet," as well as "unity in diversity."

In Acts 3, Peter clearly sets forth a two-stage fulfillment in the last days. Acts 2 highlights the present activity of the reign of the Lord Christ. Acts 3 mentions both the present and future stages in detail. Old Testament promise has not been replaced; it has been opened up, clarified, expanded, and periodized in the progress of apostolic reflection on Jesus' teaching and actions. In Acts 2 and 3, the apostolic preaching shows the presentation of God's covenant promises. They stand fulfilled or, more precisely, inaugurated in Jesus. He initiates their inauguration and will bring their ultimate consummation—better, culmination—as God brings the program of his rule to completion in the fulfillment of promises to Israel.

The use of the term *consummation* with both phases of this program, though it may be difficult for some to grasp, is appropriate simply because the consummation comes in two parts. The current kingdom phase is an *initial phase* of consummation, but it does not exhaust the promise of God. The *culmination* of God's promise, which is the ultimate consummation, comes with Jesus' return to earth, the restoration of Israel, and the display of Jesus' total authority over the entire earth.

Again, ambiguity in the use of the term *consummation* reflects the ambiguity of the two-stage presentation of the kingdom, a program that was not postponed but was always coming in two phases. That postponement is not the view of the New Testament is clear from its reading of Isaiah 53. Isaiah 53 predicted that "his own" would despise the Servant. If the Servant is Jesus the Messiah, then "his own" must refer to the expected rejection of the nation. The possibility of the nation's establishing the kingdom in Jesus' first coming is excluded according to this reading of the Old Testament.[33] The death and resurrection of Christ was seen as consistent with Old Testament expectation (Luke 24:44–47; Acts 2:23). The return of Christ was juxtaposed with the repentance of Israel (Acts 3:18–21). The kingdom has come and will come. Israel has rejected the Servant, but one day the nation will come home.

However, the appearance of delay does exist, since the ultimate culmination does not come in the current phase. When it became clear through New Testament revelation that Jesus would accomplish God's program in two stages, not one, the appearance of parenthesis could not be avoided, since the Old Testament placed the events of these periods side by side. The expectation had been that the Chosen One would bring all fulfillment in one coming. But one of the promises not integrated into the current expectation, not even by the disciples, was that the Messiah-Servant would be rejected by his own people. When one pulls apart what had appeared to be together, the gap in between the two parts inevitably looks like a parenthesis. Having made this caveat on parenthesis and delay, we nevertheless should be clear that Jesus was always coming with the kingdom, as an early passage such as Luke 4:14-30 makes clear (note also vv. 42–44). The offer of the kingdom came. This can be seen in that its fundamental benefit, the

---

[33]In fact, it seems that in Gal. 3 the Mosaic covenant is the parenthesis.

Spirit, came (Luke 3:15–17; Acts 1:6–8; 2:30–36). The offer was not withdrawn, but it did have heretofore unannounced elements in it as certain parables make clear.[34] The kingdom program of God was progressively revealed, and some of that progress came in the life and ministry of Jesus and in the period of the apostles. In this revelation, what the Old Testament meant was made clear, and some new elements of the program were also introduced.

THE REIGN OF JESUS AS DAVIDITE IN REVELATION

How does the Lukan portrait of Jesus' current role compare with that given in Revelation? Here I survey only two themes: kingdom and Davidic association. Only those passages that clearly describe Jesus' current status are considered, since any references tied to the consummative kingdom could be regarded as exclusively future.

The first text is Revelation 1:5–6. Here two points are made. First, Jesus is called "the ruler of the kings of the earth." This expression is an allusion to Psalm 89:27, a psalm about Davidic kingship and covenant. There is some discussion whether this description relates to the future or to the present. Clearly, the other two titles in this passage refer to the present period: the faithful witness and the firstborn from the dead. But the idea in Revelation 1:6 that Jesus has made us a kingdom helps to resolve the matter. The action in this verse is past, as the aorist ἐποίησεν (he made) makes clear. The text ties the kingdom to Jesus' love and our liberation from sins by his blood. The passage closes in Revelation 1:7 with the remark that he will return, demonstrating his authority against all those who pierced him. The guilty will wail on his return. What emerges is a two-stage rule: a kingdom now, and a future manifestation of judgment authority. The remark about the kingdom has a conceptual parallel in 1 Peter 2:5 and 9, though the term is not present. The point made here is like that of Matthew 28:18, where all authority resides with Jesus, who has formed a community through which he provides spiritual blessing. This is the first stage of the kingdom program. Nonetheless, the demonstration of full authority still awaits his return. The psalm allusion is key and adds to the evidence of Acts 2 and 13 that Davidic authority is applied to Jesus' work in his first coming.

Revelation 1:9 is similar in force. Here John writes to those who share with him in tribulation, kingdom, and patient endurance, three characteristics of the current period. As they await the full consumma-

---

[34]That is, the parables on the mysteries of the kingdom (e.g., Matt. 13; Mark 4; Luke 13:18–21).

tion, they are suffering for their identity with Christ, but they must also be assured of their place in God's program.

Another text that confirms the idea of total, bestowed authority to Jesus is Revelation 2:27. This text addresses those who overcome the false teaching in Thyatira. In verse 26 John promises future power over the nations as a reward for faithfulness. Jesus notes that such a reward will allow them to shepherd the nations with a rod of iron, a figure for ruling, judging authority. The power that the disciples will yield is like that Jesus *has already received* (ὡς κἀγὼ εἴληφα) from the Father.[35] This language recalls Revelation 1:5–6, Matthew 28:18, and Luke 10:22. The allusion to the power that can shatter earthen vessels recalls Psalm 2:9, a psalm about regal authority in the Davidic, messianic line. That is the authority of the overcomer in the future, which is like Jesus' authority from the Father now. Again, the visible demonstration of this power is yet to come, as Revelation 19:15 makes clear. Ruling authority is held *already* by Jesus, but it is *not yet* distributed to saints. That distribution awaits his return.

The fourth key text is Revelation 3:7. Here Jesus refers to himself as "the one who has the key of David," a phrase that contains a present participle (ὁ ἔχων, "the one who has"). This is *currently held* Davidic authority. The reference to the key is an allusion to Isaiah 22:22. There Eliakim as the chief steward has the key to the door and determines who enters and who is prevented from entering to see the treasures of the king. In Revelation 3:8–12 Jesus uses the same image. Jesus is able to open and shut the door of access to him, where he gives the crown of reward, a place in the city to come. The language of the keys also recalls Matthew 16:19. The key seems clearly to allude in part to spiritual blessing, but it also looks ahead to an ultimate place in the new rule in the new Jerusalem.

A crucial text is Revelation 3:21. Here the one who conquers is granted the right to sit on Jesus' throne, just as Jesus *conquered and sat down* (ἐνίκησα καὶ ἐκάθισα) with his Father on the Father's throne. Both of these verbs are aorist. The victory and the seating to rule are both past. This passage fits the other overcomer texts in promising future blessing to disciples on the basis of the present authority of Jesus. The picture of victory probably alludes back to the remark of John 16:33. The image of sitting on the throne is clearly an image of rule, and the description of being seated next to the Father accords with the language of Psalm 110, a messianic psalm. The previous texts in Revelation make it clear that this is an already-bestowed authority. Furthermore, this throne of the Lamb, set next to the Father, is alluded

---

[35]Note the perfect tense here. The authority already exists.

to again in Revelation 22:1. This is the same throne that Jesus occupies in the consummation! He exercises Davidic rule now, even as he will exercise it then.

Some dispensationalists attempt to avoid the force of such passages by comparing Jesus' rule now to that of David during the period of Saul. The argument is that Jesus has authority now but he does not exercise it, just as David was anointed king but did not rule until after Saul was slain. In addition, kingdom rule means coersive rule. In this view, Jesus sits passively *until* all enemies are subdued, and then he will rule. God acts in the meantime to submit the enemies to Jesus so Jesus can "coersively rule" in the future. But both arguments ignore important points. Jesus *is* at God's right hand; he is not in exile! The imagery of Psalm 110 is the imagery of installation, and the picture of Jesus seated with God pictures *currently shared rule*. It is correct to say that Jesus has not subdued all of his foes yet, since that is something that comes in the return. But the point about "until" is that the process of subjection goes on until it is completed, not that Jesus is passive on the throne waiting on the Father and doing nothing in the meantime. Jesus is neither passive nor inactive from his right-hand throne, as the many texts in Luke-Acts and Revelation show. Just because the verb for "rule," βασιλεύω, is not used of Jesus does not mean the concept is absent. Numerous other images clearly make the same point.

It also is not correct to argue that Psalm 110 refers to a heavenly throne that is distinct from the Davidic, earthly throne. In the Old Testament, these were equated (1 Chron. 29:23; 2 Chron. 9:8). Neither can one argue that the heavenly throne in Revelation 3 and Acts 2 is not Davidic. Such a distinction fails to recognize the continuity of these references to Davidic passages and their connection to events associated with Jesus' first coming, including events immediately after the Resurrection. Psalm 110 is itself a Davidic promise. Jesus links its realization to the resurrection-ascension (Luke 22:69; Acts 2:30–36). However, one other point is also crucial. Davidic images are also linked to events associated with consummation and ultimate fulfillment (Jer. 23:5–6; Ezek. 34:24–28; Rev. 19:11–16). Again, there is continuity in the kingdom reign but also distinction. Old Testament promises are ultimately fulfilled in the "earthly" terms in which the promises were expressed in the Old Testament. In fact, consummation ultimately unifies heaven and earth, so that the fulfillment occurs throughout the entire creation. The Davidic authority is now exercised in spiritual provision and blessing, but this does not exhaust the Old Testament promise. Days are coming when Jesus will consummate the promise with earthly rule and vindication. Both the hopes of present believers and the promises made to Israel come to fruition then. The Davidic throne and the heavenly throne of Jesus at the side of the Father are one and the same, but there are two stages to the rule from that throne. In this way, the earthly character of Old Testament promises made to Israel is maintained, even though their scope is broadened in the context of New Testament mystery and fulfillment. This is the portrait of Jesus' reign that emerges when one puts together the language of Acts 3:21 with Revelation.

One text remains—Revelation 5:5—and it corroborates the interpretation of present Davidic authority in the previous texts of Revelation. John weeps because there is no one worthy to break the scroll. One of the elders steps forward and tells John to stop weeping because there is one worthy to open the scrolls. It is the Lion of the tribe of Judah, the Root of David, who *has conquered* (ἐνίκησεν). He was victorious. Again the verb is aorist. The victory, or at least the decisive act, has already occurred. He is qualified to open the scrolls and the seals because of what he has already done as a Davidite. The allusions here are also key. Most see Genesis 49:9–10 as the basis of the title *Lion from Judah* and Isaiah 11:1, 10 as the allusion for the term *Root of David*. In Judaism, the Testament of Judah 24:5 uses the lion image with messianic force, as does 2 Esdras 12:31, so the allusion is clear to anyone who knows Jewish expectation. Romans 15:12 has language like Isaiah 11, where Jesus' return is described as a time when the Root of Jesse shall come and rule the Gentiles. The timing of Revelation 5:5 is crucial, since it precedes the seal judgments and the second coming, so the text shows Jesus has his regal victorious status before he returns in Revelation 19.

The portrait of these Revelation texts is consistent. Jesus rules now in spiritual-salvific terms, in a new community that is part of the kingdom program, and in a way that inaugurates Davidic promises. That kingdom exists alongside the kingdoms of earth and suffers tribulation at those kingdoms' hands, as it awaits the completion of the redemption that the King brings. So Jesus' current rule also anticipates consummation, when God delivers the rest of Old Testament hope. The believers' call in this period is to be faithful until the end. Jesus' future return brings a period when believers now and the plan for Israel are simultaneously vindicated. In it comes the visible demonstration of Jesus' universal rule. The authority of that rule is shared with those allied to Jesus. In the language of Acts 3:21, it is the time when Jesus brings "the times of restoration of all things, of which God spoke through the mouth of his holy prophets of old."

SUMMARY

The reign of Jesus Christ in the plan of God is a key concept, although a complicated one. In the gospel of Luke, it is clear that with Jesus' presence, and especially his Resurrection-Ascension, comes the beginning of Jesus' kingdom rule. The assertions of Luke's text make this evident. The nature of that kingdom rule is not really developed in Luke's gospel except that it represents the defeat of Satan and comes with the presence of Jesus. But in Acts 2 and 3, the picture of Jesus' career and rule becomes clearer. The kingdom theme reveals the stages of Jesus' rule. The covenant promises are a part of his rule. They stand inaugurated through Jesus' exaltation to heaven, which in turn leads to the distribution of the Spirit as marking the coming of God's promise. Acts 2 and 3 show a single "last days" plan laid out in two distinct stages.

First, there is an inauguration with Jesus' coming and particularly in his resurrection-ascension to God's right hand. The inauguration is not an exhaustive presence of the kingdom but looks to the ultimate consummation to come. In the initial phase, one can speak of the "already," the "sneak preview," or the "invisible" kingdom rule of Jesus. The Spirit is sent to those who believe and shows evidence of Jesus' authority to distribute the new-covenant blessings. The new covenant itself stands inaugurated, but not totally consummated. Jesus' rule from God's right hand initially yet decisively fulfills promises made to David. Jesus exercises salvation authority as people are baptized now in his name and as they call directly on him to be saved. The hope of Abraham is realized as some turn from their sins to the Servant whom God has sent. The rule of the invisible kingdom is God's rule in the Spirit through the Son in a new people gathered in a new community. Those who believe now are a picture of what will appear in grander form in the consummation. They portray in part what God will do then. Those who refuse are still subject to the Lord Christ, for they will answer one day for their rejection (Acts 10:42–43; 17:30). Jesus rules even now over all people in that salvation can be found only through him. As such, the promises are realized, and yet they still await fulfillment.

Thus the new community, the church, is the showcase of God's present reign through Messiah Jesus, who inaugurates the fulfillment of God's promises. The church is a new institution, begun at Pentecost, as Acts 11:15 shows.[36] It is a sneak preview of what is to come. Jesus reigns from heaven invisibly but powerfully, transforming people through his Spirit. Jesus also reigns in that his exaltation gives him claim and sovereignty over all. All must ultimately answer to him. He invites all

---

[36]The church's newness is also declared in Eph. 2:14–18 in the image of the new man.

into God's kingdom, where promises are beginning to be realized, a kingdom that functions *distinct from* and *in the midst of* the kingdoms of earth. The current phase of the kingdom has continuity with the kingdom to come, because it shares the call to reflect the activity and presence of God's righteousness in the world.[37] Such benefits come for the one who trusts Christ. If people now are to see God at work and humankind living in righteousness and in love, they will see it in the church, where the Spirit is the active expression of Jesus' rule. The church's mission is the expression of love and righteousness not only to its own but to all those who are in need, the "tax collectors and sinners" of the world. Jesus' own example shows the way. The pursuit is not one of secular power. The church does not seek to match the world blow for blow. Rather, moral presence and influence are shown in a life that humbly recognizes that it is dependent on the grace and forgiveness of God through the Lord Christ. So the church lives accordingly. Suffering comes with this identification with righteousness and with the effort to reflect Jesus in the world. Suffering can be endured in the face of weakness, because the Spirit is at work. The church's call and mission is to be a light and point the way to God both in its message and in the caring activity of its daily life. As well the church is to manifest his transforming presence in the moral life of its people. Confusion about the identity of the kingdom, its subjects, and its nature leads to confusion about the church's mission and mandate. Nonetheless, such is the picture of an already present kingdom that also is described in Revelation, where the Davidic note is struck even more forcefully.

In the second stage, the promise moves to ultimate consummation. Acts 3 alludes to a future visible rule. When Jesus returns, he will do all that the prophets of the Old Testament promised. The language chosen specifically ties itself to the concept of Israel's restoration, which is an element that is totally absent in the current activity of Jesus. Certain political, earthly expectations tied to Israel, such as those expressed in Luke 1 and Acts 1, are in view here. There is no indication that earthly and Israelitic elements in Old Testament promises have been lost in the activity of the two stages. In the "not yet," visible, consummative kingdom, Jesus will rule on earth. He will rule before and over all. He will rule with justice. He will restore Israel's role, as that is a characteristic of the period. He will do it as he fulfills all that the prophets have promised and as he evidences the faithfulness of his

---

[37]The two phases of the kingdom program make it clear that the church is not all there is to the kingdom. Rather, it is an institution that is a part of the kingdom program, a program that involves more institutions than just the church. In the kingdom to come, various institutions associated with the Millennium and the eternal state will be the vehicle for kingdom rule.

sovereign grace, both in his promise to all nations and in his promise to Israel.[38]

This two-stage program of kingdom-covenant fulfillment is pictured in the speeches in Acts 2 and 3. The Resurrection-Ascension is central to the plan of God and the reign of the Lord Christ. The book of Revelation confirms the picture in its various Christological statements made to the seven churches and in its heavenly proclamations about Jesus. The key to the picture is found not in a particular term but in a mosaic of concepts brought together so that a clear portrait of God's plan emerges. A careful study of the Lukan linkage of various key promise-fulfillment concepts shows that it is in Jesus that kingdom, rule, promise, and covenant come together in two clear complementary stages as Old Testament hope and New Testament realization are united without loss. In the diversity of the manifestation of rule, there is unity in the completion of promise.

---

[38]The concern to preserve God's grace and the certainty of his promise has always been central to dispensationalism and is one of the strongest elements of its approach to eschatology. It is because of God's faithfulness that promises to Israel are maintained, even though past dispensational efforts to preserve such promises have underestimated the continuity that such promises have with the current era.

CHAPTER 2

The New Covenant and the People(s) of God

Bruce A. Ware

Evangelical biblical scholars and theologians uniformly affirm that the new covenant constitutes a high point in God's redemptive and restorative program. At the heart of the new covenant is the relentless determination of a loving and gracious God to make of his people what he has called them to be. Upon examination, there can be little doubt that in speaking of the new covenant, biblical writers intended to engender hope, faith, and a longing for holiness in the hearts of God's people.

Despite this recognition, however, several questions remain. For example, what is the nature of this new covenant? Why is a *new* covenant needed? What relation exists between the old covenant and the new covenant? What is new about the new covenant? How will this new covenant be implemented? With whom is the new covenant made? Do Israel and the church both participate in the *same* new covenant? If not, what new covenant is spoken of by Jesus, Paul, and the writer to the Hebrews in the New Testament? But if so, in what way or ways do Israel and the church participate in this same new covenant? What implications might this have for our understanding of the relation between Israel and the church? When is the new covenant's anticipated fulfillment or realization? Does the New Testament teaching on the new covenant lead us to conclude that the new-covenant promises of the Old Testament are fully realized in the New Testament church? How might our conception of the people of God be informed by our understanding of the new covenant?

While each of these questions will need to be given some consideration in the process of our discussion, the purpose of this chapter is to devote particular attention to the new covenant as it relates to Israel and the church, and to do so by focusing most directly on (1) the nature of the new covenant, as given to Israel, and (2) its fulfillment or realization in relation both to Israel and the church. The main hope is that this exploration might arrive at a biblically responsible and clear understanding of the new covenant. Beyond this, though, the desire is to contribute to the formation of a framework within which we can think responsibly about the continuity and discontinuity between Israel and the church as both entities relate within the one people of God.

To accomplish this purpose, we must start with the new covenant as prophesied and envisioned in the Old Testament. I first inquire concerning the parties of this covenant, its nature, and its anticipated fulfillment. Following this, I examine the new covenant from a New Testament perspective, discussing particularly the cross of Christ, the sending of the Holy Spirit, and the new covenant's application to the church. Finally, I explore the meaning of the new covenant in relation to the broader biblical notion of the people of God.

THE NEW COVENANT IN OLD TESTAMENT PERSPECTIVE

Only one Old Testament text—Jeremiah 31:31–34—specifically mentions the new covenant that God promises to make with his people. But despite the absence of the precise phrase *new covenant* elsewhere in the Old Testament, the concept is clearly expressed in several texts. On this point, Kaiser comments:

> Based on similar content and contexts, the following expressions can be equated with the new covenant: the "everlasting covenant" in seven passages [Jer. 32:40; 50:5; Ezek. 16:60; 37:26; Isa. 24:5; 55:3; 61:8], a "new heart" or a "new spirit" in three or four passages [Ezek. 11:19; 18:31; 36:26; Jer. 32:39 (LXX)], the "covenant of peace" in three passages [Isa. 54:10; Ezek. 34:25; 37:26], and "a covenant" or "my covenant" which is placed "in that day" in three passages [Isa. 49:8; 59:21; Hos. 2:18–20]—making a grand total of sixteen or seventeen major passages on the new covenant.[1]

Kaiser is surely within legitimate bounds to cite these texts as pertaining to the new covenant spoken of in Jeremiah 31:31–34,[2] and yet we must,

---

[1]Walter C. Kaiser, Jr., "The Old Promise and the New Covenant: Jeremiah 31:31–34," *JETS* 15 (Winter 1972): 14. It appears that Ezek. 16:60–63 could rightly be added to the passages Kaiser gives under the category of "my covenant."

[2]Others have also cited several Old Testament texts in addition to Jer. 31:31–34 as examples of new-covenant passages. See, for example, H. D. Potter, "The New Covenant in Jeremiah XXXI 31–34," *VT* 33 (1983): 349; William J. Dumbrell, *Covenant and Creation: A Theology of Old Testament Covenants* (Nashville: Nelson, 1984), 164–200; Homer A. Kent, Jr., "The New Covenant and the Church," *GTJ* 6 (1985): 290–92; and Thomas E. McComiskey, *The Covenants of Promise: A Theology of the Old Testament Covenants* (Grand Rapids: Baker, 1985), 89–91.

as Kaiser also argues,[3] give primary consideration to the basic text of Jeremiah 31, incorporating other passages into our discussion as we progress. Three questions in particular need to be addressed: With whom is the new covenant made? What is the nature of the new covenant? And when is the anticipated fulfillment of the new covenant?

Parties of the New Covenant

Jeremiah 31:31 reads:

> "The time is coming," declares the LORD,
> "when I will make a new covenant
> with the house of Israel
> and with the house of Judah."

Two important observations need to be made here. First, it is clear from Jeremiah 31:31 that Yahweh promises to make a new covenant with *all* of Israel, that is, "with the house of Israel and with the house of Judah." Spoken at a time when the nation of Israel was divided into northern and southern kingdoms (Israel and Judah, respectively), and just a few years before the Babylonian exile of the southern kingdom, this pledge to make *one* new covenant with Israel *and* Judah indicates God's determined purpose to see the divided nation of Israel once again reunited as a single people. Israel and Judah are envisioned as bound under one new covenant with their God and hence bound together as his united people, so that the words will (finally!) be true, namely, "I will be their God, and they [Israel and Judah together] will be my people" (Jer. 31:33).[4] Concerning this union, Dumbrell observes:

> The twin reference to the existing geographical divisions of Israel and Judah in [Jer. 31] v. 31 recognizes the realities of the present national position or the position as it has existed since the division of the united kingdom into two entities after the death of Solomon. The new covenant will heal this breach and we thus have here a parallel to the view of Ezekiel (Ezek. 37:15−28) that in the new age the two houses of Judah and Ephraim (i.e. Israel), will be joined together by a divine grafting operation which will make them one. The point that Jeremiah is making here is a common exilic emphasis. There can be only one

---

[3]Kaiser, "Old Promise," 14.

[4]For earlier biblical indication of God's intent that he be Israel's God and they be his people, see, for example, Gen. 17:7−8; Ex. 6:7; 19:5−6; Lev. 26:12; Deut. 4:20; 7:6; 14:2; 26:18−19; 29:13; and 2 Sam. 7:22−24. And for this theme elsewhere in Jeremiah, see Jer. 7:23; 11:4; 24:7; 30:32; 31:33 (quoted in the text); and 32:38. For additional discussion and biblical references, see Walter C. Kaiser, Jr., *Toward an Old Testament Theology* (Grand Rapids: Zondervan, 1978), 33−34.

people of God and this concept will be exhibited in an inner harmony which will transcend the present geographical divisions.[5]

Here we need to explore the nature of Israel's and Judah's reunification as one people of God under the new covenant. An appropriate and important question to ask is, On what basis can a divided nation be extended a single covenant that will function to unite them again as one people of God? Most likely, our immediate response would be that their former united national identity serves as this basis. After all, God chose *Israel*, not Egypt, Babylon, Assyria, or any other nation. And God pledged himself to Israel in a manner unlike his commitments to any other nation. Surely, then, it is right to point to Israel's national identity as that which accounts for the extending of a covenant reuniting what never should have been divided.

Although the above consideration is no doubt true, it is nevertheless incomplete. For we need also to ask concerning this divided Israel: What brought about the national division that is healed under the new covenant? And here we see immediately another dimension that needs to be included.

The breach within Israel began as the people increasingly distanced themselves from their covenant God, notably with their desire to have a king over them "like all the nations" (1 Sam. 7:5, 19–20). This request displeased God greatly because it indicated a rejection of him in favor of human kings. As is clear from Israel's history, it was their sinfulness of heart producing a breach of covenant with their God that led, in due time, to the breach in their national union. But if the breach of national union results from a breach of covenant, then the remedy becomes clear. In order for God once again to unite his people, they must exhibit covenant faithfulness and so keep from the sin that resulted in their division. Under the one new covenant, then, God would so bind the people of Israel to himself and his law that they would, as a consequence, no longer and never again, break covenant with him. Thus, as a faithful people, they would again be a united people, under a new covenant promising fidelity toward God and hence fidelity toward one another.[6]

Second, an obvious observation, but one that raises serious questions about the application of the new covenant to the church, is that the new covenant of Jeremiah 31:31–34 is extended to Israel and Judah, not to

---

[5]Dumbrell, *Covenant and Creation*, 176.

[6]See Werner H. Schmidt, " 'People of God' in the Old Testament," *TD* 34 (Fall 1987): 226–31, for a defense of the view that what constitutes "the people of God" most importantly in the Old Testament is not ethnic identity but religious fidelity to the God of Israel.

71

any other nation or group. Other new-covenant passages, inside and outside of Jeremiah, also direct this new covenant to the people of Israel in a similar manner. For example, the "covenant of peace" of Isaiah 54:10 is clearly made with Zion, as is the "everlasting covenant" of Isaiah 61:8. Ezekiel 11:18–21 addresses its promised transformation to the captives of Judah who will return from Babylon, while Ezekiel 18:30–31 and 36:22–32 speak to the house of Israel; Ezekiel 34:25 and 37:26 are set in contexts describing the renewal of the rulership of David. And within Jeremiah, we see in 24:7 a promise of a new heart to be given to the captives of Judah in their return, whereas 32:36–41 and 50:4–5 speak of Israel and Judah (parallel to 31:31), while mentioning particularly the city of Jerusalem.

Despite the evidence just cited for Israel as the people with whom God pledges his new covenant in Jeremiah 31, Beckwith calls to our attention that some see the new covenant primarily having to do with Gentiles, not Jews. He comments, "One fundamental innovation is often attributed to the new covenant, however: that it is made with a new people—not the believing Jews but the believing Gentiles. This in fact is not so."[7] In support of his position, Beckwith correctly observes: "God's choice of Israel is stated in the Old Testament to be irrevocable (Jer. 31:35–37; 33:23–26), and the predictions that it makes concerning a further covenant (Isa. 42:6; 49:8; 55:3; 61:8; Jer. 31:31–34; 32:40; Ezek. 16:60; 34:25; 37:26; Mal. 3:1) represent it as a covenant made with the same people as the covenants that preceded it."[8] Furthermore, Beckwith notices, Gentiles could become members under former covenants, and they certainly are envisioned as participating along with Israel in the new covenant[9]—and this, without precluding the establishment of the new covenant particularly and directly with Israel.

One new-covenant text that seems to suggest that whereas the new covenant is given particularly to Israel, it nonetheless extends beyond Israel to the nations, is Isaiah 55:3–5:

> Give ear and come to me;
> hear me, that your soul may live.
> I will make an everlasting covenant with you,
> my faithful love promised to David.
> See, I have made him a witness to the peoples,
> a leader and commander of the peoples.
> Surely you will summon nations you know not,
> and nations that do not know you will hasten to you

[7]Roger T. Beckwith, "The Unity and Diversity of God's Covenants," *TynBul* 38 (1987): 113.
[8]Ibid., 114.
[9]Ibid.

> because of the LORD your God,
> the Holy One of Israel,
> for he has endowed you with splendor.

The everlasting covenant spoken of here is specifically said to be an expression of God's love promised to David. Israel will have its leader and commander, as promised long ago to David. But there is an additional element in this text, for this new David, who rules under a new everlasting covenant, will also summon nations and peoples Israel does not know. So while the new covenant is uniformly (here and elsewhere in the Old Testament) directed to the nation of Israel, we see from this text that the new covenant made with Israel includes a host of Gentile participants, not directly addressed as God's covenant partners.

Nature of the New Covenant

The Hebrew word for covenant, בְּרִית, although of uncertain derivation, "seems usually to carry with it," according to Dumbrell, "the note of obligation, whatever else may be implied at the same time."[10] Or, as Thompson expresses in the *Encyclopedia Judaica,* a covenant is "a general obligation concerning two parties."[11] Others also highlight the central place of obligation in the Old Testament covenant concept. For example, McComiskey states:

> The basic idea underlying the concept of *bĕrît* is that of a relationship involving obligation. When that obligation is expressed in the form of intent, the intent may be effected unilaterally or bilaterally. Parties must be involved in the *bĕrît,* but there need not always be a mutual response. Other elements, such as confirmation and explication, may be found in covenants in Scripture, but this definition represents an effort to capture the common element of all the functions of *bĕrît* in the Old Testament.[12]

And Beckwith, similarly, states: "In Old Testament usage, a בְּרִית means a league of friendship, either between man and man or between God and man, solemnly inaugurated, either by words alone or by words and symbolic ceremonies, in which obligations are undertaken on one or both sides. The obligations are often accompanied by an oath, and have the character of solemn promises."[13]

---

[10]Dumbrell, *Covenant and Creation,* 16.

[11]Norma J. Thompson, "The Covenant Concept in Judaism and Christianity," *ATR* 64 (October 1982): 502.

[12]McComiskey, *The Covenants of Promise,* 63.

[13]Beckwith, "Unity and Diversity," 96. See also the article and extensive bibliography in Elmer B. Smick, "בְּרִית," *TWOT* 1:128–30.

Two observations can be made about this sense of obligation in the new covenant. First, this obligation is expressed in a definitive and direct manner by God to his people, as is evident in the various pledges he makes to them: "*I will* make a new covenant . . ." (Jer. 31:31); "*I will* put my law in their minds . . ." (v. 33); "*I will* be their God . . ." (v. 33); "*I will* forgive their wickedness . . ." (v. 34). There can be no question but that God purposely obligates himself for the fulfillment of this covenant. The obligation expressed here is of enormous proportion, and God alone is able to ensure that his newly expressed obligations will in fact be accomplished.

Second, it is also clear from this text that the expressed obligation is unilateral or asymmetrical in its direction. That is, it is directed from God to his people with no corresponding obligation expressed on the people's part toward God. As Dumbrell notes, "What is striking and what cannot be missed in Jer. 31:31−34 is the theocentric character of the new arrangement, to which our attention is directed by the sustained series of first person divine addresses during the course of the verses. From first to last the new covenant rests upon divine initiative, and is constituted solely by a divine pardon which permits a new beginning."[14] Now, to say that the obligation is on God's side alone does not mean that Israel is excluded from any role in the covenant. In fact, the opposite is the case. Israel has a crucial role to play, but it is the role of a recipient and beneficiary, not that of an initiator or benefactor. In the new covenant, *God will act* on behalf of his people, and *they will be benefited* by his powerful and gracious work. But let us not lose sight of the fact that the obligation here is assumed by God alone, so that when the new covenant is realized, there will be absolutely no question of who is to be credited with its marvelous accomplishment.

Having seen the unilateral nature of the obligation inherent in the new covenant, a pressing question faces us at this point: What constitutes the "newness" of the new covenant?[15] While there is not complete agreement on this question,[16] various writers discuss one or

[14]Dumbrell, *Covenant and Creation,* 174.

[15]See Werner E. Lemke, "Jeremiah 31:31−34," *Int* 37 (April 1983): 184, for a discussion of the two uses of the Hebrew word חָדָשׁ, "novel; renewed." It seems best to understand the newness of the new covenant as incorporating both of these senses together: in some respects it is novel (the law's internalization), and in other respects it is renewed (the law's continued but renewed validity). See below for further discussion of these and other related points.

[16]See, for example, James Swetnam, "Why Was Jeremiah's New Covenant New?" in *Studies on Prophecy,* ed. G. W. Anderson et al., VTSup 26 (Leiden: E. J. Brill, 1974), 111−15, in which Swetnam argues the unusual view that the newness of the new covenant "consists in the fact that copies of the Mosaic Law are officially to be made available wherever Israelites are to be found, and that these copies are to figure in a [synagogue] liturgy in which knowledge of the Law is directly communicated to all" (p. 115).

more of a small collection of elements. The proposal offered here is that four such elements, taken together, describe more fully the newness of this covenant and at the same time more accurately delimit its nature. These four elements, as seen particularly in Jeremiah 31:31–34, may be summarized as follows:

1. a *new mode* of implementation, namely, the internalization of the law ("I will put my law in their minds");

2. a *new result,* namely, faithfulness to God ("they will all know me");

3. a *new basis,* namely, full and final forgiveness ("for I will forgive their wickedness"); and

4. a *new scope* of inclusion, namely, covenant faithfulness characteristic of all covenant participants ("from the least of them to the greatest").

Given this summary, we need now to discuss each of these four aspects, devoting special attention to the first of them.

The New Mode

First, there is a *new mode* by which God's covenant with his people will be implemented and carried out, namely, through the internalization of the law. That is, the new covenant differs from the former Mosaic covenant in that under the new covenant God will internalize his law within the hearts and minds of his people; the Lord now says, "I will put my law in their minds and write it on their hearts" (Jer. 31:33). Weinfeld addresses this point.

> What, then, is the novelty in the future covenant? The principal novelty is, I believe, this, that the covenant is not written on stone but on their hearts. It is this that lies behind Jeremiah's dispute with the scribes of the torah of the Lord: "How do you say, 'We are wise and the Law of the Lord is with us'? . . . In vain has wrought the vain pen of the scribes" (Jer. 8:8). Against them Jeremiah contends that all that their pen has produced has been done in vain, if they do not fulfill what is written, it is as though the Law of the Lord were written in vain. The prophet demands *the Law which is in the heart* instead of that which is written on stone tables or in a book and put in, or by the side of, the ark (Deut. 31:26).[17]

---

[17]M. Weinfeld, "Jeremiah and the Spiritual Metamorphosis of Israel," *ZAW* 88 (1976): 28. Weinfeld is not alone in singling out the law's internalization as what constitutes the newness of the new covenant. See also Robert P. Carroll, *Jeremiah: A Commentary* (Philadelphia: Westminster, 1986), 611, where he writes: "This particular instantiation of *berit* interiorizes the divine *torah* in the minds of the people, and such interiorization may constitute the new element in *berit.*"

While it may be an overstatement to call the internalization of the law the principal novelty of the new covenant, certainly it is one of the key elements contributing to its newness. For although, under the old covenant, the people were to endeavor to know the law and make it part of their minds and hearts (Deut. 6:6; 11:18), still the placing of the law on their hearts was done at best partially, and that with only a small portion of Israelites (1 Cor. 10:5). The location of the law in Israel was identified most prominently with tablets of stone (Ex. 24:12; 32:15–16; 34:27–28) or with the book of the law (Deut. 17:18; 30:10; 2 Kings 23:2), not with tablets of human hearts.[18]

But how does the new-covenant promise that God would place his law in the hearts of his people differ from the old-covenant directive that they put it there themselves (Deut. 6:6)? To answer this question we should note the complementary yet differing description of God's new dealings with Israel as given in Ezekiel 36:24–32. Although Ezekiel does not mention a new covenant, he describes a future decisive and unilateral divine action resulting in the same faithfulness as described by Jeremiah 31 and other new-covenant texts. For all the similarities of these two passages, however, there are also some differences, most notably in that, where Jeremiah speaks of God's putting his *law* within the people (Jer. 31:33), Ezekiel speaks of God's putting his *Spirit* within them (Ezek. 36:26–27). Yahweh's pledge as recorded in Ezekiel 36:24–28 reads:

> For I will take you out of the nations; I will gather you from all the countries and bring you back into your own land. I will sprinkle clean water on you, and you will be clean; I will cleanse you from all your impurities and from all your idols. I will give you a new heart and put a new spirit in you; I will remove from you your heart of stone and give you a heart of flesh. And I will put my Spirit in you and move you to follow my decrees and be careful to keep my laws. You will live in the land I gave your forefathers; you will be my people, and I will be your God.

Notice that neither in Jeremiah 31 nor in Ezekiel 36 do we find a denunciation of the law as somehow defective, requiring a new law to replace the old. Instead we find, amazingly, that the same law is carried over or maintained.[19] The problem with the old covenant, then, is not the law; the problem, rather, is with the nature of those persons who are called to covenant faithfulness but who instead transgress the law. God's

---

[18]Lemke, "Jeremiah 31:31–34," 184.

[19]On the continuance of the law in the new covenant, see, for example, Kaiser, "Old Promise," 19–20; McComiskey, *The Covenants of Promise*, 84–85; Beckwith, "Unity and Diversity," 115–16; and Thompson, "The Covenant Concept," 513.

sure and certain remedy to this problem of covenant infidelity is to effect a fundamental transformation of human agents under the new covenant, and he does this as his Spirit indwells those covenant participants (Ezek. 36:27), making his law a very part of their inner life (Jer. 31:33). Weinfeld aptly describes the complementarity of the prophetic vision found in Jeremiah and Ezekiel:

> Ezekiel does not speak of "a new covenant" but of "a new heart and a new spirit," that is, in contrast to Jeremiah, for Ezekiel the nature of the covenant does not change, but man is given the preparation and the capacity to fulfil the statutes and ordinances of the (old) covenant. The result of the giving of a new heart and a new spirit is that "they may walk in My statutes, and keep My ordinances, and do them" (11:20), or in another version, and "I will . . . cause you to walk in My statutes, and you shall keep My ordinances, and do them" (36:27). On the other hand, for Jeremiah the covenant is new, that is, it undergoes a metamorphosis in that it is not written on tables and is accordingly not set down as a formal statute but is inscribed on the heart of each one. It is thus no longer based on formal statutes. And indeed while Jeremiah speaks of *putting the Law within them,* Ezekiel speaks of *putting the spirit within them* (36:27), for the law remains as before and only the spirit of man changes.[20]

Another issue needs to be addressed within our discussion of this first element of the newness of the new covenant. It has been suggested above that the remedy for the old covenant's failure is found in the internalization of the law through the giving of the Spirit, which implies, it would seem, that this giving of the Spirit will be something new. But is, in fact, the Spirit's presence in God's people, as described in Ezekiel 36, something different from their experience of the Spirit under the old covenant? Although a full answer to this question cannot be attempted here,[21] some observations need to be made, because the answer to this question affects our understanding both of the nature of the new covenant as given to Israel and also of the realization of that new covenant in the church.

Leon Wood has observed that, in the Old Testament, the Spirit is said to come upon four different categories of people: prophets, civil leaders, judges, and craftsmen.[22] For example, the Spirit came upon

---

[20]Weinfeld, "Jeremiah and Spiritual Metamorphosis," 32.

[21]This question is taken up in more detail in Bruce A. Ware, "Rationale for the Distinctiveness of the New Covenant Work of the Holy Spirit" (paper presented at the fortieth annual meeting of the Evangelical Theological Society, Wheaton, Ill., November 1988).

[22]Leon J. Wood, *The Holy Spirit in the Old Testament* (Grand Rapids: Zondervan, 1976), 39–52.

Azariah (2 Chron. 15:1−7), before he met Asa, to prophesy God's comforting word to him (similar statements are made of Zechariah, Balaam, Amasai, Elisha, and Micah). He came upon Moses, Joshua, Saul, and David to empower them in their leadership of Israel. He came upon Othniel, Gideon, Jephthah, and Samson to empower them to preserve Israel against foreign assaults. And the Spirit came upon Bezalel to empower his craftsmanship regarding the tabernacle.

An examination of the references in the Old Testament to the actual, historical work of the Spirit leads to the conclusion that the Spirit's work was marked by three characteristics. First, his coming upon people in the Old Testament was *selective*. That is, he did not come upon all the community of faith but just on a few selected individuals. Numbers 11 is especially instructive here. Moses was convinced that he could not on his own bear the burden of all the people, so God instructed him to gather together seventy elders (v. 16) whom God would empower with the Spirit that was presently on Moses (v. 17). After receiving the Spirit, two of the seventy prophesied in the camp, distressing others who were jealous for Moses' authority. But when asked to make them stop, Moses responded, "Are you jealous for my sake? I wish that all the LORD's people were prophets and that the LORD would put his Spirit on them!" (v. 29). This account suggests that God had given his Spirit only to a select few in Israel, that Moses was fully aware of this fact, and that he even pondered longingly what it would be like if all God's people had the Spirit. The fact is that whereas the Spirit is said to be present among or in the midst of God's people during the Old Testament era (Isa. 63:11; Hag. 2:5), there is no Old Testament teaching parallel to the New Testament reality of the promised indwelling presence of the Spirit within all who believe (Acts 2:38−39; 1 Cor. 12:13).

Second, his coming was *task oriented*. This is perhaps the most important of the three characteristics in that it accounts for the other two. The Spirit came upon selected persons in order to accomplish through them some task that required supernatural empowerment. Why would the Spirit come specifically on a Moses, Saul, or David? Why are we informed of his coming upon certain prophets, judges, or craftsmen? Presumably, the answer is that these were people with particular roles to play or tasks to perform (e.g., rule the people, speak God's word accurately, deliver from threatening enemies, construct the tabernacle with care and precision), and the accomplishment of their tasks as God intended required the empowering presence of the Spirit.

Third, the Spirit's coming was, in most cases, *temporary*. This generalization cannot be made with certainty, but the evidence inclines us in this direction. The clearest example of the temporary coming of the Spirit is in the case of Saul, who, after his sin, had the Spirit taken from him (1 Sam. 16:14). In all likelihood this occurrence prompted David, after his own sin, to pray, "Do not cast me from your presence or take your Holy Spirit from me" (Ps. 51:11). So, clearly for Saul and evidently for David also, the Spirit's presence was not necessarily permanent or guaranteed. Why is this so? The answer has to do with the task-oriented nature of his coming. The Spirit comes to empower the accomplishment of some task, and when that task has been done, it stands to reason that the Spirit would leave. Even where the Spirit resides more permanently, (e.g., with Elisha or Micah), it may be due to the task-oriented purpose of his coming.

It seems, then, that the picture we have in Ezekiel 36 of the coming of the Spirit represents something dramatically new. Our question whether the actual experience of the Spirit in Israel under the old covenant differs from the prophetic vision of the coming Spirit in Ezekiel needs to be answered with a resounding yes. As will be developed below, the prophetic vision overturns all three characteristics of the Spirit's work under the old covenant. His coming will no longer be selective, but as Ezekiel 36:27 indicates (cf. Joel 2:28–29), all covenant participants will be changed as they are indwelt with God's Spirit. His coming will no longer be merely task oriented, for the purpose of his future indwelling of all God's people will be to produce a new and unfaltering covenant faithfulness characterizing the whole company of God's people. And for such faithfulness to endure, the Spirit's presence likewise must endure. Consequently, the new covenant feature of the internalization of the law through the Spirit's permanent indwelling presence in all of God's people constitutes a central element of the newness of the new covenant.

The New Result

The second aspect of newness in the new covenant is the new result that the internal work of the Spirit produces, namely, a full and lasting covenant faithfulness to God and to his law. Commenting on Jeremiah 31:32, in which Yahweh is portrayed as a faithful husband in contrast to Israel and her infidelity ("they broke my covenant, though I was a husband to them"), Dumbrell writes:

> In short the element which will characterize the new covenant and thus render it "new" will be its irrefragability [*sic*]. It will not be new because of new conditions which Yahweh will attach to it, nor because it is the product of a new historical epoch, nor because it will contain different promises, for indeed those attached to the Sinai covenant could hardly have been more comprehensive, but what will make it new is that in the new age *both* partners will keep it. In that age there will be no possibility of the new arrangements being breached

unilaterally. Thus what is being said in this dialogue of continuity and discontinuity is that discontinuity takes its rise in the nature of the human problem, in the human inability to maintain the older Sinai arrangement. Nothing short of an inward and transforming arrangement, to which Jeremiah will now refer in vv. 33–34, will guarantee continued human fidelity within the new arrangement.[23]

Other new-covenant passages confirm this glorious truth, namely, that God's intervention on behalf of his wayward people will result in their full and abiding covenant faithfulness. Jeremiah 32:39–40 presents God as promising to his people, "I will give them singleness of heart and action, so that they will always fear me . . . , and I will inspire them to fear me, so that they will never turn away from me." In Ezekiel 11:19–20, God pledges to Israel, "I will give them an undivided heart and put a new spirit in them; I will remove from them their heart of stone and give them a heart of flesh. Then they will follow my decrees and be careful to keep my laws. They will be my people, and I will be their God." Ezekiel 36:22–23, which precedes the glorious promise of the new heart and indwelling Spirit, clearly states that because Israel had profaned God's name among the nations, they had absolutely no claim on God's blessing. But despite the magnitude of their sin, God had pledged himself to these rebellious people, and he would keep his promise to bless them, lest his holiness be compromised ("It is not for your sake, O house of Israel, that I am going to do these things, but for the sake of my holy name" [36:22]). It is in this context that God comes to remake these wayward rebels into his faithful and obedient people. By giving them new hearts and the indwelling Spirit, he fulfills his pledge to them not only that he would be their faithful God but that they would truly and fully be his faithful people, for he says that they will "follow my decrees and be careful to keep my laws" (36:27). The internalization of the law by the indwelling Spirit, then, has its necessary and comprehensive change in the lives of God's people, producing in them consistent and abiding faithfulness.

The New Basis

The third aspect is the new basis for the new covenant, without which any promised covenant faithfulness would be only a vain and empty dream. This new basis would be found in the full and final forgiveness of the sin that had rendered the old covenant unsuccessful and brought about the dire need for the new covenant. In the new covenant this

---

[23]Dumbrell, *Covenant and Creation*, 178. On this aspect of the new covenant's newness, see also Lemke, "Jeremiah 31:31–34," 184–85; McComiskey, *The Covenants of Promise*, 85–86; and Thompson, "The Covenant Concept," 512.

forgiveness is of inestimable value, for without it the promised internalization of the law by the Spirit and resulting unfaltering obedience would not and could not be established. For not only did the sin of the people need to be forgiven, but beyond that, it had to be removed altogether; for unless it is *removed,* then there can be no unfaltering or fully consistent faithfulness under the new covenant. Continuing sinfulness and unfaltering covenant faithfulness are mutually exclusive modes of human existence, and since the new covenant promises the latter (see again Ezek. 11:19–20 and 36:26–27), the former must be ended.

One reason for thinking that this radical forgiveness (involving the removal of the guilt of sin and of the sin itself) is envisioned by the new covenant is that forgiveness of sin's guilt was available under the old covenant. As Kaiser correctly observes, "God's gracious forgiveness was experienced by the Old Testament man."[24] He goes on to note that God announces himself "at least eight times as 'the Lord, a God merciful and gracious, slow to anger and abounding in steadfast love and faithfulness . . . forgiving iniquity and transgressions and sins' [Ex. 34:6, 7; Num. 14:18; Deut. 5:9, 10; Ps. 86:15; Joel 2:13; Jonah 4:1; Jer. 34:18; Neh. 9:17]."[25] Therefore, it would be wrong and completely unfair to an Old Testament understanding to conclude from the promise of forgiveness in Jeremiah 31:34 that forgiveness per se would be new.

Rather, it seems that what constitutes the newness here is that forgiveness reaches a new level extending beyond the former covenant. Whereas the old covenant clearly expected and required holiness on the part of God's people, it also assumed their failure to keep the law, for an elaborate mechanism (the sacrificial system) was placed within this former covenant to deal with various instances of disobedience. But amazingly, when one looks to the new covenant for a parallel mechanism for the ongoing removal of continuing sin, one finds *no such mechanism.* Why is this so? How can this be? It can only be due to the fact that God will base his new covenant not simply on the forgiveness of past sin and its guilt but rather on the removal of all sin in all its respects, ensuring then, by his Spirit, that there will be no further need for forgiveness once sin is fully and finally abolished.

One other key to the meaning of the forgiveness spoken of in Jeremiah 31:34 is the promise not to remember Israel's sin any more. Concerning this, McComiskey comments: "Jeremiah did not deny that sin was forgiven under the old covenant. The word used here for 'forgive' (*salah*) is used throughout the Old Testament. The great

---

[24]Kaiser, "Old Promise," 20.
[25]Ibid.

difference is in the fact that God will not remember their sin. It is this blotting out of sin that is a characteristic of the new covenant."[26] And Dumbrell writes that under the new covenant,

> a situation seems to be envisaged in which sin has been once and for all dealt with. No more action in the new age will be called for against sin, for, remarks Jeremiah, "I will forgive their iniquity, and I will remember their sin no more." That parallel statement is not simply the language of prophetic hyperbole nor merely a reference to the psychological attitude of God in the new age, namely that he will "forgive by forgetting" sin. It refers rather to the new age as one in which no action (in this biblical sense of remembering) needs to be taken against sin.[27]

The forgiveness that forms the basis for the new covenant is one in which not only past sins are forgiven but the very presence of sin as an ongoing reality is removed. For only then can God fulfill in its entirety his pledge that he will be their God (in complete faithfulness) and they will be his people (in a reciprocal expression of covenant faithfulness).

The New Scope

The final element of newness is a new scope of covenant inclusiveness under the new covenant, for the internalized knowledge of God that marks the transformed quality of new covenant life will be characteristic of every covenant participant, without exception. Jeremiah 31:34 resounds with hopefulness and expectation for the multitude in Israel who never experienced the indwelling Spirit and who felt the pain of covenant infidelity. The time will come when external instruction in the knowledge of God will be unnecessary, for "they will all know me, from the least of them to the greatest."

Potter sees in the statement "from the least of them to the greatest" (31:34) an implicit denunciation of those false teachers and prophets who abused their position and led the people astray.

> Jeremiah predicts that elitism will now cease. God will give direct, intuitive knowledge of his law; he will himself write it upon men's hearts, and no longer will others be able to falsify it. No one will teach it, no one will be able, by his superior expertise, to use it to his own advantage, no one will be able to claim mitigation through ignorance. . . . This then is what is new about the covenant: it will no longer be mediated by scribes and the elite, but will be universally

---

[26]McComiskey, *The Covenants of Promise,* 87–88.
[27]Dumbrell, *Covenant and Creation,* 182.

apprehended by one and all, for the greatest to the least. God and ordinary men are linked at last.[28]

Again, while it may be overstating the case to mark this as the primary new feature of the new covenant, it nonetheless does significantly distinguish this covenant from what precedes it. Other new-covenant texts pick up the same theme. For example, Isaiah 59:21 speaks of God's Spirit and words never departing from the people's mouths, nor from their descendants' mouths. While everlasting duration is the keynote here, it is also true that this text encompasses the whole of the people of God, descendants included (cf. Acts 2:39), as having God's Spirit and word. The promise of an "everlasting covenant that will not be broken" (Jer. 50:5) is given generally to the people of Israel and the people of Judah. There is no elitism here, no selectivity regarding those who experience the full benefits of the covenant. All together will seek the Lord and bind themselves to him under this grand and everlasting new covenant. Furthermore, we are within legitimate bounds to call to mind Joel 2:28–29 in relation to Jeremiah 31:34, for Jeremiah's "least of them to the greatest" is expanded conceptually in Joel to show that neither gender distinction ("your sons and daughters will prophesy"), nor age division ("your old men will dream dreams, your young men will see visions"), nor class differentiation ("on my servants, both men and women") precludes one from being a recipient of the eschatological Spirit. The new covenant will be an inclusive covenant in which *all* God's people experience the internalization of the law by the Spirit and so know him in utter faithfulness, with sins forgiven and removed forever and ever.

Anticipated Fulfillment of the New Covenant

Having investigated the nature and participants of the new covenant, we now need to inquire what, from an Old Testament vantage point, was the anticipated time and manner of the new covenant's fulfillment. This seems an important question in light of our desire to understand just what continuity or discontinuity exists between Israel and the church regarding the new covenant.

As to the time of the new covenant's fulfillment, it appears that the phrases "the time is coming" (Jer. 31:31) and "after that time" (v. 33) are purposely ambiguous.[29] Just a few chapters before this prediction, we see Jeremiah prophesying the seventy years that Judah would serve the king of Babylon (Jer. 25:11, 12). But here in Jeremiah 31, we are

---

[28]Potter, "The New Covenant," 353.

[29]Concerning the lack of time specificity conveyed in these phrases in Jer. 31:31 and 33, see Lemke, "Jeremiah 31:31–34," 183; and Dumbrell, *Covenant and Creation*, 174.

left with only the assurance that God will enact this covenant; we have no knowledge of the time of its fulfillment.

The manner by which the new covenant would be enacted has somewhat more specificity however. It seems clear that the promised new age, in which the new covenant would finally be realized, would come only when God's king would liberate Israel from its oppressors and when God's Spirit would inhabit the whole company of the people of God. Consequently, in Old Testament perspective, while the time of the new covenant's enactment was uncertain, one thing was certain, namely, that when God would bring to his people the promised spiritual transformation, it would also be accompanied by the promised physical, national, and geographic blessings (Isa. 11:1–16; 32:9–20; 42:1–9; 44:1–8; 61:1–11; Jer. 23:5–6; 30:4–11; 33:14–18; Ezek. 34:25–31; 36:24–38; 37:24–28).

THE NEW COVENANT
IN NEW TESTAMENT PERSPECTIVE

We now turn our attention to the question of what use the New Testament makes of the new-covenant theme from the Old Testament, and more particularly whether and in what manner it envisions the new covenant to be realized in some sense within the church. That the New Testament is aware of the new covenant is beyond dispute. As Homer Kent observes, "Explicit mention of the new covenant occurs six times in the New Testament [Luke 22:20; 1 Cor. 11:25; 2 Cor. 3:6; Heb. 8:8; 9:15; 12:24], although the thought is found more frequently than these few references."[30]

New-covenant distinctives may be seen especially in the two New Testament themes of the cross and the coming of the Spirit. It would be hard to imagine any themes more important or central to the overall teaching of the New Testament than these. At the heart of each of them is the new covenant, envisioned by the prophets in the Old Testament with reference to the physical seed of Abraham (the nation Israel) but applied in the New Testament, at least in a preliminary form, to the spiritual seed of Abraham, the church.

The Cross of Christ and the New Covenant

If the newness of the new covenant is marked by the full and final forgiveness of God's people and the internalization of the law by the Spirit who indwells each participant within the covenant community, then it becomes clear that the age of the new covenant arrives in the

[30]Kent, "The New Covenant and the Church," 292.

mission of Jesus. For in Jesus we see the eschatological Spirit-anointed Messiah (Luke 4:16–21) who comes to offer his life as a ransom for all (Mark 10:45), thus securing the forgiveness of sins on which the new covenant rests (Luke 22:20). And then in his resurrection Jesus inaugurates the new covenant when he ascends to the right hand of the Father, from which place he sends his Spirit (Acts 2:33) to indwell his followers (Gal. 4:6) and make them newly transformed persons (2 Cor. 3:18) who, by the Spirit, now keep the requirement of the law (Rom. 8:2–4). Or more simply, if the new covenant is based on forgiveness and implemented by the indwelling Spirit, then we see in Jesus the beginnings of new-covenant realization.

When Jesus says, "This cup is the new covenant in my blood, which is poured out for you" (Luke 22:20), it seems clear that he meant to link together the forgiveness required for the new covenant's enactment and his blood, which would be shed in order to achieve that forgiveness (cf. Matt. 26:28). Marshall suggests that for Luke, the contents of the cup "symbolizes the new covenant, in the sense that the new covenant is brought into being by what it signifies, namely the sacrificial death of Jesus."[31] While it may be too strong to say that the new covenant is "brought into being" by Jesus' sacrificial death, nevertheless these words must at least mean that Jesus' death for sin would provide the basis for the new covenant's enactment. As noted earlier, apart from full and final forgiveness of sin, the promised transformation of life and covenant fidelity would be illusory. There could be no other way for the desired forgiveness of sin to occur than by the coming of the eternal Word (John 1:1, 14) as the Lamb of God to take away the sin of the world (v. 29).

But was the forgiveness accomplished through Christ in fact full and final in nature? This question receives special attention in the epistle to the Hebrews. Peterson suggests that the new covenant plays into the argument of Hebrews in two main ways.[32] First, Jeremiah's new covenant is employed in 8:1–9:10 to establish the inadequacies and limitations of the Sinaitic covenant. That earlier covenant ultimately pointed beyond itself to a better covenant whose promises and enablements were superior. Second, and most important for our present discussion, the writer shows how Christ's offering for sin, once for all (9:12; cf. 10:18), made a full and final payment for that sin and so fulfilled the forgiveness required for the enactment of the new covenant. Peterson's own statement of this point deserves attention:

---

[31]I. Howard Marshall, *The Gospel of Luke: A Commentary on the Greek Text*, NIGTC (Grand Rapids: Eerdmans, 1978), 806. See also L. Goppelt, "ποτήριον," *TDNT* 6:153–54.

[32]David Peterson, "The Prophecy of the New Covenant in the Argument of Hebrews 8:1—10:18," *RTR* 38 (1979): 74–81.

By his single sacrifice for sins Christ has removed the necessity for the Old Testament sacrificial system, providing that definitive cleansing of the conscience or forgiveness which is the basis of Jeremiah's prophecy (10:17f.). By that cleansing of the conscience Christ consecrates his people to God in the relationship of heart-obedience envisaged by Jeremiah (9:14; 10:10, 22). By dealing decisively with the sin problem Christ has made it possible for those who are called to receive the promised eternal inheritance (9:15).[33]

Therefore, Jesus' teaching as recorded by Luke and the argument of Hebrews both clearly establish the point that Jesus' sacrifice for sin accomplished precisely what the new covenant required. Sin's guilt (Heb. 9:14–15) and its power (2:14), and indeed sin itself (9:26), were put away and ended through Christ's death. The path has been prepared; the basis of the covenant has been secured. What remains now is to bring about the internalization of the law, by the Spirit, so that, forgiven and empowered, God's people might walk in covenant faithfulness to him.

The Coming of the Spirit and the New Covenant

In the final period of Jesus' ministry before his death, he instructed his disciples about the coming Spirit. They had seen the Spirit work through him, and they knew his testimony that he ministered by the power of the Spirit (Matt. 12:28). But they also knew that they did not have the same eschatological Spirit.

That the disciples were not indwelt by the Spirit during Jesus' earthly ministry seems clear from at least two lines of thought. First, John records an occasion when Jesus stood at the last day of the great feast and said, "If anyone is thirsty, let him come to me and drink. Whoever believes in me, as the Scriptures has said, streams of living water will flow from within him" (John 7:37–38). John interprets this statement, saying, "By this he meant the Spirit, whom those who believed in him were later to receive. Up to that time the Spirit had not been given, since Jesus had not yet been glorified" (v. 39). John's comment parallels Peter's message on the Day of Pentecost, where he claims that the risen and exalted Christ, at the right hand of God, has sent forth the Spirit on those assembled believers (Acts 2:33). Evidently, then, the Spirit is not sent upon God's people in fulfillment of Old Testament promises (Ezek. 36:27; Joel 2:28–29) until after the death, resurrection, and ascension of Jesus. The disciples who followed him during the years of his earthly

---

[33]Ibid., 81. See also Roger L. Omanson, "A Superior Covenant: Hebrews 8:1–10:18, *RevExp* 82 (Summer 1985): 370, in which he writes: "Jeremiah 31:34 (Heb. 10:17) is the main point of the claim that Christ has established the new covenant. Sin has been forgiven; there is no longer any sacrifice for sin."

ministry, by virtue of their place in history before the cross and ascension, did not at that time have the indwelling Holy Spirit.

Second, what sense would it make for Jesus to predict the coming of the Spirit to indwell his disciples if they already had the Spirit? But Jesus does in fact encourage them with this marvelous promise of the indwelling Spirit: the Spirit "lives with [παρά] you and will be in [ἐν] you" (John 14:17). In one place Jesus even assures them that it is to their advantage or for their good that he depart (16:7). Just a moment's reflection on this statement will reveal how incredulous the disciples might well have been upon hearing this. After all, they had come to realize that Jesus was none other than the long-awaited Messiah, and surely their hopes were high for his ongoing ministry and work, culminating in the full establishment of his kingdom in Israel. But now he says that he is leaving them and that it is to their *advantage* that he go. How could this be? The answer Jesus gives can be appreciated and understood fully only from a new-covenant perspective. He explains, "Unless I go away, the Counselor will not come to you; but if I go, I will send him to you" (v. 7). The implication is that though they were believers in Jesus, the disciples did not have the Spirit in John 16. Furthermore, the time would come when they would be indwelt with the Spirit, and from Jesus' perspective, having the Spirit's presence, despite his physical absence, would only enlarge their capability and spiritual well-being.

The new covenant was not inaugurated by the ministry of Jesus in the power of the Spirit or by the mere fact of his atoning death. What was lacking was the internalization of the law, by the Spirit, in all of God's people. However, this lack is quickly supplied when we turn to Acts and the Epistles. Acts 1 shows the disciples still longing for Jesus to establish his earthly kingdom—a thoroughly understandable and legitimate longing, but one whose fulfillment is not in keeping with God's immediate purposes. Instead Jesus tells them to wait for the gift of the Father, which comes in the form of the eschatological Spirit. In Acts 2 the gift comes, and his coming is with power and is extended to all those who are present. One of the features of the new covenant is that *all* those in the community of faith participate in that covenant's eschatological power and blessings, and Acts 2 makes it clear that this feature has now begun to be realized.

We must be careful, however, not to see in Acts more than is intended by its author. Stronstad has ably defended the thesis that Luke's pneumatology stresses the charismatic and vocational empowerment of the Spirit, in contrast to Paul's emphasis on the Spirit's transforming power or his use of the Spirit's filling in Ephesians 5:18.[34] Instead, in Acts, Luke's view of the filling of the Spirit shows his continuity with the dominant Old Testament conception of the Spirit's role in empowering boldness in life and witness. But while this is true, it is also the case that Peter's use of Joel 2 in his Pentecost sermon, as well as the subsequent receptions of the Spirit by different groups (Acts 8 and 10 in particular), indicate Luke's view that the Spirit who has now come in power is for *all* who believe (cf. Acts 2:38–39).[35]

If Luke's stress is on the coming of the Spirit on all in the community of faith, a coming that exhibits itself in eschatological empowerment, what is the relationship Paul sees between the Spirit's coming and the new covenant? In fairness to each, we should say that Luke and Paul present different yet complementary emphases in their pneumatology. While Luke stresses the *quantitative* expansion of the Spirit's new-covenant work (on all who believe), Paul clearly underscores the *qualitative* expansion of the Spirit's new-covenant role (effecting transformed lives by the Spirit).

The most extensive treatment Paul gives of the transforming new-covenant work of the Spirit is found in 2 Corinthians 3. There Paul clearly contrasts the inferiority of the old covenant with the grand and glorious superiority of the new covenant. For example, the old covenant is decribed variously as "the ministry that brought death" (v. 7), the ministry "engraved in letters on stone" (v. 7), "the ministry that condemns men" (v. 9), and "what was fading away" (v. 11). In deliberate contrast to this stands the new covenant, described as "not of the letter but of the Spirit; for the letter kills, but the Spirit gives life" (v. 6), the "ministry of the Spirit" with greater glory (v. 8), "the ministry that brings righteousness" as of surpassing glory (vv. 9–10), and that which is much greater because it has "the glory of that which lasts" (v. 11).

The superior glory of the new covenant is seen in its transforming power to enable its covenant participants to live increasingly righteous lives through the Spirit. In 2 Corinthians 3:18 it is the Spirit who accomplishes our transformation into the likeness of Christ, from one degree of glory to another. It seems that Paul has combined in his

[34]Roger Stronstad, *The Charismatic Theology of St. Luke* (Peabody, Mass.: Hendrickson, 1984).

[35]An interesting issue, related to our discussion, is whether the coming of the Spirit in Acts 2 parallels the giving of the law on Mount Sinai. If so, it would show the parallel between the law written on stone in the old covenant and the law written on hearts by the Spirit in the new covenant. For discussion of this issue, see, for example, I. Howard Marshall, "The Significance of Pentecost," *SJT* 30 (1977): 347–69; and R. F. O'Toole, "Acts 2:30 and the Davidic Covenant of Pentecost," *JBL* 102 (1983): 245–46.

thinking the new-covenant promise of Jeremiah 31 (see 2 Cor. 3:6, where "new covenant" is used) with the promise of the coming Spirit from Ezekiel 36,[36] for it is clearly the ministry of the Spirit that enlivens and empowers the new covenant's effectiveness.

Although the term "new covenant" is not found in Romans 8:2–4, it seems that in this text Paul is describing a new-covenant reality insofar as he contrasts the impotence of the old-covenant law with the transforming power that comes through the Spirit. In Romans 8:3–4, Paul asserts: "For what the law was powerless to do in that it was weakened by the sinful nature, God did by sending his own Son in the likeness of sinful man to be a sin offering. And so he condemned sin in sinful man, in order that the righteous requirements of the law might be fully met in us, who do not live according to the sinful nature but according to the Spirit." Paul is affirming the simple fact that the law, though it is holy, righteous, and good (Rom. 7:12), cannot enable anyone to keep it. Empowerment for keeping the law comes by the Spirit.

While the law retains its holy position, Spirit replaces flesh as the operative principle of power in the new-covenant participant and renders lawkeeping (covenant faithfulness) an expected and real possibility. Deidun comments as follows on Romans 8:3–4:

> The emphasis given to ὁ θεός in v. 3 . . . indicates that what Paul sees as the novelty of the Christian's situation is the fact that *God* has now done what man's situation (his immersion in σάρξ) had rendered altogether impossible for him. This he does by giving the Spirit, which henceforth replaces the σάρξ as the principle of man's activity. Only when God himself becomes the well-spring of man's activity can this activity save him, for *only* God can please God (contrast Rom. 8:8 with Heb. 13:21), and only when God himself energizes man's moral activity at its source can man be said to be subject to God (cf. Rom. 8:7). *This,* for Paul, is the marvel of the new covenant. Other considerations are of secondary importance.[37]

Indeed, this is a marvel, and it is the marvel of the outworking of the new covenant, based on the full and final forgiveness of sins brought at Calvary, extended to all who believe, and operative through the indwelling and life-transforming power of the Spirit of Jesus.

But having said all this, we must address a remaining question: Is Paul's theology of the Spirit distinctive new-covenant teaching, or is

---

[36]See C. J. A. Hickling, "The Sequence of Thought in II Corinthians Chapter Three," *NTS* 21 (April 1975): 389; and F. F. Bruce, *New Testament Development of Old Testament Themes* (Grand Rapids: Eerdmans, 1968), 54–55.

[37]T. J. Deidun, *New Covenant Morality in Paul* (Rome: Biblical Institute Press, 1981), 202.

Paul merely using different terminology to describe what is in fact the continuous (Old Testament and New Testament) reality of the Spirit's indwelling and transforming power? Put differently, does Paul understand the Spirit's indwelling presence and power to be new and distinctive, or is he describing, in 2 Corinthians 3 and Romans 8, for example, a reality that has always been available to those in the community of faith?

Consider again 2 Corinthians 3. Is Paul describing here the life-giving Spirit as a reality not only present now but also present under the old covenant (but which, perhaps, was not utilized as it might have been)? Or does Paul contrast eras? Does the old-covenant reality possess the letter of a law that kills, devoid of the Spirit and his life-giving power, while the new-covenant reality involves the Spirit's presence and power for life and holiness? To answer this question, it is critical to observe whether Paul sets his discussion in a historical framework, indicating that things were formerly one way but now they are different, or whether the truth he proposes is valid under both covenants. When one looks at the text in this light, it seems clear that Paul does not mean to describe some transcovenantal reality but is clearly marking off what he says about the Spirit as distinctively new covenant in reference. If any doubt exists, it is removed in 2 Corinthians 3:7–11, where Paul describes the glory of the old-covenant ministry as fading away and the glory of the new covenant as surpassing that of the old and remaining.

And what of Romans 8:2–4? An important question for us concerns not only what Paul says about the power of the Spirit to do what the law cannot do on its own but also whether Paul is saying anything new here that would not have been true under the old covenant. When one considers this question, it appears that the truth he proclaims is distinctively new covenant and hence marks a significant change from the reality that existed under the old covenant. The historical or temporal framework of these verses indicates that what was the case covenantly is no longer the case. When Paul refers to "what the law was powerless to do," he clearly implies a past reality. But that past reality of impotence and lawbreaking has now ended. How is this so? God has intervened! He sent his own Son and condemned sin, in order that a new reality might now come into existence, namely, a reality of covenant faithfulness by the power of the Spirit.

The conclusion appears to be that Paul envisions a distinctively new role for the Holy Spirit, a role he did not play under the old covenant but does so now only since the coming of Christ to conquer sin. Furthermore, this role is fundamentally characterized in qualitatively new terms. The Spirit comes to do what the law could not do. He comes to bring his indwelling power for life, righteousness, and covenant fidelity (Rom. 8:4) transforming believers into the likeness of the sin-defeating and risen Christ (2 Cor. 3:18).

THE NEW COVENANT AND ITS RELATION TO THE PEOPLE OF GOD

Having explored the meaning of the new covenant from Old and New Testament perspectives, we now want to inquire what implication this understanding might have for our conception of the people of God. Should the New Testament application of the new covenant lead us to see an identity of Israel and the church? Or should we understand the new covenant spoken of by Jesus, by Paul, and in Hebrews as a different new covenant than that which was prophesied in Jeremiah? Or is there a way of conceiving of the one new covenant in relation both to Israel and the church that, on the one hand, distinguishes them from one another while, on the other hand, unites them as one people of God? What is the relation, then, between the new covenant and Israel and the church as people of God?

Israel, the Church, and One New Covenant

First, readers are perhaps aware of an earlier dispensational view, advocated, for example, by Chafer and at one time by Walvoord and Ryrie. According to this view, in order to maintain the distinction between Israel and the church as separate peoples of God, the new covenant promised to Israel was distinct from the new covenant enacted with the church.[38] Although this view was defended vigorously by its proponents,[39] it has been uniformly abandoned by dispensationalists (including Walvoord and Ryrie),[40] who recognized, as Blaising acknowledges, that such a two new covenants view "is really a defenseless position."[41]

Homer Kent offers a helpful summary of the reasons why contempo-

[38]For brief discussions of this part of dispensationalism's history, see Craig A. Blaising, "Development of Dispensationalism by Contemporary Dispensationalists," *BSac* 145 (July–September 1988): 277–78; and Kent, "The New Covenant and the Church," 297–98.

[39]See especially Lewis Sperry Chafer, *Systematic Theology* (Dallas: Dallas Seminary Press, 1947), 4:325 and 7:98–99; and Charles C. Ryrie, *The Basis of the Premillennial Faith* (New York: Loizeaux Brothers, 1953), 105–25.

[40]See Blaising, "Development of Dispensationalism," 278; Kent, "The New Covenant and the Church," 298; and Charles C. Ryrie, "Covenant, New," in *WBE* 1:391–92.

[41]Blaising, "Development of Dispensationalism," 278. In this discussion, Blaising also says, concerning this earlier view of two new covenants: "This writer knows of no dispensational scholar who holds it today" (278).

rary dispensationalists reject the two new covenants view in favor of the one new covenant of Jeremiah 31 applying both to Israel and the church.

> First, the normal way of interpreting the various references to "the New Covenant" is to see these as one New Covenant rather than two covenants with the same name and with virtually the same contents. Second, the crucial passages on the New Covenant in Hebrews are addressed to Christians. They may well have been Jewish Christians, but the essential fact is that they were Christians. Third, it is difficult if not impossible to maintain a consistent distinction between a New Covenant for Israel and a New Covenant exclusively for the church in the reference at Heb. 12:23–24. In that passage both the church ("church of the firstborn") and Old Testament saints ("spirits of just men made perfect") are related to the New Covenant, not two covenants. Fourth, Christ's mention of the New Covenant in the upper room discourse (Luke 22:20) would certainly have caused the apostles to relate it to Jeremiah 31. Yet Christ connected it with the symbolic bread and cup which he was instituting for the church. Fifth, the apostle Paul clearly connected the upper room instruction regarding the New Covenant to the practice of the Christian church (1 Cor. 11:25). He further called himself and his associates "ministers of the new covenant" (2 Cor. 3:6). Sixth, the discussion in Hebrews 8 argues that the title "New Covenant" implies a corresponding "old covenant" which is now being superseded. The Mosaic Covenant is the old one for Israel. If the church has a totally separate New Covenant, what is the old one which it replaces?[42]

It thus seems clear that this earlier dispensational proposal for understanding the relation of the new covenant to Israel and the church as distinct peoples of God under distinct new covenants is thereby rendered unacceptable.

Inauguration and Fulfillment of the New Covenant

Having rejected the view of the two new covenants, are we then left solely with the option of understanding Israel and the church as so strictly identified under *one* new covenant as to compose *one* undifferentiated people of God? This conclusion is premature. Between the two extremes of a strict distinction between Israel and the church (two new covenants and hence two distinct peoples of God) and a strict identity of Israel and the church (one new covenant and hence one undifferentiated people of God) there is a middle position that would suggest that Israel and the church share theologically rich and important elements of commonality while at the same time maintaining distinct identities. One

---

[42]Kent, "The New Covenant and the Church," 297–98.

of these elements of theologically rich commonality is their coparticipation in the one new covenant, on the basis of which they are united as one people of God. And yet, their distinct identities should be maintained insofar as we can legitimately distinguish clearly different manners by which that one new covenant is fulfilled.

Is it legitimate, however, to claim that the one new covenant is fulfilled in distinguishable ways with Israel and the church? This question depends on two other considerations. First, what do we make of the territorial and political aspects of the new-covenant promise that clearly states that God will restore Israel to its land in prosperity and productivity and unite it again as one nation (Israel and Judah) whose center of rulership is Jerusalem? Second, is the "already–not yet" eschatological framework correct in which promises of God are understood to be realized first in preliminary (inaugurated) and then in final (future) stages? While each of these considerations deserves separate extended discussion, we must at least make some comment here to show how these considerations can help address the question of the one new covenant's varied fulfillment with Israel and the church.

First, regarding the territorial and political aspects of the new-covenant promise, it seems incorrect to disregard these or to say they are fulfilled in some spiritual manner in the church. There can be no question that the prophets meant to communicate the promise of a national return of Israel to its land. To the extent that our hermeneutics are regulated by the principle of authorial intent,[43] we are given ample reason to accept this literal rendering of what God, through the prophets, originally promised to his people Israel. Furthermore, the New Testament view does not permit a spiritual absorption of the literal promises to Israel by the church. Concerning this, Taylor correctly asserts:

> Superficial logic has continued to argue that there is no more uniqueness for the Jew and physical Israel. Since it is said Christ has broken down the barrier between Jew and Gentile [Eph. 2:11–18], Israel's election is finished. But this is not the logic of the New Testament. Although there is only one way of salvation for both Jew and Gentile, the New Testament teaches that the Jewish people do still have a unique place in the *historical* working out of God's redemption of the world in Christ. Although the Old Testament Prophecies regarding Zion and Israel do have a spiritual meaning this does not mean they have lost their literal meaning. . . .

[43]See, for example, E. D. Hirsch, Jr., *Validity in Interpretation* (New Haven: Yale University Press, 1967).

> I would rather the Church did not use the non-biblical term "New Israel" to describe itself because its implication is that physical Israel is now finished and replaced by the Church, as if the first olive tree has been chopped down and replaced by a new one (*DISCONTINUITY*). The picture of Romans 11 is of the Church ingrafted through Christ into the one olive tree. Although the tree has lost some of its old branches they will be ingrafted again to the original tree. Through Christ then, the Church belongs to the "Israel of God" [Gal. 6:15–16] (a New Testament term). It is not the "New Israel."[44]

Since, then, neither Old Testament nor New Testament teaching would allow us to understand the territorial and political aspects of God's new covenant promise to Israel in anything other than a literal fashion, we must conclude that God will yet fulfill the new covenant with the nation of Israel, precisely in the manner prophesied by Isaiah, Jeremiah, and Ezekiel.[45]

But if this is so, how can the church—a multiethnic and multinational spiritual organism, not given any such promise of national identity or land possession—participate in this same new covenant given to Israel? The answer here requires an application of the other theological consideration mentioned above, namely the "already–not yet" eschatological framework.[46]

It seems clear, from our previous discussion, that biblical teaching best supports (1) the view that the New Testament envisions the same new covenant as spoken of in Jeremiah 31 as *applied to the church,* and (2) the view that God will one day fulfill his promise of the national restoration of Israel as part of the new covenant promise as *not applicable to the church.* How can these be reconciled? They are reconciled when we permit the fulfillment of such eschatological promises to take both a preliminary and partial ("already") fulfillment as well as a later full and complete ("not yet") realization. And such in fact seems to be the case in regard to the new covenant.

The preliminary nature of the new covenant's fulfillment can be seen in two ways. First, only the spiritual aspects of new-covenant promise are now inaugurated in this age; the territorial and political aspects,

---

[44]Howard Taylor, "The Continuity of the People of God in Old and New Testaments," *SBET* 3 (Autumn 1985): 14–15.

[45]See the chapters by Burns and Bock in this volume.

[46]For the development and use of this already–not yet framework of biblical eschatology, see, for example, Oscar Cullmann, *Christ and Time,* trans. F. V. Filson (Philadelphia: Westminster, 1950); idem, *Salvation in History,* trans. S. G. Sowers (New York: Harper & Row, 1967); George Eldon Ladd, *The Presence of the Future* (Grand Rapids: Eerdmans, 1974); idem, *A Theology of the New Testament* (Grand Rapids: Eerdmans, 1974); and Anthony A. Hoekema, *The Bible and the Future* (Grand Rapids: Eerdmans, 1979).

though part of God's new-covenant promise, await future fulfillment. The fulfillment of God's new covenant thus should not now be viewed as an all-or-nothing affair. Rather, it is best seen as partially realized now (spiritual aspects of forgiveness and the indwelling Spirit for all covenant participants) and later to be realized in its completeness (when all Israel is saved and restored to its land).

This conception of a present preliminary and future complete fulfillment of God's end-of-the-age promises should not surprise us. For this is precisely the pattern we see in the eschatological promise of the coming Messiah, who came, as history has now shown, first as the suffering servant and who will come again in the future as the reigning, earthly king over all. The already—not yet nature of the new covenant's fulfillment parallels the same two-stage manner of messianic prophetic fulfillment.

Second, an understanding of the new covenant's present preliminary fulfillment is necessitated by the fact of ongoing sin and disobedience in the lives of new-covenant participants. As has been shown above, the new covenant is distinguishable from the old covenant, in part, by its pledge to bring about consistent and unfaltering covenant faithfulness in the lives of its participants. Without this feature, the new covenant's superiority over the old would be greatly jeopardized if not lost altogether. But such obedience to the law clearly is God's promise and pledge and will be accomplished in its fullness.

Now, however, we live in an age of preliminary or inaugurated new-covenant reality in which forgiveness of sin has been secured and the Spirit's indwelling presence enables covenant faithfulness. The fullness of covenant fidelity, however, awaits the end of a process of growth in holiness, rather than occurring with its fullness at the present time. The obedience that is envisioned and promised in new-covenant texts such as Jeremiah 31:31–34 and Ezekiel 36:22–32 will certainly occur in the fullest sense that those passages require. But that fulfillment in its entirety occurs, not immediately when sins are forgiven in Christ, nor immediately when the Spirit comes with his indwelling presence and power, but rather at the completion of a process by which that forgiveness and that Spirit empowerment enable progressive growth toward the goal of complete covenant faithfulness. The goal will surely be achieved in the end. At the present, however, the struggle with the world, the flesh, and the devil goes on, but it does so with the resources of new-covenant provision to enable holiness and obedience not possible prior to the coming of Christ and the sending of the Spirit. New-covenant faithfulness is expected in the New Testament precisely because we participate by faith in Christ's defeat of sin (Rom. 6) and have now his enabling Spirit (Rom. 8:3–4). But such new-covenant faithfulness will occur fully only when Christ comes again and brings to completion the new covenant, which is now inaugurated in a preliminary way.[47]

How, then, does this recognition both of the territorial and political aspects of the new-covenant promise to Israel and of the already–not yet nature of the new covenant's fulfillment help in understanding how Israel and the church can participate in the same new covenant? The church (comprising believing Gentiles and Jews) participates in the essential spiritual aspects of the new covenant in the form of a preliminary or inaugurated realization of those covenant promises, while awaiting confidently the fullness of the covenant faithfulness that it will surely realize when Christ returns. Israel still awaits a future action of God whereby he will bring "all Israel" (Rom. 11:26), or the nation of Israel as a whole, under the provision of forgiveness of sin and Spirit-indwelling as well as territorial and political restoration that it will surely enjoy in their fullness when Christ comes again. Therefore, the same new covenant, because it contains spiritual as well as physical components, and because it is inaugurated partially first and fulfilled in its entirety later, can apply both to Israel and the church but does so in a form expressing differing manners of that application.[48]

Israel and the Church as the People(s) of God

Finally, how may our conception of the people of God be informed by the theology of the new covenant and its relation to Israel and the church as presented here?

The discussion above lends support for the conclusion that Israel and the church are in one sense *a united people* of God (they participate in the same new covenant), while in another sense they remain separate in their identity and so comprise *differing peoples* of God. (Israel is given territorial and political aspects of the new-covenant promise not

---

[47]See, for example, the present reality of 1 John 1:8–10 in contrast to the future reality of 1 John 3:2.

[48]The reader will notice how similar the proposal offered here is to the one presented in brief form in Ryrie, "Covenant, New," where he writes: "Concerning the Church's relation to the [new] covenant, it seems best understood in the light of the progress of revelation. Old Testament revelation of the covenant concerned Israel alone. The believer today is saved by the blood of the new covenant shed on the cross. All spiritual blessings are his because of this, and many of his blessings are the same as those promised to Israel under the Old Testament revelation of the new covenant. However, the Christian believer is not promised blessings connected with the restoration of the Promised Land, and he is not made a member of the commonwealth of Israel. He is a minister of the new covenant, for there is no other basis than the blood of that covenant for the salvation of any today. Nevertheless, in addition to revealing these facts about the Church and the new covenant, the New Testament also reveals that the blessings promised to Israel will be experienced by her at the second coming of Christ (Rom 11:26–27)" (392).

applicable to the church.) Israel and the church are in fact one people of God, who together share in the forgiveness of sins through Christ and partake of his indwelling Spirit with its power for covenant faithfulness, while they are nonetheless distinguishable covenant participants comprising what is one unified people. As the title of this chapter suggests, they are in fact the united "people(s) of God," one by faith in Christ and common partaking of the Spirit, and yet distinct insofar as God will *yet* restore Israel as a nation to its land.

One new covenant, under which differing covenant participants join together, through Christ and the Spirit, as a common people of God—this, then, is the grace and the glory of the marvelous provision of God.

CHAPTER 3

The New Man of Ephesians 2

Carl B. Hoch, Jr.

Ephesians is critical for a theology of the relationship between Israel and the church. Markus Barth has stated that "not in all of the Pauline epistles (not to speak of all books of the New Testament) is the relationship of the church and Israel 'in Christ' described as intensively and strikingly as in Ephesians."[1] Chapters 2 and 3 are especially strategic. There Paul discusses the revolutionary soteriological and ecclesiological changes in the status of Gentiles brought about by Christ's redemptive work. Although the entire book of Ephesians will serve as a background, this chapter will concentrate on 2:11–22 as this section develops the concept of the new man.

AUTHORSHIP OF EPHESIANS

The authorship of Ephesians has been a topic of intense debate among New Testament scholars. The question is not merely a matter of historical interest but has bearing on the interpretation of the letter as well. The recent study by Lincoln is based on the premise that Ephesians is a product of an author writing during the last decade of the first century when the conflict concerning the law is over, the admission of the Gentiles is well established, Jerusalem has fallen, and Gentiles are much more numerous in the church than Jews.[2] However, I would concur with F. F. Bruce that Ephesians is "the quintessence of Paulinism."[3] It presents a consistent, coherent position with Romans on the relationship of Gentiles to Israel and clarifies this relationship even more through the use of σύν compounds.[4]

[1]Markus Barth, "Conversion and Conversation," *Int* 17 (January 1963): 13.
[2]Andrew T. Lincoln, "The Church and Israel in Ephesians 2," *CBQ* 49 (October 1987): 620.
[3]F. F. Bruce, *Paul: Apostle of the Heart Set Free* (Grand Rapids: Eerdmans, 1978), 424.
[4]The classic case against Pauline authorship was presented by C. Leslie Mitton in his

THE NEED FOR A REDEMPTIVE-HISTORICAL
APPROACH TO PAUL

Differences in the interpretation of Ephesians are due not only to a rejection of Pauline authorship but also to a lack of consensus as to proper hermeneutical method. Ridderbos has argued that unless Paul is interpreted redemptive-historically, his teaching will be distorted by categories foreign to his thought.

According to Ridderbos, the last hundred years have produced the Hegelian Paul of the Tübingen school, the liberal Paul of liberal theology, the mystical Paul of the history-of-religions school, and the existentialist Paul of the Bultmannian school.[5] One could add to this list the gnostic Paul, the rabbinic Paul, the Paul-in-process-of-theological-development, and the ecumenical Paul. Even the "devotional" Paul of popular Christianity fails to recognize that for Paul, the historic acts of God in bringing redemption to his people are the focal point of his thought. The devotional, individualistic, privatistic reading of Paul tends to miss Paul's historical orientation and his focus on groups like Jews and Gentiles, Israel and church, and the church in its corporate wholeness.

The redemptive-historical method of interpreting Paul in general has been argued in depth by Ridderbos in his masterful volume *Paul: An Outline of His Theology*. The case for this method of interpreting Ephesians in particular can be argued along three lines.

The Aorist Tenses and the Concentration
of the "In Christ" Formula

According to the writer's count, there are 125 aorist forms in Ephesians.[6] Of these, 65 are concentrated in the first three chapters.

London University dissertation, published as *The Epistle to the Ephesians: Its Authorship, Origin, and Purpose* (Oxford: Clarendon Press, 1951). Mitton advanced the work of Edgar J. Goodspeed, *The Meaning of Ephesians* (Chicago: University of Chicago Press, 1933), who argued that Onesimus was the real author of Ephesians. A good survey of work since Mitton appears in John C. Kirby, *Ephesians: Baptism and Pentecost* (Montreal: McGill University Press, 1968). A thorough defense of Pauline authorship is A. Van Roon, *The Authenticity of Ephesians* (Leiden: E. J. Brill, 1974). In the final analysis, Barth's comment on authorship is well advised: "E. Percy's study in the linguistic, thematic, and theological characteristics of Ephesians and H. Schlier's return into the camp of conservative scholars show how dispensable are the fanciful theories and how superfluous the exasperating search for an author of this epistle other than Paul" ("Conversion and Conversation," 3).

[5]Herman Ridderbos, *Paul: An Outline of His Theology* (Grand Rapids: Eerdmans, 1975), 15.

[6]The breakdown is as follows: forty-six indicatives (1:4, 6, 8, 9, 11, 13, 20, 22 [bis]; 2:1, 3, 4, 5, 6 [bis], 10, 13, 17; 3:2, 3 [bis], 5 [bis], 7, 8, 11; 4:1, 4, 7, 8 [bis], 9 [bis], 11, 19, 20, 21 [bis], 30, 32; 5:2 [bis], 25 [bis], 29; 6:22); thirty participles (1:3, 5, 9, 11, 13 [bis], 15, 20 [bis]; 2:10, 14 [bis], 15, 16, 17, 19; 3:2, 7, 9; 4:7, 10 [bis], 24, 25; 6:8, 13, 14 [bis],

There are 174 present-tense forms in Ephesians.[7] Only 52 are found in the first three chapters, whereas 122 are found in the last three chapters as compared with 60 aorists. We also note that the aorists usually mark historic, point actions of God that establish his redemptive base for the church. Present tenses express the continuing significance of these redemptive acts for the church.

A representative selection of texts illustrates this point. The *aorist tense* appears in the clauses "God blessed" (1:3), "he has freely given us" (1:6), "he lavished on us" (1:8), "we were also chosen" (1:11), "you were marked in him with a seal" (1:13), "which he exerted in Christ" (1:20), "when he raised him from the dead and seated him at his right hand" (1:20), "God placed all things under his feet and appointed him to be head" (1:22), "God made us alive with Christ" (2:5), "God raised us up with Christ and seated us with him" (2:6), "created in Christ Jesus to do good works" (2:10), "you have been brought near" (2:13), "who has made the two one and has destroyed the barrier" (2:14), and "he put to death their hostility" (2:16). The *present tense* appears in "in him we have redemption" (1:7), "we are God's workmanship" (2:10), "he himself is our peace" (2:14), "we both have access" (2:18), "you are no longer foreigners and aliens" (2:19), "the whole building is joined together and rises" (2:21), "you too are being built together" (2:22), and "we may approach God" (3:12).

The case for the redemptive-historical use of the aorists is strengthened when one observes the concentration of locative cases used of Christ in the first three chapters. The constructions "in Christ," "in him," "in the beloved," "in whom," "in the Lord," "in his blood," "in his flesh," and "in Jesus" occur a total of thirty-one times in Ephesians.[8] Of these thirty-one occurrences only two are found outside the first three

15, 16); twenty-four subjunctives (1:17; 2:7, 9, 10, 15, 16; 3:10, 16, 18, 19; 4:10, 13, 15, 29; 5:26, 27; 6:3, 8, 13, 19, 20, 21, 22 [bis]; nineteen infinitives (1:10, 18; 3:4, 8, 9, 16 [bis], 18 [bis], 20; 4:1, 22, 24; 6:11, 13 [bis], 16, 19, 20); six imperatives (4:31; 5:14; 6:11, 13, 14, 17).

[7]The count is as follows: sixty-four indicatives (1:7, 14, 16, 18, 23; 2:5, 8, 10, 14, 18, 19 [bis], 21, 22; 3:4, 12, 13 [bis], 14, 15, 20 [bis]; 4:1, 8, 9, 10, 15, 16, 17 [ter], 21, 25; 5:4 [bis], 5 [bis], 6, 10, 12, 13, 14 [bis], 15, 16, 18, 23, 24, 28 [bis], 29 [bis], 30, 32 [bis]; 6:1, 2, 9 [bis], 12, 17, 20 [bis], 21); sixty participles (1:1, 11, 16 [bis], 19, 21 [bis], 23; 2:1, 2, 3, 4, 5, 7 [bis], 11 [bis], 12, 13, 15, 20, 21; 3:4, 20 [bis]; 4:2, 3, 14 [bis], 15, 16 [bis], 18 [bis], 22, 28 [ter], 29, 32; 5:5, 10, 12, 13, 14 [bis], 16, 19 [ter], 20, 21, 27, 28; 6:6, 7, 8, 18 [bis], 24; four subjunctives (4:14, 28; 5:27, 33); eleven infinitives (1:3, 12; 3:6, 13; 4:3, 17, 23, 28; 5:12, 28; 6:11); thirty-five imperatives (2:11; 4:25, 26 [ter], 27, 28 [bis], 29, 30, 32; 5:1, 2, 3, 5, 6, 7, 8, 11 [bis], 14, 15, 17 [bis], 18 [bis], 25, 33; 6:1, 2, 4 [bis], 5, 9, 10).

[8]The locations are as follows: "in Christ," (1:1, 3, 10, 12, 20; 2:6, 7, 10, 13; 3:6, 11, 21); "in him" (1:4, 9, 10; 2:15, 16); "in the beloved" (1:6); "in whom" (1:7, 11, 13 [bis]; 2:21, 22; 3:12); "in the Lord" (1:15; 2:21; 4:1); "in his blood" (2:13); "in his flesh" (2:14); "in Jesus" (4:21).

chapters: "in the Lord" (4:1) and "in Jesus" (4:21). Even these two are related to Christ's redemptive work. It appears, therefore, that Paul was very careful to lay a solid redemptive-historical base in the first three chapters of Ephesians for the ethical exhortations he draws inferentially (οὖν 4:1) in chapters 4–6.

The We-You Contrast

It is admittedly difficult to differentiate the inclusive and exclusive uses of Paul's "we," "you," and "us" in Ephesians.[9] However, there does seem to be a contrast between Jewish Christians and Gentile Christians in 1:12, 13. The "we" of verse 12 were the first to hope in Christ (προηλπικότας), whereas the "you" in verse 13 also were included in him. Since Paul will argue in 2:12 that the Gentiles had no prior messianic hope, it would not be legitimate to include Gentiles in the "we" of 1:12. There is a historical movement, in other words, from a Jewish anticipation and realization of the messianic hope to a Gentile participation in that hope after Christ's coming and the proclamation of the gospel to them. This participation is accomplished through the sealing of the Gentiles by the promised Holy Spirit.

This redemptive-historical scheme is consistent in Paul and elsewhere in the New Testament. Romans 1:16 is not an isolated thought. The gospel was indeed first to the Jew and then to the Greek. The pattern is clear in Acts as well (10:44–48; 11:15–18, 19–21; 13:4–5, 46–48; 14:1–7; 16:13; 17:1–4, 10–12, 17; 18:1–6, 19; 19:8–10; 26:19–23; 28:26–29). The same theme is obvious in Romans 11:11–12 and 11:30–32.

The whole argument in Ephesians 2 is that Jewish privileges have been extended to Gentiles through Christ. The Messiah, citizenship, covenants, promise, hope, and knowledge of the true God belonged to "us" and not to "you." They are now available to "you" only because the Messiah sent for "us" has made them available to "you." Any exegesis that negates this movement from "us" to "you" destroys Paul's theology of Jewish advantage (Rom. 3:1-2; 9:4-5). When Schnackenburg concludes that the [non-Pauline] author of Ephesians concedes no preeminence to Israel from his theology and that the scheme of Ephesians is not salvation history but the current status of Gentile Christians individually in Christ, he ignores completely this evidence and the argument built on it.[10]

---

[9]See Koshi Usami, *Somatic Comprehension of Unity: The Church in Ephesus* (Rome: Biblical Institute Press, 1983), n. 20 with literature cited and his statement on p. 60 that "we" does not simply refer to Jewish Christians and "you" to Gentile Christians.

[10]Rudolf Schnackenburg, "Zur Exegese von Eph. 2,11–22: Im Hinblick auf das

Carl B. Hoch, Jr.

The ποτέ-νῦν Contrast

The third argument for a redemptive-historical approach to Paul and to Ephesians is Paul's use of the temporal adverbs ποτέ and νῦν. The critical point of dispute is whether these two adverbial particles refer only to preconversion and postconversion or whether they cover a more extended period (i.e., the period prior to the coming of Christ and the present interadvent period). It is the writer's contention that the wider sense was intended by Paul. Obviously, this latter sense includes the former, at least for Jews, but the former does not necessarily include the latter.

The argument for the conversion view is usually based on the Pauline association of "then" and "now" with lifestyle (2:1–3; 5:8; cf. Col. 1:21; 3:7–8; Titus 3:3; Philem. 11). However, this approach overlooks a number of significant details.

First, even though 2:1–3 is showing why God's wrath against profligate sinners is fully justified, 2:4–10 does not balance preconversion lifestyle with postconversion lifestyle. The status of being "dead" is changed only by the redemptive work of Christ, not by a change in lifestyle. In Christ, God made alive, raised up, and seated these who were "dead." The new lifestyle is a result of the new creative work of Christ in redemption (2:10).

Second, the ποτέ of 2:11 seems to be synonymous with the καιρῷ ἐκείνῳ of 2:12. "That time" was the time of alienation from Israel and all its privileges. The emphatic νυνί of 2:13 followed by another ποτέ shows a redemptive-historical change, not an existential one. It is "in Christ," "in the blood of Christ," "through the cross" that the change of status has occurred. Gentiles as a group were *once* alienated but *now* have been reconciled; they were *once* "far away" but *now* are "near."

Third, even Colossians 1:21 appears in a similar context. Christ reconciled and made peace through his cross (1:20); he reconciled Christians to God in his physical body through death (v. 22).

Fourth, other Pauline texts show that Paul conceived of the νῦν period as a redemptive-historical period. "He did it to demonstrate his justice at the present time" (Rom. 3:26); "since we have now been justified by his blood" (Rom. 5:9); "we also rejoice in God through our Lord Jesus Christ, through whom we have now received reconciliation" (Rom. 5:11); "I consider that our present [νῦν] sufferings are not worth comparing with the glory that will be revealed in us" Rom. 8:18); "so too, at the present [νῦν] time there is a remnant chosen by grace" (Rom. 11:5); "just as you who were at one time [ποτέ] disobedient to God

Verhältnis von Kirche und Israel," in *The New Testament Age*, ed. William C. Weinrich, 2 vols. (Macon, Ga.: Mercer University Press, 1984), 2:488–89.

have now [νῦν] received mercy as a result of their disobedience" (Rom. 11:30); "now to him who is able to establish you by my gospel and the proclamation of Jesus Christ, according to the revelation of the mystery hidden for long ages past, but now revealed and made known through the prophetic writings by the command of the eternal God, so that all nations might believe and obey him" (Rom. 16:25–26); "I tell you, now is the time of God's favor, now is the day of salvation" (2 Cor. 6:2); "at that time [τότε] the son born in the ordinary way persecuted the son born by the power of the Spirit. It is the same now" (Gal. 4:29).

Fifth, Peter seems to have employed the same language and time scheme: "Once [ποτέ] you were not a people, but now [νῦν] you are the people of God; once you had not received mercy, but now you have received mercy" (1 Peter 2:10).

I conclude that Paul was employing a redemptive-historical time scheme when he used ποτέ and νῦν. There was a definite status of Jews and Gentiles prior to Christ's coming. His coming has changed that status into a new man, a reality that was not historical until Christ made peace through the blood of his cross.

THE ARGUMENT OF EPHESIANS 1

Space does not permit a detailed treatment of the argument of Ephesians 1. Only the major flow of that argument will be traced.

Paul begins Ephesians with a *berakah* to God, a "praise psalm" for his grand purpose that he formulated in eternity past and has executed through the advent of Christ. Key verbs express the content and execution of the plan: "blessed" (v. 3), "chose" (v. 4), "predestined" (v. 6), "freely given" (v. 6), "lavished" (v. 8), "made known" (v. 9), "bring together under one head" (v. 10), "made heirs" (v. 11), and "marked in him with a seal" (v. 13).

Key nouns join these verbs in elucidating the redemptive plan: "blessing" (v. 3), "love" (v. 4), "adoption" (v. 5), "pleasure and will" (v. 5), "praise" (v. 6), "grace" (v. 6), "redemption" (v. 7), "blood" (v. 7), "forgiveness" (v. 7), "wisdom and understanding" (v. 8), "mystery" (v. 9), "fulfillment" (v. 10), "plan" (v. 11), "word of truth" (v. 13), "gospel" (v. 13), "salvation" (v. 13), "Holy Spirit" (v. 13), "deposit" (v. 14), "inheritance" (v. 14), and "possession" (v. 14).

It should be clear that the first fourteen verses are centered on salvation, which God planned and provided in Christ. Such salvation brings great praise (the word *praise* occurs three times in the section) from those who are recipients of it and who have received the Holy Spirit as the guarantee of the eschatological inheritance.

Verses 15 to 23 contain Paul's first prayer of the letter. The prayer is a request to God for the readers that they will know in some degree the incomprehensible magnitude of God's calling, inheritance, and power. This power has been preeminently displayed through Christ's resurrection and exaltation to authority over all created things. This authority, although cosmic in scope, is primarily displayed in the church, which is Christ's body. This church serves as the focus of attention in chapters 2 and 3.

THE ARGUMENT OF EPHESIANS 2:1–10

These verses are an indispensable prelude to the section that is the major focus of this study: 2:11–22. A summary of their importance must suffice.

The Status of Gentiles Before the Advent of Christ (2:1–2)

Paul begins his exposition of the desperate status of Gentiles before the coming of Christ with an emphatic "you" in verse 1. The Gentiles were "dead," that is, unable to respond to God.[11] This spiritual death was expressed in a life characterized by transgressions and sins. These Gentiles followed the ways of this world and were dominated by Satan, a powerful spirit being who is still energizing unbelievers. The parallel to these verses is Colossians 2:13.

The Status of Jews and Gentiles Before the Advent of Christ (2:3)

In complete agreement with his doctrine of "all under sin" (Rom. 3:9), Paul expands the alienated status of Gentiles to Jews ("all of us"). Even though Paul will present the Jewish privileges redemptive-historically in 2:12, he is careful at this point to underscore the truth that Jews had no advantage salvifically. In perfect consistency with his exposé of a Jew's guilt before God in Romans 2:17–29, he flatly states that all are by nature objects of God's wrath.

The Status of Jews and Gentiles After the Advent of Christ (2:4–10)

Verses 4–10 provide four redemptive-historical results of Christ's coming: (1) a change in salvific status from death to life and from condemnation to salvation for both Jews and Gentiles (vv. 4–5); (2) the new exalted position both have in Christ (v. 6); (3) the initial

---

[11]Johannes P. Louw and Eugene A. Nida, eds., *Greek-English Lexicon of the New Testament, Based on Semantic Domains*, 2 vols. (New York: United Bible Societies, 1988), 1:679.

realization of the eschatological purpose God has in Christ (v. 7); and (4) the contrast between the futility of works without faith in Christ and the fertility of works generated by new creation in Christ (vv. 8–10).

God's mercy and love took the initiative in reversing the alienated status of humankind. Using three σύν compounds, Paul introduces the union of Christ with his people ("made us alive with Christ," "raised us up with Christ," and "seated us with him"). This transfer from a status of condemnation to salvation has its basis in God's grace (vv. 5, 7, and 8). This grace was not in short supply but is a gift arising from God's abundant riches (vv. 7–8).

Nor was this grace an emergency measure from God. Recapitulating the stress on God's plan and purpose articulated in chapter 1, Paul uses ἵνα to underscore the fact that God's purpose is cosmic and eternal in Christ: "*in order that* in the coming ages he might show the incomparable riches of his grace, expressed in his kindness to us in Christ Jesus" (v. 7).

The transfer, although objectively provided by Christ's redemptive work, is subjectively appropriated by faith. Again the argument that works cannot justify is parallel with the extended argument in Romans 1–8. Both Jews and Gentiles must believe the gospel in order to be saved. All boasting by either group is excluded (cf. Rom. 3:27).

Although the topic of the new creation is not developed in Ephesians as extensively as in 2 Corinthians, the language in Ephesians is reminiscent of it. The verb κτίζω is used four times in Ephesians (2:10, 15; 3:9; 4:24). The reconciliation of all persons to God through Jesus Christ is proof that the new creation has been inaugurated (2 Cor. 5:16–21). Humankind's previous alienated status "in Adam" has been changed into a reconciled status "in Christ" (1 Cor. 15:22, 45). The new man is closely related to this new creation. The writer will develop this relationship in more detail in the next section. It is sufficient at this point to note that the new creation and the new man both involve a threefold change: anthropological, ecclesiological, and ethical. In 2:10 the emphasis is upon the ethical change. Good works should come from those who through faith have appropriated the anthropological transfer from "in Adam" to "in Christ" and the ecclesiological transfer from "enmity" to "peace." The new creation and the new man do not simply involve a relational change. They also demand a functional change. This functional change is a part of the same redemptive plan that God prepared in advance.

Carl B. Hoch, Jr.

THE ARGUMENT OF EPHESIANS 2:11–22

The Alienation of Gentiles (2:11–12)

Our contention that one must read Paul redemptive-historically is supported by Barclay, who entitles this section "B.C. and A.D.,"[12] and Martin, who entitles it "The Gentiles Before and After Christ's Coming."[13]

Barth, along with many others, views this section as falling into three parts: "Eph. 2:11–22 is the key and high point of the whole epistle. Its logical structure is clear, with three steps following one upon another: (a) the description of the division of mankind (vss. 11–12); (b) the praise of Christ's work of reconciliation (13–18); (c) the elaboration of the tangible result of peace, i.e. the growing church (19–22)."[14]

According to Swain, "The author now draws out the consequences of his cosmic and creative view of redemption for a new understanding of the relationship between Jews and Gentiles (Gal. 3:26–29; Rom. 9–11; Acts 15:1-29)."[15]

Scott recognizes that the alienation of the Gentiles in the period before Christ is the supposition for their reconciliation through Christ when he remarks that "in spite of their evil past they have shared in the new creation which has been effected through Christ, and are therefore on the same footing as Israel."[16]

Paul draws an inference ("therefore") in verse 11 based upon the whole preceding argument of verses 1–10.[17] The Gentiles are to recall that their new status in Christ was not always true of them. Verse 12 lists five things about their former lot that were descriptive of their alienated status. This recall is "an appeal to their background in religious history, not to their own religious experience."[18] According to Beare, the presence of the article before the word *Gentiles* is highly important, as generalizing the address—"you, the Gentiles."[19]

Eadie's assertion that "their ethnical state no longer existed"[20] is

---

[12]William Barclay, "The Letters to the Galatians and Ephesians," in *The Daily Study Bible,* 2d ed. (Philadelphia: Westminster, 1958), 124.

[13]Ralph Martin, "Ephesians," in *The New Bible Commentary Revised,* 3d ed., ed. D. Guthrie et al. (Grand Rapids: Eerdmans, 1970), 1111.

[14]Markus Barth, *Ephesians 1–3,* AB (New York: Doubleday, 1974), 275.

[15]Lionel Swain, "Ephesians," in *NCCHS,* 1186.

[16]E. F. Scott, *The Epistles of Paul to the Colossians, to Philemon, and to the Ephesians,* MNTC (London: Hodder & Stoughton, 1930), 168.

[17]T. K. Abbott, *A Critical and Exegetical Commentary on the Epistles to the Ephesians and to the Colossians,* ICC (Edinburgh: T. & T. Clark, 1897), 55.

[18]Francis W. Beare, "The Epistle to the Ephesians," in *IB* 10:649.

[19]Ibid.

[20]John Eadie, *Commentary on the Epistle to the Ephesians* (Grand Rapids: Zondervan, reprint of 1883 ed.), 161.

contested by Beare, who insists that "they were as much *Gentiles in the flesh* as they ever were."[21] It will be important to recognize that it is the soteriological status of Gentiles that is changed, not their ethnic status. Barth is correct when he writes:

> If we follow the *Haustafeln* (Col. 3:18ff.), male and female, old and young people, slave and freeman do not lose their distinctive functions when they are called "one" in Christ (Gal. 3:28; Col. 3:11; 1 Cor. 12:13) or when their life "in Christ" is described. Similarly, neither Jews nor Gentiles become colorless and meaningless internationals; both of them approach God together; circumcision and uncircumcision are now but a "so-called" barrier between God and men. Now Jews and Gentiles are joined and built together—instead of boasting at the expense of one another.[22]

Paul is not saying that the Gentiles were in the flesh in the former period but are no longer in the flesh. "In the flesh in this verse does not have its pejorative connotation of 'in a sinful state.'" It means the physical body[23] and is well translated by the NIV as "by birth." The change is not from "in flesh" to "in Spirit," as in Romans 8:9, but from "far away" to "near." In other words, the ὅτι of verse 12 is resumptive of verse 11 and describes the Gentiles' past status ποτέ in terms of καιρῷ ἐκείνῳ. The denigrating rubric "uncircumcision" is really parenthetical and is inserted to emphasize the enmity that existed between all Jews and Gentiles in the past and still continues between non-Christian Jews and Gentiles in the present. The present participles of verse 11 are descriptive of an ongoing situation: the Gentiles are still called names by Jews.

The last adjective, χειροποίητος, and its antonym, ἀχειροπόητος, are significant New Testament words (for the former, see Mark 14:58; Acts 7:48, 17:24; Heb. 9:11, 24; and for the latter, Mark 14:58; 2 Cor. 5:1; Col. 2:11). They distinguish human work from the work of God. The first is natural, the second supernatural. The one word recalls the whole discussion in Romans 2:17–29. Jews whose circumcision is only physical, the work of a knife, continue to malign Gentiles whose circumcision is spiritual and the work of God.

The five predicaments of Gentiles before Christ are now listed. They were apart from Christ, alienated from the nation of Israel, strangers to the covenants of the promise, without any eschatological hope, and without the true God in the world.

According to Beare, "separate from Christ" is the negative counter-

---

[21]Beare, "Ephesians," 650.
[22]Barth, "Conversion and Conversation," 6.
[23]S. D. F. Salmond, "The Epistle to the Ephesians," in *EGT* 3:291.

part of "in Christ."[24] Bruce says this phrase means that the Gentiles not only had not come to know Christ but also had no part or lot in the messianic people.[25] There is an *inclusio* between this phrase and the "blood of Christ" of verse 13. The Gentiles were "apart" or "separate" as long as Christ had not shed his blood. After this event, they were "near."

The next phrase has received a variety of interpretations. Many argue on the basis of the use of "fellow citizens" ($\sigma\nu\mu\pi o\lambda\hat{\iota}\tau\alpha\iota$) in verse 19 that Gentiles who before Christ were not a part of ethnic Israel have since Christ become members of the "new" or "true" Israel. Abbott is representative of this viewpoint when he asserts, "In the following verses we have two points of view combined, viz. the reconciliation of the Gentiles to God, and their admission to the $\pi o\lambda\iota\tau\epsilon\iota\alpha$ of Israel, namely the true Israel—the Christian Church."[26] Beare, however, believes that the reference is to "communion with God," which Israel had through election.[27] Dahl thinks that the author's concern is with the "roots and origin of the church in Israel."[28] Hoehner emphasizes the distinction between Israel as a national, political entity and the church as a transnational and apolitical entity with the comment, "They did not belong to the theocratic state of Israel (cf. Rom. 9:4)."[29] Scott apparently sees the statement as sociopolitical by providing a cultural background: "He is thinking of an ancient city-state which was made up of free citizens and also of resident aliens who could exercise no civic rights."[30]

With such a diversity of views among commentators, it would be unwise to attempt to be more precise concerning Paul's meaning. But the writer does not believe that Paul is presenting some kind of incorporation-into-Israel theology for Gentiles. As the later discussion will show, the key to Paul's theology is not Gentile incorporation into Israel but a new sharing with Israel in Israel's prior covenants and promise.

The third predicament or disadvantage of Gentiles before the death and resurrection of Christ was their nonparticipation in Israel's covenants and promise. Covenants and promise are found both here and in Romans 9:4 as advantages or privileges of Israel. It is my contention that Paul meant to continue his list in Romans 3 after he asked the question, "What advantage, then, is there in being a Jew, or what value is there in

[24]Beare, "Ephesians," 651.
[25]F. F. Bruce, *The Epistle to the Ephesians* (Westwood, N.J.: Revell, 1961), 53.
[26]Abbott, *Ephesians and Colossians,* 59–60.
[27]Beare, "Ephesians," 651.
[28]Nils Alstrup Dahl, "Ephesians," in *HBC,* 1217.
[29]Harold Hoehner, "Ephesians," in *BKCNT,* 625.
[30]Scott, *Colossians, Philemon, and Ephesians,* 169.

circumcision? Much in every way! First of all, they have been entrusted with the very words of God" (vv. 1–2). He really intended to write: second, the adoption as sons; third, the divine glory; fourth, the covenants; fifth, the receiving of the law; sixth, the temple worship; seventh, the promises; eighth, the patriarchs; ninth, the Messiah! But he was sidetracked by a need to expound a theodicy and did not get around to the rest of the list until chapter 9. Chapters 9–11 are not an appendix or an interruption to the argument of Romans but are a continuation of the thought begun in 3:1–2.

In either list, covenants and promise along with the Messiah appear to be the basic prerogatives of Israel's election. These three are common to both lists. Adoption, glory, law, temple worship, and patriarchs are found in Romans but not in Ephesians. Citizenship, hope, and being without God occur in Ephesians but not in Romans. It is not that the omitted items are unimportant but that covenants, promise, and Messiah are foundational. Kaiser's work on promise theology, McComiskey's work on the covenants, and Briggs's work on messianic prophecy are well known and underscore the centrality of these three terms for not only Paul but the rest of the New Testament writers.[31]

It is not possible to be sure of how many or which covenants Paul had in mind when he used the plural *covenants*. Beare names the Abrahamic, Mosaic, and new covenants.[32] Hoehner lists Abrahamic, Palestinian, Davidic, and new.[33] Mitton has Adam, Noah, Abraham, and Moses.[34] Salmond simply says it refers to Abraham and the patriarchs because they have messianic significance and not to the Mosaic because this covenant was not of the promise.[35] Scott thinks the reference is to Abraham, Jacob, Moses, and David, whose covenants were renewed and amplified from time to time.[36] I prefer Hoehner's suggestion, but it cannot be proved any more conclusively than the other lists. The consistency of Abraham in the above lists, however, shows that it would probably be unwise to eliminate that covenant from any consideration here. Its inclusion on all the lists shows the central and basic role the Abrahamic covenant plays for both Testaments.

The singular *promise* is no less problematic. Paul is not always consistent in his use of ἐπαγγελία. Sometimes he uses it in the singular

---

[31]Walter Kaiser, Jr., *Toward an Old Testament Theology* (Grand Rapids: Zondervan, 1978); Thomas McComiskey, *The Covenants of Promise* (Grand Rapids: Baker, 1985); Charles Briggs, *Messianic Prophecy* (Peabody, Mass.: Hendrickson, reprint of 1886 ed.).
[32]Beare, "Ephesians," 651.
[33]Hoehner, "Ephesians," 625.
[34]C. Leslie Mitton, *Ephesians*, NCB (Greenwood, S.C.: Attic Press, 1976), 103.
[35]Salmond, "Ephesians," 292.
[36]Scott, *Colossians, Philemon, and Ephesians*, 169.

(Rom. 4:13, 14, 16, 20; 9:8, 9; Gal. 3:14, 17, 18 [bis], 22, 29; 4:23, 28; Eph. 1:13; 2:12; 3:6; 6:2; 1 Tim. 4:8; 2 Tim. 1:1); other times he uses it in the plural (Rom. 9:4; 15:8; 2 Cor. 1:20; 7:1; Gal. 3:16, 21). The most common interpretation is that of Eadie, "The central promise here marked out by the article was the Messiah, and blessing by Him."[37]

A recent essay by Sam K. Williams has introduced some intriguing elements into the promise discussion. According to Williams, the dominant temporal scheme of Galatians is then-now (3:23-25; 4:8–9).[38] The promise is the promise of the Holy Spirit.[39] The plural "promises" refers either to the various versions of the one promise or to the promise given on more than one occasion and found in more than one scriptural text.[40] Paul can understand the promise to Abraham as the promise of the Holy Spirit because it is the Holy Spirit who begets children to Abraham and because Paul understood the γῆ of Genesis 13:15 and 17:8 (LXX) as the whole earth.[41] Romans 4:13 supports this exegesis.[42] Finally, "The view is widespread in Jewish literature that the inheritance of God's people is nothing less than the world: Ps. 36 (LXX):9, 11, 22, 29, 34; Jub. 22:14–15; 17:3; 22:29–30; 32:18–19; 1 Enoch 5:6–7; Sir. 44:21; 4 Ezra 55–59; cf. Matt. 5:5."[43]

While I would not want to exclude Christ from the promise (cf. 2 Cor. 1:20), if Williams is right about the Holy Spirit being an integral part of the promise, this would explain the central role the Spirit plays in Ephesians (1:13, 17?; 2:18, 22; 3:16; 4:3, 4, 30; 5:18?; 6:17, 18?). The Old Testament covenants are means God used to guarantee his one, comprehensive promise. For the Gentiles, their share in the promise and the covenants comes in Christ, through the Holy Spirit, not by some incorporation into Israel. Dahl sums it up well: "The reminder in Eph. 2:11–22 is, like the entire letter, addressed to Christian Gentiles who have been united with the original heirs of God's promise without becoming Jews (see 3:6)."[44]

The fourth predicament of Gentiles prior to Christ's atoning sacrifice was their lack of hope. Again, interpretations of the word *hope* are diverse. Abbott thinks hope in the widest sense is intended.[45] Beare

[37]Eadie, *Ephesians,* 166.
[38]Sam K. Williams, "Promise in Galatians: A Reading of Paul's Reading of Scripture," *JBL* 107 (December 1988): 711–12.
[39]Ibid., 712.
[40]Ibid.
[41]Ibid., 714, 717.
[42]Ibid., 718.
[43]Ibid., 719.
[44]Dahl, "Ephesians," 1216.
[45]Abbott, *Ephesians and Colossians,* 58.

suggests immortality in light of 1 Thessalonians 4:13.[46] Grassi interprets it as the messianic hope or the hope of the resurrection.[47] Since precision is not possible, a more general view of hope seems preferable. It should be broad enough to cover all the senses of hope in Paul's writings that the above interpretations isolate.

The fifth predicament of Gentiles was their estrangement from the living and true God. Paul's statement that the Gentiles were ἄθεοι (without gods) is somewhat puzzling in light of the plethora of gods in the Hellenistic world. Beare's comment is apropos: "The pagans were not 'atheists,' for they worshiped a multitude of divinities, high and low."[48] Then he adds: "Their worship of these empty creations of the human imagination could not be considered in any sense as a living communion with God."[49] This comment captures the sense Paul intended.

Their estrangement from the true God was "in the world." Mitton believes that "world" has a good sense, their "daily life on the earth."[50] Eadie, however, takes it in an evil sense: "The κόσμος is the entire region beyond the πολιτεία, and, as such, is dark, hostile, and under Satan's dominion, and, as the next verse mentions, it is 'far off.'"[51] Salmond is unsure whether the word means the world of human beings or the present evil world, but he concludes that "the latter is better."[52] Hendriksen summarizes the desperate state of the Gentiles apart from Christ with five adjectives: "Christless," "stateless," "friendless," "hopeless," and "Godless."[53]

The Reconciliation of Gentiles (2:13)

Again Paul uses the two temporal adverbs νῦν and ποτέ to underscore the redemptive-historical change made by Christ. The Gentiles experienced this change of status by virtue of being "in Christ." This is the ninth time Paul has used this phrase in these first two chapters (1:1, 3, 10, 12, 20; 2:6, 7, 10). Salmond notes that the phrase is put emphatically first.[54] Caragounis discusses its importance:

> The phrase ἐν Χριστῷ indicates at once the "sphere" in which the believer was placed by election in God's counsel (e.g. 1:4) and is now

[46]Beare, "Ephesians," 651.
[47]Joseph A. Grassi, "The Letter to the Ephesians," in *JBC* 2:345.
[48]Beare, "Ephesians," 653.
[49]Ibid.
[50]Mitton, *Ephesians,* 104.
[51]Eadie, *Ephesians,* 168.
[52]Salmond, "Ephesians," 293.
[53]William Hendriksen, *Exposition of Ephesians,* NTC, 129–31.
[54]Salmond, "Ephesians," 293.

positioned following the saving event (e.g. 1:1; 2:22), the "sphere" in which all of God's decisions were made (e.g. 1:9; 3:11) and have now in the Christ event taken effect (e.g. 1:9f.) and the "sphere" in which the salvific event with its resultant blessings become realisable for the believer (e.g. 1:7). And finally, ἐν Χριστῷ indicates also the "sphere" in which the believer shall have his future existence (e.g. 1:10).[55]

There is a difference of opinion among exegetes as to what the actual background of the terms *far away* and *near* was. Lincoln, congruent with his non-Pauline and late-date approach to Ephesians, maintains that Isaiah 57:19 is only in the remote background. The real source of the author's thought is rabbinic proselyte terminology, which has been transformed so that Gentiles are near not to Israel but to God.[56] Beare, in contrast, feels that the Old Testament background is primary and that there is only a secondary reference to current midrashic interpretation.[57] This latter view seems better in light of the definite allusion to Isaiah 57 in verse 17.

The real issue, however, is not the background of the terms. The real issues are who is "far away" and who is "near" and to what or to whom are both brought? Usami considers the omission of "we" before "the near" in verse 17 significant.[58] This, in the writer's opinion, is another in the number of futile attempts by those who want to minimize the Jew-Gentile contrast in this section and neutralize the you-we into "Christians."

That Paul intends a contrast in the entire section seems clear from the following observations. Paul has already contrasted the Gentiles with Israel in verses 11 and 12. He has used the words *uncircumcision* and *circumcision* in verse 12. He will use the word *both* three times in the following verses (vv. 14, 16, 18). He will use the word *two* in verse 15. He explicitly names the law as that which divides "both" and the "two" in verse 15. He contrasts the prior and subsequent relationships of "both" and "two" as "enmity" and "peace" in verses 14–17. He uses "one" to describe the new unity that Christ has effected (vv. 14, 15, 16, 18). He uses the definite article before both "far away" and "near" in verse 17. It would seem, therefore, to be special pleading to argue that the absence of "we" before "near" in verse 17 is significant and obliterates any distinction between Jews and Gentiles or between Gentiles and Israel. Rather, Paul is thinking of the Gentiles as "far away" and Jews/Israel as "near" throughout verses 11–22.

[55]Chrys C. Caragounis, *The Ephesian "Mysterion"* (Lund: C. W. K. Gleerup, 1977), 157.
[56]Lincoln, "Church and Israel," 610–11.
[57]Beare, "Ephesians," 654.
[58]Usami, *Somatic Comprehension*, 53–54.

Rader captures the essence of the second difficulty when he notes the pertinence of Adolphe Monod's question, "Near to whom?"[59] Certainly both Jews and Gentiles are brought (redemptively) near to God. Verse 16 clearly speaks of reconciling "both" to God, and verse 18 says that "both" now have access to the Father. But are not the Gentiles also brought near to Israel? Contrary to Lincoln,[60] Israel *is* also in view in this passage. Paul has already written of the alienation of Gentiles from Israel in verse 12. In verse 19 he will write of the changed situation from foreigners and aliens to fellow citizens. If peace and access refer only to God, then one wonders why Paul mentioned all the predicaments in verse 12. The Gentiles would have to participate in Israel's covenants, promise, hope, and God completely apart from it if Israel is not in view.

Paul, however, cannot be arguing for a Gentile incorporation into Israel similar to Jewish proselytizing. Paul never writes of Gentiles as "in Israel" in any of his letters. The key to the sense in which Gentiles are made near to Israel is the preposition σύν.[61] Paul uses six σύν compounds to express the relationship of Gentiles to Jews/Israel in these two chapters: συμπολῖται, "fellow citizens" (2:19); συναρμολογουμένη, "joined together" (2:21); συνοικοδομεῖσθε, "built together" (2:21); συγκληρονόμα, "heirs together" (3:6); σύσσωμα, "members together of one body" (3:6); and συμμέτοχα, "sharers together" (3:6). The Gentiles are brought near to Israel in Christ to share with Israel in its covenants, promise, hope, and God. They do not become Israel; they *share* with Israel.

Two more points need to be made about verse 13. "Have been brought" is aorist and looks historically to the one decisive act of Christ's redemption.[62] The phrase "the blood of Christ" indicates that redemption is possible for both Jew and Gentile only through Christ's death (cf. 1:7). Eadie comments: "The apostle's object is to show that by the death of Christ the exclusiveness of the theocracy was abolished, that Jew and Gentile, by the abrogation of the Mosaic law, are placed on the same level, and that both, in the blood of Christ, are reconciled to God."[63] According to Westcott, this blood is the blood of the new covenant.[64]

[59]William Rader, *The Church and Racial Hostility: Beiträge zur Geschichte der biblischen Exegese* (Tübingen: J. C. B. Mohr [Paul Siebeck], 1978), 152.

[60]See n. 56 above.

[61]For a discussion of the significance of the σύν compounds for Paul, see Carl B. Hoch, Jr., "The Significance of the *Syn* Compounds for Jew-Gentile Relationships in the Body of Christ," *JETS* 25 (June 1982): 175–83.

[62]Brooke Foss Westcott, *Saint Paul's Epistle to the Ephesians* (Grand Rapids: Eerdmans, 1952), 36.

[63]Eadie, *Ephesians*, 170.

THE COEQUALITY OF JEWS AND GENTILES IN CHRIST
(2:11–22)

Paul views Christ in four roles in verses 14–18: peacemaker (vv. 14–15), reconciler (v. 16), evangelist (v. 17), and accessor (or priest?) (v. 18). He, rather than Gentiles and Jews, is the focus of these five verses. (They are the focus in vv. 11–13 and 19–22.)

This change of focus is apparent from the change of person in the verb forms through the transitional verse 18, from second person plural to third person singular. The change is also emphasized by the emphatic αὐτός (he himself) at the beginning of verse 14.

The explanatory γάρ of verse 14 shows how Gentiles who were "far away" have been brought "near." Christ in his work as peacemaker, reconciler, evangelist, and accessor has brought them near. Salmond recalls the numerous Old Testament texts anticipating messianic peace: Isaiah 9:5–6; 52:7; 53:5; 57:19; Micah 5:5; Haggai 2:9; and Zechariah 9:10.[65] Eadie calls Christ the Author, Basis, Medium, and Proclaimer of peace.[66] This peace was absolutely necessary because of the severe hostility Jews had toward the *goyim*. Grassi quotes Aristeas: "Our Lawgiver fenced us round with impregnable ramparts and walls of iron that we might not mingle at all with any of the nations, but remain pure in body and soul."[67]

It is probably best, given the initial article with the first participle, to understand the three aorist participles ὁ ποιήσας, λύσας, and καταργήσας as adjectival. Rader quotes Feine, who interprets the participles adjectivally: "Christ is our peace because he, in his own person, has killed the hostility. Along with this main thought is also expressed in v. 14 what effect his act as peacemaker has brought about and in vv. 15 and 16 by what means he killed the hostility and what purpose led him in his action directed toward killing the hostility."[68]

The reference of ἀμφότερα (both) is not specifically clear. Barth suggests "things," "parties," "groups," "men," and "peoples" as possibilities.[69] Abbott, in contrast, thinks that there is no ellipsis and asserts that the neuter is used of persons in a general sense. The reference is to Jews and Gentiles.[70] Eadie argues that the word clearly means the two races, Jew and Gentile.[71] Westcott takes an entirely different approach and

---

[64]Westcott, *Ephesians*, 36.
[65]Salmond, "Ephesians," 294.
[66]Eadie, *Ephesians*, 171.
[67]Grassi, "Ephesians," 345.
[68]Rader, *The Church and Racial Hostility*, 159.
[69]Barth, "Conversion and Conversation," 6.
[70]Abbott, *Ephesians and Colossians*, 60.
[71]Eadie, *Ephesians*, 171.

feels that the meaning is two systems.[72] Whatever Paul meant exactly, it should be clear that he was thinking of two opposing entities that were relieved of this opposition through Christ.

Paul introduces at this point a contrast that is important but seldom mentioned by writers, the δύο-εἷς word pair. Although this particular word pair is unique to Ephesians, the concept is not. The fall of Adam created a terrible rift in subsequent humanity, so that people were alienated from one another and expressed this alienation through every sinful act from adultery to murder. Christ reconciled human beings not only to God but also to one another. He canceled the enmity and brought unity. Paul used various constructions to convey this unifying work: "many-one" (Rom. 5:15, 19; 12:4, 5; 1 Cor. 10:17; 12:12, 14); "all-one" (1 Cor. 10:17; 12:12, 13, 26; Gal. 3:28); "both-one" (Eph. 2:14, 16, 18); "two-one" (Eph. 2:15); or simply "one" (Rom. 15:6; Eph 4:4, 5, 6, 16; Phil. 1:17; 2:2; Col. 3:15). Beare grasps this tremendous unifying work of Christ well when he writes: "The ultimate divine purpose to bring the whole created universe into an all-embracing unity is foreshadowed, and indeed is actually begun, in the church, where a divided humanity is brought together as Jew and Gentile and united in a single worshipping community."[73]

It is not necessary to interact here with the long discussions in the commentaries as to whether or not Paul had in mind the balustrade in the Jerusalem temple. Salmond maintains that it is questionable whether there is *any* reference to the balustrade because the wall was still standing when the letter was written.[74] Grassi is correct when he points out that the "stone wall was but a token of a whole system of separation that went into every phase of life."[75]

Despite the balustrade question, all are agreed that Paul's point is that the Mosaic Law created the enmity and division between Jews and Gentiles. Hendriksen argues that Paul's emphasis is not on the Jerusalem temple but on the inveterate hostility that existed between the Jews and the Gentiles.[76]

It is now generally conceded that the first half of verse 15 is looking at the commandments of the Mosaic law as these commandments were expressed in individual decrees. Rader indicates that this understanding was not the traditional one. Until Abelard, the phrase ἐν δόγμασιν was interpreted as the new decrees that Christ himself introduced. Abelard

---

[72]Westcott, *Ephesians*, 37.
[73]Beare, "Ephesians," 648–49.
[74]Salmond, "Ephesians," 294.
[75]Grassi, "Ephesians," 345.
[76]Hendriksen, *Ephesians*, 133.

was the first to interpret the words as a further definition of the law of commandments.[77]

There has been a heated controversy in the church over just what exactly Christ "abolished" in regard to the law.[78] This is not the place to get into a discussion of the law in the New Testament or of Paul and the law. It seems best to say simply that the entire Mosaic law is no longer the rule of life for Christians. Christ abolished the entire Mosaic law. The rule of life for the Christian is the "law of Christ." This position is defended well by Moo.[79] It is supported by Abbott, who argues: "Νόμος here is not to be limited to the ceremonial law; there is nothing in the connexion to show such a limitation, which on the contrary, would make the statement very weak."[80] Martin adds, "The law's abrogation was necessary for the creation of a universal church."[81]

The barrier that was the preeminent symbol of the enmity of the old creation was the law. It had to be abolished so that the new creation might be inaugurated, in which peace and reconciliation are the order. Once the barrier was abolished, the two could be created into something new and something unified.

The object of this new creation was the new man (καινὸν ἄνθρωπον). While Barclay is correct that νέος is normally new in point of time and καινός is new in point of quality,[82] the parallel use of νέος with ἄνθρωπος in Colossians 3:10 shows that Paul did not maintain any real distinction between καινός and νέος. The new man did not exist before Christ's death on the cross. It is therefore both quantitatively *and* qualitatively new. Foulkes states this truth well when he writes: "Furthermore, Gentiles do not simply rise to the status of Jews, but both become something *new* and greater; not simply new in point of time, but as Barclay puts it 'new in the sense that it brings into the world a new kind of thing, a new quality of thing, which did not exist before'

---

[77]Rader, *The Church and Racial Hostility,* 59.

[78]See the chapters by Lowery and Martin in this volume. The literature on the subject is enormous and continues unabated mainly because of Sanders's work and the growing debate between dispensationalists and reconstructionists. For the reader who is unfamiliar with this literature, a good starting point would be the articles by Chamblin and Moo with their expansive bibliographies in *Continuity and Discontinuity: Perspectives on the Relationship Between the Old and New Testaments,* ed. John S. Feinberg (Westchester, Ill.: Crossway, 1988); and H. Wayne House and Thomas Ice, *Dominion Theology: Blessing or Curse?* (Portland, Ore.: Multnomah Press, 1988).

[79]Douglas J. Moo, "The Law of Moses or the Law of Christ?" in *Continuity and Discontinuity,* 203–18. See also the essay by Lowery in this volume.

[80]Abbott, *Ephesians and Colossians,* 64.

[81]Martin, "Ephesians," 1112.

[82]Barclay, "Galatians and Ephesians," 136. See also R. H. Mounce and Carl B. Hoch, Jr., "New; Newness," in *ISBE.*

(see also on 4:23f.)."[83] And Houlden underscores the importance of the *new* creation: "Whether there is a conscious reference to Ps. 80 or not, the background here is the common Pauline (and New Testament) idea of Christ as the new Adam (e.g. Rom. 5:12ff.; 1 Cor. 5:21ff.; Phil. 2:6ff.; Col. 3:10ff.), which is now applied to the theme in hand. Hence *create*, making the parallel with Gen. 1:26ff., the creation of Adam."[84]

Rader lists four interpretations of the new man that have been proposed historically: (1) Christ, (2) the church, (3) the Christian, and (4) all humanity.[85] While some of these suggestions relate to the new man, none of them expresses the concept fully. Rather, it seems that throughout his writings, Paul discusses three distinct comprehensive structures under the complex term *new man*. In one letter or in one section of a letter Paul will develop one structure of the new/old man. But Paul does not develop all three structures at once.

The first structure is the anthropological structure. It is best seen in the Adam-Christ contrast of Romans 5:12–21. J. Sidlow Baxter best captures the anthropological nuance of *old man* when he categorizes it as a "Paulinism meaning *the whole human race in Adam*."[86] *Old man* is a forensic term denoting the standing of humankind as "under sin" before God in Adam. This status could be changed only by the redeeming work of Christ. Christ as Redeemer creates the new category—new man— which is not "under condemnation" (Rom. 8:1). The new man now has the gift of righteousness and life through Christ (Rom. 5:17–21). This change of status is depicted by the verb *crucified* in Romans 6:6. It is unfortunate that the NIV has translated "old man" as "old self" in this verse. This makes the old man individualistic and ontic. The term, rather, is corporate and relational. The aorist passive does not mean that the "old self" continues to stir men and women to sin as in the "two natures" doctrine but that the old relationship in Adam was abrogated by Christ's work on the cross. As Dunn comments, "The societal and salvation-history dimension here should not be reduced to the pietistic experience of the individual."[87] The Pauline word equivalent to "nature" and "self" is *flesh*, not *man*.

The second structure of the new man is ecclesiological. This structure is in view in Ephesians 2:15. The new man here is the unity between Jew and Gentile through Christ. It is a reversal of the alienation of the two

[83]Francis Foulkes, *The Epistle of Paul to the Ephesians*, TNTC (Grand Rapids: Eerdmans, 1963), 83.

[84]J. L. Houlden, *Paul's Letters from Prison: Philippians, Colossians, Philemon, and Ephesians*, WPC (Philadelphia: Westminster, 1977), 291.

[85]Rader, *The Church and Racial Hostility*, 173.

[86]J. Sidlow Baxter, *A New Call To Holiness* (Grand Rapids: Zondervan, 1973), 91.

[87]James D. G. Dunn, *Romans 1–8*, WBC (Waco, Tex.: Word, 1988), 318.

ethnic and religious groups, which were polarized in the first century when Paul wrote. According to Rader the current discussion of the relationship established by the ecclesiological new man goes back to Epiphanius and Chrysostom. Rader translates Epiphanius: "If he has made both one, and has not ended the one in order to establish the other, then he has not changed the former (the Jew) into something else. Nor has he kept the second separate from the first; but he has brought the two together into one; not simply, not seemingly, but manifestly in his blood."[88] In regards to Chrysostom, however, Rader says:

> For Chrysostom both Jew and Gentile become a third entity—the Christian. This is in sharp contrast to Epiphanius who says flatly that the Jew "is not changed into something else." Chrysostom, in order to emphasize the newness of the Christian's status, minimizes the continuity between the church and Israel. For Epiphanius, by contrast, unity does not depend on a new nature or status, but on a new relationship established by Christ's death.[89]

If one asks why two such divergent views developed, Rader answers:

> Our study of Chrysostom's interpretation of Eph. 2:11–22 shows that an unfriendly attitude toward the Jewish people affected his approach to the passage. Consequently he treats it in a way which allows it little relevance for the relations of Jews and Gentiles, which is a sore subject for him. If we ask why it took until modern times before interpreters found relevance in Eph. 2:11–22 for the relation of Christians to Jews, we must answer that one of the reasons is the direction Chrysostom's exegesis of the passage took. Chrysostom's influence has continued down through the centuries.[90]

Paul's comments in Ephesians, however, exclude any salvific priority for Israel in the ecclesiological structure of the new man. Jews had just as much need of Christ's atonement as Gentiles. Both Jews and Gentiles are justified by faith. However, while there is no longer *salvific* advantage, there is still an *ethnic* distinction between Jews and Gentiles. Paul continues to speak of Jews and Gentiles as distinct ethnic groups in his letters (Rom. 1:16; 9:24; 1 Cor. 1:24; 12:13; Gal. 2:14, 15). Almost all writers now recognize a distinction between ethnic Israel and Gentiles in Romans 11. And the Jews/Israel had (and in the writer's view still continue to have) a redemptive-historical priority. While not a popular viewpoint outside of dispensational circles, Mussner's exegesis

---

[88]Rader, *The Church and Racial Hostility*, 27; Epiphanius, *Panarion Haereticorum* 42.12.3.
[89]Rader, *The Church and Racial Hostility*, 33.
[90]Ibid., 34–35.

of the relevant texts is sound. He insists that there are salvation-historical advantages of Israel according to both Romans 9:4–5 and Ephesians 2:12.[91] Although I would prefer the use of "Gentiles" instead of "Church" in the following quotation, Mussner's basic contention is true: "The Church is not the people of God which has taken the place of Israel, the Old Testament people of God. Rather, according to Rom. 11:1, the Church is only 'the participant in the root' (Israel and its forefathers), the extended people of God who together with Israel form the one people of God."[92]

The third structure of the new man is the ethical structure. Whereas the anthropological and ecclesiological structures are relational, the ethical structure is functional. The change in the anthropological structure is from "in Adam" to "in Christ." The change in the ecclesiological structure is from "enmity" to "peace." Both of these structures are fixed through the work of Christ on the cross. The ethical structure, however, is not fixed because the Christian is faced with a choice of either "walking according to the flesh" or "walking according to the Spirit." This structure is a potentiality brought into existence through Christ's death.

The major passages on the ethical structure of the new man are Ephesians 4:22–24 and Colossians 3:9–10. The aorist tenses Paul uses show that there is a sense in which the ethical new man is fixed like the anthropological and ecclesiological new man. The old man ethically was "put off" when the status "in Adam" was changed. The aorist infinitives ἀποθέσθαι and ἐνδύσασθαι in Ephesians 4:22, 24 and the aorist participles ἀπεκδυσάμενοι and ἐνδυσάμενοι in Colossians 3:9, 10 look to a point in time when these actions were accomplished. That point is the cross, where the change was effected anthropologically and ecclesiologically.

But a number of considerations show that there is an unfinished aspect to the ethical structure. Paul uses a present infinitive in Ephesians 4:23 to indicate the need for a renewal of the mind and a present passive participle in Colossians 3:10 to indicate the renewal of the image. This fits exactly with Paul's statements and imperatives in Romans 6. Christians died to sin (Rom. 6:2); the old man was crucified with Christ (v. 6). And yet they are exhorted to "not let sin reign in your mortal body so that you obey its evil desires" (v. 12). The long lists of sins in Ephesians 4–6 and Colossians 2–3 show that the ethical structure is in process of realization, at least in functional terms. The Christian is still

[91]Franz Mussner, *Tractate on the Jews* (Philadelphia: Fortress, 1984), 23–26.
[92]Ibid., 9.

in a conflict between the "works of the flesh" and the "fruit of the Spirit" (Gal. 5:16–26).

In summary, the old man–new man terminology of Paul is his way of presenting a central theme in his theology. Van Roon was right when he observed that "all of Rom. 5:12–7:24 appertains to the idea of the old man and that this idea was central to the theology of Paul and his circle."[93] This theology saw the need for men and women to be saved from sin and to be reconciled to God. It saw the need for the resolution of enmity from the fall of Adam forward, especially as this enmity existed between Jews and Gentiles in Paul's day. It saw the need for people to live righteously and stop sinning after the pattern of Adam. It saw these three needs met through the death, resurrection, and ascension of the Lord Jesus Christ, the coming of the Holy Spirit on the Day of Pentecost, and the creation of the church from a believing remnant from Israel, who shared the good news of their Messiah with Gentiles who through faith in this Messiah could now *share with* this remnant in their covenants and promise.

Christ's work as reconciler is the subject of verse 16. This time "both" is masculine and may refer to "the two," Jew and Gentile, who have become "one new man" in the previous verse. It is a mistake to attempt to bifurcate reconciliation to God and reconciliation to one another. Scripture constantly shows that enmity on the vertical axis (with God) soon produces enmity on the horizontal axis (between human beings). And enmity on the horizontal axis can never be resolved until enmity on the vertical axis is removed. If one wants to argue about order, certainly reconciliation on the vertical axis must be prior. And this is Paul's emphasis in the next three verses. Jews and Gentiles needed to be reconciled to God and to gain access to the Father. This reconciliation was provided by Christ's death on the cross. Access to the Father is through Christ. But horizontal reconciliation is also in view, for Jews and Gentiles are now members of one body (cf. 3:6) and participate in one Spirit. In chapter 4 Paul will exhort these Christians to maintain diligently the unity produced by the Spirit in the bond that the peace of Christ formed (v. 3).

The killing of the enmity shows that the reconciliation was horizontal as well as vertical. The point of verses 14 and 15 was that the Mosaic law had erected an impenetrable barrier between Jews and Gentiles. Until Christ destroyed this barrier, the enmity could not be put to death. But by his cross he did put the enmity to death.

The work of Christ as evangelist is the focus of verse 17. There is more discussion in the literature of how Christ preached peace than of

[93]Van Roon, *Authenticity of Ephesians,* 340.

the new man. The majority opinion is that this preaching took place through Christ's followers rather than through Christ himself. Hoehner's comment is typical: "Certainly this refers to the preaching of peace by the apostles rather than Christ Himself because Christ preached almost entirely to Jews (Matt. 10:5–6; 15:24–27). Also the peace that was preached was on the basis of Christ's death rather than during His life on earth."[94] Stott agrees with Hoehner: "And since the achievement was at the cross, and logically the announcement must follow the achievement, this preaching cannot refer to his public ministry. It must refer rather to his post-resurrection appearances, in which the very first word he spoke to the apostles was 'Peace be with you', and to his proclamation of the gospel of peace to the world through the apostles and through subsequent generations of Christians."[95]

However, Mitton points out that "Christ's conversations with the Syrophoenician woman, the Roman centurion, the Samaritan leper, the Samaritan woman, and the centurion at the cross show that a mission to the Gentiles was in Christ's mind during his ministry on earth."[96] Foulkes would prefer to remain uncommitted when he warns that "we are not to ask what preaching of peace this refers to—before or after the resurrection, before or after Pentecost."[97]

Whatever the resolution to this debate may be, it is clear that the gospel speaks of peace between God and humanity and between human beings as a central emphasis (Luke 2:14; John 14:27; Acts 10:36; Rom. 5:1; 14:17; 15:13; 16:20; Gal. 5:22; 6:16; Eph. 1:2; 2:14, 15, 17; 4:3; 6:15, 23; Phil. 4:7; Col 3:15; 1 Thess. 5:23; 2 Thess. 3:16; 2 Tim. 2:22; Heb. 12:14; 13:20; James 3:18; 1 Peter 3:11; 2 Peter 3:14). And Westcott is certainly right when he points out that "the record of the Acts—the Gospel of the Spirit—is the history of the extension of the message of peace to the whole world, beginning at Jerusalem and closing in Rome."[98]

Verse 18 presents Christ as the one who provides access to God. All three persons of the Trinity are present in this verse. Access is through Christ, in the Spirit, to the Father. Barth notes that Ephesians has several Trinitarian statements: 1:4–14; 4:4–6; cf. also 2 Cor. 13:13.[99] And he mentions that access "denotes the act of leading toward a

---

[94]Hoehner, "Ephesians," 626.

[95]John R. W. Stott, *God's New Society: The Message of Ephesians*, BST (Downers Grove, Ill.: InterVarsity Press, 1979), 103.

[96]Mitton, *Ephesians*, 109–10.

[97]Foulkes, *Ephesians*, 84.

[98]Westcott, *Ephesians*, 39.

[99]Barth, *Ephesians 1–3*, 268.

potentate, or granting the privilege of admission."[100] Salmond observes that the present tense "we have" denotes a present and continuing privilege and cautions that the ἐν is not *by* but *in* and refers to the element in which alone we have the access.[101] The verse affirms, then, that the source of access is the Son, the sphere of access is the Spirit, and the object of access is the Father.

Verses 19–22 draw this section of Ephesians to a close by concluding about the consequences of Christ's work. The consequences are fivefold: (1) Gentiles are no longer strangers and transients; (2) Gentiles and Jews are now members of the same household; (3) the new household is built upon Christ and the New Testament apostles and prophets; (4) the church is Christ's new temple; and (5) the church is a residence of the Holy Spirit.

In verse 19 Paul returns to the second person plural. He applies the redemptive work of Christ to the Gentiles and then to the Jews through the use of civil and architectural metaphors. As a consequence of Christ's reconciling work (ἄρα οὖν), Gentiles are no longer disenfranchised. Paul uses two nouns to describe the prior status of Gentiles: ξένος and πάροικος. According to Abbott, a ξένος is a foreigner in general; a πάροικος is a foreigner dwelling in a state who has no rights of citizenship.[102] Barth thinks that the two nouns are a hendiadys that suggests that all members of the out-group are no longer segregated from the compact in-group.[103]

The new status of Gentiles is complicated by the identification of τῶν ἁγίων in the next clause. There is no unanimity concerning their identity. In fact, some of the strongest statements are made by the various advocates of divergent theologies. Really, this one noun recycles the whole problem with which this entire letter is concerned: Gentiles and Israel or the church and Israel.

Lincoln presents the four possibilities Israel, Jewish Christians, angels, and all Christians and concludes that the reference must be to all Christians because of the consistency of usage in Ephesians of the word (1:1, 15, 18; 3:8; 4:12: 5:3; 6:18). In order to handle the σύν before πολῖται, he is forced to say that the σύν compounds have in view unity with the rest of the church.[104]

But it is details like the σύν compounds that cause other writers to identify the ἅγιοι as Israel or Jewish Christians who are a remnant of Israel. Robinson identifies them as the "holy People whose privileges

[100]Ibid.
[101]Salmond, "Ephesians," 298.
[102]Abbott, *Ephesians and Colossians,* 68.
[103]Barth, *Ephesians 1–3,* 269.
[104]Lincoln, "Church and Israel," 613–14.

they have come to share."[105] Martin believes they are Jewish Christians, as they often are in Acts.[106] And Scott combines the views of Robinson and Martin by saying that the noun refers to "those Jewish Christians who claimed, in right of their descent, to be God's people *par excellence.*"[107]

The problem is not resolved by identifying the ἅγιοι as Jewish Christians, however. The next question is usually whether this means that Gentiles are now part of "true" or "new" Israel, since συμπολῖται is a cognate of πολιτεία in verse 12. However, the term *Israel* in the New Testament is consistently reserved for physical descendants of Abraham.[108] It is not used of Gentiles. But if the Gentiles are not incorporated into the commonwealth of Israel, what citizenship do they share with Jews/Israel? Although some of Chafer's comments on this are extreme, he is basically correct when he concludes that the citizenship is "that of the heavenly city into which blessed abode the saints of all dispensations will yet be gathered (Heb. 12:22–24; Phil. 3:20)."[109]

Gentiles and Jews in Christ now form a new spiritual household. This household is a temple composed of living stones and serving as a residence of God through the Holy Spirit. There has been much discussion about verse 20. Commentators argue over whether the apostles or Christ should be the foundation, whether the prophets are Old or New Testament prophets, whether the apostles and prophets are one group or two, and whether Christ is a cornerstone or a keystone. The majority of writers conclude that both the apostles and Christ are the foundation of the new temple (the apparent conflict is just a matter of perspective); the order apostles before prophets argues for New Testament prophets; the apostles and prophets are two distinct groups; and Christ is the cornerstone rather than the keystone.[110] The fact that Paul writes here about a "foundation" and that the apostles and prophets are New Testament apostles and prophets does support my contention in this chapter that there is a real redemptive-historical change in the death of Christ and the creation of the new man.

The final difficult problem in this section is the translation of πᾶσα

[105]J. Armitage Robinson, *St. Paul's Epistle to the Ephesians* (London: James Clarke, n.d.), 163.

[106]Martin, "Ephesians," 1112.

[107]Scott, *Colossians, Philemon, and Ephesians,* 176.

[108]Carl B. Hock, Jr., "The Term *Israel* in the New Testament" (Th.D. diss., Dallas Theological Seminary, 1971).

[109]Lewis Sperry Chafer, *The Ephesian Letter* (Grand Rapids: Dunham, 1935), 94.

[110]Abbott, Barth, Beare, Bruce, and Salmond support the New Testament prophet view. R. J. McKelvey, *The New Temple* (London: Oxford, 1969), has a good discussion of Jeremias's argument for keystone in appendix C (195–204) and concludes that Paul meant a cornerstone.

οἰκοδομή in verse 21. Grammatically the combination should be translated "every building," since οἰκοδομή lacks the article. According to Abbott, the balance of the manuscript evidence is strongly against the insertion of the article.[111] But the whole flow of Paul's argument seems to demand the translation "the whole building." Commentators have taken various routes to relieve the difficulty. Bruce finds "some authority elsewhere in the New Testament for the meaning 'all' in a construction of this kind even when the definite article is absent."[112] Robinson says that Paul omits the article because he is looking at an uncompleted building growing toward completion.[113] Westcott is almost poetic when he describes the new temple in terms of the old temple, with its "council chambers, treasuries, chambers for priests, cloisters, all become part of the sanctuary."[114] Barth tries to have the best of both worlds by rendering "all that is being built."[115] Whatever the precise meaning is, all seem to agree that Paul did not have individual congregations in mind. He is looking at the new edifice that is in the process of erection after having had a solid foundation laid. This edifice is the *universal church*, with Christ as its cornerstone and head and the apostles and prophets as its foundation in the role of recipients of the divine revelation of the mystery (cf. 3:5). This universal church, then, is the "new man" of Ephesians 2.

Two more σύν compounds show the joining of the two formerly alienated groups into one new organism. Gentiles and Jews are joined together and built together into the new temple. The two σύν compound present participles and the present indicative αὔξει indicate a process that was going on in Paul's time and still has not been completed. Barth writes that αὐξάνω "means an increase in size, number, age, maturity, glory and power."[116]

This temple under contruction is holy. It is holy because God is present in it.[117] And it is "in the Lord." The "Lord" is usually Jesus Christ in Pauline usage.[118] Jesus Christ is not only the one from whom growth begins but also the one in whom growth continues (cf. 2 Peter 3:18).

With one final locative (ἐν ᾧ) Paul once again underscores the centrality of Christ in redemptive history. Gentiles and Jews are being

[111]Abbott, *Ephesians and Colossians*, 72n.
[112]Bruce, *Ephesians*, 58.
[113]Robinson, *Ephesians*, 164.
[114]Westcott, *Ephesians*, 41.
[115]Barth, *Ephesians 1–3*, 272.
[116]Ibid., 273.
[117]Ibid.
[118]Abbott, *Ephesians and Colossians*, 75.

built together in him into a dwelling in which God lives by his Spirit. Abbott supports the importance of the σύν compound: "The whole context favours the interpretation 'you together with others,' and there is no reason to give any other sense to the σύν in συναρμολογουμένη."[119] Hoehner remarks that this σύν shows that Gentiles are now one "new man" with Jewish believers.[120] No finer comment could complete this section on the new creation, on man, and on the temple than that of Stott: "He is not tied to holy buildings but to holy people, to his own new society."[121]

SUMMARY AND CONCLUSION

This chapter has argued for a number of theses that are fundamental to any discussion concerning the relationship between the church and Israel.

1. Ephesians is a key book in developing any biblical theology of Israel and the church.

2. Acceptance or denial of Pauline authorship will seriously affect the conclusions one draws about the intent of Ephesians.

3. A redemptive-historical reading of Paul is necessary if Paul's theology is to be properly understood, especially his Christology, pneumatology, soteriology, ecclesiology, anthropology, and eschatology.

4. A redemptive-historical reading of both Ephesians and Romans reveals that Paul had a consistent theology: Israel as the first elect people of God was given certain special privileges from God, which Paul names in Romans 3:2; 9:4–5; and Ephesians 2:12.

5. Ephesians 2:11–22 is a central text for the new man.

The privileges mentioned in the fourth thesis were restricted to Israel before the death of Christ and the creation of the church. Gentiles in Christ now *share with* a remnant of Israel that now exists in "the new man," the church (Rom. 11:5). Christ and this remnant carry redemptive history forward and form the bridge between the old and new covenants. The remnant of Israel together with Gentiles forms the ecclesiological *one new man*. This new man is a new creation in Christ because the death of Christ was absolutely necessary before the transfer from "in Adam" to "in Christ" could be made, before the cancellation of the enmity maintained by the Mosaic law could be accomplished, and

---

[119]Ibid., 76.
[120]Hoehner, "Ephesians," 628.
[121]Stott, *Colossians, Philemon, and Ephesians,* 110.

before the Holy Spirit became the new standard for the ethical new man, who walks "according to the Spirit" and "not according to the flesh." The ecclesiological, anthropological, and ethical structures of the new man are so intertwined for Paul that no separation of the three is possible. The three are interrelated and imply one another.

Although the primary focus of Paul in Ephesians 2 was on the ecclesiological new man, the anthropological new man was always in the background, and the ethical new man to be explicitly expounded in Ephesians 4:22–24 was anticipated. The argument of 2:11–22 moves from the alienation of the Gentiles in the ποτέ period to the current period, when they were brought near to God and to Israel through the cross of Christ.

If one asks whether "the one new man" connotes continuity or discontinuity between Israel and the church or between the Testaments, the answer is that both are found in this text. There is a strong emphasis on newness, and consequently on discontinuity. The new creation, new man, and new temple are discontinuous with Israel. But in terms of redemptive history there is continuity. The church is no accident or substitute for a failed kingdom program. Ephesians makes absolutely clear that God's plan and purpose have always been centered in Christ. The past alienation of Gentiles was only a phase of redemptive history before "the fullness of time" arrived (Gal. 4:4). The believing remnant of Israel within the church share in promises that have Old Testament roots. Through the covenants, Messiah, and promises of Israel, they experience promised blessings in which Gentiles also participate. Their new relationship resides in the new man, "the new temple" where God resides in a community of Jew-Gentile renewed by the Spirit and reconciled by Christ.

CHAPTER 4

The Church as the Mystery of God

Robert L. Saucy

The apostolic teaching in Ephesians 3 concerning the mystery has occasioned considerable disagreement between dispensationalists and nondispensationalists. Traditional dispensationalism, on the one hand, has used it to support the total discontinuity of the church with the Old Testament prophetic plan of salvation, in which the nation of Israel has the central position.[1] Nondispensationalism, on the other hand, understands the revelation of the mystery as the fulfillment of Old Testament Scriptures. While the church composed of Jew and Gentile may be viewed by some nondispensationalists as a new work of God, it is nevertheless the continuation of the divine program of salvation in such a way that it assumes the position of God's final historical channel of salvation, a position designated to Israel in the prophecies.[2]

My purpose in this chapter is not to detail the arguments of the above positions, which often entail considerable discussion of the entire biblical revelation dealing with Israel and the church. Rather, it is to focus on the apostle's more limited teaching concerning the mystery itself.

THE CONTENT OF THE MYSTERY

The General Teaching of the Mystery Passage (3:1–14)

The specific content of the mystery of the Jew and Gentile united in the church (3:6) is contained within the apostle's discussion of his own

[1]See, for example, John F. Walvoord, *The Millennial Kingdom* (Findlay, Ohio: Dunham, 1959), 232–37; Charles C. Ryrie, *Dispensationalism Today* (Chicago: Moody Press, 1965), 133–37; Lewis Sperry Chafer, *Systematic Theology,* 8 vols. (Dallas: Dallas Seminary Press, 1947), 4:71–78.

[2]See, for example, Oswald T. Allis, *Prophecy and the Church* (Philadephia: Presbyterian & Reformed, 1945), 91–108; Herman Ridderbos, *Paul: An Outline of His Theology* (Grand Rapids: Eerdmans, 1975), 46–47, 339–40.

personal ministry. This discussion enters in as a digression in relation to his prayer for his Gentile audience, which begins in verse 1 with the words "for this reason." It is resumed with the repetition of these same words in verse 14.

The digression explains Paul's description of himself as "the prisoner of Christ Jesus for the sake of you Gentiles" (v. 1) and thereby adds intensity to his prayer. According to Caragounis, the digression reflects a triangle of relationships involving Paul, Christ, and the Gentiles mentioned in the introduction: "I Paul am a prisoner *because* I serve Christ which I do *for the benefit* of you Gentiles."[3] The apostle's bonds were evidence of his faithfulness to and the success of the ministry to which God had called him. His chains were the sign of his victory and therefore should be the glory of the Gentiles rather than a cause of any discouragement.[4]

The passage may be divided into two main sections: verses 2–7, which focus on the content and divine origin of the mystery, and verses 8–12, which relate Paul's task concerning the mystery—namely, to evangelize the Gentiles and make known the administration of the mystery. These are followed by a concluding word of encouragement (v. 13).[5]

In the first section (vv. 2–7), the emphasis is upon the divine initiative and empowerment of Paul's ministry. The apostle informs his readers that a certain "administration of God's grace" had been committed to him on their behalf (v. 3). The reference is probably to the grace of apostleship, which involved, as Hodge writes, "all the gifts ordinary and extraordinary, which went to make him an apostle,"[6] and not simply the grace embodied in the gospel.[7] The ascribing of his ministry of the mystery to God's grace is also expressed in verses 7 and 8. The fact that his ministry was due solely to the grace of God continually impressed the apostle (cf. Rom. 1:5; 15:15; 1 Cor. 3:10; Gal. 1:15; 2:9).

Involved in this gift of grace was revelation from God that consisted of the mystery and its particular reference to Gentiles, who were the focus of Paul's apostolic ministry (v. 4). The language ($\kappa\alpha\tau\grave{\alpha}$

[3]Chrys C. Caragounis, *The Ephesian "Mysterion"* (Lund: C. W. K. Gleerup, 1977), 56.

[4]B. F. Westcott, *St. Paul's Epistle to the Ephesians,* reprint ed. (Grand Rapids: Baker, 1979), 43.

[5]Caragounis, *Ephesian "Mysterion,"* 73–74.

[6]Charles Hodge, *An Exposition of Ephesians,* reprint ed. (Wilmington, Del.: Associated Publishers & Authors, n.d.), 56; cf. also H. A. W. Meyer, *A Critical and Exegetical Hand-Book to the Epistle to the Galatians and Ephesians* (New York: Funk & Wagnalls, 1884), 406; Westcott, *Ephesians,* 44.

[7]F. F. Bruce, *The Epistles to the Colossians, to Philemon, and to the Ephesians* (Grand Rapids: Eerdmans, 1984), 311.

ἀποκάλυψιν, lit. "according to revelation") does not point so much to specific moments or contents of revelation (e.g., Acts 9:15; 22:21; Gal. 1:16), but rather to "the general mode of communication."[8] It denotes "revelation as a continuous and unceasing flow of information and power."[9] While the apostle emphasizes his own personal involvement in the reception and proclamation of the mystery (vv. 3, 8; cf. Col. 1:25–26; Rom. 16:25–26), revelation of it had also been given to the church at large through God's "holy apostles and prophets" (v. 5).[10]

Because of this divine revelation Paul could claim "insight" into the mystery, which his readers should be able to understand or perceive. The term *insight* (σύνεσις) signifies more than the apostle's intellectual understanding of doctrine. As Barth notes, it includes the "appropriate decision, action, attitude,"[11] and as such it encompasses the apostle's entire ministry of the mystery. The apostle's ministry of the mystery is therefore not of his own making. Since it rests solely on grace and supernaturally given insight, it is divinely authoritative and can be trusted, despite Paul's present negative circumstances.

The second section (vv. 8–12) emphasizes the specific task given to Paul as a result of God's grace. It is "to preach to the Gentiles the unsearchable riches of Christ, and to make plain to everyone[12] the administration of this mystery" (vv. 8–9). Since the riches of Christ can be nothing other than the gospel (cf. vv. 6, 7), the apostle clearly links his preaching of the gospel with the outworking of the mystery. The administration of the mystery is essentially defined in the ministry of proclaiming the gospel. The mystery is therefore not something peripheral to the entire gospel of Christ. It cannot be understood, for example, as simply an aspect of ecclesiological doctrine somewhat unconnected with the gospel. Rather, according to the apostle, the true

---

[8]Westcott, *Ephesians,* 44.

[9]Markus Barth, *Ephesians 1–3,* AB (Garden City, N.Y.: Doubleday, 1974), 330.

[10]Paul's personal prominence in the ministry of the mystery no doubt has reference to his leadership in the church's acceptance of the gospel for the Gentiles and to his special ministry to them (cf. Acts 15; Rom. 11:13; 15:15, 16; Gal. 1:16; 2:7–10).

[11]Barth, *Ephesians 1–3,* 331.

[12]The word πάντας, "everyone," is not found in some of the ancient manuscripts and is not included in some versions, for example, NASB, NEB, JB. This reading is supported by T. K. Abbott, *A Critical and Exegetical Commentary on the Epistles to the Ephesians and to the Colossians,* ICC (Edinburgh: T. & T. Clark, 1897), 87; and J. Armitage Robinson, *St. Paul's Epistle to the Ephesians* (London: James Clarke, n.d.), 170. However, with the majority of important manuscripts, it is probably to be retained; so Barth, *Ephesians 1–3,* 342; Bruce, *Colossians, Philemon, and Ephesians,* 317; and Caragounis, *Ephesian "Mysterion,"* 106 n. 36. If it is retained, the thought is the enlightenment or actual instruction of "all" as to what the administration of the the mystery is. In contrast, the omission would refer to the revelation or bringing to light of the same. As Abbott notes, "The meaning is pretty much the same with either reading, since the result of bringing the οἰκ. to light is that all men are enabled to see it."

meaning and outworking of the gospel are also the administration of the mystery.

The Specific Content

The precise content of the "mystery" in verse 4 is debated. The further statement that something had already been written briefly concerning this mystery (v. 4), does not help to decide the issue.[13] For it is not clear whether that earlier reference is only to the more immediately preceding discussion of the new relationship of Jew and Gentile (2:11–22),[14] or whether it includes both this teaching and the earlier reference to the mystery in 1:9–10.[15]

The singular reference (i.e., "the mystery") as well as its description simply as "of Christ" leads many to understand the mystery as God's whole saving action in the person and work of Christ, but with special reference here in chapter 3 to the participation of Gentiles in it. As Meyer explains, "Christ Himself, His person and His whole work, especially His redeeming death, connecting also the Gentiles with the people of God (v. 6), is the *concretum* of the Divine mystery."[16]

This broad understanding would connect the mystery of chapter 3 to the previously mentioned mystery in chapter 1. There it refers to the comprehensive plan of God "to bring all things . . . together under one head, even Christ" (vv. 9–10). Acknowledging that the accent of Ephesians is "upon the rule of Christ over all powers . . . , and upon the creation of a new man by the peace made between Jews and Gentiles and God," Barth sees the content of this first reference to mystery in Ephesians as essentially the same as in Colossians, where "Jesus Christ is the essence and contents of the revealed secret (Col 2:2)."[17] The mystery of chapter 3 thus ultimately has reference to this same broad content.

Others interpreters, focusing on the content detailed in verse 6, limit the meaning of the mystery to the incorporation of Gentiles into salvation. Viewing the mystery as only "related to Christ" rather than Christ himself, Abbott restricts its content to "the doctrine of the free

---

[13]The reference to reading that which had been written (v. 4) apparently relates to something written earlier in the Ephesian letter and not to another epistle (Abbott, *Ephesians and Colossians,* 79–80).

[14]John Eadie, *Commentary on the Epistle to the Ephesians* (Grand Rapids: Zondervan, n.d., reprint of 1883 ed.), 214; Westcott, *Ephesians,* 45.

[15]Heinrich Schlier understands Paul's reference to what he had previously written in 1:3–14, 18–23 and in chap. 2 (*Der Brief an die Epheser* [Dusseldorf: Patmos-Verlag, 1971], 149).

[16]Meyer, *Galatians and Ephesians,* 408; similar comprehensive definitions of the mystery are held by Robinson, *Ephesians,* 31, 76; and Barth, *Ephesians 1–3,* 329, 331.

[17]Barth, *Ephesians 1–3,* 125.

admission of the Gentiles."[18] Eadie similarly defines the mystery as the Gentile "admission to church fellowship equally with the Jews."[19] On the understanding that the "new revelation" composing the "mystery" was not found in the Old Testament Scriptures, Bruce identifies the mystery as the "obliteration of the old line of demarcation" in the incorporation of Gentiles and Jews into the new community of God's people. According to Bruce, Gentile blessing was part of the Old Testament promises, but this total lack of discrimination was not. This latter truth is therefore the content of the mystery that has been newly revealed.[20]

Hodge presents yet a third view of the "mystery" statements of chapter 3 by distinguishing between a broad concept of the "mystery of Christ" (v. 4), which he identifies with Christ himself and God's whole plan of salvation, and "the mystery" (v. 3) that is "the union of the Gentiles with the Jews."[21] Such a distinction seems doubtful, as the entire passage gives no hint of a different meaning to the mystery in these verses. Furthermore, it is the mention of the "mystery of Christ" in verse 4, and not "the mystery" in verse 3, which provides the nearest antecedent for the union of Jew and Gentile in verse 6, the commonly agreed central content of the mystery of this chapter. If there is any distinction between the mysteries of verses 3 and 4, it is more likely the opposite; that is, verse 3 is "a general reference to the *mysterion* and its revelation in the all-inclusive sense," whereas verse 4 points to the union of Gentiles and Jews spelled out in verse 6.[22]

In a slightly different way, Bornkamm seemingly combines both the narrow and broad interpretations with regard to the content of the mystery. After stating that the mystery in Ephesians 3:4–9 is "the share of the Gentiles in the inheritance, in the body of the Church, in the promise in Christ," he concludes that "there takes place in it already the mystery of the comprehending of the whole created world in Christ, in whom the totality receives its head and sum (Eph. 1:9, 10)."[23]

In light of the general terminology used (i.e., "the mystery" and "the mystery of Christ"), the broader interpretation of the content of the mystery seems preferable. We would conclude with Barth that Paul's reference to "the mystery" (v. 3) about which he had already written briefly is "an allusion to 1:9–10 or any other brief passage within Eph. 1–2 which speaks about the grace and power of God, his eternal

[18]Abbott, *Ephesians and Colossians*, 80.
[19]Eadie, *Ephesians*, 214.
[20]Bruce, *Colossians, Philemon, and Ephesians*, 314.
[21]Hodge, *Ephesians*, 57.
[22]Caragounis, *Ephesian "Mysterion,"* 140.
[23]G. Bornkamm, "μυστήριον," *TDNT* 4:820.

decision, revelation, the adoption of the Gentiles, the one body formed, the involvement of principalities and powers, or free access to the Father."[24] As there is no indicated difference between the content of the several references to "mystery" in these verses, it is best to see the "mystery of Christ" (v. 4) as carrying this same meaning.

Despite this broad concept of the mystery, the focus of the apostle in chapter 3 is clearly on that aspect of the mystery dealing with the unity of Jew and Gentile delineated in verse 6. How the latter relates to the broader concept will be discussed in the next section. Suffice it to say at this point that, taken together, the statements concerning the mystery in chapter 3 suggest that the apostle had "insight" into the entire mystery of Christ (v. 4) but desires to emphasize to the Ephesians the aspect that particularly distinguished his apostolic ministry, namely, the new relationship of Jew and Gentile in Christ through the gospel.[25]

Whether the beginning infinitive ($εἶναι$) in verse 6 is understood with most interpreters as epexegetical (i.e., "that is," or "namely")[26] or as fulfilling the function of a sentence describing in this instance a piece of information (i.e., "that the Gentiles . . . are . . ."),[27] verse 6 specifies the mystery's content as the truth "that through the gospel the Gentiles are heirs together with Israel, members together of one body, and sharers together in the promise in Christ Jesus."

The word $συγκληρονόμα$, "heirs together," is related to the word $κληρονομέω$, "to inherit," and signifies those who will receive or inherit something along with others.[28] The content of the inheritance is not specified here. However, it is no doubt related to the other references of an inheritance for believers in the Ephesian letter. In the first two instances the content, like this one, is not stated (1:14, 18).[29] However, in the third instance, the apostle speaks of an "inheritance in the kingdom of Christ and of God" (5:5). Other references in the New

[24]Barth, *Ephesians 1–3,* 329.

[25]Although Caragounis sees the reference to mystery in v. 4 as already the narrower content of v. 6, the relation between the broad overall mystery of God in Christ and that of v. 6 is well stated when he writes, "The *mysterion* of 1:9f. is the all-comprehending eschatological purpose of God as made known to the author (among others). In 3:4 it is that *mysterion* as proclaimed by the author to the Gentiles, applying to them in its limited aspect" (*Ephesians "Mysterion,"* 141).

[26]Abbott, *Ephesians and Colossians,* 83; Meyer, *Galatians and Ephesians,* 410.

[27]Barth, *Ephesians 1–3,* 336. Arguing that the epexegetical infinitive requires a preceding demonstrative pronoun, for example, "this is. . . ," Barth says, "The infinitive fulfills the function of a sentence that begins with 'that' and describes a perception, a belief, an utterance, or a piece of information." He prefers the paraphrase of J. B. Phillips: "This secret was hidden. . . . It is simply this: that the gentiles . . . are . . . " (vv. 5–6).

[28]Werner Foerster, "$κληρονόμος$," *TDNT* 3:781. $Συγκληρονόμα$ is found in three other instances in the New Testament (Rom. 8:17; Heb. 11:9; 1 Peter 3:7).

[29]It is possible with the NASB and the alternative translation in the NIV to see a fourth reference to inheritance in 1:11.

Testament (most of which are from the apostle Paul) reveal the content of the believer's inheritance as salvation (Heb. 1:14); glory (Rom. 8:17; cf. v. 23, "the redemption of our bodies"; Eph. 1:18); eternal life (Luke 18:18; Titus 3:7; 1 Peter 3:7); blessing (1 Peter 3:9); the promises (Heb. 6:12; cf. 10:36); and the kingdom of God (Matt. 25:34; 1 Cor. 6:19; 15:50; Gal. 5:21; James 2:5).

The final reference in the canonical Scripture to the inheritance (Rev. 21:7) describes its content as "all this," which the previous context describes as "the blessedness of God's people in the new creation."[30] This, as Foerster notes, summarizes and explains all of the other descriptions of the content above: "This tells us what is meant by the βασιλεία τοῦ θεοῦ, by ζωή, by σωτηρία and εὐλογία. In short, it tells us what the inheritance includes."[31] Without any limiting specification of the content in the previous mention of the believers' inheritance in Ephesians (1:14, 18), and given the broad content of the "kingdom" in 5:5, it seems most likely that in 3:6 the apostle intends the most comprehensive meaning of the inheritance in which the Gentiles now have a part.

To bring the Gentiles to a participation in the inheritance of God's people was in a very real sense the sum of Paul's apostolic ministry. On the Damascus road, the risen Lord sent him to the Gentiles "to open their eyes and turn them from darkness to light, and from the power of Satan to God, so that they may receive forgiveness of sins and a place [an inheritance, NASB; a share in the inheritance, JB] among those who are sanctified by faith in me" (Acts 26:17–18; cf. 20:32). The first aspect of the mystery—that is, that the Gentiles share in the inheritance of the saints—is thus nothing less than saying that they participate fully in the blessings of the ultimate salvation that God has prepared for all of his people "in Christ" (cf. Col. 1:12).

In distinction from Romans 8:17, where the apostle used the same term to teach the tremendous reality that believers are coheirs with Christ, the content of the Ephesians 3 mystery is the fact that Gentiles have become partakers of the inheritance together with Israel. While there is no mention of "Israel" (which the NIV translation might suggest), the prior context makes it clear that it is "believing Jews" with whom the Gentiles share.[32] Care must be taken at this juncture that one does not say more than the apostle. It is certainly biblical to say with Barth that according to Ephesians "no Gentile can have communion with Christ or

---

[30]G. R. Beasley-Murray, *The Book of Revelation,* NBC (Grand Rapids: Eerdmans, 1978), 313.

[31]Foerster, "κληρονόμος," 783.

[32]Abbott, *Ephesians and Colossians,* 83; cf. Barth: "together with Israel the Gentiles are now 'heirs, members, beneficiaries' " (*Ephesians 1–3,* 337).

with God unless he also has communion with Israel." But to add that Ephesians therefore agrees with Romans and Galatians that the Gentiles "are grafted onto Israel" is to go beyond the apostle's teaching.[33]

The Gentiles share with Jews, but nothing is said about their becoming Jews or part of Israel unless one reads in a new definition of Israel, which is difficult to sustain exegetically.[34] The relationship of Gentile and Jew as coheirs is seen in the teaching of the new position of Gentiles with Jews in 2:11–22. Although Gentiles are described as being formerly "excluded from citizenship in Israel" (2:12), they are not now in Christ said to be citizens of that nation. Rather, both Gentile and Jew are made into "one new man" (2:15), and both are reconciled to God and given a new intimate relationship with him through Christ and the coming of the Spirit (vv. 16–18). As Meyer explains, "This union has in fact taken place as a raising of both into a higher unity."[35] Similarly, Lincoln declares that the former disadvantages of the Gentiles "have been reversed not by their being incorporated into Israel, even into a renewed Israel of Jewish Christians, but by their being made members of a new community which transcends the categories of Jew and Gentile, an entity which is a new creation."[36] They remain Gentiles and Jews (or people of Israel), even as men and women, parents and children, slaves and masters remain what they are (5:22–6:9) while all sharing together equally as heirs of the future blessing.

Further evidence of this relationship of Jew and Gentile in the mystery as heirs together is seen when the basis of their position is considered. Believers have the status of heirs, according to the apostle, because of their relationship to Abraham. Those who belong to Christ, Jew and Gentile alike, are "Abraham's seed," and thus they are also "heirs according to the promise" (Gal. 3:29). The inheritance of which the apostle here speaks may be viewed as "all the blessing pledged to Abraham and his descendants."[37] In writing to the Romans about this same blessing of promise to Abraham and his descendants (Rom. 4:13), the apostle pointedly identifies Abraham as the father of both Gentile ("all who believe but have not been circumcised") and Jewish believers ("the circumcised . . . who also walk in the footsteps of the faith that our

[33]Barth, *Ephesians 1–3,* 337.

[34]Barth, no doubt, has such a "new" or "spiritual Israel" in mind. So also does Westcott when he says that the Gentiles are "fellow heirs with natural Israel of the great hopes of the spiritual Israel" (*Ephesians,* 46). But the Ephesian letter says nothing of such a "new" or "spiritual" Israel, nor is it clear in any other apostolic teaching. See Peter Richardson, *Israel in the Apostolic Church* (Cambridge: Cambridge University Press, 1969).

[35]Meyer, *Galatians and Ephesians,* 383.

[36]Andrew T. Lincoln, "The Church and Israel in Ephesians 2," *CBQ* 49 (October 1987): 615.

[37]Bruce, *Colossians, Philemon, and Ephesians,* 316.

father Abraham had before he was circumcised") (Rom. 4:9–11). The mystery status of the Gentiles as coheirs with Israel thus signifies their participation along with Israel in the final inheritance that God has prepared for all of his people, both those who are Gentiles and those of Israel.

The second term of the content of the mystery, σύσσωμα, "members together of one body," refers to joint incorporation of Gentiles with believing Jews "into the body of which Christ is the Head."[38] Much of the emphasis in the apostle's other teaching on the Body of Christ focuses on the incorporation of the believer into the body and the resultant relationship with the Head and the other members (cf. Rom. 12:4–8; 1 Cor. 12:12–27; Eph. 4:16). Here, however, following the teaching of the reconciliation and union of Jew and Gentile in the one body (2:15–16), the thrust is on their joint involvement in the body. Robinson aptly explains, "In relation to the Body the members are 'incorporate': in relation to one another they are 'concorporate', that is, sharers in the one Body."[39] This aspect of the mystery thus informs us that the Gentile believers share with believing Jews all that is involved with being in the body of Christ, namely, the blessings of spiritual union with him and all other believers.

The third element of the content of the mystery is that the Gentiles are "sharers together in the promise." The apostle had previously mentioned the promise in relation to the Gentiles' reception of "the promised Holy Spirit" (1:13–14), and their former existence as "foreigners to the covenants of the promise," in which Israel already participated (2:12). Now he climaxes the content of the mystery with the fact that Gentiles are full partners with Israel in God's promise. The content of "the promise" is not specified. Along with the Spirit (1:13; Gal. 3:14), the apostle in other places has identified the promise as the inheritance (Rom. 4:13; Gal. 3:18–19), life (Gal. 3:21), righteousness (Gal. 3:21), and adoption or sonship (Rom. 9:8; Gal. 4:22–31). With many interpreters, it is no doubt correct to see all of these different aspects combined as constituting the one messianic salvation that may be said to be "the promise."[40] This explains the use of both the singular "promise" (Eph. 2:12; Gal. 3:17) and the plural "promises" (Rom. 9:4; 15:8; Gal. 3:16).

Despite the comprehensive nature of the promise, the gift of the Spirit is prominent in the apostle's thinking (cf. Gal. 3:14). It is the

[38]Abbott, *Ephesians and Colossians*, 83.
[39]Robinson, *Ephesians*, 78.
[40]Julius Schniewind and Gerhard Friedrich, "ἐπαγγέλλω κτλ.," *TDNT* 2:583; cf. Meyer, *Galatians and Ephesians*, 410; Abbott, *Ephesians and Colossians*, 83.

presence of the Spirit that finally brings to reality the other dimensions of the promised salvation. If such is the case in our passage, this third statement serves to climax the previous statements of the mystery, as Westcott explains:

> There is an expressive sequence in three elements of the full endowment of the Gentiles as coequal with the Jews. They had a right to all for which Israel looked. They belonged to the same Divine society. They enjoyed the gift by which the new society was distinguished from the old. And when regarded from the point of sight of the Apostolic age, the gift of the Holy Spirit, "the promise of the Father" (Luke 24:49; Acts 1:4; 2:33, 38f.), is preeminently "the promise," to which also συμμέτοχα perfectly corresponds.[41]

The final phrases of the verse, according to the Greek text, "in Christ through the gospel," apply to all of the three previous statements and not just the last. They point out "the occasion, the means, and the condition for the whole content of v. 6."[42] The union of Gentile and Jew is effected in the person of Christ himself (2:13–16). And Christ is made available through the gospel, which at this point probably includes its powerful proclamation. Friedrich notes that in keeping with its derivation from Old Testament and rabbinic usage as a *nomen actionis,* the term *gospel* is used at times in the New Testament to describe the act of proclamation as well as its content (cf. 2 Cor. 2:12; Phil. 4:3; 1 Cor. 9:14). It includes "the dissemination, content and power of the message."[43] Thus it was through the preaching of the gospel that Gentiles and Jews were united in the new saving action of Christ. For this reason the apostle can speak later in the epistle of the "mystery of the gospel" (6:19), by which he means the mystery whose contents are proclaimed in the gospel.

The mystery of verse 6 may thus be summed up as the coequal participation of the Gentiles with Israel in the full messianic salvation that is realized in the crucified and risen Christ and made effective to both through the apostolic proclamation of the gospel. This truth of the

---

[41]Westcott, *Ephesians,* 47. Although Barth unduly restricts the promise to the Spirit, his understanding of the sequence of the terms is instructive: "More likely the three attributes of Eph 3:6 are so arranged as to lead to a climax. The last attribute is indeed a climax, if by 'promise' is meant the substance and earnest of the promise, the Holy Spirit. Because his presence manifests God's presence among his people, the Spirit is indeed the epitome of God's promise. The reference to inheritance emphasizes the hope for the future; the mention of the body alludes to the gift and task of an organic and social life; the endowment with the Spirit gives reason for joy and guarantees freedom. Through the Spirit the goods of the coming aeon are already tasted, cf. Heb 6:4" (*Ephesians 1–3,* 338).

[42]Barth, *Ephesians 1–3,* 335; cf. Abbott, *Ephesians and Colossians,* 83; Meyer, *Galatians and Ephesians,* 410.

[43]Gerhard Friedrich, "εὐαγγελίζομαι κτλ.," *TNDT* 2:729, 732.

unity of Gentiles and Israel in the church, which has already been introduced in connection with the "mystery of his will" (1:9–14, esp. vv. 12–13) and elaborated in 2:11–22, stands behind all of the teachings of the epistle as the central theme.[44]

THE MYSTERY NATURE OF THE UNITY OF GENTILE AND JEW IN THE CHURCH

Having briefly noted the place of the mystery statement in the epistle and examined its content, it remains for us to look more closely at the significance of calling the unity of Gentile and Jew in Christ a mystery. In pursuit of this issue, we will look first at the meaning of the term *mystery* and then consider its use in the New Testament and the possible relation of the Ephesian 3:6 mystery to the other uses. The information derived from these inquiries will then help us determine the meaning of *hiddenness* and *revelation* associated with this and other New Testament mysteries. This meaning in turn will be applied to the issue of the continuity and discontinuity of this mystery as it relates to the church and to God's plan for biblical history.

The Biblical Concept of Mystery

In its earliest known occurrences the word *mystery* ($\mu\nu\sigma\tau\eta\rho\iota\sigma\nu$) was used as a Greek religious term denoting "secret rites or the implements or teaching connected with them."[45] Subsequently the term was used more generally among the Greeks for philosophical problems and secrets of any kind.[46]

In the Greek Old Testament (LXX), *mystery* occurs in the canonical books only in Daniel 2, where it translates the Aramaic רָז. It is also used quite frequently in the apocryphal books, where it at times translates the Hebrew word סוֹד, which is used for various kinds of secrets, both human (e.g., Tobit 12:7, 11; Judith 2:2; 2 Macc. 13:21; Sir. 22:22) and divine (Wisd. Sol. 6:22; 8:4).[47] This same Hebrew term, סוֹד, is found in the canonical Scriptures for God's secret (e.g., Amos 3:7; Ps. 25:14; Prov. 3:32; Job 15:8), but there it is always translated by Greek words other than $\mu\nu\sigma\tau\eta\rho\iota\sigma\nu$.[48]

---

[44]Schlier, *Epheser,* 151.

[45]C. F. D. Moule, "Mystery," in *IDB* 3:479. For a fuller discussion of these Eleusinian mysteries, see Caragounis, *Ephesian "Mysterion,"* 3–19.

[46]Caragounis, *Ephesian "Mysterion,"* 20–22.

[47]$M\nu\sigma\tau\eta\rho\iota\sigma\nu$ occurs in the LXX "mostly in the books written in Greek or with lost or only fragmentary Hebrew originals" (Moule, "Mystery," 479).

[48]Later Greek versions do occasionally use $\mu\nu\sigma\tau\eta\rho\iota\sigma\nu$ to translate the Hebrew סוֹד (e.g., both Symmachus and Theodotion [second century] use it in Job 15:8). It has been surmised that earlier translations of the Old Testament avoided this term because of its

The use of μυστήριον in Daniel provides the first use of that term in the sense of an eschatological mystery, which Bornkamm defines as "a concealed intimation of divinely ordained future events whose disclosure and interpretation is reserved for God alone . . . and for those inspired by His Spirit."[49] This meaning is developed in the later Jewish apocalyptic writings, where the "mysteries" refer to God's counsels outlining "the final events and states which are already truly existent in heaven and may be seen there and which will in the last days emerge from their concealment and become manifest events."[50]

The concept of mysteries plays an important role in the Qumran literature dated around the first century B.C. In the writings of this sectarian community, we find further use and development of the term in the sense of divine mysteries, which is closely related to the New Testament and especially the Pauline usage (e.g., 1QH 5:36; 1QpHab 7:4–5; 1Q27 1:1, 2–4).[51] Coppens describes the Qumran use of *mysteries* as "an ensemble of knowledge, of decrees, and of the riches of grace which are beyond human understanding. No one has access to them except through revelation and divine generosity."[52]

It is now generally agreed that this Semitic meaning of the term— namely, a secret of God that he alone makes known through revelation at the appointed time—rather than its meaning in the Greek mystery religions provides the background for the New Testament understanding of mystery.[53] Thus the basic idea of a secret, or something that had previously been hidden but now is made known, has come to be the generally accepted meaning of the term *mystery* in the New Testament. As a result μυστήριον when not translated "mystery" is frequently rendered "secret" (NEB, NIV; cf. German *Geheimnis*). The language related to the central mystery of the New Testament—namely, Christ himself (cf. Col. 2:2; 4:3)—provides clear support for this basic

pagan religious association but that once it passed into common use with a neutral meaning, it came to be used quite freely.

[49]Bornkamm, "μυστήριον," 814–15.

[50]Ibid., 816.

[51]Cf. Joseph Coppens, " 'Mystery' in the Theology of Saint Paul and Its Parallels at Qumran," in *Paul and Qumran,* ed. Jerome Murphy-O'Connor (Chicago: Priority Press, 1968), 132–58; Franz Mussner, "Contribution Made by Qumran to the Understanding of the Epistle to the Ephesians," in ibid., 159–67; Raymond E. Brown, *The Semitic Background of the Term "Mystery" in the New Testament* (Philadelphia: Fortress, 1968), 22–30.

[52]Coppens, " 'Mystery' in the Theology of Saint Paul," 135.

[53]Caragounis notes that in view of recent studies in the Jewish apocryphal and pseudepigraphal writings and especially the Qumran materials, "it has become increasingly more usual to sever the ties of contact between the New Testament *mysterion* and the Mystery Religions, and establish them, instead, with the Jewish background" (*Ephesian "Mysterion,"* 119). Caragounis makes a good case for showing that Daniel's use in particular stands behind the use of mystery in Eph. 1 and 3 (121–26).

meaning. It was prepared before the world was created (1 Cor. 2:7), hidden in God in the past (1 Cor. 2:8; Eph. 3:9; Col. 1:26; Rom. 16:25), and now made known through revelation by the Spirit (1 Cor. 2:2–10; Eph. 3:5).

It might be noted in passing that this simple meaning of secret (without any connotations of something mysterious or incomprehensible), which is based largely on the authority of Lightfoot and followed by Abbott and others,[54] has been called into question by Caragounis. Caragounis has amassed considerable evidence for the element of mysteriousness or that which is unfathomable in the original religious meaning of mystery. Acknowledging that its meaning broadened in subsequent nonreligious usage to include mere secrets, he maintains that the New Testament continues the uniform meaning of mysterious truth from its prior religious use. It is mysterious and incomprehensible as far as human understanding is concerned, for only those whose minds are enlightened by the Spirit can know it.[55] While Caragounis's thesis adds a dimension to the meaning of the term, it is not determinative for understanding the apostolic teaching concerning the divine mysteries.

The Use of Mystery in the New Testament

The term μυστήριον appears only twenty-eight times in the New Testament, twenty-one of which are in the Pauline writings.[56] While all of the uses refer to divine secrets, following Moule, we may divide the nature of the mysteries into three broad categories.[57] By far the most significant use, both in terms of number and content, is for what may be called the divine plan of salvation that is now revealed in Christ. This category would obviously include the teaching of Christ concerning the

---

[54]J. B. Lightfoot says, "Of the nature of the truth itself the word says nothing. It may be transcendental, incomprehensible, mystical, mysterious, in the modern sense of the term (1 Cor. xv.51, Eph. v.32): but this idea is quite accidental, and must be gathered from the special circumstances of the case, for it cannot be inferred from the word itself" (*Saint Paul's Epistles to the Colossians and to Philemon* [Grand Rapids: Zondervan, reprint of 1879 ed.], 168). Abbott similarly says, "We may conclude that μυστήριον was an ordinary, or rather the ordinary, word for 'a secret'" (*Ephesians and Colossians,* 16).

[55]Along with the history of the term, Caragounis adduces as evidence for the meaning of incomprehensibleness the fact that the term *hidden* is used as a qualifier along with *mystery* in several instances (Eph. 3:9; Col. 1:26), which is considered redundant, and that even after its revelation, the mystery is still called mystery (*Ephesian "Mysterion,"* 1–26). The truth that the understanding of the mystery comes only through the revelation of the Holy Spirit may also argue for something of an incomprehensible nature of the truth to people at large.

[56]These totals include the variant reading in 1 Cor. 2:1. In addition to the twenty-one in Paul's writings, the term is found three times in the Synoptic Gospels, all of which are parallel passages concerning the mysteries of the kingdom (cf. Mark 4:11 and par.), and four times in Revelation (1:20; 10:7; 17:5, 7).

[57]Moule, "Mystery," 480.

kingdom of heaven (Mark 4:11 and par.) and the apostolic teaching related to God's dealing with Israel and the Gentiles (e.g., Rom. 11:25; Col. 1:26, 27; Eph. 3:3–10). The broad descriptions such as "the mystery of Christ" (Eph. 3:4; Col. 4:3) and "the mystery of the gospel" (Eph. 6:19), which are central to God's plan of salvation, are also related to this group.

Second, *mystery* is used for various divine secrets that are divulged to given individuals. The references to knowing and speaking mysteries in 1 Corinthians 13:2 and 14:2 belong in this category. Moule would also include in this usage Paul's reference to the mystery of the bodily transformation at the coming of Christ (1 Cor. 15:51).

Finally, in three instances *mystery* is used for the hidden meaning found in symbols and types, such as the seven stars and lampstands (Rev. 1:20; cf. also mystery Babylon, in 17:5, 7) and marriage (Eph. 5:31–32). In these instances the term probably refers both to the symbols and to their hidden meanings.

While not all of the mysteries can be shown to be related except by the concept of mystery itself (e.g., "the mystery of lawlessness," 2 Thess. 2:7; and the mystery of the transformation of the body at the coming of Christ, 1 Cor. 15:51), there is general agreement that many of the individual references are in fact aspects of one central mystery centered in Christ and the gospel.[58] In the preaching of the crucified Christ to the Corinthians, the apostle claimed to be speaking "the mystery of God" (1 Cor. 2:1)[59] or "God's wisdom in a mystery" (2:7, NASB). The latter expression and the context make it evident that "mystery" is here equivalent to the wisdom of God, which is nothing less than "the divine will to save fulfilled in the crucifixion of Christ (1:24),"[60] or "the gospel and . . . Christ, the content of the gospel."[61] Summing up the apostle's teaching concerning the mystery in 1 Corin-

---

[58]Bornkamm argues in addition that in the New Testament the term "always has an eschatological sense" ("μυστήριον," 822).

[59]This is the meaning if we accept the reading μυστήριον over μαρτύριον. In support of the former reading, see UBS text, 3d ed. (corrected); Barth, *Ephesians 1–3*, 125; Bornkamm, "μυστήριον," 819; Brown, *Semitic Background of the Term "Mystery" in the New Testament*, 48–49; William F. Orr and James Arthur Walther, *1 Corinthians*, AB (Garden City, N.Y.: Doubleday, 1976), 156; Caragounis, *Ephesians "Mysterion,"* 28. For the preference of μαρτύριον, see C. K. Barrett, *A Commentary on the First Epistle to the Corinthians*, NTC (New York: Harper & Row, 1968), 62–63; Gordon Fee, *The First Epistle to the Corinthians* (Grand Rapids: Eerdmans, 1987), 91; F. W. Grosheide, *Commentary on the First Epistle to the Corinthians* (Grand Rapids: Eerdmans, 1953), 58.

[60]Bornkamm, "μυστήριον," 819; cf. also Brown: "As the succeeding verses [2:9ff.] make clear, it is the economy of salvation prepared beforehand for those whom God loves, and now at last revealed. In other words *sophia en mysterio* covers much of the same conceptual territory that we shall later see covered by *mysterion* alone" (*Semitic Background of the Term "Mystery" in the New Testament*, 41).

[61]Seyoon Kim, *The Origin of Paul's Gospel* (Tübingen: J. C. B. Mohr, 1981), 75.

thians 2, Kim says, " 'Christ crucified' is God's wisdom ἐν μυστηρίῳ because he embodies 'God's wise plan of redeeming the world through a crucified Messiah', 'which God foreordained for our glory before the course of ages began' (1 Cor. 2.7), and salvation 'which God prepared for those who love him' (1 Cor. 2.9)."[62]

It seems there is a similarity between the Corinthian use of mystery and the idea of mystery tied to Christ (Col. 2:2; 4:3; Eph. 3:9; 1 Tim. 3:16) and to the gospel (Rom. 16:25–26; Eph. 6:19). These statements would also appear to be connected to the "mystery" of God's will to bring all things together in Christ (Eph. 1:9–10).

This brings us to the question of whether and how the mystery of Ephesians 3 is also related to this one comprehensive mystery. I have argued previously that the terminology "the mystery" (v. 2) and "the mystery of Christ" (v. 4) are in fact related to the apostle's earlier mention of the broad concept of the mystery of God's will to bring all things together in Christ in 1:9. The unity of Gentile and Jew in Christ, which is the focus of the discussion of the mystery in chapter 3, is therefore in reality an aspect of this one broader mystery. This relationship between the Ephesians references to mystery is expressed by Caragounis, who states that "the mystery which deals with the universal *anakephalaiosis* in Christ stands hierarchically above the other μυστήριον concepts in this Epistle and includes them as parts of a whole." The mystery of chapter 3 dealing with the unity of the Gentiles and Jews, he says, is simply "a more particular facet of the general, programmatic use of the concept in ch. 1."[63]

Barth likewise relates the Ephesian 3 mystery to the one great mystery of Christ, declaring, "The one mystery is the mystery of Christ the preexistent, the revealer, the savior, the regent of church and world, the one to unite Jews and Gentiles." Specifically with regard to the inclusion of the Gentiles into God's people, he goes on to say that this "is not a further mystery added to the mystery of Jesus Christ. . . . Rather to speak of the savior Messiah who includes Gentiles in his body is to speak of the one revealed secret of God."[64]

In addition to defining the one mystery as "Christ and God's plan of salvation that Christ embodies," Kim goes on to show the developing relationship between the references to this mystery in 1 Corinthians 2, Colossians 1, and Ephesians. The "mystery of God, or God's wisdom" (1 Cor. 2:1, 7), is "simply Christ or God's plan of salvation embodied in Him." In the apostle's teaching to the Colossians (1:27), God's salvation

[62]Ibid., 76–77.
[63]Caragounis, *Ephesian "Mysterion,"* 29, 118.
[64]Barth, *Ephesians 1–3,* 331.

141

is defined more specifically as a salvation that includes the Gentiles. The teaching of Ephesians 3 simply makes this more explicit. These different passages, according to Kim, are not dealing with three mysteries, but only one—Christ.[65] To these passages, we might also add the reference to mystery in Romans 16:25, which is paralleled to the gospel and the proclamation of Jesus Christ. Thus the Ephesians 3 mystery is part of the one comprehensive mystery of the plan of God's salvation through Christ.[66]

The Hiddenness and Revelation of the Mystery

The relation of the mystery of Ephesians 3 to the larger mystery of God's salvation plan in Christ elicits the question of the nature of this relationship. More specifically, how is it related to the total revelation of that plan in Scripture? Is the truth of the unity of Gentiles and Jews in the church revealed in the preaching of the gospel a totally new aspect of the salvation plan? Or does its relation to the one mystery suggest a connection between this more specific aspect of the mystery and the Scriptures dealing with the comprehensive mystery of Christ?

Basing their interpretation on Paul's teaching of a mystery as that which has been hidden prior to its present revelation through the proclamation of the gospel (cf. Rom. 11:25–26; 1 Cor. 2:7; Eph. 3:9; Col. 1:26), traditional dispensationalists have understood the revelation of a mystery as entailing truth not previously found in Old Testament revelation. Chafer, for example, states, "The sum total of all the mysteries in the New Testament represents that entire body of added truth found in the New Testament which is unrevealed in the Old Testament."[67]

In contrast, nondispensationalists view the New Testament revelation of a mystery as clearly related to Old Testament prophecies. Regarding the mystery of Ephesians 3, some limit the revelation to new details of Old Testament prophecies.[68] Others place the emphasis on a new

---

[65]Kim, *Origin of Paul's Gospel,* 82; Schlier similarly says, "The mystery . . . is the mystery of God in Christ, his wisdom, the mystery of Christ as his wisdom and the mystery of the Church as the body of Christ and his wisdom, not, however, as three mysteries, but as one and the same" (*Epheser,* 61–62).

[66]A rather comprehensive definition of the one Pauline mystery is provided by Hugo Rahner: "The character of the 'mystery' of New Testament revelation, as we encounter it in St Paul (Rom. 16.25ff., 1 Cor. 2.7–10, Col. 1.25ff., Eph. 1.8–10 and 3.3–12), can be summarized as follows. The 'mystery' is the decision to save man when man had become separated from God by sin, a decision made since all eternity in the depth of the Godhead's being and hidden from all eternity. This hidden resolve is made manifest in the God-man Christ, who through his death brings the gift of 'life' to all men" (*Greek Myths and Christian Mystery* [New York: Harper & Row, 1963], 28).

[67]Chafer, *Systematic Theology* 4:76; cf. Walvoord, *Millennial Kingdom,* 232.

[68]Bruce, *Colossians, Philemon, and Ephesians,* 314. Peter O'Brien seems to suggest the

understanding of previously revealed truth.[69] Both, however, view the reality of the mystery—that is, the union of Gentiles and Jews in the church—as the fulfillment of Old Testament Scripture.

The various New Testament uses of *mystery* suggest that there are several different senses in which a mystery may be said to have been hidden and subsequently revealed. First, as we have seen, a mystery may be hidden in symbol or language with an inner meaning (cf. Rev. 1:20; Eph. 5:32). In this instance the revelation of the mystery consists in the unveiling of the meaning of the symbol or language that has already been given. Second, a mystery may be hidden because its truth has never been the subject of objective revelation. The mystery of the instant change of believers at the coming of Christ (1 Cor. 15:51) provides an example of this type. Nothing concerning this phenomenon had been included in any prior revelation.

The use of *mystery* in relation to Christ and the divine plan of salvation in him demands a third dimension of hiddenness and revelation. While there is no doubt that this use of the term involves disclosure of details concerning the person and saving work of Christ that are absent from the Old Testament prophecies, it is impossible to see these additional truths as constituting all that is meant in the hiddenness and revelation of this mystery.

Frequently the apostles asserted that the gospel that they preached and taught concerning Jesus as the Messiah was grounded in the Old Testament Scriptures. In Romans 1:1–2, Paul states that the "gospel of God," for which he was set apart, was "promised beforehand through his prophets in the Holy Scriptures" (cf. Titus 1:1–3). This is surely the same message that he called, later in Ephesians 6:19, "the mystery of the gospel." On his first missionary journey the apostle proclaimed to those at Pisidian Antioch, "We tell you the good news: What God promised our fathers . . ." (Acts 13:32). Even the inclusion of the Gentiles in the salvation of Christ was part of the Old Testament promise that was being fulfilled through the apostle's ministry. Before Festus and Agrippa, Paul testified, "I am saying nothing beyond what the prophets and Moses said would happen—that the Christ would suffer and, as the

---

same interpretation of the related mystery teaching in Colossians 1:27: "The manner in which that purpose [the Old Testament prophetic purpose of salvation for the Gentiles] would come to fruition—by the incorporation of both Jew and Gentiles into the body of Christ—was not made known. That had remained a mystery until the time of its fulfilment, and Paul, as apostle to the Gentiles and first steward of this mystery, has the privilege of unfolding its wonder to his readers" (*Colossians, Philemon*, WBC [Waco, Tex.: Word, 1982], 86).

[69]Allis, *Prophecy and the Church*, 94–97; Ridderbos, *Paul*, 339–40; Meyer, *Galatians and Ephesians*, 409; Abbott, *Ephesians and Colossians*, 82.

first to rise from the dead, would proclaim light to his own people and to the Gentiles" (Acts 26:22–23).

Finally, evidence may be seen in the apostle's statement that his "gospel and the proclamation of Jesus Christ [is] according to the revelation of the mystery hidden for long ages past, but now revealed and made known through the prophetic writings" (Rom. 16:25–26). Just how the mystery may be said to be revealed through the prophetic writings is explained by Cranfield:

> The manifestation, which has taken place in the gospel events and their subsequent proclamation, and is contrasted with the hiddenness of the mystery in the past, is a manifestation which is properly understood in its true significance only in the light of its Old Testament foreshadowing and attestation. It is when the manifestation of the mystery is understood as the fulfilment of God's promises made in the Old Testament (cf. 1:2), as attested, interpreted, clarified, by the Old Testament (cf., e.g., 3:21; 9:33; 10:4–9, 11, 13, 16, 18–21; 11:2, 26f), that it is truly understood as the gospel of God for all mankind.[70]

If the mystery of Christ and that of the divine plan of salvation has already been the subject of Old Testament prophecy, then in what sense can it be said to have been hidden and only now revealed by the New Testament apostles and prophets? Reflecting on this question brings us to a third and perhaps primary understanding of the hiddenness and revelation of a mystery. A mystery may be hidden in the sense that its truth has not yet been realized. The corresponding revelation consists not in making the truth known in an objective or propositional sense but in bringing it to reality or existence. In this instance the truth of the mystery may be the subject of previous prophecy, but it is said to be hidden until in God's appointed time it becomes a manifest event.

Ridderbos explains this concept of hiddenness and revelation when he says:

> "Hiddenness," "mystery," etc., has therefore, in addition to a noetic a plainly historical connotation; it is that which has not yet appeared, that which still exists in the counsel of God and has not yet been realized in

[70]C. E. B. Cranfield, *A Critical and Exegetical Commentary on the Epistle to the Romans,* ICC, 2 vols. (Edinburgh: T. & T. Clark, 1975–79), 2:812. Similarly William Sanday and Arthur C. Headlam state, "All the ideas in this sentence are exactly in accordance with the thoughts which run through this Epistle. The unity of the Old and New Testament, the fact that Christ had come in accordance with the Scriptures (Rom. i.1, 2), that the new method of salvation although apart from law, was witnessed to by the Law and the Prophets [cf. Rom. 3:21] . . . , the constant allusion esp. in chaps. ix–xi to the Old Testament Scriptures; all these are summed in the phrase διὰ γραφῶν προφητικῶν" (*A Critical and Exegetical Commentary on the Epistle to the Romans,* ICC, 5th ed. [Edinburgh: T. & T. Clark, 1902], 434).

history as fulfillment of that counsel. Accordingly the corresponding word "reveal" not only means the divulging of a specific truth or the giving of information as to certain events or facts, but the appearance itself, the becoming historical reality of that which until now did not exist as such, but was kept by God, hidden, held back.[71]

Similarly, Grosheide says, "Hidden does not mean 'totally unknown,' but 'not yet existing.' "[72]

This sense of hiddenness and revelation is seen in the Lord's statement concerning the revelation of truth that the Father was making through him. To his disciples, who were recipients of his teaching of the mysteries of the kingdom, Jesus said, "Blessed are the eyes that see what you see. For I tell you the truth that many prophets and righteous men longed to see what you see but did not see it, and to hear what you hear but did not hear it" (Matt. 13:17; cf. Luke 10:21–24). "Seeing" and "hearing" in this beatitude of Jesus clearly refers not to the reception of new information as such but to the actualization and experience of prior prophecy. As Manson explains, "The point of the saying is that what for all former generations lay still in the future is now a present reality. What was for the best men of the past only an object of faith and hope is now a matter of experience."[73] These eschatological blessings had been revealed to the prophets, at least to some extent, but they had not yet seen or heard them because they were "hidden" in the counsel of God until the coming of Christ.

This teaching of Jesus brings us to a further significant dimension of this sense of the hiddenness and revelation of a mystery. The mystery is made known or revealed only through the enlightening power of the Spirit and is understood only by those of faith. According to the apostle the mystery of the wisdom of God, the message of Christ crucified, was not understood by the rulers of this age (1 Cor. 2:7–8). Their failure was due to the fact that the mystery was " 'hidden in God' and could only be grasped by a revelation of the Spirit (v. 10)."[74] This "hiddenness" continues for those whose minds are blinded by the god of this age

[71]Ridderbos, *Paul*, 46–47.

[72]Grosheide, *First Corinthians*, 64. Compare the comment by Meyer on "mystery" in Eph. 1:9: "And the mystery with which the divine will is occupied, is the counsel of redemption accomplished through Christ, not in so far as it is in itself incomprehensible for the understanding, but in so far as, while formed from eternity, it was until the announcement of the gospel hidden in God, and veiled and unknown to men. See Rom. xvi.25f.; Eph. iii.4f., 9, vi.19; Col. i.26. By the prophets the mystery was not disclosed, but the disclosure of it was merely predicted, here at the proclamation of the gospel the prophetic predictions became the means of it being disclosed" (*Galatians and Ephesians*, 320; cf. also Ernst Käsemann, *Commentary on Romans* [Grand Rapids: Eerdmans, 1980], 312; Bornkamm, "μυστήριον," 816, 822).

[73]T. W. Manson, *The Sayings of Jesus* (London: SCM, 1949), 80.

[74]Fee, *First Corinthians*, 105–6; cf. Orr and Walther, *1 Corinthians*, 165–66.

(2 Cor. 4:3–4). Thus even with the proclamation, the mystery "remains hidden, in so far as . . . its truth remains beyond human comprehension and can only be laid hold of by faith."[75]

The hiddenness and revelation of the mystery in this third sense may thus be summarized as entailing two dimensions. First, it is hidden and revealed with regard to its realization in God's historical plan of salvation. It may have been a part of previous prophecy, but it was hidden until the time came for its actualization. Second, it is hidden and revealed even then in relation to the reception of the Spirit's enlightening ministry to human hearts. Even in this last instance, the full knowledge of the mystery awaits the final day of the believer's perfection, as Bornkamm notes: "For the coming glorification of believers is only intimated in the μυστήριον. The riches of glory are already included in it, but they are still included in it, Christ being the 'hope' of glory in whom the treasures of wisdom and knowledge are still concealed, Col. 2:3. Hence the revealed mystery still conceals the final consummation. The eschatological enactment is still only in word, the fulfilment of all things is as yet only through the Church, δόξα is only in the concealment of θλίψεις, Col. 1:24f.; Eph. 3:13."[76]

It should be noted in passing that even in this third sense the contrast between the hiddenness and revelation of a mystery is best understood as absolute rather than relative. On the basis that the Old Testament Scriptures were not silent on the mystery of Christ (Rom. 16:25-26), Murray states concerning the revelation that "the contrast is not absolute but . . . *relative,* and this relative contrast must not be discounted."[77] Cranfield, however, sees in the contrastive words "but [δέ] now revealed" (v. 26), a much sharper discontinuity. It is "the contrast between the ages before Christ's incarnation and the period which began with it. It was in the gospel events, the life, death, resurrection and ascension of Jesus Christ, that the mystery was manifested decisively."[78] According to Cranfield, the fact that Christ was foretold and even in a sense present in the Old Testament "must not be distorted into a denial of the utterly decisive nature of the event indicated by the statement ὁ λόγος σάρξ ἐγένετο [the Word became flesh]."[79] The apostle's language in connection with the Ephesians 3 mystery is therefore best interpreted as contrastive rather than comparative. When it is stated that the mystery "was not made known to men in

[75]Rahner, *Greek Myths and Christian Mystery,* 29.
[76]Bornkamm, "μυστήριον," 822.
[77]John Murray, *The Epistle to the Romans,* 2 vols., NICNT (Grand Rapids: Eerdmans, 1965), 2:242.
[78]Cranfield, *Romans* 2:811.
[79]Ibid., 810, n. 3.

other generations as it has now been revealed" (v. 5), it does not mean that it is simply better known now, but that it was not known previously and is now revealed.[80]

Of the various senses of hiddenness and revelation found in New Testament concepts of mystery, which one most appropriately characterizes the mystery of the new union of Jew and Gentile in Ephesians 3? Is this aspect of the mystery an example of the second type of meaning for mystery, that there was no prior mention of this truth in the prophetic Scriptures? Or does it belong in the third category along with the mystery of Christ and of the gospel, according to which revelation, although including the addition of new details, signifies primarily the actualization of that prior prophecy? In short, in what sense is the revelation of this mystery related to earlier prophetic truth in the Old Testament?

Without going into all the details in the Old Testament, it is clear that the prophecies did look forward to a time when God's salvation would extend to the nations. The prophet Isaiah wrote of the time when God's people would "with joy . . . draw water from the wells of salvation" and proclaim the name of God and his acts among the nations (Isa. 12:2–4). This salvation was to come through the messianic servant, whom God would appoint as "a covenant for the people and a light for the Gentiles" (Isa. 42:6). Zechariah likewise sees the coming king as speaking peace to the nations (Zech. 9:9–10). Finally, this predicted salvation is brought about in union with Israel. For the promises anticipated the time when the nations would be united with Israel in the worship of the Lord (Isa. 2:2–4), and God's house would be "a house of prayer for all nations" (Isa. 56:7). In this way, the original promise to Abraham would be fulfilled: through him, that is, through his seed, Messiah (Gal. 3:16), "all peoples on earth will be blessed" (Gen. 12:3).

Not only is a salvation predicted that is common to Israel and the nations, but there are indications of its attainment through spiritual union with the Messiah. While there are no explicit references in the prophecies to the Messiah indwelling his people, there are concepts pointing in this direction. Shedd examines the teachings of the corporate unity of humankind found in the Old Testament (e.g., corporate involvement in blessing [Gen. 18:23–32] and sin [Josh. 7:16–26]) and the early Jewish conception of the solidarity of Israel and humankind, the latter based primarily on the oneness of creation (cf. *b.Qid.* 40b, 39b; *m.'Abot* 3:18) and sin (cf. *Sipra Lev* 27a; *Secrets of Enoch* 41:1–2). He concludes that "the doctrine of the Body of Christ is . . . an explicit application of the Hebraic conception of corporate personality."

[80]Schlier, *Epheser*, 150.

147

This corporate relationship is not the kind of spiritual union that is found in Christ, but it nevertheless provided the type of which "the unity of the Church is the anti-type, the real thing."[81]

The solidarity becomes more explicitly related to the Messiah in the apocalyptic writings. According to Davies, "It is now generally accepted that the idea of a Messiah in apocalyptic did involve the idea of a community of the Messiah; and whether we trace this conception, as it is found in Jesus, to the Book of Enoch or to Dan. 7, or to Isa. 53, it is a fact that Jesus was aware that he was gathering around Himself a community of people pledged to loyalty to Him above all else."[82] Although the apocalyptic references do not ground this community in a spiritual union, Schweitzer rightly speaks of this eschatological concept as the "union of those who are elect to the Messianic Kingdom with one another and with the Messiah."[83] Something of the union between Jesus and his people, although short of the body truth of the church, is similarly taught in Jesus' teachings of a peculiar intimacy between himself and his disciples. Those who accept the disciples are said to accept Jesus himself (Matt. 10:40). To help one of the brothers of Christ is, in fact, to help him (Matt. 25:40).

More directly related to the spiritual union of the body of Christ taught in the mystery of Ephesians 3 is the prophetic teaching of the indwelling Spirit. Not only would the promised Spirit of the new covenant be poured out on his people (e.g., Joel 2:29; Isa. 44:3; Ezek. 39:29), but he would live within them. According to Ezekiel, God promised, "I will put my Spirit in you" (36:27; cf. 37:14). The effect of obedience to the law through the indwelling of the Spirit (cf. 36:27) indicates that the same indwelling is meant in Jeremiah's statement of the new covenant that God would put his law within his people and write it on their hearts (Jer. 31:33).

When we come to the New Testament, we find that this indwelling of the Spirit is directly related to the indwelling of Christ. After saying that he would ask the Father to send the Paraclete, Jesus goes on to say, "I will not leave you as orphans; I will come to you." Obviously connecting his statement with the coming of the Spirit, he then adds, "On that day you will realize that I am in My Father, and you are in me, and I am in you" (John 14:16, 18, 20).[84]

This same teaching of the indwelling of Christ as a result of the

[81]Russell Phillip Shedd, *Man in Community* (Grand Rapids: Eerdmans, 1964), 165, 199.
[82]W. D. Davies, *Paul and Rabbinic Judaism* (London: SPCK, 1965), 99–100.
[83]A. Schweitzer, *The Mysticism of Paul the Apostle* (New York: Henry Holt, 1931), 101.
[84]See Raymond E. Brown, *The Gospel According to John XIII–XXI*, AB (Garden City, N.Y.: Doubleday, 1970), 644–47; J. H. Bernard, *A Critical and Exegetical Commentary on the Gospel of St. John*, 2 vols. (Edinburgh: T. & T. Clark, 1928), 2:548.

indwelling of the Spirit is found throughout the New Testament. The Spirit comes as the Spirit of Christ (e.g., Rom. 8:9; Acts 16:7), so that the apostle can say by means of a functional identity, "Now the Lord is the Spirit" (2 Cor. 3:17). In other words, the Lord carries on his ministry in his people through the indwelling Spirit.[85] This is nowhere seen more clearly than in the apostle's prayer that the Ephesian believers might be strengthened with power through the Spirit in the inner being in order that Christ might dwell in their hearts by faith (Eph. 3:16–17). The linking of the indwelling Christ with the presence of the Spirit is also evident when Paul ties together the concepts of the "Spirit of God" who "lives in you," "having the Spirit of Christ," and "Christ . . . in you" (Rom. 8:9–10).

The evidence from the Old Testament prophecies and in some cases their later Jewish interpretation shows a relationship between what was promised and what is now revealed. Specifically, the promises concerning the salvation of the Gentiles along with Israel, a certain solidarity between the promises concerning the Messiah and his people, and, perhaps most important, the prediction of the indwelling Spirit of God, make it difficult to deny some connection between this Old Testament hope and the mystery of the union of Gentiles and Israel in Christ found in Ephesians 3. To be sure, there are new truths involved in the outworking of the mystery in the church that are not evident in the Old Testament. In particular, the nature of the fulfillment of this truth during this age is not apparent in the Old Testament. The prophecies pictured God's salvation flowing to the Gentiles after Israel as a nation had been restored to her Messiah, who was reigning on the earth. Now in the church, the mystery is being fulfilled when Israel as a people has largely been set aside. This change corresponds with Christ's revelation of the mysteries of the kingdom. The Old Testament had pictured one coming of Christ to establish his kingdom reign, but Christ in the mysteries predicts a time when the kingdom would be operating on earth in power with spiritual salvation before his actual reign (cf. Matt. 13). Accordingly, the revelation of the mystery in the apostolic era relates to this new interim phase of kingdom salvation.

Despite the unrevealed time of this age to which the revelation of the mystery of Ephesians obviously refers, it is clear that the truth of this mystery of the union of Gentiles and Israel in Christ's salvation does relate to Old Testament prophecy. Consequently, the revelation of this

---

[85]Other references indicating a functional identity between the exalted Christ and the Spirit are Luke 12:11–12 par. 21:14–15, and Acts 10:13–14 par. 10:19. Compare the letters to the seven churches in Revelation 2–3, where the message is both from Christ and from the Spirit (2:1, 7, etc.).

previously hidden mystery relates primarily to the actualization or realization through Christ of that which the prophets foretold and longingly anticipated. This actualization also brought fresh detail and more focus to what had been promised.

The connection between Paul's mystery, the preaching of Jesus, and Old Testament prophecy appears in the concluding doxology of the epistle to the Romans (16:25–26). This is especially noteworthy in light of that letter's discussion of the historical development of God's salvation plan involving Israel and the Gentiles. Although it is implied earlier in the letter, chapters 9–11 focus directly on this issue with frequent appeals to the Old Testament. Specifically, the apostle teaches the equal participation of Gentiles and Jews in the blessing of God through the metaphor of the olive tree (Rom. 11:16–24), a truth that is clearly related to the mystery of Ephesians 3. And in chapter 15 just preceding the reference to the mystery in chapter 16, the apostle speaks at length concerning the salvation of the Gentiles, quoting as support four passages from the Old Testament stating that the Gentiles will worship God. These truths, which constitute the mystery of Paul's gospel in Romans, are thus clearly related to the content of the mystery in Ephesians 3. As Sanday and Headlam note, the apostle's conclusions developed in Romans form the basis on which his ideas of the church are developed in Ephesians.[86] Since the apostle declares that the mystery of Romans is made known through the prophetic writings, these same prophetic writings must be related to the expression of the mystery further developed in Ephesians 3.

The revelation of the equal participation of Israel and the Gentiles in God's salvation through union with Christ is a realization of Old Testament prophecy. But this association should not lead us to the conclusion that these prophecies are fully realized, or completely fulfilled, in the content of the Ephesian 3 mystery. Neither the primary statement of the content of the mystery in 3:6 nor the earlier development of the similar truth in 2:11–22 goes beyond teaching a new spiritual salvation that brings a consequent new relation to God and to each other. In teaching this new and present work of God in the church, there is no denial of the previous teaching of Romans 11:25–26 in which the apostle looked forward to the future salvation of the nation Israel.

By way of analogy, although the apostle teaches that the new union of Jew and Gentile constitutes "a holy temple in the Lord" (Eph. 2:21), there is no reason to deny future significance for the temple at Jerusalem in which, according to the same apostle, the man of

---

[86]Sanday and Headlam, *Romans*, 434.

lawlessness will exalt himself as God (2 Thess. 2:4). McKelvey's comment in this regard is a caution worth considering in all of the apostle's teaching. "While one may say with certainty that the apostle thought of God's dwelling in the Church in parallel fashion to his dwelling in the temple of Jerusalem, one is reluctant to deduce that (therefore) the temple of Jerusalem ceased to have religious significance for him. . . . A straightforward reading of Paul's own writings can hardly be said to bear this out."[87]

Our examination of the mystery in Ephesians 3 leads us to a mediating position between traditional dispensational and nondispensational views. The unity of Jews and Gentiles in Christ is taking place in the church in partial fulfillment of Old Testament promises. Messianic days have dawned, albeit in a way not clearly anticipated in the prophecies. Rather than one grand age of fulfillment under the messianic reign, the prophetic fulfillment has been divided into two ages related to the two comings of Christ. In this first age of fulfillment, the spiritual messianic salvation is already present in the gospel. This gospel is broadly spoken of as the mystery, or the mystery of Christ, or the mystery of the gospel. The specific spiritual unity of all peoples entailed in this gospel is the content of the mystery of Ephesians 3.

THE SITUATION OF THE CHURCH IN GOD'S PURPOSE

After discussing the revelation of the mystery and its content (Eph. 3:1–7), the apostle goes on to speak of its actual administration and purpose (vv. 8–13). Since the mystery in its content refers to the reality of the church with its Jew-Gentile unity, the expression of its purpose provides insight into the place and purpose of the church in the divine plan of salvation. In the present administration of the mystery God intends "that now, through the church, the manifold wisdom of God should be made known to the rulers and authorities in the heavenly realms, according to his eternal purpose which he accomplished in Christ Jesus our Lord" (vv. 10–11).

The Display of Wisdom to the Heavenly Powers

According to the purpose statement in 3:10, God aims to make his "manifold wisdom" known to the heavenly powers through the church, the new reality created by the unification of Gentile and Jew in Christ. Disagreement exists over whether this cosmic audience of "rulers and

---

[87]R. J. McKelvey, *The New Temple* (London: Oxford University Press, 1969), 123.

authorities" refers to good spirits[88] or evil spirits[89] or both.[90] According to Scripture, both good and evil spiritual forces need enlightenment concerning the working of divine wisdom in Christ (cf. 1 Peter 1:12). In addition, the apostle's earlier statement in this same epistle concerning the exaltation of Christ "far above all rule and authority, power and dominion" (1:21) is no doubt intended to declare his supremacy over all spiritual powers, both good and evil. It is probably best, therefore, to understand the intended audience as all spiritual intelligences.

The "heavenly realms" to which these "powers" belong refers to the higher, spiritual plane above the earthly and the physical. It is from this realm that the "powers and authorities" exert their influence in the affairs of human history both for good and for evil. It is also in this realm that the ultimate victory of salvation took place with the defeat of the opposing forces (cf. Col. 2:15), so that believers are already seated victoriously "in the heavenlies" with Christ (2:6).[91] Thus it is to the powers of this heavenly realm, who are bound up with salvation history, that the church created by the mystery reveals the mystery and displays God's wisdom.

The divine wisdom on display is the content of the mystery (cf. "God's wisdom in a mystery," 1 Cor. 2:7 NASB) that was hidden in the divine counsels until the present apostolic proclamation of the gospel (cf. "now" in v. 10). It is the same divine wisdom that in its "much variegated" nature manifests itself in creation and in the person of Christ and in God's dealings throughout history.[92] The immediate context, however, demands that the particular aspect of this wisdom being made known to the heavenly powers be understood "as the divine plan of salvation which has been fulfilled with the common entry of both Jews and Gentiles into Jesus Christ."[93]

According to the apostle, this wisdom is exhibited not simply through the proclamation of the gospel by the church but through the very reality of the church herself. Meyer declares, "The Christian church . . . is, in its existence and its living development, as composed of Jews and Gentiles combined in a higher unity, the medium *de facto* for the divine wisdom becoming known. . . . the church of the redeemed is therefore, as it were, the mirror, by means of which the wisdom of God exhibits

---

[88]Meyer, *Galatians and Ephesians*, 414–15; S. D. F. Salmond, "The Epistle to the Ephesians," in *EGT* 3:309.
[89]E. F. Scott, *The Epistle of Paul to the Colossians, to Philemon, and to the Ephesians* (London: Hodder & Stoughton, 1930), 189–90; Schlier, *Epheser*, 155.
[90]Bruce, *Colossians, Philemon, and Ephesians*, 321; Robinson, *Ephesians*, 20–21.
[91]Caragounis, *Ephesian "Mysterion,"* 146–52.
[92]Bruce, *Colossians, Philemon, and Ephesians*, 320; cf. Schlier, *Epheser*, 165.
[93]Ulrich Wilckens, "σοφία κτλ.," *TDNT* 7:523.

itself."[94] While the emphasis is certainly on the unity of Gentile with Jew in the display of wisdom through the church, it is probably not going beyond the apostle's thought (as evidenced in the entire discussion of the salvation enjoyed by Gentile and Jew in Christ, cf. chap. 2) to say with Barth that "in her total being . . . as founded and ruled by the Messiah; as composed of Jews and Gentiles formerly dead in sins and divided in hostility; as a people daring to live on the basis of forgiveness; as a community boldly looking into God's face and speaking to him; as a suffering and struggling, poor and yet enriched nation—this way the church is God's display, picture window, legal 'proof' (2:7), lighthouse (5:8), for the benefit of the world."[95]

The Mystery of the Church in the Plan of Salvation

The unity of Gentiles with Israel in the church, as the manifestation of the mystery that had been for long ages hidden, raises the question of the place of this present divine work in the total plan of salvation history. We have seen that the mystery of the church is vitally related to the Old Testament promises of spiritual salvation in the messianic era. It is part and parcel of the one great mystery of Christ—namely, God's eschatological salvation through his Son.

Having said this, however, we may still ask the question as to how fulfillment in the church is related to the complete fulfillment of God's mystery of salvation in Christ. Does the divine work of building the church through the revelation of the mystery of Ephesians 3, the union of Gentile and Jew in Christ, constitute the complete soteriological fulfillment of the divine mystery? Is the realization of this mystery in the church "the epitome of the whole structure of God's purposes on the earth"?[96] Or is it only the beginning of a messianic salvation that entails additional steps in the unfolding and completion of the divine mystery in Christ? For the purpose of this chapter, our response to this question (which entails much of Scripture) must be limited to Ephesians 3.

Nothing in the apostle's teaching concerning the mystery of the unification of Gentiles and Israel in Christ suggests that what is presently taking place is the last phase of messianic salvation. Instead, when the entire teaching concerning the divine mystery in Ephesians is considered, there is evidence that the work noted in chapter 3 is only the first step toward the final goal of God's purpose in Christ. That goal expressed in the revelation of "the mystery of his will" is "to bring all

[94]Meyer, *Galatians and Ephesians,* 415–16.

[95]Barth, *Ephesians 1–3,* 364.

[96]Clarence B. Bass, *Backgrounds to Dispensationalism: Its Historical Genesis and Ecclesiastical Implications* (Grand Rapids: Baker, 1960), 9.

things in heaven and on earth together under one head, even Christ" (1:9–10).

One great obstacle to the consummation of all things was the great divide in the human race evident in the alienation between Jew and Gentile. The focus of the mystery of Ephesians 3 is the overcoming of this obstacle. The realization of the mystery through the proclamation of the apostolic gospel has united them into one new humanity with Christ as its Head. In Christ the hostility that divided humankind has been resolved through people's reconciliation to God and consequently to each other.

But the resolution of this first obstacle is not the complete fulfillment of the summation of all things together in Christ. The rebellious powers represent a further problem. The letter to the Ephesians makes it clear that Christ has been exalted above all powers, whether good or evil (1:20–22). But in God's administration of the mystery, the time has not yet arrived for their hostile activity to be silenced. They remain as powerful opponents of the believer in the church (6:11–12). In Colossians 1:20 a thought similar to the union of all things in Christ is expressed with the reconciliation of all things to God. Although this reconciliation has been effected through the peace made at the cross, its ultimate outworking will occur only with the final subjugation or forced "peace" (i.e., pacification), when they will be compelled to acknowledge Jesus as Lord (Phil. 2:10–11).[97] The church today is not given the task of subjugating the powers, but of being "strong in the Lord and in his mighty power" and equipping itself with divine armor so that it can "stand against the devil's schemes" and "stand" against the onslaughts "when the day of evil comes" (Eph. 6:10–13). The ultimate victory will be accomplished only through the personal intervention and reign of Christ (cf. 1 Cor. 15:24–25).

The present outworking of the mystery in the church is therefore not the final completion of the mystery of Christ to bring all things together in him. Rather, in the words of Meyer, it is "a voucher of the redemption which embraces all mankind," "the highest manifestation of divine wisdom."[98] In short, the present outworking of the Ephesians 3 mystery in the constitution of the church is the initial stage in the realization of the divine plan of salvation in Christ, which is the comprehensive mystery of God.

As such, the church already witnesses to that wisdom of God manifest in the mystery. Although Scott focuses only on the evil powers, he explains that through the church, created as a result of Christ's death,

[97]O'Brien, *Colossians, Philemon*, 55–57.
[98]Meyer, *Galatians and Ephesians*, 416.

the powers can now perceive the hidden purpose of God to unite all things in Christ. "They knew that God had willed to restore a universal peace by Christ, and that through the Church His plan was already on the way to fulfilment."[99] The church is thus not the conclusion of the program, but "a functional outpost of God's kingdom,"[100] with further kingdom activity to come in the future.

CONCLUSION

Our discussion of the apostle's teaching concerning the Ephesians 3 mystery leads to several conclusions. First, the unity of Gentile and Jew in Christ is the fulfillment of the divine salvation promised for messianic times, when the nations along with Israel would enjoy God's blessing. As such, this reality is permanent. Jew and Gentile will from now on stand together equally in their spiritual relation to God. They both will have access to the Father through the Son in the Spirit (cf. 2:18). It should be noted that nothing in the discussion of the mystery goes beyond this equality of spiritual position in Christ. Thus the unification of Gentile and Jew in the church does not rule out the possibility of *functional* distinctions between Israel and the other nations in the future, even as there are functional distinctions among believers in the church today without impairing spiritual equality.

Second, the mystery's revelation is a new action of God. Despite the fact of Old Testament promise, the mystery was hidden in the counsel of God and hence unknown or not yet actualized. According to the mystery, the church unifies Gentile and Jew in Christ and is therefore truly a new work. It rests upon the New Testament work of Christ's first coming and the bestowal of the Spirit.

Finally, although the mystery's present manifestation is an eschatological fulfillment of the promised salvation, it is not the completion of the mystery of God's salvation program for the world and the universe. The church's situation in relation to the powers described in this epistle makes it evident that the final summing up of all things in Christ is yet to come. The remainder of that plan is not detailed in connection with the present revelation of the mystery in Ephesians. But nothing precludes its harmonization with the apostle's other teaching of the divine mystery concerning a future work with Israel (Rom. 11:25–26). Such a hope for Israel fits many Old Testament promises that remain as yet unfulfilled.

---

[99]Scott, *Colossians, Philemon, and Ephesians,* 190.
[100]Barth, *Ephesians 1–3,* 364.

CHAPTER 5

The Israelite Imagery of 1 Peter 2

W. Edward Glenny

The use of the Old Testament in the New is one of the most fruitful and promising areas of study for evangelical scholars today. It is at the center of current discussion concerning hermeneutics, inerrancy, and the relationship between the Testaments. The application to the church of Old Testament passages that speak of the nation of Israel is also an important factor in the question concerning the relationship of Israel and the church. First Peter is often overlooked in this discussion,[1] yet it has a contribution to make because this epistle not only applies the Old Testament to its recipients, but it also addresses them with epithets and imagery used to describe Israel in the Old Testament. J. Ramsey Michaels notes that "no New Testament letter is so consistently addressed, directly or indirectly, to 'Israel,' that is (on the face of it) to Jews."[2]

Applying the Old Testament to the recipients of 1 Peter is

---

[1]John H. Elliott, "The Rehabilitation of an Exegetical Step-Child: 1 Peter in Recent Research," *JBL* 95 (1976): 243–54. Elliott laments the neglect of 1 Peter by New Testament exegetes. This neglect is obvious when one surveys studies of the use of the Old Testament in the New Testament. See D. Moody Smith, "The Use of the Old Testament in the New," in *The Use of the Old Testament in the New and Other Essays,* ed. James M. Efird (Durham, N.C.: Duke University Press, 1972), 20–65. Smith surveys the use of the Old Testament in Acts, by Jesus, Paul, Mark, Matthew, Luke, John, and in Hebrews and Revelation, but there are no major works that survey 1 Peter. Two recent studies of the use of the Old Testament in 1 Peter are the author's dissertation, "The Hermeneutics of the Use of the Old Testament in 1 Peter" (Th.D. diss., Dallas Theological Seminary, 1987), which is the basis for much of this study, and William L. Schutter, "The Use of the Old Testament in the Composition of 1 Peter" (Ph.D. diss., Cambridge University, 1985).

[2]J. Ramsey Michaels, *1 Peter,* WBC (Waco, Tex.: Word, 1988), xlv. The unity, Petrine authorship, and predominantly Gentile Christian audience of the epistle are assumed in this study. In spite of the Old Testament Israelite descriptions of the addressees, "there is a near consensus that 1 Peter was in fact directed to a predominantly Gentile Christian audience" (xlvi). Passages such as 1:14, 18; 2:10; 4:3, 4 support this viewpoint. This does not rule out the presence of some Jews among the addressees however (cf. Acts 2:9).

foundational for the entire epistle and is developed in 2:4–10.[3] In this passage Peter takes the central concept of Israel's self-understanding, their status as the elect people of God, and using Old Testament texts that originally spoke of Israel, he transfers this status to his recipients.[4] What implications does this imagery have concerning the relationship of Israel and the church? Does the use of the Old Testament in 1 Peter 2:4–10 allow us "to say with assurance that the church has now become the true Israel of God"?[5] Or, is it more correct to say that "nowhere in 1 Peter are the readers addressed as a *new* Israel or a *new* people of God, as if to displace the Jewish community"?[6]

This essay will address these questions by studying the method used to apply the Old Testament in 1 Peter 2:4–10. To do this it will be necessary to consider the context of each citation in the Old or New Testament as well as the tradition history of each of the texts in Judaism and the New Testament. Our goal is to demonstrate that Peter applies Old Testament imagery in 1 Peter 2:4–10 to his recipients by the use of typological-prophetic hermeneutics.[7]

There are four components in typological-prophetic associations:

1. The Old Testament type must be based on "historical facts— persons, actions, events and institutions," not hidden meanings found in the text.[8]

---

[3]John Hall Elliott, *The Elect and the Holy* (Leiden: E. J. Brill, 1966), 217.

[4]Valdir R. Steuernagel, "The Exiled Community as a Missionary Community: A Study Based on 1 Peter 2:9, 10," *ERT* 10, no. 1 (1986): 11.

[5]Wayne Grudem, *1 Peter,* TNTC (Grand Rapids: Eerdmans, 1988), 113.

[6]Michaels, *1 Peter,* 107.

[7]See Glenny, "Hermeneutics in 1 Peter," esp. 192–288, for a more thorough treatment of the topic of this chapter. For a bibliography on typology, see Henning Graf Reventlow, *Problems of Biblical Theology in the Twentieth Century,* trans. John Bowden (Philadelphia: Fortress, 1986), 14–37. A key work on typology is Leonhard Goppelt, *Typos: The Typological Interpretation of the Old Testament in the New,* trans. Donald H. Madvig (Grand Rapids: Eerdmans, 1982). Other works that have been especially helpful on defining typology are Douglas J. Moo, *The Old Testament in the Gospel Passion Narratives* (Sheffield: Almond, 1983), 30–34; and Darrell L. Bock, *Proclamation from Prophecy and Pattern* (Sheffield: JSOT Press, 1987), esp. 49–52. The designation *typological-prophetic* is sometimes used rather than *typology* to emphasize the prophetic aspect of typology. Bock explains that "although typology is often retrospective, that is, often the pattern cannot be recognized until it is repeated, it is still prophetic because at its foundation is the idea that God works in certain patterns in working out his salvation. This pattern is fulfillable and is recognized as a fulfillment in an event or person. Also many of the initial Old Testament texts found in the typological category are texts of promise tied to ideas of deliverance, kingship, or other key concepts that have eschatological overtones and suggest patterns of salvation in themselves. As a result of these factors, 'typological-prophetic' is an accurate description of this class of texts, although the nature of the prophetic connection often is different from purely prophetic texts. It would be accurate to say that typology is a way of thinking about God's work in history as it moves to consummation" (291–92).

[8]Goppelt, *Typos,* 17. See also his discussion on pp. 5–6.

2. The link between the type and the antitype must be identifiable in Scripture.

3. A pattern or correspondence must exist between the Old Testament type and the New Testament antitype.[9]

4. There must be an escalation or heightening from the Old Testament type to the greater New Testament antitype.[10]

Typology is distinguished from analogy by the fact that analogy involves a less distinct pattern and the absence of both escalation and a prophetic element. Typology is differentiated from direct prophecy by the fact that in the latter the text looks exclusively to a future event or figure, while with typology the Old Testament text "looks to a pattern within events that is to culminate in a final fulfillment in light of the passages and the Old Testament's context of hope and deliverance."[11] In typology the Old Testament facts provide a context for understanding God's greater redemptive work in the New Testament. The correspondence or pattern seen between the type and antitype demonstrates the continuity of God's work of salvation, while the escalation indicates progression and advancement.[12]

After an introduction to the structure of 1 Peter 2:4–10, this chapter will examine the context of 1 Peter 2:4–5, the *stone* quotations of 1 Peter 2:6–8 and the *people of God* allusions of 1 Peter 2:9–10. In conclusion it will consider the application of the *people of God* references in 1 Peter 2:9–10 to Peter's recipients and the importance of the Old Testament imagery in these verses for our understanding of the relationship between Israel and the church.

THE STRUCTURE OF 1 PETER 2:4–10

Peter describes the contents of his first epistle in 5:12b, which states, "I have written to you briefly, encouraging you and testifying that this is the true grace of God. Stand fast in it." This summary statement as well as the details of the epistle suggest that the tribulation of the recipients of 1 Peter made them question their election and the validity of the message that had been preached to them, which in turn led to a decline in their commitment to Christ and to one another. In 2:4–10, Peter uses Old Testament citations describing the election, honor, and

---

[9]See the helpful discussion of this point in Richard Longenecker, *Biblical Exegesis in the Apostolic Period* (Grand Rapids: Eerdmans, 1975), 94–95.

[10]Goppelt, *Typos*, 18; Glenny, "Hermeneutics in 1 Peter," 65.

[11]Bock, *Proclamation from Prophecy and Pattern*, 50.

[12]I am indebted to one of my students, Richard Leo Schwagel, for some ideas in this paragraph.

privilege of Christ, God's "stone," and of God's "people," the nation of Israel, to describe the elect and honored position of believers in Christ, and in so doing to make the foundational theological statement of the epistle.[13] This section is marked off by a change in mood from the preceding section, as well as the clear break between 2:10 and 2:11.[14] The interrelationship between verses 4–5 and 6–10 leaves no doubt that verses 4–10 should be considered as a unit.[15]

Elliott has demonstrated that, as verse 4 is apparently "a condensation and reformulation" of verses 6–7, so verse 5 is also "a condensation and modification" of verse 9.[16] The connection of verse 4 and verses 6–7 is clear from the repetition of concepts and terminology therein (λίθον, vv. 4b, 7b; ἀποδεδοκιμασμένον, v. 4b, and ἀπεδοκίμασαν, v. 7b; ἐκλεκτόν, vv. 4b, 6b; ἔντιμον, vv. 4b, 6b). The connection of verse 5 and verses 9–10 is perhaps not as clear; the repetition of ἱεράτευμα and ἅγιον in verses 5b and 9b is the clearest example of it. The repetition of ἱεράτευμα is especially noteworthy, since these are the only two occurrences of the word in the New Testament. Elliott also suggests a connection between οἶκος πνευματικός in verse 5 and βασίλειον in verse 9.[17]

This interrelationship between the Old Testament quotations and allusions in 1 Peter 2:6–10 and the statements in 2:4–5 suggests that the introductory formula in 2:6a refers to all the Old Testament references in verses 6–10. The content of the introductory formula, "For in Scripture it says" (διότι περιέχει ἐν γραφῇ), supports this same understanding. The verb περιέχω is often used of something contained in a document,[18] and it is best to understand ἐν γραφῇ as meaning "die Schrift als ganze, nicht eine Schriftstelle."[19] Warfield notes that the singular γραφῇ in 1 Peter 2:6 refers to the Old Testament "in its completeness as a unitary whole."[20] Thus this formula, which introduces

---

[13]See Glenny, "Hermeneutics in 1 Peter," 328–42, for the development of the argument of 1 Peter.

[14]Elliott, *Elect*, 217; cf. 199.

[15]See ibid., 16–23 on the structure of 1 Peter 2:4–10.

[16]Ibid., 19–20.

[17]Ibid., 20, 149–69. On p. 153, Elliott states that "οἶκος πνευματικός, therefore, is Peter's explanation of βασίλειον as an attribute for the Christian body of the faithful. That this house is a 'house of the Divine King' means that it is a 'Spiritual house,' 'a house in which the Divine Spirit resides.'"

[18]BAG, s.v. "περιέχω"; and F. J. A. Hort, *The First Epistle of St. Peter I.1–II.17* (Minneapolis: James & Klock, 1976), 114–15.

[19]Leonhard Goppelt, *Der erste Petrusbrief* (Gottingen: Vandenhoeck & Ruprecht, 1978), 147, n. 44. So also BAG, s.v. "γραφή"; E. Earle Ellis, *Paul's Use of the Old Testament*, TBS (Grand Rapids: Baker, 1957), 21; Benjamin Breckinridge Warfield, *Revelation and Inspiration* (New York: Oxford University Press, 1927), 140–41; and G. Schrenk, "γραφή," TDNT 1:754.

[20]Benjamin Breckinridge Warfield, *The Inspiration and Authority of the Bible* (Grand Rapids: Baker, 1948), 238.

the support or reason for the statements in verses 4–5, allows for a diversity of support from various portions of the Old Testament Scriptures.

Another aspect of the form of the Old Testament citations in 1 Peter 2:6–10 that should be considered is the similarity to rabbinic methodology. This is seen first in the collection of the three quotations in verses 6–8, which are united by the common key word *stone*, λίθος (Isa. 28:16; Ps. 118:22; Isa. 8:14).[21] Also the collection of allusions and descriptions in verses 9–10 is united around the word *people*, λαός (Ex. 19:5–6; Isa. 43:20–21; Hos. 1–2). This methodology is an example of *gezerah shawah*,[22] Hillel's second rule of interpretation, which is based on "verbal analogy from the one verse to another; where the same words are applied to two separate cases, it follows that the same considerations apply to both."[23] Furthermore, midrashic comments on the Scripture references in verses 6–10 are interspersed among those references.[24] Elliott has demonstrated the verbal correspondence of these Scripture references and the interspersed comments on them in the following chart.[25]

6b τίθημι	8c ἐτέθησαν
6b ἔντιμον	7a ἡ τιμή
6c ὁ πιστεύων	7a τοῖς πιστεύουσιν
	7b ἀπιστοῦσιν
8a λίθος προσκόμματος	8b οἳ προσκόπτουσιν
9a ὑμᾶς	9b ὑμᾶς
	7a ὑμῖν
10a οἳ ποτε οὐ λαός	10a νῦν δὲ λαὸς θεοῦ
10b οἱ οὐκ ἠλεημένοι	10b νῦν δὲ ἐλεηθέντες

Each item in the left-hand column is in a quotation or allusion to the Old Testament; the words in the right-hand column are contained in the midrashic comments interspersed among the Scripture references as "a

[21]Elliott, *Elect*, 21.

[22]There is further explanation of rabbinic exegetical practices in Longenecker, *Biblical Exegesis in the Apostolic Period*, 20–45; and Walter C. Kaiser, *Toward an Exegetical Theology* (Grand Rapids: Baker, 1981), 52–57. For a bibliography of more technical material, see Merrill P. Miller, "Targum, Midrash, and the Use of the Old Testament in the New Testament," *JSJ* 2 (1971): 48–49.

[23]Longenecker, *Biblical Exegesis in the Apostolic Period*, 34.

[24]Elliott, *Elect*, 22. Cf. three commentators who use the term *midrash* to explain these comments: Edward Gordon Selwyn, *The First Epistle of St. Peter*, 2d ed., TC (Grand Rapids: Baker, 1981), 164, 269; Goppelt, *Der erste Petrusbrief*, 148; J. N. D. Kelly, *A Commentary on the Epistles of Peter and Jude* (Grand Rapids: Baker, 1981), 93.

[25]Elliott, *Elect*, 18.

kind of running commentary."[26] Elliott concludes his study entitled
"The Structure of Verses 4–10" by stating:

> According to these facts two strata of material are evident: the Old
> Testament references and the commentary upon these texts (vv. 4f.
> and the midrash within vv. 6–10). Whereas the former are passages
> close to the LXX in formulation, the latter are reformulations and
> reflections upon the same, dependent upon and secondary to the
> former. These reformulations are specifically Petrine, that is, from the
> hand of the author of 1 Peter, and hint that herein lies the clue to the
> intent and purpose of this pericope."[27]

One other factor that must be emphasized is the movement from
Christology (vv. 6–8) to ecclesiology (vv. 9–10) in these verses.[28] The
purpose of the section is to establish the identity or self-understanding
of the recipients of the epistle as the people of God, and this identity,
described in verses 9–10, is based upon their relationship with the
stone in verses 6–8. This same development is seen in verses 4–5.
Furthermore, the focus on the people of God described in verses 4–10
is not a focus on their individual identity; rather, as Selwyn notes, "the
words effect a swift transition from the individual to the institutional
aspect of religion, which is nevertheless kept personal throughout."[29]

THE CONTENT OF 1 PETER 2:4–5

Unlike 2:9–10, these verses do not contain the Israelite imagery that
is the main focus of the study. However, verses 4–5 are important for
the understanding of verses 9–10 because they establish the context for
the Old Testament quotations in verses 6–10 and because the Old
Testament quotations in verses 6–10 are given to support the
statements in verses 4–5.

In 1 Peter 2:4 there is a change in emphasis "from individual to
corporate Christian experience"[30] and a change in the description of the
Christian life from the metaphor of a child, used in the previous context
(1:14, 17, 23; 2:2), to a building (2:4–8). The description of Jesus Christ
as a "living stone" (2:4) refers to his resurrection (1:3) and life-giving

---

[26]Ibid., 22.

[27]Ibid., 22–23. Cf. Ernest Best, "1 Peter II.4–10—a Reconsideration," *NovT* 2 (1969):
270–93, who feels the quotation of Isa. 28:16 in 1 Peter 2:6 is confirmatory and the
quotation of Ps. 118:22 in 2:7b both confirms v. 4 and advances the author's argument.
According to Best, all the other quotations and allusions in vv. 8–10 carry forward the
author's argument.

[28]Michaels, *1 Peter*, 93.

[29]Selwyn, *First Peter*, 157.

[30]Michaels, *1 Peter*, 97.

nature.[31] Wayne Grudem notes that "the fact that Christ is the *living* stone shows at once His superiority to an Old Testament temple made of dead stones and reminds Christians that there can be no longing for that old way of approach to God, for this way is far better."[32] The contrasting treatment of this stone, "rejected by men but chosen by God and precious to him," is a main point of this section and of Peter's preaching in Acts 4:11–12. These truths from 1 Peter 2:4 will be supported by the three Old Testament quotations in verses 6–8.

Verse 5 connects Peter's recipients with Christ by describing them as "living stones"[33] in "a spiritual house."[34] In calling believers a spiritual house, Peter means that they are the temple of God, the place where God dwells in this age.[35] Furthermore, as believers continue to "come" in worship to Christ,[36] "the cornerstone" (v. 6) of their "house," God builds them up[37] into a "holy priesthood offering spiritual sacrifices acceptable to God by Jesus Christ." Thus believers,[38] who constitute this house, also minister in the house as priests. The sacrifices of this new priesthood, composed of all believers, are not the Old Testament animal sacrifices but sacrifices inspired by the Spirit of God (Rom. 12:1; Phil. 4:18; Heb. 13:15–16),[39] which are acceptable to God on the basis of Christ's work and the believer's union with him.[40] The understanding of

[31]For further discussion of the background of Peter's stone imagery, see N. Hillyer, " 'Rock-Stone' Imagery in 1 Peter," *TynBul* 22 (1971): 58–81.

[32]Grudem, *1 Peter*, 98.

[33]The adverb ὡς is used regularly in 1 Peter to indicate characteristics or characteristic qualities of those to whom it is referring. Elliott states that this particle is regularly used in 1 Peter "to identify the hearers themselves from a certain point of view" (*Elect*, 36 n. 2). "As living stones" in 2:5 does not distinguish between Jesus ("the living stone") and believers; rather, it states a fact (i.e., "being living stones"). See Elliott's discussion on p. 36 and BAG, s.v. "ὡς."

[34]"Spiritual house" in the nominative case does not function as the direct object of this clause but rather is a "predicative amplification" of the subject "you." D. Edmond Hiebert suggests the translation "yourselves are being built up, a spiritual house" (*First Peter* [Chicago: Moody Press, 1984], 122 n. 23). See also A. T. Robertson, *A Grammar of the Greek New Testament in the Light of Historical Research*, 4th rev. ed. (New York: Hodder & Stoughton, 1923), 401.

[35]See Kelly, *Peter and Jude*, 90; and Grudem, *1 Peter*, 99, 102–4, for a discussion of temple imagery in the New Testament and at Qumran.

[36]The context (v. 3), the present tense of the participle, and the use of the verb "come" in the New Testament (esp. Heb. 4:16; 7:25; 10:1, 22; 11:6; 12:18, 22) all suggest that the coming spoken of here is coming in worship.

[37]Since the builder in this context is God, the verb must be an indicative, not an imperative.

[38]Elliott's argument that this passage does not teach a universal priesthood of all believers is not convincing in light of the clear teaching of vv. 4–5, 9 (*Elect*, 1–15, 219–26).

[39]For further discussion of these spiritual sacrifices, see Kelly, *Peter and Jude*, 91–92; and Hiebert, *First Peter*, 124.

[40]"Through Jesus Christ" could modify the verb "offering" or the adjective "acceptable."

spiritual house and priesthood in verse 5 is especially important to the interpretation of the Old Testament imagery in verse 9 if, as argued above, verse 9 is the scriptural support for verse 5.

THE STONE QUOTATIONS IN 1 PETER 2:6–8

The three Old Testament citations and the commentary on them found in these verses not only substantiate verse 4 but also set the immediate context for the Old Testament imagery in verse 9. The development of this section will be according to the three Old Testament quotations; the midrashic commentary on them will be discussed with each quotation.

The Quotation of Isaiah 28:16 in 1 Peter 2:6

The first stone quotation comes from a context in which Isaiah delivers a message of judgment against the drunken leaders of Judah, who were relying on an alliance with Egypt or Assyria to protect them, rather than trusting in God's provision (Isa. 28:14–22). Isaiah prophesies that they will be swept away by the overwhelming scourge of the Assyrians, but those who put their trust in the "tested stone" God has laid in Zion will be delivered (v. 16).

The identification of the stone in Isaiah 28 is extremely difficult, as the number of interpretations given by the commentators suggests.[41] I propose that this tested stone,[42] which is also described as a cornerstone, is the Davidic monarchy.[43] The message of Isaiah 28:16 for the people

---

The latter agrees best with the emphasis of the passage, but there is little difference in meaning between the two options.

[41]For a survey of the various interpretations of this verse, see Otto Kaiser, *Isaiah 13–39*, OTL (Philadelphia: Westminster, 1974), 252–54; John N. Oswalt, *The Book of Isaiah, Chapters 1–39*, NICOT (Grand Rapids: Eerdmans, 1972), 2:301–3.

[42]M. Tsevat, "בחן," *TDOT* 2:71–72. He suggests that the *'ebhen bochan* was a foundation stone used in a fortress (cf. 1QS 8:7ff., 1QH 6:26, 7:9) and that the statement in Isa. 28:16d was the inscription on the stone. This interpretation of *bochan* is not considered in more detail here because whether it is accepted or not, it does not change the referent Isaiah had in mind for the stone in the Old Testament context.

[43]The following facts support this interpretation. First, the stone is established "in Zion." In this context, which speaks of rulers making covenants with other nations, Zion must be a reference to Jerusalem, the political capital of Judah and united Israel and the seat of the Davidic monarchy (cf. 30:19; 33:20, etc.). Second, the only other occurrence of פנת ("cornerstone") in Isaiah is in 19:13, where it refers to the princes of Egypt. For Isaiah to use it in 28:16 to refer to the Davidic monarchy is consistent with 19:13. Third, the covenant and promises God made to David are regularly connected with the call to trust in God in Isa. 1–39 (cf. 9:7; 11:1; 16:5; 22:21–22; 37:35). Fourth, this interpretation of Isa. 28:16 is consistent with the context, which condemns the leaders of Jerusalem for making worthless covenants with other nations when God has established an eternal covenant with David (2 Sam. 7). This eternal covenant promised a "house" (2 Sam. 7:11–12) to David, and David and the Davidic monarchy that follows him are the cornerstone upon which

---

of Judah is to look to God,[44] who has established a secure foundation for his people. All who are rightly related to God and believe the promises he made to David are secure and will be a part of the eternal house that God promised David (2 Sam. 7:16).

Peter's quotation of Isaiah 28:16 faithfully renders the conceptual meaning of the Hebrew and the LXX text, though it is closer to the LXX, and especially LXX-A with its reading ἐπ' αὐτῷ.[45] The referent of the stone in 1 Peter 2 is clearly Jesus the Messiah.[46] Furthermore, verses 6b–7a teach that because of their relationship with Jesus Christ, the Christian community enjoys great privilege. The reason there is blessing for those who trust in Christ and stumbling for those who do not trust in him is that he is elect and precious to God (vv. 4, 6). They have believed in Christ, so they are privileged and will be delivered.

Peter uses Isaiah 28:16 in 1 Peter 2:6 as proof to confirm his statements in verses 4–5. This is most clearly seen by the formula used to introduce this citation in verse 6a ("For in Scripture it says"). However, this Old Testament quotation is more than a proof text; it also indicates that Christ is the fulfillment of the prophecy in Isaiah 28:16. The Davidic kings whom God placed on the throne in Jerusalem were a pattern and type of Christ, who is the ultimate fulfillment of the promises made to David (2 Sam. 7). This typological-prophetic understanding of the use of Isaiah 28:16 in 1 Peter 2:6 is bolstered by the messianic and eschatological emphasis of the tradition history of the

God builds that house. Fifth, this interpretation fits nicely with the past tense verb יסד in 28:16b. As Franz Delitzsch says, "What is historically realized has had an eternal existence, and indeed an ideal re-existence even in the heart of history itself (ch. xxii.11, xxv.1, xxxvii.26). Ever since there had been a Davidic government at all, this stone had laid in Zion. The Davidic monarchy not only had in this its culminating point, but the ground of its continuance also. . . . Whatever escaped from wrath, even under the Old Testament, stood upon this stone" (*Isaiah*, trans. James Martin, COT, reprint ed., 2 vols. [Grand Rapids: Eerdmans, 1969], 2:10). Cf. Edward J. Young, *The Book of Isaiah* (Grand Rapids: Eerdmans, 1964–71), 2:286.

[44]The verb אמן used absolutely, as in the MT of Isa. 28:16, is, as Walther Eichrodt says, "a comprehensive term for the total God man relationship" (cf. 7:9). He suggests that this verb "expresses a total spiritual attitude which is absolutely determinative for the relationship of the individual with God" (*Theology of the Old Testament*, 2 vols. [Philadelphia: Westminster, 1967], 2:283–84). See also A. Jepsen, "אמן," *TDOT* 1:292–309, esp. 307–8.

[45]Ellis (*Paul's Use of the Old Testament*, 19) and R. T. France (*Jesus and the Old Testament* [Grand Rapids: Baker, 1971], 31) both found this same tendency toward LXX-A in their studies.

[46]The meaning of ἀκρογωνιαῖον in 1 Peter 2:6 has no significance concerning the hermeneutics employed in the use of the quotation in 2:6. R. J. McKelvey argues convincingly that it means a cornerstone at one of the corners of the foundation and also gives a summary of the discussion concerning the meaning of this Greek word ("Christ the Cornerstone," *NTS* 8 [1961–62]: 352–59). Hillyer gives further evidence of the same (" 'Rock-Stone' Imagery," 70–72). The main question concerning the meaning of this term involves its use in Eph. 2:20.

stone passages in Judaism and the New Testament.[47] This verse means that Christ is the fulfillment of the divine prophetic pattern established in God's promise to David, and therefore through him (1 Peter 1:21) God offers salvation. The fulfillment of God's program of salvation has come in Christ, and Peter's recipients are experiencing it.

The emphasis of this stone quotation is not Christological. Rather, by building upon the already-accepted messianic interpretation of these texts, Peter uses them to teach the elect and privileged position of believers in Christ. The emphasis in this passage is on the recipients of the epistle who have put their trust in this elect and honored stone. They will be delivered (v. 6b),[48] even as they are presently honored (v. 7a).[49] The meaning for Peter's recipients is clarified and emphasized in verse 7a (emphatic ὑμῖν, "to you") and in verse 5a (emphatic αὐτοί, "you").

The Quotation of Psalm 118:22 in 1 Peter 2:7b

After Peter has described the honor and deliverance of believers in Christ in 1 Peter 2:6–7a, he goes on to contrast their position with that of unbelievers in verse 7b. The midrashic note "But to those who do not believe" that introduces verse 7b establishes the "parallelism and antithesis" of one of the two groups.[50] The quotation from the LXX text of Psalm 118 (117):22 in verse 7b[51] means that Christ, the rejected

---

[47]See Elliott, *Elect,* 26–33; Hillyer, " 'Rock-Stone' Imagery," 58–81; Klyne R. Snodgrass, "1 Peter II.1–10: Its Formation and Literary Affinities," *NTS* 24 (1977–78): 97–106; J. Jeremias, "λίθος," *TDNT* 4:268–80; Str-B 3:276, 593, 763; Matthew Black, "The Christological Use of the Old Testament in the New Testament," *NTS* 18 (1971): 1–14, esp. 11–14; and C. H. Dodd, *According to the Scriptures* (New York: Scribners, 1963), 41–43. This material is summarized in Glenny, "Hermeneutics in 1 Peter," 204–13. The key representative texts are *Tg. Jon.* Isa. 28:16, *Targum of Isaiah,* trans. and ed. J. F. Stenning (Oxford: Clarendon, 1949); 1QS 8:5–10; Matt. 21:33–46; Mark 12:1–12; Luke 20:9–19; Acts 4:8–12; Rom. 9:33; and Eph. 2:20. Each time a stone text is used in the New Testament, Jesus is identified as the stone. As Snodgrass maintains, because of the accepted messianic interpretation of these texts in Judaism and because of Christ's interpretation and use of them, "the stone testimonia were used to help the church express her Christology, her understanding of Christ's rejection and exaltation, her soteriology, her ecclesiology and her understanding of judgment" ("1 Peter II.1–10," 105).

[48]To "not be put to shame" was a common description of God's salvation in the early church. See Rom. 10:11.

[49]Many translations (KJV, ASV, RSV, NIV, NASB) understand v. 7a to teach that Christ, the cornerstone, is precious to believers. This understanding is highly unlikely; it is better to translate v. 7a, "Therefore, the honor (or 'privilege') [is] to you, the believers." This is more consistent with the context and emphasis on "you" (ὑμῖν) in the Greek text; it correctly translates τιμή as "honor" or "privilege" and not "preciousness," which sense it never has in any of its forty-one New Testament occurrences (Grudem, *1 Peter,* 104); also it allows τιμή to function as the subject of the sentence, which seems necessary, since it has the definite article preceding it.

[50]Elliott, *Elect,* 38, n. 1.

[51]There is no doubt that this quotation is closer to the LXX than to the Hebrew. The

stone,[52] has been exalted by God to be the most important and foundational stone in the spiritual house God is building in this age.[53] The effect of unbelief in Christ and rejection of this stone is described further in verse 8.

The basis of the use of Psalm 118 (117):22 in this passage is the typological connection between the stone in the Old Testament context and the stone (Christ) in the New Testament context. The stone in Psalm 118 is a representative of the nation, most naturally understood as the king of Israel. The bulk of Psalm 118 (vv. 5–19, 21, 28) is in the form of a psalm of individual thanksgiving.[54] The changes from plural to singular throughout the psalm reflect the fact that a spokesman is representing the nation (vv. 19–20, 21),[55] and the language of the psalm suggests the original context of this psalm followed a military victory (vv. 9–14).[56] If the stone is the king of Israel, the builders are most naturally understood as "the empire builders of the day"[57]—"the super powers that controlled the destinies of lesser nations, especially those they considered insignificant."[58] The king, on behalf of the nation, praises God for the nation's deliverance from these empire builders. This deliverance means that God's program focuses on the nation of Israel and more specifically the Davidic dynasty in Israel, even though this king (and the nation he represents) is considered worthless by the "super powers."[59]

---

only difference between the LXX and New Testament is the case of λίθος, which is accusative in the LXX. See Glenny, "Hermeneutics in 1 Peter," 230.

[52]It is doubtful whether "the builders" are Jewish leaders, as in the Gospels (Mark 12:11; Matt. 21:43; Luke 20:17) and in Acts 4:8–12. Cf. Goppelt, *Der erste Petrusbrief,* 149, which sees the builders as the men who would build their own world, according to v. 4a. The general term ἀνθρώπων which describes these men in v. 4a supports this interpretation.

[53]J. Jeremias states, "The early community found in Ps. 118 (117):22 scriptural evidence for the death and resurrection of Jesus. The Crucified One is the rejected stone which in the resurrection is made by God the chief cornerstone in the heavenly sanctuary (Acts 4:11), to be manifested as such in the parousia. First Peter 2:7 interprets Psalm 118:22 in terms of the σκάνδαλον which Jesus is for unbelievers. In other words, the κεφαλὴ γωνίας is not so much the final stone but a sharp stone at the corner of the building against which men stumble and fall. This interpretation is suggested by the quotation from Isaiah 8:14 which immediately follows (1 Peter 2:8)" ("κεφαλὴ γωνίας," TDNT 1:793). Therefore, the NIV marginal reading "cornerstone" is preferred over the textual reading "capstone."

[54]Leslie C. Allen, *Psalms 101–150,* WBC (Waco, Tex.: Word, 1983), 122–23. This conclusion is supported by Claus Westermann, *Praise and Lament in the Psalms* (Atlanta: John Knox, 1981), 102–11.

[55]See H. C. Leupold, *Exposition of the Psalms* (Grand Rapids: Baker, 1969), 811–12.

[56]Allen, *Psalms 101–150,* 123.

[57]Leupold, *Exposition of the Psalms,* 818.

[58]Thanks goes to Allen P. Ross for the description of the passage.

[59]Leupold shows that this psalm fits nicely into the period after the return from captivity because of the clear allusions to building (*Exposition of the Psalms,* 810–21). Some who

The typological connection between the Old Testament and the New Testament is evidenced by the pattern or correspondence between the Davidic king and the greatest or ultimate Son of David, Christ the Messiah. Thus there is not only a divinely ordained pattern and identifiable link between the type and antitype but also an escalation in meaning. God's pattern of working in the life of the Davidic king is being seen again in his working in and through the Messiah. Psalm 118 celebrates the Lord's deliverance of a historical Davidic king who represented the nation of Israel. First Peter 2:7 celebrates the Lord's deliverance of the ultimate Davidic king, the Messiah, a fact that has present and future implications for Christians, whom he represents. The typological-prophetic classification of this use of the Old Testament is further supported by Christ's use of this passage in the Gospels and Peter's use of it in Acts;[60] both see the rejection of Jesus by the Jewish leaders and his exaltation by God as fulfillment of Old Testament prophecy.

The Quotation of Isaiah 8:14 in 1 Peter 2:8

The quotation from Isaiah 8:14 in 1 Peter 2:8 is the only quotation in 1 Peter that is closer to the Hebrew text than it is to the LXX. First Peter shortens the "loose paraphrase"[61] that the LXX makes of the Hebrew text into a rendering that "corresponds almost perfectly to the MT."[62]

This quotation further describes the cornerstone in 2:7b as "a stone that causes men to stumble and a rock that makes them fall" and thus further emphasizes the negative and destructive result of not believing in the stone. Verse 8b identifies stumbling over the stone with disbelief of the word, thus connecting the complex with 1:22–23.[63] Furthermore, verse 8b indicates that stumbling over the stone is in accordance with God's sovereign purpose ($\dot{\epsilon}\tau\dot{\epsilon}\theta\eta\sigma\alpha\nu$), just as the fact that the stone is

---

understand the stone in Psalm 118:22 to be Israel are Leupold (ibid., 811); Selwyn (*First Peter*, 158); Derek Kidner (*Psalms 1–72*, TOTC [Downers Grove, Ill.: InterVarsity Press, 1973], 23); Stewart Perowne (*The Book of Psalms*, reprint ed. [Grand Rapids: Zondervan, 1976], 343); and Franz Delitzsch (*Psalms*, trans. Francis Bolton, BCOT, 3 vols. [Grand Rapids: Eerdmans, 1970], 3:141). Others understand the stone to be the king of Israel, who represents the nation: see Allen, *Psalms 101–150*, 118–25; and A. A. Anderson, *The Book of Psalms*, NCB, 2 vols. (Greenwood, S.C.: Attic Press, 1972), 797–805.

[60]Matt. 21:33–46; Mark 12:1–12; Luke 20:9–19; Acts 4:8–12.

[61]Hort, *First Peter*, 121.

[62]Gleason L. Archer and G. C. Chirichigno, *Old Testament Quotations in the New Testament: A Complete Survey* (Chicago: Moody Press, 1983), 97. Two who agree with this assessment are Gene L. Green ("Theology and Ethics in 1 Peter" [Ph.D. diss., University of Aberdeen, 1979], 18–19) and W. Howard Burkeen ("The Use of the Old Testament in Selected Passages in 1 Peter" [M.A. thesis, Trinity Evangelical Divinity School, 1973], 52). G. Stählin, "σκάνδαλον," TDNT 7:341, notes that the terms in 1 Peter 2:8 are appropriate for a translation of the section of the MT quoted there.

[63]Elliott, *Elect*, 38.

the basis of salvation to those who believe in him is according to God's sovereign purpose (τίθημι, v. 6).[64] As in this whole context, the stone is Jesus, the Messiah. The fact that such disobedience and stumbling of unbelievers are according to God's plan is meant to be a comfort to Peter's recipients.

The hermeneutical classification that best identifies the use of the Old Testament in the New Testament in this instance is again typological-prophetic. The Old Testament text shows that the prophecy in Isaiah 8:14 did not look exclusively to a future event as in direct prophecy. It promised deliverance or stumbling for Isaiah's audience as well as for Peter's. There is a clear, divinely ordained pattern between stumbling over Yahweh in the Old Testament and stumbling over Jesus in the New Testament, just as there are other links between Yahweh in the Old Testament and Jesus Christ in 1 Peter (1:25; 2:3; 3:14). In fact, the connection between Yahweh and Jesus may be the basis for the quotation of Isaiah 8:12 in 1 Peter 3:14. The use of Isaiah 8:14 in 1 Peter 2:8 not only honors the meaning of the Old Testament context but also deepens and specifies the referent of the stone, clearly identifying it as Christ.

Summary of the Use of the Old Testament in 1 Peter 2:6–8

The hermeneutical classification that best describes the appropriation of the three stone quotations in 1 Peter 2:6–8 is typological-prophetic. It involves a divinely ordained and orchestrated historical correspondence (pattern) between a person, persons, or event in the Old Testament and Christ the greater antitype in the New Testament. Furthermore, the link between the type and antitype is clearly identifiable in this passage of Scripture.[65] Midrashic technique is present here, but typology is really the means by which texts are linked.[66] The emphasis of the stone complex is not Christological, however, as are other stone complexes in the New Testament; rather, it is soteriological, describing believers and unbelievers. Elliott states that "the λίθος complex has not been cited merely to make a Christological statement but to provide the basis for a description of the believing community."[67] Peter is now ready to develop further the identity of the believing community in verses 9–10, on the basis of their connection with the stone described in verses 6–8.

---

[64]Grudem, *1 Peter*, 106–10, has a helpful discussion on 2:8 and on election and reprobation in Scripture.

[65]Glenny, "Hermeneutics in 1 Peter," 65–66.

[66]See ibid., 225–28, for a discussion of the possibility of a midrash or pesher method of hermeneutics in 1 Peter 2:6.

[67]Elliott, *Elect*, 38.

THE PEOPLE OF GOD ALLUSIONS IN 1 PETER 2:9–10

The connection between the stone (λίθος) quotations in verses 6–8 and the people (λαός) allusions[68] in verses 9–10 is based on the fact that both the stone and the people are elect.[69] Peter adapts the LXX quotation from Isaiah 28:16 in 1 Peter 2:6 by omitting "costly" (πολυτελῆ), which modifies "stone" in the LXX, so that "elect" (ἐκλεκτόν) is the first modifier of stone or cornerstone in the New Testament text. He also modifies the allusion in 1 Peter 2:9, inserting the comma "chosen people" (γένος ἐκλεκτόν) in the allusion from Exodus 19:6, making this the first description of the people in verses 9–10. As Elliott suggests, "The concept of election and the adjective ἐκλεκτόν is the sole medium of correspondence" between the stone (vv. 6–8) and the people (vv. 9–10).[70] Such a "transference of attributes"[71] between Christ and the church is common in 1 Peter.[72] Shrenk states that "the similarity of designations is intentional. In content a total view of the images suggests that the λίθος ἐκλεκτός creates and upholds the γένος ἐκλεκτόν."[73]

The election of believers and Christ is a major emphasis from the very beginning of 1 Peter (1:1, 2, 20). Because of their connection with Christ, believers (1:21; 2:6) and their sacrifices (2:5) are acceptable to God. In 2:7a, Peter infers from the preceding discussion "that the honour which Christ had by virtue of God's choice is imparted to, and shared by, the faithful."[74] The quotations in verses 6–8 give Old Testament support for the fact that Christ is the honored and elect Messiah. The honor and election of believers, described in verses 6–8, is based on their corporate identity with Christ.[75]

[68]For this study, if the Old Testament reference is more than a phrase and is a close reproduction of the Old Testament text, it is classified as a quotation. An allusion is "a verbal or material parallel to a specific Old Testament passage" (Bock, *Proclamation from Prophecy and Pattern,* 57) which "utilizes Scripture *words* and *phrases* without introduction and without disrupting the flow of the narrative" (Moo, *The Old Testament in the Gospel Passion Narratives,* 20, emphasis added).

[69]Elliott, *Elect,* esp. 141–45, demonstrates the importance of the theme of election in 1 Peter.

[70]Ibid., 144.

[71]Dodd, *According to the Scriptures,* 105–6. Elliott, *Elect,* 143, n. 4, notes that the δέ in 1 Peter 2:9 is not used in the original adversative sense it had in Ex. 19:6; rather, it effects "a relation between two similar objects."

[72]Elliott, *Elect,* 144, n. 3.

[73]G. Schrenk, "ἐκλεκτός," *TDNT* 4:191.

[74]Selwyn, *First Peter,* 164.

[75]On the concept of corporate identity, see H. W. Robinson, *Corporate Personality in Ancient Israel* (Philadelphia: Fortress, 1964); E. Earle Ellis, *Prophecy and Hermeneutic in Early Christianity* (Grand Rapids: Eerdmans, 1978), 170–71; and G. K. Beale, "Did Jesus and His Followers Preach the Right Doctrine from the Wrong Texts? An Examination of the Presuppositions of Jesus' and the Apostles' Exegetical Method," *Themelios* 14 (April 1989): 90–92.

The three allusions to the Old Testament in 1 Peter 2:9–10 are taken from Exodus 19:5–6, Isaiah 43:20–21, and Hosea 1–2. As in verses 6–8, these allusions are interspersed with Peter's comments. In 1 Peter 2:9 the language of Exodus 19:6 and Isaiah 43:21 is combined to present a series of epithets used to describe the believers referred to in verses 6–8, who, instead of stumbling over the stone, trust in him. Just as the three quotations in verses 6–8 are united in their application to Christ by the common term *stone*, so the three allusions in verses 9–10 are united in their New Testament application by the term *people* found in each context.[76] In each of these Old Testament contexts the word *people* is used to refer to Israel as the people of God. The phrase *people of God* was used in the Old Testament, especially Deuteronomy, to designate Israel as God's elect people (Deut. 7:6; cf. 4:37; 10:15).[77] Thus, Peter's description of his recipients by three passages speaking of people of God in the Old Testament further emphasizes the election and honor of his recipients. The application of these Old Testament texts to his recipients also has importance in the discussion concerning the relationship of Israel and the church.

The Use of Exodus 19:5–6 in 1 Peter 2:9

Exodus 19 is an account of the proposal by God and acceptance by Israel of the covenant at Mount Sinai. At this time Israel not only becomes a national entity but also enters into a unique relationship with God. God declares to the nation in 19:4 that their redemption from Egypt manifested his choice of them (cf. Deut. 4:37). In light of this election, God initiates a special covenant relationship with Israel and then outlines the unique relationship the nation will enjoy with him if they obey him and keep the stipulations of this covenant (19:5–6). First, Israel will be God's "treasured possession" out of all of the nations of the earth. The LXX reads, "You shall be a special people to me of all the nations" (ἔσεσθέ μοι λαὸς περιούσιος ἀπὸ πάντων τῶν ἐθνῶν). This phrase is the basis for the connection of this passage with the other people of God passages. The description emphasizes God's election of Israel and the unique position Israel possesses by virtue of the fact that they are God's property.[78] The second description of Israel, "kingdom of priests" (ממלכת כהנים), emphasizes God's kingship over the covenant nation, the holiness of the nation as priests, the nation's access to God, and the collectivity of the nation in its relationship with God through this covenant. The Old Testament context (Ex. 3:12; 6:6–8) suggests that the main emphasis in this epithet is not Israel's mediatorial function to the Gentile nations but rather its worship and priestly service to Yahweh.[79] The third description of Israel in this passage, which identifies them as a "holy nation," emphasizes the fact that the nation was to be set apart to God from all that was profane.[80] The motivation for this holy lifestyle was God's election of the nation (Deut. 14:2). These epithets in Exodus 19:5b–6 are "one of the central and dominant expressions of the theology and faith of the Old Testament People of God."[81]

In Exodus 19 Israel agrees to obey God and enter this covenant relationship with him, and they become special people of God (Deut. 7:6–16). It should be emphasized that God's choice of Israel was an expression of his remembrance of the covenants he had made with their fathers (Ex. 2:24; 6:2–8; Ps. 105:8–15).[82] Furthermore, Israel's obedience to the covenant stipulations God had given them had nothing to do with his choice of them, and their eventual disobedience would not annul God's original choice but instead would result in the curses of the covenant (Lev. 26; Deut. 28). When Israel failed to keep the Mosaic covenant, God in love and faithfulness promised a "new covenant" with the nation (Jer. 31:31–34).

Peter uses the LXX as the source for his quotation of Exodus 19:5–6.[83] The most convincing proof of this is the correspondence of words in the difficult phrase βασίλειον ἱεράτευμα. Peter does not include the phrase λαὸς περιούσιος ἀπὸ πάντων τῶν ἐθνῶν from the LXX text of Exodus 19:5, even though *people* (λαός) is the common term that unites the three allusions in 1 Peter 2:9–10. Perhaps this first of three descriptions of the Old Testament covenant people found in Exodus 19:5b–6 is not included in 1 Peter because it is a comprehensive

---

[79]The mediatorial office of the members of the nation may be implicitly included in Ex. 19:6, but it is not emphasized as it is later in Isa. 61:1–9. Cf. Martin McNamara, *Targum and Testament* (Shannon, Ireland: Irish University Press, 1972), 149–51; and Elliott, *Elect*, 50–63. McComiskey and Kaiser see Israel's mediatorial work to other nations as part of the meaning of Ex. 19:5–6 (McComiskey, *The Covenants of Promise*, 68–69; Kaiser, *Old Testament Theology*, 108).

[80]See Gordon J. Wenham, *The Book of Leviticus*, NICOT (Grand Rapids: Eerdmans, 1979), 18–25, for a helpful discussion of the term *holiness* in the Old Testament.

[81]Elliott, *Elect*, 62.

[82]William Dyrness, *Themes in Old Testament Theology* (Downers Grove, Ill.: InterVarsity Press, 1979), 120. Cf. Dyrness's discussion entitled "The Covenant," on pp. 112–26.

[83]Elliott, *Elect*, 50, n. 1.

description, encompassing the more particular concepts found in the individual epithets used in 1 Peter 2:9–10. Peter does include the two descriptions of the Old Testament covenant people found in Exodus 19:6. Thus the introductory words, "But you are" (ὑμεῖς δέ), and the words "royal priesthood" (βασίλειον ἱεράτευμα) and "holy nation" (ἔθνος ἅγιον) come from Exodus 19:6 and are used in this passage of 1 Peter to express Peter's theology of the New Testament people of God.

A major problem in understanding the LXX text quoted in 1 Peter 2:9 is the meaning of the phrase βασίλειον ἱεράτευμα, translated "royal priesthood," which renders the Hebrew ממלכת כהנים, "kingdom of priests." This phrase could be understood as two substantives ("a royal residence [and] a body of priests")[84] or as an adjective and a substantive ("a royal priesthood").[85] The evidence suggests that the former option is the best understanding of the phrase both in the LXX and the New Testament. First, the vast majority in the tradition history of the LXX phrase βασίλειον ἱεράτευμα understood these words as two independent nouns.[86] Also if, as argued above, the Old Testament references in verses 6–10 are the basis for the statements in verses 4–5, then it would be natural for the noun "royal residence" (βασίλειον) to

---

[84]Ibid., 63–76. Perhaps βασίλειον would be better translated as simply "kingdom," used "in the sense of the people under the rule of God the king (as intended in the MT)" (ibid., 73). On p. 72, Elliott gives the evidence for the adjectival function of βασίλειον in Ex. 19:6. He goes on to show that the evidence for a substantival function of βασίλειον is stronger. Best takes βασίλειον as a noun meaning "group of kings." See Ernest Best, 1 Peter, NCBC (Grand Rapids: Eerdmans, 1971), 107–8; and idem, "1 Peter II.4–10."

[85]Hort, First Peter, 125–26; and Michaels, 1 Peter, 108–9.

[86]Glenny, "Hermeneutics in 1 Peter," 245–60; Elliott, Elect, 63–76. Kelly, in Peter and Jude, 97, summarizes the main evidence for this interpretation: "(a) The Hebrew lying behind the first of the two words is, as we have explained, a noun, viz., 'kingdom.' (b) While basileios can mean 'royal,' its use as an adjective is exceedingly rare in Biblical Greek (twice only in the LXX, if we exclude Ex. xix.6: xxiii.22 as being subject to discussion). (c) Much the most common use of the word in the LXX is as a neuter noun basileion, and this is found frequently in secular Greek too. In the latter it generally has the sense of 'royal residence' (Xenophon, Cyrop. ii.4.3; Herodotus, Hist. i.30.178—in plural), or else 'royal capital' (Polybius, Hist. iii.15.3); while in the LXX the meanings 'sovereignty', 'crown', 'monarchy' (2 Sam. i.10; 1 Chron. xxviii.4; Wis. 1.14; 2 Macc. ii.17), or (mostly in plural) 'palace' (Esth. i.9; ii.13; Prov. xviii.19; Nah. ii.7; Dan. vi.19), predominate. (d) In the exegesis of Hellenistic Judaism basileion in LXX Ex. xix.6 was interpreted as a substantive: cf. 2 Macc. ii.17 ('kingdom'); Philo, De sobr. 66 and De Abr. 56 ('royal house'). (e) The author of Rev. 1.6; v. 10 also seems to have read the relevant words of Ex. xix.6 as two independent nouns (cf. 'a royal house, priests to God . . .'; 'a royal house and priests'). (f) Stylistic considerations in fact favour our taking basileion as a substantive, for had it been an adjective we should have expected it to be placed, like the other adjectives in the sentence, after its noun." Charles August Briggs suggests that the two nouns in the Hebrew phrase "kingdom of priests" (Ex. 19:6) functioned more like a compound noun than a construct relation (Messianic Prophecy [New York: Charles Scribner's Sons, 1902], 102–3, n. 2). However the phrase is understood, it includes royal and priestly concepts.

be the basis for the phrase "spiritual house" (οἶκος πνευματικός) in verse 5.[87] The noun ἱεράτευμα speaks of the privilege of Peter's recipients in approaching God as well as their ministry as God's representatives.[88]

Not only does the epithet *holy nation* (ἔθνος ἅγιον) emphasize the positional holiness of Peter's recipients, but *nation* (ἔθνος) also indicates their common origin and their unity as one group of people. It is obvious that the national and political aspects of the Hebrew term גוי communicated in the original Old Testament context are not carried over literally to the New Testament context. The meaning of ἔθνος in the New Testament context is a people who have certain characteristics of a nation (unity and common origin).[89] These epithets, which are applied to the church as a corporate body, indicate the position, privilege, and purpose of this elect body of believers, who are the people of God in the "last times" in which Peter writes (1:18).

Perhaps the most important part of the allusion to Exodus 19:6 in 1 Peter 2:9 is the first phrase, "But you are" (ὑμεῖς δέ). This equative clause, which identifies Peter's believing recipients as the people described in the following epithets, replaces the future tense in the LXX and Hebrew texts. While Israel was promised that they *would be* God's people and a kingdom of priests and a holy nation if they would obey him and keep covenant with him, Peter's recipients *are* all of these things now; they have obeyed God (1:2, 22–23), and they are participants in the new covenant sealed with his blood (vv. 2, 18–21).

Although there is an analogy between the way Exodus 19:6 was used in its original context and its use in 1 Peter, there is also an advancement of the meaning in the New Testament context beyond the Old Testament, which is seen in each of the three phrases used in 1 Peter 2:9.

The Use of Isaiah 43:20–21 in 1 Peter 2:9

The expressions in 1 Peter 2:9 that reflect Isaiah 43:20b–21 are "chosen people" (γένος ἐκλεκτόν) and "a people belonging to God, that you may declare the praises" (λαὸς εἰς περιποίησιν ὅπως τὰς ἀρετὰς ἐξαγγείλητε). The repetition in these phrases of γένος ἐκλεκτόν, λαός,

---

[87]This parallels the meaning of 1 Cor. 3:16–17 and Eph. 2:14–22, and in the immediate context it makes sense of the "honor" that belongs to believers in v. 7a.

[88]Kelly states, "Even so, a body of priests seems to convey something more than the idea of a community enjoying unique closeness to God; the idea of performing holy service in His honor (cf. 'spiritual sacrifices' in 5) must also be included as a subordinate but none the less consciously intended motive" (*Peter and Jude*, 98).

[89]G. Bertram and K. L. Schmidt, "ἔθνος," *TDNT* 2:364–72, esp. p. 369 on the New Testament meaning.

περιεποιησάμην (περιποίησις), and ἀρετάς[90] from the LXX text of
Isaiah 43:20b–21 points to an LXX source for Peter's words.[91]

The LXX text of Isaiah 43:20b–21 has been adapted by Peter to fit his
purposes, and it is possible that he was influenced by other Old
Testament texts in his formulation of these phrases. The phrase "a
people belonging to God" may have been influenced by Exodus 19:5
(LXX: λαὸς περιούσιος) and Malachi 3:17 (LXX: εἰς περιποίησιν).[92]
The phrase "of him who called you out of darkness into his wonderful
light" in 1 Peter 2:9b may be a reflection of several Old Testament
texts, among them Isaiah 40:1–3, 14–15; however, since the connection is not certain, it will not be considered in this chapter.[93] Also, as
noted above, the phrase "chosen people" (γένος ἐκλεκτόν), based on
Isaiah 43:20b, is inserted into the citation from Exodus 19:6 in 1 Peter
2:9a between "but you are" (ὑμεῖς δέ) and "royal priesthood"
(βασίλειον ἱεράτευμα), with the result that "chosen people" is the first
epithet used to describe the church in 1 Peter 2:9.

Isaiah 40–48, the Old Testament context of this citation, develops
the theme that in contrast to powerless idols, the incomparable
sovereign Lord will deliver and restore his people, Israel, by the power
of his word. In chapter 43 the Lord promises to regather and renew his
created, elect, and witnessing Servant, Israel. A key idea in this chapter
is redemption (vv. 1, 3, 14). Although the promises of redemption have
a primary reference to God's deliverance of Israel from Babylonian
captivity, the language of the chapter implies that a greater return prior
to the second advent of Christ is also intended (vv. 5, 6). The clearest
promise of Israel's deliverance from the Babylonian captivity found up
to this point in the second part of Isaiah is 43:14–21 (cf. 48:14–22).
Here God promises he will deliver Israel out of Babylon (43:14–15) as
he delivered them from Egypt (43:16–17); furthermore, God promises
this will be a safe second exodus that will be much greater than the
exodus from Egypt (43:18). This deliverance is described as a "new
thing" (v. 19; cf. 41:22; 42:9; 43:9; 46:9; 48:6), which shows not only
that it is future to the original recipients (cf. "former things" describing
God's past accomplishments and sovereignty in 43:18; 41:22; 42:9;
46:9; 48:3) but also that it has clear eschatological force, which
eventually ties it to Christ's first advent (Isa. 42:1–9), as well as going
beyond anything accomplished at that first advent (Isa. 65:17–25; cf.

[90]Selwyn, First Peter, 165.

[91]Elliott implies a LXX source but does not state it explicitly (Elect, 39–44). Best states
that the Old Testament phrases in vv. 9–10 are from the LXX (1 Peter, 107). Peter's
tendency to use the LXX would also suggest this conclusion.

[92]See Hort, First Peter, 127–28, for his discussion of this phrase.

[93]See Kelly, Peter and Jude, 100, for a summary of the background of 1 Peter 2:9b.

Jer. 16:14–15; 23:7-8). Verse 20 states that the jackals, owls, and other wild animals in the desert will glorify God because of his glorious works on behalf of his chosen people, indicating that all of creation will be blessed at this time. Also language such as "water in the desert" and "streams in the wasteland" (vv. 19, 20) is often used in Isaiah to describe the blessing of the eschatological kingdom (35:1, 6–7; 44:3-5).[94] Isaiah 43:20–21 emphasizes God's choice of Israel as the basis for his deliverance of them. The result of the Lord's deliverance and provision for his people is that these people, whom he formed for himself, will fulfill the purpose of their election by praising him (43:21).

The epithet "chosen people" (γένος ἐκλεκτόν) is applied to the church in 1 Peter, indicating that all believers have a common ancestry and unity.[95] Peter's phrase "a people belonging to God" (λαὸς εἰς περιποίησιν) abbreviates the LXX's λαόν μου ὃν περιεποιησάμην of Isaiah 43:21a.[96] In 1 Peter this phrase indicates "a community which God has singled out and made peculiarly His own and which finds the end of its existence in this fact."[97] In the LXX, *people* (λαός) "became the *terminus* par excellence for the People of God."[98] In the New Testament it was used "as an ethnic designation for Jewish Israel and as a title for the true people of God."[99] In its use as a designation for Israel in the LXX and for the true people of God in the New Testament, it indicates election, covenant status, holiness, and redemption.[100] In the New Testament the requirement for belonging to this true people of God is purely religious: faith in Jesus as the Messiah, or "coming to the stone" (1 Peter 2:4).

The following clause, "that you may declare the praises" (ὅπως τὰς

---

[94]In Isa. 44:3–5 the thought of 43:19–21 is picked up and continued after God's declaration of Israel's sins in 43:22–28. In chap. 44 the promise of physical blessing ("water") is combined with spiritual blessing ("Spirit") for Israel. At that future time Gentiles (44:5) will be attracted to Israel and the Lord because of God's blessing on Israel. The combination of spiritual and physical blessing as well as the coming together of Israel and the Gentiles suggests not only a future time of blessing for ethnic Israel but also a literal fulfillment of these promises.

[95]BAG, s.v. "γένος."

[96]The LXX text of Ex. 19:5 and Mal. 3:17 may have influenced Peter's wording here.

[97]Kelly, *Peter and Jude*, 99. See Elliott, *Elect*, 40; and Beare, *The First Epistle of Peter*, 3d ed. (Oxford: Basil Blackwell, 1970), 105. Elliott, *Elect*, 41, n. 2, shows that in the New Testament the idea of becoming God's possession was closely related to redemption (cf. Titus 2:14; Eph. 1:14; Acts 20:28).

[98]Elliott, *Elect*, 40; R. Meyer and H. Strathmann, "λαός," *TDNT* 4:29–57.

[99]Elliott, *Elect*, 40. Elliott has two different groups in mind in this statement, as his previous discussion indicates. He states that λαός had a twofold significance in the LXX: "semantically it served as the ethnic designation for Israel; theologically there was implied, in addition, the religious character of Israel, her election and covenantal status with JHWH, her holiness, and her redemption."

[100]Ibid. Elliott's brief discussion of λαός was especially helpful for the development of this section.

ἀρετὰς ἐξαγγείλητε), shows the purpose or task of this chosen people. The connection between verses 5 and 9 of 1 Peter 2 suggests that this purpose is a further development of the purpose stated in verse 5: "offering spiritual sacrifices." The verb "declare" (ἐξαγγέλλω) means to "proclaim"[101] or "report"[102] and is used often in the Psalms for praising God; its only other possible New Testament occurrence in the short ending of Mark may indicate that the early church associated it with proclamation concerning salvation.[103] The noun "praises" (ἀρετάς), which translates the Hebrew תהלה in the LXX and is used in the New Testament quotation in 1 Peter 2:9, seems to mean more than God's "virtues," "excellencies," or "powers"; instead, it refers to his "mighty deeds" or "saving acts."[104] The context of verses 9–10 as well as the following section supports this understanding of the noun (cf. 2:12; 3:1–4). Thus the proclamation in 2:9 is the church's proclamation of God's saving acts to the world around them. This proclamation involves a person's whole lifestyle (ἀναστροφή, 1:15, 18; 2:12; 3:1–2, 16); it is a "living sacrifice" as described in Romans 12:1–2. Peter calls it a "spiritual sacrifice" (2:5) because it is a sacrifice of the lives of these Spirit-indwelt (cf. "spiritual house," 2:5), Spirit-empowered (4:10–11) believers. The mighty acts and deeds of God that the church is to proclaim are described further in verse 9 by the phrase "of him who called you out of darkness into his wonderful light," words having clear election and salvation significance for the church.[105]

Thus the allusions from Isaiah 43:20b–21 are used by Peter to show that his recipients are the elect, peculiar people of God who have been redeemed by him and given an elect, covenant status and holy standing. Furthermore, the purpose of this people of God extends beyond that of Old Testament Israel. They are to proclaim the "redemption brought about by Christ's death and resurrection."[106] This is to be done by word and also by life, as the connection with "offering spiritual sacrifices" in verse 5, as well as the following context (2:11–4:11), indicates.[107]

The Use of Hosea 1–2 in 1 Peter 2:10

The description of believers in Jesus that began in 1 Peter 2:9 continues in verse 10, which presents a conflation of terms and concepts

---

[101]BAG, s.v. "ἐξαγγέλλω."

[102]Grudem, *1 Peter,* 112.

[103]Elliott, *Elect,* 42.

[104]Ibid.; Selwyn, *First Peter,* 167; O. Bauernfeind, "ἀρετή," *TDNT* 1:457–61; BAG, s.v. "ἀρετή." Also BDB, s.v. "תהלה," suggests this idea for the MT of Isa. 43:21.

[105]Elliott, *Elect,* 43–44.

[106]Selwyn, *First Peter,* 167.

[107]The emphasis upon service as well as speech may be a reflection of the emphasis on service in the interpretation of Isa. 43:20b–21 in *Tg. Jn.*

from the LXX text of Hosea 1–2.[108] This manner of citation is often found in rabbinic writings,[109] where Hosea 1–2 was used to show God's love for his people, Israel, and his desire to restore Israel to a right relationship with him. Paul used some of the same passages in Romans 9:25–26. In Romans 9:25 he conflates phrases from Hosea 1:6, 9, and the Vaticanus text of 2:23 (LXX), and he quotes Hosea 1:10 in Romans 9:26. Peter's use of Hosea in 1 Peter 2:10 is not based upon this passage in Romans because 1 Peter has the phrase "not received mercy" (οὐκ ἠλεημένοι), while Paul uses the Vaticanus reading of Hosea 2:23 (LXX), "not my loved one" (οὐκ ἠγαπημένη). Furthermore, Peter leaves out Romans 9:26c, "There they will be called 'sons of the living God.'"[110] Apparently both authors worked independently and very possibly relied on a common tradition that, as Dodd says, treated Hosea 1–2 "as a description of the way in which God, of His sheer grace, adopted as His people those who formerly were no people of His—for Hosea, repentant Israel, for Christian teachers, the Gentiles."[111]

It is also noteworthy that in the stream of tradition Hosea 1–2 was always used as a reference to Israel. An exception occurs in Romans 9 and in 1 Peter 2. In Romans 9 Paul uses the promise from Hosea 2:23 to confirm the fact that God was calling people from among the Gentiles to salvation. F. F. Bruce states, concerning Paul's use of Hosea in Romans 9, "Great numbers of Gentiles, who had never been 'the people of God' and had no claim on His covenant mercy, were coming to be enrolled among His people and to be the recipients of His mercy. The scale of the divine action was far wider than in Hosea's day, but the same *pattern* and *principle* were recognizable."[112] Kelly notes that, whereas Paul uses Hosea 1–2 to stress the universal nature of salvation, Peter uses it to stress "the eschatological blessedness which his readers now

[108]Since the chapter and verse numbers of the MT and LXX do not always correspond with the English versions, this chapter will use the English text locations of verses from Hosea. Those using the MT or LXX should note that Hosea 1:10 and 2:23 in the English are 2:1b and 2:25 in the MT and LXX.

[109]Rather than having any single text in mind, Peter may have "had in mind the whole episode of Lo-Ammi and Lo-Ruhamah as it developed in chapters i–ii" (Dodd, *According to the Scriptures*, 75).There was a tradition in the rabbinic writings of combining texts from Hos. 1–2. See Elliott, *Elect*, 45; Str-B 3:273–74; Dodd, *According to the Scriptures*, 75; see also *b. Pesaḥ* 87, *Num. Rab.* xxiii.8, and *Ex. Rab.* xlviii.6. Although much of this material was written after 1 Peter, it may indicate an earlier oral tradition.

[110]See Kelly, *Peter and Jude*, 101–2; Selwyn, *First Peter*, 280–82; and Dodd, *According to the Scriptures*, 75.

[111]Dodd, *According to the Scriptures*, 75.

[112]F. F. Bruce, *The Epistle of Paul to the Romans*, TNTC (Grand Rapids: Eerdmans, 1963), 196. C. E. B. Cranfield, *A Critical and Exegetical Commentary on the Epistle to the Romans*, ICC, 2 vols. (Edinburgh: T. & T. Clark, 1975–79), 2:500, suggests a typological application of Hosea in Rom. 9:25.

enjoy as a result of accepting the gospel."[113] Both writers use these two chapters in Hosea in passages emphasizing God's sovereign election of people to salvation.

The first three chapters of Hosea describe Hosea's marriage to Gomer, her unfaithfulness to him, and his steadfast love for her. God uses this account of their domestic life as a dramatization of his steadfast love for Israel and Israel's unfaithfulness to him. The fact that Gomer severs her relationship with her covenant partner is used by Hosea to picture Israel's disruption of its covenant relationship with God. Because of Israel's disobedience, this nation that had previously been the people of God in covenant relationship with him (Lev. 26:12; Ex. 6:7; Deut. 26:17–18) is now called "not my people," and God is no longer their God (1:9). Although Gomer commits adultery, Hosea never seeks to divorce her but instead seeks to restore her to a proper relationship with him. In the same way, God's ultimate purpose in his relationship with disobedient Israel is to heal their relationship rather than terminate it (2:2b, 7, 14–23; 3:5; 14:1–2). The reason given in Hosea for God's faithfulness to Israel and his final restoration of Israel is his love (2:19; 3:1; 11:1–11). In 11:1 this love is clearly seen in his election of Israel and displayed in the exodus from Egypt (cf. 12:9, 13; 13:4).[114]

The verses from Hosea alluded to in 1 Peter 2:10 voice God's promise that in a future day these people who were "no longer loved" (Hos. 1:6) and "not my people" (1:8) would receive God's love (2:23) and be called "my loved one" (2:1), "my people," (2:23) and "sons of the living God" (1:10).[115] These promises in Hosea are given to Israel and will be fulfilled in "that day" (2:21; cf. 2:16, 18; 3:5) when God will make them as the "sand on the seashore" in number (1:10), and they will be gathered together in the land (1:11; 2:23). The day when these promises will be fulfilled will also be the day when the nation of Israel acknowledges Yahweh as "my God" (2:23). In "that day" God will establish an eternal unbreakable relationship with Israel (2:19).

The allusion to Hosea 1–2 in 1 Peter 2:10 concludes the description of believers in Jesus in 1 Peter 2:6–10 by two antithetical descriptions of them. In both instances Peter begins with the negative, which describes these people before they believed in Christ, and then

---

[113]Kelly, *Peter and Jude*, 102.

[114]Cf. Ex. 19:4. In Deut. 7:7–8, God's choice of Israel is based on his love for them. The "love" (חסד in Hos. 2:19), which is one of the characteristics of God's future relationship with Israel, involves a loyal love that is the response to a (covenantal) relationship. See Nelson Glueck, *Hesed in the Bible* (Hoboken, N.J.: KTAV Publishing House, 1975).

[115]Elliott, *Elect*, 44–45, was helpful for this section.

contrasts that condition with their present position in Christ ("not a people . . . people of God," "not received mercy . . . have received mercy"). In both antitheses, following the pattern in verses 6–8, the first description is an allusion to the Old Testament text ("not a people," "not received mercy") and the second is "a secondary adaptation"[116] ("people of God," "have received mercy"). As the people of God, Peter's recipients are elect, redeemed, and holy.[117] The fact that they have received mercy refers to their regeneration and new life, which are based upon Christ's resurrection (1:3).

Another important aspect of this verse is Peter's emphasis on what Elliott calls the "eschatological now." He states that "the formulation ποτε . . . νῦν and/or τοτε . . . νῦν as well as the terms νῦν, νῦν δέ, νυνί δέ enjoyed wide usage in Christian parlance for designating the 'eschatological now,' the occurrence of the messianic age of salvation, in contrast to the former age of sin, darkness, and alienation from God."[118]

The allusion to Hosea 1–2 in 1 Peter 2:10 is the conclusion of Peter's doctrinal statement in 2:4–10 and the goal toward which all of the Old Testament quotations, allusions, and comments on them in verses 4–10 have been directed. The point of Peter's catena of Old Testament references is that by virtue of their relationship with Jesus, the elect Messiah, his recipients are the elect people of God in these last days. He does not explicitly call them the *new* or the *true* Israel; instead he shows that they are the *people of God,* whose salvation and spiritual benefits under the new covenant follow a pattern established in God's promised relationship with his chosen people, the nation of Israel. However, although their relationship with God follows a pattern seen in the nation of Israel, the spiritual aspect of their relationship with God and their relationship with the resurrected Christ surpass the experience of Old Testament Israel.

THE APPLICATION TO PETER'S RECIPIENTS OF THE OLD TESTAMENT REFERENCES IN 1 PETER 2:9–10

Crucial in determining the meaning that the Israelite imagery in 1 Peter 2 has for the church is the manner in which Peter appropriates

---

[116]Ibid., 46. See p. 35, n. 2 for evidence that this negative-positive antithetical arrangement is a characteristic of Petrine style.

[117]Ibid., 40. See the helpful discussion of the term λαός in Meyer and Strathmann, "λαός."

[118]Elliott, *Elect,* 46. He gives the following as examples: Rom. 11:30–31; Eph. 5:8; Gal. 4:8–9; Rom. 3:21; 7:6; 16:26; 1 Cor. 15:20; 2 Cor. 6:2; Gal. 2:20; Eph. 2:13; 2 Tim. 1:10 (46 nn. 2–3). See also R. Russell, "Eschatology and Ethics in 1 Peter," *EvQ* 47 (1975): 78–84.

these passages to his recipients. If these passages are appropriated to Peter's recipients by analogy, it would indicate that his recipients were like Israel in their analogous circumstances but not necessarily connected in any other way and thus not in any way fulfilling prophecies concerning Israel in these verses. The New Testament context of these allusions indicates they are not appropriated to Peter's recipients by analogy. If these passages are appropriated to Peter's recipients by direct prophetic fulfillment, it would mean that Peter's recipients are the final fulfillment of the prophecies in the Old Testament context and that the prophecies had no historical reality in the original Old Testament context in which they were given but instead looked exclusively to a future event or figure. Furthermore, if this is a direct fulfillment of the Old Testament in 1 Peter 2:9–10, then this is the final fulfillment, and there is no future fulfillment of these prophecies for ethnic Israel. The Old Testament context of the passages quoted in 1 Peter 2:9–10, however, indicates that they are not direct prophecies. If, however, Peter's appropriation of these passages to his recipients is accomplished by means of typological-prophetic hermeneutics, then these passages are linked by the divinely ordained pattern between Israel and the church (as the people of God), and there is escalation or advancement in God's program of salvation history from the lesser Old Testament type to the greater New Testament antitype. Such a typological-prophetic fulfillment is seen in the *stone* quotations in 1 Peter 2:6–8, and the previous discussion of the *people of God* references suggests they are applied to Peter's recipients by this same hermeneutical method.[119]

It should be noted that there are many similarities between the Old Testament contexts of these references and the situation in 1 Peter. The pattern common to each of these passages in its Old Testament context and in its use in 1 Peter 2:9–10 is that each context describes the relationship of the subjects of the passage (Israel in the Old Testament, the church in 1 Peter) to God. In each passage this relationship is described in terms of the elect people of God. In Exodus 19:4–6 Israel's potential relationship as the people of God under the Mosaic covenant, and the descriptions of that relationship in these verses, is a pattern for God's relationship with the church under the new covenant.[120] These verses are not a direct prophecy concerning the

---

[119]This historical context of the Old Testament passages quoted from Ex. 19:5, 6, and Isa. 43:21 indicates that they cannot be direct prophecies. Israel's historical situation described in Hosea also argues against a direct prophecy in the appropriation of it in the New Testament. This is supported by the fact that the Old Testament passages used in 1 Peter 2:6–8 were appropriated to Christ by means of typology.

[120]McComiskey, *The Covenants of Promise*, 153–61, has a helpful discussion on the present validity of the new covenant. See also the chapter by Ware in this volume.

church because Israel realized this relationship under the Mosaic covenant (Deut. 7:7–8; 14:2). Furthermore, the prediction that God would make a new covenant with Israel, because they broke the Mosaic covenant (Jer. 31:32), indicates that there is still the future potential for the application of Exodus 19:5–6 to the nation (Jer. 31:31–34; 32:37–40; Isa. 59:20–21; Ezek. 16:60–63; 37:21–28).[121]

In Isaiah 43, God promises to bring Israel back from captivity in Babylon because the nation is "the people I formed for myself that they may proclaim my praise" (v. 21). The elect status of the nation of Israel and their resulting responsibilities are a pattern for the church. Once again, however, as this elect relationship of Israel was the foundation for their release and return from the Babylonian captivity, the context indicates that the prophecy also refers to a yet future supernatural restoration of Israel (Deut. 30:3; Jer. 32:37–44; Hos. 1:11).

An analogous pattern exists between Hosea 1–2 and Peter's recipients. Just as Israel in Hosea was not currently in faithful covenant relationship and yet was promised to be restored to such a relationship, so also Peter's recipients had not been God's people, and yet they had become his in Christ. Once again, although Israel's experience is a pattern for New Testament believers, the context of Hosea 1–2 prophesies a future fulfillment of this pattern in the nation of Israel. The parallels and similarities between the original recipients of these Old Testament passages and the recipients of 1 Peter suggest that 1 Peter is using these Old Testament references to show that the church is analogous to Israel and that he is therefore merely comparing the two. However, the context in 1 Peter indicates that Peter is doing more than simply comparing Israel and the church; the context of 1 Peter demonstrates a divinely ordained historical correspondence and an escalation from lesser to greater, which indicates a typological-prophetic connection between Israel and the church.

The first indication of a typological-prophetic appropriation of the Old Testament references in 1 Peter 2:9–10 is the fulfilled prophecies in the stone complex in verses 6–8. Peter's recipients are the elect people (vv. 9–10) by virtue of Christ, the elect stone who fulfills the prophecies in verses 6–8. They become the elect people through their belief in him. They are recipients of the benefits poured out on God's people "in these last times" (1:20). Thus they have something more than Old Testament Israel.

---

[121]The application of Isa. 59:20–21 to Israel in Rom. 11:26–27 supports this point. In the next verses (Isa. 60–61) is one of the clearest passages in the Old Testament concerning Israel's future ministry to the Gentiles (cf. Ezek. 37:28). See the chapter by Burns in this volume.

Another indication of fulfillment of prophecy in 1 Peter 2:9–10 comes in the allusion to Exodus 19:6 that introduces 1 Peter 2:9—"But you are." This equative clause, which identifies Peter's believing recipients as the people described in the following epithets, replaces the future tense in the LXX and Hebrew texts. While Israel was promised that they *would* be God's people, a kingdom of priests, and a holy nation if they would obey him and keep covenant with him, Peter's recipients *are* all of these things now; they have obeyed God (1:2; 2:22–23), and they are participants in the new covenant sealed with his blood (1:2, 18–21). Furthermore, the certainty of this fact for the church, in contrast with the conditional statement in Exodus, indicates an escalation or advancement in God's relationship with the church, compared with his relationship with Israel.

Peter's use of Exodus 19:5–6 escalates or advances its meaning in its original context. Not only is the potential ("you will be") of the Old Testament a certainty in the New Testament ("you are"), but the epithet "kingdom of priests" becomes "a royal residence" and "a body of priests," emphasizing God's residence in his people by means of the Spirit in the New Testament context. The New Testament context also suggests that the priestly ministry of New Testament believers exceeds that spoken of in Exodus 19:6. Each believer, not just a priestly family, ministers to others as God's representative. Also the national or political connotations of the Old Testament words *kingdom* and *holy nation* are not carried over into their New Testament application.

In the use of Isaiah 43:20–21 in 1 Peter, there is also evidence of escalation or advancement in meaning beyond its Old Testament context. In Isaiah 43:21 the purpose of Israel is described as praising the Lord, whereas in 1 Peter the purpose of the church is the telling forth of God's saving deeds, apparently to other people. Also while the context of Isaiah 43 (v. 14) promises redemption from captivity in Babylon for Israel, Christians "have been called out of moral darkness into the marvelous light of salvation in Christ" (1 Peter 2:9).

There are several indications that Peter's use of Hosea 1–2 in 1 Peter 2:10 also involves fulfillment of prophecy. First, Paul uses the same context and concepts from Hosea in Romans 9:25–26 to show that the conversion of Gentiles fulfills these prophecies in Hosea. Another indication of fulfillment in the use of Hosea in 1 Peter 2:10 is the "once . . . now" language, which, as Elliott suggests, designated for the first-century Christians "the 'eschatological now,' the occurrence of the Messianic Age of salvation."[122]

Another support for typological-prophetic hermeneutics in the use of

[122]Elliott, *Elect*, 46.

the Old Testament in 1 Peter 2:9–10 is the explanation in 1 Peter 1:10–12 of how the words and promises of the Old Testament function in the New.[123] These verses show that the intended meaning of the Old Testament prophet did not always exhaust God's intended meaning.[124] The use of the Old Testament in 1 Peter suggests that the fuller meaning of an Old Testament text, which it sometimes has in the New Testament, is rather a further referent, to which the conceptual sense of the Old Testament passage is applied through pattern.[125]

Peter is teaching that the church represents a pattern and thus is a fulfillment of the promises made to Israel in these Old Testament passages. He is not saying the church equals Israel; instead he is saying that as Israel in the Old Testament was the people of God by virtue of its relationship with Yahweh, so the church is the present people of God by virtue of its relationship with Jesus, the elect Messiah of God. As Israel could be God's elect people if they would keep the Mosaic covenant, so the church is God's elect people in these last days by virtue of its participation in the new covenant (Ex. 19:6; 1 Peter 1:3–12). As Israel will be restored to a covenant relationship with God as his people in the future (Hos. 1:7; 2:23), so the church has entered into a covenant relationship with God on the basis of its union with Christ (1 Peter 1:13–20). Peter uses Israel's historical situation as the people of God as a pattern of his recipients' relationship with God; he is not saying that the church is a new Israel replacing the nation.[126]

[123]See Glenny, "Hermeneutics in 1 Peter," 343–62, for an exegetical discussion of 1 Peter 1:10–12.

[124]See ibid., 38–60; Darrell L. Bock, "Evangelicals and the Use of the Old Testament in the New," parts 1–2, *BSac* 142 (1985): 209–23, 306–18; and Douglas J. Moo, "The Problem of Sensus Plenior," in *Hermeneutics, Authority, and Canon,* ed. D. A. Carson and John D. Woodbridge (Grand Rapids: Zondervan, 1986), 179–211. These sources will serve as an introduction to this whole subject. For a summary of the meaning of 1 Peter 1:10–12, I recommend Grudem, *1 Peter,* 74–75, which summarizes the meaning of the difficult phrase τίνα ἢ ποῖον καιρόν in 1 Peter 1:11. See G. D. Kilpatrick, "1 Peter 1:11 TINA 'Η ΠΟΙΟΝ KAIPON," *NovT* 28, no. 1 (1986): 91–92, for a summary of the New Testament use of τίς and ποῖος.

[125]See Glenny, "Hermeneutics in 1 Peter," 287, 291, for a summary of my study. I suggest that as God's revelation progresses, the conceptual sense of the Old Testament author is applied to a further referent. This is done without violating the conceptual sense of the original human author. This is what takes place in the divinely ordained correspondence and pattern between Israel and church in 1 Peter 2:9–10 and between Christ and the original referent of the stone passages cited in 1 Peter 2:6–8.

[126]See Peter Richardson, *Israel in the Apostolic Church* (Cambridge: Cambridge University Press, 1969), for a discussion of the use of the term *Israel* in the New Testament. He argues that this term is not used for the church in the New Testament. Many of the arguments used to suggest the church is a new Israel replacing the nation are based on parallels and correspondences between the two; the obvious error is the belief that such a correspondence or parallel proves identity. Michaels, *1 Peter,* xlix, states that "the actual Jewish community is simply ignored" in 1 Peter. He goes on to say, "In this respect, 1 Peter stands in contrast to most other early Christian uses of such biblical texts

A further question about the typological pattern that I trust will clarify this relationship is whether the New Testament application of the text is its final or ultimate application, or whether the pattern has further application and fulfillment. This is the crucial question raised by the people of God texts in 1 Peter 2:9–10. If these Old Testament texts are appropriated to Peter's recipients by typological-prophetic hermeneutics as this study has argued, then is this the final and exhaustive fulfillment of them, or is it an initial fulfillment that does not exhaust the prophetic intent of the original type?

There are many indications that even though the church fulfills these Old Testament prophecies, it does not exhaust them. These indications mean that an initial fulfillment in the church does not eliminate the final and complete fulfillment of the pattern in the future for the nation of Israel. First, the fact that a pattern of God's activity can find more than one fulfillment is seen in Isaiah 43, where God uses the exodus from Egypt (vv. 15–17; cf. v. 2) as a pattern, not only of Israel's deliverance from Babylonian captivity, but also for a future supernatural regathering of the nation, which, as was suggested above in the discussion of this context, goes beyond the historical details of the return from Babylon.[127] Second, it is even clearer with Hosea 1–2 that the details of those prophecies are not completely fulfilled in the church.[128] Third, this understanding of these passages is consistent with the historical interpretation of many Old Testament prophecies, which speak of Israel's future restoration to the land of Palestine (Isa. 11:1–12; Jer. 31:10; 32:37, 42; Ezek. 37:21–28), their eternal inheritance of the land (Gen. 17:7–8; cf. 12:7; 13:15, 17; 15:18–21), and their spiritual restoration to God and participation in the new covenant (Jer. 31:31–34; 32:37–40; Isa. 59:20–21; Ezek. 16:60–63; 37:21–28).[129]

as Ps. 118:22. The same text is cited in Matt. 21:42–43 to prove that 'the kingdom of God will be taken from you (i.e., the Jewish "high priests and Pharisees," v. 45) and given to a nation (i.e., the Gentile Christian churches) accomplishing its deeds' (the displacement tendency is carried still further in early Christian redaction of the Jewish apocalypse of 4 Ezra: e.g., 4 Ezra 1:24–25, 35; 2:10). Even though Peter designates his Gentile Christian audience as a 'holy nation' (2:9), he has no equivalent theme of displacement. Nor does he link his two quotations (28:16 and 8:14) to Israel's failure to attain its own standards of righteousness (as Paul did in Rom. 9:31–33)."

[127]John S. Feinberg, "Systems of Discontinuity," in *Continuity and Discontinuity*, ed. John S. Feinberg (Westchester, Ill.: Crossway, 1988), 118, suggests the same idea in Jer. 31:1, 2, 12, 13. He calls it multiple fulfillments of a single, determinative Old Testament meaning. The biblical motifs of the messenger of Yahweh (Mal. 3:1), Antiochus-Antichrist, the abomination of desolation, and the destruction of Jerusalem provide other possible examples of multiple fulfillment of a pattern in Scripture.

[128]As discussed above concerning Ex. 19:5–6, some of the aspects of Israel's relationship to God, as described in the old covenant, will be more fully realized in their new-covenant relationship.

[129]See Alva J. McClain, *The Greatness of the Kingdom* (Chicago: Moody Press, 1959),

The prospect of a future for ethnic Israel is essential for Peter's argument. Peter's purpose in this epistle is to demonstrate to his original readers that they are recipients of the grace of God and to exhort them to stand fast in this grace (5:12). He uses the Old Testament in 2:4–10 to demonstrate that their position in Christ (2:6–8) is that of the elect people of God in these last times (1:20).[130] Peter's argument does not suggest or necessitate that his recipients replace Israel in God's program. Peter's point is that their relationship with Christ represents a continuation of the pattern God established in his election of Israel to be his people. So if God's election of Israel in the Old Testament was somehow annulled and therefore not an eternal election, it would destroy the argument of 2:4–10 as well as that of the whole epistle (cf. 1:1, 2, 5). What encouragement and comfort could the recipients of 1 Peter have in God's election of them if it is patterned after his retracted election of the nation of Israel?[131] God's promise and faithfulness are clearly at stake, and Peter's argument is vacuous if Israel has no future.

A fifth argument brings final confirmation to this position. Peter's own teaching in Acts 3:19–21 indicates that there is still going to be a future restoration of the nation of Israel. In verse 21 Peter states that when Jesus comes again, God will "restore everything, as he promised long ago through his holy prophets." The word "restore" in Acts 3:21 is the Greek noun ἀποκαταστάσεως, the verbal form of which (ἀποκαθιστάνεις) is used in Acts 1:6 in the disciples' question to Jesus, "Lord are you at this time going to *restore the kingdom to Israel?*" The repetition of this terminology for the restoration of Israel in 1:6 and 3:21, the repetition of the term χρόνος in both contexts (1:6 and 3:21), and the fact that the restoration spoken of in 3:21 was "promised long ago through his holy prophets" all indicate that the restoration mentioned in 3:21 is associated with Christ's return and refers to the

135–254, for a discussion of prophecies concerning the nation of Israel in the Old Testament prophetic writing.

[130]Cf. Acts 2:17; 1 Tim. 4:1; 2 Tim. 3:1; Heb. 1:1; 1 John 2:18.

[131]In Romans 11:25–29 Paul concludes his argument that "all Israel will be saved" with the principle that "God's gifts and his call are irrevocable" (v. 29). Therefore, the reason God cannot forsake the nation of Israel is that his election is irrevocable. Grudem's argument that "the nation blessed by God is no longer the nation of Israel, for Christians are now God's true 'holy nation' (v. 9)" (*1 Peter*, 113) misses not only the point of Peter's argument concerning election but also the meaning of election. His later statement that the Old Testament references (apparently in 2:4–10) come from contexts repeatedly warning "that God will *reject* his people who persist in rebellion against him" (emphasis added) misses the point of the Old Testament passages and the meaning of God's election. Cf. Michaels, *1 Peter*, xlix, for a response to the so-called displacement theory (see n. 126 above).

future fulfillment of the Old Testament prophecies concerning Israel.[132] The fact that this promise (Acts 3:21) follows the Day of Pentecost shows that the final fulfillment of the Old Testament promises to the nation of Israel is not found in the application of these Scriptures to the church (cf. Joel 2:28–32 in Acts 2:17–21). Furthermore, the fact that Peter is the one who uses Joel 2 in his sermon in Acts 2 and makes the statements in Acts 3:19–21 indicates that the author of 1 Peter did not understand the church to be the final fulfillment of Old Testament prophecies concerning Israel.

This approach recognizes one major difference between the fulfillment of prophecy in Christ in 1 Peter 2:6–8 and the fulfillment in the church in 1 Peter 2:9–10. Whereas Christ is the ultimate or final fulfillment of the pattern in the typological prophecies of 2:6–8, the church is the initial fulfillment of the pattern in the typological prophecies in 2:9–10. There were many Davidic kings before Christ, but there will never be another after him. There will be, however, a future exhaustive fulfillment of the typological prophecies in 2:9–10 in the nation of Israel.

CONCLUSION

The evidence from the use of the Old Testament in 1 Peter 2:6–10 suggests that the Old Testament imagery used to describe the church in 1 Peter 2:9–10 does not present the church as a new Israel replacing ethnic Israel in God's program. Instead, Old Testament Israel was a pattern of the church's relationship with God as his chosen people. Therefore Peter uses various aspects of the salvation, spiritual life, and service of Israel in its relationship with Yahweh to teach his recipients the greater salvation, spiritual life, and service they enjoy in Christ. In his use of the three *people of God* citations in 1 Peter 2:9–10, the apostle is teaching that there are aspects of the nation of Israel's experience as the people of God that are also true of the New Testament church. These elements of continuity include the election, redemption, holy standards, priestly ministry, and honor of the people of God. This continuity is the basis for the application of the title *people of God* to the church in 1 Peter 2:9–10.

The escalation or advancement of meaning in Peter's application of these passages to his recipients emphasizes the distinction between Israel and the church. Israel is a nation, and the national, political, and geographic applications to Israel in the Old Testament contexts are not

[132]See Darrell Bock's chapter above for a fuller development of the argument of Acts 3:19–21.

applied to the church, the spiritual house, of 1 Peter. Furthermore, the initial application of these passages to the church by typological-prophetic hermeneutics does not negate the future fulfillment of the national, political, and geographic promises, as well as the spiritual ones, made to Israel in these Old Testament contexts.

Such a typological-prophetic understanding of the use of the Old Testament in 1 Peter 2:6–10 is judged to be superior to other approaches used by major groups of evangelical Christians because it avoids two common errors. On the one hand, it avoids the denial of the historical meaning of the Old Testament prophecies, which is the error of those who see a final fulfillment of these prophecies in the church. On the other hand, it avoids the denial of the historical meaning of New Testament fulfillment language, which is the error of those who see in this context a mere analogy between Israel and the church.

CHAPTER 6

The Future of Ethnic Israel in Romans 11

J. Lanier Burns

Robert Brawley concludes his study of Lukan theology as follows: "The Jews in Luke-Acts play out their roles enmeshed in an intricate pattern of theme and plot development. Little wonder that ambiguity smudges the colors scholars paint onto their portrait. Little wonder also that oversimplification engraves one outline of the images in stronger relief than another."[1] Brawley defined his task as the breaking down of hardened stereotypes, such as Luke's rejection of Jews, and the offering of a new portrait of conciliation. But this task needs to be extended to the interpretation of the people of God elsewhere in Scripture and in history. It applies to other texts such as Romans 9–11, to theological debates between viewpoints that differ substantially on the relationships of Israel and the church, and to Christian tradition with its various anti-Semitic tendencies and movements.

This chapter is about eschatology, ethnic Israel, and Romans 11. The text is a central passage on the relationship between Jews and Gentiles in Pauline theology. It is one of the central passages in the theological debate between covenantal and dispensational theologians on the identity and destiny of the people of God. And it is the central text for symposiums on historical dysfunctions between the church and Jews, especially in ecumenical discussions in the shadows of Holocaust's nightmare.[2] These perspectives raise many questions about Romans 9–11. What does Paul mean by the fullness of Jews and Gentiles and the salvation of all Israel? How does he understand and relate Jew, Gentile, and church in the olive tree metaphor? Are they two distinct peoples of God or parts of only one people? Does Israel have unique

---

[1]Robert L. Brawley, *Luke-Acts and the Jews: Conflict, Apology, and Conciliation*, SBLMS 33 (Atlanta: Scholars Press, 1987), 155.

[2]For example, Robert A. Guelich et al., "Symposium on the Church and Israel: Romans 9–11," *ExA* 4 (1988); K. E. Skydsgaard et al., "Symposium on the Church and Israel: Romans 9–11," *LW* 10 (1963).

purposes and promises through history that are not fulfilled in any other people? Is there a future for ethnic Israel at the end of the twentieth century? How should the church relate to Israel: by a pluralistic model of mutual coexistence with recognition of equal validity, or by a conversionistic model of mission in behalf of truth overcoming error?

While recognizing relevance to these questions, this chapter will address primarily the future of ethnic Israel in Pauline theology. To limit the scope, I focus on an exposition of Romans 11. Retrospect has shown that this is the indispensable first step, because superficial exegesis has been used as theological camouflage in an almost innumerable list of vanities and biases. Paul himself identifies crucial parts of his teaching in Romans 11 as "mystery," demonstrating that we need revelation for accurate understanding. I limit discussion to Romans 11 as much as possible and focus on what it does say rather than what it could imply.

We will consider the use of the chapter in the covenantal and dispensational traditions. This seriatim treatment is designed to show variations and developments in those traditions. More briefly treated is the revisionist use of Romans 11 in light of concerns raised by the Holocaust. It is relevant to the subject, but less relevant to this volume as a whole, and the Jewish apostle to the Gentiles, who pleaded for a unity that has been notably lacking, would not approve of its neglect. Finally, some lessons and suggestions from this study will conclude the chapter.

A necessary preliminary is the meaning of "ethnic Israel." The *Oxford English Dictionary* (1971) defines "ethnic" with emphasis on nationhood and, in the second sense, "pertaining to race; peculiar to a race or nation; ethnological." Most English dictionaries add the nuance of Gentile nations as distinct from Israel that is derived from גּוֹיִם. In Paul's own words, ethnic Israel will be used of "his brethren, my kinsmen according to the flesh" (9:3; 11:1). On the one hand, Israel was an ancient nation among empires with the customary theocratic structures. In this synchronic sense, it was distinguished only by its elect position under the only living and true God. Because he is living and true, Israel alone could claim to be a valid theocracy (Deut. 32:21 in Rom. 10:19). But human need and national functions were continuous with Egyptian, Mesopotamian, Phoenician, and Hellenistic peoples. On the other hand, in a diachronic sense, Israel was the unique recipient of sovereign divine favor that placed the covenants and the Messiah in its tradition (9:4–5; 11:2). Divine חֶסֶד and Israelite faith sustained this blessed relationship and, at the same time, prevented it from being automatic. Thus, Israelite unbelief generated probably the most profound theodicy of history

(9:6–8, 25–26, 30–33; 10:1–4; chap. 11). In this sense of the need for faith, "there has been no distinction between Jew and Greek" (10:12).

Ethnic Israel is also connected with λαός, so that they are "God's people" (11:1–2), who have been "a disobedient and obstinate people" (10:21). This term denotes a sense of racial cohesion. "In most cases ἔθνος is used of men in the sense of a 'people.' Synon. are φυλή (people as a national unity of common descent), λαός (people as a political unity with a common history and constitution) and γλῶσσα (people as a linguistic unity). The term ἔθνος is the most general and therefore the weakest of these terms, having simply an ethnographic sense and denoting the natural cohesion of a people in general."[3] Schmidt concludes that in Romans 11 "Jewish people is meant in the same sense as others" and that ἔθνος and λαός are practically interchangeable.[4]

THE EXPOSITION

Paul argues for a future for ethnic Israel in Romans 11 under his stated theme in verse 2a: "God has not cast off his people whom he foreknew." This theme is developed in three subthemes: Israel has always had an elect remnant by the grace of God (vv. 1–10); the unbelief of the majority of Israelites will not last forever (vv. 11–24); and the mystery and mercy of the divine plan will result in a fullness of salvation for Gentiles and Jews (vv. 25–32). A closing doxology concludes chapters 9 through 11 with praise for God in view of his mysterious ways (11:33–36). The first subtheme *looks back to the Old Testament* to demonstrate God's ubiquitous grace through a faithful remnant in spite of Israel's persistent hardness. Thus, the hardness of Israel is only partial. The second section *explains the present phase of the divine plan* in terms of a metaphor of branches of a living olive tree. It emphasizes that the hardness is only temporary. The third subtheme *sets forth the mystery of the future fullness of Israel's faith.* It promises, according to God's merciful plan, that Israel in some sense will be saved.

Paul begins the chapter with an emphatic denial of the possibility that God has cast off Israel (11:1). Λέγω . . . μή introduces a rhetorical question four times in the context, anticipating in each case a negative answer with contrast (ἀλλά in 10:18–19) or inference (οὖν in 11:1, 11). The verbal form and the particle connect 11:1 with the preceding chapter. In 10:18–21 Paul had confirmed from Psalm 19:4, Deuteronomy 32:21, and Isaiah 65:1–2 that Israel had heard and understood "the word of Christ" and had obstinately refused to believe and obey. The

---

[3]K. L. Schmidt, "ἔθνος," *TDNT* 2:369.
[4]Ibid.

nation was therefore clearly without excuse. The question that remained was whether Israel's willful disobedience and the Gentiles' acceptance of the gospel reflected God's exclusion of Israel from his plan of salvation. Had Israel disqualified itself, prompting God's rejection of his people?

Paul emphatically denies the idea, as he had previously done in 3:3–4 with μὴ γένοιτο, with language that recalls God's inviolable commitment to Israel, and with an affirmation in verse 2 that uses the same words that were used in the question. The force of μὴ γένοιτο is evident to all interpreters.[5] The verb ἀπώσατο and the relative clause ὃν προέγνω can be linked with Old Testament passages that categorically promise that God will not repudiate his people (1 Sam. 12:22 and Ps. 94:14).[6] In 1 Samuel 12:22 Samuel was speaking to "all Israel" about the evil of requesting a king. His exhortation to serve God and reject useless idols was followed by an assurance that the Lord will not reject (לֹא־יִטֹּשׁ) his people. Yahweh had made Israel his own people for his great name's sake. However, persistence in doing evil would result in disciplinary judgment on the people and the king.[7] Psalm 94:14, in a context of vindicated justice, affirms Yahweh's inviolable commitment to his people, his inheritance. These allusions are important for Romans, because one must ask whether Paul used προγινώσκω in 11:2 to refer to an elect remnant as in verses 4–6 or to refer to the ethnic nation as God's chosen people. Calvin interpreted the clause as a restrictive reference to the elect remnant of grace.[8] However, the ties to verse 1 and the Old Testament allusions would favor the general election of ethnic Israel as God's chosen people. The phrase λαὸν αὑτοῦ, in view of these details, offers a clue to the direction that the chapter will take.

---

[5]One could note, however, the strength of the exclamation from the repetition of the denial in 3:3 and 11:11. According to BAG, 157: "μὴ γένοιτο strong negation, in Paul only after rhet[orical] questions . . . *by no means, far from it, God forbid,* lit. 'may it not be.'" With the strong emphasis on divine sovereignty and its vindication in the chapter, the force of the negation is that such an idea about God's plan should not even be entertained.

[6]Str-B 3:286: "Midr Ps. 94 §3 (209b): Jahve wird sein Volk nicht verstoßen u. sein Erbe nicht verlassen Ps 94,14; u. eine (andre) Schriftstelle sagt: Denn Jahve wird sein Volk nicht verstoßen לֹא יִטֹּשׁ um seines großen Namens willen 1 Sm 12,22." On ἀπωθέω, see K. L. Schmidt, *TDNT,* 1:448; and James D. G. Dunn, *Romans 9–16,* WBC (Waco, Tex.: Word, 1988), 634.

[7]The MT in 1 Sam. 12:22 uses נטשׁ of Yahweh's faithfulness to Israel's calling, but it uses סָפָה of the consequence of Israel's persistent unbelief. In Ps. 94:14 נטשׁ is used again of divine commitment in parallel with עזב. The future tense has the force of divine resolve.

[8]John Calvin, *Commentary upon the Epistle of Saint Paul to the Romans,* trans. C. Rosdell and ed. H. Beveridge (Edinburgh: Calvin Translation Society, 1844), 309. The key clause is "quin semper Ecclesiam conservet quandiu superstites manent electi" (T. H. L. Parker, ed., *Iohannis Calvini: Commentarius in Epistolam Pauli ad Romanos* [Leiden: E. J. Brill, 1981], 241).

Cranfield correctly summarizes Paul's argument in these verses: "The question is thus tantamount to asking, 'Had God broken His explicit promise not to cast off His people?' So we may say that the first ground of the μὴ γένοιτο which follows is the one which, though unexpressed, is implicit in the language used, namely, that Holy Scripture testifies that God will not cast off His people. . . . The fact that God foreknew them (i.e., deliberately joined them to Himself in faithful love) excludes the possibility of His casting them off."[9]

The second and third grounds for Paul's emphatic denial follow. The second ground of the denial of μὴ γένοιτο is Paul's own apostolic ministry: "I myself am an Israelite, a descendant of Abraham, of the tribe of Benjamin."[10] Various interpretations of this appeal have been that Paul's conversion from Judaism proved that the Jewish people as a whole had not been rejected,[11] or that since Paul the persecutor above all would have been rejected, therefore, his salvation proves that less wicked Jews would not necessarily have been cast away.[12] Cranfield is more correct in adding Gentile apostleship to the notion of a converted Jewish persecutor of the church: "Were God intending only to save a mere handful of Israel, had he really cast off the people of Israel as a whole, should he have chosen an Israelite to be the apostle to the Gentiles and the chief bearer of the gospel message? In his person the missionary vocation of Israel is at last being fulfilled and Israel is actively associated with the work of the risen Christ."[13]

This perspective better accords with the emphatic character of the verse and passage. Cranfield further argues with Calvin that Ἰσρα- ηλίτης . . . ἐκ σπέρματος Ἀβραάμ has its ordinary sense of "descend- ant" (9:7a) as distinguished from the spiritual sense of children of faith

[9]C. E. B. Cranfield, *A Critical and Exegetical Commentary on the Epistle to the Romans,* ICC, 2 vols. (Edinburgh: T. & T. Clark, 1975–79), 2:544–45.

[10]William Sanday and Arthur C. Headlam, *A Critical and Exegetical Commentary on the Epistle to the Romans,* ICC, 5th ed. (Edinburgh: T. & T. Clark, 1902), 309, incorrectly viewed this self-appeal as offended patriotic sentiment: "All his feelings as an Israelite make it disloyal in him to hold it. . . . he reminds his readers that he is an Israelite, and that therefore to him, as much as to them, the supposition seems almost blasphemous." This shifts the emphasis to Paul's sentiment rather than God's sovereign plan.

[11]C. K. Barrett, *A Commentary on the Epistle to the Romans,* HNTC (New York: Harper & Row, 1957), 207: "It is much more likely that he means, 'God cannot have cast off his people (as a whole), for I myself am both a Jew and a Christian; this proves that Christian Jews may exist.' "

[12]Martin Luther, *Luther's Works,* vol. 25, *Lectures on Romans,* ed. H. C. Oswald (St. Louis: Concordia, 1972), 95: "I would have been rejected if He had rejected His people."

[13]Cranfield, *Romans* 2:544. Note as well, Karl Barth, *CD* II/2, *The Doctrine of God,* trans. G. W. Bromiley et al. (Edinburgh: T. & T. Clark, 1957), 268: "To admit that God has rejected His people would mean the annulment, not only of Paul himself, but above all (and this alone is absolutely 'impossible') of his office, his commission, and its whole content."

(9:7b−8).[14] Similarly, Cranfield rejects interpretations of φυλῆς Βενια-μίν that play on Old Testament details such as near extermination (Judg. 20−21), the tribe of Saul, or Benjamin's being the first tribe to enter the Red Sea in rabbinic tradition.[15] This view, however, does not go on to explain why three designations are used for the simple meaning of "true Israelite," when one of them would have sufficed. One can best argue that Paul could only be referring to physical descent from ethnic Israel. Precisely because he often juxtaposes ethnic and spiritual senses (1:16; 4:9−25; 9:1−9; Gal. 3:14), he would be expected to clarify that he is talking about God's abiding commitment to ethnic Israel with special reference to his own tribe for emphasis. The keynote of the chapter links it ultimately to "his own race, the people Israel" (9:3). The implication for following verses is that we would expect ethnic Israel to be included in eschatological fulfillments. "His people" is not the church in these two verses.

The third ground of Paul's denial is a reminder that God has always had his λεῖμμα κατ᾽ ἐκλογὴν χάριτος, even in periods of profound ethnic unbelief. His Old Testament illustration is Elijah and the remnant of seven thousand (11:2b−6).[16] Specifically, he refers to Elijah's imprecation against Israel in 1 Kings 19:10, 14, which he abbreviates in verse 3.[17] Out of the emphatic repetition of question and answer in the Elijah account, Paul retains (with transposition) only the evil deeds of the Israelites in killing the prophets and tearing down the altars, leaving Elijah with the impression that he was alone (as reflected earlier at the Carmel confrontation in 18:22) and would soon die as well. Paul

---

[14]Cranfield, *Romans* 2:545; cf. Calvin, *Romans*, 308.

[15]Cranfield, *Romans* 2:545.

[16]On the reference to entitled sections of Scripture according to their subject matter, see Str-B 3:288. Cf. Mark 12:26; Luke 20:37. Sanday and Headlam list several examples from talmudic, Homeric, and patristic sources (*Romans*, 310−11).

[17]The episode seems to have acquired an almost proverbial significance. See 1 Macc. 8:32; 10:61, 63; 11:25. The infamy of Ahab and Jezebel's Baal cult is probably an important aspect of Elijah and Paul's connection and the respective remnants. E. F. Harrison, "Romans," in EBC 10 (Grand Rapids: Zondervan, 1976), 117, suggests: "It is just possible that Paul likewise persecuted by his own countrymen, felt a special kinship with Elijah, and this may help to account for his mention of himself in v. 1." In an excellent note, Sanday and Headlam see the Elijah narrative as the inception of the remnant idea in prophetic narrative (*Romans*, 316). If it was not the beginning of the idea, it was at least a significant point in its development. They summarize the idea on p. 317: "This doctrine of a Remnant implied that it was the individual who was true to his God, and not the nation, that was the object of the Divine solitude; that it was in this small body of individuals that the true life of the chosen nation dwelt, and that from them would spring that internal reformation, which, coming as the result of the Divine chastisement, would produce a whole people, pure and undefiled, to be offered to God (Isa. lxv.8, 9)." The implication of these thoughts on Elijah and the remnant tradition is that Paul would be building his case of a future for ethnic Israel on a commonly understood tradition that was as well known as his own apostleship.

omitted the preceding clauses that referred to Elijah's own zeal and the Israelites' rejection of Yahweh's covenant, though these elements can be inferred in the explicit references to their deeds and his solitude. Both elements were crucial in Paul's use of the passage. He will emphasize the continuation of God's revealed will by sovereign grace rather than works or zeal (11:6–7). The Israelites' unbelief had resulted in idolatrous and murderous behavior. The remnant would obviously have reflected gracious intervention rather than ethnic nurture and influence. Less obvious was Elijah's zeal, which drove him to plead his case before Yahweh God of Hosts at Horeb, the place of Israel's national establishment. A number of parallels between Moses and Elijah would have made the narratives suitable for Paul's purpose: the condition of the people (1 Kings 19:10, 14 with Ex. 33:4–6), the miraculous fast of forty days and nights (1 Kings 19:8 with Ex. 24:18 and 34:28), an intimate encounter with God (1 Kings 19:11–13 with Ex. 33:12–23), and the reception of verbal divine guidance (1 Kings 19:15–18 with Ex. 34:1–7). Elijah's despair, in turn, paralleled the tensions in Rome. His complaint was that God's will in the Sinaitic covenant had apparently come to nought, leaving his own calling in shambles. An important contrast was his condemnation of the Israelites, while Moses had earlier interceded for the stiff-necked idolaters (Ex. 32:32 with Rom. 10:1–5). Elijah's zeal reflected a rather self-righteous posture that discounted the grace of God. The remnant was not called in response to Elijah's prayer. The sizable remnant had apparently already been graciously called and preserved (1 Kings 19:18). God sovereignly directed Elijah to crucial people who would take the nation, the remnant, and the prophetic office forward by his grace.[18] The calling of Elisha as a willing apprentice validated all of this for his mentor (19:19–21).

Paul parallels the situation of Elijah and his own circumstances (οὕτως οὖν, 11:5). One can certainly infer that a large majority of Israelites had resisted the gospel with misdirected zeal (10:1–4). Theirs were the covenants, law, and promises. Theirs were the temple and the *shekinah.* Theirs were the patriarchs, the privileged relationship, and the ancestry of Christ—a tradition that had blinded them to their need of faith. Paul's passion (9:1–5) seems to imply further his own persecution at the

---

[18]God's answer (χρηματισμός is a hapax legomenon in the New Testament) was an authoritative oracle, reminding Paul's Roman readers (in question form) that the answer to the Israel question (11:1) was God's faithfulness to his revealed will (note Paul's addition of ἐμαυτῷ) as viewed in an elect remnant. Cranfield relates the significance of seven thousand as symbolic of completeness to its place in the mysterious oracle: "God's statement that He is preserving for Himself seven thousand men in Israel amounts to a declaration of His faithfulness to His purpose of salvation for His people, a declaration that that purpose will continue unchanged and unthwarted to its final goal" (*Romans* 2:547). Cf. K. H. Rengstorf, "ἑπτά κτλ.," *TDNT* 2:629–30.

hand of his unbelieving countrymen (2 Cor. 11:21–29). However, as in Elijah's day there is a λεῖμμα κατ' ἐκλογὴν χάριτος. This is the most important parallel in Paul's argument. God's gracious reservation of a remnant for himself existed as an earnest of ethnic promises and a divinely assured inheritance. The certainty of God's commitment was grounded in the gracious exercise of his will—not (οὐκέτι, logically) works, because grace would then no longer (οὐκέτι) be grace. "The remnant has its origin, not in the quality of those saved, but in the saving action of God."[19] Thus, concludes Barrett, " 'remnant' is a word that spells grace, as the distinction (see chap. 9) between Isaac and Ishmael, Jacob and Esau, spells mercy. In itself the remnant is not 'better' than the rest of Israel, any more than Isaac was 'better' than Ishmael, or Jacob than Esau; but it consists of the 'vessels of mercy' (9:23), whom God chose as the vehicles of his glory."[20]

The perspective of works grounded in a superior law had led to the national hardening and the consequential question of 11:1. It would have resulted in an affirmative answer, but it would not have been able to explain the continuum of Israel's history (particularly episodes like Elijah) in spite of national unbelief, the messianic fulfillments, and the present Hebrew-Christian remnant of grace including Paul, who had been graciously called in the midst of his fierce opposition to the gospel. The perspective of grace, on the contrary, suggests "an open number, and so eloquent for the people as a whole."[21] The emphatic point of verse 6 also has prepared the way for Paul to argue that Gentile and Hebrew believers (in the church, which is not mentioned because of the ethnic emphasis of the chapter) are the present channel (or perhaps agency or people) of God's grace, far from being contrary to God's will as the unbelieving majority had evidently supposed.

Paul's conclusion (11:7) to his "remnant according to grace" argument (τί οὖν) was that ethnic Israel had not obtained the righteousness of God (ὅ . . . τοῦτο) that it had so zealously sought through the law. In contrast (δέ), the elect had obtained it by grace (11:5) through faith (10:6–13). The majority of Israel was hardened in unbelief as predicted in the Old Testament (vv. 8–10). The effect of this closing point of the section is that there had been a continuum of an unbelieving majority, just as there had been a continuum of God's people by remnant. Contrary to "democratic" expectations in the broadest sense, the

[19]V. Herntrich, "λεῖμμα," *TDNT* 4:203.

[20]Barrett, *Romans*, 209. To underscore Paul's emphasis on grace, Barrett makes vv. 5b–6 parenthetical.

[21]Cranfield, *Romans* 2:548. He earlier paraphrased the same idea as "full of promise for the rest of the nation, a pledge of God's continuing interest in those λοιποί who have indeed been hardened by a divine hardening such as is spoken of in Scripture."

unbelief of the majority of Israel did not cancel the faithfulness of God to his people.

Israel's vain zeal in law and the elect's attainment of salvation by faith summarize 9:30–10:6 with the more abstract ἐκλογή focusing on divine grace that determined the elect (11:7). The unbelieving majority were hardened in accordance with prior teaching (cf. 9:18) and the Old Testament.[22] The hardening of the heart is a metaphoric use of πωροῦν that was derived from the progressive formation of a stone in the bladder or a callous or a healing bone, thus encompassing both Israel's progressively blinding unbelief (chap. 10) and sovereign divine choice (chap. 9).[23] The formation of a stiffening condition and its divine sanction are both emphasized in Paul's thinking. This also accords with the general principles of the letter, whereby humankind's knowledge without excuse is juxtaposed with God's giving them over to their ungodly lusts (1:18–32). The passive voice in 11:7 supports the divine aspect of hardening; however, ἐπέτυχεν and ἐπωρώθησαν mutually develop the mercy of God in the progression of the chapter. Everyone deserves rejection (Rom. 3; 10:11–13, with 11:1–10), regardless of ethnic heritage. Divine hardening is not God's last word to the λοιποί; in the second section, the same grace that secured the remnant will also work for the others in their jealousy over the salvation of the Gentiles (vv. 11–24).

Paul quotes Deuteronomy 29:4 and Psalm 69:22–23 to show that Israel had been characterized by an ἐκλογή-λοιποί from the days of Moses to the present (ἕως τῆς σήμερον ἡμέρας). In other words, a present majority of unbelievers should not provoke presumptuous questions (11:1), because God's faithfulness is the continuing issue (cf. 3:1–4).

Paul strengthened Deuteronomy 29:4 to highlight the thought of divine hardening. He replaced the negative verb and positive infinitival phrases with a positive verb and negative infinitival phrases. He replaced the second-person pronominal address in Deuteronomy with the third person in Romans to highlight his reference to the λοιποί. In place of "a mind to understand," he substitutes "spirit" (πνεῦμα) and a rare term "stupor" (κατανύξεως) that occurs elsewhere in Isaiah 29:10. The Deuteronomic context is a covenant renewal of Sinai (29:1–2) prior to Israel's entry into the land (vv. 27–28). Yahweh's goodness to Israel is reviewed, even in the wilderness, where the majority of his people did

---

[22]The aorist passive verbal form (ἐπωρώθησαν) should be connected with the substantival πώρωσις in 11:25 as well.

[23]K. L. and M. A. Schmidt, "πωρόω (πηρόω), πώρωσις (πήρωσις)," TDNT 5:1025–28.

not have an understanding mind, seeing eyes, or hearing ears "to this day," in spite of their abundant knowledge (vv. 3–5). The faithfulness of Yahweh and the inviolability of his covenantal word are stressed (vv. 12–15). A forfeiture of blessing for unbelief (or exile from the land) completes the chapter. The specific manifestation of unbelief is idolatry (vv. 16–18, 25–26). The Isaianic context contains the fulfillment of Moses' prediction in the second "woe" oracle of the section, chapters 28–35. It portrays the Lord's people as zealous but rebellious: the clay denying its potter (29:16; cf. Rom. 9:19, 21), pious language hypocritically masking an unbelieving heart (29:13), and sacrifices betraying empty festivals (29:1–2).[24] Yahweh has imposed on the false worshipers רוּחַ תַּרְדֵּמָה, so that they will be judged (29:3–10). However, that is not the last word, for Yahweh "in a short time" will turn his people to himself (29:17–24). From Isaiah 29:10 Paul used the emphasis on divine hardening and the descriptive condition of "a spirit of stupor."[25] By combining Deuteronomy 29 and Isaiah 29, he establishes a continuum of the remnant-majority motif and the inviolability of God's faithfulness to his covenantal word that extends from Israel's *Urzeit* (Deut. 29:14–15) to its exilic *Endzeit* (Isa. 29:17–24) and by extension through Paul's own day (σήμερον).[26] Furthermore, the combined quotation becomes a basis for Israel's mysterious future fulfillment in 11:25–32, as Isaiah had similarly predicted.

Paul quotes David as well in Romans 11:9–10, his continuative καί connecting the Old Testament quotations. Psalm 69 is an imprecation of a godly king who was suffering unjustly from an oppressive conspiracy (vv. 1–21), perhaps at a time of national defeat (vv. 34–36). The psalm was frequently quoted in the New Testament with reference to Christ's sufferings, as in Romans 15:3. The imagery of the table has been variously interpreted, usually referring to Israel's privileges (9:1–5; 10:1–4).[27] At the least, the imagery suggests a people who were feasting

---

[24]On Jerusalem as Ariel, meaning "altar hearth," see G. W. Grogan, "Isaiah," in EBC 6 (Grand Rapids: Zondervan, 1986), 187: "The true poignancy of the 'woe' here lies in the fact that the God who had enabled David to take it would now besiege this city himself, through its enemies (v. 5), and cause its destruction by fire just as if the whole city had become an extension of the altar hearth within its temple." In other words, its idolatrous worship would consume it.

[25]Cranfield, *Romans* 2:550, correctly renders κατάνυξις: "Some such meaning as '*torpor*' would seem most satisfactory. In any case, πνεῦμα κατανύξεως here in Romans, as in Isa. 29:10, must denote a state of spiritual insensibility."

[26]Sanday and Headlam, *Romans,* 315, insightfully cross-reference Paul's emphasis with Acts 7: "St. Stephen's speech illustrates more in detail the logical assumptions which underlie St. Paul's quotations."

[27]Ibid.: "So to the Jews that Law and those Scriptures wherein they trusted are to become the very cause of their fall and the snare or hunting-net in which they are caught"; Barth, *CD* II/2, 278: "God's table (the sum and substance of all his favours) remains in

on prosperity that had been gained through compromising unbelief. Paul, who was allied with the godly remnant past and present, prays that "their table" (the alleged advantage of the unbelieving majority) might become a trap (snare or offense with just retribution), that their eyes might be blinded, and that their backs might become bent in oppression, so that their unbelief might be broken.[28] Thus, the quotation becomes another descriptive preview of the restorative jealousy to follow. The use of σκάνδαλον in this messianic text brings to mind 9:30–33, where Paul's generation stumbled (προσέκοψαν) over "the stumbling stone," with messianic quotations from Isaiah 8:14 and 28:16. Thus, he seems to be alluding to the recent division of Israel over Messiah, which prompted the section (9:1) on natural children versus children of promise and on explanations involving the majority versus the remnant. The specific similarity of the citations in 11:8–10 is the majority's blind condition, so that Paul is using the psalmist's prayer to bring about conditions of oppression that would cause them to see their true condition and to turn to Messiah in faith (10:1). This positive hope is validated not only by his previously expressed desires for the salvation of Israel (9:1–4) but also by his assurance that the divine plan will be effective (11:26). This is the redemptive aspect of the implication with implied reversal. Paul's quotation of Psalm 69 emerges as ironic; may Israel see that in seeking its best apart from Christ, it had attained the burden of the messianic rock (9:33). May Israel's crushing burden make it realize that its stumbling block is self-imposed, so that the unbelievers might turn in faith to the rock that would remove their shame. The "bending of the backs" could refer to an oppressive burden or to a random groping on the ground because of blindness. In either case it is part of the ironically merciful imprecation and is the reason why διὰ παντός must mean "continually" (until faith) rather than "forever." Cranfield's point on the duration of the curse is crucial to the argument of the chapter:

> The recent tendency to translate διὰ παντός by "forever" (e.g., Moffatt, Weymouth, RSV, Barclay, Barrett, NEB, JB) is surely mistaken. The meaning, rather, is "continually." The point here is not that the bowing down of the backs is to go on forever but that as long as it does go on, it is not to be intermittent but continuous and sustained. This

their midst—even if it causes their downfall"; Barrett, *Romans,* 211: "Their table is their table-fellowship: the unity and interrelatedness created by the law and so highly valued in Judaism were no more than a delusion since they were a union in sin (iii.20), not righteousness."

[28]The elements of the imprecation change the LXX reading in v. 9, so as to focus on the idea of reversal or trap. Καὶ εἰς θήραν is added, and ἀνταπόδομα is substituted for ἀνταπόδοσιν and transposed with σκάνδαλον.

explanation is supported by consideration alike of the usage of *tāmîd* (the RV correctly renders it "continually" in the psalm), of the usage of διὰ παντός both in the Bible and in secular Greek, and of the context in Romans (vv. 11ff.).[29]

In other words, if Paul had not meant an intensive yet temporary condition, he would have contradicted both what he had said and what he was about to say.

We began this section with Paul's stated theme for the eleventh chapter: God had not rejected his people whom he foreknew. That theme answered the rhetorical question in 11:1 that was raised on the basis of the preceding chapters. Chapter 9 clearly identifies "his people" as ethnic Israel (9:3), Paul's own race according to his Benjamite lineage (11:1). God had not rejected them, in spite of their willful preferences of law to the righteousness of faith (chap. 10). The first of these explanatory subthemes in the chapter is that Israel had always had an elect remnant by the grace of God (11:1–10). Paul appealed to God's inviolable commitment to Israel in passages like 1 Samuel 12:22 and Psalm 94:14. He appealed to his own ministry as an Israelite apostle to Gentiles, a converted persecutor of the church, as proof of God's abiding commitment to ethnic Israel. Hebrew Christians were merely the most recent remnant of God's gracious preservation of his people in spite of unbelieving majorities, as proved by quotations and allusions to Elijah, Moses, Isaiah, and David. The section closes with an imprecation that Israel can be brought to its senses by faith through the faithfulness of God on its behalf. This section focuses on the continuity of God's commitment to his people, ethnic Israel. It is an abiding commitment to the Jew first (1:16) in which Paul and Hebrew Christians inherit the missionary vocation of the nation. Nothing is said about a discontinuity of Pentecost or of the church as a new people of God or a successor to Israel. Instead, the section closes with a prayerful hope that the present remnant might be instrumental in God's gracious salvation of the unbelieving majority. The second subtheme (11:11–24) will explain that God has not rejected his people because the unbelieving majority of ethnic Israel will not last forever. His focus moves from the *past* in the Old Testament to the *present* plan of God in which ethnic Israel will be regrafted into God's fulfilling promises.

The second section begins in 11:11 with the same form (λέγω οὖν, μή) and emphatic denial (μὴ γένοιτο) as in verse 1. The third person plural reference links this section to the λοιποί preceding (11:7–10). With these connections in mind, one must determine the relationship

---

[29]Cranfield, *Romans* 2:552. He refers as well to an article of his ("The Significance of διὰ παντός in Romans 11:10") in *SE* 2 (1964): 546–50.

between their stumbling and their falling (with the ἵνα). Was the *result* of their stumbling their irreversible ruin, which would support a meaning of "forever" for διὰ παντός in 11:10? This understanding would contradict the emphatic denials of 11:1 and 11. Instead, the emphasis is on the reversibility of the majority's stumbling.[30] The focus is on the reality of stumbling in sin rather than the possibility of falling permanently, a very real stumbling from stupor rather than irreversible ruin, as the two terms would respectively connote.

With strong contrast (ἀλλά) the result of their stumbling-trespass is that salvation in God's sovereign plan has come to the Gentiles (ἔθνεσιν) in order to provoke the unbelieving Israelites to jealousy. Paul's use of ἔθνος in juxtaposition with λοιποί and ἐκλογή indicates that he has ethnic entities in mind. He may be writing to the Romans in the context of the church, but he does not emphasize or even mention the church, any kindred organism, or the singleness of body as in Ephesians 2. With the introduction of the Gentiles he has introduced an ethnic discontinuity that will be maintained to the end of the passage and the chapter. At the same time, with παραπτώματι he focuses the majority's unbelief on their recent rejection of Christ and the gospel: "Paul's meaning by the statement as a whole is generally explained by reference to Acts 8:1ff.; 13:45–49; 18:6; 28:24–28; and it is indeed likely that Paul did have in mind the fact that it was the rejection of the gospel message by the Jews which compelled the messengers to turn to the Gentiles."[31] The divine intention was not the rejection of his people but rather their jealousy unto salvation (Deut. 32:21 with Rom. 10:19). In Cranfield's words, "Thus that hardening of which v. 7 spoke has for its ultimate purpose the salvation of those who are hardened."[32]

If the unbelief of the majority of Jews meant riches of salvation for the Gentiles merely to make God's people jealous, then one could question whether the divine plan might be more capricious than

---

[30]Cf. K. L. Schmidt, "πταίω," *TDNT* 6:883–84, who, like many commentators, relates it to the sense of 9:32 (προσκόπτω). The nuance of purpose is preferred here for ἵνα, because of the general emphasis in the passage on sovereign will (retrospective) or mysterious plan (prospective).

[31]Παράπτωμα is frequently used by Paul to denote a sinful act. For πίπτω and παράπτωμα, see W. Michaelis, *TDNT* 6:164, 172; cf. Cranfield, *Romans* 2:556. Along with the reversibility of the majority's standing, one may note an apparent finality on more specific cases like Matt. 21:42–43. Barth, *CD* II/2, 279, with distinctive emphasis, extends the "trespass" to the Jews' specific rejection of Jesus himself, which then led to his death for the world (Jews and Gentiles). Cf. Rom. 5:10.

[32]Cranfield, *Romans* 2:556. Perhaps there is an allusion to covenantal jealousy with a marriage analogy in this statement of purpose. We know from vv. 26–27 that Paul had the new covenant in mind. Israel had made God jealous with the idolatry of the nations (Jer. 31:32 with Deut. 32:31 and Rom. 10:19). Conversely, God would make Israel jealous with ethnic favor to the Gentiles.

beneficently purposeful. Verse 12 begins to qualify Paul's theodicy by showing not only that God is not frustrated by Israel's unbelief but also that he is able to accomplish his will with blessings for the world in spite of it. From a believer's perspective, the majority's unbelieving transgression and consequent loss has meant riches for the world and Gentiles in particular.[33] The blindness of the unbelievers' perspectives shields them from such a view of Calvary. It is their recognition and acceptance of truth that Paul has prayed for in verses 9 and 10. The blessing of the world is the saving work of Christ (Rom. 3:22–26; 5:9–11; 10:12–13), which provided the new outpouring of divine grace on Gentiles as an ethnic people.[34] The apodosis of the verse extols the greater blessing of the ultimate conversion of the majority.[35] "Their fullness" refers to "the unbelieving majority's being brought up to its full numerical strength (i.e., the full strength of Israel as a whole, which is the relevant strength that a loyal Jew could properly be concerned with) by being reunited with the believing minority through its own (i.e., the majority's) conversion."[36] The issue of divine hardening in verse 25 is what makes this interpretation difficult to comprehend for a people accustomed to believing in a "now or never" decision.

The same emphasis on divine blessing for the world is found in verse 15. With explanation of the parenthetical exhortation in verses 13 and 14 and with reaffirmation of the blessing in spite of unbelief in verse 12, Paul states that the unbelieving majority's ultimate reception means "life from the dead." Again, Paul's condition means that if the unbelieving majority's temporary rejection (ἀποβολή, cf. v. 1) meant the reconcilia-

[33]Πλοῦτος is a descriptive effect, substantially synonymous with σωτηρία above. Cranfield, *Romans* 2:557, has an important remark on ἥττημα: "The substantive ἥττημα is known to occur in only two other places, Isa. 31:8 and 1 Cor. 6:7, in both of which it may be translated 'defeat,' which is the sort of meaning one would expect it to have, since it is derived from ἡττᾶσθαι, which can mean 'be less' or 'weaker (than someone).' . . . And this meaning suits the context here perfectly well." The point is that when unbelieving Israelites thought that they had "won" at the crucifixion, they lost the riches of salvation. This view is to be distinguished from Barrett, *Romans,* 214, who contrasts "diminution" to the later "fullness" rather than paralleling it with παράπτωμα.

[34]If *world* means Gentiles, then the two conditional protases are redundant, and the use of different terms is unexplained. Thus, the respective riches are distinguished above. The Gentiles are a part but not the whole of the world, which will include the transformed Israel of the eschaton.

[35]P. M.-J. Lagrange, *Saint Paul Épître aux Romains* (Paris: Librairie Lecoffre, 1950), 275–76: "Dans le v. 11, la balance paraissait pencher, du côté des Juifs, puisque, si leur chute était ordonnée au salut des gentils, le salut des gentils était à son tour ordonné au salut des Juifs. Paul rétablit ici l'équilibre, en montrant que la conversion des Juifs aura elle aussi de bons résultats pour les autres."

[36]This interpretation is necessitated by the need for a consistent antecedent for αὐτῶν in vv. 11–12, which is the preceding λοιποί. Extolling an undefined "fullness" of the λοιποί seems strange until one finds the same anticipation for the Gentiles (11:25). Obviously, Paul has in mind the beneficent, mysterious sovereignty of the divine plan.

tion of the world through the death of Christ (5:10–11), then what does its reception mean (climactically) other than resurrection itself at the end of the age?[37] The noun πρόσλημψις is a hapax legomenon in the New Testament (although its cognate verb appears in 14:1, 3; 15:7, and Philem. 17). Thus, its meaning in contrast with ἀποβολή must be "God's final acceptance of what is now unbelieving Israel."[38] Some have taken ζωὴ ἐκ νεκρῶν in a figurative sense.[39] With that nuance, the expression must mean a spiritual vivification of the world as a result of the conversion of Israel en masse. However, this reverses the order of 11:25–26, where the fullness of the Gentiles precedes the salvation of all Israel. Thus, with Cranfield, the term *life* would associate the faith of Israel in the community of believers with eschatological resurrection in principle and a blessed fulfillment of the divine plan.[40]

Verses 13 and 14 express Paul's personal wish relative to the divine plan. These verses in the development of this section parallel the contribution of 11:1 to the first section, expressing Paul's personal interest in the ultimate salvation of his people. The emphatic ὑμῖν in verse 13 marks Paul's specific address to the Gentile Christians at Rome that continues to his closing doxology. Contrary to their expectation that he might turn his back on the unbelieving Jews as apostle to the Gentiles, Paul states that he honors his office and hopes its saving riches among the Gentiles might provoke some of his fellow Jews to jealousy and salvation. In other words, Paul hopes that his ministry might be "a precious foretoken"[41] of the eschatological harvest that is referred to in 11:26. Particularly important in the parenthesis are the careful ethnic distinctions that Paul makes for himself and his converts. He, a Hebrew Christian, is an apostle to Gentiles, whose salvation will hopefully provoke some Jews to salvation. Elsewhere he can speak of organic unities in the present age (as in Eph. 2), but here all time periods demonstrate that neither God nor Paul has rejected the foreknown people. Paul now develops illustrative metaphors that lead to the hope of Israel's fullness.

[37]An association of Israel's fullness with resurrection and Parousia (v. 26) is the point. Any attempt to distinguish resurrections on the basis of this passage would be unwise.
[38]Cranfield, *Romans* 2:562.
[39]Calvin, *Romans*, 320–21 (Grand Rapids: Eerdmans, 1965). F. Godet, *Commentary on St. Paul's Epistle to the Romans*, trans. A. Cusin (Edinburgh: T. & T. Clark, 1881), 2:243: "A powerful spiritual revolution which will be wrought in the heart of Gentile Christendom by the fact of the conversion of the Jews." See also Leon Morris, *The Epistle to the Romans* (Grand Rapids: Eerdmans, 1988), 411; John Murray, *The Epistle to the Romans*, NICNT, 2 vols. (Grand Rapids: Eerdmans, 1965), 2:82–84.
[40]For "life from the dead" as an eschatological reference, see Cranfield, *Romans* 2:562–63. For the noneschatological view, see William Hendriksen, *New Testament Commentary: Exposition of Paul's Epistle to the Romans* (Grand Rapids: Baker, 1981), 370.
[41]The phrase is Cranfield's, *Romans* 2:561.

Two illustrations confirm Paul's argument that ethnic Israel has a future, in spite of present unbelief; the first a brief one about a representative consecration of the harvest in the firstfruit cake (v. 16a), and the second a lengthier one about the holiness of olive branches because of their root (vv. 16b–24). The point of the firstfruit cake offering (ἀπαρχὴν φυράματος, Num. 15:20 LXX) is that a representative portion could dedicate the full harvest to the Lord, a part (or remnant) as representative for the whole.[42] In Numbers 15:17–21, the firstfruit instruction is the second of three authoritative commands from the Lord (cf. the introductory formula in 15:1, 17, 37). Several elements of the passage would have made it suitable for Paul's purposes in Romans 11. First, the firstfruit principle and the illustration emphasize God's faithfulness to his stated promises: in Numbers to the provision of the land, and in Romans to his provision of fullness of people (Rom. 11:4–5, 21–29). Second, the Numbers passage applies to both Jews and Gentiles, as it does in Romans (Num. 15:15–16 with Rom. 11:21). Paul chose an illustration of dedication in faith that was more than a national command, the same reciprocation that was needed in the Roman church. Third, the command was to be perpetual, "throughout the generations to come" (Num. 15:21), so that Romans became a specific instance mutatis mutandis with its focus on people.

Who or what, then, is the firstfruits and the root? The problem is descriptively complex: it depends on preceding and on following details; on other metaphoric elements such as the role of the branches, faith, and God in the illustration; and on both its constant and its dynamic aspects. The firstfruits illustration is brief and undeveloped. The choice

---

[42]Explanations of holiness (ἀγία) here sometimes confuse purification, which is more apropos for the accompanying bloody sacrifice (as in Lev. 23:9–14). According to Sanday and Headlam, "By the offering of the first-fruits, the whole mass was considered to be consecrated; and so the holiness of the Patriarchs consecrated the whole people from whom they came" (*Romans*, 326n). However, an excursus in the same commentary (330–32) summarizes the evidence for a vicarious-merit view of the patriarchs in contemporary Judaism (i.e., purification by lineage) and distinguishes it from Paul's emphasis on faith, lest Paul seem to be advocating what he often condemned, that the descent of the Jews from Abraham is sufficient for their salvation. According to Lagrange, *Romains*, 279: "Les Juifs sont toujours, d'une certaine maniére un peuple consacré à Dieu, un peuple dû à Dieu. Il le prouve par deux comparaisons. D'abord les prémices." It may have been natural for the Jew to think of the cake as purifying the dough, but the firstfruits offering was an acknowledgment that "all blessing is from the Lord and all produce belongs to him. . . . his people are ever dependent on his largess" (Ronald B. Allen, "Numbers," in EBC 2 [Grand Rapids: Zondervan, 1990], 828). Cranfield makes the same point, *Romans* 2:563, when he states: "Its purpose seems rather to have been to free the rest of the dough for general consumption (cf. Lev. 23:14)." However, the parallel of firstfruits and root would seem to be evident in the word by proximity and illustrative purpose. The grain was to be not only choice (Ex. 23:19) but also coarse and from the threshing floor (Num. 15:20–21). Thus, one was to think first of God's rich provision and of his stated will for obedient dedication.

part (the remnant in context) sanctifies the whole harvest (the fullness to come). The olive tree metaphor is an extended passage that bridges the second and third subthemes of the chapter, God's abiding commitment to his people that will achieve his eschatological promises. His plan relates the root and the branches of an olive tree to his mysterious use of Jews and Gentiles in his provision of salvation for the world (vv. 16b–24). Several questions surface.

First, are ἀπαρχή and ῥίζα parallel? If they are, then the metaphors can be used to interpret one another. The form (parallel conditions) and content (part for whole) indicate parallelism, which does not mean that Paul's emphasis in the metaphors is necessarily identical. Paul could have developed the olive tree because it was familiar to his audience. Or the firstfruits could emphasize awareness of fulfillment (that is, nonrejection of ethnic Israel leading to future fullness), while the two could emphasize progress of fulfillment. The part-for-whole parallel is clear. Analogous to the firstfruits illustration, if the root is holy, so are the branches. The firstfruit and the root set the harvest and the tree apart in God's progressive accomplishment of salvation.

It is less certain that the parallel means that ἀπαρχή and ῥίζα refer to the patriarchs per se: "There is a very widespread agreement that it [ῥίζα] must refer to the patriarchs and that Paul's meaning is that the unbelieving majority of Jews are hallowed by their relation to the patriarchs."[43] Admittedly, the patriarchs are at least an aspect of the illustration as the progenitors of the "natural" lineage (9:5; 11:28). Also the extended metaphor concludes with an explicit allusion to them in 11:28–29.[44] In those verses the unbelieving ("they are enemies on your

[43]Cranfield, *Romans* 2:565.

[44]The patriarchal interpretation is shared by Calvin, *Romans,* 322; Sanday and Headlam, *Romans,* 326; Lagrange, *Romains,* 279; Murray, *Romans* 2:85. A second favored interpretation takes ἀπαρχή to be the Jewish Christian remnant (11:5), with particular reference to the first converts of an area (Rom. 16:5 and 1 Cor. 16:15). Cranfield, *Romans* 2:564, sees "no sufficient reason for assuming ἡ ἀπαρχή and ἡ ῥίζα must have the same application" and concludes that "the existence of Jewish Christians serves to sanctify the unbelieving majority of Israel, and the faith of one partner in a marriage sanctifies both the other partner and the children." See also C. H. Dodd, *The Epistle of Paul to the Romans* (London: Fontana, 1959), 188–89; Dunn, *Romans 9–16,* 659; F. F. Bruce, *The Epistle of Paul to the Romans,* TNTC (Grand Rapids: Eerdmans, 1963), 217; Barrett, *Romans,* 216. However, the parallel of firstfruits and root would seem to be evident in the verse by proximity and illustrative purpose. The metaphor looks to the following context rather than to 11:5, and the emphasis is not the believing remnant so much as the ultimate life of the unbelieving majority (the antecedent of the "theirs" preceding; cf. Hermann Olshausen, *Romans,* BCNT (Edinburgh: T. & T. Clark, 1871), 367–68. A third view that is found in several Fathers and Barth is that the firstfruit is Christ himself (1 Cor. 15:20). Barth would include patriarchs and Jewish Christians in his eclectic view (*CD* II/2, 285). Cranfield, *Romans* 2:564, mentions Clement of Alexandria, Origen, and Theodore of Mopsuestia. This truth of Paul's theology, however, is too direct and is less satisfactory for the contextual parallelism and metaphors than the preceding view. Note E. M. Embry, "Tree,

account") majority ("they are loved on account of the patriarchs") is stylistically subordinated to the new-covenant deliverer who forgives in accordance with God's irrevocable gifts and calling. In other words, God's plan of salvation is based on gracious permanent covenants (11:1, 11), particularly the new covenant, with the patriarchs. Thus, we would equate the notion of gifts and calling with the notion of covenant.

But the root of the tree could not mean any human claim on God's blessing, even for the patriarchs: "The patriarchs are a holy root, not because of any innate worth or merit of their own, but by virtue of God's election of grace."[45] However, even this true statement focuses more on root as divine initiative and abiding commitment, the covenantal basis of God's saving plan. If the patriarchs are the *living* root ("the nourishing sap"), then their physical lineage would seem efficacious and the brokenness of unbelieving Jews as natural branches would be inexplicable. In other words, if Paul was emphasizing that the patriarchs were holy, were their branches necessarily holy? This simple condition must be qualified. The background problem involved is rejection of grace because of pride in tradition without faith in God, physical relationship without covenantal promise. Because Abraham was progenitor of flesh and faith (Rom. 4), there is overlap on a critical question when one would wish for strict separation for clarity's sake. The people of promise are the people of faith, which points beyond themselves to God. The covenants were the progressively revealed words of promise. They spelled out the terms of faith for the elect. Relationship by faith (vv. 20–23) with God's covenantal commitment is the basis of the branches' blessing ("riches," v. 12) and the nourishing kindness of God (vv. 17, 22). This emphasis on a covenantal saving plan accords better with the chapter's priority on God's sovereign grace that the majority of his people had rejected with consequent removal (v. 17). He had not rejected them, however, and mercifully awaited their regrafting (vv. 11, 17). Therefore, the concept of covenant best explains the various aspects of "root" in the illustration.

A second question concerns God's role in the illustration. Is he the root and perhaps the firstfruits? Even more prominent in context than the patriarchs, he is the author of covenantal decrees and the object of faith. However, he is distinguished from the root (and could hardly be firstfruits in any sense). He is hardly the one who maintains the

---

Plant, Root, Branch," in *DNTT* 3:869. One must note in conclusion that one's interpretation of this point does not affect the validity of a present remnant of Hebrew Christians that will ethnically come to fullness, nor does it affect God's abiding covenantal commitment to ethnic Israel on the basis of their patriarchal promises.

[45]Cranfield, *Romans* 2:565. On the olive tree metaphor, note as well Dunn, *Romans 9–16*, 659–75; and Morris, *Romans*, 411–17.

fruitfulness of the tree (11:21) by pruning unfruitful (i.e., unbelieving) branches. He, like the patriarchs, seems to be an aspect of the root element but not identical with it. If the root is his covenantal relationships with the patriarchs, then that aspect is satisfied and his blessing and discipline operates according to that particular standard (e.g., Gen. 17).

A final question concerns the human aspect of the metaphor and its bearing on constant versus dynamic elements. Paul seems to limit the people(s) of God to two branches. He carefully distinguishes the root and the branches. The former is always holy (v. 16), a constant source of nourishment (v. 17), and a traditional support for the people of faith (v. 18). It is not subject to change such as ingrafting or regrafting. It is the source of life for the tree. The latter are carefully distinguished as wild and natural branches. The two types are never mixed or confused. They are respectively removed, added, or restored. This point can hardly be overemphasized, because the characteristics of one cannot be ascribed to the other without destroying the argument of the metaphor (vv. 26–29). They would seem to apply to the past on a remnant-majority basis (vv. 1–10) as distinguished from the Gentiles' ingrafting aspect, which is new in biblical revelation. Therefore the root would seem to refer not so directly to the people of God as to the covenant basis of their relationship, involving faith in the immutable author as the governing standard of acceptance and blessing. Crucial to this context is the standard of faith that marked believers as "offspring of the promise" (9:8) and "a chosen remnant" (9:7–13 and 11:5). "That holy stock" and "that holy stem"[46] would thus include the word of God that recorded his gracious saving will for history, that decreed justification by faith (1:16–17; chap. 4), that made Abraham the recipient of covenant promises and the father of God's family (4:16–17 and 9:7–9), and that mercifully calls and uses faithful branches to fulfill the blessing of the earth.[47] The root, then, would be God's covenants (cf. 9:1–2), and supremely his word about Christ (9:5; chap. 10; cf. Heb. 1:1–2) that determines one's relationship (or lack of it) with the tree.

I would conclude that the root focuses on divine grace, on God's initiative and commitment—in other words, his loyal love to covenantal stipulations and promises. An equation of root and patriarchs does not

[46]The phrases are taken from Cranfield, *Romans* 2:570, 572. He comes close to the desired emphasis on p. 567: "If the root signifies the patriarchs, then we may understand its fatness to signify the divine election in which alone their special worth consists."
[47]The olive tree in the prophets is a metaphor for the beauty of believing Israel (Jer. 11:16; Hos. 14:6; cf. Judg. 9:8–9. Interestingly, Jeremiah's passage refers not to an ingrafting for fruitfulness like Paul's but rather to an annihilating judgment by fire and a disaster of brokenness. Each passage is appropriate to its context.

necessarily violate the emphasis on covenants. However, it does remove the emphasis on divine faithfulness that is central to the chapter. Perhaps the patriarchs would be an appropriate emphasis for the firstfruits. Even there, however, a case could be made for the remnant concept that is the earnest for the harvest to come. The human aspect of the illustration is the branches that focus on the stipulations of faith for the inclusion in the tree. The tree, accordingly, would refer to a saving program that would be theocratically based on Israel's covenants. In Romans 11 the new covenant is more relevant, because it incorporated Gentiles under Messiah's forgiveness, and its misapplications led to the ethnic tensions in the Roman church.

With the context in view, it is germane to note that Paul is talking not only about saving faith as acceptance of truth but also about a God-centered attitude of faith that would promote ethnic humility and healing among Roman Christians. In verses 17–24 Paul used the metaphor to address the need for believing Gentiles to "fear in faith" and not to boast divisively against the lost position of unbelieving Jews.[48] The passage emphasizes faith as the basis of the branches' position in the tree. Thus, unbelieving Jewish branches had been broken off. Some believing Gentiles had been grafted in to share acceptance and blessing with God ($\pi\iota\acute{o}\tau\eta\tau\sigma\varsigma$) with Jewish Christians (cf. 10:12). The unnaturalness of grafting a wild branch into a natural tree, contrary to the usual procedure for enhancing fruitfulness, will be used by Paul to argue for the plausibility of restoring natural branches that come to faith into their own tree (11:24).

This view can be clarified by comparing it with the interpretation of Sanday and Headlam, who see the live tree as "the Church of God, looked at as one continuous body; the Christian Church being the inheritor of the privileges of the Jewish Church."[49] The roots are the "Patriarchs, for whose faith Israel was originally chosen (vv. 28–29)."[50] The branches are "the individual members of the Church who derive their nourishment and virtue from the stock or body to which they belong."[51]

Sanday and Headlam have blurred the distinctives of the passage by confusing the parts and the whole. First, by making tree equal church and branches equal individual believers as *one continuous* body, they have

---

[48]The second person plural is used in vv. 13 and 25. This is changed to the second person singular in vv. 17–24. Paul makes a direct appeal to the ethnic problems in the Roman church by addressing them in terms of their individual need to promote unity in the church.

[49]Sanday and Headlam, *Romans*, 327.

[50]Ibid.

[51]Ibid.

blurred the ethnic distinctions that are central to the problems in the Roman church (11:18–19), to Paul's distinctive ministry in the present age (vv. 13–14), and to the ingrafting and regrafting processes. The Gentile believers are never identified as natural branches in the chapter; therefore, though there is one body (as explicitly taught in Eph. 2), it is not "one and continuous" ethnically.

In a summary of their commentary, Sanday and Headlam acknowledge that Paul is concerned with God's election of ethnic entities rather than with individual salvation: "It undoubtedly represents the main lines of the Apostle's argument and his purpose throughout these chapters."[52] Their explanation of the branches is a two-stage succession (natural = Old Testament Jewish church, wild = New Testament Christian church) rather than a complementary relationship on the premise that "Israel as a nation was rejected from the Christian Church" because they had rejected the Messiah.[53] It is difficult to reconcile Sanday and Headlam's affirmation of ethnic Israel ("as a nation") and their interpretation of πᾶς Ἰσραὴλ σωθήσεται: "[All Israel] 'shall attain the σωτηρία of the messianic age by being received into the Christian Church': the Jewish conception of the Messianic σωτηρία being fulfilled by the spiritual σωτηρία of Christianity."[54] Such a position, however, removes any meaningful notion of ethnicity. In the redefinition of salvation, consistency is lost. Paul, in contrast, argues for a complementary relationship between Israel and the church in which a present remnant (v. 5) results in a future fullness for Israel by provocation of the Gentiles. There is a regrafting of natural branches that Sanday and Headlam ignore. Sanday and Headlam's interpretation of the future is that it will be a time when the whole earth (the kingdoms = πλήρωμα of the Gentiles plus the nation of Israel) will be united in the church of God (p. 336). This removes the third stage of the mystery because the union of ethnic Jew and Gentile in principle has already been accomplished. The future may involve "ways other than we can follow."[55] However, we do know the three successive stages of verses 25–26 that relate past, present, and future in God's one irrevocable plan of salvation.

Second, by taking "for whose faith" in reference to the patriarchs, Sanday and Headlam have weakened Paul's emphasis on sovereign divine grace (vv. 5–6) as if their faith was a meritorious cause of God's election rather than a response to it.

---

[52]Ibid., 341 with 335–36.
[53]Ibid., 342.
[54]Ibid., 336.
[55]Ibid., 342. Dunn, *Romans 9–16*, 691, is wise: "Again in this summary statement Paul does not say how it will come about, but again he does not need to."

Third, it does not follow from Paul's argument that "inheritor of the promises" establishes ethnic identity. In summary, if Jews and Gentiles are "one and continuous" without ethnic distinctions, then there is no point in the urgency of the initial question about rejection and the progression to the future salvation of all Israel (v. 26).

Because acceptance with God is based on faith in Jewish covenantal promises that were fulfilled in Christ, the Gentile Christians should not boast (or gloat) over the rejected branches (11:19), as if God had rejected his foreknown people (vv. 1–2, 11) out of preference for Gentiles (v. 18). They are indebted to Israel; Israel owes them no debt. The skewed, anti-Semitic perception of some in the church reflected an attitude of superiority over "saving" the root rather than gratitude over sharing blessings in the patriarchal tradition (v. 18 and chap. 4).[56] The metaphor stresses Gentile incorporation into the stock of God's elect people ("first for the Jew," 1:16), the recipients of the promise of the seed in whom all nations would find blessing. Faith is decisive for positional acceptance (11:20; cf. "stand" here and 5:2); therefore, arrogance is out of place. Humility as an accurate perception of oneself (cf. 12:16) and as fear of divine justice is critical, because if God did not spare his traditional people in their unbelief, he would surely break off Gentile branches for the same reason (11:21).

Faith calls for reflection on the kindness (4:2) and severity (1:18) of God. There has been severity of "fallenness and brokenness" (the stupor) toward the λοιποί; there have been riches of gracious vitality

---

[56]Cranfield, *Romans* 2:568: "And to such an egotist this half-truth seems a conclusive proof of his own superior importance and a sufficient justification for his contemptuous attitude." The attitude of arrogance in believing Gentiles supports the notion that Paul wrote Romans in response to background pressures. For an excellent, provocative exposition of this aspect of the letter, see E. P. Sanders, *Paul, the Law, and the Jewish People* (Philadelphia: Fortress, 1983), 31: "I am on the whole persuaded by those who, following the lead of T. W. Manson, view Romans as primarily coming out of Paul's own situation." Sanders constructively emphasizes the apostolic ministerial connection of 11:13–14 and chap. 15 (esp. v. 17); see pp. 171 and 184 on Paul's tireless work for "the third race," the church. One will not agree with Sanders's helpful synthesis on every point. On p. 197, he struggles: "He [Paul] thought that the only way to be saved was through Christ Jesus. If it were to be proposed that Christians today should think the same thing, and accordingly that the Jews who have not converted should be considered cut off from God, and if such a proposal come before a body in which I had a vote, I would vote against it. I still would. I am now inclined to think that perhaps Paul would too." This writer, with similar struggles, would think that Paul would not, because of his pride in his heritage and his urgent longing for them to trust in the saving faith of our common Messiah.

A second suggestive study of the background with application to the Holocaust and the mutuality of Jews and Gentiles is H. M. Rumscheidt, " 'Do Not Live in Fear, Little Flock!': The Interpretation of Romans 9–11 of Georg Eichholz," *ExA* 4 (1988): 85–94. Also, Halvor Moxnes, *Theology in Conflict: Studies in Paul's Understanding of God in Romans* (Leiden: E. J. Brill, 1980), esp. chaps. 2 and 4. Moxnes is concerned with how conflict in Rome affected Paul's (traditional) language about God.

bestowed on believing Gentiles. If the Gentiles do not abide in faith (with secondary application to their own ungracious, severe attitudes toward Jewish people), then they will be justly cut off from the tree. If the unbelieving Jews believe, then God is able to graft them in again.[57] Again, Paul underlines the divine standard and prerogative instead of human worth and ability. His argument moves from an implausible fact (wild branch, natural tree) about which the Gentiles boast to its plausible counterpart that they have been less prone to accept. Thus, he demonstrates the absurdity of their high-mindedness.

An important fact about the metaphor is that the wild and natural branches are never mixed or confused. For an apostle who proclaims the church as an indivisible unity (Eph. 4), the careful ethnic distinctions of Romans 11 are extraordinary. One may have expected the grafting process to blend the branches, so that the root would enrich hybrid (*agriekallious,* wild-natural) branches. Or one may have expected the grafting process to be permanent and secure, so that the removal of branches would threaten the life of the root. Or one may have expected the contextual problem that Israel in unbelief had forfeited her national privileges under God. However, these inferences are precisely what we do not find, because of the mysteriousness and certainty of God's plan in verses 25–36.

Without compromising the principle of faith, God will accomplish the fullness of salvation (11:25–32). This passage concludes the preceding "fullness" (v. 12) by "regrafting" (v. 24) with a mysterious, merciful salvation of "all Israel" and summarizes the substance of the preceding three chapters. Paul stresses his conclusion with an emphatic formula (οὐ ... θέλω ὑμᾶς ἀγνοεῖν) and the vocative (cf. 1:13), emphasizing the familial unity of believers in Christ. The conclusion's referent is to τὸ μυστήριον τοῦτο, teaching that could be known only by revelation. In effect, it is God's own statement through Paul of how past, present, and future contribute to his salvation.[58] A specific connection with preceding verses is the need for godly fear (v. 20), lest

---

[57]Cranfield's emphasis is precisely correct in *Romans* 2:569 n. 1: "Paul does not think of standing as a reward for faith and there is no good reason for reading into the other dative the idea of 'as a punishment for.' It is rather by the very fact of their unbelief, and by the very fact of their faith, that the ones are cut off and the others stand." This also remains, a charge of divine bias, pro or con, toward Jews and Gentiles. The issue is sovereign justice (the passives ἐξεκλάσθησαν [v. 20] and ἐγκεντρισθῶ [v. 19] connote divine action) rather than ethnic superiority (cf. vv. 7 and 11). Somehow Paul is speaking primarily of ethnic entities. However, he continues to address individual Gentiles (v. 13). I cannot develop the latter exhortation for this passage, but discipline for sedition could be in view.

[58]An inference of mystery as new revelation seems to be unwise in view of the composite Old Testament allusion that follows. Better is an emphasis on fresh insights about Old Testament predictions in view of the gospel events.

ungodly (and ethnically biased) conclusions (vv. 1 and 11) demean other believers and the character of God (vv. 33–36).

The content of the mystery carries Paul's preceding argument to its conclusion in a three-part sentence, containing three successive stages in God's plan of salvation: the divine hardening of the majority in Israel (vv. 5, 7, 17), the coming in of the full number of Gentiles, and, finally, the salvation of all Israel. The composite Old Testament quotation in verses 26b and 27 and the emphatic οὕτως clearly prioritize the salvation of Israel as the emphasis and the terminus ad quem of Paul's argument. Thus, the future progression of salvation is a rather striking reversal of the past order in 1:16. The reversal means that Israel's salvation can be explained only as "an act of divine mercy . . . not the recognition and satisfaction of human claims."[59] God's sovereignty alone is able to accomplish salvific good out of the unbelief of his people. So wonderful is the mercy of God in this mystery that Paul closes the chapter with praise for God's wisdom and knowledge (vv. 33–36). Human interpretation reasoned that the principle of faith would necessitate rejection of the unbelieving nation, even if it was the traditional people of God. Divine revelation reinterpreted the rejection of Israel as the reconciliation for the world without compromising principles of faith and promise. But the accomplishment of such a plan necessitates (οὕτως) glory that is from him, through him, and to him forever: "Far from any arbitrariness, there is liturgical order in the sequence of these pronouncements: they begin with lamentation, proceed to thanksgiving (related to the function entrusted to Paul), and conclude with adoration."[60]

The hardening (πώρωσις) of Israel's part refers to the unknowably mysterious divine aspect of its unbelief (cf. 11:7), a condition that would continue until the inclusion of the fullness of the Gentiles. The temporal implication is that once Gentile fullness is attained, Israel's hardness will end.[61] Πλήρωμα is best explained as the full number of elect Gentiles that constitutes a representative remnant of the "Gentile world" as is similarly "the fullness" of all Israel (vv. 12 and 26).

The meaning of πᾶς 'Ισραήλ is a much-debated *crux interpretum* that must be understood in light of the emphases of the passage:[62] divine faithfulness to his saving plan, ethnic remnants in the church, and the relationship of the present to an unspecified future fullness. The

---

[59]Barth, *CD* II/2, 300.

[60]Marcus Barth, "One God, One Christ, One People," *ExA* 4 (1988): 9.

[61]"The verb [εἰσέρχεσθαι] is seldom used by Paul, and he uses it in this pregnant sense nowhere but here" (Cranfield, *Romans* 2:576).

[62]Morris, *Romans*, 420, does not overstate the case when he describes "unending disputation" and "notoriously difficult."

interpretation of this passage generally reflects one's interpretation of the chapter. Therefore, specific issues will be mentioned here and discussed further in the following section.

Two views have been commonly held with variations: the elect (of both Jews and Gentiles or, rarely, only of Israel)[63] or the nation (rarely every individual of Israel, usually the whole of Israel but not every individual).[64] Cranfield carries forward Sanday and Headlam's criticisms of the election views: it "is not feasible to understand Ἰσραήλ in v. 26 in a different sense from that which it has in v. 25, especially in view of the sustained contrast between Israel and the Gentiles throughout vv. 11–32," and πᾶς must mean more than "what would simply amount to the salvation of the elect remnants of Israel of all the generations."[65] One must agree that "all Israel" as the elect including Gentiles contradicts the sustained ethnic contrast in verses 11–32, and equally implausible is the inclusion of every individual member, certainly for the past and probably for the future, since the chapter includes unbelieving generations of Israelites as majorities. Therefore, the answer would seem to lie in the other options: the elect of Israel or a whole nation but not every member. A consensus of scholars agrees that "Israel" must mean the ethnic nation.[66] Πᾶς cannot be comprehensive in

---

[63]Cranfield, *Romans* 2:578, lists Calvin as representative for the election of both Jews and Gentiles, and Bengel as representative of the view that the elect refers only to Israel. Bruce, *Romans,* 223, notes: "There is an unmistakable universalism here, even if it be an eschatological universalism and not a present one, or a representative rather than an individual universalism." Barth, *CD* II/2, 300, joins Calvin, *Romans,* 330, in understanding "all Israel" as the church, the elect from Jews and Gentiles. Cf. Ludwig Ott, *Fundamentals of Catholic Dogma,* 4th ed., ed. J. Bastible, trans. P. Lynch (Rockford, Ill: Tan, 1960), 486, for a similar Catholic interpretation. See also Karl Kertelge, *The Epistle to the Romans* (New York: Herder & Herder, 1972), 126; and D. J. Harrington, *God's People in Christ* (Philadelphia: Fortress, 1980), chap. 5. Paul J. Achtemeier, *Romans: Interpretation: A Biblical Commentary for Teaching and Preaching* (Atlanta: John Knox, 1985), 188, interprets the passage nonethnically in terms of the general principle of the book: "God hardens the very people he intends to save!" (cf. 177–78). Ordinarily, the "elect of Jews and Gentiles" interprets "Israel" as spiritual Israel with reference to Gal. 6:16. A helpful summary of interpretations can be found in Hendriksen, *Romans,* 379–82.

[64]LaGrange, *Romains,* 285; Godet, *Romans,* 256, interprets the phrase as a collective movement of the nation in general, with allowances for individual unbelief. In contrast, πᾶς denotes "every element of which the totality of the object is composed." An "elect" interpretation, in his opinion, would be tautological with σωθήσεται. Godet's discussion illustrates the difficulty of being consistent on this matter. See also Barrett, *Romans,* 223–24; and Dodd, *Romans,* 192–93.

[65]Cranfield, *Romans* 2:576–77. Cf. H. P. Liddon, *Explanatory Analysis of St. Paul's Epistle to the Romans,* reprint ed. (Minneapolis: James & Klock, 1977), 217. In support of a national, eschatological conversion of Israel, see Charles Hodge, *A Commentary on the Epistle to the Romans* (Philadelphia: Grigg & Elliot, 1835), 474–77.

[66]Cranfield and Sanday and Headlam have already been noted. We may add Johannes Munck, *Christus und Israel: Eine Auslegung von Röm 9–11* (Copenhagen: Ejnar Munksgaard, 1956), 102: "Sanday und Headlam fassen πᾶς Ἰσραήλ auf als 'Israel as a whole, Israel as a nation, and not as necessarily including every individual Israelite.' Dies ist

past and present perspectives, and it probably is not comprehensive in the future any more than the fullness of Gentiles would mean all (each and every one of the) Gentiles. Such an understanding of πᾶς would involve a universalism that is alien to the severity of God against unbelief in context.[67] The text suggests that the divine hardening ends with the fullness of the Gentiles, which accordingly provides the occasion for the conversion of the fullness of Israel's elect.[68] The notion that "all Israel" could be the elect of Israel (an unspecified number) should not be objectionable in view of the prior emphasis on the doctrine (v. 7) and the preceding metaphors (v. 16) that emphasize in principle that the holy part sanctifies the whole. Therefore, in my opinion, the third stage is the conversion of the full number of Israel's elect as preparation for the cleansing of the nation by its Deliverer in fulfillment of the new covenant.

Paul confirms the future salvation of Israel with a composite quotation from Isaiah that also gives some basis and description of the promise. Isaiah 59:20 emphasizes the deliverance of Zion by its just and righteous Messiah. The focus of his coming is the forgiveness of those who repent of their sins. In verse 21 this forgiveness is related to the new-covenant promises (cf. Jer. 31:31–34, esp. v. 34). The verse goes on to elaborate a permanent relationship with the Holy Spirit, but Paul alludes instead (ὅταν) to a similar emphasis on forgiveness in Isaiah 27:9. This is consistent with the emphasis throughout Romans 11 on Israel's unbelieving stupor. In Isaiah Jacob will be atoned by the Lord's purifying judgment of Leviathan "in that day." Israel will blossom and fill the world with fruit (27:6), which reminds us of Romans 11:12 as the effect of Israel's regrafting into its own olive tree (v. 24).[69] The force of Paul's argument and use of the Old Testament underlines the fact that

---

richtig. 'Ganz Israel' bezeichnet den 'Rest,' aber es ist nicht die Rede von einer Vollständigkeit. Alle heilsgeschichtlichen Kategorien wie die Heiden und Israel, der 'Rest' und die Kirche werden errettet oder verworfen in ihrer Gesamtheit, aber das Heil des Einzelnen ist nicht verbürgt mit Gottes Auserwählung und Errettung der betreffenden Totalität, der dieser Einzelne angehört." See Bruce, *Romans*, 220, who does not specify whether every individual is included.

[67]No other eschatological text that points to future conversions such as Rev. 7:9–10 or 11:13, assuming a futurist interpretation, indicates such a universalism either (cf. Rev. 16:8–21). Discussion about Daniel's seventieth week (Dan. 9:24–27), Jeremiah's "time of Jacob's trouble" (Jer. 30:7), and distinctions between resurrections require detailed study of other texts. Rom. 11 establishes only the fact that there is a future for ethnic Israel in fulfillment of Old Testament promises, particularly in the new covenant.

[68]John Witmer, "Romans," *BKCNT*, 2.483.

[69]Cranfield, *Romans* 2:577–78, summarizes the composite nature of the quotation: "ἥξει . . . agrees with the LXX version of Isa. 59:20–21a exactly, except that ἐκ is substituted for the ἕνεκεν of the LXX, perhaps under the influence of Ps. 14 [LXX: 13].7; 53:6 [LXX: 52.7] or 110 [109].2, and the καί before ἀποστρέψει is omitted." Cf. Str-B 4:981.

Israel's salvation is dependent on the mercy of God alone, apart from any claim on God or any notion of meritorious obligation.

Paul's use of the Old Testament seems to offer additional insight into the phrase "all Israel." The tendency is to interpret the phrase quantitatively (or numerically), which has created as many questions as it has resolved. We have noted Paul's emphasis on God's sovereign purpose(s) in history, his commitment to the patriarchal covenants of Israel, his consistent ethnic distinctions, and his careful synthesis of new-covenant texts in a composite quotation. Without losing the aspect of a future elect remnant in continuity with Israel's history (v. 5), I wish to suggest two additional aspects in this composite idea. First, "all Israel" seems to include its Messiah, who expresses its corporate ideal in his person. The focus in the Isaiah passages is not so much on the people (although the repentant ones are explicitly mentioned) as on the Deliverer.[70] This nuance of corporate salvation in Christ is supported by the subtle change of Isaiah 59:20 from advent (to Zion) to lineage (from Zion) with an explicit new-covenant accomplishment of forgiveness of sins. This accords with Paul's Christological emphasis in Romans 9–11 (esp. 9:5; 10:4) rather than a pneumatological emphasis, as expounded, for example, by Paul in 2 Corinthians 3 (esp. v. 16).[71]

Second, the salvation of Israel is described as the future part of a history-long progression that is identified in Old Testament texts as "the day" of the Lord's vindication and cleansing of Jacob from the idolatry of the nations. In Jeremiah 31, "the time is coming" for the ratification of a new covenant with the house of Israel, when their sins will be forgiven and they will be "my forgiven people" (vv. 31–34). In other words, Paul seems to be teaching that Messiah's eschatological Parousia will be the time of God's sovereign ratification of the new-covenant promise with Israel.[72] This is consistent with his strong emphasis on divine purpose in

---

[70]For a similar suggestion, see J. M. Stifler, *The Epistle to the Romans* (Chicago: Moody Press, 1960), 196. For a similar sense of Christ as Israel, the true Jew, see Barth, "One God, One Christ, One People," 15–16.

[71]The identification of the covenant as the new covenant is generally accepted; see Barrett, *Romans,* 224; Ernst Käsemann, *Commentary on Romans,* trans. and ed. G. W. Bromiley (Grand Rapids: Eerdmans, 1980), 314; Rainer Schmitt, *Gottesgerechtigkeit— Heilsgeschichte—Israel in den Theologie des Paulus* (New York: Peter Lang, 1984), 111.

[72]For a similar suggestion, see Harrison, "Romans," 124. An additional consideration is that the differences between Paul's treatments of the new covenant in Gal. 3 and 4 and Rom. 11 reflect the respective Gentile and Jewish enjoyment of covenantal blessings. Galatians views the new covenant as a present reality with focus on the presence of the Spirit. The recipients are primarily Gentiles who receive its blessings by faith in Christ. In Rom. 11 it is a future expectation for Israel at the Parousia. The covenant will be effected with all Israel in connection with the removal of Israel's stupor. Either Paul's presentation of the covenant is inconsistent, or eschatological progression in this age has "already" and "not yet" aspects. The latter understanding is best. A few interpreters, such as R. C. H. Lenski, *The Interpretation of St. Paul's Epistle to the Romans* (Minneapolis: Augsburg, 1936),

history in Romans 9–11 (cf. Gal. 4:4; 2 Cor. 6:2) and the mysterious historical inversion of "fullnesses" in response to gospel proclamation (Rom. 1:16; 11:11–32). Paul probably did not mean for later interpreters to quantify fullness. And he seems to have wanted us to include elements of remnant, Messiah, and covenant ratification in "all Israel."

The next five verses develop the implications of the new-covenant promise of ethnic regrafting to a bold conclusion in which human disobedience is contrasted with God's overcoming mercy. The mystery of the progress of gospel ministry relates God's loving election of the patriarchs to his use of Gentile salvation to bring mercy to Israel. The gracious gifts and calling of God are unchangeable (not repentable), so he has not and will not reject his chosen, ethnic people (vv. 28–29).[73] The progression of gospel ministry is explained with a carefully balanced parallelism ($\ddot{\omega}\sigma\pi\epsilon\rho\ \gamma\dot{\alpha}\rho\ \ldots\ o\ddot{v}\tau\omega\varsigma\ \kappa\alpha\dot{\iota}$) in verses 30–31 that Cranfield has critically analyzed in all of its narration: "Paul draws a comparison between the cases of the Gentile Christians and the unbelieving Jews, in which he brings out . . . the fact of their interrelatedness . . . and affirms with special emphasis—it is the climax of the whole comparison—that the final destiny of the still disobedient Jews is that they too, like those Gentile Christians who were once disobedient, should receive mercy."[74]

Mysteriously, behind the present disobedience of the majority of Jews is the merciful providence of God, who will certainly accomplish their fullness as proved by his blessing of the Gentiles. The end of Paul's argument (v. 32), which has now come full circle (10:21), is an affirmation of freedom from the bondage of merits in a disobedient world: "This is the fundamental thing—mysterious though God's ways are and dark and indeed forbidding though they may sometimes seem to us to be, the end of them is mercy, mercy pure and uncompromised."[75] Therefore, there is no room in the church for high-mindedness toward God, other believers, or different ethnic groups.

728, interpret the advent of the deliverer as Christ's first advent. However, the future tense of $\sigma\omega\theta\dot{\eta}\sigma\epsilon\tau\alpha\iota$ in v. 26 and the prediction of v. 25 prohibit this. On the coherency of Paul's argumentation in vv. 25–32, see E. P. Sanders, *Paul* (Oxford: Oxford University Press, 1991), 124–26.

[73]$E\dot{v}\alpha\gamma\gamma\dot{\epsilon}\lambda\iota o\nu$ in this review statement must refer to the ministry and saving work of Christ and the ministry and reconciling work of the church as discussed from chap. 9. $'E\chi\theta\rho o\dot{\iota}$ refers to Israel's state of being cut off from her tree, justly experiencing the severity of God for disobedience. We must not diminish the form of $\chi\alpha\rho\dot{\iota}\sigma\mu\alpha\tau\alpha$ or the copulative $\kappa\alpha\dot{\iota}$. God's dealings with Israel have all been unmerited from Abraham's calling to be his special family in behalf of all the families of the earth (Gen. 12:1–4; Rom. 11:1). $'A\mu\epsilon\tau\alpha\mu\dot{\epsilon}\lambda\eta\tau\alpha$ is emphatic by position, thus necessitating a future for ethnic Israel, the particular people who have enriched the world as the wayward vassal of their faithful sovereign.

[74]Cranfield, *Romans* 2:585.
[75]Ibid., 587.

This section has developed the thesis that Paul teaches a future for ethnic Israel in Romans 11 under three subheadings. First, he emphatically denied that God had rejected "his people" because of their unbelief, referring to ethnic Israel. Paul supported his emphatic negation with Old Testament language and quotations that recalled God's inviolable commitment to Israel, his own apostolic ministry, and an ever-present remnant by grace. In brief, history proves that God has an ongoing covenant relationship with the nation Israel. An unbelieving majority in any generation does not cancel that commitment. Particularly interesting is the fact that Paul in the church age, the premier apostle to the Gentiles, refers to Israel as God's people (v. 1), focuses on a special, distinctive remnant in the church (v. 5), and combines election with imprecation out of a special concern for the unbelieving majority of Israel (vv. 7–10).

Second, ethnic Israel has a future because the unbelief of the majority of Israelites will not last forever (vv. 11–24). Israel's stumbling in unbelief will not last forever, because in God's plan the spiritual riches of Gentiles will cause the Jews to be jealous of their special covenantal relationship with their "root." God's covenant with the patriarchs guaranteed the sacredness of his harvest, the regrafting of his people into a fulfilling position of fruitful service. In sovereign wisdom he is able to translate the evil of unbelief into life for the world without compromising his saving plan. In this extraordinary passage about ethnic problems in the Roman church, Jews and Gentiles are not mixed or confused ethnically or temporally.

Third, the mystery and mercy of the divine plan will result in salvation of the elect fullness for Gentiles and Jews (11:25–32) and a doxology. Ethnic Israel has a future, because God will accomplish salvation for Israel according to his new-covenant promise. This awaits the fullness of the Gentiles, when Israel's hardening will be removed and when Gentile provocation will have taken its course. All Israel will be saved in such a way that God's mercy will be evident to all.

THE ISSUE OF ETHNIC ISRAEL
IN THEOLOGICAL INTERPRETATIONS

As mentioned in the introduction, three views of the people(s) of God have been set forth that are based on various emphases in Romans 11. They are the supersessionists of covenant theology, the distinctionists of dispensational theology, and the revisionists of various contemporary theologies. Here I list and briefly discuss representatives and issues in this order.

Supersessionist positions affirm that the church is "the community of believers, and this community existed from the beginning of the old dispensation right down to the present time and will continue to exist on earth until the end of the world,"[76] in accordance with the Belgic Confession (art. 27) and the Heidelburg Confession (art. 21). Concomitant with the one community of believers is an overarching covenant of grace between God and his church after the Fall.

John Calvin's view of the church and Israel reflects the characteristic emphases of his Reformed theology. He tended to be more favorable to the Jews than "traditional medieval anti-Judaism" (which was maintained by Luther), because of the diasporalike existence of Calvinists and his theological perception of the unity of the covenants. "Nevertheless, the general perception that Calvin stressed the unity of the covenants and accordingly the *substantial* unity of law and gospel, broadly conceived, more than Luther is an accurate one."[77] In the *Institutes* he has comparatively little to say except to compare the two Testaments and conclude: "The covenant made with all the patriarchs is so much like ours in substance and reality that the two are actually one and the same. Yet they differ in the mode of dispensation," because Christ is the

---

[76]L. Berkhof, *Systematic Theology*, 4th ed. (Grand Rapids: Eerdmans, 1949), 571. Berkhof's key discussion is entitled "The Church in the Different Dispensations." In the patriarchal period the church was represented in pious households, where patriarchs were priests. When Israel became a nation, the "people of Israel were not only organized as a nation but were also constituted the Church of God. . . . The Church has its institutional existence in the national life of Israel . . . the whole nation constituted the Church" (570). "In essence Israel constituted the Church of God in the Old Testament, though its external institution differs vastly from that of the Church in the New Testament" (572). One wonders how one essence could have such vast institutional differences? He distinguished the Roman Catholic view from the Reformed view by its emphasis on visible hierarchy instead of its spiritual "preaching of the Word and the right administration of the Sacraments" (572–73). On this point, he concludes, "We cannot agree with those premillennarians who, under the influence of divisive dispensationalism, claim that the Church is exclusively a New Testament institution, which did not come into existence until the outpouring of the Holy Spirit on the day of Pentecost and will be removed from the earth before the beginning of the millennium" (571). Similarly, Martin J. Wyngaarden, *The Future of the Kingdom in Prophecy and Fulfillment* (Grand Rapids: Zondervan, 1934), 24–25, 151–54, and 187, who appealed for a "natural" interpretation of Rom. 9–11; and Oswald T. Allis, *Prophecy and the Church* (Philadelphia: Presbyterian & Reformed, 1947), 108–10, who affirmed Berkhof's theological position under the olive tree metaphor and his rejection of Darby and Scofield. See also, C. I. Crenshaw and G. Gunn, *Dispensationalism Today, Yesterday, and Tomorrow* (Memphis: Footstool, 1985), 40–57; C. M. Horne, "The Meaning of the Phrase 'And Thus All Israel Will Be Saved' (Romans 11:26)," *JETS* 32 (December 1978): 330.

[77]The phrase is from Heiko A. Obermann, *The Roots of Anti-Semitism: In the Age of Renaissance and Reformation* (Philadelphia: Fortress, 1984), 22. The quotation is from I. John Hesselink, "Calvin's Understanding of the Relation of the Church and Israel Based Largely on His Interpretation of Romans 9–11," in *The People of God*, ed. Markus Barth, JSNTSup 5 (Sheffield: Sheffield Academic Press, 1983), 60. For an interesting complement to Obermann's views, see P. D. L. Avis, *The Church in the Theology of the Reformers* (Atlanta: John Knox, 1981), chap. 13, entitled "The Conversion of the Jews."

substance and foundation of both.[78] Toward the end of his discussion, Calvin introduced his point of critical tension between the persistent unbelief of the Jews and the secure election of the patriarchs: "By this public calling the Gentiles not only were made equal to the Jews, but it also was manifest that they were, so to speak, taking the place of dead Jews."[79] Further development of his position must be derived from his commentary on Romans.[80] There he focuses on tensions between national response and general election as distinguished from individual response and particular election. Key are verses 11, 12, and 26. He stresses both the banishment of Israel because of unbelief and the abiding validity of the inviolable covenant because of God's faithfulness, being expressed through a remnant: "Then they are fallen, and fallen to destruction, who were obstinately offended at Christ, yet the nation is not so fallen, that it should follow of necessity whosoever is a Jew he is lost, or fallen away from God."[81] This can be true, because there is a general election of Israel after the flesh and a particular election of Israel after the Spirit, the former being judicial and the latter effectual.[82] On this basis, Calvin interestingly argues from the olive tree metaphor that all Israel has been generally sanctified in Abraham: "Because the Lord sanctified to himself Abraham upon this condition, that his seed also should be holy, and so put sanctity not only into the person of Abraham, but also into the whole kindred, thereupon Paul doth not reason amiss, that all the Jews were sanctified in their father Abraham."[83] To reconcile the particular aspect of remnant and the general calling of verse 26, Calvin explained "all Israel" as the whole "Israel of God," consisting of

---

[78]John Calvin, *Institutes of the Christian Religion,* ed. J. T. McNeill and trans. F. L. Battles (Philadelphia: Westminster, 1960), 2.9–11, esp. 2.10.2 for the quotation. One of the most important topics for further study is antecedents to the Reformers, notably Augustine. One may consult Larry V. Crutchfield, "Israel and the Church in the Ante-Nicene Fathers," *BSac* 144 (July–September 1987): 254–76; and P. J. Gorday, "The Place of Chapters 9–11 in the Argument of the Epistle to the Romans: A Study of the Romans Exegesis of Origen, John Chrysostom, and Augustine" (Ph.D. diss., Vanderbilt University, 1980). It is generally acknowledged that Justin Martyr was the first author to identify the name *Israel* with the church. See Peter Richardson, *Israel in the Apostolic Church* (Cambridge: Cambridge University Press, 1969), 1, 9–18.

[79]Calvin, *Institutes* 2.11.12.

[80]Hesselink, "Calvin's Understanding," 62, notes that Calvin probably utilized commentaries of Melanchthon, Bullinger, and particularly Bucer. The final edition of the *Institutes* coincided with the final editions of Romans, thus "both have roots in the thought of the young Calvin, but the final editions of both reflect the experience and thought of the reformer at the height of his career."

[81]Calvin, *Romans,* 318.

[82]Ibid., 309 and 312–13; *Institutes* 3.21.6. This distinction corresponds to his agreement with Augustine on a distinction between the visible and invisible church.

[83]Calvin, *Romans,* 322. Though consistent with his theological premises, one wonders how Calvin can maintain the general-particular distinction with the cutting off and regrafting processes? Ultimately, it must be explained as a spiritual people as Calvin does.

the Jewish and Gentile elect: "I extend the name of Israel unto all the people of God, to this sense, when the Gentiles shall be come in, the Jews shall also turn from their defection unto the obedience of faith. . . . In the same manner, to the Galatians, he calleth the Church, consisting together of Jews and Gentiles, the Israel of God, by that opposing the people gathered from the dispersion to the carnal sons of Abraham, who were fallen away from his faith."[84] Thus, Calvin worked from the unity of the covenants to the union of spiritual Israel.

A number of contemporary Reformed scholars agree with the identification of Israel and the church as a single people of God. Their differences are usually on millennarian issues. Millard Erickson's view is that spiritual Israel has "taken the place" of literal Israel, fulfilling some of the promises to literal Israel (e.g., Rom. 9:24–25): "To sum up, then: the Church is the new Israel. It occupies the place in the new covenant which Israel occupied in the old. . . . There is a special future coming for national Israel, however, through large-scale conversion to Christ and entry into the church."[85] Similarly, Anders Nygren states: "According to Paul, the Christian church has its roots in the Old Testament, in God's choice of the fathers. . . . Christians are not a new race; they are rather

---

[84]Ibid., 230. Murray, *Romans* 2:96–97, n. 51, objects to Calvin's appeal to Gal. 6:16, because there is no sustained contrast there between Jews and Gentiles such as we have in Romans. Donald Bloesch, " 'All Israel Will Be Saved': Supersessionism and the Biblical Witness," *Int* 34 (1980): 134: "When Paul confesses that 'all Israel will be saved,' he is indubitably thinking of the future restoration of ethnic Israel. Calvin erred when he interpreted 'all Israel' to mean the sum total of the complete church, Gentile Christians and the remnant of believing Jews." Also, S. Lewis Johnson, Jr., "Paul and 'The Israel of God': An Exegetical and Eschatological Case-Study," in *Essays in Honor of J. Dwight Pentecost,* ed. Stanley D. Toussaint and Charles H. Dyer (Chicago: Moody Press, 1986), 181–96.

[85]Millard J. Erickson, *Christian Theology,* 3 vols. (Grand Rapids: Baker, 1985), 3:1043. Remarkably similar to Erickson is Hans K. LaRondelle, *The Israel of God in Prophecy: Principles of Prophetic Interpretation* (Berrien Springs, Mich.: Andrews University Press, 1983), 125–26, 129–31, and 210. LaRondelle, a Seventh-day Adventist, begins his discussion of Rom. 9–11 by taking issue with dispensationalism's distinction between Israel and the church. The olive tree demonstrates their unity and continuity; however, it is only a spiritual replacement: "It is not correct, therefore, to state that the Church has replaced Israel. Rather, the Church is the continuity of the Old Testament Israel of God; it has only replaced the Jewish nation. Gentile Christians do not constitute a different or separate entity from the faithful remnant of Israel. They are ingrafted into the messianic Israel" (210). LaRondelle places great emphasis on the Hebrew Christian remnant, the people of God, whose increase in the church will be Israel's eschatological fullness through faith in the Deliverer who has come (11:26–27; pp. 130 and 132). See also G. C. Berkouwer, *The Return of Christ,* trans. J. Van Oosterom (Grand Rapids: Eerdmans, 1972), chap. 11, who removes "end-time" apocalyptic mystery. On p. 358 he concludes, "In this outlook on the church as a living sign lies the actuality of Paul's expectation for all Israel in the last days—and the failure of the church to live up to it."

the continuation, the legitimate continuation, of God's Old Testament people."[86]

Anthony Hoekema interprets Romans 11 as a simultaneous tension of Jewish unbelief and jealousy that will result in their mutual salvation with Gentiles, culminating in the Parousia. "The main point of Paul's previous discussion in Romans 11 has been to indicate that God, who in times past dealt almost exclusively with Israel as far as the bringing of salvation to his people was concerned, is now dealing with Jews and Gentiles together."[87] Thus the ingrafting and regrafting occur simultaneously. This is a continual process of faith that is based on the first coming of the Deliverer.[88] Similarly, Palmer Robertson attempts to demonstrate that the chapter's primary focus is on God's dealings with Israel in "the present era of gospel proclamation":[89] "Nothing in the figure of ingrafting necessarily communicates the idea of a distinctive and corporate inclusion of the Jews at some future date."[90] And " 'All Israel' describes all elect people within the community of Israel"[91] that are saved in present-age gospel ministry.

Willem VanGemeren sees an already–not yet tension in Romans 11:

> On the one hand, the apostle Paul clearly saw continuity in the church's relation to the covenants, redemptive history, and the Old Testament people of God. In this sense, the church is the Israel of God (Gal. 6:16). On the other hand, Paul had not yet witnessed the separation of church and synagogue, of Christians from Jews. . . . In the sense of historic and national continuity, Israel is still the people of God, even in their rejection of the Messiah (Rom. 11:15–16). The hope of Israel's repentance and faith in Jesus the Messiah comes from Paul's understanding of Isaiah, according to whom the eschatological moment brings Jews and Gentiles together into one body.[92]

He places the "eschatological moment" beyond the present rejection of Israel to a future acceptance that will usher in a new era.

[86]Anders Nygren, *Commentary on Romans* (Philadelphia: Fortress, 1949), 399–400.

[87]Anthony A. Hoekema, *The Bible and the Future* (Grand Rapids: Eerdmans, 1979), 146.

[88]Ibid., 142–47. Hoekema's distinctive amillennialist position on the new earth came from his recognition of the connection between the people and their promised land (205–13).

[89]O. Palmer Robertson, "Is There a Distinctive Future for Ethnic Israel in Romans 11?" in *Perspectives on Evangelical Theology: Papers from the Thirtieth Annual Meeting of the Evangelical Theological Society* (Grand Rapids: Baker, 1979), 207–27.

[90]Ibid., 216.

[91]Ibid., 225.

[92]William VanGemeren, *The Progress of Redemption: The Story of Salvation from Creation to the New Jerusalem* (Grand Rapids: Zondervan, 1988), 400.

We also note a covenant premillennialist who is relatively close to the dispensational interpretation. George Ladd distinguished "empirical" Israel (the people as a whole, Israel according to natural descent) and "spiritual" Israel (the faithful remnant, the true Israel of faith). Believing Gentiles have been added to the believing remnant, and the olive tree is the union of Israel and the church. "The olive tree is the one people of God. . . . Thus, while God has not finally and irrevocably cast away his people Israel, the church consisting of both Jews and Gentiles has become the branches of the olive tree—the people of God—the true Israel. . . . In view of such statements, it is highly probable that when Paul speaks of the 'Israel of God' (Gal. 6:16) he is referring to the church as the true spiritual Israel."[93] Nevertheless, and here he agrees with dispensationalists, Ladd retains a future fulfillment for ethnic Israel, an eschatological event at the end of the age.

Finally, Vern Poythress concludes that "there is only one holy (cultivated) olive tree, hence one people of God, and one root."[94] However, there is dichotomy at the cross, which establishes a great historical distinction between Israel and the church: "It is the distinction between before and after Christ's resurrection, not a distinction between heavenly and earthly."[95] We must acknowledge that Jews have not lost their distinctive status, and Christ is "Lord of the *community* of God's people, not simply Lord of the individual soul."[96]

Dispensationalists have strongly emphasized distinctions between Israel and the church.[97] But these were dependent upon the more foundational bifurcation between heavenly and earthly people of God.[98]

[93]G. E. Ladd, *A Theology of the New Testament* (Grand Rapids: Eerdmans 1974), 538–39. With VanGemeren, Ladd prefers to avoid explanation of detailed future prophecies. This becomes a rather significant difference with dispensationalists, who emphasized issues like the covenantal land promises. This difference is evident in Daniel Fuller's *Gospel and Law* (Grand Rapids: Eerdmans, 1980), 189–97.

[94]Vern S. Poythress, *Understanding Dispensationalists* (Grand Rapids: Zondervan, 1987), 44.

[95]Ibid., 43.

[96]Ibid., 44.

[97]This has been evident not only to adherents of the system but also its opponents; see Clarence Bass, *Backgrounds to Dispensationalism* (Grand Rapids: Eerdmans, 1960), 18, 24–27. Bass's discussion relates the distinction to two other crucial issues: literal interpretation and God's covenantal commitment to Israel. See Daniel Fuller, "The Hermeneutics of Dispensationalism" (Th.D. diss., Northern Baptist Theological Seminary, 1957), 25. Fuller's *Gospel and Law*, 3, adds the separation of law and grace as the motive behind distinguishing Israel and the church.

[98]J. N. Darby, *The Collected Writings of J. N. Darby*, 34 vols., reprint ed., ed. W. Kelly (Sunbury, Pa.: Believers Bookshelf, 1971), 2:266. According to Craig Blaising, "Developing Dispensationalism" (unpublished paper, Dallas Theological Seminary, 1986), 16, this is the essential doctrine that gives meaning to all of Darby's thought. Blaising's treatment of the subject can also be found in "Development of Dispensationalism by Contemporary Dispensationalists," *BSac* 145 (1988): 133–40 and 254–80.

The church, a heavenly people, is a mystery that could not have been known in the Old Testament era. The present age of the church is a "parenthesis" in God's dispensational economies on earth.[99] Old Testament promises that speak of an earthly kingdom will be fulfilled by Israel, an earthly people, in a millennial kingdom under Christ. But the heavenly church has a different destiny. It will displace wicked angelic hosts and share heavenly glory with Christ as his bride (Ephesians).[100] Thus, the two peoples have a larger comprehensive unity in their destiny in Christ, "mutually enhancing the blessing and joy of each other, yet each has its respective sphere."[101]

Darby's contemporaries generally agreed with him on the heavenly-versus-earthly principle; however, variation in details began to surface. Some, including Darby himself, seemed to have included Old Testament saints in the heavenly realm. And others, such as F. W. Grant, seemed to consider the possible merger of the two peoples in eternity.[102]

Prophecy conferences disseminated the dispensational viewpoint, usually with characteristic unanimity on the two peoples and variations in details. Brookes and Gaebelein, for example, maintained the eternal distinction of the peoples.[103] An author known only as H. W. H., in contrast, taught that the church is revealed in Old Testament types and denied that the church is a mystery or that it exists in a parenthetical period.[104]

The *Scofield Reference Bible* and Chafer's *Systematic Theology* hardened the principle of two peoples for traditional dispensationalism. The strict dichotomies between Israel and the church with distinctive purposes and destinies were more vigorously emphasized.[105] And even the

[99]Darby, *Writings* 14:19; 2:376; 32:41; 33:2. At one point, Darby suggests the death of Stephen as the beginning of the church (1:130).

[100]Ibid. 2:81–82, 267–83, 378; 11:119, 125, 153, 265.

[101]Ibid. 2:123. See also 2:56 and 11:42.

[102]Edwards Dennett, *The Blessed Hope,* reprint ed. (Denver: Wilson Foundation, 1879), 125–26; and F. W. Grant, *The Lessons of the Ages* (New York: Loizeaux Brothers, n.d.), 46–57.

[103]James Brookes, *Maranatha* (New York: Fleming H. Revell, 1899), 401–2 and 521–23; Arno C. Gaebelein, *The Harmony of the Prophetic Word* (New York: Fleming H. Revell, 1907), 167–68. Brookes, *Maranatha,* (pp. 522–23), is emphatic: "If we forget the distinction between an earthly and heavenly people, or in other words, if we lose sight of dispensational truth, where everything is beautiful and well-ordered in its season, we will be thrown into inextricable confusion in attempting to understand the Scripture."

[104]H. W. H., *The Church and the Great Tribulation* (Dublin: R. Stewart, 1906), 18–20 and 42–44. (H. W. H. is all we have of the author's name; such abbreviation was common among some earlier dispensational writers.)

[105]Lewis Sperry Chafer, *Systematic Theology,* 8 vols. (Dallas: Dallas Seminary Press, 1948), 4:34, 47–53; C. I. Scofield, *Rightly Dividing the Word of Truth,* reprint ed. (Findlay, Ohio: Fundamental Truth, 1947), 6; idem., *Scofield Bible Correspondence Course,*

perception of the present age as a parenthesis was felt to be too soft. Chafer preferred to call it an intercalation: "A parenthetical portion sustains some direct and indirect relation to that which goes before or that which follows; but the present age-purpose is not thus related and therefore is more properly termed an *intercalation*."[106] Blaising has noted that Chafer's dualistic synthesis wove his doctrines of ecclesiology, eschatology, and sanctification together with a problematic law-grace result: "Thus for Chafer, a distinction between Israel and the Church *is* a soteriological doctrine (and this in spite of the fact that he has been vindicated, with some difficulty, from the charge of teaching two ways of salvation)."[107] The intercalation, in turn, led to Chafer's advocating two separate new covenants: one for Israel and a present one for the church.[108]

The *New Scofield Reference Bible* and Ryrie's *Dispensationalism Today* refined the system in the 1950s and 1960s. Ryrie asserts an eternal contrast between Israel and the church, but he softens Chafer's strong expression of the dichotomy.[109] He maintains, however, that the distinction is "probably the most basic theological test of whether or not a man is a dispensationalist, and it is undoubtedly the most practical and conclusive."[110] Sauer, McClain, and Pache, however, diminished future distinctions of the two peoples.[111] Blaising records the direction of development in this period precisely:

> What is most amazing is that when we come to the writings of Walvoord, Pentecost, Ryrie, and McClain, which were published in the 50s and 60s, the heavenly/earthly dualistic language is gone! A distinction between Israel and the church is vigorously asserted and all

19th ed. (Chicago: Moody Bible Institute, n.d.), 23–25. In this period, an "ultradispensationalism" also appeared, which subdivided the church in Acts according to ethnic periods. See, for example, E. W. Bullinger, *Foundations of Dispensational Truth* (London: Eyre & Spottiswoode, 1930).

[106]Chafer, *Systematic Theology*, 4:41. See also Charles Ryrie, *The Basis of the Premillennial Faith* (Neptune, N.J.: Loizeaux Brothers, 1953), 127.

[107]Blaising, "Development of Dispensationalism," 275; Chafer, *Systematic Theology*, 4:41.

[108]Chafer, *Systematic Theology* 4:32 and 2:98. Scofield, in contrast, held that the one new covenant had two aspects (*The Scofield Reference Bible* [New York: Oxford University Press, 1909], 1297).

[109]Charles Ryrie, *Dispensationalism Today* (Chicago: Moody Press, 1965), 137–40 and 146–47.

[110]Ibid., 45.

[111]Erich Sauer, *From Eternity to Eternity* (Grand Rapids: Eerdmans, 1951), 82, 89, and 93, held that the Millennium is the inheritance of the church, which will be a "ruling aristocracy" in it. Alan McClain, *The Greatness of the Kingdom* (Winona Lake, Ind.: BMH Books, 1959), 439–41, makes the church the "spiritual nucleus of the Kingdom." René Pache, *The Return of Christ* (Chicago: Moody Press, 1955), 418, suggests that temporal distinctions will disappear in eternity.

the theological structures of distinction are present except that the eternal destinies of the two people now share the same sphere. Consequently, the heavenly/earthly description of the two peoples is dropped."[112]

Contemporary "moderate" dispensationalists have diminishing unanimity about details to the extent that the dichotomy between Israel and the church is "softening."[113] In general, the systemic premises still apply: Israel is not the Old Testament church, and God will fulfill ethnic Israel's promises in the future. Saucy noted that contemporary dispensationalists are united in their insistence on a distinction between Israel and the church, but they are not united on what the distinction is: "There are significant differences as to the extent of their separation in the purposes and programs of God. These differences focus on the relationship of the present Church age with the messianic promises of the Old Testament."[114] In other words, the issue of distinction has been complicated by the increased interest of evangelical scholars in the use of the Old Testament in the New Testament and the hermeneutical implications of the first advent of Christ. Saucy himself denies the existence of two programs for the two peoples, affirming instead that both contribute to God's unified historical purposes.[115]

Robert Gundry has questioned the point of eternal distinction by affirming that the final destinies of Israel and the church converge in the eternal state: "The Scriptures also teach the essential unity of all saints. Dispensational distinctions between God's people are economical and transitory. At a deeper level, all saints enjoy unity in Christ."[116] Affirming this deeper unity, Gundry further argued that ingrafted Gentile believers in Romans 11 "scarcely bespeaks a discrete position

[112]Blaising, "Development of Dispensationalism," 17.

[113]Kenneth L. Barker, "False Dichotomies Between the Testaments," *JETS* 25 (1982): 4, may have been speaking for others in saying, "As I perceive the grand sweep of what God is doing, the old sharp distinction between Israel and the Church begins to become somewhat blurred."

[114]Robert Saucy, "Contemporary Dispensational Thought," *TSFB* 7 (1984): 10. Following this quotation, Saucy used Rom. 11 and Jer. 31 to support his point. See also Blaising, "Development of Dispensationalism," 15.

[115]Robert Saucy, "The Crucial Issue Between Dispensational and Non-Dispensational Systems," *CTR* 1 (1986): 149–65. However, he opts in the end for the "Focal Issue" being "the understanding of that historical plan and the goal of that plan through which God will bring eternal glory to Himself" (156). The plan is "the comprehensive mediatorial kingdom, finally fulfilled through the reign of Christ" (164). One should compare these positions with his earlier work, *The Church in God's Program* (Chicago: Moody Press, 1972), chap. 5.

[116]Robert Gundry, *The Church and the Tribulation* (Grand Rapids: Zondervan, 1973), 21–22. See also W. Robert Cook, *The Theology of John* (Chicago: Moody Press, 1979), 90.

for the Church."[117] He builds on this unity in maintaining a posttribulational Jewish conversion and rapture of the church (11:26–27).[118]

Walvoord, however, uses the same passages from Romans 11 to argue that Israelite believers and Gentile believers are contrasted (9:11), the one never becoming the other, and that Romans 9:6 contrasts spiritual Israel and Israel according to the flesh. Therefore, Israel is to be restored, nationally delivered, and covenantally fulfilled at the Parousia without Gentiles or the church, which will have been raptured before the Tribulation period.[119]

The end of this survey shows that dispensational theologians have consistently distinguished Israel and the church, while dispensationalism has undergone remarkable developments over time in terms of a common destiny in the city of God, a shared new covenant, and, most recently, a recognition by many scholars of a present form of messianic kingdom that removes the parenthetical idea. The dispensational position as a whole must now precisely redefine the distinctiveness and interrelationships of the church within the progressive historical phases of God's kingdom.[120]

Still another approach, the revisionist position, has been concerned with the dysfunctional relationships between Jews and Christians through the centuries. The topic received its impetus in this century from the Holocaust and has focused on Romans 11 in ecumenical discussions.[121] The arrogance that Paul condemned is particularly noted. The tendency has been to redefine the Jewish and Christian vocations away from the supersessionist view toward a position of mutual acceptance and respect.[122] Thus, "nach älterer Tradition (v. Hoffmann,

---

[117]Gundry, *The Church and the Tribulation,* 22.

[118]Ibid., 24, 82, 132, 147 n. 1, 169, 182.

[119]John F. Walvoord, *The Nations, Israel, and the Church in Prophecy* (Grand Rapids: Zondervan, 1988), 57–61; idem, *The Millennial Kingdom* (Grand Rapids: Dunham, 1959), 118, 166–73, 187–92, 213–15, 273–74.

[120]A constructive attempt to wrestle with these issues and to deal with dispensationalism's denigration of the church as God's agency of earthly sanctification is Michael D. Williams, "Where's the Church? The Church as the Unfinished Business of Dispensational Theology," *GTJ* 10 (Fall 1989): 165–82. Craig Blaising, "Dispensationalism at the End of the Twentieth Century" (paper presented to the Evangelical Theology Group of the American Academy of Religion, November 1990), 8, stated: "But the church is seen less and less as a parenthesis in the divine program. Instead it is seen as vitally linked to and comprehended in the plan of God revealed in the Old Testament. It is the next stage, the next dispensation in the accomplishing of that plan and is itself vitally linked to the next historical phase of redemptive history which begins at the second advent of Jesus Christ."

[121]Marcus Barth, ed., *The People of God* (Sheffield: Sheffield Academic Press, 1983), chap. 1, surveys traditional attitudes behind contemporary dialogue and the many approaches, Jewish and Christian, that have been advanced to bridge the gaps.

[122]Bloesch, "All Israel Will Be Saved," 130–31, 136–40; W. D. Davies, *Jewish and Pauline Studies* (Philadelphia: Fortress, 1984), 134ff., which is a reprint of "Paul and the People of Israel," *NTS* 24 (1978): 4–39.

Fr. Delitzsch) war es der besondere Beruf Israels, in seiner alttestament-
lichen Geschichte den Weg Jesu und der christlichen Gemeinde
vorzubereiten."[123] And, "J. Moltmann . . . Israel bleibt, wo es seiner
Berufung treu bleibt, ein Stachel in der Seite der Kirche. Das Dasein
des Juden zwingt dem Christentum den Gedanken auf, daß es selbst
nicht am Ziel angelangt ist, sondern stets auf dem Wege bleibt."[124]
Finally, with reference to Karl Barth, "Für ihn ist das 'Geheimnis' von
Röm 11,25f. wichtig, sowohl seine Zukünftigkeit wie auch sein
Nochnichtgeschehensein."[125]

Barth's position is close to Calvin and the supersessionists, but one
senses a spirit of openness and conciliation. The "great miracle" is the
conversion of the Gentiles after the Resurrection, which was "the event
of the fulfillment of every promise of Israel."[126] It is incomprehensible
that "Israel in its totality is not yet gathered to the Church," because
"Israel is foreordained to be the Church, and finally to be revealed as the
Church, with the revelation of its Messiah, being merged in the Church
as its proper and final form."[127]

An interesting result of the revisionists' work is a renewed interest in
the apostolic setting that has elevated Romans 9–11 to a position of
central importance for Paul's self-perception.[128]

CONCLUSION

In expounding Romans 11, we have seen the text used as support for
very different and sometimes polarizing positions. This or any similar
study will not solve the problems or bridge the gaps for more than a few
readers. However, I wish to encourage every reader to believe that
Romans 11 will yield the riches of God's wisdom. Everyone acknowledges its importance, but in Christian traditions it has been proof-texted
or neglected more than it has been thoughtfully interpreted and applied.
With a more profound reading, one could expect a renewed appreciation of the roots of Israel for all believers and a measure of
rapprochement for the many groups that love their Messiah with their
hearts, souls, and minds.

---

[123]Otto Michel, *Der Brief an die Römer* (Göttingen: Vandenhoeck & Ruprecht, 1955),
362.
[124]Ibid.
[125]Ibid.
[126]Barth, *CD* II/2, 298.
[127]Ibid.
[128]Krister Stendahl, *Paul Among Jews and Gentiles* (Philadelphia: Fortress, 1976). For
critique of Stendahl, note Scott Hafemann, "The Salvation of Israel in Romans 11:25–32:
A Response to Krister Stendahl," *ExA* 4 (1988): 38–58; S. R. Haynes, " 'Recovering the
Real Paul': Theology and Exegesis in Romans 9–11," ibid., 70–84.

We leave the study with a sense of the need for newness as we think further about the people of God in this chapter. First, there is the need for *a new terminology* that more adequately expresses the complexity of Romans 9–11. One senses that there is a fear of "complexity" in some circles because it might interfere with "clarity" and the perspicuous understanding of various constituencies and their traditional conflicts. However, complexity does not militate against clarity, especially if it more precisely describes the Scriptures. Are Israel and the church one or two peoples? We began the chapter with a definition of ethnic Israel. There one could begin to see the different levels of meaning in the name *Israel*. Likewise, this question contains different categories like times and history, theological differences in purpose, and personal and corporate identities. This can be seen in the relationship of past and present ages. The remnant is historically continuous, but its stages are distinctive. Paul's reference to Elijah was designed to prove the continuity of past and present remnants (v. 5). This, in turn, proved that Israel's hardening was only partial. When Gentiles were grafted into the olive tree, God was sovereignly working in continuity with his saving plan. There is only one olive tree in Paul's metaphor. However, in time and history the Gentile ingrafting was discontinuous (vv. 16–21). There was a time when they were not in the tree as an ethnic people. Since Paul is addressing Jewish unbelief in Messiah's and his own generations, Pentecost can be implied with its consequences for Jewish and Gentile perceptions of the people of God (cf. Acts and Eph. 2). This discontinuity was so profound that it raised questions about God's rejection of his covenant people (Rom. 11:1, 11). It provided the background situation in the Roman church for the composition of the letter. Also, when the Gentiles were grafted into the tree, they did not assume the historical purpose of Israel. Israel's purpose by implication (cf. 9:3–8) was to bring salvific riches to this fallen world. If Israel was to provoke Gentiles to faith (in a sense like Deut. 4:5–8), it still did not result in God's rejecting his covenant nation forever. The Gentile and apostolic provocation assumes the unique aspects of Israel's history that cast a covenantal, sovereign commitment over the whole chapter. Jews and Gentiles are united in the same body of Christ (by implication here), but they are mutually dependent and ethnically distinct.[129] Their identities, even in the church, do not merge. The ingrafting does not take the place of a necessary regrafting in the plan of God. Thus, one must be careful to use terminology that precisely describes both the continuities and discontinuities of the tree. One must avoid a simplistic either-or that dishonors the text when both-and is more precise.

---

[129]Barth, "One God, One Christ, One People," 11.

227

Second, the latter point leads us to the need for *a new sophistication* in thinking about the people(s) of God. Again, we face a both-and situation. The chapter clearly teaches a single people of God in three senses. First, there is a single covenantal base. Father Abraham is the basis of children of the flesh, children of the promise, and children of faith (cf. 9:6–8 with Gal. 3:6–9). There may be many branches, but there is only one root. In the plan of God it was apparently necessary for the apostle to the Gentiles to be a Hebrew Christian (Rom. 11:13). Second, there is only one elect people of faith. The basis of salvation can only be by grace through faith in God (v. 1). Works *never* work for salvation. There is only one true, living God. There can, therefore, be only one way to relate to him salvifically. Third, related to the above, Paul strategically uses "all" people to refer to a state of disobedience that is dependent on the mercy of God (v. 32).[130]

Just as surely, however, the chapter clearly teaches a diverse people of God. To compare Israel and the church in terms of Romans 11 can be a category mistake, unless one carefully qualifies the comparisons. For example, does Israel equal the Jews in Romans 9–11? Israel as a national entity is bifurcated at least once (9:8). One can hardly overemphasize the fact that the church is never mentioned per se in this chapter. The chapter is about how ethnic parts of the church related to each other in the history of salvation, and the parts are never confused; the natural branches never become wild branches or vice versa. It is simplistic to say that the church and Israel are the same except for institutional differences, or that the distinction between Jew and Gentile has been abolished in the one body of Christ. The church and Israel are the respective theocratic agencies in their respective ages, but they have substantial differences that must be integrated into any comparison. It is best to say that Israel did not become the church. Jews and Gentiles were uniquely joined as believers in a new entity that did not abolish distinctive identities and purposes.

Paul is a specific case in point. In the church age, when Gentiles are fellow heirs, fellow members, and fellow partakers (Eph. 3:6), he still referred to the Jews and "his people" (Rom. 11:1–2), identified himself as a Hebrew Christian (v. 1), and prioritized the Jews in ministry (1:16; 11:14).[131]

Third, there is the need for *a new perspective* in view of the progression of Romans 11. This can be seen in the relationship of

---

[130]Leon Morris, *New Testament Theology* (Grand Rapids: Zondervan, 1986), 31.

[131]Cf. Barth, "One God, One Christ, One People," 9. Contra Moxnes, *Theology in Conflict*, 86, Paul does not seem to be concerned with whether Jews or Gentiles have a greater advantage in position. He seems to be concerned that both entities come to faith.

present and future ages. The present Jewish remnant is part of the church (i.e., Hebrew Christians). It represents the residual continuum that Israel's hardness is only partial. The ingrafting process relates the riches of the Gentiles to their fullness (vv. 12, 25). The fullness of the Gentiles signals the fullness of the Jews (vv. 12, 26). In the process, in Barth's words, they are "a people in contradiction,"[132] beloved enemies (v. 28). The present ingrafting by provocation leads to regrafting (v. 24). Thus, there is an "already" dimension to a necessary future, when God's irrevocable promises are fulfilled. It is reasonable to infer (cf. 2 Cor. 3) that a significant part of the provocation of Israel is the present blessing of Gentiles under the new-covenant provisions of Calvary. Again, there is only one covenantal basis for blessing the world.

Again, like Pentecost, there is discontinuity in the future. An indefinite fullness of the Gentiles must occur before all Israel is saved. Israel's history is not yet fulfilled. There is a future transition in history at the Parousia when the nation will enjoy what only a remnant has presently experienced. By the mercy of God, it will be all of that and more.

Therefore, I would suggest constructive writing and dialogue that will align theological commitment and text in a greater sophistication of terminology, especially when one discusses the topics of the people of God and eschatology. With Paul, one best closes with doxology, trusting him for his sovereignty over these and other matters.

---

[132]Barth, "One God, One Christ, One People," 12.

CHAPTER 7

Christ, the End of the Law in Romans 10:4

David K. Lowery

Paul uses the word *end* in this passage in the sense of supersession. The "law," the focus of righteousness in the old-covenant era of salvation history, has been superseded by the revelation of Christ and the era of the new covenant that he instituted.

Israel failed in refusing to recognize Christ as the righteousness of God, revealing in word and deed the will of God in a new era of salvation history. As Paul sees it, this shows that Israel misunderstood the provisional nature of the law and, by clinging to the precepts of a former era, failed to obtain the righteousness of God.

THE MEANING OF SIGNIFICANT TERMS

The meaning of Romans 10:4 is a great stimulus for discussion among students of the New Testament.[1] As in any kind of interpretation, particular terms require definition before significant discussion can take place. I discuss here the meaning of five key words that are relevant to an understanding of Paul's statement.

Christ

What Paul means by *Christ* is clear enough.[2] It is that Jesus is the Messiah, the promised son of David (Rom. 1:3), whom Israel, for the most part, rejected. As Paul says in the context preceding his statement in 10:4, drawing a phrase from Isaiah 8:14, Israel stumbled over the "stumbling stone" (Rom. 9:32). They turned away from Jesus and his

---

[1]Cf. R. Badenas, *Christ the End of the Law: Romans 10.4 in Pauline Perspective* (Sheffield: JSOT Press, 1985).

[2]The Christology of Romans, however, is not without controversy. Cf. C. E. B. Cranfield, "Some Comments on Professor J. D. G. Dunn's Christology in the Making, with Special Reference to the Evidence of the Epistle to the Romans," in *The Glory of Christ in the New Testament*, ed. L. Hurst and N. Wright (Oxford: Oxford University Press, 1987), 267–80.

message and failed to recognize him as the Christ, the one who in the purpose of God accomplished redemption for all humankind (3:24–25).

Righteousness

The meaning of *righteousness* is somewhat more complex, since it can refer either to an attribute that is characteristic of a person or to an attribute that is ascribed to a person. In the first instance, the character of both God and humankind can be described as righteous to the extent that they do what they say they will do. In this sense, righteousness "is a concept of relationship and he who is righteous has fulfilled the demands laid upon him by the relationship in which he stands."[3] In the context of the Old Testament, the Mosaic covenant gave definition to that relationship. The righteousness of the community was manifested when they carried out their covenant obligations, and the righteousness of God was reflected similarly.[4]

Righteousness as a characteristic or manner of life is therefore determined by faithfulness to revelation. In the era of the old covenant, although the expectation for Israel is expressed at various places in the literature of the Old Testament, it is primarily embodied in the Mosaic legislation. The expectations for the church are variously set forth in the literature of the New Testament.

When Paul considers righteousness as an attribute of God, he finds it demonstrated in various ways. The fact that God is true to his word despite human unfaithfulness is, for Paul, an illustration of God's righteousness (3:3–5). So too, God punishes sin, as he said he would do, and this also, for Paul, serves as a demonstration of God's righteousness (3:25–26; cf. 2:5–6).[5]

With human beings the situation is different. At the beginning of a summation concluding his argument about the guilt before God of all humanity, Jew and Gentile alike, Paul quotes Ecclesiastes 7:20, "No one is righteous, not even one" (3:10). An unrelenting catena of Old Testament texts follows, portraying the desperate plight of humankind (3:19–20). It is a polemical portrait, meant to undermine any sense of presumption about one's standing before God and to elicit from all the cry, "Have mercy on me, a sinner" (Luke 18:13).

Paul does believe that people are able to live righteously (6:18), but it is due to the enablement of God (15:5; 16:25–26), which in the present era derives from unity with Christ (8:1–2) and the provision of the

---

[3]E. Achtemeier, "Righteousness in the Old Testament," in *IDB* 4:80.

[4]Cf. W. Eichrodt, *Theology of the Old Testament*, trans. J. A. Baker, 2 vols. (London: SCM, 1961), 1:241–42.

[5]Certainly in this sense at least, the gospel that Paul proclaims "upholds the law" (3:31).

Spirit (8:4, 13). One can therefore live a life that is pleasing to God and in accordance with his will (14:17–18); to a large degree the substance of chapters 12–16 provides definition concerning the form that this righteousness should take in the course of everyday life.

The first part of this letter, however, of which 10:4 is a part, is primarily occupied with righteousness as an ascribed attribute (though cf. 6:12–13, which anticipates 12:1–2). That is, it is God who credits righteousness to believers, a declaration by grant, as it were, of right standing before him (3:22, 26). It is not something that can be humanly achieved (3:20, 28; 4:2). Rather, it must be received (5:17).

Faith

The means by which this righteousness (in both its aspects) is received from God is faith (3:22, 28; 6:11). Faith accepts as true the revelation of God, trusting that God will do what he says he will do despite circumstances or appearances to the contrary (e.g., 4:18–21).

Faith has both internal and unseen dimensions as well as external and verifiable dimensions. Paul refers to aspects of both at 10:10: "It is with your heart that you believe and are justified, and it is with your mouth that you confess and are saved." In this instance, confession is cited as one expression of faith, the external corollary to the unseen and internal belief of the heart.[6]

With regard to both aspects of righteousness (ascribed or as a manner of life), faith accepts as true what God says. With regard to righteousness as an ascription, faith acknowledges human failure to do the will of God ("all have sinned and fall short of the glory of God," 3:23) and the necessity of relying upon God's mercy, expressed in Jesus' sacrifice of atonement (3:24–25; 4:25), to escape condemnation (in brief, calling on the name of the Lord to be saved [10:13]).

With regard to righteousness as a manner of life, faith accepts as true the fact that to be united with Christ means that one has been set free from the authority of sin so that one is able to live a life characterized by righteousness (6:6, 18). The enabling agent for this manner of life is the Spirit (7:6; 8:2).

In short, Paul sees righteousness as a manner of life, or obedience to the will of God, as the external aspect of faith. That is why he can speak of his ministry as calling people to "the obedience that comes from faith" (1:5; 15:16–17). That he thinks of faith and obedience as two aspects of a single reality is also illustrated by a comparison of his words of commendation to the Romans. In 1:8, he expresses thanks to God

---

[6]His word to the Galatians about "faith expressing itself in love" (5:6) is another illustration of faith's visible corollary.

that their "faith is being reported all over the world." In the parallel word of commendation at 16:19, he says that "everyone has heard about your obedience, so I am full of joy over you."

Faith, therefore, is the means by which both aspects of righteousness are experienced, because both derive from God. This is so not only with regard to righteousness as a declaration of right standing before God but also with regard to righteousness as a manner of life that corresponds to or fulfills the will of God. This is summarized at 1:17, where Paul refers to the righteousness that comes from God as a "righteousness that is by faith from first to last, just as it is written: 'The righteous shall live by faith.'"[7]

Law

What Paul usually means when he refers to the law is illustrated at 7:7, where he says, "I would not have known what it was to covet if the law had not said, 'Do not covet'" (Ex. 20:17; Deut. 5:21). The "law" is the legislation belonging to the old covenant, primarily contained in the Pentateuch, though expressed in other parts of the Old Testament as well. It is, however, a term with more controversy regarding its meaning than those previously considered.

In some passages, for example, Paul seems to use *law* to refer to a norm or principle, similar to the way one might refer to the "law of gravity" (e.g., 7:21: "So I find this law at work: when I want to do good, evil is right there with me").[8] This use of the term is debated, however, and for purposes of this chapter may be left aside, since it does not figure in the discussion of the meaning of "law" at 10:4 (or in the immediate context, 9:30–10:13).

What Paul means by *law* and how he understands its role is discovered both by what he says about it and also by how he uses it in the development of his message. A passage such as 3:10–18, for example, shows that Paul can use the term with reference to the testimony of the Old Testament generally concerning human behavior.[9]

---

[7]It is common in Greek syntax to find that the prepositional phrase ("by faith") modifies the verb ("shall live") rather than the noun ("the righteous"). Although the prepositional phrase has been seen as functioning adjectivally ("the righteous by faith," e.g., C. E. B. Cranfield, *A Critical and Exegetical Commentary on the Epistle to the Romans*, ICC, 2 vols. [Edinburgh: T. & T. Clark, 1975–79], 1:101–2), which gives more of an eschatological orientation to the verb, the arguments put forward for this reading are not compelling. Cf. H. Cavallin, "The Righteous Shall Live by Faith," *ST* 32 (1978): 33–43.

[8]Cf. H. Räisänen, "Sprachliches zum Spiel des Paulus mit Nomos," in *Glaube und Gerechtigkeit*, ed. J. Kiilunen et. al. (Helsinki: PFES, 1983), 131–54.

[9]The judicial connection to thought or deeds is noteworthy, since apart from this function Paul seems to avoid using the term *law* with reference to the Old Testament Scriptures as a whole. Paul's reference in 1 Cor. 14:21, in which he cites Isa. 28:11–12 with the words "in the Law it is written," is no exception to this, since the passage in Isaiah

The texts cited are drawn from the Psalms, Proverbs, Ecclesiates, and Isaiah, but when he refers to their cumulative message at 3:19, he uses the phrase "whatever the law says."

He uses the law, in this instance, in what might be called a diagnostic sense, to show the guilt of all humankind before God. It is an illustration of his understanding that "through the law we become conscious of sin" (3:20). Or as he says at 7:7, "I would not have known what sin was except through the law." The law thus primarily serves to specify the will of God, and to define the weal or woe that accompanies its performance. Paul also refers to some of the ethical stipulations of the law to give definition to his contention that Christian behavior is not contrary to the law ("he who loves his fellow man has fulfilled the law," 13:8–10; cf. Gal 5:14, 22).

Despite these instances where the continued relevance of the law's message seems to be accepted, Paul says things elsewhere that suggest that he regards the law as provisional, as inextricably linked to an era of salvation history that has been superseded by the coming of Christ and the ministry of the new covenant, mediated by the Spirit.

His remarks at 7:4 and 6 are a case in point. He says that Christians have "died to the law through the body of Christ," and "by dying to what once bound us, we have been released from the law so that we serve in the new way of the Spirit, and not in the old way of the written code." It might be suggested that Paul is not here speaking of the law as it is, but of the law misunderstood or misapplied.[10] However congenial this explanation might be for harmonizing Paul's varied statements about the law,[11] it fails in at least one respect with regard to his remarks at 7:4 and 6—the references to the law are unqualified. He speaks simply of being released from the law, without qualification or modification.[12]

---

echoes Deut. 28:49 concerning the consequences of disobeying the law. When this distinction is lost sight of and "law" is equated with the Old Testament Scriptures generally (e.g., Cranfield, *Romans* 2:845–70), no little confusion results.

[10]It has been argued, for example, that when Paul uses the phrase "works of the law," he is not referring to sincere acts of devotion to God but rather to legalistic abuse of the law (D. Fuller, *Gospel and Law: Contrast or Continuum?* [Grand Rapids: Eerdmans, 1980], 89–102). It is problematic, however, that no pejorative sense is attached to the use of similar phrases in the literature of Judaism (cf. D. Moo, " 'Law,' 'Works of the Law,' and Legalism in Paul," *WTJ* 45 [1983]: 73–100).

[11]As one who once maintained this position has said, "It is tempting to try to reconcile his statements by saying that what he abandons is not the Torah itself but a 'legalistic' abuse of it." He thinks now, however, that "it is doubtful whether this proposal can be sustained" (C. F. D. Moule, "Jesus, Judaism, and Paul," in *Tradition and Interpretation in the New Testament,* ed. G. Hawthorne and O. Betz [Grand Rapids: Eerdmans, 1987], 48).

[12]This lack of qualification is a problem also for the view that Christians are released from the curse of the law (F. Thielmann, *From Plight to Solution: A Jewish Framework to Understanding Paul's View of the Law in Galatians and Romans* [Leiden: E. J. Brill, 1989],

The illustration from marriage that begins the chapter (7:1−3) shows that being released from the law means being released from the authority, or the rule and reign (κυριεύει, v. 1), of the law. When he says that the authority of the law has come to an end for the Christian, he does so in language reminiscent of his assertion that the authority of sin has been broken, expressed in the immediately preceding section of the letter (6:6, 18; cf. 5:21).

So analogous is this development of thought, in fact, that a reader might conclude that Paul thinks of the law and sin as one and the same thing (7:7). But Paul seeks to avoid this fallacy by showing that while he may regard the relationship of the Christian to sin and to the law as analogous, he does not regard sin and the law as equal (in this case, equally pernicious) entities. On the contrary, the law as a revelation of the will of God is "holy, righteous and good" (7:12). The problem or deficiency is anthropological; it is human, not revelatory or divine. For Paul, the problem is that while the law reveals the will of God for humankind, its subjects are constitutionally incapable of carrying it out, and it has not within itself the capacity to endue its subjects with the ability to perform its directives (cf. 8:3). The dilemma is summarily stated in 7:14: "the law is spiritual; but I am unspiritual."

The result, according to Paul, is that while the law shows sin to be sin (3:20; 4:15b; 5:13; 7:7, 13), it also exacerbates the dispositon to sin that characterizes the human condition (5:20; 7:5, 8−9) and lays bare the wretchedness of humanity's plight (3:19; 4:15a; 7:23−24).[13] This is of course but one aspect of the law's function. Yet the recurrence of this theme (notably in the passages mentioned in the previous paragraph) underscores the importance that Paul attaches to rightly appreciating human impotence in the face of divine revelation and must be borne in mind when a statement like 10:4 is considered.

End

The word commonly translated "end" (*telos*) in the statement of 10:4 can be understood in the sense of "termination"[14] or "conclusion," or "goal" or "result." The alternatives are not entirely disparate. The meaning "goal" or "result" might also carry with it some sense of

72−76, 116−19) or from its condemnation (B. Martin, *Christ and the Law in Paul* [Leiden: E. J. Brill, 1989], 144).

[13]The recognition of this dilemma was not unique to Paul. Israel's failure to fulfill the law is regularly addressed in the Old Testament and Jewish literature. Cf. Thielmann, *From Plight to Solution*, 28−45.

[14]*Telos* occurs thirteen times in literature traditionally regarded as Pauline, but only once (1 Tim. 1:5) does it clearly mean "goal."

"termination" or "conclusion," since the realization of a goal often implies the obsolesence of the antecedent(s).[15]

A prophecy, for example, that found its fulfillment in the life and ministry of Jesus would, in the achievement of its end, at the same time be rendered obsolete. Such is the case with Micah 5:2, for example, which Matthew (2:6) cites in connection with Jesus' birth in Bethlehem of Judea. In achieving its "goal," the applicability of the prophecy has come to an "end"; it no longer awaits fulfillment and to that extent can be spoken of as "prophetically obsolete" (cf. Luke 22:37, "It is written: 'And he was numbered with the transgressors'; and I tell you this must be fulfilled in me. Yes, what is written about me is reaching its fulfillment [*telos*]").

If the law is to be understood as that which defined righteousness in one era in the history of salvation, as Paul seems to describe it in 5:14, it can similarly be said to be "salvifically obsolete" in view of Christ's coming and the ministry he carried out. The old covenant has been superseded by the new. With the initiation of the new, the old is rendered obsolete. Therefore, one can agree with the affirmation that "in Christ the law in its promise of righteousness reaches its goal,"[16] while also understanding that the implications of that fact mean that an era characterized by the authority of the law has come to an end.[17]

This seems to be Paul's viewpoint in 7:4 and 6, illustrated by the woman who remarried after the death of her former spouse (7:1–3). The death of the spouse brought one marital era to an end. That being the case, she could enter freely into another relationship.

A similar viewpoint, though employing a different illustration, is expressed in the letter to the Galatians (3:24–25). There Paul compares the law to a schoolboy's overseer, whose authority ends when the era of tutorial instruction comes to close. The law, says Paul, functioned in a similar capacity until the coming of Christ.[18] With the coming of Christ, what he said and did became the focus of faith, and the authority of the

---

[15]Cf. BAGD, 811(1c). E. Käsemann in his *Commentary on Romans* (Grand Rapids: Eerdmans, 1980), 282, rightly says that "the message of the New Testament soon would no longer be recognizable if exegesis were allowed to exploit every linguistic possibility," but he overstates the matter when he says that "Paul does not leave the least room for attempts of this kind," with regard to *telos* here. Cf. S. Wedderburn ("Paul and the Law," *SJT* 38 [1985]: 613–22, esp. 615) on this point and the acknowledgment by H. Räisänen (*Paul and the Law*, 2d ed. [Tübingen: Mohr, 1987], 53).

[16]C. T. Rhyne, "Nomos Dikaiosynes and the Meaning of Romans 10:4," *CBQ* 47 (1985): 493. "Promise" should be read in light of the conditional sense attached to legislative statements like Lev. 18:5 (the one who does this [i.e., if you do this, then you] will live).

[17]Cf. W. Gutbrod, "νόμος," *TDNT* 4:1075–78; Käsemann, *Romans*, 282–83; J. Dunn, *Romans 9–16*, WBC (Waco, Tex.: Word, 1988), 596–97.

[18]Cf. D. Lull, "The Law Was Our Pedagogue," *JBL* 105 (1986): 481–98, esp. 497–98.

law came to an end. Paul puts it summarily to the Galatians this way: "Now that faith has come, we are no longer under the supervision of the law" (Gal. 3:25).

The contrast between faith and law recurs also in the context surrounding Romans 10:4, and attention ma ; now be turned to the hermeneutical issues that come to bear upon Paul's statement.

A DISCUSSION OF ROMANS 10:4 IN ITS CONTEXT

The statement in 10:4 occurs in the context of a discussion concerning the contrasting situation of Israel and the Gentiles with regard to righteousness (9:30–10:13). Some Gentiles, Paul says, find themselves in the position of receiving by faith that for which they did not strive (9:30; cf. 10:20), while many in Israel, although diligently pursuing this same goal, do not attain it (9:31; cf. 10:21). Why not? The answer is that in the purpose of God the righteousness made possible by Christ is not something to be achieved (5:17). It may be received, and the instrumentality for doing so is faith (3:22); but it cannot be achieved.

This contention seems to be at the heart of Paul's contrast of faith and works (9:32). Many in Israel are diligently pursuing the law, which gives definition to what constitutes a status of righteousness before God (9:31).[19] But the stipulations of the law are not attained (cf. 3:23).

These verses (9:30–32) are a demonstration of the thesis stated previously in the letter: "Now when a man works, his wages are not credited to him as a gift, but as an obligation. However, to the man who does not work but trusts God who justifies the ungodly, his faith is credited as righteousness" (4:4–5). There are Gentiles who do not work, but they obtain righteousness.[20] In contrast, many in Israel show great zeal in the pursuit of righteousness (cf. 10:2) but do not attain to it. This is related to the conviction, affirmed earlier in chapter 9, that the plan and purpose of God is not something that is subject to the dictates of human will or endeavor. Without equivocation, Paul says simply that what God does is not a matter of human will or effort (9:16).[21]

In the purpose of God, Jesus became the agent of God's righteousness in the present time (3:25–26). It is the failure to recognize this, however, which Paul regards as the singular failing of Israel. As he says at 10:3, "Since they did not know the righteousness that comes from

---

[19]The relative clause in this sentence is an attempt to express the meaning of the genitive "righteousness" in the phrase "law of righteousness."

[20]The "righteousness" that the Gentiles obtain is synonymous with "salvation" (10:1, 10).

[21]Note the use made of athletic terms in both passages to underscore the level of exertion (cf. τρέκω, v. 16, and διώκω, vv. 30–31).

God and sought to establish their own, they did not submit to God's righteousness." Yet the citation of Isaiah 28:16 and 8:14 at 9:33 is a reminder that though Israel is responsible for failing to recognize Jesus as the Christ, their situation is nevertheless part of the plan of God ("I lay in Zion a stumbling stone"; cf. 9:6).[22]

The contrast of faith and works shows up also in the verses that immediately follow 10:4. According to Paul (at 10:5, citing Lev. 18:5), "Moses describes in this way the righteousness that is by the law: 'The man who does these things will live by them.' But the righteousness that is by faith says . . . ," and there follows a selection of Old Testament citations that ends with Isaiah 28:16 (earlier cited at 9:33): "Everyone who trusts in him will never be put to shame" (10:11).

It seems clear that Paul regards the law as fundamentally concerned with "doing," but the gospel, which has Christ as its object, essentially a matter of "believing." This is borne out by comparison with a kindred passage in Galatians where Paul also cites Leviticus 18:5 to the same effect: "The law is not based on faith; on the contrary, 'The man who does these things will live by them'" (Gal. 3:12).[23]

Paul's handling of the texts from Deuteronomy 30:12–14 at Romans 10:6–8 is also relevant to the thesis that what Christ said and did supersedes the role performed by the law in ministry of the old covenant. In the passage from Deuteronomy, Paul has replaced a focus on the law with a focus on Christ and the gospel.[24] While this may seem to be a curious method of scriptural citation,[25] it is entirely consistent with Paul's conviction that the role and place of the law has been superseded by Christ and the gospel.

His discussion of the old and new covenants in 2 Corinthians 3 illustrates this as well. In the time frame of salvation history, the law had, as it were, its day in the sun. As Paul says, "It came with glory, so that the Israelites could not look steadily at the face of Moses because of its glory, fading though it was. . . . If the ministry that condemns men is glorious, how much more glorious is the ministry that brings righteous-

---

[22]The affirmation of both human responsibility and also divine intent is similarly expressed at 1 Peter 2:8, where these texts from Isaiah are again collocated with this commentary: "They stumble because they disobey the message—which is also what they were destined for."

[23]Cf. H. D. Betz, *Galatians* (Philadelphia: Fortress, 1979), 147–48.

[24]Cf. J. Aageson, "Typology, Correspondence, and the Application of Scripture in Romans 9–11," *JSNT* 31 (1987): 51–72, esp. 63.

[25]Dunn gives examples of the free handling of this passage in Jewish literature (*Romans 9–16*, 604–5) and thinks that "although Paul clearly does rechannel the thrust of the passage in accordance with his own theological insight, the possibility and propriety of his so doing would therefore not necessarily have been a subject of controversy" (605). Cf. J. Aageson, "Scripture and Structure in the Development of the Argument in Romans 9–11," *CBQ* 48 (1986): 265–89, esp. 274–76.

ness" (2 Cor. 3:7, 9). In its day, the law was a glorious phenomenon, the focus of God's revelatory self-disclosure to humankind. But the focus has changed. It has moved on or progressed to Christ, to what he has said and done. The idea of supersession is contained in these words of Paul from the same passage: "And if what was fading away came with glory, how much greater is the glory of that which lasts!" (v. 11).

Israel's pursuit of a righteousness in accordance with the stipulations of the law (Rom. 9:31; 10:3) is related to another question concerning the relationship of Christ and the law: Does Paul think it is humanly possible to obtain a status of righteousness according to the law? The answer is no, if two passages in Romans are taken at face value.[26] At Romans 3:19–20 he says this: "Now we know that what the law says, it says to those who are under the law, so that every mouth may be silenced and the whole world held accountable to God. Therefore no one will be declared righteous in his sight by observing the law; rather, through the law we become conscious of sin." The phrases "every mouth," "whole world," and "no one" express the universal dimension of Paul's conviction. More individualistic, but equally dire, is the portrayal of human inability to fulfill the law given at 7:7–25, which contains these words: "For in my inner being I delight in God's law; but I see another law at work in the members of my body, waging war against the law of my mind and making me a prisoner of the law of sin at work within my members. What a wretched man I am! Who will rescue me from the body of this death?" (vv. 22–24).

Some interpreters of Paul, however, find him equivocal on the issue of human ability to carry out the stipulations of the law, pointing to his remarks in Romans 2 as an indication of the fact that he believed some people (in this case, Gentiles) could do so.[27] Confusion on this point, however, may be due to a failure both to grant Paul some recognition of ethical gradation in his comments on humanity and also to see that his reference to ethical Gentiles occurs in the context of an accusatory passage focusing on Israel, the purpose of which is to substantiate the just condemnation of all people.

When, for example, he says that "all have sinned and fall short of the glory of God" (3:23), it need not be presumed that he regarded all humanity as failing in the same degree. Some individuals may plumb the depths more profoundly than others. Or to put it more positively, some

---

[26]Two passages in Galatians are equally to the point: "if righteousness could be gained through the law, Christ died for nothing" (2:21); and "if a law had been given which could impart life, then righteousness would certainly have come by the law" (3:21).

[27]Cf. Räisänen, *Paul and the Law*, 94–127; K. Snodgrass, "Justification by Grace—To the Doers: An Analysis of the Place of Romans 2 in the Theology of Paul," *NTS* 32 (1986): 72–93.

may rise to higher ethical planes than others, yet still fail to gain the approval of God.

In the nature of the case, some people will therefore exhibit a higher degree of conformity to the law than others. This seems, in fact, to be the gist of his argument in chapter 2 when he maintains that there are Gentiles whose manner of life, though unenlightened by a written revelation, more clearly manifests the will of God than some of those in Israel.[28] It is not necessary to conclude that Paul regards the more ethical manner of life of these Gentiles as in fact gaining thereby the approval of God, since in the development of his brief argument, he intends to arrive at the conclusion that "there is no one righteous, not even one" (3:10).

It does seem, however, that at one time Paul regarded the stipulations of law as achievable. What he wrote to the Philippians suggests this. In the third chapter of that letter is a passage that is remarkably similar in style and substance to what he says in Romans 10:2–5. In Philippians he writes with regard to himself, but what he says there about his former beliefs and manner of life he says also with regard to the situation of his kinsman in Israel, whose plight is the object of his concern in Romans 10. As Paul sees it, they retain the viewpoint that he himself maintained before his encounter with Christ on the Damascus road. He says, for example, in Philippians 3:6, that at one time he regarded himself, in terms of the righteousness stipulated by the law, as blameless (ἄμεμπτος).[29] A few verses later (3:9), he refers to "a righteousness of my own which comes from the law,"[30] an echo of the sentiments expressed in verse 6. Similar phraseology is employed at Romans 10:5, "the righteousness that is by the law," whereupon Leviticus 18:5 is quoted, "The man who does these things will live by them." It would appear, on the basis of his statement in Philippians 3:6,

---

[28]Reference to Gentiles whose manner of life serves to condemn Israel is found also in the teaching of Jesus (Matt. 12:41–42; Luke 11:31–32). In similar fashion (though stated negatively), Ezekiel (16:51–52) says that in comparison to Israel the Samaritans "appear righteous."

[29]There is no reason to regard this assessment as extraordinary. Luke says the same thing about Elizabeth and Zechariah (1:6), though Zechariah is censured subsequently for lack of faith (1:20). Read as a statement of scrupulosity on matters subject to measurement, the tithers of mint and cummin, who are warned at Matt. 23:23, might also be called blameless, though obviously remiss in grander, unquantifiable matters—justice, mercy, faithfulness. Cf. J. Espy, "Paul's 'Robust Conscience' Re-examined," *NTS* 31 (1985): 161–81.

[30]In both Phil. 3:6, 9 and Rom. 10:5 Paul uses an article to show that the prepositional phrases which follow the noun *righteousness* should be construed as modifying the noun in an adjectival sense (rather than the modification of the verb, which prepositional phrases more commonly do). At Phil. 3:6, 9 he uses the phrases *en nomō* and *ek nomou* respectively, with similar meaning. At Rom. 10:5 the phrase is *ek tou nomou*, as at Phil. 3:9 (since the article with *nomos* does not materially affect the meaning of the term).

that Paul believed he did this. His statement to the Philippians suggests that he had no reservations about himself in this regard. He gives no indication that it was pangs of conscience or dismay at his inability to fulfill the law that brought him to recognize Jesus as the Christ. Instead, as he says to the Philippians (3:6), his zeal for God led him to persecute the church (cf. Acts 22:3–4). Similarly at Romans 10:2, Paul says with regard to his kinsman in Israel, "I can testify about them that they have a zeal for God, but their zeal is not based on knowledge." It is a zeal Paul knew well, related to a refusal to recognize that Jesus was the Christ, in and through whom the will of God was being carried out. As Paul before his conversion did not know the righteousness that comes from God through faith in Christ and sought to establish his own, so too his kinsman "did not know the righteousness that comes from God and sought to establish their own, [and] they did not submit to God's righteousness" (Rom. 10:3).

The whole situation began to change for Paul when he encountered the risen Lord on the Damascus road.[31] The confidence that characterized his former way of life underwent a dramatic alteration. As he says to the Philippians (3:7), "whatever was to my profit I now consider loss for the sake of Christ." Indeed, he says with regard to former things, "I consider them rubbish, that I may gain Christ and be found in him, not having a righteousness of my own that comes from the law, but that which is through faith in Christ—the righteousness that comes from God and is by faith" (3:8b–9).

It would be difficult to state the disjunction any more radically than he does here in these verses in Philippians. A righteousness "that comes from the law" ($\tau\grave{\eta}\nu$ $\grave{\epsilon}\kappa$ $\nu\acute{o}\mu o\upsilon$) is contrasted with a righteousness "which is through faith in Christ" ($\tau\grave{\eta}\nu$ $\delta\iota\grave{\alpha}$ $\pi\acute{\iota}\sigma\tau\epsilon\omega\varsigma$ $X\rho\iota\sigma\tauo\hat{\upsilon}$, Phil 3:9). If the statement of Romans 10:4 had appeared at the end of this testimony in Philippians, there would be little reason to doubt that "end" meant something that was over and done with. The similarity of the ideas and the manner of their expression, the way the reading of Philippians as an individual testimony coheres with what Paul sees in Romans as a viewpoint widely shared by his kinsman, suggests strongly that reading "law" in 10:4 as a way of life in contrast to "faith in Christ" corresponds to the line of Paul's thinking in the passage. And given that what Paul says in 10:4 is sandwiched in between statements evocative of the sentiments conveyed to the Philippians, such a reading of the passages is made even more compelling.

---

[31]The time frame in which Paul came to these conclusions remains a matter of speculation. His writings are a witness to what he thought at a particular point in time, but they do not specify when he first arrived at these convictions.

If this is the correct reading of 10:4, it does not mean, of course, that the alternative idea that Christ is the goal or aim of the law is incorrect. It is simply to suggest that that particular idea is not the point that Paul is making in this passage. The overriding contrast, from the passage 9:30–10:13, is a righteousness by faith versus a righteousness by law. For better or worse, that is the contrast that Paul develops in this passage, an antithesis that coheres with similar convictions stated elsewhere in his letters.

THE QUESTION OF COHERENCE

To suggest that in the statement of Romans 10:4 Paul means to say that the role formerly played by the law has come to an end for the Christian because of the work of Christ raises the question of whether Paul had a coherent viewpoint in light of his reference to the law elsewhere (e.g., the notion that Christian love fulfills the law, Rom. 13:8–10; Gal. 5:13–14, 22).

Without minimizing the complications faced in comprehending Paul's view of the law, the least problematic approach remains the examination of individual statements, asking in each case what is meant and allowing a conclusion to develop from an analysis of the data and the context without immediate regard to the difficulties such an approach may create for subsequent synthetic or harmonizing concerns.[32]

Developing a conception of Paul's overall view of the law is a troublesome task, since it seeks to do something that he himself does not undertake. Paul's letters are examples of occasional writing with pastoral aims that address particular issues. They are not characterized by the nuanced discussion usually present in a monograph or treatise. They are polemical in parts and employ hyperbole.[33] As such, his comments on a given issue are often partial, and the attempt to reconstruct his viewpoint on the subject as a whole is a bit like trying to put together a puzzle for which some of the pieces are missing. It should not be surprising if the finished effect is less than satisfying or that one is left holding a few pieces that seem not to fit anywhere among the partly assembled sections. Given this situation, however, the awkward pieces

[32]One such concern is expressed by Cranfield ("St. Paul and the Law," *SJT* 17 [1964]: 43–68, esp. 64), who thinks that viewing the law as provisional or inadequate is "theologically grotesque." While this may be so (the problem may be a matter of definition, see n. 8), it does not seem to be a sentiment shared by the writer of Hebrews, who unabashedly says, "If there had been nothing wrong with that first covenant, no place would have been sought for another" (8:7). Cf. H. Marshall, "Some Observations on the Covenant in the New Testament," in *Context: Essays in Honour of Peder Johan Borgen*, ed. P. Bøckmann and R. Kristiansen (Trondheim: TAPIR, 1987), 121–36.

[33]Cf. J. Barclay, "Mirror-Reading a Polemical Letter," *JSNT* 31 (1987): 73–93.

should not be ignored and tossed aside,[34] nor is it acceptable to trim the available pieces in order to fit them together. At best, only a caricature can be produced.

Also one must resist the temptation to force the available pieces together into a makeshift composite and then discuss the incoherent nature of the resulting picture.[35] One can sympathize with the frustration that comes from working with partial material. But such conclusions do not follow necessarily from the information available. If the evidence is partial, coherent synthesis may simply be impossible.

Some of the tensions that exist in Paul's statements concerning the law perhaps are due in part to the fact that he sees Christian experience as a process with a definite beginning that awaits a future consummation. There is therefore a "now but not yet" aspect to his understanding of Christian realities. This way of viewing Christian experience may also affect his understanding of the role of the law.

With the coming of Christ a new era in the history of salvation dawned. Jesus' death and resurrection made redemption possible for all people, Jew or Gentile. As Paul sees it, the present reality of this redemption is that the declaration of righteousness is given to those who believe (Rom. 3:22–24). Yet this very real beginning awaits a future consummation. He expresses his longing for this consummation at 8:23 when he says, "We ourselves, who have the firstfruits of the Spirit, groan inwardly as we wait eagerly for our adoption as sons, the redemption of our bodies." This "now but not yet" aspect applies both to redemption and also to sonship (cf. 8:14–15).

It has application to the reality of sin as well. While Paul can speak unequivocally about the authority of sin being broken in the life of a Christian (Rom. 6:6–7), the exhortation to "not let sin reign in your mortal body" (v. 12) is a reminder that the presence and power of sin is a continuing danger for mortal beings until the awaited "redemption of our bodies" (Rom. 8:23; cf. vv. 10–11) is realized.

So too, although Paul can speak about the authority of the law as something that has ended for the Christian ("you are not under law," Rom. 6:14; Gal. 5:18), he does not preclude the possibility that individuals can reenter the sphere of its authority (Gal. 4:21: "you who

---

[34]Interpreters, like lawyers, may understandably wish to prevent the admission of evidence deemed detrimental to their case, but the temptation to vindicate a thesis at the expense of accounting for all the evidence must be resisted by the exegete.

[35]Though Räisänen's exegesis (in *Paul and the Law*) is often to the point, it is difficult to escape the notion that occasionally the vindication of a thesis (the incoherence of Paul's view of the law) is a constraining factor in the process (e.g., the exegesis of Rom. 2) or that sometimes the capacity to tolerate theological tension is unusually low or missing altogether.

want to be under the law") and be burdened again, to borrow Paul's metaphor, by a bond of their own making (Gal. 5:1: "Do not let yourselves be burdened again by a yoke of slavery"). The law thus retains a validity and authority for those outside the community of faith in Christ.[36]

Yet elsewhere Paul can speak of his own submission to the law with no fearsome consequences in view. In writing to the Corinthians, he says, "To those under the law I became like one under the law (though I myself am not under law), so as to win those under law" (1 Cor. 9:20). That Paul believes he can do this with impunity doubtless stems from his conviction that he observes the law voluntarily,[37] motivated by missionary concerns, as he says, "to win those under the law."

This way of viewing the law is traceable to the life and teaching of Jesus (though Paul has obviously applied it more widely). To what extent Paul knew about the teaching of Jesus is difficult to determine. His actual references to Jesus' teaching are relatively rare (e.g., 1 Cor. 7:10, 12, 25) in comparison to his frequent appeals to Jesus' self-sacrificial manner of life, which Paul takes as an example for himself and others to follow (1 Cor. 10:33–11:1; 2 Cor. 8:9; Rom. 15:2–5; Phil. 2:1–11). It is for this reason more likely that it is this self-sacrificial manner of life, characterized by a concern for the well-being of others, that Paul has in mind when he mentions the "law of Christ" (1 Cor. 9:21; Gal. 6:2).[38]

In any case, there are as well indications in the accounts of Jesus' teaching that make the position to which Paul ultimately came an understandable development. The account of Jesus' instruction concerning the payment of the temple tax (Matt. 17:24–27) sets out the same approach to and rationale for observance of the law that characterize Paul's statements in his letter to the Corinthians. In this particular case, the law stipulates the payment of a sum to the temple (Ex. 30:11–16).[39] Matthew portrays the collectors of this tax approaching Peter with the question, "Doesn't your teacher pay the temple tax?" (17:24). Peter

[36]That the law is valid for Jewish Christians but not Gentiles (e.g., A. Schweitzer, *The Mysticism of Paul the Apostle*, trans. W. Montgomery [New York: Macmillan, 1931]) has recently been contended by P. Tomson, *Paul and the Jewish Law* (Assen: Van Gorcam, 1990), 261. But such a view falls foul of what Paul says about his behavior at Antioch (Gal. 2:11–14). That the study takes no account of Rom. 10:4 may skew the conclusion as well.

[37]His observance of the law, it could also be said, is sporadic. His continued table fellowship with Gentiles in Antioch when the other Jewish Christians had withdrawn is a case in point (Gal. 2:11–14).

[38]Cf. O. Hofius, *Paulusstudien* (Tübingen: Mohr, 1989), 50–74.

[39]For historical considerations regarding this tax and the conclusion that the discourse is dominical, see W. Horbury, "The Temple Tax," in *Jesus and the Politics of His Day*, ed. E. Bammel and C. F. D. Moule (Cambridge: Cambridge University Press, 1984), 265–86.

answers affirmatively, but later Jesus poses this question to him: "From whom do the kings of the earth collect duty and taxes—from their own sons or from others?" "From others," Peter answers. "Then the sons are exempt," is Jesus' reply (vv. 25–26). In effect, Jesus says that he and those identified with him are free from the authority of the law (at least in this instance). However, he advises payment of the tax so as not to cause offense (v. 27); but it is clearly a voluntary act.

Paul's behavior is similarly rooted in the conviction that he is free from the authority of the law ("I am free . . . I myself am not under law," 1 Cor. 9:19–20), yet to maintain opportunity for ministry he willingly restricts his liberty ("I make myself a slave . . . I became like one under law"). Consistent with his approach to ministry ("Follow my example, as I follow the example of Christ," 1 Cor. 11:1) he advises Christians in the various churches likewise to adopt this principle when faced with individuals struggling with scruples related to matters of the law (e.g., Rom. 14:20; 1 Cor. 8:13). In truth, the sentiments found in Matthew's account of the temple tax are so similar to those applied by Paul that one might conclude he is the author of both. No one does, of course, nor is their certain evidence Paul was aware that instruction of this kind was linked to Jesus other than the fact that his own recommendations and practice reflect the principle found in Matthew's narration of this event.

One further account in the Gospels may be mentioned as relevant to the question of Paul's view that Christ was the end of the law in the sense that he superseded and thereby freed people from its authority. Matthew (8:21–22) and Luke (9:59–60) record the words of Jesus to a disciple who asks to defer following him until he has discharged his duty to his parent (cf. 1 Kings 19:20), a duty linked to the fifth commandment: "Honor your father and your mother" (Ex. 20:12).[40] But Jesus denies this request with the words: "Let the dead bury their own dead." In effect, what Jesus says takes precedence over the stipulations of the law. It is an indication, as E. Sanders puts it, "that Jesus was prepared, if necessary, to challenge the adequacy of the Mosaic dispensation."[41]

But it is not only the issue of freedom from the law that has roots in the accounts of Jesus' teaching. Paul's references to Christians fulfilling the law also have conceptual antecedents in the teaching ascribed to Jesus. According to Matthew, Jesus told his disciples that to enter the kingdom of heaven their righteousness must surpass that of the scribes and Pharisees (5:20). The subsequent discourse gives greater definition to that expectation by calling for a manner of life that not only exceeds

[40]Cf. M. Hengel, *The Charismatic Leader and His Followers* (Edinburgh: T. & T. Clark, 1981), 8.
[41]E. P. Sanders, *Jesus and Judaism* (Philadelphia: Fortress, 1985), 255.

the stipulations of the law of God (5:21–48) but also is characterized by a thoroughgoing righteousness of life that God alone sees (6:1–6, 16–18).

This same conviction, that righteousness is fundamentally inward rather than external, is given expression by Paul in Romans 2:28–29, employing words ("in secret" and "inwardly"; ἐν τῷ κρυπτῷ) and ideas (cf. reward and praise) similar to those found in Matthew 6. But Paul's contrast of the Spirit and the letter looks forward to 7:6, where it is clear that it is not by means of the law but by the agency of the Spirit that, as he says, Christians are able to "bear fruit to God" (7:4).

It is in this light that we should understand Paul's references to the fulfillment of the law (Rom. 8:4, 13:8–10; cf. Gal. 5:13–14, 6:2).[42] The Spirit does what the law was not able to do. The "fruit of the Spirit" (love, joy, peace, patience, kindness, goodness, faithfulness, gentleness, self-control [Gal. 5:22–23]) amply fulfills the summary of the law (love of God and neighbor, Matt. 22:34–40; Mark 12:28–34; Luke 10:25–28). Although the leading of the Spirit renders the law obsolete (Gal. 5:18, 23a), this does not mean that Paul preaches an ethically inferior gospel (cf. Rom. 3:8). On the contrary, the way of the Spirit is ethically superior by virtue of its more excellent product.

CONCLUSION

In the progress of salvation history the beginning of the end of the role of law is in the coming of Christ. Its end is based on the work he effected and applied to the church he established. Although indications of this change of eras are evident in the ministry of Jesus, its implications are more clearly manifested in the subsequent ministry of a spokesman like Paul, whose ministry is portrayed as an extension of that which Jesus began (cf. Luke 2:32 and Acts 13:47).

That the law as a body of stipulations defining righteousness is no longer applicable to the church does not mean that the church is left without guidance or commandments. In the same sentence in which Paul affirms that circumcision is a matter of indifference, he states the importance of keeping the commandments of God (1 Cor. 7:19), a statement given definition by the dominical (v. 10) and personal (v. 12) stipulations regarding Corinthian concerns that immediately precede. Though one body of legislative material may no longer be applicable, it does not mean the church is without guidance. Certainly Paul's own expectation is that Christians will see themselves as "slaves to righteous-

[42]Cf. S. Westerholm, *Israel's Law and the Church's Faith* (Grand Rapids: Eerdmans, 1988), 201–5.

ness" (Rom. 6:18) with "Christ formed in you" (Gal 4:19). But it is God by means of the Spirit who accomplishes this in the context of the Christian's faith.

Faith is the recurring medium in salvation history. Paul finds in Abraham an example of faith in God and his Word (Rom. 4:18–22) that illustrates the principle of righteousness by faith expressed in Habakkuk 2:4. In the progress of salvation history the focus of faith changes. Abraham accepted as true that God would fulfill the promise of descendants. With the coming of Christ, faith finds its focus in what he said and did.

CHAPTER 8

Christ, the Fulfillment of the Law in the Sermon on the Mount

John A. Martin

Perhaps no section of Scripture reveals the changing nature of the dispensationalist approach to the Bible as much as the interpretation of the Sermon on the Mount in Matthew 5:1–7:29. At the very heart of the issue and the foundation of the sermon are Jesus words, "Do not think that I have come to abolish the Law or the Prophets; I have not come to abolish them, but to fulfill them" (5:17).

STATEMENT OF THE PROBLEM

The purpose of this chapter is to delve into the issue of the relationship of Jesus to the law. The question to be explored is, What was Jesus' relationship to the law? In what manner could he say that he "fulfilled" it? The discussion is not new.[1]

Although important in its own right for the interpretation of the gospel of Matthew, the issue is raised in this chapter because of a discussion about the relationship between the two Testaments. This

---

[1]Robert A. Guelich divides general interpretations on this issue into three groups: (1) Jesus "brought the law to its full expression," "established the Law's true meaning," "set forth its ultimate intention," and thus "completed the Law" generally through his own teaching about the law; (2) Jesus came to "establish" or "validate" the law; (3) Jesus' ministry fulfilled the law by fulfilling the "Covenant promise" of the total realization of the right relationship between God and his people. It appears that Guelich's overview of interpretations is complete. However, as will be argued below, the first and third categories have much in common and can be united. Guelich went on to note concerning the term *fulfill* as used by Matthew, "The question of the Law's continuing validity now becomes a part of the larger context of Jesus' coming as the one who brings that new relationship between God and humankind promised in the Scriptures. The normative character of the Law remains in the picture (5:18, 19) but set within the broader panorama of Jesus' coming as the Bringer of the age of salvation to fulfill the Scriptures (cf. 5:18)" (*The Sermon on the Mount: A Foundation for Understanding* [Waco, Tex.: Word, 1982], 138–42).

matter arises because of an "older dispensational" understanding that there are very few meaningful links between the law and the New Testament. A statement like our Lord's therefore casts a shadow over the interpretation of the text for many. This has left a number of dispensational authors groping for ways to explain Jesus' words.[2] The issue under discussion is, How could Jesus say that he had come to fulfill the law if there is little connection between the law and Jesus' ultimate work in the church?[3]

A number of dispensational authors have sought to uncover Jesus' meaning in these words. These interpretations have been documented in a brief way elsewhere, but it will be helpful for the discussion to review them here.[4]

The Kingdom View

This view was espoused by "older" dispensationists,[5] who sought to reconcile the Sermon on the Mount and in particular Jesus' words about the law with a strict separation of the Testaments. Most notably, but not alone by any means, Lewis Sperry Chafer was a proponent of this view. In his *Systematic Theology* Chafer sought to explain Jesus' words in the Sermon on the Mount. He noted: "The Bible provides *three complete and wholly independent* rules for human conduct—one for the past age (there was no need of recording such rules as held good for people who lived before the Bible was written) which is known as the Mosaic Law and is crystallized in the Decalogue; one for the future age of the kingdom which is crystallized in the Sermon on the Mount; and one for the

---

[2]Dispensational thought has often been misunderstood in a variety of ways. One of the greatest misunderstandings is an assumption that there is a single "dispensational interpretation" of every passage. As will be seen below, this is not the case. The system of interpretation has been evolving and, I assume, will continue to evolve. Perhaps the misconception grew up because of the dearth of material that has been produced by dispensational interpreters in the past four decades. One theory as to why this is the case is that younger scholars have been reluctant to produce material that would be perceived as "going against" the older established works.

[3]In my opinion, dispensationalism has changed greatly over the last two decades. This matter has been dealt with in a brief manner by Craig Blaising, "Developing Dispensationalism," *BSac* 145 (July–September 1988): 254–80. The general trend is to see more continuity between the two Testaments. Therefore it is very difficult to talk about "the" dispensational approach to a particular passage of Scripture. This was mentioned in John A. Martin, "Dispensational Approaches to the Sermon on the Mount," in *Essays in Honor of J. Dwight Pentecost,* ed. Stanley D. Toussaint and Charles H. Dyer (Chicago: Moody Press, 1986), 35–36.

[4]Martin, "Dispensational Approaches," 38–48.

[5]By "older dispensationalists" I do not mean the age of the interpreter. Rather, I am referring to a group of dispensationalists who were writing in the 1930s through the 1950s on the relationship between the Testaments. At the same time there were other dispensationalists who would not agree with the "older dispensational" camp on many issues.

present age which appears in the Gospel by John, the Acts, and the Epistles of the New Testament."[6]

Chafer's words sound almost "ultradispensational."[7] Because of his wide distinction between the Testaments, Chafer could not understand Jesus' fulfilling the law in any way in his role as head of the church. The statement under discussion was made, according to this older dispensational view, in the context of Jesus' offer of the kingdom.[8] In that view, Jesus was speaking only to the nation of Israel in the first half of the gospel of Matthew. At that point his offer of the kingdom had not yet been rejected, and therefore the kingdom was assumed to be coming. Jesus' statements about the "ethic of the kingdom" fit into that context, not into the context of the church, which came about because of the rejection of Jesus' offer of the kingdom.[9] Chafer's words about the distinction between these two time periods, which have very little to do with each other, are stark and to the point.[10]

Other interpreters followed the same line of thought. Donald Campbell, current president of Dallas Seminary, picked up this theme in

[6]Lewis S. Chafer, *Systematic Theology* (Dallas: Dallas Seminary Press, 1948), 5:98, emphasis added.

[7]The term *ultradispensational* is normally reserved for those who break the New Testament into various dispensations. Chafer is not normally classified in this way. However, these words seem to imply that the Synoptic Gospels do not contain an ethic that is to be part of the lifestyle of the church.

[8]The concept of the "offer of the kingdom" is a difficult and complicated one that is currently under much debate in dispensational circles. For a critique of the view by a dispensationalist of a previous generation, see Erich Sauer, *From Eternity to Eternity* (Grand Rapids: Eerdmans, 1954), 175–77.

[9]That statement is an oversimplification of the view but is faithful to its character. I have never found any dispensationalist who would deny that the church would have come into existence even if the nation of Israel had accepted Jesus' offer (as this view supposes). Usually the assumption is that the "church age" would be extremely short and would be the "cause" of the beginnings of the tribulation.

[10]"Let it be dogmatically asserted at this point that those who hold such views either have failed to recognize the hopeless, blasting character of the law which this discourse announces and from which the Christian has been saved (Rom. 6:14; Gal. 5:1), or they have failed to comprehend the present position and perfection in Christ which is the estate of every believer. Apparently the two great systems—law and grace—become so confused that there could be no order of thinking possible. Distortions of the divine revelation are due, it would seem, to a slavish adherence to traditional interpretation and not to any unbiased personal investigation into the problems that are involved. Accompanying this inattention to the exact character of doctrine is, too often, the blind assumption that the student who does observe the patent character of this discourse and who therefore cannot give it a primary application to the Church is striking hands in agreement with the destructive critic who boldly rejects Scripture altogether. To give this discourse a primary application to the Church means that it is made to be, word for word, the rule of life prescribed for the child of God under grace. A secondary application to the Church means that lessons and principles may be drawn from it, but that, as a rule of life, it is addressed to the Jew before the cross and to the Jew in the coming kingdom, and is therefore not now in effect" (Chafer, *Systematic Theology* 5:97).

a dissertation written under Chafer.[11] He developed the kingdom approach throughout the entire Sermon on the Mount to its logical conclusion. Perhaps best known is the original *Scofield Reference Bible* note on the Sermon on the Mount.

The kingdom view was undoubtedly the predominant dispensational approach to the Sermon on the Mount at one time. In Kissinger's wonderful classification and bibliography, the kingdom view is the only dispensational approach presented.[12] However, in the last generation of dispensational interpreters, questions about the viability of this view have been asked. Other interpretive models began to take shape.

The Penitential View

A second view espoused by some dispensationalists is the penitential view, also called the repentance view by some individuals. Although this view has long been associated with Lutheran theology, it also has found a place in modern dispensational thought. The most notable dispensational author to espouse it is J. Dwight Pentecost, who has taught for many years at Dallas Theological Seminary. Pentecost's interpretation of the Sermon on the Mount is somewhat confusing and disjointed. At times he appears to take the kingdom view.[13] At other times he has clearly stated that the purpose of the Sermon on the Mount is similar to the purpose of the law in the Old Testament, which was, in his view, to lead people to repentance through recognition of their inability to live according to the perfect law of God.[14] The penitential view posits that in the Sermon on the Mount Jesus was calling the people of Israel to repentance. The listeners were to respond by noting that they could not possibly live in their own strength according to the lifestyle that Jesus was promulgating. The purpose of the sermon was to make the people realize that they needed to depend on some other source for salvation.[15]

[11]Donald K. Campbell, "Interpretation and Exposition of the Sermon on the Mount" (Th.D. diss., Dallas Theological Seminary, 1953).

[12]Warren S. Kissinger, *The Sermon on the Mount: A History of Interpretation and Bibliography* (Metuchen, N.J.: Scarecrow Press, 1975). Dispensationalism is one of thirty-three schools of interpretation listed and is dealt with on pp. 61–66. Notably, it is one of the longest treatments, since the author felt the need to explain what dispensationalism is and why it arose.

[13]See Pentecost's treatment in his *Design for Living: The Sermon on the Mount* (Chicago: Moody, 1975). Pentecost strongly believes in the kingdom offer–rejection approach to the gospel of Matthew. In private conversation he has noted to the author that he is deeply disturbed by developing trends in dispensationalism. However, although he is committed to the underpinnings of Chafer's kingdom view, he himself does not rigidly hold to all of Chafer's inferences about the value, or lack thereof, of the Sermon on the Mount. The very fact that Pentecost published a book on the Sermon on the Mount with application to Christians shows that he broke sharply with the kingdom view.

[14]This is taken especially from the epistle to the Galatians.

[15]"This view draws heavily on Matthew 5:17–20 in which Jesus noted that he had not

Proponents of this view would state that when Jesus compared the righteousness of the listeners to that of the scribes and the Pharisees, the response would have been amazement by the crowds.[16] The listeners would never have thought that they could live up to the righteous standards of the religious leaders.

Several problems surface with this view. First, is the primary purpose of the law in the Old Testament to show an individual that an alien righteousness is needed for salvation? If that can be demonstrated, does it follow that the Sermon on the Mount has the same purpose? There is serious difficulty with the idea that the Old Testament law was designed primarily to cause people to repent. Those who take this view must rely heavily on Paul's teaching in Galatians that it is impossible to fulfill the law completely. However that view ignores the fact that Paul also taught that an Old Testament believer did live according to the law in daily life. In fact, the prophets of the Old Testament not only called on people to live that way but expected them to live according to the law. To make righteousness impossible in the Old Testament is to imply that the prophets were mocking their listeners with standards that could not be achieved. It appears from the text that the prophets sincerely expected listeners and readers to be able to live according to the law. If that is granted to be true, then Jesus, speaking as a prophet, must also have expected his listeners to be able to live according to the law.

Another problem with the repentance view is the supposition that the original listeners would question their ability to live righteously compared to the scribes and the Pharisees. It is doubtful that John the Baptist was the only one who observed the failings of the religious class. Jesus' words recorded in Matthew 5:20 may have evoked loud laughter from his hearers, not silent amazement.

The absence of any other "salvation" formula in the sermon also calls into question the penitential view.[17]

---

come to 'abolish the Law or the Prophets' but 'to fulfill them.' If Jesus was speaking in a legal setting, the effect of the Sermon would be the same as the effect of the law—no one can be justified by the law and therefore there has to be some other means of salvation. People of faith in the Old Testament realized that they needed to depend on the mercy of God for their salvation" (Martin, "Dispensational Approaches," 43).

[16]This interpretation seems to be taken from Matt. 7:28–29. However, it ignores the irony with which the religious establishment is treated and the lack of faith that is noted throughout the rest of the gospel.

[17]Walvoord stated, "That the Sermon on the Mount presents ethical content all agree. That it delineates the gospel that Jesus Christ died and rose again, that it presents justification by faith, or is suitable to point an unbeliever to salvation in Christ is plainly not the intent of this message" (*Matthew: Thy Kingdom Come* [Chicago: Moody Press, 1974], 44).

The Interim Ethic View

Another view that has some acceptance in dispensational circles is the interim ethic view. It is espoused by Toussaint in his commentary on Matthew.[18] This view frees one from the shackles of teaching that the Sermon on the Mount is not applicable for the church today. Toussaint states: "All these events of Matthew 1–4 form the background for the Lord's Sermon on the Mount (Matt. 5–7). That famed discourse sets forth His ethics for the interim until the kingdom should come and establishes the kind of righteousness God has always expected from His followers. Most agree the theme of Matthew 5–7 is genuine righteousness as God sees it."[19] This view notes that the demands of the Sermon on the Mount, while severe, are livable, like martial law during a time of war. The demands are special considerations for a specific group of people during a difficult time.

It is interesting to note how far removed this view is from the kingdom view. In Chafer's theology anyone who would say that Jesus' words in the Sermon on the Mount composed an ethic for today did not understand the "blasting character of the law." Now in this view, advocated by a thoroughgoing dispensationalist, the sermon is accepted as the norm for daily life in the church.

There are some serious problems with the outworking of this view. The interim ethic view assumes that Jesus went beyond the ethic of the law. It deems the words of Jesus as new revelation to people of faith.[20] However, rather than being radically different, it appears that Jesus taught the same truths as are found in the Old Testament. The demands

---

[18]Stanley D. Toussaint, *Behold the King* (Portland, Ore.: Multnomah Press, 1980). Basically this commentary is an updating of Toussaint's doctoral dissertation written at Dallas Theological Seminary. Toussaint has served for many years as chairman of the Bible exposition department at Dallas. He related to the author in private conversation that, while a student at Dallas Seminary, he found the arguments for the prevailing kingdom view extremely weak. While pondering this question, he came across Albert Schweitzer's interim ethic view (found in *The Mystery of the Kingdom of God*, trans. Walter Lowrie [New York: Dodd & Mead, 1914]), adapted it to his evangelical dispensational understanding of Matthew, and saw it as the key to understanding the Sermon on the Mount. Actually the author questions whether Toussaint really holds to a strict interim ethic view. It appears that Toussaint really sees the Sermon as a believer's ethic.

[19]Stanley D. Toussaint, "The Kingdom and Matthew's Gospel," in *Essays in Honor of J. Dwight Pentecost,* ed. Stanley D. Toussaint and Charles H. Dyer (Chicago: Moody Press, 1986), 24–25.

[20]By this I do not mean new revelation in terms of the recording of the gospel of Matthew. Rather, the new revelation spoken of is in the form of added ethical demands on the "people of God." This point brings up another question that cannot be developed in this chapter, one currently in flux in dispensational circles: "Who are the people of God?" See the chapter by Glenny in this volume.

on the follower seem to be no greater than for an Old Testament woman or man who had a "prophetic" understanding of the law.[21]

JESUS AS PROPHET

The Believer's Ethic View and Jesus as Prophet

A fourth view in dispensational circles has been called the believer's ethic.[22] This view is, by far, the predominant view in dispensational circles today.[23] Before the fourth view is explained, it is necessary to give some background on the Sermon on the Mount. It appears that the solution to the problem of Jesus' fulfilling the law is not nearly as difficult as many interpreters make it out to be—certainly not as difficult as the dispensational interpretations (especially those that held the kingdom view) seem to indicate.

Jesus was clearly acting like a prophet in the gospel of Matthew. As a prophet, he had a special relationship to the law that he wanted to clarify to his listeners. Before that prophetic voice of Jesus can be delineated, another issue must be settled. One of the major issues arises because of a common misunderstanding of the meaning of "the law."

Jesus and the Meaning of "the Law"

The structure of the Sermon on the Mount is very important in the interpretive process. This writer will assume that the Sermon on the Mount as found in the gospel of Matthew is a structural unit. Undoubtedly, the text of the sermon as it appears today is the product of the author of the gospel. Whether it is a condensation of a longer body of teaching from the lips of Jesus or a compilation of Jesus sayings cannot be clearly demonstrated.[24]

The main body of the Sermon on the Mount is framed in an *inclusio* with the terms "Law or Prophets" and "Law and Prophets" as the framing units. In 5:17 Jesus said, "I did not come to abolish the Law or the Prophets." In 7:12 he again referred to the Law and the Prophets. As is usually the case, so here the *inclusio* denotes the subject matter of the entire section. The subject matter of the entire body of the Sermon

---

[21]This matter will be discussed in some detail below.

[22]Martin, "Dispensational Approaches," 46.

[23]I realize that this is a subjective statement and that no hard data exists to back it up. The statement is made because of my fifteen years of traveling and teaching in those circles. Rarely does one come across anyone who believes the kingdom view. Those who take that view often are those who were trained under Chafer or exclusively use the *Scofield Reference Bible.*

[24]An attendant interpretive problem is the relationship between the Matthean record of the Sermon on the Mount and the record in Luke's gospel, which appears primarily in chap. 6 but also has remnants spread throughout the record.

on the Mount is Jesus' interpretation of the Law and the Prophets, as almost all interpreters agree.

In the canon of Scripture current in Jesus' day (as well as in the Hebrew Old Testament today), three divisions existed: the Law, the Prophets, and the Writings. Jesus clearly thought of the canon in this tripartite way, as is evidenced in his statement "This is what I told you when I was still with you: Everything must be fulfilled that is written about me in the Law of Moses, the Prophets, and the Psalms" (Luke 24:44). This understanding of the canon is also evident in Jesus' statement in Matthew 23:35 in which Jesus obviously was speaking literally rather than chronologically.[25]

In the paragraph in question Jesus then shortens "Law or Prophets" (5:17) to "Law" (v. 18). Sometimes the Old Testament was referred to by all three names (Law, Prophets, Writings), sometimes by a shortened form of Law and Prophets, and sometimes simply by Law. It is clear in this passage that Jesus was not speaking of simply the legal sacrificial system. The Law in the canon was much more than the legal system. It also was a record of the dealings of God with humankind, culminating in his dealings through Abraham with the nation of Israel. Jesus also included the term *Prophets* to make sure that his listeners understood that he was not simply referring to the "rules" of the Law. This makes sense in the context of Matthew's gospel because a prophetic interpretation of the Law is one of the issues that Matthew was concerned about in his interpretation of Jesus' life and ministry.

The Prophetic Understanding of the Law

One of the difficulties in dispensational interpretation of the Old Testament is a misunderstanding and oversimplification of the role of the prophet in Old Testament society. The prophets were not primarily interested in the future. Very little new revelation was given by the prophets when they spoke about the end times. When various prophets spoke about the end times or the consummation of the age and the coming kingdom of God, it was almost always in the context of the moral life of the people of that present generation. The prophets were primarily interested in their present day in the light of the past. The past

---

[25]In my opinion, this is the most difficult textual statement in the entire gospel of Matthew. Jesus is clearly referring to the death of Zechariah recorded in 2 Chron. 24:21. Speaking of the canon in a literary way, Jesus was reminding his hearers of the deaths of righteous people from the beginning of the Old Testament (Abel) to the end of the Old Testament (Zechariah). Since the book of Chronicles was placed last in the canon, he was using these accounts as a merism. The difficulty comes with the fact that the Zechariah noted in 2 Chron. 24 was the son of Jehoiada the priest, not the son of Berekiah. Zechariah the son of Berekiah was the prophet who wrote the book of Zechariah.

concerned the law that had been given through Moses and was contained in the Pentateuch. The present was the moral life of the generation in which that particular prophet ministered. In effect, the books of the prophets were commentaries on both the law and on the people of the prophet's day. The prophets were applying the law to the life of the nation. In most cases the nation came up lacking before the revealed law of God.

However, it is misleading to think that because the nation of Israel and Judah rarely pleased the prophets that the prophets thought the people were excused from the necessity of living according to the law. The prophets never seemed to think that the people could not live by the law. Just the opposite appears to be true, as they expected the people of the nation to live under the law of God. The prophets constantly were exhorting the people to internal righteousness and not merely external adherence to the law.

Isaiah, who we might call the dean of the prophets, was very concerned about the moral fiber of the nation of Israel and Judah. Even a cursory reading of chapter 1 shows that he was facing a generation that was involved in outward adherence to the law but was not internally righteous. In the midst of the discipline of the Lord (the Assyrian invasion that was to eventuate in the fall of the northern kingdom in 722),[26] the people refused to turn to the Lord with inward worship. The plaintive terms found in Isaiah 1 resound again in Matthew 23, where Jesus excoriates his generation in a very Isaianic manner. Isaiah 1 is also reminiscent in Matthew 5, especially "hands full of blood" while involved in praying (Isa. 1:15) and being guilty like a murderer while going to the altar (Matt. 5:21–23).

Micah wrote a similar message calling for internal repentance rather than mere outward adherence to the law. If one sacrificed large gifts or if one could even give his children as a sacrifice, it would not be sufficient. Instead, the Lord desires justice, kindness, and the fear of the Lord (Mic. 6:6–8). This message is very similar to Jesus' words in the Sermon on the Mount and his words in Matthew 23:23–24: "You have neglected the more important matters of the law—justice, mercy, and faithfulness. You should have practiced the latter, without neglecting the former."[27]

---

[26]Although some debate exists, it seems certain that Isa. 13–23 describes the Assyrian invasion that culminated in the fall of Samaria and the kingdom of Israel. Isaiah used the fall of Israel as a case study for the kingdom of Judah, exhorting that nation to turn back to God.

[27]This statement against the religious establishment is intriguing in view of its placement within the gospel. It is understood that Jesus was addressing Jewish legalists who were refusing to see him as Messiah. However, it is placed in the last half of the book, in which

Jesus in the Role of Prophet

Jesus' role in the gospel of Matthew varies. Obviously he is the teacher of righteousness (the terms *righteousness* and *unrighteousness* occur more in the gospel of Matthew than in all of the other gospels combined). However, in the early chapters of the gospel one role stands out above all of the rest. Jesus is linked by Matthew with the prophetic tradition. This can be seen from a number of lines of evidence.

First, John the Baptist was the forerunner of Jesus. John, in Matthew's account, is clearly linked to Elijah. Matthew used the same description of John the Baptist in chapter 3 that the author of Kings used of Elijah in 2 Kings 1. John the Baptist appeared and began to preach at the place from which Elijah disappeared. He preached the same message of repentance, excoriating the religious leaders for coming to him and thinking that they could be right with God without bringing fruit in keeping with their repentance (Matt. 3:8). John's message was, "Repent, for the kingdom of heaven is near" (v. 2). Jesus' message was the same (4:17). Jesus taught his disciples to preach the same prophetic message of repentance (10:7).

On the Mount of Transfiguration the great triad Moses, Elijah, and Jesus were together. Moses was the lawgiver. He had uncontested authority in the minds of the people of Jesus' day. Elijah was the prototype prophet who preached a message of repentance to an unlistening generation. The lawgiver and the "prophet to the prophets" were united with Jesus as he began a new phase of his ministry.[28]

Second, the early chapters of Matthew are filled with "fulfillment passages" from the prophets. These fulfillment passages are not at all easy and have been grossly misunderstood by many. Although the intent of this chapter is not to discuss these fulfillment passages, several points do need to be made about them. First, in the early chapters of Matthew and again in Matthew 26:56, it was the prophets who were being fulfilled in the life of Jesus. Matthew went out of his way to record Jesus' words linking himself to the prophets and the prophetic tradition. Second, "fulfill" means several things in the gospel of Matthew. This has been pointed out thoroughly elsewhere.[29] It is important to interpret terms within the viewpoint of the author using those terms. In this case, as noted above, the crucial terms occur in 5:17 and 7:12. These phrases

---

(according to the kingdom-offer view) Jesus has turned his attention to the coming church age.

[28]The transfiguration scene is recorded by the synoptics after the "great confession" by the disciples framed by Peter. At that same time Jesus began to tell his disciples about his impending death. Apparently they were not ready to receive news about his death until that point in their development.

[29]See, for example, R. Schippers, "Fulness," in NIDNT 1:733–41.

form a merism that bound everything else in the sermon within its concept. It would be logical to see these boundaries as parallel to one another. In the first one (5:17) Jesus was not abolishing but was fulfilling. In the second, after a person has understood Jesus' teaching (not only by hearing but also by doing),[30] that person's actions (doing to others what one would have others do to oneself—7:12) sum up (NIV) the Law and the Prophets (lit. "this *is* the Law and the Prophets"). Thus, "fulfilling" and "summing up" (or "being") are parallel thoughts in the sermon.

DID JESUS AGREE WITH THE OLD TESTAMENT PROPHETS?

Many commentaries on the Sermon on the Mount note the parallels between Jesus' teaching and various passages in the Old Testament. One such work is the extensive study of Friedlander, who posited that all material in the Sermon on the Mount came either from the Old Testament canon or from early Jewish literature.[31] There was nothing new or unique in Jesus' teaching.[32] Friedlander gives many examples throughout his book.[33] The point that must be concluded is that Jesus' words agreed with the Old Testament in striking ways. Although Friedlander wanted to belittle the influence of Jesus, this in no way diminishes Jesus' unique role or undermines his messiahship. Jesus was

---

[30]Matt. 7:24–27. This occurs outside of the merism but was a natural outgrowth of the sermon bounded by the Law and the Prophets.

[31]Gerald Friedlander, *The Jewish Sources of the Sermon on the Mount*, prolegomena by Solomon Zeitlin (New York: KTAV, 1969).

[32]"Israel's heroic suffering during the last nineteen hundred years is an actual parallel to the words of Jesus. The persecution by the Church is the living commentary on the higher morality said to have been enunciated by her founder. Deeds speak louder than words. The Beatitudes have undoubtedly a lofty tone, but let us not forget that all that they teach can be found in Isaiah and the Psalms. Israel finds nothing new here. The Jew rejoices to think that such fine teaching is common to Judaism and Christianity. Would that the practice of these noble words were realized by all the children of men, then would happiness be established in the Kingdom of God on earth" (ibid., 23).

[33]Just a few examples will suffice. The purpose of this note is not to agree or disagree with all of the examples but to note that there are striking parallels.

Matt. 5:3: cf. Ps. 34:18; 41:1; Isa. 11:4; 57:15
Matt. 5:4: cf. Ps. 94:13; Isa. 61:3
Matt. 5:5: cf. Ps. 25:13; 37:11
Matt. 5:6: cf. Ps. 42:2; Jer. 23:6
Matt. 5:7: cf. Ps. 41:1; Prov. 14:21
Matt. 5:8: cf. Ps. 24:4
Matt. 5:9: cf. Isa. 52:7
Matt. 5:10: cf. Isa. 50:6–7; 51:7, 12

These examples are all taken from the Beatitudes but could be extended throughout each section of the sermon.

giving a prophetic interpretation of the law. An often-overlooked clue in the text for this interpretation is found in Matthew 5:1, where it is recorded that Jesus "sat down" to talk to the disciples. Sitting down would be the normal position for a teacher or rabbi when explaining the law.[34] This can be coupled with the fact that Jesus was compared with "their teachers of the law" (Matt. 7:29) when he had finished his explanation. The text seems to indicate that at least those hearers considered Jesus to be explaining the law.

It seems likely that the term *Prophets* (5:17; 7:12) must be understood in a broad sense. At a later time Peter called David a "prophet" (Acts 2:30). If the broader sense of the word is granted, then Jesus was not only speaking of the Law and the Prophets but was using those divisions to speak of the entire canon of his day.

THE BELIEVERS' ETHIC INTERPRETATION

With the foregoing background it appears that the ethic that Jesus promulgated is an ethic for all time.[35] That is why the name *believers' ethic* was chosen. Whether a person was a believer prior to the coming of Jesus Christ or after his coming, the ethic applied.

The Sermon Addressed to Believers

Although there is an invitation section at the end (Matt. 7:13–27), the major part of the sermon is addressed to disciples. Although *disciple* can mean different things in various contexts, here it seems to apply to those who have followed Jesus because they have seen a series of messianic miracles and are being persuaded that he might be the promised king (Matt. 4:23–25).

The people to whom the sermon is addressed are called salt and light (5:13–16); God is their Father (5:9, 16, 45, 48; 6:1, 4, 6, 8, 9, 14, 15, 18, 26, 32; 7:11, 21); the sermon is concerned with service (5:10–16, 19–48; 6:1–18, 19–34; 7:1–12, 15–23, 24–27). The sermon seems to be looking at the entire life of a believer, which begins by repentance and is marked by good fruit. The subject is good fruit—that is, the fruit of repentance that was demanded by John the Baptist (3:8).

The Setting of the Sermon

Jesus was in the process of announcing the coming kingdom of heaven. John, the forerunner, had been preaching, "Repent, for the

---

[34]See Jesus' words in Matt. 23:1–4 about the religious leaders that have seated themselves in the "chair of Moses," the position in the synagogue from which one promulgated the law.

[35]This section is an expansion of my "Dispensational Approaches," 46–48.

kingdom of heaven has drawn near" (3:2). Jesus had been announcing the same message (4:17). Jesus performed miracles (messianic signs) to authenticate his message (vv. 23–25). Crowds came to Jesus in anticipation of the beginning of the kingdom (vv. 24–25).

Placed in this setting, the sermon thus can be seen to refer not primarily to the kingdom but to the time in preparation for that coming kingdom. Jesus was giving an ethic in light of the fact that the kingdom was going to be established but was not yet present.

However, the ethic is one that would apply to all ages. Jesus did not give a new ethic. It was an ethic that fulfilled the law and that will endure throughout the time of preparation for the kingdom into the kingdom age itself. It is historically conditioned, but it is an enduring ethic.

"Fulfilling the Law" and the New Testament

Another aspect of this discussion that is troubling to some is the question of how the sermon fits into the rest of the New Testament. Six observations are relevant here.

First, many have noted the similarity of the Sermon on the Mount to the book of James and its concept of good works. In the Sermon on the Mount good works are a result of true repentance (Matt. 5:17–20; 7:16–23). This is also reflected in John the Baptist's words recorded in the gospel (3:1–12). For James, good works are an evidence of genuine faith (James 2:18). The concepts are very much the same.

Second, just as the Epistles set forth "unattainable" standards for the Christian life (1 Peter 1:15; 1 John 2:1; Col. 3:13; Phil. 3:12, to name just a few), so Jesus set forth the life that is to be the mark of a believer. It is "unattainable,"[36] but nevertheless it is to be attempted by his disciples in dependence on God.

Third, the sermon is primarily addressed to disciples, exhorting them to a righteous life in view of the coming kingdom, which will include judgment as well as blessing. The rest of the New Testament is also, for the most part, addressed to disciples, who are urged to live a holy life in view of the coming consummation of the age.

Fourth, when Jesus spoke these words, he was still living in the time of the Mosaic law. In the present day some situations of the law no longer exist. For example, no longer are offerings taken to the altar (Matt. 5:23–24). However, the change of situation[37] in no way

---

[36]Unattainable in the sense of completeness. However, in any given situation the believer has the choice of following the word of God in obedience or of turning away. When failure does occur, the grace of God in the context of God's forgiveness operates on behalf of the believer and provides the basis for restoration because of Jesus' work on the cross.

[37]Or, one could read, "the change of dispensation."

invalidates the principle for which Jesus used the example. It would have been nonsense for Jesus to give the sermon in terms of the church, for the church did not exist at that time. It is interesting to note that either Jesus did not use, or Matthew did not include, examples that came from the dietary and ceremonial aspects of the law. Almost exclusively, basic issues of morality were discussed.

Fifth, although Jesus spoke during the time of the law, Matthew recorded the sermon during the time of the church. Matthew was a churchman, most likely firmly entrenched in a local church situation. Presumably he wrote his gospel not only as an evangelistic tool but also, and maybe primarily, as a teaching tool for church people. Many interpreters have noted that there are five major teaching sections in the gospel of Matthew. If it is read as a literary unit, when one comes to the end of the gospel and reads Jesus' words, "teaching them to obey everything I have commanded you," it is obvious that the author wanted his readers to recall the teaching sections contained in the book. Although some of the commands of Jesus were abrogated later in the book,[38] the commands given in the sermon appear to have a timeless quality.

Sixth, no doubt the audience to which Jesus was speaking had the same questions that readers have today—how far do we go with this teaching?[39]

RELATING THE OLD TESTAMENT TO CURRENT BELIEVERS

This subject has been neglected by most dispensational authors. Although it needs a much fuller treatment, a broad framework is presented here. With the strict division between the Testaments by older dispensationalists, it became popular to say that the law has been "cut off" and that the believer is under no obligation to the law any more. It also became popular to note that nine of the Ten Commandments are "repeated" in the New Testament, the one not repeated being the Sabbath law. Thus the model grew up that the law existed until Jesus' death and was completely abrogated. A new ethic began at the cross with the "repeating" of the commands that God wanted in effect

---

[38]For instance in Matt. 10:5–6 the disciples were told to go and preach the message of the kingdom only to Israel and not to the Samaritans and the Gentiles. Later in the book this command is changed and the disciples were charged with the task of going to the whole world (Matt. 28:19).

[39]This is especially true with Matt. 5:38–42, which, in my opinion, causes more people to want to abandon a direct application of the Sermon on the Mount than any other part of it.

for this new group of believers. This view is very common in "popular preaching" dispensationalists.

There are serious weaknesses with that approach to the commands of God. The two Testaments are connected by the same God, whose attributes do not change. His attributes are the basis of the Law, the Prophets, the Writings, and the New Testament. All of the parts of Scripture demand a surrender of the will to a holy God. The will of God remains the same, but the manifestations of that will vary according to historical development. It is important to understand the concept of progressive revelation, which gives historical conditioning to the revelation of God. It is also important to explore higher criticism of both Testaments to understand fully the dates, authors, settings, and purposes of individual portions of the Bible.

Rather than a complete break between the Testaments, it seems preferable to see continuity and modification.[40] The outworking would be as follows.

The Law

The law can be broken down in a variety of ways. In *the Book of the Covenant* (Ex. 20–23) are found the Ten Commandments, which were foundational for Israel. These commands are repeated in the New Testament (except for the commandment regarding the Sabbath), which shows continuity between the Testaments in matters of basic morality for God's people. Although the Sabbath is not repeated for the church,[41] the principle of one in seven for rest is found throughout the Bible, both before the law as well as after the Mosaic law during the church age. The civil legislation is also found in this section. One must determine what is eternal from what is historically conditioned. The moral law never passes away. It continues to make sin, sin (Rom. 7). The law was never intended as a means of salvation and never had the power to change a person's heart. That change could come only by God's grace and the faith of the responder. To the man or woman of faith, the law does have the power to sanctify (Pss. 1, 19, 119; 2 Tim. 3).

The *cultic legislation* (Ex. 25–Leviticus) was modified by the sacrificial fulfillment in Jesus Christ as explained in the epistle to the Hebrews. However, the moral truths underpinning these laws continue because of the attributes of God.

The *dietary and ceremonial legislation* (Leviticus) was abrogated for the church in Acts 15, 1 Corinthians 6–10, and 1 Timothy 4:1–5.

---

[40]For a similar treatment of this area, see Kenneth Barker's chapter in this volume.
[41]Now all days are holy to the Lord, not just one day.

The Prophets

The words of the prophets are to be believed. The character of God is unchanging and is to be acknowledged by all believers. God's justice and holiness obligate the person of faith to be just and holy. The words of the prophets are historically conditioned for the people of their day and the obligations under which they operated. The prophets were explaining the law to their generations and were commanding their people to live by God's standard.

The Writings

The character and demands of God are constant, although much of the material is historically conditioned. The Wisdom material is an expression of the moral ordering of the creation of God. One needs to submit in any given situation to the eternal truths of God. If one orders one's actions this way, life is "easier" because the consequences of the actions will be good.

SUMMARY

This chapter has argued that Jesus fulfilled the law by reiterating a believers' ethic for the generation in which he lived. The ethic was not new. It was prophetic in that it explained the demands of a righteous and moral God in the context of the Mosaic law. Matthew recorded this ethic in the context of the church. The ethic, although historically conditioned, is applicable to all ages. Jesus fulfilled the law by maintaining that the listeners must do to others what they want to have done for them. They are to be internally motivated to keep the law.

CHAPTER 9

The New Jerusalem in Revelation 21:1–22:5: Consummation of a Biblical Continuum

David L. Turner

The theme of the new Jerusalem suggests the motif of the ideal city, a subject that could profitably be examined sociologically,[1] theologically,[2] or missiologically.[3] This chapter, however, will consider the ideal city from the perspective of biblical theology. Viewed within the canon of Scripture, the new Jerusalem of Revelation 21:1–22:5 appears as the consummation of a complex biblical continuum reaching all the way back to the book of Genesis. Revelation 21–22 is truly "the end of the beginning."[4]

Years ago the Lutheran minister J. A. Seiss (1823–1904) eloquently articulated the theological perspective shared by the present study:

If the nature of the fall was to destroy the existence of man as a race
and to dispossess him of his habitation and mastery of the earth, the

[1]See, for example, two works of L. Mumford: *The City in History* (New York: Harcourt, 1961) and *The Culture of the Cities* (New York: Harcourt, 1938). Studies more directly related to the present chapter include F. E. Peters, *Jerusalem and Mecca: The Typology of the Holy City in the Near East* (New York: New York University Press, 1986); and F. S. Frick, *The City in Ancient Israel* (Missoula, Mont.: Scholars Press, 1977).

[2]Augustine, *The City of God.* Augustine's theological use of the biblical material is sharply critiqued by H. Strathmann in "πόλις," *TDNT* 6:533. Also contrast the pessimism of Jacques Ellul, *The Meaning of the City* (Grand Rapids: Eerdmans, 1970), with the optimism of Harvey Cox, *The Secular City* (New York: Macmillan, 1965). See also Daniel Callahan, ed., *The Secular City Debate* (New York: Macmillan, 1966).

[3]For example, see K. B. Cully and F. N. Harper, eds., *Will the Church Lose the City?* (New York: World, 1963); D. Frenchak and S. Keyes, eds., *Metro-Ministry* (Elgin, Ill.: David C. Cook, 1979); R. S. Greenway, ed., *Discipling the City* (Grand Rapids: Baker, 1979); and R. S. Greenway and T. Monsma, eds., *Cities: Missions' New Frontier* (Grand Rapids: Eerdmans, 1989).

[4]W. J. Dumbrell, *The End of the Beginning: Revelation 21–22 and the Old Testament* (Homebush West N.S.W.: Lancer; Grand Rapids: Baker, 1985). See also G. Lindeskog, "The Theology of Creation in the Old and New Testaments," in *The Root of the Vine* (London: Dacre, 1953), 1–22; and C. Westermann, *Beginning and End in the Bible,* trans. K. Crim (Philadelphia: Fortress, 1972).

nature and effect of the redemption must necessarily involve the restitution and perpetuation of the race, as such, and its rehabilitation as the happy possessor of the earth; for if the redemption does not go as far as the consequences of sin, it is a misnomer, and fails to be redemption. The salvation of any number of individuals, if the race is stopped and disinherited, is not the redemption of what fell, but only the gathering up of a few splinters, whilst the primordial jewel is shattered and destroyed, and Satan's mischief goes further than Christ's restoration.[5]

In Revelation 21:1–22:5 the vision of the new Jerusalem coming down from heaven to the new earth represents the culmination of the eschatological hope of the Old Testament viewed from the perspective of the Lamb's victory. The cosmic effects of Christ's work are portrayed elsewhere in the New Testament,[6] but never so vividly as in the apocalyptic imagery of Revelation 21:1–22:5. Poythress is certainly correct in calling for further exploration of this passage in the dialogue between dispensationalists and covenantalists.[7]

This chapter seeks to avoid both an insensitive approach to apocalyptic imagery and a spiritualizing, Platonistic approach to redemption. It is argued that Revelation 21:1–22:5 portrays the ultimate destiny of the present universe when it is renovated by the redemptive power of the death and resurrection of Jesus Christ. Such a renovation involves both continuity and discontinuity as the old Adamic order is transformed into the new messianic order. There is continuity in that the new heaven and new earth will be substantially one with the present heaven and earth. There is also discontinuity in that the new heaven and earth will be radically transformed from the bondage of the disobedience of the first Adam to the freedom of the obedience of the second Adam, Jesus Christ. The new universe in Christ is none other than the old Adamic universe gloriously liberated from its cacophonous groan to a harmonious song of praise to the One who sits on the throne.

To demonstrate this position we will first trace the development of *the city* in Scripture, with emphasis upon Jerusalem, the city of the great king (Ps. 48:2). Then, turning to Revelation 21:1–22:5, we will seek to

---

[5]J. A. Seiss, *The Apocalypse* (London: Marshall, Morgan, & Scott, n.d.), 483. See also E. Sauer, *The Triumph of the Crucified*, trans. G. H. Lang (London: Paternoster, 1951), 181–82.

[6]See Matt. 6:9–10; 19:28; 28:18; Acts 3:21; Rom. 8:18–25; 16:20; 1 Cor. 15:20–28; 2 Cor. 5:17; Phil. 2:6–11; Col. 1:20; 2:15; Heb. 2:5–9; 2 Peter 3:13. R. Webber is convinced that the cosmic implications of Christ's work are being increasingly recognized in such divergent theological circles as Anabaptist, Reformed, and Roman Catholic. See his *Church in the World* (Grand Rapids: Zondervan, 1986), 267–69, 273–75.

[7]Vern S. Poythress, *Understanding Dispensationalists* (Grand Rapids: Zondervan, 1987), 130–31.

establish a hermeneutical approach to Revelation as apocalyptic literature. Next the passage under consideration will be set into the literary
structure of the Apocalypse. Then selected exegetical problems will be
addressed. Finally, the conclusion will suggest a comprehensive biblical
theology of newness as it applies to the universe.

THE NEW JERUSALEM ANTICIPATED:
THE CITY IN THE BIBLE

The apocalyptic image of the holy city, new Jerusalem, represents the
culmination and transformation of the hopes of the people of God from
long ages past. Because of sin, the Jerusalem of biblical history never
attained the ideal status it was meant to have as the city of the great king
(Ps. 48:2). The Old Testament prophets confronted the sin of the
historical Jerusalem and spoke predictively not only of its Babylonian
captivity but also of its restoration to God's favor. The New Testament
teaching on Jerusalem depends upon these Old Testament prophecies to
show that the church of Jesus Christ will share in the glorious future of
the heavenly Jerusalem that God has planned for all the nations through
the Messiah.

Jerusalem in the Old Testament

To follow the city in the Old Testament is to recognize first the
process of urbanization in the ancient Near East as nomadic existence
gave way to settlements and walled cities.[8] This should not be viewed as
necessarily antithetical to the Creation mandate regarding the settlement of the earth (Gen. 1:28). However, Cain's building the city of
Enoch seems to be in rebellion against God's verdict that he should be a

---

[8]Several studies from various perspectives provide historical and theological discussions
of the city and Jerusalem in the Old Testament: J. B. Bauer and J. Marböck, eds., *Memoria
Jerusalem: Freundesgabe Franz Sauer zum 70 Geburtstag* (Graz: Druk, 1977); A. Finkel,
"Jerusalem in Biblical and Theological Tradition: A Jewish Perspective," in *Evangelicals
and Jews in an Age of Pluralism*, ed. M. Tanenbaum et al. (Grand Rapids: Baker, 1984),
140–59; F. S. Frick, "The City of God in the Old Testament" (Ph.D. diss., Princeton
University, 1970); J. M. Halligan, "A Critique of the City in the Yahwist Corpus" (Ph.D.
diss., University of Notre Dame, 1975); A. Holtz, *The Holy City: Jews on Jerusalem* (New
York: Norton, 1971); D. S. Lim, "The City in the Bible" *ERT* 12 (1988): 138–56;
M. Noth, "Jerusalem and the Israelite Tradition," in *The Laws in the Pentateuch and Other
Essays*, trans. D. R. Ap-Thomas (Edinburgh: Oliver & Boyd, 1966), 132–44; D. C. Pellett,
"Jerusalem the Golden: From the Earthly City to the Heavenly Holy City," *Enc* 34 (1973):
272–81; N. W. Porteous, "Jerusalem-Zion: The Growth of a Symbol," in *Living the
Mystery* (Oxford: Basil Blackwell, 1967), 93–111; S. Talmon, "The Biblical Concept of
Jerusalem," *JES* 8 (1971): 300–316; G. Von Rad, "The City on the Hill," in *The Problem of
the Hexateuch and Other Essays*, trans. E. Dicken (Edinburgh: Oliver & Boyd, 1966), 232–
42; and R. R. Wilson, "The City in the Old Testament," in *Civitas: Religious Interpretations
of the City*, ed. P. Hawkins (Atlanta: Scholars Press, 1986), 3–13.

wanderer (4:12, 17). If the boast of Cain's descendant Lamech is any indication, Cain's city was a place of vengeful violence (vv. 23–24). After the Flood Cush's descendant Nimrod built several cities, including Babel and Nimrod (10:8–12). The motivation for founding Babel was to create a secure environment for the exercise of human autonomy in violation of God's law (11:1–4). Therefore God judged the city by scattering its inhabitants and confusing their language. Later the wicked "cities of the valley," including Sodom and Gomorrah, were destroyed (13:12; 19:25, 29). Thus God's plan for humankind to scatter and subdue the earth led to urbanization, a process that should not be viewed as evil in itself. Rather, the divine intent for humankind was perverted as people used the city to assert autonomy against God and to oppress other human beings.[9]

In the conquest of the land Joshua and the Israelites captured and destroyed the cities of the wicked Canaanite civilization (Num. 13:19, 28; 21:2–3, 25; Deut. 1:28; Josh. 10:37; 11:12–14, 21; etc.). Under the kingship of David, the capital city of Israel was moved from Hebron to a site that was more geographically central and politically neutral— Jebus.[10] This Jebusite city was conquered in spite of great difficulty and became Jerusalem, David's residence, a place where he began to enjoy great prosperity (2 Sam. 5:5–10; 1 Chron. 11:4–9).[11] Jerusalem emerged as Israel's ultimate symbol of God's power and presence as the first temple was built during Solomon's reign (2 Sam. 7:12–13; 1 Kings 5:3–8:66; 1 Chron. 17:11–12; 22:6–19; 28:6–25; 2 Chron. 2–7).[12] However, as sin increased in the life of King Solomon, it also increased in the kingdom (1 Kings 11:1–8). When the kingdom split during the time of Jeroboam and Rehoboam, the significance of Jerusalem was rivaled by holy places in the north and tarnished by apostasy in the south (1 Kings 11:32, 36). From this point the checkered history of Jerusalem

[9]Lim correctly analyzes this process by stating that "God intends urbanization," but "humanity misuses urbanization" ("The City in the Bible," 141–42). A similar perspective is found in W. C. Kaiser, "A Biblical Theology of the City," *UM* (September 1989): 7–17.

[10]"Jebus" or "Jebusites" (יְבוּס or יְבוּסִי / יְבֻסִי) occurs in Gen. 10:16; 15:21; Ex. 3:8, 17; 13:5; 23:23; 33:2; 34:11; Num. 13:29; Deut. 7:1; 20:17; Josh. 3:10; 9:1; 11:3; 12:8; 15:8, 63; 18:16, 28; 24:11; Judg. 1:21; 3:5; 19:10, 11; 2 Sam. 5:6, 8; 24:16, 18; 1 Kings 9:20; 1 Chron. 1:14; 11:4, 6; 21:15, 18, 28; 2 Chron. 3:1; 8:7; Ezra 9:1; Neh. 9:8; Zech. 9:7.

[11]It is possible that earlier events in Genesis typify the theological significance that Jerusalem was to attain under David. Consider Salem, the city over which Melchizedek ruled (Gen. 14:17–20; cf. Ps. 76:1–2; 110:4), as well as Mount Moriah, the site of Abraham's near sacrifice of Isaac (Gen. 22:1–19; cf. 2 Chron. 3:1).

[12]Several passages from the Psalms extol the central role of Jerusalem and Mount Zion as the site of the temple, the place where God uniquely manifested his power to his people through the Davidic dynasty. See Ps. 2:6; 46:4–7; 68:29; 69:34–36; 87:1–7; 122:1–9. It is also remarkable that Ps. 55:9–11 seems to portray David's enemies and their mischief against Jerusalem in terms that recall God's judgment on Babel in confusing its language (cf. Gen. 11:1–9).

is a period of decline, as various kings either obey or disobey the law of God and experience the blessing or discipline promised in the Davidic covenant (2 Sam. 7:14–15; Ps. 89).

During this time of the ebb and flow of godliness, the prophets inveighed against the city with all their might (e.g., Isa. 1; 3; 22:2, 9; 29:1–16; 48:1–2; Jer. 6:1–8; 17:19–24; 19; 20:5; 21:3–10). Though Jerusalem had sinned, it would not be conquered by Sennacherib of Assyria (Isa. 36–37). But later when its sin (esp. idolatry and oppression of the poor) became unbearable, God would give the city over to the Babylonians (Jer. 20:4–6; 21:7; 22:6–10, 25:1–11). While captive in Babylon, God's people should continue to seek the welfare of the city from which they were taken (Jer. 29:7) because God would bring his people back to the land and the city under the auspices of Cyrus the Persian (Isa. 44:24–45:7; 46:11; Jer. 29:4–14; 30:3, 18; 31:38).[13] God will once again bless his city Jerusalem and his people who live in the land in obedience to the covenant (Isa. 1:26–27; 2:1–4; 4:2–6; 24:23; 26:1–2; 35:1–10; 37:30–32; 46:13; 59:20–60:22; 62:1–12).[14] While these promises of future blessing were given in the historical context of the return from Babylon, their language goes beyond the relatively modest prosperity experienced at that time. These promises ultimately are consummated in the new earth (Isa. 65:17; 66:22; 2 Peter 3:13; Rev. 21:1).

The visions of Ezekiel corroborate the stress just noted on judgment (Ezek. 4:1–3; 5:2–17; 7:2–3; 22:2–3; 24:6, 9) and restoration (11:19–20; 16:60–63; 20:40–44; 28:25–26; 36:4, 10, 22–38; 37:21–28; 39:25–29; 40–48). Judgment upon Jerusalem's sin is so strong that the prophet cries out in anguish that it appears that not even a remnant will survive (9:4, 8; 11:13). It is Ezekiel's emphasis upon both the destruction of the corrupted temple and the restoration of the future temple that makes his contribution unique. The judgment of the present temple and the blessing of the restored temple are pictured vividly as God's glory departs from the temple because of the abominations that are being committed in it (8:3–6, 9, 13, 15; 9:3; 10:4, 18–19; 11:22–23) and then later reappears in the restored temple (43:2–5; 44:4). This concept of the glory of God is important for the understanding of the

---

[13]Two psalms also speak about Israel's captivity experience. Ps. 74 recalls the utter destruction of Mount Zion and asks God to judge Israel's enemies and to restore the nation and the city to the praise of God. Ps. 137 strikes a more personal note of devotion to Jerusalem as the psalmist's highest joy and recognition that the songs of Zion cannot be sung in a strange land. Here there is no explicit plea for restoration but instead an imprecation against Edom and Babylon for their respective roles in Jerusalem's destruction.

[14]Isa. 26:1–2 is significant for this study because of its mention of the city, its walls, and its gates (cf. Rev. 21:10–21).

book of Revelation (cf. 15:8; 21:11, 23). Ezekiel's vision of the restored temple is tied to the vision of the old temple by its date (40:1) and by the manner in which the vision was received (40:2; cf. 8:3; 11:1; Rev. 21:10).

Another unique perspective on the place of Jerusalem in the Old Testament is found in Daniel. The author of Daniel acknowledged that God in judgment had given Jerusalem into the hand of Nebuchadnezzar (Dan. 1:1–2). Nevertheless, Daniel still dared to believe in God's promise regarding the sacred inviolability of Jerusalem and prayed toward it daily (Dan. 6:10). This habit was based upon Daniel's faith that God would honor the prayer of Solomon on the occasion of the temple's dedication (1 Kings 8:1–53; esp. vv. 46–50; cf. 2 Chron. 6:14–42). Daniel confronted Nebuchadnezzar's oppression of the poor and his egotistical pride in his magnificent city, Babylon the great (Dan. 4:27, 30). Later under Belshazzar's regime, the Babylonian Empire came to an inglorious end as Daniel announced that God's patience with its arrogance had been exhausted (5:17–28; cf. Isa. 14:4–23). Thus the Neo-Babylonian Empire should be viewed in theological continuity with the past rebellious city of Genesis 11 and with the eschatological oppressors of God's people (Dan. 4:30; Rev. 14:8; 16:19; 17:5).

Later, during the regime of Darius, Daniel learned from Jeremiah that God would restore his people to his city (Dan. 9:1–2; cf. Jer. 25:11–12; 29:10). In this context the seventy-year captivity becomes the basis of the prophecy of the seventy weeks regarding the ultimate removal of sin from Jerusalem and its reestablishment as God's holy city (Dan. 9:24–27). In this connection Israel's return to Judah and Jerusalem under Cyrus occurs, and the second temple is built (see Ezra, Nehemiah, and Esther).[15] The prophet Haggai alludes to the fact that this temple was unimpressive when compared with the first. However, the word of the Lord confirms to Zerubbabel the promise that God is with the nation. With words that anticipate Revelation 21:24–26 and 22:2, Haggai 2:6–9 promises that God's judgment of heaven and earth (cf. Heb. 12:26) will result in the nations' bringing their glory to the temple. Thus its latter end will be characterized by a greater peace and glory than that of the first temple.

Micah 3:9–4:13 provides a summary of prophetic denouncement and promise regarding Jerusalem. Jerusalem will be plowed like a field because of the sin of its leaders, who built it with injustice and violence. It will become a heap of ruins. Nevertheless, the heap of rubble will

---

[15]Ps. 126 provides insight to the joy of Israel at their return to the land and to the effect that the return had upon the surrounding nations. Rebuilding the land is likened to a painful sowing process that will result in a bountiful harvest.

become the mountain of the house of the Lord, and this mountain will be raised over all the nations of the earth. The nations will go up to Jerusalem to learn from the God of Jacob, and the nations will live in peace forever. God will take the outcasts of Israel and transform them into a strong nation. Though Israel's travails because of its sin and captivity in Babylon were like those of a woman giving birth, it will be victorious over its enemies and will use their wealth in the service of God.

Jerusalem in the New Testament

Not surprisingly, Jerusalem also figures prominently in New Testament theology.[16] It is the city to which the magi came seeking the king of the Jews, the city of Herod's temple, the city where Jesus was crucified and resurrected, the city where the Spirit gave birth to the church, and the city where Christian mission began. Its place in the hopes of God's people in both Old Testament and New Testament is not lost but transformed as it continues to be the ultimate symbol of communion with God in eschatological *shalom*. Jerusalem is the central city of the entire New Testament. As the gospel moves outward to Antioch and then to Rome, the center of Christian mission shifts geographically but not theologically.

In the Gospels Jerusalem is featured as the place where the Father's house, the temple, still stands. The birth of Jesus' forerunner, John, is announced to his father, Zechariah, a priest, while Zechariah is serving in the temple burning incense (Luke 1:5, 8–11). As a newborn infant, Jesus is brought to the temple to be initiated into the covenant community of God's people (Luke 2:21–38). Mysterious Gentiles from a distant land traverse many miles to learn more of Jesus, but the king who rules in Jerusalem will have nothing to do with the infant who was born King of the Jews (Matt. 2:1–18). The gospel of Luke makes Jesus' resolve to go to Jerusalem the organizing feature of the central section of his gospel (Luke 9:51–19:28). John portrays four occasions when Jesus visits Jerusalem (John 2:23; 5:1; 7:10; 12:12).

When he comes to the temple, the One who is greater than the temple must purge it of unethical profiteers who oppress religious pilgrims (Matt. 12:6; 21:12–13). Jesus' enigmatic temple teaching that he is the true locus of communion between God and humankind goes

[16]See E. Asante, "The Theological Jerusalem of Luke-Acts," *ATJ* 15 (1986): 172–82; A. Bandstra, "Jerusalem and Rome in the Apocalypse," *CTJ* 1 (1966): 67–69; S. G. F. Brandon, *The Fall of Jerusalem and the Christian Church* (London: SPCK, 1951); J. C. DeYoung, *Jerusalem in the New Testament: The Significance of the City in the History of Redemption and in Eschatology* (Kampen: J. H. Kok, 1960); J. T. Townsend, "The Jerusalem Temple in New Testament Thought" (Ph.D. diss., Harvard University, 1959).

unheeded (John 2:18–22). At the end of his ministry, multitudes of people acknowledge him as Messiah upon his entrance to Jerusalem, but their grasp of his messiahship is only superficial (Matt. 21:8–11). Israel's leaders, charged with the spiritual oversight of God's chosen people, refuse to acknowledge the divine authority of Jesus, even though his miraculous works occur within the very temple of God (Matt. 21:14, 23–27; Luke 20:1–8). Jesus weeps over Jerusalem because it has lost its opportunity for genuine peace. Because it has not recognized the day of its visitation by God's Messiah, it will be razed to the ground (Luke 19:41–44). Sadly, the city that rejected the prophets also rejects the ultimate prophet (Matt. 23:29–37). The leaders of Israel prefer the rule of the Romans to the rule of great David's greater son (John 19:15, 19–22). Such is the sad story of Jerusalem's response to Jesus in the Gospels.

Nevertheless, Jerusalem remains "the holy city," even though it was the scene of Jesus' temptation and his crucifixion (Matt. 4:5; 27:53). Jesus' teachings support the Old Testament view of Jerusalem as the city of God in at least three respects. First, Jesus' allusion to Psalm 48:2 in Matthew 5:35 assumes that Jerusalem, despite its many failures, remains in the present "the city of the great king."[17] Jesus' ethical teachings reject the casuistry of the Pharisees, who profane Jerusalem and the temple by wrongfully using them in oaths. Swearing by the temple is just as serious a matter as swearing by God himself, since he manifests his earthly presence in the temple. Second, by his cleansing of the temple Jesus renews the claim of his Father upon it: the temple is still the Father's house (Matt. 21:13; Mark 11:17; Luke 19:46; John 2:16; cf. Isa. 56:7; Jer. 7:11). The abominations of Ezekiel's day may have ceased, but unethical business dealings have taken their place. Third, it is likely that Jesus is thinking of Jerusalem when he speaks of "a city set on a hill" as an image of the testimony that disciples of the kingdom are to exhibit to the world at large (Matt. 5:14–16). Jerusalem's purpose as a light to the nations is thus the basis of Jesus' image stressing the necessity of good works that glorify the heavenly father. Such a testimony to the world is a token of the ultimate purpose of the new Jerusalem in the new heaven and new earth.[18]

The epistles of Paul also make use of the theological implications of both the earthly and the heavenly Jerusalems in at least two ways. First, Paul's teaching on the Christian's heavenly citizenship or commonwealth

---

[17]DeYoung cogently remarks that this text indicates a "present realization of God's kingly rule from Jerusalem" and concludes that "it would be hard to overestimate the latent significance of this text within the total picture of Jesus' positive attitude toward Jerusalem" (*Jerusalem in the New Testament*, 38–39).

[18]K. M. Campbell, "The New Jerusalem in Matthew 5:14," *SJT* 31 (1978): 335–63.

(seen most clearly in Phil. 3:20–21) assumes that the believer's genuine homeland is not the present world with its lusts and demonic influences (Gal. 1:4; Eph. 2:1–3; Phil. 3:18–19; Col. 2:20). Instead, the believer's identity is tied to Christ's present heavenly session, which will be followed by his return to rule the earth (Eph. 1:20–23; 3:10; Phil. 3:20–21; Col. 3:1–4). Through Christ's redemptive victory over the evil powers, believers already have a measure of victory that will be totally actualized at Christ's return (Rom. 8:37–39; 2 Cor. 10:5; Eph. 6:10–12; Col. 1:13; 2:15). In all of this the undergirding idea is the identification of the believer with Christ in a heavenly citizenship (πολίτευμα, Phil. 3:20). Believers constitute a colony of heaven on earth, which is not so much to say that Christians should desire to be in heaven as it is to say that believers should desire heaven on earth. As part of the new creation (2 Cor. 5:17), believers long for the time when the universe will be reconciled to God.[19]

A more explicit Pauline use of the heavenly Jerusalem is found in Galatians 4:21–5:1. Here Paul develops a contrast between his gospel of freedom in Christ and bondage to the teachings of the circumcision party. Finding his principle of spiritual freedom in the Old Testament, Paul develops a detailed analogy between the situation of Abraham beginning in Genesis 17:16 and that of the Galatians. Abraham's son Ishmael by Hagar the slave is contrasted with Abraham's son Isaac by Sarah the free woman. The circumcision party with its emphasis on works of the flesh is tied to Hagar/Ishmael, Mount Sinai, and the present Jerusalem. The Galatians, born in freedom according to the promise and the Spirit, are tied to Sarah/Isaac and the Jerusalem that is above. Here Paul works with the Old Testament in a typological manner,[20] taking latent Old Testament principles and expounding them in a patent manner for the Galatians. The Galatians will maintain their freedom in Christ by looking back to Isaac the promised child and by looking up to their mother or homeland, the Jerusalem that is above.

The book of Hebrews also makes much use of Jerusalem and Old Testament history. This begins in the rehearsal of the pilgrim faith of

---

[19]David L. Turner, "Paul and the Ministry of Reconciliation in 2 Corinthians 5:11–6:2," *CTR* 4 (1989): 77–95.

[20]Paul's words in Gal. 4:24 (ἅτινά ἐστιν ἀλληγορούμενα) do not introduce an ahistorical speculative spiritualization of the Old Testament but the development of a theological principle from the historical narrative on the assumption that the Old Testament and Christ are in basic continuity. The point is that it is the Pharisees and the circumcision party who are discontinuous with the Old Testament, not Paul and his gospel. See J. Calvin, *The Epistles of Paul the Apostle to the Galatians, Ephesians, Philippians, and Colossians,* trans. T. H. L. Parker (Grand Rapids: Eerdmans, 1965), 84–85; F. F. Bruce, *The Epistle to the Galatians,* NIGTC (Grand Rapids: Eerdmans, 1982), 217–19.

the Old Testament worthies in chapter 11.[21] Those to whom the epistle is written need to endure severe trials (10:36), and the author supplies encouragement by alluding to the faith of prominent Old Testament saints. These serve as witnesses (12:1) whose lives demonstrate the very virtues needed by the audience. Jesus himself is the ultimate example of such a life of faith (12:2–4). In this context Abraham's search for a city with foundations, designed and prepared by God (11:10, 16; cf. 10:34), serves as a model of faith in the promise of God. Abraham and the others who lived as pilgrims on earth died in faith before they actually experienced the promised city (11:13). They would be made perfect only in connection with the followers of Jesus Christ (11:39–40).

A second allusion to the heavenly Jerusalem occurs in Hebrews 12:22. Here the author is characteristically warning the audience not to miss God's grace (v. 15). The awesome visible circumstances associated with the giving of the law to Moses on Mount Sinai (vv. 18–21) are compared to the even more awesome yet invisible circumstances which accompany the church's reception of the gospel (vv. 22–25). The lesser-to-greater comparison escalates the guilt of those who refuse the warning of the heavenly voice (v. 25; cf. 2:1–3). Mount Zion, the city of the living God, and myriads of angels are the spiritual entities that believers in Jesus have encountered. The heavenly Jerusalem is the homeland of the church of the firstborn, which includes the people of God of every dispensation. "Just men made perfect" (12:23) describes the faithful saints of the old-covenant era (cf. 11:40), whose destiny is incomplete apart from the culmination of the ages in the ultimate redemption wrought by Jesus Christ (cf. 1:1–3; 2:5–8).

The last reference to the heavenly Jerusalem in Hebrews is found in 13:14. Here the pilgrimage motif appears again as the author contrasts the sacrificial trappings of the old covenant with the spiritual realities experienced by the believer in Jesus. The sufferings of Jesus occurred outside the city of Jerusalem, and the believer likewise finds it necessary to suffer with Jesus "outside the camp" (v. 13). As pilgrims on earth, believers seek a coming city, not lasting identification with a present one. This coming city should not be contrasted with earthly existence, however, since that would render the analogy with Abraham in 11:10 meaningless. The new Jerusalem, the better, lasting city with founda-

---

[21]W. G. Johnson, "Pilgrimage Motif in the Book of Hebrews," *JBL* 97 (1978): 239–51; L. F. Mercado, "The Language of Sojourning in the Abraham Midrash in Hebrews 11:18–19" (Th.D. diss., Harvard University, 1967); L. M. Muntingh, "Hebrews 11:8–10 in the Light of the Mari Texts," in *De Fructu Oris Sui: Essays in Honor of Adrianus Van Selms,* ed. I. H. Eybers et al. (Leiden: E. J. Brill, 1971), 108–20; A. Richardson, "Whose Builder and Maker Is God," *TToday* 8 (1951–52): 155–56; G. Spicq, "La Panegyrie de Hebr 12:22," *ST* 6 (1953): 30–38.

tions, designed and made by God, is a city that is to come to the new earth as a kingdom that cannot be shaken (12:28).

The final New Testament passage to be discussed is 2 Peter 3:13, where the prospect of the new heavens and new earth is presented to motivate believers to live holy lives in the present. The mockery of biblical eschatology by skeptics overlooks the fact that God has already once judged the present heavens and earth (vv. 3–7). God's patience with sinners should not be interpreted as if it militated against his promise to return in judgment (vv. 8–9). The judgment of the day of the Lord will certainly come, and with it the present heavens and earth will be purified by a fiery judgment that results in new heavens and a new earth that will be characterized by righteousness (vv. 10–13). The prospect of this future conflagration must motivate believers to present holiness and godliness (vv. 11, 14). The vivid language of incineration presented here should not be taken as a total annihilation of the present universe because there is no corresponding picture of the creation ex nihilo of the new heavens and earth. As the flood of Noah's day purified the old earth and prepared it for Noah's family, so eschatological fire will radically purify the present universe from the effects of sin and renovate or transform it so that it will be a suitable dwelling for the returning Lord and his people (vv. 5–7).

The New Testament theology of Jerusalem must be seen from the vantage point of inaugurated eschatology. As citizens of the heavenly Jerusalem, believers have already experienced the transforming vision of the new Jerusalem in the new heavens and earth. Though the present Jerusalem has failed to exemplify the character of its God and will be destroyed, the city remains as a symbol of God's eschatological salvation. Believers are already citizens of the heavenly Jerusalem, so they recognize themselves as pilgrims in the present world system. But their prospect is not so much to leave the present earth as it is for the present state of affairs on earth to leave them. That is, believers are already a colony of the new earth as they live on the present earth. The righteousness that will characterize the future new Jerusalem must now be manifested to the present Babylon. As DeYoung puts it, "Present continuing realization" of union with the heavenly Jerusalem will lead to the "future culmination" when the New Jerusalem descends to the renewed earth.[22] Believers must pray and act so that God's rule may be advanced as his will is increasingly done on earth as it is in heaven (Matt. 6:10). The values of the eschaton are to be seen already in all the relationships that believers sustain with each other, with their neighbors, and with nature. Communities of believers must begin now to mimic the

---

[22]DeYoung, *Jerusalem in the New Testament*, 163.

ultimate community of God on the new earth. The present groanings of believers and of the earth itself are not for the earth to be eliminated but for it to be set free from the debilitating effects of sin.[23] Between the already and the not yet comes the inescapable duty of perseverance (Rom. 8:18–25) as believers anticipate the consummation of history in Revelation 21:1–22:5.[24]

THE HERMENEUTICS OF THE NEW JERUSALEM

How should one interpret the pervasive symbolic imagery of apocalyptic literature in general and of the book of Revelation in particular? There appear to be three major approaches. First, some take the imagery quite literally, at face value. The reasoning seems to be that the reality and truth of the passage depend upon this approach. Apocalyptic visions are viewed as if John were viewing photographic prints of the reality envisioned. Either everything will literally occur just as in the details of the vision, or the passage totally loses its force. Though he acknowledges the symbolic nature of the passage, Walvoord seems to reason that it accurately describes the actual details of the eternal state upon the new earth: "It is probably a safe procedure to accept the description of this city as corresponding to the physical characteristics attributed to it."[25]

A very different approach argues from the visionary nature of the passage that its details do not correspond to earthly reality. Indeed, there is doubt that the passage describes physical or material reality at all. In this view the concept of an eschatological, temporal, spatial locale is replaced by the idea of a mystical portrait of timeless spiritual blessing. According to Wilcock, the final vision of Revelation "has no meaning *on earth:* it deals entirely with heaven."[26]

---

[23]Here the conclusions of DeYoung (ibid., 116–17, 128) assume too much discontinuity between Old Testament and New Testament eschatological hope. The New Testament is just as interested in an earthly city as the Old Testament is. The new Jerusalem's heavenly origin does not rule out its earthly destination. Christians have been ethically united with the new Jerusalem as a present spiritual reality, but their hope is ever for this ethical-spiritual union to be manifested temporally and physically (Matt. 6:10).

[24]This view of Jerusalem in biblical history and eschatology will go far to blunt the cogent but overgeneralized critique of dispensationalism found in D. F. Wells, "The Future," in *Christian Faith and Practice in the Modern World,* ed. M. A. Noll and D. F. Wells (Grand Rapids: Eerdmans, 1988), 290–91.

[25]J. F. Walvoord, *The Revelation of Jesus Christ* (Chicago: Moody Press, 1966), 320. This approach is developed in detail by G. G. Cohen, who calculates the square miles covered by the city as well as its potential population ("Some Questions Regarding the New Jerusalem," *GJ* 6, no. 3 [Fall 1965]: 26–28). More calculations of a similar sort are found in H. M. Morris, *The Revelation Record* (Wheaton: Tyndale House; San Diego: Creation Life, 1983), 450–52.

[26]M. Wilcock, *I Saw Heaven Opened: The Message of Revelation* (Downers Grove, Ill.:

Neither of these views is accepted in the present study. The first view is weakened by its insensitive hermeneutical approach to apocalyptic imagery, and the second has an inadequate grasp of the biblical theology of creation and redemption. While the first view handles the symbolism woodenly, the second takes it merely as poetic license or hyperbole. What is needed is an approach that does justice to apocalyptic symbolism without evaporating the earthiness of biblical protology and eschatology.

A wooden approach to apocalyptic imagery tends to put the question of interpretation too simply: either the passage describes material reality just as the images literally portray it, or it does not describe reality at all. Tan, who argues that an actual literal city is portrayed just as it is, never seems to grasp the fact that an actual literal city may be portrayed through symbols.[27] Few would argue that the four different metals of the statue that appeared to Nebuchadnezzar in Daniel 2 are the literal descriptions of the four kingdoms symbolized there. Nevertheless, this does not mean that actual, literal kingdoms are not found in the passage. A similar argument could be made from the four vicious beasts, which symbolize the same four nations in Daniel's dream in Daniel 7. Indeed, if the nations literally conform to the imagery, the perspectives of Daniel 2 and Daniel 7 would be contradictory instead of complementary pictures of the four nations.

Just as the four actual kingdoms of Daniel 2, 7 do not literally correspond to the imagery that portrays them, so the new Jerusalem does not literally correspond to the imagery of Revelation 21–22. Though it is an actual literal city, its glory will far surpass the language that John uses to portray it. John's language is an attempt to describe what is in one sense indescribable.[28] His language adequately and genuinely describes what he saw, but what he saw, characterized as it is as "having the glory of God" (21:11), cannot be fully described by finite human beings in a vision. If that were the case, the new Jerusalem would be considerably less glorious than it is. Recognizing that John's language does not literally correspond to the actual description of the holy city hardly lessens its glory. On the contrary, the approach that limits the glory of the city to John's finite imagery is the approach that is guilty of diminishing its magnificence.

InterVarsity Press, 1975), 203. Elsewhere Wilcock indicates that he views Rev. 20 as symbolic and timeless (181) and that the city in Rev. 21 is the church (207).

[27]P. L. Tan, *The Interpretation of Prophecy* (Winona Lake, Ind.: BMH Books, 1974), 285–92.

[28]According to E. Sauer, the angel who mediated the vision to John "employed human measures and forms, so as to bring the infinite to the consciousness of the finite spirit" (*The Triumph of the Crucified*, 193–94).

The point being made here can be demonstrated by noting John's characteristic language of visionary correspondence. John often uses the words ὅμοιος and ὡς to describe the realities he is envisioning. In the passage under consideration, 21:1–22:5, ὅμοιος occurs in 21:11, 18,[29] and ὡς occurs in 21:2, 11, 21; 22:1.[30] In these instances John compares what is seen to an object with which he is familiar in the present world. What he sees is "like" that object; the visionary detail corresponds to the physical object from everyday life, but it is hardly to be equated or identified with that object. This is tacitly admitted even by some who argue for a totally literal approach. One commentary, billed as the most literal interpretation of Revelation available,[31] describes each "pearly gate" (21:21) as "one magnificent shimmering pure body of flawless pearl."[32] The problem here is that the text does not speak of a "body" of pearl material; it affirms that each gate is from one pearl. Along the same lines, the streets of gold are taken to be "lined with" gold,[33] but the text literally indicates that the streets are gold in their entirety. Perhaps the absence of oysters large enough to produce such pearls and the absence of sufficient gold to pave such a city (viewed as literally 1,380 miles square and high) is viewed as sufficient reason not to take these images as fully literal!

If the preceding discussion serves to warn against a "hyperliteral" approach to apocalyptic imagery, what follows serves to avoid a "hypoliteral" approach. It should be noted first that the Apocalypse should not be viewed as a nonprophetic piece of imaginative speculation.[34] The book repeatedly claims to be prophetic (1:3; 10:7, 11; 22:6, 7, 9, 10, 18, 19). As such, it confronts the people of God in terms of ethical obedience to their present covenant obligations and speaks of the future in order to serve the present ethical goal. The author of Revelation intended to speak to God's people in the same way that the Old Testament prophets spoke to God's people. He intended to interpret the historical experiences of his audience in the light of the

---

[29]Other uses of ὅμοιος for visionary correspondence in Revelation are 1:13; 4:3, 7; 11:1; 13:2; 14:14.

[30]Other uses of ὡς for visionary correspondence in Revelation are 1:10, 14–17; 2:18, 27; 3:3; 4:1, 6, 7; 5:6; 6:1, 6, 12–14; 8:8, 10; 9:2, 3, 5, 7–9, 17; 10:1, 9, 10; 12:15; 13:2, 11; 14:2; 15:2; 16:3, 13; 18:21; 19:1, 6, 12; 20:8.

[31]Morris, *The Revelation Record*, 9, 12, 14, and dust jacket.

[32]Ibid., 454.

[33]Ibid., 455.

[34]D. Hill, *New Testament Prophecy* (London: Marshall, Morgan, & Scott, 1979), 86. Hill develops several similarities between Revelation and prophecy. See also G. E. Ladd, "Why Not Prophecy-Apocalyptic?" *JBL* 76 (1957): 192–200; and idem, "Apocalyptic and New Testament Theology," in *Reconciliation and Hope,* ed. R. Banks (Grand Rapids: Eerdmans, 1974), 285–96. Ladd's argument that biblical apocalyptic is ethically prophetic is crucial for the present discussion.

two epochal comings of Jesus Christ, the Lamb-Lion of God, to the earth. Whatever Revelation is about, it is about the existence and destiny of God's people on earth as defined by both comings of Jesus Christ to the earth. Therefore, to interpret Revelation 21:1–22:5 merely as a symbolic picture of the church's blessings is to remove the church from its redemptive historical context in space and time history on the earth. As Adam's disobedience wrought catastrophe upon the earth, so the second Adam's obedience will accomplish reconciliation upon the earth. To take the vision of the new Jerusalem merely as an ideal symbol of the church's blessing fails to reckon with the earthly character of Old Testament eschatological hope and the full cosmic effects of Christ's redemption.

To conclude, the hermeneutical approach to Revelation 21:1–22:5 must be informed by sensitivity to apocalyptic imagery and acceptance of the cosmic nature of eschatology and redemption. Sensitivity to the imagery will help to avoid an excessive literalism that paradoxically can only limit the glory of the city. Accepting the earthiness of biblical eschatology will help to avoid the opposite error of spiritualizing the imagery in a Platonistic dualism between matter and spirit. The dualism of apocalyptic is a dualism of ethics, not ontology. Biblical eschatology involves an ethical renewal, not an ontic renewal. The eschatological hope of the Bible is not for deliverance from the earth, but from sin. Creaturehood inevitably involves physical existence, and the redemption of creatures includes the redemption of creation. The creation is good (Gen. 1:31), though it is terribly marred by human sin. The work of Christ will ultimately be applied to this present groaning earth, and then it will be brought to a new level of goodness in reflecting the glory of God (Rom. 8:18–25). God's character will be holistically integrated into every facet of life in God's world. Thus the approach of this study stresses sensitivity to apocalyptic imagery coupled with the conviction that cosmic redemption is pictured by that imagery.[35]

THE NEW JERUSALEM IN LITERARY CONTEXT

There is no escaping the fact that the literary background for Revelation in general and for Revelation 21:1–22:5 in particular is the Old Testament. There are over fifty allusions to the Old Testament in

---

[35]Such an approach is well articulated by George Ladd's "biblical realism" in *The Presence of the Future* (Grand Rapids: Eerdmans, 1974), 62–64. It is interesting that Ladd's theological opponent, A. J. McClain, makes essentially the same point in *The Greatness of the Kingdom* (Chicago: Moody Press, 1968), 519–26. For discussion of Ladd's and McClain's differences, see D. L. Turner, "The Continuity of Scripture and Eschatology," *GTJ* 6 (1985): 275–87, esp. 287.

this section of thirty-two verses. Old Testament books cited most frequently are Isaiah, Ezekiel, Psalms, Genesis, and Zechariah. Though the limited purpose of this study precludes a detailed study, the following is presented as an overview of the material in Old Testament order:

OT Passage		Found in Rev.	Concerning
Gen.	2:9; 3:22	22:2	Tree of Life
	19:24	21:8	fire and brimstone
Ex.	28:21	21:12–13	(verbal parallel)
	32:32–33	21:27	Book of Life
Lev.	26:11–12	21:3	God with his people
2 Sam.	7:14	21:7	God and his sons
1 Kings	22:19	21:5	God sits on his throne
2 Chron.	6:18	21:3	God dwells on earth
	18:18	21:5	God sits on his throne
Ps.	11:6	21:8	fire and brimstone
	17:15	22:4	God's face seen
	36:9	21:6	spring of life
	42:2	22:4	God's face seen
	47:8	21:5	God sits on his throne
	69:28	21:27	Book of Life
	72:10–11	21:24, 26	nations serve God
	89:26	21:7	God and his sons
	89:27	21:24	kings of the earth
Isa.	6:1	21:5	God sits on his throne
	25:8	21:4	tears wiped away
	30:33	21:8	fire and brimstone
	35:10	21:4	sorrow passes away
	42:9; 43:19	21:5	God renews
	44:6	21:6	God is first and last
	48:12	21:6	God is first and last
	52:1	21:2, 10	the holy city Jerusalem
	54:11–12	21:19	precious stone found
	55:1	21:6	thirsty drink at no cost
	58:8; 60:1–2	21:11	glory of God
	60:3, 5	21:24	wealth of nations
	60:19–20	21:11, 23; 22:5	God's glory illumines
	61:10	21:2	bride adorned
	65:17	21:1	new heavens and new earth
	65:19	21:4	no more weeping
	66:22	21:1	new heavens and earth
Jer.	2:13	21:6	spring of water
	31:16	21:4	no more weeping
Ezek.	1:26–27	21:5	throne of God
	37:27	21:3	God with his people
	38:22	21:8	fire and brimstone
	40:2	21:10	vision from mountain

	40:3, 5	21:15	measurement
	43:16	21:16	12 x 12 dimension
	47:1, 7	22:1	flowing water
	47:12	22:2	leaves for healing
	48:16–17	21:16–17	measurements
	48:31–34	21:12	twelve gates of the city
Dan.	7:18	22:5	the saints reign forever
	12:1	21:27	Book of Life
Joel	3:18	22:1	flowing waters
Amos	3:13; 4:13	21:22	Lord God of Hosts
Zech.	2:10	21:3	God with his people
	14:7	21:25; 22:5	no night
	14:8	22:1	flowing waters
	14:11	22:3	no more curse[36]

While some of the allusions summarized above may be no more than verbal parallels, it remains true that every major feature of the vision in 21:1–22:5 is drawn from the Old Testament. In Revelation 21:1–22:5 is found the full flowering of Old Testament eschatological hope.

Another matter of note in a literary study of Revelation 21:1–22:5 is that several of its key images are anticipated earlier in Revelation. Thus the reader of Revelation is prepared for the consummation of God's salvation by the mention of some of the key features of that salvation earlier in the book. In this connection one notes terms related to Jerusalem such as "the holy city" (11:2; 21:2, 10; 22:19) and "the new Jerusalem" (3:12; 21:2). God's people are described as the bride (19:7; 21:2, 10) and as overcomers (2:7, 11, 17, 26; 3:5, 12, 21; 12:11; 15:2; 21:7). Similarly, descriptions of the blessing of God's people are found earlier in Revelation: tears will be wiped away (7:17; 21:2); the water of life will be available for those who thirst (7:17; 21:6; 22:1, 17); the Tree of Life supplies food (3:7; 22:2, 14); God's name will identify them (2:17; 3:12; 7:3; 13:16–14:1; 22:4). In addition, the judgment of unbelievers is also featured, including the lake of fire (19:20; 21:8) and the second death (2:11; 20:6, 14; 21:8). The Book of Life shows who is and who is not a genuine follower of Jesus (3:5; 13:8; 17:8; 20:12, 15; 21:27). The measurement of the new Jerusalem, which has no temple (21:22), is anticipated by the earlier measurement of the temple (11:2; 21:15).

The extent to which the imagery of Revelation 21:1–22:5 has been anticipated earlier in the book is underlined by the fact that even the eternal reign of God's people with which 21:1–22:5 concludes has been clearly mentioned earlier in the Apocalypse (1:6; 2:26–27; 3:21; 5:10;

---

[36]This table was constructed by collating data from the apparatuses of the standard editions of the Greek New Testament.

20:4, 6; 22:5). Thus it is clear that 21:1–22:5 presents the climactic resolution of much that has been presented only partially earlier in the book. All of this is clear testimony to the literary unity of Revelation and to the continuity of the believer's present hope with future consummation.

The third literary matter to be discussed is structure. For the Apocalypse the matter of literary structure is crucial because it is so closely tied to exegesis and the development of the book's theology.[37] As might be expected, scholars are not agreed on this matter. Elaborate schemes involving chiasm, dramatic scenes, recapitulated cycles, and the number seven are common. However, a more simple approach has the most to commend it, and it does not rule out the legitimate insights of the other approaches. It recognizes four main visions, each of which is marked by the expression ἐν πνεύματι (1:10, 4:2; 17:3; 21:10).[38] Generally John's ἐν πνεύματι experience is accompanied by an angelic visit and promise to show (δείξω; 4:1; 17:1; 21:9) the new vision. The repetition of these features is very likely John's own method of structuring the visions he has received. Construed on the basis of these revelatory experiences, this outline of the Apocalypse follows:

Prologue (1:1–8): Announcement of the prophecy

First vision (1:9–3:22): Christ's counsel to the churches living in Babylon

Second vision (4:1–16:21): Christ's judgment on Babylon

Third vision (17:1–21:8): New Jerusalem replaces Babylon

Fourth vision (21:9–22:5): Details of the new creation

Epilogue (22:6–21): Reaffirmation of the prophecy

Thus the section of Revelation chosen for this study, 21:1–22:5, includes the final section of the penultimate vision as well as the totality of the ultimate vision. The section 21:1–8 concludes the vision that began in 17:1, and 21:9–22:5 forms the final vision, which arguably ends at 22:5, where the epilogue takes up several themes from the prologue in *inclusio* fashion.[39]

---

[37]M. Rissi is correct: "In scarcely any other biblical book are the method of exposition and the understanding of the book's literary structure so thoroughly intertwined as they are in the Revelation to John. The question of construction deeply touches the highly problematic character of the book. The organization of the total work itself discloses a distinctive theological interpretation of history (*Time and History: A Study of the Revelation*, trans. G. C. Winsor [Richmond: John Knox, 1966], 1).

[38]M. C. Tenney, *Interpreting Revelation* (Grand Rapids: Eerdmans, 1957), 32–33.

[39]Some of the more prominent themes of the *inclusio* are the following:

Revelation 21:1–8 concludes the third vision with two statements introduced by the characteristic formula καὶ εἶδον (vv. 1–2).[40] Here John sees that the new heaven and the new earth have replaced the old heaven and earth, and that the new Jerusalem is descending from heaven from God. Following this statement of the content of the vision is an interpretive comment on its significance (vv. 3–8). John hears (καὶ ἤκουσα) a voice from the throne that announces the presence of God with his people to remove all of their pain (vv. 3–4).[41] Then the One who sits on the throne proclaims the renewal of the universe, accompanied by the reward of overcomers and the punishment of sinners (vv. 5–8). In this fashion John concludes his account of the judgment of the great prostitute, Babylon (17:1), and also introduces the reader to the theme of newness, which pervades the final vision. Revelation 21:1–8 is thus a hinge passage that interrelates the final judgment of the city of man with the eternal blessedness of the city of God.[42]

The final vision of Revelation begins characteristically in 21:9–10 by describing the occasion of the vision. This introduction to the final vision is closely modeled upon 17:1–2 and is clearly intended to contrast with it. As John sees what the angel "shows,"[43] there follows first a general description of the new Jerusalem, emphasizing the glory of its wall, gates, and foundations (21:11–14). Then the angel mediating the vision uses a gold measuring rod to reveal the measurements and

1:1/22:6	Things about to occur are revealed from God through an angel to servants.
1:3/22:7	Promise of blessing to those who heed the prophecy.
1:3/22:10	The time is near.
1:4, 9/22:8	John the author.
1:7/22:7	Jesus Christ is coming quickly.
1:8/22:13	I am the Alpha and the Omega.
1:17/22:13	I am the first and the last.

[40]The phrase καὶ εἶδον occurs around almost forty times in the Apocalypse: 1:12, 17; 5:1, 2, 6, 11; 6:1, 2, 5, 8, 9, 12; 7:2; 8:2; 9:1, 17; 10:1; 13:1, 11; 14:1, 6, 14; 15:1, 2, 5; 16:13; 17:3, 6; 19:11, 17, 19; 20:1, 4, 11, 12; 21:1, 2, 22. The verb εἶδον occurs without καὶ six times: 4:1; 7:1, 9; 10:5; 13:2; 18:1.

[41]This is the first time in the apocalypse where God himself speaks. The twenty-seven occurrences of ἤκουσα generally involve angelic voices, frequently described as loud. See 1:10; 4:1; 5:11, 13; 6:1, 3, 5, 6, 7; 7:4; 8:13; 9:13, 16; 10:4, 8; 12:10; 14:2 (bis), 13; 16:1, 5, 7; 18:4; 19:1, 6; 21:3; 22:8 (also ἀκούων in this verse).

[42]The pattern of the final words of a preceding section serving to anticipate or introduce the main theme of the following section is common in the Apocalypse. Examples include 1:19–20 leading into 2–3; 1:21 leading into 4–5; 8:1–2 leading into 8:3–9:21; 11:15 leading into 15–16; 16:19 leading into 17–20; and 21:1–8 leading into 21:9–22:5. See I. T. Beckwith, *The Apocalypse of John,* reprint ed. (Grand Rapids: Baker, 1967), 241–47.

[43]The verb δείκνυμι occurs at several strategic places in the literary structure of Revelation in description of the revelatory nature of the book. See 1:1; 4:1; 17:1; 21:9, 10; 22:1, 6, 8.

shape of the city (vv. 15–17). The precious stones that are the materials of the city are described next (vv. 18–21). Then John "sees" that there is no temple in the city as his vision turns to the religious life of its inhabitants (vv. 22–26), along with the sources of that life, the river and Tree of Life (22:1–2). The vision concludes with interpretive commentary reminiscent of 21:3–4 that describes the everlasting felicity of God's people as they serve and reign with him forever (22:3–5).

When the passage is understood in this fashion and viewed as a unit, the following outline results:

I. General introduction of the new heavens, the new earth, and the new Jerusalem (21:1–8)
   A. Description of the vision by John (21:1–2)
   B. Interpretation of the vision by the One on the throne (21:3–8)

II. Specific description of the glorious new Jerusalem (21:9–22:5)
   A. Occasion of the vision (21:9–10)
   B. Summary of the glory of the city, wall, gates, and foundation (21:11–14)
   C. Measurement of the city (21:15–17)
   D. Materials of the city (21:18–21)
   E. Life in the city (21:22–27)
   F. Sources of the city's life: the river and the tree (22:1–2)
   G. Eternal reign of God's servants (22:3–5)

The final vision of the Apocalypse concludes on the note of the eternal reign of God's people (22:5; cf. Dan. 7:18, 27; Rev. 1:6; 5:10; 20:4, 6). The remainder of the book serves as an *inclusio*-style epilogue that underlines key themes from chapter 1 and warns the reader that the prophecies just concluded are inviolable, on pain of divine punishment (22:18–19).

KEY EXEGETICAL ISSUES IN THE NEW JERUSALEM

Since the exegesis of Revelation 21:1–22:5 is exceedingly complex, only selected matters of crucial relevance to the theme of this study can be addressed.[44] The first of these must be the question of recapitulation.

---

[44]Specialized studies of this passage include G. Dieter, "Die Visionen vom himmlischen Jerusalem in Apk 21 v 22," in *Kirche: Festschrift für G. Bornkamm,* ed. D. Lührmann (Tübingen: Mohr, 1980), 351–72; L. J. Garrett, "The New Jerusalem: A Study in Jewish and Christian Apocalyptic" (Ph.D. diss., Harvard University, 1957); R. H. Gundry, "The New Jerusalem: People as Place, Not Place for People," *NovT* 29 (1987): 254–64; L. D.

Simply put, after addressing the eternal state in Revelation 21:1–8, does 21:9–22:5 return to the matter of the Millennium, previously addressed in 20:1–6? Those who advocate the view that 21:9–22:5 recapitulates 20:1–6 seem to depend upon two very different lines of reasoning. Some, such as Charles and Ford,[45] argue on the grounds of supposed interpolations from various sources by a later scribe into the original form of the vision. Others, such as Darby, Kelly, Phillips, and Scott,[46] argue that the description of the nations' bringing their glory into Jerusalem and being healed by the leaves of the Tree of Life (21:24, 26; 22:2) fits the millennial state, not the eternal state.

Those who advocate the view that the passage contains interpolations by a later editor assume the incompetence of that editor and their own ability to detect that incompetence. Both assumptions are dubious. There is no textual evidence that such interpolations have occurred, and the passage makes plausible sense without resorting to the theory of interpolations.

Those who argue that a single author has recapitulated his earlier description of the Millennium seem to work from two misconceptions. The first misconception posits excessive discontinuity between the Millennium and the eternal state and assumes an ability to divide the two neatly. However, the Old Testament passages that form the basis of Revelation 20–22, especially Ezekiel 40–48 and Isaiah 60–66, make no neat break between the Millennium and the eternal state.[47] The heightened blessings of Christ's millennial reign will be further intensified to their ultimate degree in the eternal state, but the difference is only in degree, not in kind. Thus features of the new

Melton, "A Critical Analysis of the Understanding of the Imagery of the City in the Book of Revelation" (Ph.D. diss., Southern Baptist Theological Seminary, 1978); M. Rissi, *The Future of the World: An Exegetical Study of Revelation 19:11–22:15,* SBT, 2d ser., 23 (Naperville, Ill.: Allenson, 1966); F. Zeilinger, "Das himmlische Jerusalem: Untersuchungen zur Bildersprache der Johannesapokalypse und der Hebräerbriefs," in *Memoria Jerusalem: Freundesgabe Franz Sauer zum 70 Geburtstag,* ed. J. B. Bauer and J. Marböck (Graz: Druk, 1977), 143–65.

[45]R. H. Charles, *A Critical and Exegetical Commentary on the Book of Revelation,* ICC (Edinburgh: T. & T. Clark, 1920), 2:144–54; J. M. Ford, *Revelation,* AB 38 (Garden City, N.Y.: Doubleday, 1975), 360–70.

[46]J. N. Darby, *Notes on the Apocalypse* (London: G. Morrish, n.d.), 149–50; W. Kelly, *Lectures on the Revelation* (London: G. Morrish, n.d.), 460–61; J. Phillips, *Exploring Revelation* (Chicago: Moody Press, 1974), 267; and W. Scott, *Exposition of the Revelation of Jesus Christ* (London: Pickering & Inglis, n.d.), 440–41.

[47]H. M. Wolf's study *Interpreting Isaiah* (Grand Rapids: Zondervan, 1985) is helpful here. Wolf notes that "some of the features of Isaiah's description of the messianic age seem to look ahead to the eternal state" (251) and that "it is somewhat artificial to distinguish the new heaven and new earth from . . . the rule of the Messiah. Isaiah understood all of them as the consummation of God's work of salvation, and it is difficult to divide them into separate categories" (300).

heavens and new earth that are similar to the Millennium do not justify supposed sharp distinctions and recapitulations. Second, a misconception of the nature of life in the eternal state may also be at work here. This misconception assumes that there will be no need for growth in redemptive grace in the eternal state. However, the consummation of redemption, often referred to as glorification, does not obliterate the Creator-creature distinction and make finite humans suddenly possess infinite knowledge and holiness. Believers will be set free from sin at the consummation but will still need to exercise faithful stewardship of the God-given means of grace in order to serve God and reign with him. The attempt to separate glorified believers from responsible obedience to God is mistaken.

Both the interpolation view and the recapitulation view attempt to move away from the more natural reading that Revelation 19:11–22:5 is a sequential picture of the end times. The return of Jesus to the earth (19:11–16), the war with the beast's forces (19:17–21), the binding of Satan (20:1–3), the rule of the saints (20:4–6), the last rebellion (20:7–10), the great white throne judgment (20:11–15), and the inauguration of the eternal state (beginning in 21:1) follow a natural sequential progression. Each of these units except the last rebellion begins with John's characteristic καὶ εἶδον, a phrase that implies sequence. Thus the interpolation and recapitulation views are faced with a burden of proof that they cannot bear.[48]

Another important exegetical question concerns the nature of the newness spoken of in 21:1, 2, 5. Some take this newness in terms of renovation or renewal of the old universe,[49] while others insist that an entirely new creation replaces the old order, which has evidently been entirely annihilated.[50] The word in question is καινός, which describes

---

[48]The recapitulation view is well refuted by G. G. Cohen, *Understanding Revelation* (Chicago: Moody Press, 1978), 167–77; and J. D. Pentecost, *Things to Come* (Grand Rapids: Zondervan, 1958), 563–80. However, Pentecost's preference (580) for the mediating view that 21:9–22:5 describes the eternal state of the resurrected saints during the Millennium is puzzling.

[49]Ford, *Revelation,* 364–65; A. A. Hoekema, *The Bible and the Future* (Grand Rapids: Eerdmans, 1979), 280–81; Sauer, *The Triumph of the Crucified,* 178–79; Seiss, *The Apocalypse,* 483–89; H. B. Swete, *Commentary on Revelation,* reprint ed. (Grand Rapids: Kregel, 1977), 274–75.

[50]G. R. Beasley-Murray acknowledges that Old Testament eschatological hope looked for a renewal of the present earth but thinks that Revelation speaks of the creation of a new earth that replaces the old one. See his *Revelation,* NCBC (Grand Rapids: Eerdmans; London: Marshall, 1981), 306–7. The language of Morris (*Revelation Record,* 436) and Walvoord (*Revelation,* 315–16) is unclear but seems to imply a new creation in the strict sense of the words. J. Ellul's rigid antithesis between the city of man and the city of God seems to leave him with no choice other than to argue that there is absolutely no continuity between the old and new worlds (*Apocalypse: The Book of Revelation,* trans. G. W. Schreiner [New York: Seabury, 1977], 214–31).

the nature of the heavens and the earth, Jerusalem, and indeed the entire universe. Though some would contrast καινός with νέος, according to Harrisville both words can "connote a temporal as well as a qualitative significance."[51] Thus the question cannot be solved merely by debating the dubious nuances of words that are synonyms.

It seems clear that the former view of newness is to be accepted; God radically renews the present system but does not entirely obliterate or annihilate it. Such annihilation would be foreign to Old Testament eschatological hope and to the teaching of the New Testament as well. The "making new" of all things (καινὰ ποιῶ πάντα, Rev. 21:5) is equivalent to the "regeneration" (παλιγγενεσία, Matt. 19:28) or "restoration" (ἀποκατάστασις, Acts 3:21) of the universe through Christ's redemptive work. It is not that God does away with the creation that he once pronounced exceedingly good (Gen. 1:31). The physical, material world is not the source of sin. If it were, redemption could never be pictured as a cosmic reconciliation or pacification (Col. 1:20). Indeed, there would be no such thing as redemption for the physical creation, and Paul's thought in Romans 8:21–22 would be absurd. Rather than annihilating the present universe and performing a re-creation ex nihilo, God will radically transform the universe, which has been ravaged by the sin of human beings driven on by evil supernatural powers by removing from it all that constitutes sin. Cosmic renewal is no more an annihilation of the old world than personal regeneration is an annihilation of the old person. Ethical rather than ontological transformation is in view. The vivid imagery that describes the passing away of the old order (2 Peter 3:10, 12; Rev. 20:11; 21:1) describes the radical nature of its renewal, not its obliteration. Inasmuch as the physical universe did not commit sin, there is no reason to suppose that it must cease to exist because of sin.

The third exegetical matter to be discussed is the close association of the bride of Christ with the new Jerusalem (21:9–10). In an important article R. H. Gundry has argued that the new Jerusalem is simply a symbol for the people of God and not a place at all. According to Gundry, John "transforms Jerusalem into a symbol of the saints themselves. . . . John is not describing the eternal dwelling place of the

---

[51]R. A. Harrisville, *The Concept of Newness in the New Testament* (Minneapolis: Augsburg, 1960), 106. Harrisville's conclusions dispute the views of R. C. Trench, who argued that only καινός possessed qualitative significance. See Trench's *Synonyms of the New Testament*, 9th ed. (Grand Rapids: Eerdmans, 1948), 221. J. P. Louw and E. A. Nida also doubt that this possible distinction between the words should always be pressed (*Greek-English Lexicon of the New Testament, Based on Semantic Domains*, 2 vols. [New York: United Bible Societies, 1988], 1:594).

saints; he is describing them, and them alone."[52] No doubt this is an intriguing suggestion, but under scrutiny it does not hold up.

To support his thesis, Gundry asserts that "Rev. 21:1–22:5 does not describe the new earth, . . . it only mentions it."[53] This is not true, however, for 21:22–22:5 describes several features of the new earth, the Water of Life and the reappearing pre-Fall Tree of Life being particularly noteworthy. The Water of Life was mentioned previously in 21:6 as a reward of God's people, part of the inheritance promised to them in 21:6. This inheritance is no doubt to be connected to the new earth. Thus Gundry's assertion that the new earth is not described is overstated.

Gundry also argues that the marking of God's servants on their foreheads with the name *new Jerusalem* (Rev. 3:12) "identifies the New Jerusalem with the person who overcomes."[54] It is not clear what Gundry means here by "identifies," but to support his contention it would have to mean "equals," and that is doubtful here. John does not mean to assert that the overcomer is the new Jerusalem but rather that the overcomer is associated with his or her ultimate destiny, the new Jerusalem, as well as with Christ and God. Gundry also argues that in Revelation 20:9, "the beloved city" is parallel with "the camp of the saints."[55] This of course is true, but the parallelism is between the city and the camp, not the city and the saints.

The initial association of people and place occurs in 21:2, where John envisions the holy city, new Jerusalem, prepared as (ὡς) a bride for her husband. Here it is clear that "as" introduces a simile that compares the city to a bride, but this is a far cry from identifying or equating the city and the bride. Granted, there is an association of people and place in the vision as it alternates between city and bride imagery, but Gundry has overstated this metaphoric comparison in equating the place with the people of God. Also, Gundry's view results in a truncation of the cosmic effects of Christ's redemptive work, since the renewal of creation itself is minimized if not omitted entirely (whereas Revelation leads us to expect such renewal by numerous references to the earth prior to chapter 20).

The interpretation of the numbers used in 21:1–22:5 is another knotty exegetical problem. There are many numbers here: twelve gates and foundations (21:12, 14, 21), the dimensions of the city as twelve thousand stadia (21:16), the city wall of 144 cubits (21:17), and the

[52]Gundry, "The New Jerusalem," 256.
[53]Ibid.
[54]Ibid.
[55]Ibid., 256–57.

twelve fruits and leaves of the Tree of Life, which heal the nations (22:2). Earlier in the section on the hermeneutics of apocalyptic literature, it has been argued that these numbers are not the equivalent of the dimension specifications on an architect's blueprint. But what is intended?[56]

It is clear that all of the above items are connected to the number twelve or to a multiple of twelve (cf. Rev. 7:5–8; 12:1, 12).[57] This number is perhaps the most familiar number in the Bible, most frequently associated with the sons of Jacob, the twelve tribes of Israel, and the twelve apostles of the "new Israel," the church. The mention of the twelve tribes as the gates of the city would seem to underline the fact that access to salvation is through Israel's covenant promises in general and through Israel's promised Messiah in particular (Isa. 49:5–6; 51:4; John 4:22; Rom. 11:16–25; Eph. 2:11–22). The mention of the twelve apostles as the foundations of the city would seem to indicate that they are the foundation of the church as they confess the Lamb, Jesus, as the Messiah, the Son of God (Matt. 16:18; Eph. 2:20). Taken in tandem, the twelve tribes/gates and the twelve apostles/foundations clearly portray the essential transdispensational continuity of Israel and the church as the one people of God.[58]

From here on things get more difficult. Concerning the city dimensions of twelve thousand stadia in 21:16, if the number twelve is the number of God's people and if multiplying it by one thousand implies vast magnitude,[59] then the twelve thousand stadia would appear to indicate that the city is sufficient to accommodate an infinite number of God's people. The city can handle the full company of God's elect, though their number includes the total complement of the remnant of the nation of Israel (Rev. 7:1–8; 14:1) as well as innumerable multitudes of people from every nation on earth (7:9). The number describing the wall (144 cubits—height or thickness?) is much smaller than that describing the city as a whole. Perhaps the significance of the wall's dimension pertains to the full protection of God's people from the

---

[56]For a cautious approach to numbers in the Bible, see J. J. Davis, *Biblical Numerology* (Grand Rapids: Baker, 1973).

[57]This fact is obscured in the text of the NASB with its translation "fifteen hundred miles" in 21:16, though the marginal note has "twelve thousand stadia," as it literally appears in the text. The KJV, NIV, and RSV render the number correctly and use the marginal note to supply the equivalent in miles.

[58]This fact has not been sufficiently acknowledged by traditional dispensationalism. Perhaps the twenty-four elders (Rev. 4:4, et al.) are meant to picture the same truth. The people of God, composed of Jews and Gentiles who confess Jesus as Messiah, could be conceived here as the unity of Israel, represented by the twelve tribes, and the church, represented by the twelve apostles.

[59]So G. B. Caird, *The Revelation of St. John the Divine*, HNTC (New York: Harper & Row, 1966), 273.

evil and pain that were experienced during their sojourn on the old earth. The final use of the number twelve is found in the twelve fruits of the Tree of Life in 22:2. This seems to indicate that the provisions of the city for the nurture of its people are adequate. Just as its people are twelve, so is its capacity to sustain the life of those people. But this feature of the city anticipates the final exegetical matter to be discussed: the nature of life in the city.

A final question concerns the nature of life in the new Jerusalem. This matter is particularly challenging because of the mention of such features as the glory of earthly kings being brought into the city (21:24–27) and the evident need for the healing of the nations (22:3). It has already been argued at the beginning of this section that these words do not interpolate or recapitulate millennial conditions. It is the eternal state that is being described—the golden age, not the silver age, or Millennium. Therefore it is necessary to reexamine and rethink traditional concepts of life in the eternal state.

One possible approach to this question would be that the saved individuals who survive the Tribulation and enter the Millennium in an unglorified state will remain in such a state when the Millennium gives way to the new heaven and earth. If that were the case, however, all things would not have been made new (21:5), and flesh and blood would have inherited the kingdom of God (1 Cor. 15:50). A more plausible approach involves rethinking the concept of glorification and distinguishing it from an unbiblical deification in which believers are seemingly made into little gods who automatically have all the answers to all the problems that plagued them on the old earth. Such a view compromises the crucial biblical and theological distinction between Creator and creature. Even in the eternal state the infinite Creator will be far above his finite creatures, though they are no longer plagued by sin. Glorified individuals will no doubt be sinless individuals (Rom. 8:29; 1 Thess. 5:23; 1 John 3:2), but this does not mean that glorified individuals will cease to need and long for the continuing application of the means of grace.[60] Glorification does not mean that every person in the eternal state will possess equal knowledge of God, Christ, the Spirit, and the Scriptures or equal capacities for every task. Rather, glorification means that believers will not be hindered in their earthly pursuits by personal or structural sin, demonic influence, or a "groaning" earthly environment.

Believers will evidently be assigned duties based upon their gifts and

---

[60]Harrisville understands the healing of the nations to imply that "the memory of what occurred in the old aeon is gradually banished in the full enjoyment of the new life" (*The Concept of Newness,* 104).

their faithfulness in the development and application of those gifts prior to death or rapture (Matt. 19:27–30; 25:14–30; Luke 19:11–27; 1 Cor. 6:2–3). Therefore, the nations will still need to seek the light of the city and will still be required to bring their best achievements into it. Healing will be necessary not in the sense of taking away sickness or sin but in the sense of developing physical, social, and spiritual capacities to serve God, neighbor, and nature more lovingly and faithfully.[61]

CONCLUSION: THE NEW JERUSALEM
AND BIBLICAL THEOLOGY

It has been said that the Bible begins with a garden but ends with a city.[62] However, this seeming discontinuity is only superficial because the eschatological city retains some of the key features of the protological garden. The image of the river or spring of the water of life (Rev. 22:1, 2) may be traced ultimately to Genesis 1:9; 2:10 and is also found in Psalm 46:4 and Ezekiel 47:1. The same image occurs elsewhere in Revelation in 7:17; 21:6; 22:17. The accompanying image of the Tree of Life is found for the first time in Genesis 1:11–12, 29; 2:9; 3:22–24, and is also found in Ezekiel 47:12, as well as in noncanonical Jewish literature (2 Esd. 8:52; 2 Enoch 8:3–4). Because of the fall of human beings in Adam and Eve, access to the Tree of Life was barred, but because of the Lamb's victory, access is once again available, as is made clear elsewhere in Revelation 2:7; 22:14, 19.

All of this means that by the grace of God and through the redemption of Jesus Christ, God's people and God's universe will one day fully experience harmonious mutual relationships that far exceed even the relationships that once characterized the universe before the Fall.[63] In Christ's obedience God's people are graciously given far more than they gave up in Adam's disobedience (Rom. 5:12–21). Their experience of this gift comes in three phases: a preliminary and anticipatory bronze stage brought to earth by the first coming of Christ,

---

[61]For an innovative if not entirely convincing approach to this problem, see R. J. Mouw, *When Kings Come Marching In: Isaiah and the New Jerusalem* (Grand Rapids: Eerdmans, 1983).

[62]E. L. Copeland speaks in this disjunctive vein but then moderates the discontinuity considerably by noting that the new Jerusalem is a garden city. See his "Urbanization and Salvation: Can the City Be Saved?" in *Discipling the City,* ed. R. S. Greenway (Grand Rapids: Baker, 1979), 67–70.

[63]E. Sauer states it well: "The end of history and the beginning of history belong together. The last leaf of the Bible corresponds with the first. Holy Scripture begins with Paradise (Gen. 1:2); and with paradise it ends (Rev. 22). But the conclusion is greater than the beginning. The Omega is greater than the Alpha. The future paradise is not only the lost and regained, but above all it is the heavenly and eternally glorified paradise" (*The Triumph of the Crucified,* 199).

an intermediate silver age brought to earth at Christ's second coming, and an ultimate, golden age, consummated when all opposition to God's rule has ceased. Those who believe in the Lord Jesus Christ are already ethically transferred into his kingdom and live on earth as the redeemed community, an earthly colony of the coming heavenly city, the new Jerusalem (Gal. 4:26; Col. 1:13; Heb. 12:22). These colonies endure many trials in anticipation of Christ's return to rule on the earth for a thousand years (Matt. 25:31–46; Rev. 20:1–6). This Millennium is an intermediate transitional stage of God's kingdom that further extends his rule over the entire earth, not just the colonies of the redeemed. However, because of the continuing presence of sinners, there are still difficulties and problems that finally erupt in the rebellion of Revelation 20:7–9. The ultimate extension of Christ's rule involves the exclusion of all sinners from the renewed heavens and earth (Rev. 20:10–12; 21:8, 27; 22:15, 19).[64]

These three stages of the extension of God's rule are characterized by a corresponding decline in the extent of the rule of the great adversary, Satan. The preaching and power of the gospel of the kingdom are already binding Satan as individuals submit to kingdom authority and live under God's rule in their homes, churches, and cultures (Matt. 12:28–29; Col. 1:13; 3:5–17). At Christ's return Satan is effectively banished as the Millennium begins, and righteousness increases, even though Satan still has many who are ready to follow him at his release (Rom. 16:20; Rev. 20:1–9). The total removal of Satan's influence from the earth occurs when he and all his angelic and human followers are put under eternal punishment in the lake of fire, outside the new Jerusalem (Rev. 20:10–12; 21:8, 27; 22:15, 19).

When all evil supernatural powers and all humans who were subject to these powers are removed from God's new heaven and earth, the people of God will be freed to live in mutually loving harmonious relationships with God, neighbors, and nature. Gone will be all social, ethnic, and sexual biases. The removal of the curse (Rev. 22:3) will mean that the physical universe will no longer terrorize humans with earthquakes, hurricanes, floods, blizzards, plagues, famines, and the like.[65] Instead, harmony will be the rule, and there will be absolutely no exceptions. In this age of total newness, believers will finally be able to

---

[64]Poythress is correct in stating that some dispensationalists have overemphasized the penultimate Millennium at the expense of the ultimate renewed heavens and earth (*Understanding Dispensationalists*, 130–31; cf. 47–51). However, the transitional and penultimate nature of the Millennium is articulated well by E. Sauer, *The Triumph of the Crucified*, 152–53, and 169, where Sauer strikingly comments that "even the Millennium is still but a portico to eternity."

[65]Ladd, *The Presence of the Future*, 62–64.

realize the unhindered use and blessing of their God-given skills (Rev. 21:24–22:2). There will be unending growth in creaturely godliness as each person becomes in the end what God had intended from the beginning. To the extent that finite creatures can share with the infinite Creator, God's people will "participate wholly in the activity of the Godhead, for they will reign for ever and ever."[66]

Such a prospect ought to affect profoundly the believer's view of life in the present world. Alva J. McClain put it this way: "The premillennial philosophy of history makes sense. It lays a Biblical and rational basis for a truly optimistic view of human history. Furthermore, rightly apprehended, it has practical effects. It says that life here and now, in spite of the tragedy of sin, is nevertheless something worth-while. All the true values of human life will be preserved and carried over into the coming kingdom; nothing worthwhile will be lost."[67]

---

[66]Harrisville, *The Concept of Newness,* 105.

[67]McClain, *The Greatness of the Kingdom,* 531. While McClain would not have stressed continuity to the degree that it has been advocated here, his thoughts at this point concur remarkably.

The Scope and Center of Old and New Testament Theology and Hope

Kenneth L. Barker

Since it would be impossible for anyone to deal, even cursorily, with the topic assigned to me within the limits of a single chapter, it will be necessary to take a highly selective approach. After all, Peters devoted three massive volumes to the same general subject![1] So I propose to make this chapter, first, an expansion of, and sequel (or postscript) to, some of the issues I touched on in a previous article on relationships between the Testaments.[2] In that article I expressed the hope that I could develop the false dichotomies (i.e., the true continuities) between the Testaments more fully in the future. This chapter is a step in that direction. Incidentally, in that same article I also issued a challenge for an amillennial, covenant theologian to respond with an article stressing the *legitimate* discontinuities between the Testaments. The challenge was accepted by Karlberg,[3] but he did not really argue the case for the discontinuities I had in mind. In fact, he in essence denied some of the continuities I had emphasized.[4] Thus I have decided to direct attention to one of the major discontinuities under the sections "Old Testament Expectation" and "Progressive Fulfillment" below.

The selectivity mentioned above will focus primarily on the themes

---

[1]G. N. H. Peters, *The Theocratic Kingdom*, 3 vols. (New York: Funk & Wagnalls, 1884; reprint, Grand Rapids: Kregel, 1988). In my judgment, no amillennial, covenant theologian has ever made a serious attempt to rebut this cogent case for premillennialism.

[2]K. L. Barker, "False Dichotomies Between the Testaments," *JETS* 25 (March 1982): 3–16.

[3]M. W. Karlberg, "Legitimate Discontinuities Between the Testaments," *JETS* 28 (March 1985): 9–20. On this whole subject, see now J. S. Feinberg, ed., *Continuity and Discontinuity: Perspectives on the Relationship Between the Old and New Testaments* (Westchester, Ill.: Crossway, 1988).

[4]Basically, I agree with W. VanGemeren's evaluation that "Mark W. Karlberg has made an attempt at defining 'legitimate discontinuities,' but fails to be convincing because of his prior understanding of typology" ("Systems of Continuity," in *Continuity and Discontinuity*, ed. J. S. Feinberg [Westchester, Ill.: Crossway, 1988], 330, n. 54).

of law and grace, and Israel and the church. After such a follow-up to my earlier article (see "Orientation" below), I will address the related subjects of God's rule as the center (or at least the dominating theme) of biblical theology, the nature of Old Testament expectation and the tension created when that expectation is compared with New Testament fulfillment, and the resolution of that tension through the progressive fulfillment of prophecy. Because of certain points made in discussing progressive fulfillment below, my subtitle for this whole chapter could be "Not Either-Or but Both-And."

ORIENTATION

In my article entitled "False Dichotomies Between the Testaments,"[5] I discussed the need for a mediating position between traditional dispensational premillennialism and traditional covenant theology. Some significant developments and refinements have been occurring within both schools of theological thought. Since I wish to build on that article, a review and further development of what I wrote there are in order. Here, then, somewhat expanded at certain points, are some of the more salient features of that article. (In order to make it easier to follow, I present these in the order in which they appear in the article.)[6]

1. *Dispensational premillennialists and amillennial, covenant theologians of orthodox persuasion should treat each other more like brothers in Christ and less like adversaries or even heretics.*[7] I still stand behind that statement, and I believe I do so on biblical grounds.

2. *Personally, I classify myself as at least a moderate dispensationalist.* I do so, first, because I maintain that Israel is not the Old Testament "church." To hold that Israel is the church is almost to imply that the center of biblical theology is the church. Moreover, it is not certain or clear that the church is the new or spiritual Israel, or the Israel of God. All passages on which such terminology is based can be just as satisfactorily explained otherwise. Second, I remain convinced that God's future program includes ethnic or national Israel (see below). Third, I hold that Christ will reign literally on this earth in space-time history (see below).

---

[5]See n. 2.

[6]Appreciation is hereby expressed to R. Youngblood, editor of *JETS*, for permission to refer to so much of that material. For support, see the details in that article.

[7]Cf. R. P. Lightner, *Prophecy in the Ring* (Denver: Accent Books, 1976). Lightner advocates that we take prophecy of "things [still] to come" (other than the doctrines of the second coming, the final resurrection, the final judgment, and the eternal state, on which all agree) out of the boxing ring. His book closes with a quotation of these appropriate maxims: "In essentials unity, in uncertainties freedom, in all things love" (120).

The reason for the qualifier "moderate" is likewise threefold. First, I stress only two major dispensations—the old-covenant era and the new-covenant era. This appears to be in harmony with the argument of Hebrews 8–10. The present and future forms of the messianic era (church and Millennium) both fit within the time when the new covenant is in force. Second, I believe that several passages that other dispensationalists relegate solely to the future received a literal fulfillment in the New Testament period or are receiving such a fulfillment in the continuing church age—in addition to a final, complete fulfillment in the future in the case of some of those passages (see "Progressive Fulfillment" below). Third, I prefer to think in terms of an inaugurated eschatology rather than an exclusively futurist eschatology (again, see under "Progressive Fulfillment").

3. *To say that the Old Testament knows only of the circumcision of the flesh, while the New Testament speaks of the circumcision of the heart, is a false dichotomy.* The truth of the circumcision of the heart, often considered to be New Testament teaching, is very much present in the Old Testament (e.g., Deut. 10:16).

4. *To say that the Old Testament presents the letter of the law, while the New Testament reveals the spirit of the law, is a false dichotomy.* A proper interpretation of passages like Psalm 50, Matthew 5:21–48, Romans 2:17–29, and 2 Corinthians 3:6–18 will demonstrate the validity of this assertion.[8] Actually, both Testaments speak with a united voice on the importance and necessity of adhering not only to the letter of the law but also to its spirit.

5. *To say that the Old Testament is the testament of law but the New Testament is the testament of grace is a false dichotomy.* Any consideration of the scope of biblical theology (such as in this chapter) must include some discussion of the law, since it played such a significant role during the old-covenant era. Then there is the question of continuity and/or discontinuity between law and grace, or law and gospel.

It must first be borne in mind that the law was given to the *redeemed* people of God as a means of expressing their love to God as well as a means of governing their relationship to God and to each other. It was not a way of salvation but a way to enjoy an orderly life and God's fullest blessing within the covenantal, theocratic arrangement. Thus God's grace precedes the covenantal law he gave to his people and represents a use of salvation history to inspire grateful obedience. Passages such as Deuteronomy 4:37–40 and 7:6–11 are saying: Because God has loved you and shown grace to you, you ought to obey him (cf. John 14:15).

[8]See, for example, the study notes on these passages in *The NIV Study Bible*, ed. K. L. Barker et al. (Grand Rapids: Zondervan, 1985).

According to Jesus, the ultimate key to the understanding of the Ten Commandments (Ex. 20; Deut. 5) is not law but love—love for God (Matt. 22:37, quoting Deut. 6:5 and summarizing the first four commandments) and love for others (Matt. 22:39, quoting Lev. 19:18 and summarizing the last six commandments; similarly Paul in Rom. 13:8–10).

The negative attitude toward the law in certain New Testament references is due to an unlawful use of the law. Jesus' conflict in, for example, Matthew 5 and 23 was not with the law and the Old Testament but with the "letter-of-the-law" interpretations and accretions made by some of the Pharisees and the teachers of the law.[9] Similarly, what Paul condemned in Romans and Galatians was not the law or obedience to the law but the use of the law in a legalistic manner to merit salvation or sanctification or both.

The only proper role the law can play for unregenerate people is to reveal the darkness of their sin against the backdrop of the radiant light of God's holiness and point them to the Savior (Rom. 3:20; Gal. 3:24; 1 Tim. 1:8). But for the person of faith it is the gracious revelation of God's righteous will and is to be followed as the grateful and joyful expression of that faith (cf. Pss. 1, 19, and 119). There are, however, certain obvious exceptions, such as the purely ceremonial laws—those types and shadows that found their fulfillment and reality in Christ (see Hebrews).

Even if τέλος in Romans 10:4 means "termination" instead of something like "completion," the statement that Christ is the termination of the law must still be qualified. Otherwise, one cannot account satisfactorily for the numerous instances where the New Testament uses the Law (as well as other parts of the Old Testament) for exhortation and for application of eternal truths and principles, particularly in the areas of spiritual life, morality, and ethics (cf., e.g., Matt. 4:4, 7, 10; 15:4; 19:5, 18–19; 22:37–40; Acts 23:5; Rom. 4:3; 7:7; 9:15; 12:19; 13:9; 1 Cor. 5:13; 9:9; 2 Cor. 4:6; 6:16; 8:14–15; 13:1; Gal. 3:6; 4:30; 5:14; Eph. 6:1–3; 1 Tim. 5:18; Heb. 10:30; 13:5; James 2:8–11, 20–24; 1 Peter 1:15–16—the selections here were deliberately restricted to uses of the Pentateuch). If the ethical and moral law reflected in the Torah has been abrogated, how can New Testament writers legitimately use the references listed above to express, substantiate, support, reinforce, or give authority to the points they make? Surely this common New Testament practice strongly implies that the cited passages are authoritative for the church today.

---

[9]Cf. P. Fairbairn, *The Revelation of Law in Scripture* (Edinburgh: T. & T. Clark, 1869; reprint, Grand Rapids: Zondervan, 1957), 227–29, 275.

Besides, if the Old Testament moral law is no longer in force, how can "all Scripture" (referring primarily to the Old Testament at that stage of progressive revelation) be "useful for teaching, rebuking, correcting and training in righteousness" (2 Tim. 3:16)?[10] One of the legitimate continuities, then, between the Old and New Testaments is God's moral law expressed *throughout* Scripture. It transcends dispensational (or any other) discontinuities. In fact, if the Old Testament moral law is not applicable to us today or if we are no longer under it, how can the references given above and below (as well as passages like Rom. 15:4 and 1 Cor. 10:1–14) be true? It is more in keeping with the totality of biblical teaching to insist that the ethical and spiritual commands of the Old Testament, the numerous moral imperatives of the New Testament, and Christ (or the law of Christ, or the royal law of love) are *all* part of the believer's rule of life. After all, the commandments (as well as other material) are reiterated in the New Testament and are presented as part of the permanent spiritual and moral (and divine) standard that Christians are to follow. Motivation and enablement may change, but the standard continues because it expresses the immutable moral nature of God and can change only if God's character can change.

As I understand Paul, he condemns not only legalism (and "nomism," according to some) in Romans and Galatians but also antinomianism and libertinism (Gal. 5; Phil. 3). The gracious liberty we enjoy in Christ is not to be (mis)construed as license to do as we please. Rather, our liberty is limited by God's *eternal* moral law, which includes Exodus 20 and its expositions in the Pentateuch and later Old Testament literature, notably the prophetic books. Perhaps one of the reasons for the lamentable behavior of many Christians today—including leaders—is that they do not take the abiding moral, ethical, and profoundly spiritual commands of the Old Testament seriously enough.

But, someone may object, what about those references to believers' being "not under (the) law" (Rom. 6:14–15; 1 Cor. 9:20; Gal. 5:18)? In my opinion, a careful study of those passages in their context (e.g., Rom. 6–8) will indicate that what Paul means fundamentally is that we believers have been delivered from the law as a system or from the law's sentence of death because of our sins. (Because of Christ's work for us, we are no longer under the threatening condemnation or tyranny of death pronounced against us by the law.)

Such an understanding seems more in harmony with passages such as the following:

---

[10]On 2 Tim. 3:16–17, see W. C. Kaiser, Jr., *Toward Rediscovering the Old Testament* (Grand Rapids: Zondervan, 1987), 26–32.

Matthew 5:17–19. Jesus made it clear that he had not come to abolish the Law and the Prophets but to fulfill them (fill them to the full), and that "whoever practices and teaches these commands will be called great in the kingdom of heaven."

Romans 3:31. Paul claimed to uphold the law.

Romans 7:12. The law is described as "holy, righteous, and good" because it presents God's *eternal,* moral, ethical, and spiritual standard.

Romans 8:1. Paul declared that while the law brings condemnation (including death) because it points out, stimulates, and condemns sin, "there is now *no condemnation* [not 'no law'] for those who are in Christ Jesus."

Romans 13:8–10. Paul applies several of the commandments to Christians.

2 Corinthians 3:6–18. The law is described as the "ministry that brought death" and the "ministry that condemns." (The believer in Christ, however, indwelt by the life-giving Spirit, is no longer "under the law" in that sense.)

Colossians 2:13–15. Paul makes the point, not that the law has been abolished, but that God canceled the law's accusations against Christians because of their union with Christ, who paid sin's penalty on the cross.

1 Timothy 1:18. The law is described as "good if one uses it properly."

Hebrews 8–10. Rightly understood, this passage means, not that the law has been done away with, but that the old (Sinaitic)-covenant arrangement has been superseded by the new-covenant arrangement.

The correct interpretation of "not under (the) law," then, is "not that the Christian has been freed from all moral authority. He has, however, been freed from the law in the manner in which God's people were under law in the Old Testament era. Law provides no enablement to resist the power of sin; it only condemns the sinner. But grace enables."[11] The life-giving Spirit, "in fulfillment of the promise of the new covenant, writes that same law inwardly. . . . He thus provides the believer with love for God's law, which previously he had hated, and with power to keep it, which previously he had not possessed."[12]

P. P. Bliss put it correctly when he proclaimed:

---

[11]*NIV Study Bible,* 1714, note on Rom. 6:14.

[12]Ibid., 1766, note on 2 Cor. 3:6. I am not certain that I would go as far as David H. Stern, who translates *erga nomou* (works of law) as "legalistic observance of Torah commands" and *hypo nomon* (under law) as "in subjection to the system which results from perverting the Torah into legalism," but it seems to me that he at least is moving in the right direction. See his *Jewish New Testament* (Clarksville, Md.: Jewish New Testament Publications, 1989), xxiv. Cf. also C. E. B. Cranfield, *A Critical and Exegetical Commentary on the Epistle to the Romans,* ICC, 2 vols. (Edinburgh: T. & T. Clark, 1975–79), 2:845–62.

> Free from the law, O happy condition,
> Jesus hath bled, and there is remission;
> *Cursed by the law* and bruised by the fall,
> *Grace hath redeemed us* once for all.
>
> Now we are free—*there's no condemnation,*
> *Jesus provides a perfect salvation;*
> "Come unto Me," O hear His sweet call,
> Come, and He saves us once for all. (emphasis added)

Believers, then, are not "free from the law" per se. Rather, as those who are under God's redemptive grace in Christ, they have been liberated from the *curse* of the law; see Galatians 3:10–14, where the subject, in context, clearly is justification, which cannot be earned—for that would be legalism—but is received as the free gift of God "by grace through faith" (Eph. 2:8–9). This does not mean, however, that Christians are under no obligation to follow the moral imperatives of the law.

Fairbairn commented perceptively on Colossians 2:14: "[Christ] *wiped out* the writing [the Mosaic law] . . . that is, in effect deleted it . . . in the respect in which it formed an accusing witness against us. . . . the law itself in its condemnatory aspect toward men was brought to an end."[13] Leslie Flynn's words are likewise apropos:

> An erroneous dichotomy equates the Old Testament with law, and the New Testament with grace. But the Old Testament is full of God's grace in dealing with the penitent, and the new Testament is full of moral law. When Paul tells children to obey their parents, he reinforces the injunction by quoting the fifth commandment "Honor thy father and mother," and adds, "which is the first commandment with promise" (Eph. 6:1, 2). Does not this strongly suggest that the Decalogue continues as a regulator of Christian behavior?
>
> To preach justification by law is legalistic, voiding the Gospel. To preach the non-validity of the law for today is antinomian, voiding the law. To preach obedience to the law for the Christian, who has been justified apart from the law, is evangelical, voiding neither grace nor law.
>
> Though the believer is not under the law's condemning power, he is under its commanding power. The law does not give, but it does guide, life.[14]

---

[13]Fairbairn, *Revelation of Law*, 467. For our deliverance from the curse of the law, but at the same time the law's application to and validity for believers today, see also Calvin, *Institutes* 2.7.12–15; D. Clowney, "The Use of the Bible in Ethics," in *Inerrancy and Hermeneutics*, ed. H. C. Conn (Grand Rapids: Baker, 1988), 214–18.

[14]L. Flynn, letter to the editor, *Moody Monthly*, December 1976, p. 6; see also S. Bolton, *The True Bounds of Christian Freedom* (Edinburgh: Banner of Truth, 1964), 9–109.

This line of thought ultimately means that the Christian Bible, for faith and practice (with the qualifications and exceptions we have noted), is not just twenty-seven books but sixty-six books. McComiskey is certainly correct when, after providing an exegesis of Micah 6:8, he writes:

> The standards of this verse are for those who are members of the covenantal community and delineate the areas of ethical response that God wants to see in those who share the covenantal obligations. These standards have not been abrogated for Christians, for the New Testament affirms their continuing validity. We are still called to the exercise of true religion, to kindness, and to humility (1 Cor. 13:4; 2 Cor. 6:6; Col. 3:12; James 1:27; 1 Peter 1:2; 5:5). Christians are in a covenant relationship with God in which the law (*torah*) has been placed within their hearts (Jer. 31:33; cf. Heb. 10:14–17), not abrogated.[15]

I take this position because I sincerely believe it to be the biblical view. Some, however, argue against it based on James 2:10: "For whoever keeps the whole law and yet stumbles at just one point is guilty of breaking all of it." The argument is that, since the law is a unit, one cannot distinguish the moral law from the ceremonial law and claim that the former applies to us while the latter does not. The most obvious answer to this line of reasoning is that Scripture itself makes the distinction (Ex. 20:1; 21:1; 35:1; see also other sections of legal literature, where there are clear formulaic demarcations between apodictic [basically moral and spiritual] law, casuistic [essentially civil, social, and ethical] law, and ceremonial law). In the New Testament compare, for example, the abrogation of dietary laws in 1 Timothy 4:3–5 with the application of the moral law to the church by the same writer (Eph. 6:1–3). Clearly such distinctions are scriptural.[16]

Others argue from Galatians 3:15–4:7 that the law is done away with. But regardless of the meaning of this much-debated passage (the commentaries and journal articles differ), it relates to only one purpose of the law. According to Pentecost, there are no less than ten purposes of the law![17]

Still others maintain that the *regulatory* purpose of the law was

---

[15]T. C. McComiskey, "Micah," in EBC 7 (Grand Rapids: Zondervan, 1979), 436–37.

[16]For additional support, see R. A. Cole, "Law in the Old Testament," in ZPEB 3:883–94; K. L. Barker, "Ordinance," in ibid. 4:543–44; R. K. Harrison, "Law in the Old Testament," in ISBE 3:76–85; J. E. Hartley, "*yārâ,*" in TWOT 1:403–5; J. R. W. Stott, *God's New Society: The Message of Ephesians* (Downers Grove, Ill.: InterVarsity Press, 1979), 99–101.

[17]J. D. Pentecost, "The Purpose of the Law," BSac 128 (July–September 1971): 227–33.

temporary and ceased when the church began, while the *revelatory and pedagogical* purpose of the law (revealing the eternal, moral character and will of God) can still be used to guide the Christian's moral and ethical conduct; indeed, the law is so quoted and applied in the New Testament. If this distinction is helpful to some, I have no strong objection to it, though I must confess that it is difficult for me to conceive of laws revealing God's will in the moral, ethical, spiritual, and theological spheres that at the same time do not also regulate and even dictate our beliefs and behavior. The most satisfying approach to me personally and, I believe, the one most consistent with the precepts and practice of Scripture as a whole is simply to hold that, in the area under discussion, whatever the New Testament has not clearly abrogated or modified in Old Testament revelation is for us today.[18]

In commenting on Matthew 12:5, 7, F. B. Meyer put it this way: "All through the Old Testament you may detect the spirit of the New; the mercy in which God delights. . . . The New Testament is in accord with the Old. . . . Is it likely that He will contradict his original design, and undo what cost Him thought and care? Surely not; He is pledged only to undo the evil which has marred his work."[19] "Or haven't you read in the Law? . . . If you had known what these words mean . . ." (Matt. 12:5, 7).

What I am pleading for is an approach that does justice, not simply to two or three references (such as James 2:10; Gal. 3:15–4:7—after all, there is always the possibility that our understanding of such passages may be somewhat deficient), but to the literally hundreds of instances where the New Testament uses the Old Testament (including the moral law) as authoritative for believers today. That is to say, I am appealing for an approach that recognizes the Old Testament moral law for what it appears to be—part of God's timeless moral standard that can no more change than God's eternal moral character can. While we are no longer under the Mosaic law as a whole or as a system,[20] we are certainly under

---

[18]By "abrogated or modified" I have in mind primarily ceremonial laws, laws of cleanliness, and types as discussed elsewhere in this chapter. Civil law is a more complex category, which needs to be assessed on a case-by-case basis. That which is in harmony with God's moral character should continue.

[19]F. B. Meyer, *Great Verses Through the Bible* (Grand Rapids: Zondervan, 1966), 373. On the relationship and application of Old Testament law to New Testament believers, see further Kaiser, *Toward Rediscovering the Old Testament*, 147–90; T. E. McComiskey, *The Covenants of Promise* (Grand Rapids: Baker, 1985), 76–137.

[20]In view of parallel passages, the meaning here may even be that we are no longer under the curse or condemnation of the law (i.e., death), for Christ redeemed us from that. See further Moo's discussion of Rom. 6:14 and 7:4 in D. Moo, "Romans 1–8," in *WEC*, 405–8, 411, 438–42, 446–48. He interacts well with the recent views of Sanders, Dunn, and others and provides an essentially balanced treatment of the law and the Christian, though my position is probably somewhat stronger than his and closer to that of W. C. Kaiser, Jr., as expressed in his book *Toward Old Testament Ethics* (Grand Rapids:

the moral and ethical part of it. In other words, "don't throw the baby out with the bath water." While some claim that the Old Testament moral law is valid for us only because most of it is sanctioned by the New Testament, I maintain instead that it is more logical (and theological!) to hold that the reason such law is repeated in the New Testament is that it is inherently transdispensational, transcovenantal, transcultural, and thus eternal. Even if the Old Testament moral law had not received the approbation of the New Testament, it would still have been binding on us today because of its very nature.

Thus we must not interpret two or three passages in Romans, Galatians, or James in a manner that conflicts with the way the rest of the New Testament clearly uses the Old Testament (its moral law in particular) as authoritative for believers today. I have personally heard some pastors and professors preach and teach these passages in such an unqualified manner that they leave the impression that today we are free to discard the entire Old Testament (including its moral imperatives) because it allegedly contains only material no longer applicable to us in any sense—other than as stories from which we can draw some practical lessons.

Before leaving the discussion of this false dichotomy, I wish to make it clear that the approach I am advocating is not the same as the so-called theonomic model or the Christian reconstructionist movement, which does not adequately distinguish between the old covenant and the new covenant, or between Israel as a theocracy and the church as a "mystery" form of God's kingdom (e.g., Matt. 13), or between Israel as a covenant nation and the United States as a pluralistic society.[21]

6. *To say that the Old Testament is concerned with Israel but the New Testament is concerned with the church is a false dichotomy.* Any treatment of the scope of Old and New Testament theology (as in this chapter) must involve some consideration of Israel and the church, since they are the two primary entities of the old- and new-covenant eras. Then there is the issue of continuity or discontinuity between them. There is some truth to the discontinuity position, but it also contains some error. Certain both-and situations are often forced into either-or ones, as though there are no alternatives. Two either-or extremes are to be

Zondervan, 1983), 307–14. See also Kaiser, "Legitimate Hermeneutics," in *Inerrancy,* ed. N. L. Geisler (Grand Rapids: Zondervan, 1979), 143–44; cf. J. W. Wenham, "Christ's View of Scripture," in ibid., 13.

[21]For works defending this movement, see, for example, G. L. Bahnsen, *Theonomy in Christian Ethics* (Phillipsburg, N.J.: Presbyterian & Reformed, 1984); G. North, *Conspiracy: A Biblical View* (Fort Worth, Tex.: Dominion, 1986); R. J. Rushdoony, *The Institutes of Biblical Law* (Phillipsburg, N.J.; Presbyterian & Reformed, 1973). For a critique, see H. Wayne House and Thomas Ice, *Dominion Theology: Blessing or Curse?* (Portland, Ore.: Multnomah Press, 1988).

avoided with respect to the relationship between Israel and the church: (1) their complete amalgamation by many in the ranks of covenant theology, and (2) their almost total separation by most traditional dispensationalists. In my view, the truth lies somewhere between such a polarization. That the church in some sense is latent in the great promises of Gentile blessing in the Old Testament seems clear from Paul's use of such promises in, for example, Romans 9:24–26; 15:8–12. That ethnic Israel in some sense continues in the present and future aspects of the new-covenant (i.e., messianic) era likewise seems clear from the most natural exegesis and understanding of such passages as Leviticus 26:40–45; Deuteronomy 30:1–10; Psalm 89:28–37; Jeremiah 31:36–37; 32:37–41; Ezekiel 11:17–21; 36:24–31; 37:24–28; Romans 11:11–29. At the same time, since Romans 11 indicates that Gentiles (in the church) have been, by sovereign grace, grafted into Israel's olive tree, by so much it stresses the continuity of the people of God (see "Progressive Fulfillment" below). I am in essential agreement with Saucy, who takes the position that "the Scriptural concept of the people of God supports both a certain continuity and discontinuity."[22]

Snaith's statement about Israel's new covenant (Jer. 31:31–40) bears on the question of the perpetuity of national Israel (or at least a remnant thereof): "God's sure, unswerving love will find a way by which even stubborn, unrepentant Israel can turn. It will mean new hearts, but God will accomplish even this. Then there will be a turning to God in all sincerity, and loyal obedience to His law."[23] Such a future fulfillment of the new covenant for Israel also appears evident from Zechariah 12:10–13:1.

As I perceive the grand sweep of what God is doing, the old sharp distinction between Israel and the church begins to become somewhat blurred. In my understanding of Romans 11 and other passages, both entities are involved in the present and future forms of God's kingdom as well as in the eternal state (in my view 1 Cor. 15:20–28 teaches that the messianic, or mediatorial, or millennial aspect of the kingdom merges into the eternal kingdom). Strictly speaking, it is incorrect to call Israel God's earthly people and the church God's heavenly people, since in the eternal state we will all be together, sharing in the blessings of the new Jerusalem and the new earth (Rev. 21:2–3; cf. Heb. 12:22–24). As far as the eternal state is concerned, it appears that there will be no

---

[22]R. L. Saucy, "Israel and the Church: A Case for Discontinuity," in *Continuity and Discontinuity: Perspectives on the Relationship Between the Old and New Testaments: Essays in Honor of S. Lewis Johnson, Jr.*, ed. John S. Feinberg (Westchester: Crossway, 1988), 240.

[23]N. H. Snaith, *The Distinctive Ideas of the Old Testament* (New York: Schocken, 1964), 122.

heavenly people in the sense of living somewhere off in space or even beyond it.

There is thus a greater unity or integration in God's grand design, overall purpose, and comprehensive program for this earth and its people than many dispensationalists have been willing to acknowledge. In the past, some of us have not been able to see the forest for the trees. We have compartmentalized too much.[24]

Finally, in considering Israel and the church, what becomes of Israel's land promises? Fuller rightly maintains that "ethnic Israel will some day inhabit the land that God marked out for Abraham's descendants."[25] Van Ruler, who is not a dispensationalist, concurs: "For the consciousness of the Christian church throughout the centuries there has always been a surplus in the Old Testament that it could not assimilate."[26] He then raises some searching and humbling questions: "Does everything end in the church? Does everything, not only Israel, but history and creation, exist for the sake of the church? Or is the church only one among many forms of the kingdom of God, and does its catholicity consist precisely in the fact that it respects, acknowledges, and holds dear all forms of the kingdom, for example, even the people of Israel?"[27]

Recognizing that Israel's great land promises are part of the "surplus" that the church is not now assimilating, Hoekema solved the problem by relegating such promises to the new earth in the eternal state.[28] His position marks an advance over the old amillennial view that argued that the land and kingdom promises either were forfeited through Israel's disobedience or are all now being spiritually fulfilled in the church. But my hermeneutics still will not let me agree with his expungement of national Israel (or a remnant thereof) from God's future program, or with his elimination of a literal, visible reign of Christ on this earth in time-space history.[29]

7. I reiterate my call for more dialogue and discussion in facing together the key problems in biblical hermeneutics, biblical exegesis, and biblical theology. I

---

[24]Cf. W. R. Cook, *The Theology of John* (Chicago: Moody Press, 1979), 90–91, n. 35.

[25]D. P. Fuller, *Gospel and Law: Contrast or Continuum?* (Grand Rapids: Eerdmans, 1971), 89.

[26]A. A. van Ruler, *The Christian Church and the Old Testament* (Grand Rapids: Eerdmans, 1971), 89.

[27]Ibid., 98.

[28]A. A. Hoekema, *The Bible and the Future* (Grand Rapids: Eerdmans, 1979), 205–13.

[29]See further M. Weinfeld, "The Covenant Grant in the Old Testament and in the Ancient Near East," *JAOS* 90 (1970): 184–203; W. C. Kaiser, Jr., "The Promised Land: A Biblical-Historical View," *BSac* 138 (October–December 1981): 302–12, and, more recently, idem, *Toward Rediscovering the Old Testament*, 46–58; *NIV Study Bible*, 19; J. L. Townsend, "Fulfillment of the Land Promise in the Old Testament," *BSac* 142 (October–December 1985): 320–37.

have become convinced that if all of us could approach the text of Scripture as honestly and objectively as possible, without being unduly influenced by our conscious or unconscious presuppositions from systematic or dogmatic theology, we would move even closer in our theological positions. As I wrote in the ICBI volume on hermeneutics:

> Even the church must be prepared, if necessary, to modify its traditions, creeds and confessions if biblical exegesis and biblical theology clearly dictate that it should. I personally do not believe that this will ever need to happen in the case of commonly accepted cardinal doctrines of the Christian faith, but it could easily happen in the case of the church's understanding of other doctrines and specific passages of Holy Scripture. . . . we must be willing to revise and refine our systematic theology if biblical exegesis and biblical theology indicate that we should do so. If this means that systematic theology (other than in the areas of universally acknowledged cardinal doctrines of historic Christianity) must, at least to some extent, be always in a state of flux, so be it. . . . Otherwise, inerrancy no longer attaches to the text of Scripture but to our understanding of it. After all, this is the International Council on *Biblical* Inerrancy, not the International Council on *Ecclesiastical* Inerrancy. Therefore, in the final analysis, Scripture itself, when interpreted properly through the process of biblical exegesis and when synthesized legitimately through the process of biblical theology, must stand in judgment on all our humanly devised systems of dogmatic theology.[30]

Goldingay's assertion is valid: "Dogmatic theology has often imposed its own concerns on biblical study and hindered the Bible's own concerns and categories from emerging."[31]

GOD'S RULE:
THE CENTRAL FOCUS OF BIBLICAL THEOLOGY

Our chapter title demands that we consider the center or unifying theme of biblical theology. In my "False Dichotomies" article, I offered this attempt at stating such a center (German *Mitte*): God is asserting and establishing his kingdom or rule over all that he has created, thus bringing all creation, through the mediatorial work of his Son, into complete submission and order under his sovereignty in order to bring the highest possible glory to himself. Most statements of a theological

[30]K. L. Barker, "A Response to Historical Grammatical Problems," in *Hermeneutics, Inerrancy, and the Bible,* ed. E. D. Radmacher and R. D. Preus (Grand Rapids: Zondervan, 1984), 139–40.

[31]John Goldingay, *Approaches to Old Testament Interpretation* (Downers Grove, Ill.: InterVarsity Press, 1981), 21.

center are too limited (e.g., promise or covenant), too broad (e.g., God), or too anthropocentric (e.g., redemption or salvation history).

Numerous other attempts have been made to discover and formulate the center of biblical theology. These have been conveniently summarized by Hasel: covenant; theocracy (God's rule); God's holiness; God's lordship; God's kingship; Israel's election as God's people; God's kingdom; the rule of God and communion between God and man; promise and fulfillment; God in his relations to man, Israel, and the world; Yahweh the God of Israel, Israel the people of Yahweh; salvation history; covenant-kingdom; and others. Hasel claims that none of these is comprehensive enough to describe the multiform and multiplex nature of the biblical materials. He therefore opts for the statement that the Old Testament is theocentric and the New Testament is Christocentric. In short, for him God is the unifying center of the Old Testament, and Christ is the center of the New Testament.[32]

If the proposed theological centers that Hasel rejects seem to him too limited, his resolution of the debate appears to be too broad. A central focus of biblical theology should state something active and specific about God and Christ. In other words, a subject needs a complement. Something should be predicated of God and Christ. It is instructive that most of the proposed centers listed above relate in some way to the rule or kingdom of God; hence the heading "God's Rule: The Central Focus of Biblical Theology." At the very least, God's rule is a dominant theological theme in the Bible.[33] Unfortunately, we can only trace the outlines of such a theme here, and even then we are being very selective with the biblical materials.

It is significant that the Bible begins (Gen. 1–2) and ends (Rev. 19–22) with royal motifs. As I have indicated elsewhere, "Statements like 'The LORD will be king over the whole earth' stand at the very center of a truly biblical theology."[34] Indeed, the theological subject matter of all the biblical books may be delineated along theocratic (kingdom-covenant) lines.

The Torah/Law/Pentateuch

Genesis. The origins of the theocracy are traced, particularly the origins of its people and land. Concerning the concept of creation by the word as a royal motif, as in Genesis 1:3 (cf. Ps. 33:6–9), I have written:

---

[32]G. F. Hasel, *Old Testament Theology: Basic Issues in the Current Debate* (Grand Rapids: Eerdmans, 1975), 77–103; idem., *New Testament Theology: Basic Issues in the Current Debate* (Grand Rapids: Eerdmans, 1978), 140–70. Cf. also D. L. Baker, *Two Testaments, One Bible* (Downers Grove, Ill.: InterVarsity Press, 1977), 377–86.

[33]K. L. Barker, "Zechariah," in EBC 7 (Grand Rapids: Zondervan, 1979), 664–65, 697.
[34]Ibid., 693.

In the ancient Near East, the word of a god was thought to possess inherent power, guaranteeing its effect. The Akkadian epic Enuma Elish (4:19–28) illustrates this (cf. *ANET*, p. 66). In this passage the destructive and creative or restorative power of the Babylonian god Marduk's word is related to his right to rule above all others. Similarly, the Lord's efficacious word, which can both destroy and deliver or restore, suggests his right to absolute sovereignty. He alone is the Great King, and he reigns supreme. One of the ways he demonstrates his sovereignty and superiority, then, is by speaking and fulfilling his dynamic word. The power of God's word, of course, resides in his will, not in magic.[35]

According to Genesis 1:26–28, the very purpose of God's creation of human beings in his image and likeness was that they (male and female) might rule over all that God had created. Here I agree with von Rad that the Hebrew conjunction ו in verse 26 should be understood syntactically as having the sense of purpose ("*so that* they may rule").[36] Such rule is further developed in Psalm 8:5–8 and Hebrews 2:5–9 (cf. Heb. 10:12–13). Then, in Genesis 2:15, God placed the man in the Garden of Eden to exercise dominion over God's good creation. God also gave the man a test of obedience under God's sovereignty. The first man and woman failed in their responsibility (Gen. 3), but Hebrews 2:5–9 indicates that all is not lost—thanks to the intervention of the ultimate Son of Man.

The Abrahamic covenant (Gen. 15:9–21) was cast in the form of ancient Near Eastern royal land-grant treaties and contained a perpetual and unconditional divine promise to fulfill the grant of land to Abraham and his descendants (Gen. 17:1–19; 1 Chron. 16:15–18; Ps. 105:8–11). Near the end of the book of Genesis, Jacob prophesied that the scepter (i.e., the rule) would not depart from Judah "until he comes to whom it belongs [the Messiah ultimately] and the obedience of the nations is his" (49:10; cf. Ezek. 21:27).

Exodus. The theocratic nation is founded and redeemed, and the Sinaitic/Mosaic/old covenant is established with them. As a result of the Lord's redemption of his people, Moses celebrated the majesty, power, faithful love, and eternal reign of the Great King (Ex. 15:1, 3, 6–7, 11–13, 17–18). Israel was to be "a kingdom of priests and a holy nation" among the nations of the world (19:5–6).

The Sinaitic covenant (established originally in Ex. 19–24, with renewals in Ex. 35, the whole book of Deuteronomy, and Josh. 24) was cast in the form of ancient Near Eastern suzerainty-vassal treaties (of the

[35]Ibid., 605.
[36]G. von Rad, *Genesis: A Commentary*, OTL (London: SCM, 1963), 57.

second millennium B.C.) and contained the divine pledge to be Israel's God/Suzerain-Protector if it would be faithful to him as its covenant Lord and obedient to the stipulations of the covenant as the vassal-people of his kingdom. There would be blessings for such obedience but curses for disobedience (Deut. 27–30). The ark of the covenant in the tabernacle (Ex. 25–40) represented the earthly throne of the Suzerain (Yahweh) among his subjects (Israel).

Leviticus. A manual of regulations enables the holy King to set up an earthly throne/dwelling among the people of his kingdom and explains how they are to be his holy people and to worship him in a holy manner. Holiness, or sanctification, in this sense means to be separated from sin and set apart exclusively to the Lord for his holy purposes and functions in his service and for his glory.

Numbers. The Lord's army marches forth to possess the Promised Land, with the ark of the covenant, representing the throne of their King, among them. Although Israel failed at first (Num. 13–14), the Balaam oracles (chaps. 22–24) indicate that God's promise in the Abrahamic covenant cannot finally be frustrated, despite Israel's failures (note particularly 23:19–23). These oracles also contain the beautiful prophecy that an ultimately messianic Star would come out of Jacob and crush all antitheocratic forces (24:17–19; cf. Rev. 22:16).

Deuteronomy. The Sinaitic covenant is renewed (see above).[37]

The Nebi'im/Prophets

Former Prophets: Joshua. The Great King's promise to the patriarchs and Moses to give the land of Canaan to the chosen people of his kingdom by "holy war" is historically fulfilled (Josh. 1:1–6; 11:43–45).

Judges. "Judges" fail as mediators of the theocracy, thus anticipating the rise of kings as mediators (note 8:23; 17:6; 18:1; 19:1; 21:25).

Samuel. Kings are established as mediators of the theocracy (note 1 Sam. 8 and 12). The royal epithet *Yahweh Sabaoth* occurs for the first time in 1 Samuel 1:3.[38] The Davidic covenant was established in 2 Samuel 7 and was cast in the form of ancient Near Eastern royal grant treaties. It contained a perpetual and unconditional divine promise to fulfill the grant of dynasty, kingdom, and throne to David and his descendants, culminating in the Davidic Messiah (2 Sam. 7:16; 23:5;

---

[37]For the evidence, see K. A. Kitchen, *Ancient Orient and Old Testament* (Chicago: InterVarsity Press, 1966), 90–102; M. G. Kline, *Treaty of the Great King* (Grand Rapids: Eerdmans, 1963).

[38]For its significant contribution to the concept of Yahweh as King, see K. L. Barker, "YHWH Sabaoth: 'The LORD Almighty,'" in *The NIV: The Making of a Contemporary Translation*, ed. K. L. Barker (Grand Rapids: Zondervan, 1986), 109–10; and the works cited on p. 163, nn. 10–18.

Pss. 89:3–4, 28–37; 132:11–18; Isa. 55:3; Matt. 1:1; Luke 1:32–33; Rom. 1:3; Rev. 3:7; 5:5; 22:16).

Kings. Kings fail as mediators of the theocracy, thus anticipating the need, and creating an even more intense desire, for the appearance of the Davidic Messiah as the ideal Mediator of God's kingdom on earth.

Latter Prophets: Isaiah. All things—especially Israel—will be restored to the divine ideal of submission and order under Yahweh's, and ultimately the Messiah's, rule. This royal theme is developed in the book through the use of the theocratic-covenant name *Yahweh* (421 occurrences),[39] the appellative or generic term *Elohim/El* (stressing the Great King's sovereign power in creation and history), royal epithets (such as *King, Lord, Shepherd* [a royal metaphor, Isa. 40:11; 49:8–10], and *Divine Warrior*)[40], divine royal attributes (sovereignty, incomparability, holiness, righteousness [one of the qualities or characteristics of the ideal ruler in the Old Testament], loyal covenant love, etc.),[41] and divine royal actions (judging, saving/redeeming, restoring, etc.).[42] The Servant Songs are also part of the royal motif in Isaiah, for to be the Servant of Yahweh is to be a member of the Great King's royal administration—something like "trusted envoy" or "confidential representative."[43] Other Isaianic references to royal terminology that should be studied are 9:6–7 (note the four "throne names" in v. 6); 24:23; 33:22 (four royal functions are mentioned here); 40:10; 43:15 (four royal titles); 44:6 (several more royal titles); 52:7 ("your God reigns!"— ultimately messianic, Rom. 10:15). These names and descriptions make clear that, according to Isaiah, Yahweh, the holy and all-glorious King, will acquire a holy people after he purges out the wicked rebels. Yahweh's kingdom on earth, with its righteous Ruler and his righteous subjects, is the goal toward which the book of Isaiah (and all Scripture) steadily moves. This divine ideal for the earth will be realized through the mediatorial work of his Son, the Davidic Messiah.

Jeremiah. The divine Suzerain issues a warning that the royal city,

[39]Ibid., 106–9.

[40]Cf. P. D. Miller, Jr., *The Divine Warrior in Early Israel* (Cambridge: Harvard University Press, 1973), 154–65, 170–75.

[41]On incomparability, see C. J. Labuschagne, *The Incomparability of Yahweh in the Old Testament* (Leiden: E. J. Brill, 1966). On holiness, see my discussion in "Zechariah," 621. (One of the chief characteristics of Isaiah is the use of "Holy One of Israel" as a title for the Lord. Indeed, this epithet is distributed about equally between the so-called two Isaiahs; thus it is strongly indicative of the book's unity, authenticity, and single authorship.) On righteousness, see Snaith, *Distinctive Ideas,* 73–74. On covenant love, see Barker, "False Dichotomies," 6–8, 10–11.

[42]For a study of Hebrew words for salvation, see J. F. A. Sawyer, *Semantics in Biblical Research* (London: SCM, 1972), 28–88.

[43]For a modern study of the Servant Songs, see F. D. Lindsey, *The Servant Songs* (Chicago: Moody Press, 1985).

Jerusalem, will fall and the vassal people will suffer the curses for covenant disobedience if they do not repent and become faithful once again to the terms of the covenant. This they refused to do, so the curses were carried out and Jerusalem fell, resulting in the Babylonian exile (586 B.C.). Nonetheless, God's rule and the triumph of his kingdom were assured by the promise of the new covenant. Key passages in Jeremiah include 8:19 ("Is the LORD not in Zion? Is her King no longer there?"); 10:7 ("Who should not revere you, O King of the nations?"), 10:10 ("The LORD is the true God; he is the living God, the eternal King"); 23:5–6 (clearly messianic, with the references to David's righteous Branch, King, and the LORD Our Righteousness—thus the ideal King; the passage is echoed in 33:15–16); 46:18; 48:15; 51:57 (the latter three verses all refer to "the King, whose name is the LORD Almighty"). Certainly the most important passage theologically is 31:31–40, announcing the new covenant. It was cast in the form of ancient Near Eastern royal grant treaties and contained unconditional, gracious, and profoundly spiritual, moral, ethical, and relational promises. For a fuller treatment, see the discussion below.

Ezekiel. "The theme of Ezekiel's prophecy is that the fall of Jerusalem and the Babylonian captivity are necessary measures for the God of grace to employ if He is to correct His disobedient people and draw them back from complete and permanent apostasy. But the day is coming when Jehovah will restore a repentant remnant of His chastened people and establish them in a glorious latter-day theocracy with a new temple."[44]

In 20:33 Yahweh announced that he would rule over his chosen people. This announcement is then followed by the promise to regather the entire nation (including the northern kingdom) from the Diaspora, to purge them of all rebels, to bring them "into the bond of the covenant" (v. 37), and to restore them fully to kingdom blessing in the Promised Land (vv. 34–44; cf. chaps. 40–48). The government of Israel may be removed from King Zedekiah, but it will be restored when "he comes to whom it rightfully belongs" (21:25–27, referring to the Messiah and alluding to Gen. 49:10; cf. Ezek. 34:23–31, another passage anticipating the coming kingdom with the use of the messianic titles *Shepherd* and *my Servant David*).

The Twelve: Hosea. Yahweh's restoring love triumphs in spite of Israel's unfaithfulness to the covenant. It was a divine, covenant love that would not—indeed, could not—let Israel go.

Joel. Both the negative (judgment) and positive (blessing) aspects of

---

[44]G. L. Archer, Jr., *A Survey of Old Testament Introduction* (Chicago: Moody Press, 1974), 368.

the eschatological "day of the LORD" are unfolded.[45] (For the exegetically and theologically significant passage 2:28–32, see below.)

Amos. God will judge his disobedient, covenant-breaking people but will also establish his rule over Israel and the world through the revived house of David. (For comments on 9:11–15 and its use in the New Testament, see below.)

Obadiah. Antitheocratic forces such as Edom will be destroyed, but God's kingdom will triumph.

Jonah. The Lord expresses concern for his whole creation and desires that all peoples (not just Israel) worship him as universal Savior and Sovereign (note particularly 1:9; 2:9; 4:2, 11).

Micah. Yahweh registers his complaint against his covenant people. His punishment of their sin is certain, but so are his sure salvation and the restoration to come, centering in the appearance of the Davidic messianic Deliverer (e.g., 2:12–13; 4:1–8; 5:2–5).

Nahum. God's judgment on the wicked Neo-Assyrian empire is proclaimed, and the ultimate triumph of his own righteous and ideal kingdom is implied.

Habakkuk. Hindrances to the full expression of the theocracy will eventually be removed. The covenant people are exhorted to live by faith (and faithfulness) in the face of such hindrances.

Zephaniah. Both the negative (judgment) and positive (blessing and restoration) aspects of the Day of the Lord—who is "the King of Israel" (3:15), "mighty to save" (3:17)—are prophesied.

Haggai. The truth is demonstrated that if God's covenant people would only seek first his kingdom and his righteousness, all necessary temporal things would be given to them as well (Matt. 6:33).

Zechariah. The returnees from Babylonian exile are encouraged to complete the rebuilding of the temple, leading to even grander pictures of the final, full establishment of God's rule on earth through the Messiah.[46]

Malachi. The Great King (1:14)—ultimately the Messiah—is coming to judge (3:1–5; 4:1) and to bless and restore (3:6–12; 4:2).

The Kethubim/Hagiographa/Holy Writings

Psalms. Hymns and prayers celebrate the kingship of Yahweh, who is establishing his righteous and wise rule on earth in and through his covenant people and ultimately through the messianic Mediator of that kingdom and covenant. His people pray for the realization of the

---

[45]For an exegetical and theological summary of this concept, see my "Zechariah," 619–20.

[46]See further, ibid., 623, 626–27, 638–41, 650–52, 662–65, 672, 690, 695–97.

theocracy, and they exhort one another and others to praise, trust in, and serve the Great King. Even the lament psalms are primarily prayers that Yahweh will intervene and fully establish his kingdom on earth. In the royal psalms, kings in the Davidic dynasty are typical and/or prophetic of David's great, messianic Son. Regarding the so-called enthronement psalms, I have written elsewhere:

> One of the four major categories of messianic prophecy is indirect messianic prophecy. . . . [It] refers to passages that can be literally and fully realized only through the person and work of the Messiah—e.g., passages that speak of a personal coming of God to his people. . . . The same is true of references to the expression "the LORD reigns" or "will reign," so characteristic of the so-called Enthronement Psalms (e.g., 93, 95–99). These "eschatologically Yahwistic" psalms are probably best labeled theocratic, "Rule-of-God" Psalms. The point is that all passages that speak of a future coming of the Lord to his people or to the earth, or that speak of a future rule of the Lord over Israel or over the whole earth, are ultimately messianic—indirectly or by extension—for to be fully and literally true, they require a future, literal messianic kingdom on the earth.[47]

Key theocratic references in the Psalter include 2:6, 9; 7:7; 9:7; 10:16; 22:28; 24:10; 29:10; 47:2, 6–8; 48:2; 59:13; 66:7; 67:4; 68:16; 72:8; 93:1; 95:3; 96:10; 97:1; 99:1; 103:19; 110:2; 145:13; 146:10.

Proverbs. Instruction is given on how to live wisely and successfully in the "fear of the LORD" within the covenantal, theocratic arrangement. Wisdom is basically following the benevolent King's design for an orderly life—resulting in quality of mind (1:2) and quality of life (1:3). The "fear of the LORD" (1:7; 9:10) includes reverence for, trust in, and commitment to the Lord and his will as revealed in his Word.

Job. Here is presented a philosophical and theological, but painfully practical, drama (perhaps more accurately, theodicy) that wrestles with the wisdom and justice of the Great King's rule. Righteous sufferers must trust in, acknowledge, serve, and submit to the omniscient and omnipotent Sovereign, realizing that some suffering is the result of unseen, spiritual conflicts between the kingdom of God and the kingdom of Satan—between the kingdom of light and the kingdom of darkness (cf. Eph. 6:10–18).

Song of Songs. The readers are taught how to live lovingly (8:7) within the covenantal, theocratic arrangement. Such marital love is designed by the Creator-King to come to natural expression within his realm (see Gen. 1:26–31; 2:24).

Ruth. The importance of faithful, covenant love within the theocracy

---

[47]Ibid., 619; cf. *NIV Study Bible*, 784–86.

is beautifully illustrated. Because of her selfless, complete devotion (1:16–17), "Ruth the Moabitess" (1:22) became a true daughter of Israel and a worthy ancestress of King David (4:18–22). Similarly all peoples, through the "obedience that comes from faith" (Rom. 1:5), will participate in the kingdom of David's greatest Son (cf. Rev. 5:9–10; 7:9).

Lamentations. Here is a lament over the destruction of the capital of the theocracy in 586 B.C. because of covenant-breaking rebellion, but also hope for restoration (5:19–22) because of "the LORD's great love" and "faithfulness" (3:21–33).

Ecclesiastes. Instruction is given on how to live meaningfully, purposefully, and joyfully within the covenantal, theocratic arrangement—primarily by placing the covenant Lord at the center of one's life, work, and activities; by contentedly accepting one's divinely appointed lot in life; and by reverently trusting in and obeying the Creator-Shepherd (a royal metaphor). Note particularly 2:24–26; 3:11–14, 22; 5:18–20; 8:15; 9:7–10; 11:7–12:1; 12:9–14.

Esther. The Great King exercises his providence and sovereign control over all the vicissitudes of his beleaguered covenant people (cf. 4:12–16).

Daniel. "The Most High God is sovereign over the kingdoms of men" (5:21), and he "will set up a kingdom that will never be destroyed" (2:44; see also 4:17, 25–26, 32, 34, 37; 7:26–27; 9:24–27; cf. Rev. 11:15).

Ezra-Nehemiah. The Jews return from exile, rebuild the temple, and are restored to a relative theocracy while also under Gentile rule. Later, Ezra himself returns and institutes certain theocratic reforms. Still later, Nehemiah returns, leads the people in rebuilding the walls of the capital city (Jerusalem), and institutes more theocratic reforms.

Chronicles. A strongly theological account of the history of the theocracy is intended to encourage the restored community of Israel as it sought to reorient itself as God's covenant people in a different and difficult situation. The Chronicler focuses primarily on David and Solomon, portraying them in such a manner as to prefigure more aptly the ideal messianic King. He similarly presents the other good kings of the Davidic dynasty—and for the same reason. Note particularly 1 Chronicles 16:31; 17:14; 28:5; 29:11–12, 23; 2 Chronicles 9:8; 13:8; 20:6.

The New Testament

In a similar fashion, all the New Testament books—the Gospels, Acts, Paul's Letters, Hebrews, the General Letters, and Revelation—can be related to the Lord's kingdom program. Key references to include in such a study are Matthew 1:1; 2:2, 6; 3:2; 4:17; 5:35; 6:10; 13; 21:5; 24:30; 27:11, 37; Mark 1:15; 9:1; 13; 15:26; Luke 1:32–33; 17:21; 19:38; 23:3, 38; John 1:49; 12:13, 15; 18:37; 19:19; Acts 2:34– 39; 3:19–21; 8:12; 19:8; 20:24–27; 28:23, 31; Romans 11:25–29; 15:12; 1 Corinthians 15:24–25; Ephesians 5:5; Colossians 1:13; 1 Thessalonians 2:11–12; 2 Thessalonians 1:5; 1 Timothy 1:17; 6:15; 2 Timothy 2:12; Hebrews 2:5–10; 10:12–13; 12:28; James 2:5; 1 Peter 2:9–10; 2 Peter 1:10–11; Jude 4; Revelation 1:5; 2:27; 3:14; 11:15; 12:5, 10; 15:3; 17:14; 19:6, 15–16; 20:4, 6; 21:1–5; 22:3, 5, 16. Most interpreters agree that the kingdom (or rule) of God was the central thrust of Jesus' preaching and teaching, but many deny that this was the main emphasis of Paul's message. Yet Paul himself summarized what he had been preaching and teaching under the concept of "the kingdom" (Acts 20:25).

God's Kingdom, the Central Theme in Biblical Theology

The purpose of the following catena (a method employed also in Scripture; e.g., Rom. 3 and Heb. 1) is to demonstrate the widespread agreement on this point. Such synthesizing declarations on the theological unity of Scripture by authors who generally concur with the basic position taken here (based on exegetical theology) include the following:

> The two Testaments are organically linked to each other. . . . *And the bond that binds them together is the dynamic concept of the rule of God.* . . . The Old Testament is illumined with the hope of the coming Kingdom, and that same Kingdom lies at the heart of the New Testament as well.[48]

> [Because] *law* and *warfare* are functions of the Giver of the covenant the religion of Early Israel can best be interpreted under the rubric of *Israel as the kingdom of Yahweh* . . . the covenant between Yahweh and Israel at Sinai is an adaptation of the vassal treaty, most clearly extant in the Hittite Suzerainty Treaty. . . . Yahweh is King, and Israel is His kingdom in law and warfare. . . . Yahweh's covenant with Israel created a unique kingdom where faith and the inner experiences of people became the world of supreme value. The accumulated community experience of Yahweh's rule was codified ultimately in the collections of "law" and extended historical accounts recalling Yahweh's success against Israel's enemies and, with astonishing honesty, her own frequent disloyalty. Everywhere in the Kingdom the impact of the covenant and its formulas is unmistakable. . . . [The Decalogue's] purpose is to protect the rulership of Yahweh, who is the source of all authority in Israel. . . . Interpreting the relations between Yahweh and

[48]J. Bright, *The Kingdom of God* (Nashville: Abingdon, 1953), 196–97.

Israel by means of the vassal treaty model strongly suggests that the covenant was the core of the kingdom in Early Israel. . . . Moran has shown that "love" in Deuteronomy owes nothing to the metaphor of conjugal love in Hosea but is rather the "love" shown by a subject to a king. . . . To "love" the king is to be a loyal and obedient servant. . . . Israel was the kingdom of Yahweh. In that community the exercise of His rulership was meaningful in all areas of life.[49]

Thus, by God's grace, we have passed over the great, leading Biblical doctrine of the Kingdom of God—a Kingdom covenanted, established, overthrown, predicted, preached, postponed,[50] and finally gloriously re-established under the mighty Theocratic King. We have, logically and consecutively, traced the Kingdom of God, finding it based upon the covenants, instituted in an initiatory form, modified in the Davidic incorporation, overthrown for man's sinfulness, tendered to the elect nation, but rejected, postponed[51] to the period of the Sec. Advent, and finally re-established with great power and glory by David's Son and Lord. . . . The Kingdom embraces all our desire—the King, the Princes, the Angels, the restored Jews, the admiring Gentiles, the released Creation, the Millennial gladness, the Eternal Ages, and God over all, blessed forevermore. Dr. Bonar . . . [concluded]: "Our doctrine, as Millenarians, pervades the whole Word of God, from Genesis to Revelation. . . . It is no dream of carnal enthusiasts, enamored of materialism, and anticipating a paradise of gross delights. It is the calm belief of spiritual men, resting upon God's sure promise, and looking forward to a Kingdom of 'righteousness, peace, and joy in the Holy Ghost.' ". . . the precious doctrine of the Kingdom is undoubtedly true, because based on the plain grammatical sense of that which *"is written," "the word of the Lord."*[52]

The kingdom of heaven or kingdom of God is the central theme of Jesus' preaching, according to the Synoptic Gospels. While Matthew, who addresses himself to the Jews, speaks for the most part of the "kingdom of heaven," Mark and Luke speak of the "kingdom of God," which has the same meaning as the "kingdom of heaven," but was more intelligible to non-Jews. The use of "kingdom of heaven" in Matthew is certainly due to the tendency in Judaism to avoid the direct use of the

---

[49]A. E. Glock, "Early Israel as the Kingdom of Yahweh: The Influence of Archaeological Evidence on the Reconstruction of Religion in Early Israel," *CTM* 41 (October 1970): 564, 577, 589, 591–93.

[50]I would not use such terminology. The omniscient, sovereign God never "postpones" anything. Israel's rejection of their Messiah at his first advent—and, along with him, the full expression of the theocratic kingdom at that time—was foreseen by God and, in fact, was part of God's plan to accomplish redemption through the "sufferings of Christ [= the Messiah]" (1 Peter 1:11; cf. Ps. 22; Isa. 53). Thus the Lord knew that the final, complete fulfillment of the "glories that would follow" must await the Messiah's second advent for their greatest manifestation.

[51]See n. 50.

[52]Peters, *Theocratic Kingdom* 3:603–4; cf. 3:382–88, 460, 544, 548, 582.

name of God. In any case no distinction in sense is to be assumed between the two expressions (*cf., e.g.,* Matt. 5:3 with Luke 6:20).[53]

God is the ruling Lord: that is the one fundamental statement in the theology of the Old Testament. . . . Everything else derives from it. Everything else leans upon it. Everything else can be understood with reference to it and only it.[54]

That which binds together indivisibly the two realms of the Old and New Testaments—different in externals though they may be—is the irruption of the Kingship of God into this world and its establishment here. This is the unitive fact because it rests on the action of one and the same God in each case; that God who in promise and performance, in Gospel and Law, pursues one and the selfsame great purpose, the building of his Kingdom. This is why the central message of the New Testament leads us back to the testimony of God in the old covenant.[55]

Could the ancient Near Eastern literature which unites the ruling, judging, and warrior concepts around the central ideology of the kingship of the gods, be a conceptual framework which will unite the biblical functions of God into an overarching framework? . . . the idea of the covenant is of prime importance to Israelite theology, but it is not inclusive enough a theme to encompass the universal activity of God. . . . The study of the ancient Near Eastern literature puts the concept of Yahweh into perspective, and the biblical literature suggests that the kingship or sovereign rule of Yahweh is of central importance in developing a biblical theology of the Old Testament.[56]

According to the testimony of the first three Gospels the proclamation of the kingdom of God was Jesus' central message. . . . The mystery of the kingdom (Matt. 13:11; Mark 4:11) is precisely this: that prior to its eschatological consummation, the kingdom has come in an unexpected form in the historical mission of Jesus. . . . The church is not the kingdom. The kingdom is the rule of God and the sphere in which his rule is experienced. In this age it is an altogether invisible, spiritual realm (cf. Col. 1:13); at the eschatological consummation the sphere of his rule will be universal. . . . the whole gospel conceives of the coming of the eschatological kingdom *only* because the kingdom had first come in history in the person and mission of Jesus.[57]

[53]H. Ridderbos, "Kingdom of God, Kingdom of Heaven," in *NBD* (Grand Rapids: Eerdmans, 1962), 693.

[54]L. Kohler, *Old Testament Theology* (Philadelphia: Westminster, 1957), 30.

[55]W. Eichrodt, *Theology of the Old Testament,* 2 vols. (Philadelphia: Westminster, 1961), 1:26.

[56]G. V. Smith, "The Concept of God/the Gods as King in the Ancient Near East and the Bible," *TJ,* n.s., 3 (Spring 1982): 38.

[57]G. E. Ladd, "Kingdom of God (Heaven)," in *BEB* 2:1269, 1276–77.

[The] kingdom of God is the central theme which ties together everything, both in the Old Testament and in the New.[58]

Biblical Theology is the knowledge of God's great operation in introducing His kingdom among men, presented to our view exactly as it lies presented in the Bible.[59]

"The K. [kingdom] of God" is the central theme of the teaching of Jesus, and it involves his whole understanding of his own person and work.[60]

The proclaiming, making possible, and bringing to completion of this kingly rule of God was the entire purpose of the work of Christ; the proclaiming was His work as Prophet, the making it possible He effected as Priest, the completing will be His work as King. . . . The kingly rule of God is the final goal of salvation's history. "That God may be all in all" (1 Cor. 15:28). The kingdom is therefore the real basic theme of the Bible.[61]

The New Testament is no less theocratically undergirded and no less eschatologically oriented toward the Kingdom of God than the Old Testament.[62]

The kingdom of God is, in a certain and important sense, the grand central theme of all Holy Scripture. . . . we are not forgetting the person and work of our Lord Jesus Christ. For *He* is the King eternal, and there could be no final Kingdom apart from him and His work as the Lamb slain from the foundation of the world. . . . This reign of God arises out of His own sovereign nature, was reflected in the "dominion" bestowed by God upon the first Adam, was forfeited quickly by reason of the sin of man, has been restored judicially in the Last Adam, will be realized on earth in the final age of human history, and reaches out endlessly beyond history where we behold a throne which, as John explains, is "the throne of God and of the Lamb" (Rev. 22:3). . . . In the Biblical doctrine of the Kingdom of God we have the Christian philosophy of history.[63]

Mark's introductory summary of Jesus' message makes it plain that the kingdom of God was His central theme (Mark 1:15; cf. Matt. 4:17). Jesus stated that His task was to preach the Gospel of the kingdom (Luke 4:43), and the evangelists echo His words. . . . He appointed His disciples to proclaim the same message. . . . There can, therefore,

[58]R. F. Lovelace, *Renewal as a Way of Life* (Downers Grove, Ill. InterVarsity Press, 1985), 40.

[59]A. B. Davidson, *The Theology of the Old Testament* (Edinburgh: T. & T. Clark, 1904), 1.

[60]A. Richardson, *A Theological Word Book of the Bible* (New York: Macmillan, 1950), 119.

[61]E. Sauer, *The Triumph of the Crucified* (Grand Rapids: Eerdmans, 1951), 23, 144.

[62]T. C. Vriezen, "Theocracy and Soteriology," in *Essays on Old Testament Hermeneutics,* ed. C. Westermann (Atlanta: John Knox, 1979), 217–18.

[63]A. J. McClain, *The Greatness of the Kingdom* (Chicago: Moody Press, 1968), 4–5.

be little doubt that the phrase "the kingdom of God" expresses the main theme of His teaching.[64]

> The goal toward which all history moves is the coming of God to manifest his glory and establish his holiness among his people and throughout the whole world. All phases and programs, including God's dealings with Israel, the church, and the nations, culminate in this end. . . . This world destiny is expressed in a variety of themes that provide the fundamental structures of biblical eschatology. The most prominent of these is the coming of God's rule or kingdom. . . . There is general agreement among biblical scholars that the overriding theme of all Scripture is the kingdom of God.[65]

> The ministry of Jesus revolves around a fascinating term—"the kingdom of God." Everything else is related to it and radiates from it.[66]

It seems clear, then, that although there are several great theological themes in the Bible, the central focus of biblical theology is the rule of God, the kingdom of God, or the interlocking concepts of kingdom and covenant (but not covenant alone). This theocratic kingdom is realized, completed, and consummated chiefly through the mediatorial work of God's (and David's) messianic Son. Significantly, Ephesians 1:9–10 appears to indicate that God's ultimate purpose in creation was to establish his Son—the Christ—as the supreme Ruler of the universe.

THE NATURE OF OLD TESTAMENT EXPECTATION

In view of all the previous data, plus other considerations and additional Scripture passages, it becomes clear that an unbearable tension is created between what the Old Testament anticipated and what actually happened at the first advent of the Messiah and in the New Testament period. To illustrate, the Old Testament envisioned an era of unparalleled material and spiritual blessing in the Promised Land for Israel (e.g., in the Abrahamic covenant), a universal kingdom of peace and righteousness under the Davidic Messiah ruling from Jerusalem (as promised in the Davidic covenant), and a time when all would know the Lord and the earth would be filled with the knowledge of the glory of the Lord (a provision of the new covenant; cf. Hab. 2:14). In further

---

[64]I. H. Marshall, "Kingdom of God, of Heaven," in *ZPEB* 3:804; cf. also the discussion of the kingdom of God, the messianic kingdom, Israel, and the church in W. VanGemeren, *The Progress of Redemption: The Story of Salvation from Creation to the New Jerusalem* (Grand Rapids: Zondervan, 1988), esp. 460–64.

[65]R. L. Saucy, "The Eschatology of the Bible," in *EBC* (Grand Rapids: Zondervan, 1979), 1:105.

[66]L. Goppelt, *Theology of the New Testament*, 2 vols. (Grand Rapids: Eerdmans, 1981), 1:43.

describing the future, visible aspect of the messianic kingdom, Sauer wrote:

> [The] peoples of the world reach the promised blessings, and there will be effected: their final admission [i.e., to the blessings promised]—through the judgment in the valley of Jeshoshaphat (Joel 3:12; Matt. 25:31–46); their spiritual renewal—through national conversion (Isa. 2:3; 19:21, 24, 25); their political ordering—through the Divine Redeemer (Rev. 1:5; Isa. 2:2; 45:22, 23); their international concord—through the award of the King of the world (Isa. 2:4; Zech. 9:10); their civil harmony—through just social measures (Isa. 11:3–4; 29:19–21); their outward happiness—through everyday blessings [which he enumerates in a footnote as bodily health (Isa. 35:5, 6), patriarchal longevity (Isa. 65:20), successful labor (Isa. 65:21–23), avoidance of giant cities (Zech. 3:10), and fruitfulness of nature (Isa. 30:23, 24; 41:18, 19; 43:20; 55:13)]; their inward sanctification—through fellowship with the Eternal (Zeph. 3:9; Hab. 2:14; Isa. 11:10); their common worship—through pilgrimages and Divine service (Mic. 4:2; Zech. 8:21; 14:16; Isa. 56:7; 60:3; 66:23).[67]

McClain delineates the nature or blessings of the prophesied kingdom along these lines: (1) the coming kingdom will be basically spiritual, centered in the royal Man; (2) it will be moral and ethical in its effects; (3) it will have social effects: all military warfare will be abolished, complete social justice will become a reality, social wastes in human life will be reclaimed, everything worthwhile in human life will be tenderly fostered, and every legitimate interest of human life will receive its due; (4) it will be political in its effects, with an international authority, a world capital, a settlement of the Jewish problem, a righting of political wrongs, and a removal of the language barrier; (5) it will have physical effects, with beneficial climatic changes, waste places becoming fruitful, increased fertility and productiveness, changes in the animal world, the disappearance of physical disease and deformity, and freedom from ordinary hazards; (6) it will have ecclesiastical effects, with a Priest-King, Israel as the religious leader, Jerusalem as the religious center, the union of "church and state" under the personal rule of the messianic King, a future temple, forms of worship, and pilgrimages to the world center of worship.[68]

Nothing like this has yet happened. This obvious disparity between Old Testament prophecy and New Testament fulfillment is one of the great apparent discontinuities in the study of the relationships between

---

[67]Sauer, *Triumph of the Crucified*, 166–67.

[68]McClain, *Greatness of the Kingdom*, 218–53; see also pp. 527–31 for a premillennial philosophy of history.

the Testaments. It has caused such difficulty that many, particularly in the ranks of covenant amillennial theology, maintain that the land and kingdom promises either were forfeited through Israel's disobedience or are all now somehow being spiritually fulfilled in the church. As observed earlier, however, there are hermeneutical problems with such an elimination of ethnic Israel from God's future program and of a literal, visible reign of Christ in time-space history. Ladd argues for such a future reign of Christ on this earth:

> One of the most debated passages in Revelation is the "millennial" passage in 20:1–6. The most natural exegesis of these verses finds in them a series of events that will follow the second coming of Christ, who is pictured in military idiom in 19:11–16 as a conqueror victorious over his foes. This is followed by a binding of Satan in the abyss, the resurrection of the saints, and the reign of Christ with His saints over the earth for a thousand years. At the end of this millennial reign occurs the resurrection of the rest of the dead, the final judgment, the destruction of Satan and death, and the inauguration of the eternal state of the age to come. This is called the premillennial interpretation for the return of Christ is followed by a literal, temporal, millennial kingdom on earth.[69]

Some amillenarians, however, would agree with Zorn. In arguing his case that the New Testament church is the successor and embodiment of true, spiritual Israel, he goes so far as to declare, "National Israel might even cease to exist as a nation."[70] Such a position, however, is flatly contradicted by several Old Testament passages, discussed below.

Leviticus 26:40–45

In this chapter containing blessings and curses for covenant obedience and disobedience, the indication is that Yahweh will not reject his old-covenant people *in spite of* (v. 44) their rejection of his laws. Rather, he will remember the covenant with their ancestors and will not break his covenant with them.

---

[69]G. E. Ladd, "Kingdom of God, Kingdom of Heaven," in *ISBE* 3:29. Ladd deals adequately with objections to premillennialism in his *Crucial Questions About the Kingdom of God* (Grand Rapids: Eerdmans, 1952), 153–83. Finding it more hermeneutically consistent and satisfying, I concur with Ladd's defense of premillennialism. But whatever one's view of Rev. 20:1–6 may be, Warfield's treatment is certainly inadequate, with its flights of fancy and giving free rein to an unbridled imagination (see his *Biblical Doctrines* [New York: Oxford University Press, 1927; reprint, Edinburgh: Banner of Truth, 1988], 643–64). To their credit, most of Warfield's modern counterparts do utilize more hermeneutical controls than he did in his treatment of Rev. 20:1–6.

[70]R. O. Zorn, *Church and Kingdom* (Philadelphia: Presbyterian & Reformed, 1962), 23.

Jeremiah 31:31–40

In context, the promise of the new covenant occurs in the Book of Comfort, or consolation section of Jeremiah, namely, chapters 30–33, which basically depict the future messianic kingdom. Chronologically, a time of trouble for Jacob (the tribulation period, 30:4–11) is followed by Israel's return to the land (30:12–31:30), which is followed by their experience of the new covenant (31:31–40). Thus the prophetic setting of the new-covenant announcement is Israel's final restoration to the land after the tribulation period and at Christ's second coming to the earth. Significantly, the same sequence is discernible in Matthew 24 and Revelation 6–20. This reveals when the new covenant is to be fulfilled in the life of Israel as a whole. Such an understanding is confirmed by Zechariah 12:10–13:1[71] and by Romans 11:11–29 (see below).

The *people* of the new covenant are identified as the house of Israel and the house of Judah (Jer. 31:31). The *reason* for the new covenant is that God's people Israel broke the covenant he made with them at Sinai (v. 32). The *provisions* of the new covenant are: (1) enablement by the Holy Spirit to obey his law (v. 33a; Ezek. 36:26–27; cf. Rom. 8:3–4)—the significance of this should not be overlooked by those who now live in the first stage of the new-covenant era and who draw the lines too sharply between law and gospel, or law and grace (cf. Ezek. 37:24); (2) an intimate personal relationship and fellowship with God (v. 33b); (3) a saving knowledge of the Lord (v. 34a; Rom. 11:26a); and (4) the forgiveness of sins (v. 34b; Ezek. 36:25; Zech. 3:4, 9).

The *nature* of the new covenant is that it is unconditional and eternal, hence immutable and irrevocable (vv. 35–37; 32:40; Ezek. 37:26). This obtains in spite of Israel's failure (v. 37b). It then becomes a question of God's faithfulness to his Word. Munck asks a pertinent question: "If God has not fulfilled his promises made to Israel, then what basis has the Jewish-Gentile church for believing that the promises will be fulfilled for them?"[72] Finally the *city* of the new covenant is Jerusalem—to be rebuilt for the Lord, to be purified, and never to be overthrown again (vv. 38–40). Then it will be the *Holy City* in truth.

It is true that the church—believing Gentiles and the spiritual remnant of Israel (Rom. 11:1–16)—is today the recipient of the benefits promised to Israel in the new covenant (Matt. 26:28; Luke 22:20; 1 Cor. 11:25; Heb. 8–10). This is possible only by God's sovereign, gracious grafting of Gentiles into that place of blessing (Rom.

---

[71]Barker, "Zechariah," 685.

[72]J. Munck, *Christ and Israel: An Interpretation of Romans 9–11* (Philadelphia: Fortress, 1967), 35.

11:17–24). These blessings will yet be experienced by ethnic Israel at their Messiah's return (Rom. 11:25–29).

Romans 11:11–29

Here Paul expounds the doctrine of the ingrafted church. The result of such ingrafting is that the church, along with Israel, becomes an heir of the promises in Israel's great unconditional covenants—the Abrahamic, the Davidic, and the new. These promissory covenants provide assurance that God will establish his rule throughout the earth when all Israel is saved (note that Israel's hardening is only partial and temporary). The church, then, while not clearly and specifically envisioned in the Old Testament and though being a new creation consisting of Jews and Gentiles, nonetheless by God's sovereign grace also inherits the covenanted promises (see, in addition to this passage, Gal. 3:29; Eph. 2:11–19; 3:6). That is why Israelite terminology is applied to the church (1 Peter 2:9), but the church does not supplant Israel. Indeed, one of the purposes of the ingrafted church is to provoke Israel to exercise saving faith in their Messiah for their salvation.

In view of all this, the new-covenant era must be divided into two stages: (1) the period of the ingrafted church (the "mystery" form of the kingdom, Matt. 13), introduced by the first advent of the Messiah ("inaugurated eschatology"), and (2) the period of the messianic kingdom consummation, introduced by Christ's second advent. The sequence of redemptive events in Romans 11:11–15 supports such an understanding: "The 'transgression' and 'loss' (v. 12) of Israel leads to the salvation of the Gentiles, which leads to the jealousy or envy of Israel, which leads to the 'fullness' (v. 12) of Israel when the hardening is removed, which leads to even more riches for the Gentiles. . . . the conversion of the Jews . . . will result in even greater blessing for the world" (see further Rom. 11:25–29).[73] Reventlow adds:

> Most Christian attitudes to the problem of the church and Judaism begin from a dialectical presupposition on the basis of the New Testament evidence: on the one hand the period of Old Testament Israel as the chosen people of God and bearers of the promise has

---

[73]*NIV Study Bible*, 1723, note on Rom. 11:15. For more evidence of a future for Israel in a literal messianic kingdom on the earth, see my commentary "Zechariah," 627, 651, 672; R. B. Girdlestone, *The Grammar of Prophecy* (London: Eyre & Spottiswoode, 1901; reprint, Grand Rapids: Kregel, 1955), 134–40; E. D. Radmacher, "The Current Status of Dispensationalism and Its Eschatology," in *Perspectives on Evangelical Theology*, ed. K. S. Kantzer and S. N. Gundry (Grand Rapids: Baker, 1979), 171–75; R. L. Saucy, "A Rationale for the Future of Israel," *JETS* 28 (December 1985): 433–42; idem., "Eschatology of the Bible," 115; E. Sauer, *From Eternity to Eternity* (Grand Rapids: Eerdmans, 1954), 185–94. The last-named work builds a good case not only for a future for Israel but also for premillennialism.

come to an end through the testimony of Christ and the time of the church, in which the promises once made to Israel have been fulfilled . . . , and a new community has come together made up of Jews and non-Jews (Gentiles). On the other hand (as is stressed with especial reference to Paul's remarks in Rom. 9–11), the election of Israel, once made, is not simply done away with, since God faithfully keeps his promises, once made, despite all human disobedience (and after the rejection of the sending of Jesus). . . . even in the light of the New Testament it is hardly possible to justify a simple "substitution theory" . . . according to which the church has solely and completely taken over the role of the elect people.[74]

Thus the tension spoken of earlier remains.

PROGRESSIVE FULFILLMENT OF PROPHECY

The tension referred to above is best relieved, in my judgment, by acknowledging the validity of the principle of the progressive fulfillment of prophecy. I first alluded to this principle in print in my "False Dichotomies" article.[75] There I indicated that several passages that other dispensationalists relegate solely to the future received a literal fulfillment in the New Testament period or are receiving such a fulfillment in the continuing church age—in addition to a final, complete fulfillment in the future in the case of some of those passages. Classic examples would be the fulfillment of Joel 2:28–32 in Acts 2:17–21 and of Amos 9:11–12 in Acts 15:16–17—without denying a final, future stage to complete the fulfillment with respect to Israel (see below). That is to say, these propositions are not either-or but both-and.

This approach I prefer to think of as "progressive fulfillment," an expression I first encountered in Beecher, who also refers to the principle as manifold fulfillment, generic prophecy, and cumulative fulfillment.[76] As I conceive it, it means that prophecies quite frequently include two or more stages (not the same as double or multiple sense) in the progressive fulfillment of the whole picture seen by the prophet. One might say by way of analogy that just as revelation came in progressive stages, so prophecy is often fulfilled in progressive stages. Conceptually, each stage is necessary in order to fulfill completely (i.e.,

---

[74]H. G. Reventlow, *Problems of Biblical Theology in the Twentieth Century* (Philadelphia: Fortress, 1986), 80, 85. It is significant that John Murray, a Reformed covenant theologian and exegete, was compelled by his Greek exegesis of Rom. 11 to insist on a future for Israel. See his *Epistle to the Romans*, NICNT, 2 vols. (Grand Rapids: Eerdmans, 1968), 2:100; similarly Cranfield, *Romans* 2:572–77.

[75]Barker, "False Dichotomies," 4, n. 5.

[76]W. J. Beecher, *The Prophets and the Promise* (New York: T. Y. Crowell, 1905; reprint, Grand Rapids: Baker, 1975), 127–31.

fill to the full) the total content of what the prophet envisioned or foretold. Kaiser refers to this phenomenon as prophetic foreshortening. He explains: "The perspective of the prophet in certain predictive passages often simultaneously included two or more events that were separated in time at their fulfillment, yet, there often was no indication of a time lapse between these various fulfillments in the predictive word as they were originally given."[77] He elaborates:

> The fundamental idea here is that many prophecies begin with a word that ushers in not only a climactic fulfillment, but a series of events, all of which participate in and lead up to that climactic or ultimate event in a protracted series that belong together as a unit because of their corporate or collective solidarity. In this way, the whole set of events makes up one collective totality and constitutes *only one idea,* even though the events may be spread over a large segment of history by the deliberate plan of God. The important point to observe, however, is that all of the parts belong to a single whole. They are generically related to each other by some identifiable wholeness.[78]

I might add that the fulfillment of any part is part of the fulfillment of the whole—an earnest or guarantee that the remaining events will, in fact, follow. Furthermore, each stage of progressive fulfillment becomes typological of the later stage(s), that is, of the fulfillment(s) yet to come.[79] Also involved in first-advent fulfillment of prophecy is the phenomenon of inaugurated eschatology, or of prophecy already in process of realizing itself. From the Old Testament perspective, the messianic or eschatological era has already begun, as Hebrews 1:2 makes clear. Many messianic prophecies, however, involve two stages in the progressive fulfillment of the whole, and these stages correspond to the two advents of the Messiah and to both the present and future aspects of the messianic kingdom.[80]

What I have labeled progressive fulfillment Kaiser prefers to call generic fulfillment,[81] a term that in my opinion is more applicable to promise than to fulfillment. In other words, it seems to be more natural usage to state that generic prophecy is progressively fulfilled. But this is only a minor difference between us.

Examples of such progressive fulfillment of certain prophecies

---

[77]W. C. Kaiser, Jr., *The Uses of the Old Testament in the New* (Chicago: Moody Press, 1985), 63.

[78]Ibid., 67–68.

[79]On typology, see S. L. Johnson, Jr., *The Old Testament in the New* (Grand Rapids: Zondervan, 1980), esp. 55–57, 69–71, 78–79, 93–94.

[80]On the future and present aspects of the kingdom, see D. L. Turner, "The Continuity of Scripture and Eschatology: Key Hermeneutical Issues," *GTJ* 6 (Fall 1985): 286.

[81]Kaiser, *Uses of the Old Testament,* 66–68.

abound. We have already noted the involvement of the church, including Gentiles, in the progressive fulfillment of the great promises in Israel's unconditional covenants, but not excluding Israel in the future.[82] Another obvious classic illustration is the promise of the coming of the Messiah. If I had been living in the old-covenant era, I am quite certain that I would have anticipated only one messianic appearance and fulfillment. In the new-covenant era, however, we discover through the unfolding progress of revelation and fulfillment that there are actually two advents of the Messiah. Moreover, it becomes clear that, in order to fulfill everything predicted of the Messiah and his work, both stages of the Messiah's coming are absolutely essential. Thus the promise of the advent of the Messiah is progressively fulfilled in two stages.

Similarly, Isaiah 40:1–5 is progressively fulfilled in *three* stages: (1) the restoration from Babylonian exile through Cyrus the Great; (2) the deliverance and restoration through the Messiah, the great King, announced by John the Baptist at Christ's first advent (Luke 3:3–6); and (3) the return of Christ, when the glory of the Lord will be even more fully revealed (Matt. 24:30) and "all mankind together will see it" (Isa. 40:5; cf. Rev. 1:7). Another example of progressive fulfillment is Malachi 4:4–5, fulfilled through John the Baptist as well as through Elijah the prophet (or through another who will come in the spirit and power of Elijah) in the eschaton (cf. Rev. 11:6).

To conclude this section, I wish to focus briefly on the use of Joel 2:28–32 in Acts 2:17–21 and of Amos 9:11–12 in Acts 15:16–17. I do not have space to discuss all the text-critical, exegetical, hermeneutical, and theological considerations that normally should be woven into my treatment. In the Joel 2 and Acts 2 passages the main subject is the outpouring of God's Spirit. The *time* of the Spirit's outpouring is announced as "afterward" (Joel 2:28a), which is defined in the *inclusio* (v. 29b) as "in those days." The previous verses make it clear that the phrase refers to the eschatological day of the Lord and is basically equivalent to "in the last days" (Hos. 3:5), which is essentially the same as the messianic age. Such an understanding is confirmed by the exposition in Acts 2:17. The *recipients* of the Spirit's outpouring are identified in vv. 28b–29. Combining these two verses, we may say that all members of the covenant nation will participate in this outpouring, regardless of sex, age, or rank (cf. Num. 11:29; Gal. 3:28). The

---

[82]For several examples of progressive fulfillment in the book of Zechariah, see my "Zechariah," 613, 616–17, 620, 650, 663, 666, 670, 679–80, 683–84, 687. For example, Zech. 9:9–10 is fulfilled in two stages, involving both advents of the Messiah.

characteristics and/or *results* of the Spirit's outpouring are delineated as prophecy, dreams, and visions (v. 28c).

The *signs* accompanying the Spirit's outpouring include cataclysmic phenomena or cosmic signs to herald the day of Yahweh (Joel 2:30–31; cf. Isa. 13:9–10; Matt. 24:6–8, 29; Rev. 6:12; 8:8–9; 9:1–18; 14:14–20; 16:4, 8–9). While certain wonders did occur at Calvary and on the Day of Pentecost—darkness, earthquake, and "tongues of fire"—nothing on the scale of what is described in the above passages took place. So these "wonders" that did occur are but a harbinger, earnest, foretaste, down payment, or prefiguration of the future complete fulfillment in the eschatological aspect of the Day of the Lord (Joel 2:31). The *deliverance* accompanying and/or following the Spirit's outpouring is announced in Joel 2:32. The most important result of the future repentance of Israel, described in the preceding verses of Joel 2, is their spiritual transformation, predicted by Joel in this passage (see also Jer. 31:33–34; Ezek. 36:26–27; 39:29; Zech. 12:10–13:1). Peter apparently extends the "all flesh" of Joel 2:28 and the "everyone" of verse 32 to the Gentiles in Acts 2:39; so the Gentiles are not excluded from the Spirit's outpouring or from the deliverance mentioned here—in harmony with the doctrine of ingrafting traced above in Romans 11.[83]

When we turn to the New Testament passage, I am in essential agreement with Ladd's exposition.[84] Basically, he argues for two stages in the progressive fulfillment of the prophecy, with the still-future stage having special reference to Israel (Rom. 11:25–29). The traditional dispensational approach maintains that Peter merely used Joel's prophecy as an analogy or illustration of what was happening in his day and that the prediction was not even partially fulfilled in Acts 2.[85] However, it seems more natural to understand Acts 2 as a valid part of the fulfillment of Joel 2, particularly in view of the use of "this is that" (Acts 2:16). The latter expression certainly appears to be asserting that "this" at least partially fulfills Joel's words. Here I agree with Carson: "This is not an identity statement, since the antecedent of 'this' is the set of phenomena associated with that first Christian Pentecost, not the

---

[83]For another dispensational handling of this text like the one I suggest here, see Darrell L. Bock, *Proclamation from Prophecy and Patterns: Lucan Old Testament Christology,* JSNTSup 12 (Sheffield: Sheffield Academic Press, 1987), 166–69, 346–47; and idem, "The Reign of the Lord Christ," chap. 1 above.

[84]G. E. Ladd, "Acts," in *The Wycliffe Bible Commentary* (Chicago: Moody Press, 1962), 1127–29.

[85]*The Ryrie Study Bible,* with notes by C. C. Ryrie (Chicago: Moody Press, 1985), notes on Joel 2:28 and Acts 1:16–21; C. L. Feinberg, *The Minor Prophets* (Chicago: Moody Press, 1976), 81–82.

prophecy itself. The statement really means, 'This fulfills what was spoken by the prophet.' "[86]

Acts 2, then, is a direct, initial, partial fulfillment of Joel 2, but it is not the final and complete fulfillment. Joel 2 promised the outpouring of the Spirit, spiritual transformation, and enablement for all. The fulfillment came, in part, at the first advent of the Messiah and on the Day of Pentecost. The second advent and accompanying events will bring the final, complete outpouring of God's Spirit on all, including Israel.

The use of Amos 9:11–12 in Acts 15:16–17 should be handled similarly. Although one encounters a few fairly substantial textual differences in comparing the Hebrew Old Testament, Septuagint, and Greek New Testament texts of the passage, the general sense is clear in all of them and is ultimately the same. James quoted Amos 9 at the Jerusalem Council (Acts 15) basically to show that Gentiles were included in God's program, as also was promised in the Abrahamic and Davidic covenants (cf. Isa. 55:3–5; Acts 13:32–39). The Davidic dynasty will become lowly, but it will be restored through the Messiah and his mission. The comprehensive or expansive purpose of his mission includes his rule over Gentiles—that aspect of his mission has already begun. Romans 11 allows for such Gentile inclusion with its doctrine of the ingrafted church.

My understanding is again essentially the same as Ladd's: "This does not mean that Israel as a nation has no future. Romans 11 clearly affirms that all Israel shall be saved; God yet has a future for national Israel. However, this was not James' concern; he was citing Amos to prove that the successful mission to the Gentiles is in the purpose of God and was predicted by the Old Testament."[87] As I have expressed it elsewhere, "The present ingathering (Acts 15:12–18) is but a stage in the complete fulfillment (cf. Matt. 24:14; Rev. 7:9; 21:24, 26)."[88] In other words, what happened in Acts 15 constitutes a stage in the progressive fulfillment of the entire prophecy in Amos 9 (cf. Acts 15:12–15). It is an instance of direct fulfillment, but not the final and complete fulfillment, as the following verses in Amos (9:13–15) plainly indicate.

Additional examples could be given, but these should suffice to validate the principle of progressive fulfillment in understanding and explicating the phenomena of biblical prophecy.[89] The principle demon-

---

[86]D. A. Carson, *Exegetical Fallacies* (Grand Rapids: Baker, 1984), 61; see also R. D. Patterson, "Joel," in EBC 7 (Grand Rapids: Zondervan, 1979), 257–58.

[87]Ladd, "Acts," 1152.

[88]Barker, "Zechariah," 620.

[89]A few more illustrations of the principle may be found in E. J. Young, *My Servants the Prophets* (Grand Rapids: Eerdmans, 1952), 29, 34–35; Saucy, "Eschatology," 104.

strates that many issues should not be reduced to either-or propositions but instead should be regarded from a both-and perspective. Many traditional dispensationalists of the past seemingly have not paid enough attention to *first*-advent fulfillment of prophecy, and many traditional covenant theologians and exegetes have not made enough allowance for the possibility of *second*-advent fulfillment.

CONCLUSION

One way to summarize the major emphases of this chapter is to view them as suggesting that certain potentially dichotomous concepts are not either-or but are both-and. For example, we are to base our faith and practice, not on *either* the New Testament ("gospel") *or* the Old Testament ("law"),[90] but on both the New Testament and the Old (with minor, obvious exceptions as previously noted). We are to interpret prophecy as fulfilled, not either in the church or in Israel, but both in the church and in Israel. We are to see prophetic fulfillment, not in either the first advent or the second, but in both. We are to consider the great promises in Israel's unconditional covenants (Abrahamic, Davidic, and new), not as either spiritual or national, but as both.[91] (Of course, certain aspects of those same promises are also universal.)

I conclude with words I have used elsewhere:

> It is my belief that, within God's comprehensive purpose and unified program, the present form of his kingdom is moving toward the grand climax of history when that kingdom will find expression in a visible reign of Christ that will include elect Israel, the true Church, and elect Gentiles who may not fit into either of the two previous categories. The future kingdom of history will then merge into the eternal kingdom, and the Lord God Omnipotent will rule forever. This overall program of God is all of grace from start to finish (including the Old Testament part of it), and all will redound to the praise and glory of God through Jesus Christ our Lord and King.[92]

---

[90]See J. H. Gerstner, "Law in the New Testament," in *ISBE* 3:85–91.

[91]See, for example, W. C. Kaiser, Jr., "Kingdom Promises as Spiritual and National," in *Continuity and Discontinuity*, ed. J. S. Feinberg (Westchester, Ill.: Crossway, 1988), 289–307, in contradistinction to B. K. Waltke, "Kingdom Promises as Spiritual," in ibid., 263–87.

[92]Barker, "False Dichotomies," 15–16.

Part 2

Responses

A Response

Willem A. VanGemeren

MY BACKGROUND

My response to the above chapters comes from a personal pilgrimage that has led me to a twofold commitment. As a minister in a Reformed denomination (PCA) and as a teacher at a Reformed seminary (RTS), I am committed to the system of doctrine contained in the Westminster standards. Through my graduate studies (Westminster Theological Seminary [Philadelphia], Hebrew University [Jerusalem], University of Wisconsin [Madison]) and in my professional pursuit of Old Testament theology, I have become more committed to the need for growth in the understanding of Scripture.

I have also been well acquainted with the development of dispensationalism for nearly fifty years. Let me explain how. I was born in Boskoop, the Netherlands, during World War II. Contrary to many expectations, I do not come from a Reformed family and was not a member of any Reformed body until I came to the United States. Instead, I was raised in a Plymouth Brethren home, and my parents are still committed to the principles of the Plymouth Brethren (closed communion), an assembly of believers with a dispensational framework of interpretation and practice that goes back to J. N. Darby (1800–1882). My grandfather was the unofficial leader of a small assembly in Boskoop. When I was five years old, my family moved to Alphen aan den Rijn, a town located near Leiden. This town had the unique distinction of having the largest assembly in all of the Netherlands, possibly even Europe. Very few people outside the assembly were aware of this distinction, nor did they notice that once a year the brethren from all over Europe came for fellowship, Bible study, and lectures in our assembly hall. The day sessions were restricted to the Brethren, but the evening sessions were open to the public. I was encouraged—with due persuasion—to attend the evening sessions in which renowned Brethren spoke regarding the last days (Israel, the church, and the Millennium). The Brethren may not have been able to define dispensationalism, but each one of them was clear in his own mind that Reformed theology confused law and grace, material and spiritual, B.C. and A.D., Israel and the church.

As I grew up, I raised questions about these distinctions. The Brethren tried to answer my questions. One after the other could not help me because each one of them was operating from his own hermeneutical circle. They could not step out of it, even when they wanted to bring back this questioning soul.

After I came to the United States in 1962, I remained committed to dispensational theology, as best as I understood it. My studies at Moody Bible Institute (1963–66) opened up the theological and hermeneutical circle of dispensationalism. Most of my teachers were graduates of Dallas Theological Seminary and encouraged me to read widely. I spent many happy hours in extracurricular reading: *Things to Come,* by J. Dwight Pentecost, and the voluminous writings of Lewis Sperry Chafer (1871–1952), including his multivolume *Systematic Theology.* While some of my questions were answered, others came to the surface. I devoured Charles C. Ryrie's *Dispensationalism Today* as it came hot off the press. He settled some questions, but many lingered on.

I extended my reading list to include Reformed theologians, including the Dutch theologians, notably Abraham Kuyper and Herman Bavinck. They opened up a different approach to the Bible and to my unresolved theological and exegetical questions. I did not know the goal of my pilgrimage but became more and more aware that I was leaving dispensationalism, however defined, for Reformed theology. Under professors Cornelius Van Til, Paul Woolley, Edmund Clowney, Clair Davis, Norman Shepherd, Richard Gaffin, and others of Westminster Theological Seminary (1968–71), I learned to explore the history, hermeneutics, and theology of the Reformed tradition. These teachers helped me to develop a confessional framework, to understand the Reformed heritage, and to think exegetically. They blended together the great doctrines of the truly catholic church, the reformational emphases, and the Reformed distinctives into a harmonious whole: *tota Scriptura,* the Holy Trinity, the unity of the covenant of grace, the sovereignty and grace of God, the plan of redemption, the nature of man, the communion of the saints, Christian ethics, a Christian world and life view, and eschatology.[1]

<hr/>

[1] I am indebted to my teachers in my article entitled "Systems of Continuity" (in *Continuity and Discontinuity: Perspectives on the Relationship Between the Old and New Testaments: Essays in Honor of S. Lewis Johnson, Jr.,* ed. John S. Feinberg [Westchester, Ill.: Crossway, 1988], 37–62). Regrettably, Mark Karlberg's criticism of my position in his review of this article arose from misleading citations and deductions ("Israel and the

A Response

As a transplant in the soil of Reformed theology, I had to make new points of reference, develop a new framework, and open up many exegetical issues. Later I learned that others who had remained faithful to dispensationalism had undergone similar struggles. I was first surprised when I discovered that dispensationalism was changing. Since then I have enjoyed many occasions of close fellowship with my dispensational brothers. We speak with mutual respect and with a common commitment to the Holy Trinity and to the Scriptures. As I reflect on my dispensational background, I am grateful to the Plymouth Brethren who taught me to know the Scriptures and the Savior. They encouraged me to live by *sola Scriptura*, to hold to the authority of God's Word, and to ascertain that my faith and practice are grounded in Scripture.

DISPENSATIONALISM AS A DEVELOPING SYSTEM

When Craig Blaising first asked me to write a response to this book, he had just delivered a major paper before the "Dispensational Theology Pre-Meeting" (November 20, 1986) in Atlanta, Georgia. In his paper, "Developing Dispensationalism," he advanced the thesis that any theological system develops organically and that dispensationalism, as a theological system, is in "the process of doctrinal development in the work of contemporary dispensational scholars." Blaising isolated several areas for specific attention: (1) the place of the church in the unfolding program of God's kingdom; (2) the relation of law, grace, and the work of the Spirit; (3) the nature of man; (4) the doctrine of dispensations; and (5) the study of all doctrines in the light of a Christocentric and eschatological present-future kingdom. These five areas are more fully, even though unevenly, developed in this book.

The four respondents to his paper raised fundamental issues. Stanley N. Gundry called for humility in "doing theology" by stressing that the goal of theology is to bring us to the reality of God himself, not the details of eschatology. Gerry Breshears sought to correct a possible misunderstanding of Blaising's paper by stressing the penultimate importance of the Millennium: "The christological focus of God's working is climaxed in the millennium." Stephen R. Spencer made the relation of Israel and the church the sine qua non of dispensationalism.

Eschaton," *WTJ* 52 [1990], 119–21). More regrettable is the ad hominem argument from a Reformed theologian. My intent was to set forth the variety and unity of Reformed theology against its critics. For my position on covenants, see *The Progress of Redemption: The Story of Salvation from Creation to the New Jerusalem* (Grand Rapids: Zondervan, 1988), esp. 230–39, 454–55; *Interpreting the Prophetic Word* (Grand Rapids: Zondervan, 1990), esp. 314–16, 332–37.

He noted that dispensationalism "affirms one people of God, however, redemptively and eschatologically. Even as there is continuity as well as expansion between the family of Abraham and the nation of Israel, so there is continuity as well as expansion between the nation of Israel and the Body of Christ, the Church." Finally, David L. Turner called on dispensationalists to listen to their critics, to restudy fundamental concepts, to evaluate their hermeneutic in the light of culture, and to develop a holistic approach to the unfolding plan of God in Scripture.

DISPENSATIONALISM ON ISRAEL AND THE CHURCH

The contributors to this present volume were given the difficult task of distilling the distinct hermeneutic and theology of dispensationalism. I commend them for not working out a programmatic approach. As the chapters stand, readers must discern for themselves the nature of the dispensational assumptions, hermeneutic, and view of history.

I greatly appreciate this opportunity of writing a response to these essays. This response is an expression of gratitude to my parents and to my dispensational teachers and friends. It is also an unambiguous statement of my commitment to Reformed theology. The response will be in the form of a consideration of seven (yes, the symbolic number) major areas and an assessment of dispensationalism as a theological system.

The Kingdom of God: Spiritual and Political

Darrell L. Bock ("Reign of Christ") focuses on the theology of the kingdom from the vantage point of Luke's presentation of Jesus "as the fulfillment of promises and covenants made to Israel." He maintains that Luke develops four stages within the one kingdom program: (1) the inauguration of the "initial stages" of the kingdom during Jesus' earthly ministry when the kingdom was within the reach (*entos humōn*, Luke 17:21) of his contemporaries; (2) the inauguration of the kingdom at Jesus' resurrection; (3) the present rule of Christ in the church; and (4) the millennial reign as the culmination of the kingdom.

Bock agrees with covenant theology that the eschatological kingdom was inaugurated in the ministry of Jesus and is evidenced in his rule over the church. Gentiles share with Jews in the spiritual benefits of Jesus' kingdom (forgiveness, Spirit, new covenant). This view of the kingdom stands in clear contrast to the older thesis that the offer of the kingdom was withdrawn.

While I appreciate Bock's holistic approach to the Bible as unfolding the one plan of God (covenants and promises), his exegesis is controlled by prior assumptions. He argues that the kingdom has two aspects—

national-political and spiritual—and that these aspects are temporally juxtaposed: the church age and the Millennium. For Bock, the former is a dim reflection—a "sneak preview"—of the visible, millennial rule of Christ over the earth. For me, the present age is the era of the Spirit of restoration.[2] The Spirit is constituting a community of believers who live in anticipation of the consummation and who have the assurance by the presence of the Spirit that they belong to the new humanity who will enjoy the eternal fulfillment of God's promises and covenants in the new state of restoration. This new humanity consists of Jews and Gentiles, as I have expressed in an exegetical study on Joel 2:28–32:

> The inclusion of the Gentiles need not be interpreted to the exclusion of the Jews. That is the point of Paul's argument in Romans 9–11, and especially as he develops the application of Joel 2:32 in Rom. 10:14– 11:32. . . . the fidelity of God and the promise-word of God sustain us with hope that a great number of Israel will be saved. They will join together with Gentile Christians in the worship of the Father and his Messiah, our Lord Jesus Christ. How this will come about is hidden in the wisdom of God (Rom. 11:33–36). Thus, the newness of the age of the Spirit lies in the all-inclusive formation of the new humanity.[3]

Pentecost marks the coming of the "Spirit of restoration," whose presence assures the believers of the fullness of restoration. As the Spirit of restoration, he encourages the faithful to persevere in the hope of the restoration to come:

> The Holy Spirit is Guarantor and Reconciler. On the one hand, he guarantees and applies the words of blessing to all of God's children. He brings them comfort, counsels, gives life and peace (John 14:15– 19, 26–27) and assures the adoption to sonship (Rom. 8:14–17, 23). However, it is a serious mistake to limit the work of the Holy Spirit to the individual, to Christian ministry, or to the church. The ministry of the Holy Spirit is co-extensive with the building of the kingdom of God and with progress of restoration. He points beyond the renewal of life, beyond ministry, and beyond ethics to the eschaton. The Holy Spirit pushes us not to be content with the present experience of the Christian life, because the fulfillment of the promises is not ours as yet. The apostle Paul explains that in the Spirit we wait with eager anticipation for "our adoption as sons," for "the redemption of our bodies" (Rom. 8:24).[4]

Furthermore, I question the present limitation of Jesus' authority to spiritual-salvific in the church, or as Bock writes, "the new community,

---

[2]Willem A. VanGemeren, "The Spirit of Restoration," *WTJ* 50 (1988): 81–102.
[3]Ibid., 92.
[4]Ibid., 100.

the church, is the showcase of God's present reign through Messiah Jesus." This separation of Jesus' authority may be explained by a self-imposed limitation. I believe that the evidence of Luke-Acts must be taken in totality, including (1) Peter's vision and the conversion of Cornelius; (2) the progressive revelation entailed in Paul's conversion, call, and mission to the Gentiles; (3) Luke's presentation of the Acts of the apostles in the context of tension and of development, as the mantle of apostolic authority goes from Peter to Paul;[5] and (4) Paul's preaching that Christ is the head of the church *and* the ruler over creation (Acts 17:24–26, 29–31; 1 Cor. 15:25; Col. 1:1–17).[6] At the end of the apostolic age, the apostle John still bears witness to Christ's sovereignty and to the present rule of Christ over this world in judgment and vindication (Rev. 1:6, 16–18).[7]

The placement of the millennial reign with its distinct program for the Jewish people introduces a discontinuity between the church age and the era of consummation. The *present "salvific" rule* of Jesus Christ is separated from the "judgment authority" to be exercised in the *future millennial rule* when he will vindicate Israel. In essence, a shift takes place from looking at the church as a parenthesis to treating the Millennium—the era of restoration and vindication—as a parenthesis between the church and the consummation.

Bock's hermeneutic controls his exegesis in that it dictates the fulfillment of the promises and the covenants to be in a particular period of time (millennial reign) and for a particular people (the Jews). I believe that Bock is well aware of this assumption, as he writes, "Acts 3 *alludes* to a future visible rule. . . . *There is no indication* that earthly and Israelite elements in Old Testament promises have been lost in the activity of the two stages" (emphases mine). I am reminded of Stan Gundry's remarks in his 1986 response to Craig Blaising's presentation: "We have tended to be preoccupied with the details of our dispensational schemes and eschatological maps. Too often this preoccupation with the details of the map has detracted from the experience of traveling through the territory itself."

The New Covenant: Spiritual and Political Blessings

Bruce A. Ware ("New Covenant") opens up a profitable approach of relating Old Testament and New Testament by a study of Jeremiah 31:31–34. Since the older dispensational distinctions between a new covenant for the church and another new covenant for Israel have

---

[5]VanGemeren, *The Progress of Redemption,* 369–70.
[6]Ibid., 387–95.
[7]Ibid., 458.

apparently been abandoned, how can a distinction between Israel and the church be maintained? If this distinction were to be abandoned, is there still a sine qua non of dispensationalism? Ware, as can be expected, affirms a distinction between Israel and the church. He does so by a study of Jeremiah 31:31–34, the classic new-covenant text in the Old Testament.

The context of these verses is very relevant. It constitutes a small part of the hope that Jeremiah gave the preexilic community in the Book of Consolation (Jer. 30–33). In these chapters, Jeremiah confirms the continuity of the promises and of the covenants—with creation, Abraham, Israel, the priesthood, and David—to those in exile or going into exile.[8] The prophet had declared that the people would go into exile on account of their breaking the covenant. They would no longer enjoy the realization of the promises and the assurance of the covenants because of their sins, not because of God's infidelity.[9] He also proclaimed that because God is faithful, he will preserve a remnant; he will restore the exiles to the land; he will constitute a new community; and he will renew the covenants and the promises!

Indeed, the postexilic community tasted the benefits of God's fidelity. In the progress of redemption,[10] the Lord renewed his promises and covenants to Israel after the Exile. They tasted the fulfillment of the "physical, national and geographical blessings" as well as the spiritual blessings.[11] In the progress of redemption the Lord renewed his promises and covenants in Jesus Christ, the fountainhead of all the promises and covenants. He is the key to both the spiritual and the material blessings because he is the Mediator of the new covenant, the covenant of grace, whose benefits extend backward to the saints under the old covenant, and forward to all the saints under the new.

In the light of this postulate, I cannot agree with the bifurcation of the new covenant into two stages: the territorial and political blessings to be given to the Jews in the millennial kingdom, and the spiritual benefits already inaugurated in the church. Does Jeremiah's prophecy not apply to the postexilic community? Were the territorial and political blessings not realized in principle upon the return of the Jews after the decree of Cyrus (538 B.C.)?

---

[8]VanGemeren, *Interpreting the Prophetic Word*, 313–17.

[9]VanGemeren, *The Progress of Redemption*, 290–99; idem, *Interpreting the Prophetic Word*, 183, 302–9.

[10]I owe the language of progress to Geerhardus Vos, who likens this development to that of a seed (*Biblical Theology* [Grand Rapids: Eerdmans, 1947], 15).

[11]VanGemeren, *The Progress of Redemption*, 300–312; idem, *Interpreting the Prophetic Word*, 182–210.

I hold to Calvin's sense of progressive hermeneutic,[12] according to which the postexilic events, the coming of Christ, the church age, and the consummation organically and progressively unfold the plan of God. "When he restored the Jews to liberty, and employed the ministry of Zerubbabel, Ezra, and Nehemiah, these things were fulfilled. Yet at the same time they ought to be continued down to the coming of Christ, by which the Church was gathered out of all parts of the world. But we ought also to go forward to Christ's last coming, by which all things shall be perfectly restored."[13]

Calvin's comments on Jeremiah 31 (vv. 5, 24) are quite relevant:

> Hence the Prophet here intimates that God's favour would be certain, because he would not only give leisure to the Jews, when they returned, to plant vines, but would also cause them to enjoy the fruit in peace and quietness. . . . He extends God's favour to the country and the villages, as though he had said, that the land would be filled with inhabitants, not only as to the fortified towns, but as to the fields. . . . Now, were one to ask, when was this fulfilled? We must bear in mind what has been said elsewhere,—that the Prophets, . . . included the whole kingdom of Christ from the beginning to the end. . . . But the Prophets, as it has been said, include the whole progress of Christ's kingdom when they speak of the future redemption of the people. The people began to do well when they returned to their own country; but soon after distresses came. . . . It was, therefore, necessary for them to look for the coming of Christ. We now taste of these benefits of God. . . . *We hence see that these prophecies are not accomplished in one day, or in one year, no, not even in one age, but ought to be understood as referring to the beginning and the end of Christ's kingdom.*[14]

Because Ware applies Jeremiah's prophecy to the fulfillment in the first coming, he defines the essence of the new covenant as the "*new mode* by which God's covenant with his people will be implemented and carried out, namely, through the internalization of the law." I believe that it is not the mode but God's *deeper commitment* to the new community that defines the essence of the new covenant. Moreover, I believe that the postexilic community already enjoyed some realization of these promises.

> The Spirit of God will affect a change in their hearts, so that more than ever before and in greater number the godly will persevere in doing God's will by the power of the Spirit. Internalization does not remove

---

[12]VanGemeren, *Interpreting the Prophetic Word,* 86–92.

[13]John Calvin, *Commentary on the Book of the Prophet Isaiah,* trans. W. Pringle (Grand Rapids: Baker, 1979), 4:101.

[14]John Calvin, *Commentaries on the Book of the Prophet Jeremiah and the Lamentations,* trans. J. Owen (Grand Rapids: Baker, 1979), 4:62, 116–18 (emphasis added).

the legitimate place of intermediaries (priest, king, prophet), but puts a greater *responsibility* on individuals. . . . The hope of *democratization* of the covenant community goes back to God's promise to Israel at Sinai, where he promised to make Israel a holy and royal nation, distinct from and favored above all nations (Ex. 19:5–6). As God's *segullâ* ("treasured possession," v. 5), they were to be the *servants* of the living God, that is, called and commissioned by the Lord to establish his kingdom on earth (Deut. 26:18–19; Ps. 114:2). Jeremiah spoke of a new era that Yahweh sovereignly, monergistically, freely, and graciously opens up. . . . Yahweh will renew the covenant administration and offer the members of the new community even greater privileges.[15]

Consequently, I have grave reservations with Ware's treatment of the Holy Spirit in the Old Testament. Was the Spirit not involved in the regeneration and sanctification of the Old Testament saints? Did they not experience internalization of the law of God (cf. Ps. 37:31; 40:8)?[16] Was the Spirit not involved in helping the Old Testament saints persevere in their longing for the day of redemption? It appears to me that the prophetic hope lies in a *numerical extension* of the covenant community by the Spirit's transformation of Jews, Gentiles, and their offspring, in an *intensification* of the relationship between God and the new community, and in a *radical transformation* of creation.

> The Spirit of God strives at bringing about the fullness of God's kingdom on earth by restructuring human values and structures to correspond with God's values and structures. He is independent from human organizations and systems, but also freely uses them to accomplish God's purposes. From the prophetic perspective, Israel could not function within God's purposes unless the Spirit of the living God was in them. The purpose of God's revelation through Moses was to continuously involve the Spirit of God in renewing the hearts of human beings (Deut. 10:16; 30:6).[17]

Moreover, what is there to gain by separating the present inaugurated reality (forgiveness of sin; the Spirit's indwelling presence) from the political and territorial blessings? Since the goal of redemptive history lies in the new creation, over which God is the sovereign ruler, the promises of Jeremiah 30–33 point to that eschatological kingdom in which all things cohere in Jesus Christ.[18] Why not speak of the present inaugurated political and territorial blessings in the light of Colossians 1, according to which Christ is the Ruler and Sustainer of all creation? Are

---

[15]VanGemeren, *Interpreting the Prophetic Word,* 315–16.

[16]Willem A. VanGemeren, "Psalms," in EBC 5 (Grand Rapids: Zondervan, 1991), 184–86, 303.

[17]VanGemeren, *Interpreting the Prophetic Word,* 236.

[18]VanGemeren, *The Progress of Redemption,* 460–64.

both the spiritual and physical not united in Christ at the present time in principle, and in reality in the eternal state? Does the church not share in principle in the "political" aspects of the promises (Rev. 5:10; cf. Matt. 5:5)?

The Unity and the Diversity of the People of God

Covenant theologians will appreciate the change in dispensational teaching regarding the church. According to Carl B. Hoch ("The New Man"), the church is an important stage in the unfolding of God's plan as Gentiles are incorporated in the new humanity. He defines "the new man" (Eph. 2) as a participant in Israel's heritage, which includes the covenants, the promises, and the revelation of God (2:12; cf. Rom. 3:2 [divine oracles]; 9:4–5 [divine glory, covenants, law, worship, patriarchs]). This "new man" walks by the Spirit and represents the new Jewish-Gentile community. Hoch observes: "Their new relationship resides in the new man, 'the new temple' where God resides in a community of Jew-Gentile renewed by the Spirit and reconciled by Christ."

Robert L. Saucy's essay ("Church as the Mystery of God") develops a similar argument along two lines: continuity and discontinuity. He defines *mystery* as a secret, that is, a truth that was previously hidden and subsequently revealed by God's Spirit to the apostles. This mystery concerns the new act of God in saving Gentiles and in endowing them with the Holy Spirit. The outworking of "God's historical plan of salvation" involves the salvation of Gentiles and Jews, their incorporation in the church as a "partial fulfillment" of the promises, and their being filled with the Holy Spirit.

Yet, Saucy keeps the Gentiles distinct from the Jews. On the one hand, he defends the thesis that Gentiles share in the "full messianic salvation that is realized in the crucified and risen Christ and made effective to both [Gentiles and Jews] through the apostolic proclamation of the gospel." On the other hand, the Jews have not lost their identity. They remain distinct, even as members of the church. They are heirs of other aspects of the unfolding of God's mystery, namely "a future work with Israel." After all, he argues, the church age is "the beginning of a messianic salvation."

W. Edward Glenny ("Israelite Imagery of 1 Peter 2") also maintains the clear distinction between Israel and the church. He concludes that the "prospect of a future for ethnic Israel is essential for Peter's argument." Here he agrees with Bock that Peter's position is consistent (cf. Acts 3) in that the apostle confirms the hope for "a future restoration of the nation of Israel." The church does share with Israel in the promises of God's election and redemption, in the holy standards, in the priestly ministry, and in the honor of belonging to the people of God (1 Peter 2:6–10), but it has a separate existence from national Israel, to whom belong the prophetic words of national restoration. Did I miss something in the logic of Glenny's argument? The argument as it stands is not persuasive because it is essentially an argument from silence, a hidden agenda, or a hermeneutic that posits a programmatic platform for Israel's future. Again, Glenny ends up with three stages of fulfillment: (1) the church as the initial stage, (2) a "future exhaustive fulfillment" in the nation of Israel, and (3) Christ as the ultimate fulfillment.

The Future of the Jews

J. Lanier Burns ("The Future of Ethnic Israel in Romans 11") clarifies the piece of the argument that is assumed by Hoch, Saucy, and Glenny. He defines "ethnic" as the "racial cohesion" of the Jewish people in contrast to the church (Rom. 11:1; cf. 9:3) and from the other (Gentile) nations. He specifies that the existence of this remnant is a guarantee for the fulfillment of God's word, "an earnest of ethnic promises and a divinely assured inheritance." Consequently, he concludes in favor of "a continuum of the remnant-majority motif and the inviolability of God's faithfulness to his covenantal word that extends from Israel's *Urzeit* . . . to its exilic *Endzeit* . . . and by extension through Paul's own day."

While I am open to consider a place for ethnic Israel in the unfolding progress of redemption,[19] I have reservations in reading a definite program of fulfillment according to which at the coming of the Lord Jesus "the nation will enjoy what only a remnant has presently experienced."

I agree with Burns's final suggestion that much "constructive" dialogue is requisite, but I wonder whether a "greater sophistication of terminology" (regarding the oneness and diversity of the one people of God) will bring the various theological camps any closer together.

The Law and the Spirit

David K. Lowery ("Christ, the End of the Law") perpetuates the distinction between law and Spirit. According to him, the law is negative (demonstration of sin) and temporary (till Christ). It was an external and negative bond by which God taught righteousness. Since Jesus' coming, God teaches righteousness by faith and by his Spirit.

Lowery creates a "false dichotomy" between the Old Testament as "external" and the New Testament as "internal." At least, so it appears:

---

[19]W. A. VanGemeren, "Israel as the Hermeneutical Crux in the Interpretation of Prophecy," *WTJ* 45 (1983): 132–45; 46 (1984): 254–97.

"Although the leading of the Spirit renders the law obsolete (Gal. 5:18, 23a), this does not mean that Paul preaches an ethically inferior gospel (cf. Rom. 3:8). On the contrary, the way of the Spirit is ethically superior by virtue of its more excellent product." Lowery relativizes the law of Moses to the administration of the old covenant without extensive qualifications. He writes, "The law as a body of stipulations defining righteousness is no longer applicable to the church."

I am left with several questions. What about those Old Testament saints who walked with God and experienced the internalization of the law?[20] What about the struggle within Paul between the flesh and the Spirit, between the present age and the age to come? What about Paul's argument against the Judaizers? Lowery interprets Romans 7:7–25 and Philippians 3:9 as illustrative of the contrast between the two ages: righteousness that comes from the law versus a righteousness that comes through faith in Christ. Instead of appreciating the historical context of Paul's argument against the law,[21] he defines Paul's view of the law as "provisional, as inextricably linked to an era of salvation history that has been superseded by the coming of Christ and the ministry of the new covenant, mediated by the Spirit." I agree that Christ, not the law, is "the goal" (Lowery's rendering of *telos*). But are we beyond the positive use of the law as an instrument of righteousness as we await the coming of Christ? Lowery answers in the affirmative, "Paul has replaced a focus on the law with a focus on Christ and the gospel." The law was never intended to be a focus.[22]

John A. Martin ("Christ, the Fulfillment") sets up a disjunction between the Law and the teaching of Jesus but is more cautious by discussing elements of continuity and discontinuity. While I appreciate Martin's concern in listening to Jesus' teaching as representative of the prophetic tradition,[23] he holds that Jesus taught "the believers' ethic." The basis of this ethic is the moral law of God (the Ten Commandments), but Martin makes a distinction between the law as "historically conditioned" and the moral order rooted in creation and in the character of God. This distinction may have some merit but must be more

---

[20]VanGemeren, "Psalms," 184–86, 303.

[21]See James D. G. Dunn, *Romans 1–8*, WBC (Waco, Tex.: Word, 1988), 318.

[22]VanGemeren, *The Progress of Redemption*, 158–61. See Knox Chamblin, "The Law of Moses and the Law of Christ," in *Continuity and Discontinuity: Perspectives on the Relationship Between the Old and New Testaments: Essays in Honor of S. Lewis Johnson, Jr.*, ed. John S. Feinberg [Westchester, Ill.: Crossway, 1988], 181–202; W. A. VanGemeren, "The Grace of Law: A Reformed Perspective," in *Law, Gospel, and the Modern Christian: Five Views*, ed. Wayne G. Strickland (Grand Rapids: Zondervan, forthcoming).

[23]VanGemeren, *Interpreting the Prophetic Word*, 354–63.

carefully argued, lest dispensationalism be charged with latent antino-mianism.[24]

The Church Age, the Millennium, and the Consummation

David L. Turner's study ("The New Jerusalem") is essentially a sound biblico-theological development of the biblical teaching of the city of God as a symbol of the new creation. It is an image that "represents the culmination and transformation of the hopes of the people of God from long ages past." After a study of this image in the Old and New Testaments, he turns to the hermeneutical significance of this theme, calling for a "sensitivity to apocalyptic imagery and acceptance of the cosmic nature of eschatology and redemption." He argues that Revelation 21:1–22:5 is in fact "the full flowering of Old Testament eschatological hope." Furthermore, he concludes that Revelation 21:1 introduces a new, eternal, and transformed state in which all the elect have a share.

So far I am in agreement. Then Turner sets the eternal state in the context of the progress of redemption. To this end, he distinguishes between three distinct, though organically related, stages. He begins with the first coming of Christ (why not go back to Eden?), calling it the bronze age. The Millennium is the intermediate state, the silver age. Finally, comes the golden age: the eternal state. Many readers of this volume agree with Turner's optimistic view of history. I, for one, remain unconvinced.

> Regrettably, evangelical Christians have locked horns on the precise details of interpretation and, even more regrettably, have defined Evangelicalism in terms of a particular millennial perspective. Each of the millennial positions suffers from not hearing the whole prophetic and apostolic witness. . . . Depending on our position, we have various vantage points from which we look at eternity as the one horizon and at the interpretation of the Bible as the other horizon.[25]

Continuity and Discontinuity

Kenneth L. Barker's essay ("The Scope and Center") covers significant areas of past discussion between dispensational and covenant theologians. I appreciate his restatement and further development of "false dichotomies."[26] The irenic spirit of Barker will go far in opening up dialogue on the "false" dichotomies among the representatives of the

---

[24]John H. Gerstner, *A Primer on Dispensationalism* (n.p., 1982).

[25]VanGemeren, *The Progress of Redemption,* 474.

[26]Kenneth L. Barker, "False Dichotomies Between the Testaments," *JETS* 25 (1982): 3–16.

various theological perspectives. His concern for love for brothers in Christ is coupled with a desire to listen to the whole Bible (*tota Scriptura*).

Barker affirms "a greater unity or integration in God's grand design, overall purpose, and comprehensive program." He does so by a reduction in the number of "dispensations," by an inclusion of the church "in some sense" in the application of the prophecies, and by the unifying principle of God's rule in both Testaments. This "central focus of biblical theology" avoids separating the Old Testament too radically from the New.

Moreover, he properly concludes that the law was an expression of God's grace teaching the regenerate how they might please him, while condemning the unregenerate for their sinful rebellion against the Holy One of Israel. Barker rightly insists on the place of the moral law in the new covenant. After all, the Old Testament saints also experienced the work of the Spirit in regeneration.

Yet, there is a major area of disagreement in that Barker distinguishes between Israel and the church. He defines *Israel* as a political body in which the redeemed often formed a minority, and the *church* as an organic, transcultural, transnational body of believers. I believe that the members of the church are called by the Father, regenerated by the Spirit, in union with the glorious Son of God, justified by the Father, sanctified by the Spirit, and await the coming of the kingdom in its full splendor. The status of Israel, apart from Jesus Christ, is ambivalent. The Jews as a people are *lo-ammi* because of their rejection of the Messiah; nevertheless, they are still the beloved of God on account of Abraham (Rom. 11:28). The future of Israel is hidden in the wise counsel of God (vv. 33–36). Consequently, I am open to God's way in Israel because he is sovereign and free, but I remain unconvinced that a premillennial reign, including the land promises, is necessary within the framework of the progressive hermeneutic.

BRONZE, SILVER, AND GOLD

Blaising has raised the important issue of the sine qua non of dispensationalism. The growing corpus of dispensational studies and distinctions has created some bewilderment, especially since there is no confessional framework by which conclusions may be tested. No doubt, dispensationalism has been developing as any vital theological system does. Blaising, Bock, and the contributors to this volume are to be commended for providing fellow dispensationalists and nondispensationalists an update of what dispensationalism is today.

The title of this volume—*Dispensationalism, Israel and the Church*—

suggests that the answer to the question, What is the sine qua non of dispensationalism? can be found in defining the relationship of Israel and the church. While Gentiles as the people of God share many benefits with the Jews through the covenant, the Jews have a distinct place within God's program and receive a different fulfillment of the promises (national, political).

At a deeper level, the dispensational approach to the relationship between the two Testaments creates a hermeneutical framework. This hermeneutical assumption appears in two ways. First, *the place of the law* in the church remains an area for disagreement between covenant and dispensational theologians. Over against the dispensational ambivalence on the relation of the law to the Spirit, covenant theologians hold that the law is vitally important in the process of sanctification by the Holy Spirit. For the covenant theologian, the three—law, the presence of the Holy Spirit, and personal sanctification—are interrelated.

Second, the *focus of Christian hope* remains an area for disagreement between covenant and dispensational theologians. It still appears to me that the focus of dispensationalism lies in the second coming of Christ, the Jews, and the Millennium. While I am not opposed to a millennial kingdom, I favor an openness to the details of eschatology, keeping in mind past mistakes in interpreting and misapplying God's revelation.[27] For this reason, I prefer a broad center—the Christological and eschatological focus of Scripture, which I developed in *The Progress of Redemption*.[28] The Bible unveils one grand design gradually and progressively. Everything coheres in Jesus Christ the Redeemer, who accomplished the work of redemption during his earthly ministry and who applies the benefits of the covenant of grace to the saints under the old-covenant administration *and* to the saints under the new-covenant administration.

In my evaluation the dispensational hermeneutic of progressive fulfillment bypasses the realization of God's promises after the Exile, distinguishes between the spiritual and the politico-judicial aspects of Jesus' ministry, and tends to dwarf the importance of the eternal state. On the one hand, dispensationalism treats the postexilic events as relatively insignificant to the unfolding of God's promises made through the preexilic and the exilic prophets.[29] On the other hand, dispensationalism projects a program of restoration during the Millennium. These words may seem harsh, but I must wonder whether, after all the

[27]W. A. VanGemeren, "Prophets, the Freedom of God, and Hermeneutics," *WTJ* 52 (1990): 79–99; idem, *Interpreting the Prophetic Word*, 80–85.

[28]VanGemeren, *The Progress of Redemption*, 25–27.

[29]See my plea for a study of the postexilic era in ibid., 300–324; idem, *Interpreting the Prophetic Word*, 87–92, 183–87.

qualifications, the sine qua non of the dispensational hermeneutic is *a distinct view of history.*

If this is the case, God's program for Israel ("the silver age") is the focus of redemptive history, and the place of the church is relegated to that of a "bronze age." Is this not another way of maintaining a parenthesis, whether it be the church age or the millennial age? Certainly, dispensationalists have significantly polished the bronze of the church age within God's program, but bronze is still bronze, and silver is silver.

In conclusion, the following citation from my article in *Continuity and Discontinuity* is to encourage my dispensational brothers to live with tensions in the exegesis of the Bible:

> The Bible unfolds the development of the plan of salvation through time in diverse *stages.* The progression of redemptive history in distinct epochs (*dispensations*) testifies to the variety of God's works and to the continuity of his love and fidelity to man. These epochs are organically related to each other, corroborating to the fact of the single plan of God, confirmed in the one mediator, Jesus Christ.
>
> The appreciation of unity amidst variety arises from a profound recognition of the *variety,* magnificence and mystery of divine revelation. The revelation of God witnesses to the acts of God (creation, the history of redemption, in Christ) and the *acts* of God witness to his *promises, kingship, covenants, commitment* to Israel and to the nations, *communion with his people, grace and fidelity,* and to the fullness of finality of *redemption of heaven and earth.* These are a few of the many motifs of Scripture and in their variety, they find their *focus* in Jesus Christ.
>
> The task of biblical theology concerns both the study and appreciation of the many themes of Scripture and their inner *relationships.* The task of Reformed Theology further involves a deepening sense of the *unity* and *continuity* of God's plan in the history of redemption, while maintaining the tensions of: material and spiritual, time and eternity, law and gospel, token and reality, promise and fulfillment, old and new, Israel and the Church, this world and the world to come.
>
> Each of these areas reveals an inner dynamism, requiring careful attention to all the biblical data and motifs. Calvin never gave a simple answer to these complex issues, and his heirs too admit their humanness in not always being able to find the balance.[30]

---

[30]VanGemeren, "Systems of Continuity," 59.

A Response

Bruce K. Waltke

This book signals a significant restructuring of dispensationalism within the framework of inaugurated eschatology. According to historic dispensationalism, the church is unrelated to God's program for ethnic Israel and so does not fulfill the Old Testament's covenants and promises. Christ offered, it taught, the prophesied messianic kingdom to ethnic Israel, but when that nation rejected him and his rule, he inaugurated a heretofore hidden form of the kingdom, the church. This radical separation between God's program for the Jews and for the church was heretofore a sine qua non of dispensationalism.

Although not monolithic, as these chapters show, reconstructed dispensationalism essentially believes that Christ inaugurated the fulfillment of Israel's covenants and promises and that the church actualizes them. It denies that the church is a parenthesis within God's program for Israel. At the same time, however, it continues historic dispensationalism by its adherence to the notions that God has two peoples with two distinct programs, ethnic Israel/the Jews and the church, and that the future of the former can be found in a literalistic interpretation of the Old Testament, entailing a restoration of the house of David in the land.[1] All of this, dispensationalism contends, will occur during the Millennium. It does not affect dispensationalism as such to incorporate these two distinct programs for Israel and the church within an all-embracing eternal program.

David Turner says that the prophesied kingdom will be consummated in two stages: in the Millennium, "an intermediate silver age brought to earth at Christ's second coming," and in the new heaven and new earth, "an ultimate, golden age, consummated when all opposition to God's rule has ceased." He refers to the present stage of Christ's rule as "a

---

[1]See George Eldon Ladd, "The Revival of Apocalyptic in the Churches," *RevExp* 72 (Summer 1975): 268.

preliminary and anticipatory bronze stage brought to earth by the first coming of Christ." From his distinguished study of Revelation 21–22 he draws the conclusion that the description of the heavenly Jerusalem in the new heaven and new earth "clearly portray[s] the essential transdispensational continuity of Israel and the church as the one people of God." That position is closer to covenant theology than to dispensationalism.

This revised dispensationalism significantly affects hermeneutics. Although insisting on a future literalistic interpretation of Old Testament covenants and prophecies when God restores the kingdom to Israel (Acts 1:6), Bock's careful exegesis of Acts 2 leads him to draw the conclusion that Christ's present, "invisible" reign fulfills the Old Testament's Davidic covenant and prophecies, which represent David's future kingdom as visible and carnal. In other words, Peter resignified the earthly, visible representations of the Davidic kingdom in the Old Testament to denote Christ's present, spiritual, invisible rule from his Davidic, heavenly throne. Likewise, from his excellent exegesis of 1 Peter 2, Glenny teaches that Peter used a typological-prophetic hermeneutics of Old Testament imagery. The patterns within the types described in Isaiah 28:16, Psalm 118:22, Isaiah 8:14, Exodus 19:5–6, Isaiah 43:20–21, and Hosea 1–2 find an escalated fulfillment in their antitype, Christ and his church. Nevertheless, according to Glenny, Peter does not rule out the possibility that God will again restore the type when he restores ethnic Israel.

This already—not yet model of dispensationalism, entailing a less than one-for-one correspondence between Old Testament covenants and prophecies and their partial fulfillment in the church, shakes the very foundations of dispensational hermeneutics, which includes a *consistent* literalistic interpretation of the Old Testament, another sine qua non of the system. Traditional dispensationalism's inconsistent use of types for ecclesiology in narrative, because it still preserved the "mystery" character of the kingdom, but not in Old Testament covenants and prophecies, is now extended by Glenny to a consistent use of types of Christ and his church in the whole Old Testament.

The revised model removes other benchmarks of dispensationalism. Hoch says that "the whole argument in Ephesians 2 is that Jewish privileges have been extended to Gentiles through Christ" and that the Gentiles now share with Israel in their prior covenants and promise, not restricting with historic dispensationalism the Gentiles' inheritance to the "spiritual" blessings of the Abrahamic covenant in contrast to its "national and political" aspects. Saucy makes explicit what Hoch implies: "The inheritance of which the apostle here [Gal. 3:29] speaks may be viewed as 'all the blessing pledged to Abraham and his descendants.'"

On the basis of circumspect exegesis of Ephesians 3:1–14 and Romans 16:25–26, Saucy interprets *mystery* as "the actualization or realization through Christ of that which the prophets foretold and longingly anticipated," dismissing the traditional dispensational understanding of *mystery* as the revelation of truth not previously found in the Old Testament. Nevertheless, "the unification of Gentile and Jew in the church does not rule out the possibility of *functional* distinctions between Israel and the other nations."

This remarkable development within dispensationalism also breaks down other distinctions between what historic dispensationalism designated as the earthly people of God versus the heavenly people of God. According to the new view, Christ inaugurated the new covenant at his first advent, and both Israel and the church share in it. Both also participate in the new Jerusalem.

The modernized model also has raised new questions about the church's relationship to the law. Whereas historic dispensationalism contended that the unified Mosaic law has been done away with, Martin, in his original study on the Sermon on the Mount, contends that Jesus based his ethic on his authoritative, prophetic interpretation of the Mosaic law and that Matthew recorded his ethic in the context of the church. Consequently, although both are historically conditioned, it follows that the Mosaic law and Jesus' interpretation of it are "applicable" to the church. In his marvelously felicitous study of Romans 10:4, Lowery argues that the Mosaic law has been superseded by the new covenant instituted by Christ. Barker, following McComisky, qualifies this emphasis, noting that the law has not been abrogated because in the new-covenant arrangement the law is now written on the heart, not on rock. It provides the "enablement by the Holy Spirit to obey his law."[2] Their excellent studies present a healthy tension, not a contradiction.

After this setting forth of the system, I critique first the book and

---

[2]Importantly—and this would help refine Glenny's excellent essay—the Old Testament uses "people of God" in two ways: for the elect nation, the "outward" people of God (Ex. 6:7; Deut. 7:6), and for "true Israel," the inward people of God characterized by faith and obedience (Ex. 19:6; Lev. 26:3–12). The former is circumcised only in the flesh, the latter in the heart (Deut. 10:16; 30:6). The church, also characterized by faith and obedience, continues the latter, not the former. The "root" of both "branches," as Burns says so well, is "God's covenants (cf. [Rom.] 9:1–2), and supremely his word about Christ (9:5; chap. 10; cf. Heb. 1:1–2)." God and his true people are united by the work of Christ and their faith in Christ (Gal. 3:16, 26–29). In the Old Testament true Israel looked forward to the unfolding promises of his coming (Gen. 3:15; 15:6; Matt. 13:17; John 8:56) and sang of him (Pss. 2; 16; 110; Isa. 52:13–53:12). In the New Testament the church, composed of true Israel and believing Gentiles, looks back upon his coming and sings of him (1 Tim. 3:16). Together they look forward to his Parousia (Heb. 11:10, 39–40; 12:22–23; 13:14; Rev. 21:9–17).

then the system (the two, of course, are somewhat inseparable). I salute the editors and contributors for their openness, honesty, scholarship, and irenic tone. This new perestroika within dispensationalism augurs well for the future of dispensational schools, especially for Dallas Theological Seminary, with which most of them (as well as myself) are related as former students and/or faculty members. In the best traditions of that institution, they are committed to accurate exegesis of the Holy Bible, not confessions or doctrinal statements, and are willing to revise them if necessary in light of their research. Older dispensationalists in that institution, who had no firm pedagogical heritage from historic Christian doctrine,[3] were convinced that accurate exegesis would bear out their system. These younger dispensationalists, having come under the impact of realized eschatology, especially in renowned universities, know that careful exegesis must lead at the least to this restructuring of the historic model. Without that openness, honesty, and careful exegesis, dispensational schools would betray their commitment to inspired Scriptures rightly interpreted above uninspired confessions and would fail to attract bright, young minds and to raise up theologians to lead them. I should like to take this opportunity to thank the editors for inviting me to participate in their "ongoing work of interpreting the Scripture."[4]

Significantly, these younger dispensationalists cite older dispensationalists mostly to distance themselves from them. In truth, however, they are desperately trying to retain their heritage. I found the exegesis by Bock, Glenny, Turner, Martin, Hoch, Lowery, Saucy, and Burns (on Rom. 11:1–25, not 26–32) outstanding. (Barker's good work is theological, not exegetical.) Some marred their studies, however, by adding to their texts material from their dispensational heritage. In my opinion, however, the chapters contain serious flaws.

The book of Hebrews is critical to the topic of the relationship of Israel and the church. Turner does not fail us in his treatment of Jerusalem in that book, but Ware does. Ware's studies of other New Testament texts, establishing that Jesus inaugurated the new covenant with his blood and Spirit, are helpful, but his study of Hebrews 8–10 is deficient. Whereas other contributors rightly started with the New

[3]See the brilliant dissertations by Alan Patrick Boyd, "A Dispensational Premillennial Analysis of the Eschatology of the Post-Apostolic Fathers (Until the Death of Justin Martyr)" (Th.M. thesis, Dallas Theological Seminary, 1977), and by John Hannah, "The Social and Intellectual History of the Origins of the Evangelical Theological College" (Ph.D. diss., University of Texas, 1988), reprinted UMI Dissertation Information Service (1991).

[4]Craig A. Blaising, "Development of Dispensationalism by Contemporary Dispensationalists," *BSac* 145 (July–September 1988): 255.

Testament and worked their way back into the Old, Ware begs the issue by starting with the Old and uses the book of Hebrews selectively to substantiate his interpretation.[5] In other words, he autonomously eisegetes Hebrews, not submissively exegetes it. What is needed is a careful exegesis of this inspired interpretation of the two testaments, the Old and the New. An inductive, historical approach, I suggest, will not corroborate Ware's distinction between spiritual aspects of the new covenant already realized in the church and its alleged national aspects not yet fulfilled for Israel. The writer of Hebrews was intimately acquainted with expectations in the Old Testament. If there was ever a passage where the distinction Ware wants to draw is to be found, it is here.[6] The absence of Ware's distinction in Hebrews disproves him. His distinction is flatly contradicted in Revelation 5:9–10. Furthermore, Ware fails to realize that if in fact Ryrie, with whom he says he is in agreement, allowed that Christ inaugurated or fulfilled *for the church* the "spiritual" blessings of the new covenant promised exclusively to the house of Israel and to the house of Judah, Ryrie would have prepared the way for revised dispensationalism and ultimately for amillennialism.[7]

Burns, in spite of much excellent material on Romans as a whole and on Romans 11:1–25 in particular, let this reviewer down when he came to the crucial verses 26–32. All dispensationalists depend on these verses to establish a future program for national Israel in contrast to the church. In an obiter dictum Burns refers "all Israel shall be saved" to a future time when "the full number of Israel's elect [shall be saved] as preparation for the cleansing of the nation by its Deliverer in fulfillment of the new covenant." Burns later associates Israel's future salvation

---

[5]Ladd correctly noted that the starting point—a literal interpretation of the Old Testament, into which the New is then fitted versus the New Testament teaching—is the watershed between dispensational and nondispensational theologies (see George E. Ladd, "Historic Premillennialism," in *The Meaning of the Millennium: Four Views,* ed. Robert G. Clouse [Downers Grove, Ill.: InterVarsity Press, 1977], 20–21).

[6]See Robert H. Gundry, *The Church and the Tribulation* (Grand Rapids: Zondervan, 1973), 16–17, for a list of parallels between Jeremiah's new covenant and its description in the New Testament.

[7]Ware ambiguously shifts his terms from *inaugurate* and *fulfill* to *apply.* Is Ryrie, who is a master of definition, deliberately elusive in using a precise term to describe the relationship of Israel and the church to one new covenant? Historic dispensationalists are well aware that if the church is "fulfilling" the new covenant promised to Israel, the door is wide open to an amillennial interpretation of the rest of the Old Testament. Ryrie wrote: "If the Church is fulfilling Israel's promises as contained in the new covenant or anywhere in Scripture, then [dispensational] premillennialism is weakened. One might well ask why there are not two aspects to one new covenant. This may be the case, and it is the position held by many premillennialists, but we agree that the amillennialist has every right to say of this view that it is 'a practical admission that the new covenant is fulfilled in and to the Church'" (C. C. Ryrie, *The Basics of the Premillennial Faith* [Neptune, NJ: Loizeaux Bros., 1953], 118). Hence, unlike Ware, he avoids the term *fulfill,* though this is the obvious concept in the New Testament, as Ware validates.

with the "Messiah's eschatological Parousia." I agree with Burns's identification of "all Israel" as "the full number of [ethnic] Israel's elect," but I am less than convinced from Burns's exegesis that this *crux interpretum* refers exclusively to the Parousia, and I reject as eisegesis his addition that Israel's salvation in turn prepares the way for a further national salvation. Burns's eschatological interpretation is less than convincing because he leaves unexegeted the critical adverbs *houtos*, "thus; in this way" ("and so," NIV), not "then," in verse 26; and *nun*, "now," not "then," in verse 31. Furthermore, his comment on the change of prepositions from "the deliverer will come *to* Zion" (Isa. 59:20 MT) to "the deliverer will come *from* Zion" is not cogent with reference to the time when true Israel's full salvation and its experience of the new covenant will come. Helpfully, he gives the interpretation of others, supported by this unexegeted data, that refer these words to elect Israel in the present age up to the Parousia.

To his great credit Burns does not fall headlong into the historic dispensational trap of falsifying Paul's teaching that God is restoring and will restore Israel into the kingdom into the error that God will restore the kingdom to Israel. Correlatively, dispensationalists read into the text Israel's national-political salvation in the land. Paul adds nothing of the sort to Israel's salvation in the very passage where dispensationalism rightly expects it. The salvation of all Israel is the same as that which the Gentiles presently enjoy in the new covenant—the removal of godlessness and sin.

An objective essay is also needed on Galatians, Paul's epistle that rebuts the Judaizers, who wish to reestablish the beggarly rudiments, that is, the ceremonial demands of the law (Sabbath observance, kosher foods, circumcision, a distinction between clean and unclean). Only Saucy comments on Galatians 3:29, and Burns mentions 3:6–9. Galatians 3, however, is a pivotal chapter for deciding the relationship of Israel and the church. What is needed is a detailed exegesis of the entire chapter; for example, of "those who believe are children of Abraham" (vv. 6–9), of "the Scripture does not say 'and to seeds,' meaning many people, but 'and to your seed,' meaning one person, who is Christ" (v. 16), and of "if you belong to Christ, then you are Abraham's [and implicitly Israel's and Judah's] seed" (v. 29). I interpret Paul to mean that the true seed of Abraham comprises those in Christ who have an inward commitment to God's promise analogous to that of Abraham before he had received circumcision or Israel was given the law.

Other passages in Galatians needing detailed study are 4:21–31, apparently denying ethnic, unbelieving Israel any claim to its covenants of promise, and 6:15–16. In light of the rest of the book as a whole that in Christ there is neither Jew nor Greek and of the preceding verse in particular, "neither circumcision nor uncircumcision means anything; what counts is a new creation," Paul cannot have intended in verse 16 to contrast "those [Gentiles] who follow this rule" with "the Israel of God." The NIV rightly reads "even the Israel of God," a reference to the church.

Finally, a detailed exegesis of Revelation 20:1–10 is a must. Revised dispensationalists assume the Millennium as the "not-yet" stage of the kingdom, but none validates it from the New Testament. This hypothetical assumption, enabling dispensationalists to project a national Israel into the future, has far-reaching hermeneutical implications, for it enables them to maintain their cherished, literalistic interpretation of Israel's covenants and prophecies.

In addition to neglecting these crucial New Testament texts, the contributors ignore both the classic comprehensive critique of dispensationalism by Oswald T. Allis (*Prophecy and the Church* [Philadelphia: Presbyterian & Reformed, 1945]) and the superb book by Hans K. LaRondelle (*The Israel of God in Prophecy: Principles of Prophetic Interpretation* [Berrien Springs, Mich.: Andrews University Press, 1983]). Let none be put off by LaRondelle's ecclesiastical affiliation. Astonishingly, none of the contributors takes note of W. D. Davies, *The Gospel and the Land: Early Christianity and Jewish Territory Doctrine* (Berkeley: University of California Press, 1974). This is the most comprehensive work in English on the subject of the land, so critical to this discussion. I find myself in agreement with Anthony A. Hoekema, *The Bible and the Future* (Grand Rapids: Eerdmans, 1979), who is not answered adequately. In my opinion, the works by LaRondelle and Hoekema remain the best on the topic.

Disappointingly, none of the contributors engages my essays "Kingdom Promises as Spiritual," in *Continuity and Discontinuity: Perspectives on the Relationship Between the Old and New Testaments: Essays in Honor of S. Lewis Johnson, Jr.*, ed. John S. Feinberg (Westchester, Ill.: Crossway Books, 1988), 263–88; and "Theonomy in Relation to Dispensational and Covenant Theologies," in *Theonomy: A Reformed Critique* (Grand Rapids: Zondervan, Acadamie Books, 1990), 59–88. In the former essay I argued among other things that if there is any tension in one's interpretation between the Old Testament and the New, priority must be given to the New; that Revelation 20:1–10 cannot be linked textually with Israel's covenants and promises; that no New Testament passage clearly teaches a future Jewish millennium; and that the New Testament interprets the imagery of the Old Testament with reference to the present, spiritual reign of Christ from his heavenly throne. In the latter essay I validated exegetically the point that the unified law has at least three aspects: the Ten Commandments (the eternal, moral law), the judicial (the application of the Ten Commandments to a specific historic situation), and the cultic (transitory symbols of the heavenly reality). I further argued along the lines proposed by Barker for the relationship of the old and new covenants. Contributors should have dialogued with, not ignored, the influential and well-researched work by Curtis I. Crenshaw and Grover E. Gunn III, *Dispensationalism: Today, Yesterday, and Tomorrow* (Memphis, Tenn: Footstool Publications, 1985). I agree essentially with the substance, not always the style, of this book.

I turn now to comments on revised dispensationalism as a system. If the book augurs well for the future of dispensational schools, it does not augur well for the future of dispensationalism. What remains distinctive to dispensationalism pertains to the "not-yet" aspect of the kingdom. The truth that ethnic Israel retains a place in God's redemptive history is not distinctive, as John Feinberg correctly noted.[8] At issue is whether or not God has two "true peoples" (true Israel and the church) and whether true Israel has a future role in redemptive history different from the church. If one envisions a Jewish millennium in which the kingdom will be restored to ethnic Israel in the land, the term *dispensationalism* will still be useful. If ethnic Israel's role is only its remnant status on a permanent equality with the Gentiles in the one true people of God with no distinctive role in the land beyond the Parousia, then the term *dispensationalism* is misleading and ought to be dropped.

To be sure, Jews and Gentiles are distinct peoples in redemptive history, but there is only one true people of God united in their faith in Messiah. William Hendriksen said it well: "The New Testament recognizes only *one* vine, *one* good olive tree, *one* body, *one* elect race, *one* royal priesthood, *one* holy nation, *one* people for God's own possession, *one* bride, *one* holy city, having the names of the apostles written on its foundations and the names of the tribes on its gates."[9] Our Lord clearly taught that when the Jews rejected him, God set aside national Israel as the distinctive, favored expression of his kingdom (Matt. 8:1–12; 21:43). Though many Jews are yet to be saved and become part of the one true people of God in Christ, the new man, God will never set them either apart from or above saved Gentiles in Christ or restore to them the "weak and beggarly" shadows of the Old Testament.

What strikes one dramatically in reading these chapters is the

---

[8]See John S. Feinberg, "Systems of Discontinuity," in *Continuity and Discontinuity: Perspectives on the Relationship Between the Old and New Testaments: Essays in Honor of S. Lewis Johnson, Jr.*, ed. John S. Feinberg (Westchester, Ill.: Crossway, 1988), 71.

[9]William Hendriksen, *And So All Israel Shall Be Saved* (Grand Rapids: Baker, 1945), 16.

overwhelmingly convincing evidence in the New Testament for the "already" fulfillment of Israel's covenants and promises in Christ and his church and the lack of *any* convincing exegetical evidence from the New Testament that the "not-yet" fulfillment of the kingdom will be realized by ethnic Israel in the land according to a literalistic interpretation of the Old Testament.

Bock rests his case for the restoration of the kingdom to national Israel on the verbal linkage of "restore" in Acts 3:21 and Acts 1:6. The former passage, however, speaks of the "restoration of everything" at the Parousia, not the restoration of the kingdom to national Israel. The restoration foreseen by the prophets includes among other things "the sun will no more be your light by day, nor will the brightness of the moon shine on you, for the LORD will be your everlasting light, and your God will be your glory" (Isa. 60:19). Amazingly, Bock ignores Peter's own mature reflections on what the prophets promised about the restoration of everything in 2 Peter 3:13: "But in keeping with his promise we are looking forward to a new heaven and a new earth, the home of righteousness." Significantly, on the basis of the Old Testament promises, Peter and the church were not looking for the restoration of national Israel in an alleged millennium before the new heavens and new earth. To introduce a millennium into Petrine theology is based on eisegesis, not exegesis. Turner rightly comments: "The 'making new' of all things (. . . Rev. 21:5) is equivalent to the 'regeneration' (. . . Matt. 19:28) or 'restoration' (. . . Acts 3:21) of the universe through Christ's redemptive work. . . . Cosmic renewal is no more an annihilation of the old world than personal regeneration is an annihilation of the old person." In sum, Bock is not convincing in his exegesis of Acts 3:21. After Acts 7 the territorial limits of Palestine are transcended. In fact, instead of jumping to Revelation, readers would have been better served by tracing the developing controversy in Acts in which the Gospel superseded the territorialistic, nationalistic, and cultic interests of Hebraic Christianity.

Also Bock dodges the logical conclusion from his study that the church's hermeneutics should conform to that of the apostles; namely, that visible representations of the kingdom in Old Testament covenants and prophecies should be interpreted as having an invisible, spiritual fulfillment. I argued in "Kingdom Promises as Spiritual" that prophecies finding fulfillment up to the ascension of Christ, such as his birth in Bethlehem, will have an earthly, visible fulfillment, and those pertaining to the church formed with the coming of the Spirit at Pentecost from Christ's heavenly Davidic throne will have an invisible, spiritual fulfillment.

Glenny bases his thesis that the nation of Israel, not the church, fulfills Old Testament prophecy on the fact that a type can have more than one fulfillment, that the details of the prophecies in Hosea 1–2 are not completely fulfilled in the church, that such an interpretation is consistent with a historical (?) interpretation of many Old Testament prophecies, that Peter does not suggest or require that his recipients replace Israel in God's program, and on Bock's faulty interpretation of Acts 3:21. He misses the obvious point, however, that Peter does not teach what he alleges. These arguments are all dragged in at the end of his otherwise superb paper without any exegetical validation. His arguments here are largely negative, not positive, and these can be satisfied by Hoekema's model that the "not-yet" aspect of prophecies finds its fulfillment in the new heavens and new earth. Furthermore, if Glenny accepted Hoekema's model, rather than the old dispensational model, he would avoid the obviously embarrassing entailment that God will walk back from an escalated fulfillment of typical prophecy in the antitype, Christ his church, to the shadow, earthly Israel. According to Hebrews, God does not walk backward.[10]

Turner essentially agrees with Hoekema (see his n. 49), though he throws in an unsubstantiated millennium between the present age and the age to come. This responder is in total agreement with Turner's chapter, aside from his unproved hypothesis that Revelation 20:1–10 pertains to a future, Jewish millennium. For a better interpretation of this *crux interpretum,* see Meredith Kline's magnificent exegesis, establishing what Jay Adams calls a "now-millennium," in "First Resurrection [Rev. 20, 21]," *WTJ* 37 (1975): 366–75.

Hoch's exegesis of Ephesians 2 is well done, and he wisely restrains from adding to Paul a future program for ethnic Israel distinct from the church. In Ephesians Paul speaks only of the permanent unity of Jews and Gentiles in Christ, "the new man." Ethnic Israel's privileges, says Hoch, "were restricted to Israel before the death of Christ and the creation of the church." This is a far cry from historic dispensationalism.

After his admirable demonstration that the church inherits "all the blessing pledged to Abraham and his descendants" and that the church actualizes the Old Testament prophecies, Saucy curiously reverses himself, introducing without any exegetical warrant the conclusions that "rather than one grand age of fulfillment under the messianic reign, the prophetic fulfillment has been divided into two ages related to the two comings of Christ" and that "nothing in the discussion of the mystery goes beyond this equality of *spiritual* [emphasis mine] position in

---

[10]John Wilmot, *Inspired Principles of Prophetic Interpretation,* foreword by D. M. Lloyd-Jones (Swengel, Pa.: Reiner Publications, n.d.), esp. 99–105. I commend this book to readers of this volume.

Christ. Thus the unification of Gentile and Jew in the church does not rule out the possibility of *functional* distinctions between Israel and the other nations in the future, even as there are functional distinctions among believers in the church today without impairing spiritual equality." What these functional differences may be he wisely does not speculate. The New Testament does not validate his hypothetical two stages of the "not-yet" aspect of the kingdom, and his restriction of the mystery blessings for the unified church to spiritual does not derive from his exegesis of Ephesians. Again, the "already" realization of the kingdom is based on solid exegesis of that book; the alleged "not-yet" national Israel stage is based entirely on eisegesis.

Barker helpfully holds that generic prophecy is progressively fulfilled. He focuses on the fulfillment begun by the first advent of Christ, but in truth the land promises began to be fulfilled in Israel's successive returns to the land from 538 B.C. on. To be sure, these fulfillments do not mean that these prophecies concerning Israel's restoration are now finished; that must be established from the New Testament. Barker's hermeneutics "will not let [him] agree with [Hoekema's] expungement of national Israel . . . from God's future program, or with his elimination of a literal, visible reign of Christ on this earth in time-space history." But he ignores the well-accepted fact that the New Testament, though produced by Jewish Christians who lived in a time when the land was of constant concern for most Jews, shows no interest in it. If revised dispensationalism produced one passage in the entire New Testament that clearly presents the resettlement of national Israel in the land, I would join them. But I know of none! Blanchard in his doctoral dissertation on the land comments: "Despite much popular opinion to the contrary, the New Testament is strangely silent about the rebuilding of Israel as a political nation in The Land."[11] Its silence is even more striking when one considers that *land* is the fourth most frequent term in the Old Testament. In fact, as Hoch points out, Paul resignifies *gē* from "land" in the Abrahamic covenant to "earth." This is more than an argument from silence. Jesus promised the apostles: "But when he, the Spirit of truth, comes, he will guide you into all truth. He will not speak on his own; he will speak only what he hears, and he will tell you what is yet to come. He will bring glory to me by taking what is mine and making it known to you" (John 16:13–14). Is it creditable that Jesus withheld from "all things" and from "what is yet to come" that his consummate, glorious kingdom will occur in a future millennium with a Jewish flavor?

---

[11]See William Maurice Blanchard, Jr., "Changing Hermeneutical Perspectives on 'The Land' in Biblical Theology" (Ph.D. diss., Southern Baptist Theological Seminary, 1986).

If there be any passage where Paul should have singled out the land for special mention it is Romans 9–11. But nowhere, especially here, as Burns should have pointed out, does Paul claim that the Jews will once again establish a nationalistic, territorial kingdom in the land. Dispensationalists put these words into the inspired apostle's mouth. In truth, none of the epistles—not those of Paul, of John, of Peter, or of the other Catholic Epistles of Hebrews and James—teach a future for national Israel in the land. The book of Hebrews denies it. The dispensationalist's case from the New Testament rests chiefly on the symbolic imagery of the Apocalypse, not on its clear letters and epistles.

What is needed to understand the Old Testament teaching about the land, on which revised dispensationalism heavily rests, is an essay on linguistic and social structuralism and hermeneutics.[12] I have in view Martin Heidegger's emphasis on the priority of language and his stress that we are at the disposal of language (rather than language being at our disposal), and the sociologist's emphasis that language signifies the culture of which the speaker is mostly unaware.[13] In brief, Israel's covenants and promises were unconsciously expressed in the symbols and imagery of the Old Testament dispensation(s). There was no other language in which to write. This approach provides a firm foundation for the hermeneutics of men like A. B. Davidson.[14] E. F. Kevan wrote: *"Interpretation must emerge from the dispensational character of prophecy as determined by the Covenant. . . .* This [old] dispensation determines the outward material forms of prophecy. . . . This means that we take the prophet to mean exactly what he says—'literalistically' (except in cases of obvious and declared metaphor)—though the *fulfillment* of what he says may greatly transcend both what he knows and the terms he uses."[15]

With the death, resurrection, ascension, and coming of Christ in the Spirit (i.e., the inauguration of the new covenant), a new social reality broke into the remnant's reluctant consciousness, namely, Christ's invisible, spiritual rule from his heavenly throne. Only the coming of the Spirit removed the veil of their old literalistic hermeneutics. No longer was the opposition, so necessary for meaning, between Jerusalem and pagan capitals but between heavenly and earthly Jerusalem. In that new light the images of the old dispensation were resignified to represent the

---

[12]See John Barton, *Reading the Old Testament: Method in Biblical Study* (Philadelphia: Westminster, 1984), 104–39.

[13]Peter Berger and Thomas Luckmann, *The Social Construction of Reality: A Treatise in the Sociology of Knowledge* (New York: Anchor, 1966). Personally, I discount the relativism of this work. The authors seem totally unaware that they themselves write in their inherited myth of secularism.

[14]A. B. Davidson, *Old Testament Prophecy* (Edinburgh: T. & T. Clark, 1904), 169.

[15]E. F. Kevan, "The Covenants and the Interpretation of the Old Testament," *EvQ* 26 (1954): 24.

heavenly reality of which they always spoke. As W. D. Davies expressed it, "The Land" was "Christified."[16] The writer of Hebrews warns his generation not to go back to these images that have been abolished forever; he implicitly cautions us against projecting them imaginatively into the future. The concern of the New Testament is a relationship with Jesus Christ, not a restoration of the types of the Old Testament.

Nevertheless, these images still await their even greater fulfillment in the new heaven and earth. As the writer of Hebrews expressed it: "These were all commended for their faith, yet none of them received what had been promised. God had planned something better for us so that only together with us would they be made perfect" (Heb. 11:39–40). If God promised the fathers $5 and he rewards them with $5,000, is he unfaithful?

---

[16]W. D. Davies, *The Gospel and the Land: Early Christianity and Jewish Territory Doctrine* (Berkeley: University of California Press, 1974), 367–68. In the New Testament the holiness of places and things, including the land, is replaced by holiness in the person of Jesus Christ. By Christifying space, the land as such became irrelevant. Instead, I suggest, the land becomes a type of the Christian's life in Christ. For old Israel the land was a gift, accepted by faith, where one met God, and in which one remained through persevering faith; for new Israel it is a type of Jesus Christ.

An Epangelical Response

Walter C. Kaiser, Jr.

There are three major types of theology that describe the relationship of Israel to the church, though countless shades and combinations exist within and between these three.[1] The three may be described as follows:

1. The *new Israel* view holds that geopolitical, national Israel was replaced by the church, which is now the new, spiritual Israel. There is no need to wait for any material or physical aspects to the fulfillment of God's promises to the patriarchs and David, or to expect a physical and real presence of Christ as he reigns from Jerusalem over all nations, for there will be no millennium.

2. The *covenant* view maintains that Israel and the church are one and the same throughout all of history: namely, they are the faithful from all of humanity. This one body is embraced in a covenant, not precisely referred to in Scripture, but surely one that embodies the essence of salvation described in the Bible: namely, the "covenant of grace" or the "covenant of redemption." All the promises, covenants, and prophecies are fulfilled in the gospel, which gospel is climaxed in the church, as God's covenant people. Thus individual believing Jews are grafted into the church.

3. The traditional *dispensational* view holds that Israel and the church have separate and distinct identities, destinies, and promises. During the so-called church age, Israel as a nation has been set aside, and the program of God has gone into a parenthesis or an intercalation. After this church age parenthesis comes to an end, God will resume relations

---

[1]My organization and basic pattern for the identification of these three types and my analysis of their positions has been substantially aided by the work of Daniel Gruber, *"That They Might Be One": The Biblical Relationship of Israel and the Church* (Hanover, N.H.: Privately published, April 1990), 27ff.; 94ff. This work is currently being published under the title *The Church and the Jews: The Biblical Relationship* (Springfield, Mo.: General Council of the Assemblies of God, Intercultural Ministries Department, 1991).

with the nation Israel once again and restore the Davidic kingdom to its greatest height ever.

In my view, however, each of these views, as stated in their classic forms, is seriously flawed. The most basic problem is that each begins with the church and then considers Israel from within the church, trying to fit the Jews within this framework. This accusation may sound most distorted when applied to dispensationalism; however, the above chapters will demonstrate how significant, for example, the Ephesian letter is for this system and how central a role the issue of "mystery" plays in it.

Each of these three solutions to the relationship of Israel to the church fails to reckon with one or more of the following three primary assertions of Scripture:

1. The church is grafted into Israel, not Israel into the church.

2. The new covenant of Jeremiah 31:31–34 was made with "the house of Judah and the house of Israel," not with the church. It is not a covenant made with all humanity, but all humanity may be grafted into it.

3. God has had a faithful remnant ever since the beginning of the human race. The church is that portion of the faithful remnant that was called out of the Gentiles, since Pentecost, to be grafted into the faithful remnant in Israel. There is a distinction between Israel and the church, but not a separation; there is oneness in which distinguishable aspects of that oneness may be seen without implying or necessitating a division of identity or destiny.

THE ANTI-ISRAEL POSTURE OF THE THEOLOGY OF THE CHURCH

It is sad to note that somewhere around the time of Eusebius Pamphili in the fourth century of the Christian era, the church began to adopt an anti-Jewish stance that had an enormous effect on its theological constructions. Fortunately, modern dispensationalism has not been part of this general movement within the church. This is the reason why it has presented such a strong position, especially when it came to handling such key texts as Romans 9–11 and the numerous Old Testament prophecies about the kingdom and related topics.

Most readers of the first four centuries of the Christian church realize that almost without exception, the church espoused and vigorously taught that Christ would return to earth in the Millennium to rule and reign over all the nations of the earth from Jerusalem. The major break with this theology came in the the fourth century A.D. during the reign of Emperor Constantine in the work *Ecclesiastical History* by Eusebius

Pamphili. Eusebius did not believe that there was a distinct future for the Jews; rather, the church was God's new Israel. Any proposal about a millennium was thought by Eusebius to be heretical.

Eusebius was aware that his view of Israel and the Millennium was not the one embraced by Papias (c. A.D. 60–c. 130), a student of the apostle John and Philip the Evangelist. In one place Eusebius praised this associate of the church father Polycarp (c. A.D. 60–155) by saying, "At this time, Papias was well known as bishop of the church at Hierapolis, a man well skilled in all manner of learning, and well acquainted with the Scriptures."[2] However, when Eusebius came to Papias's exposition of the Millennium, all of a sudden he started to heap scorn on him, almost as if he had forgotten the high words of praise he had given to him in another connection.

> He [Papias] says there would be a certain millennium after the resurrection, and that there would be a corporeal reign of Christ on this very earth; which things he appears to have imagined, as if they were authorized by the apostolic narrations, not understanding correctly those matters which they propounded mystically in their representations. For he was very limited in his comprehension, as is evident from his discourses; yet he was the very cause why most of the ecclesiastical writers, urging the antiquity of the man, were carried away by a similar opinion; as, for instance, Irenaeus, or any other that adopted such sentiments.[3]

It is clear, however, that Eusebius granted the apostolic case for the Millennium, as he allowed that Papias learned this doctrine from the apostles. Moreover, Papias was praised for his learning and understanding until the subject of the doctrine of a millennial rule and reign of Christ on the earth arose. Why the sudden shift in Eusebius's attitude and estimate of Papias as a scholar? What Papias taught happened to be the same teaching shared by "most of the ecclesiastical writers," Eusebius agreed, even though he tried to blame the ready acceptance of this teaching on "the antiquity" (i.e., the advanced years) of Papias. Most startling of all is the fact that Eusebius could not produce a single writer from that period who held his view. It was the support of Emperor Constantine that spirited Eusebius's position into the view that eventually was adopted by an astonishing number of contemporary theologians.

Previous to Eusebius's work, the industrious church father Origen (c. A.D. 185–c. 254) had set the scene for much that was to follow. He had

---

[2]Eusebius Pamphili, *The Ecclesiastical History of Eusebius Pamphili*, trans. Christian Frederick Cruse (Grand Rapids: Baker, 1989), 3.36 (120).
[3]Ibid. 3.39 (126).

championed the allegorical system of interpretation as the best way to handle most of the Old Testament. If some did not wish to interpret the text allegorically, as he did, they were nothing more than a "Jew" who did not belong in the church. In fact, "If anyone wishes to hear and understand these words [of the Old Testament] literally he ought to gather with the Jews rather than with the Christians. But if he wishes to be a Christian and a disciple of Paul, let him hear Paul saying that 'the Law is spiritual' [thereby] declaring that these words are 'allegorical' when the law speaks of Abraham and his wife and sons."[4]

But it was the Emperor Constantine that set this theology in concrete for many generations to come. In his letter to the churches over the Passover Controversy, he drew the line at the altar that had been abolished when Christ tore down the middle wall of partition. He referred to the Jews as "polluted wretches," whose hands were "stained . . . with a nefarious crime," "parricides and murders of our Lord."[5] In addition, the foundations for an anti-Jewish attitude were laid, a contempt and separation from everything connected with the Jews was forged, and the will of the bishops in council was now equated with the will of God, with any dissent being regarded as a criminal act—all by edict of the emperor! It was at this point that theology decided no longer to affirm that the gospel of God was "to the Jew first" (Rom. 1:16).

It is no wonder, then, that any system of interpretation that espouses a return of the geopolitical unit of a real Israel back to its land, an actual, future rule and reign of Christ on earth, or a real millennial reign of all believers of all ages with Christ on earth is still regarded with deep suspicion by all of the more highly recognized theologians and ecclesiastical fellowships of our day. But the roots of this illness are easily traced. Origen, Eusebius, and Constantine must be given most of the credit for turning the tide against the first three or four centuries and for making the point so strenuously that to this day few have dared even to whisper any thought of reversing it.

In this regard, however, dispensationalism along with historic premillennialism stand out as unique and as conservators of the original teaching of the apostles and the church fathers of the first three or four centuries of the Christian era.

METHODS OF HANDLING THE COVENANTS

Over the course of the Christian centuries, five different methods for relating Israel and the church may be distinguished, which I label as

---

[4]Origen, *Homilies on Genesis and Exodus,* trans. Ronald E. Heine, in *The Fathers of the Church,* vol. 71 (Washington, D.C.: Catholic University Press, 1982), homily 6 (121–22).
[5]Eusebius, *Ecclesiastical History,* 51–54.

(1) the replacement covenant, (2) the super covenant, (3) the dual covenant, (4) the separate covenant, and (5) the renewed covenant. Each must be examined in order to understand what the options are for solving this key problem of relationships between Israel and the church. This in turn will set the background for my evaluation of the chapters in this volume.

The Replacement Covenant

Simply stated, this option declares that the church, Abraham's spiritual seed, has replaced Israel, since it failed to keep the terms of the covenant. Thus, if anything is attributed to Israel that still remains to be fulfilled, the interpreter must read "church" in place of "Israel."

There are at least six serious flaws with this solution.

1. God never made a formal covenant with the church.
2. The failure of the Jews, like the failure of the Gentiles, was included and calculated in the plan of God (Rom. 11:8).
3. Even now there is a faithful remnant of Jewish believers who are part of Israel *and* part of the church (Rom. 9:6–8; Gal. 3:16).
4. The New Testament clearly teaches that God has not cast off disobedient Israel (Rom. 11:1, 25–26).
5. The church is never called the "new Israel" of God in the Bible.
6. The claim that the promises about the land were fulfilled long ago, thus making the present state of Israel irrelevant to the plan of God, is unsupported by Scripture. Zechariah 10, for example, written after the return from Babylonian exile, is still looking forward to the regathering of Jews from the four corners of the earth.

To argue that God replaced Israel with the church is to depart from an enormous body of biblical evidence. No covenant ever stated such a replacement. No textual clues were ever given for reading "church" or "spiritual seed" when "Israel" or "physical seed" were being discussed.

The Super Covenant

In the sixteenth century of the Christian era, a theology arose that would eventually be labeled covenant theology. In its mature form, it viewed Israel and the church as one and the same throughout all of the history of the human race. The covenant that united them was the "covenant of grace" or the "covenant of redemption," neither of which is explicitly revealed in Scripture, but whose contents are partially found in the succession of covenants in the Bible. While this covenant of redemption had, according to this system, been preceded by the covenant of works made with Adam in the Garden of Eden, the covenant of redemption came with the fall of humankind and will last up to the final consummation. The stress here is on the *sign* of the covenant, the *people* of the covenant, and the *grounds* of the covenant: the sign now is baptism, the people are the church, and the grounds are grace alone.

This view also has some major problems.

1. The Bible never mentions such a "covenant of grace" or "covenant of redemption" that embraces all the other covenants.

2. The "new covenant" was made with "the house of Judah and the house of Israel," not with the church.

3. The apostle Paul, as a New Testament believer, can still identify himself with his physical kinsmen (Phil. 3:4–6; Rom. 11:1).

4. The salvation of the New Testament is not generic but Jewish (John 4:22).

5. Jesus did not disavow the restoration of the kingdom to Israel but instead specifically affirmed it (Acts 1:6–7; 3:21; 15:13–18).

6. The "all Israel shall be saved" of Romans 11:25–26 refers to Jewish, not church, people.

The supercovenant view has depended more on theological inference and implication than it should, in that it has built one all-embracing plan of redemption out of the shape and the form of the covenant itself along with a synthesis of some of the contents of covenantal teachings. It has caught the unity of the plan of redemption, but it has reduced all of revelation to soteriology and missed the centrality of the Jew in God's plan of salvation. It would have been better to focus on the content of the covenant, rather than on its shape and form (thereby building out of the sign, the people, and the grounds of the covenant), staying with the covenants themselves rather than adding an unmentioned, alleged overarching covenant.

The Dual Covenant

As a response to various forms of anti-Semitism and false Christian charges that contemporary Jews are responsible for killing Christ, Franz Rosenzweig (d. 1929), a Jewish philosopher, argued that Jewish people are saved through the promise God left Abraham. Therefore Jews do not need the gospel offered to the Gentiles, which is a separate covenant. Evangelicals may evangelize anyone, according to the dual covenant view, except Jews; they are already delivered and are "saved" by virtue of their identification with the patriarch's covenant.

Although this position earnestly attempts to offer a new route for smoothing relationships between Jews and the evangelical church, it too fails at several critical points.

1. The gospel offered to Abraham is the same one offered today in the church (Gen. 12:3; 15:6; Luke 1:73; Gal. 3:6–9; Rom. 4:13).

2. The object of faith in both the Old Testament and the New is the same: the "Seed," "Christ," the Man of Promise who was and who now has come (Gen. 15:1–6; John 14:6; Acts 4:12).[6]

3. All of history and all the promises in the Old Testament point to Jesus (Acts 2:37–40; 3:25–26).

4. The "new covenant" that the church has already begun to enjoy was made originally with the Jewish nation (Jer. 31:31–34; Ezek. 36:22–30).

5. The "olive tree" into which the church was grafted was Jewish; it does not have a distinct and separate existence apart from the Jews (Rom. 11:20–23).

The dual covenant theory is a subbiblical view. What the church has come to enjoy was originally made and then maintained for Israel. Instead of a dualism, Scripture insists on a unity.

The Separate Covenant

Traditional dispensationalism affirmed that Israel and the church had separate identities, promises, and destinies. To a large degree, it would appear that what has created this enmity and division between Jew and Gentile for dispensationalism in its classic forms of the past was its view of the Sinaitic covenant.

Dispensationalism was correct in recognizing that Israel and the church were not the same, but it failed when it went beyond this point of distinguishing between the two to say they were distinct and separate. It was correct when it affirmed that the fullness of the promises made to Israel would not be realized until the future, but it exceeded the requirements of the biblical text when it claimed that God was not dealing with Israel and fulfilling some of the promises, even if they were fulfilled only in part, in the present era of the church.

Here are some of the criticisms that must be raised against separating too sharply the covenants, and therefore the peoples and the programs of God:

1. The church has no other covenant than the one our Lord made with Israel (Luke 22:20; Heb. 7–10).

2. The early church preached the gospel from the Old Testament, not from the New; it was not written as yet.

---

[6]For a fuller substantiation of this bold claim, see Walter C. Kaiser, Jr., *Toward Rediscovering the Old Testament* (Grand Rapids: Zondervan, 1987), 121–28.

3. The church is not an interruption, a parenthesis, or even an intercalation in the plan of God but part of its continuation (Acts 26:22–23).

4. Israel was not set in limbo for a parenthetical period of intercalation but continues both through a remnant (Rom. 11:5) and through God's determination to bring them back to their land.

5. Israel and the church are not to be regarded as separate and distinct from one another but as one body of believers with one way of salvation (Eph. 2:14–16; 4:4–6; Acts 15:11).

6. Both believing Jews and Gentiles are to try to bring unbelieving Jews to the gospel even during this present age (Rom. 1:14–16; 11:11).

7. The New Testament does not teach that the kingdom was "postponed" when Israel refused to believe in Jesus while he was on earth; thus the cross was not a backup plan in the divine order of things (Acts 4:27–28; Ps. 110:1).

8. The church is part of the same kingdom plan Jesus related to the Jews (Matt. 8:11–12; Luke 13:28–29; Acts 8:5, 12; 28:23, 28).

Dispensationalism valiantly and rightfully held the line on maintaining a future for Israel, but it did so, at times, at the cost of schematizing too sharp a division between an earthly and a heavenly people, a program that hypothetically offered salvation by works (i.e., if a person kept the law perfectly), versus a salvation by grace alone. But Scripture failed to substantiate the fact that there were two peoples, two programs, and two types of destinies. A good distinction had been overdrawn, presumably in an effort to popularize and to capture the hearts of Bible readers as to the significance of the true observation that had been found in the text.

The Renewed Covenant

Following Willis J. Beecher's fine 1905 Stone Lectures at Princeton Seminary, I have recently proposed "promise theology," or "epangelicalism" (from the Greek root *epangel-*, meaning "promise"). In the main, this view agrees with the distinction between Israel and the church. But instead of continuing to say, as classical dispensationalism did, that there are two separate peoples (Israel and the church) with two separate programs (the earthly kingdom and the heavenly kingdom of our Lord), this view stresses that there is one people ("the people of God") with a number of discernable aspects within that one people (such as Israel and the church), and there is only one program of God (the "kingdom of God") with numerous aspects under that single program.

Moreover, promise theology, or epangelicalism, noticed that the contents of the covenants God had made with Abraham, Isaac, Jacob,

Moses, David, and the "house of Judah and the house of Israel" (i.e., the new covenant) shared a progressively enriched and developing body of specifications and contents while maintaining the foundational residual truths. Even the name *new covenant* could be rendered just as well by "renewed covenant," since Hebrew had no separate words to distinguish between the idea of being "brand new" and being "renewed." In fact, the larger part of the contents of the new covenant was but a repetition of what had already appeared in the covenants that had preceded it.[7]

Most important, in the view of the renewed covenant, the law of Moses was never intended as a temporary or even a hypothetical substitute for the divine promise to Abraham. Instead, it was intended to fit along with the promise by giving guidance to all as to how those under promise should live. It was meant to supplement the promise, not to supplant it. The law no more supplanted the promise to Abraham than the new covenant replaced Abraham's promise.

True, some parts of the Sinaitic covenant, in contradistinction to the Abrahamic, Davidic, and new covenants, did have some built-in portions of obsolesence, in which it recognized part of its own temporal limitations. For example, when the instructions about the tabernacle and its services were given in Exodus 25–40 and Leviticus 1–27, God deliberately told Moses that what he was to make was only a "copy," a "pattern." It was not the real thing but only imitated what at that time was in heaven (Ex. 25:8, 40).

But this did not prevent our Lord from giving guidance that had an abiding value to all who asked, "How, then, shall we live in the promise"? Surely, it is for this reason that many of the principles found in the moral aspect of the Mosaic legislation are given proverbial status in the book of Proverbs and, to some degree, in Ecclesiastes and the Psalms.

God kept enlarging the sphere and the contents of his covenant promises while maintaining the base and the foundational realities that were at the heart of it all. Those foundational truths might be reduced to three principial matters: (1) *an heir:* the messianic seed would come from Abraham, enlarged to the whole nation of Israel, and narrowed again to David's family; (2) *an inheritance:* the land of Israel would be given to the Jews as an everlasting inheritance without any conditions attached for its ultimate fulfillment; and (3) *a heritage:* the gospel is as

[7]For a development of these points, see Walter C. Kaiser, Jr., "The Old Promise and the New Covenant: Jeremiah 31:31–34," in *The Bible and Its Literary Milieu: Contemporary Essays,* ed. Vincent L. Tollers and John R. Maier (Grand Rapids: Eerdmans, 1979), 106–20.

old as Genesis 12:3, namely, "in [Abraham's] seed, all the nations of the earth would be blessed."

AN EVALUATION OF MODIFIED DISPENSATIONALISM

An enormous amount of water has gone under the bridge in more than a quarter of a century since Charles Ryrie's *Dispensationalism Today* was published in 1965 by Moody Press. In fact, somewhere in the decade of the 1960s, one of the most significant developments in dispensationalism took place. It happened so quietly, but so swiftly, that it is difficult to document, even to this day. This is what changed the whole course of dispensationalism: the view that there were *two* new covenants, one for Israel and one for the church, was decisively dropped. The implications of such a move are enormous, as the events that followed duly testified.

The Address of the New Covenant

The new covenant was made with "the house of Israel and the house of Judah," yet the church was obviously enjoying the benefits of this same covenant. They drank the "blood of the covenant" in the Lord's Supper, and they had "ministers of the new covenant."

But when Israel and the church were viewed as sharing one and the same covenant, the possibilities for major rapprochement between covenant theology and dispensationalism became immediately obvious. Moreover, that one factor ended the major roadblock in a key hermeneutical rule that dispensationalism had repeatedly stressed in the past: keep Israel's mail separate from the mail that was written for the church. Thus, 2 Chronicles 7:14 ("If *my people,* which are called by my name, shall humble themselves . . ."), for example, did not need to be restricted, as had been taught, solely to Israel but could now be addressed to the whole church. On the same bases, the Sermon on the Mount was released from its future kingdom setting for use by the whole body of Christ now.

Old Testament Prophecy

The results of deleting two new covenants from the system were all to the good. But in reading the new set of essays in this volume, one is immediately struck by the overwhelming emphasis on New Testament biblical theology. Except for some survey material on the scope and center of Old Testament theology, dispensationalism (if one is to judge simply from the chapters in this book) seems to have shifted from its former strength in making its case from the kingdom and restoration promises in the Old Testament to a biblical theology that is satisfied to rest the majority, if not all, of its case on the New Testament texts alone. If history is any kind of guide to the future, that could be a bad omen for the future of dispensationalism and the church at large. History has shown this to be the first step in capitulating to the anti-Israel mood of post-Constantine theology. This lacuna in this set of essays needs to be remedied.

Inaugurated Eschatology

These chapters do, nevertheless, witness some exceedingly important exegetical and theological advances over what more classical forms of dispensationalism had argued for. One of the most commonly shared advances was the advocacy of a carefully defined inaugurated eschatology, wherein both the "already" and the "not yet" fulfilled were provided for, just as Scripture so clearly demonstrated. As Darrell Bock concluded so well, covenant theologians have tended to stress the "already" features of prophecy in their rebuttals of dispensationalism, and dispensationalists tended to focus on the "not yet" portions of prophecy in their responses to their covenant brethren—often minimizing that portion of the prediction that God was already carrying out. The advocacy of a balance between the two is no small gain for the whole body of Christ and for a more balanced understanding of Scripture.

The Abandonment of the Interim Ethic View

Traditionally, many dispensationalists have taught that the Sermon on the Mount was not applicable to the church today, but this view again reflected the fact that the relationship between law and grace was still seriously in need of theological development. But on this point another real advance can be seen in these chapters. Instead of regarding Jesus' teaching on the Sermon on the Mount as an interim ethic, a new predominate view is emerging that proclaims the Sermon on the Mount to be the ethic for believers today. This new revelation of Jesus, it is rightly argued, taught the same truths as the Old Testament taught; in fact, it gave them the same poignancy that the Old Testament prophets gave to the law. Only when we misunderstand the meaning and the purpose of the law can we misjudge the meaning and purpose of the Sermon on the Mount.

The Mosaic Law and the Christian

One of the most heated controversies in the Christian church concerns the question, What did our Lord "abolish" in the law? Dispensationalism in the past has tended to answer that he abolished the entire Mosaic law. In this view, Christians no longer find any guidance for their life from the law of Moses; instead, Christians' rule of life is to be found solely in the "law of Christ." In some of the essays, this same Achilles' heel of interpretation can still be detected. This conclusion is not one that is distinctively and uniquely owned by dispensationalists. I hear and read many Reformed and covenant theologians who will place just as strong a disjunction between law and promise as many of their dispensational colleagues.

The heart of this false opposition between law and grace is the old saying, repeated by David Lowery, that the law was fundamentally concerned with "doing," but the gospel, which has Christ as its object, was essentially a matter of "believing." Most will turn, at this point, to Leviticus 18:5 and its citation in Romans 10:5 and Galatians 3:12. These New Testament passages are then interpreted as showing how Christ replaced the old program of "doing" with the new program of "believing." Is it any wonder that we have difficulties in convincing Christians to study the "inerrant," "inspired," and "profitable" word of God in the Old Testament if it offers merely a heuristic advantage?

The major source of trouble here is not, as Lowery contends, that Israel's pursuit of righteousness was in accordance with the stipulations of the law. To advocate this point of view, a point widely affirmed but most assuredly one hundred miles off target from what Paul is teaching in Romans 9:30–10:13, is to demonstrate the precise area of the difficulty that has been fostered for so long in our circles. Instead, Paul four times emphasizes the point that the Jews failed to achieve God's righteousness, not because they inadvisedly obeyed what the law of Moses taught (as if it were only Moses' teaching and God had nothing to do with it), but simply because it was a *homemade kind of righteousness.* The key phrases that prove that it was miles away from what God taught and only what they had devised for themselves are:

> Rom. 9:31–Israel made a law [out of] righteousness. (Note the order of the Greek words.)

> Rom. 9:32–Israel pursued this righteousness, "as if it were possible, by works." Paul's point is that it was not possible; that is why the Gentiles received it by faith and Israel lost it.

> Rom. 10:2–Israel was zealous enough, but it was a "zeal not based on knowledge" of the Word of God.

> Rom. 10:3–Israel sought to establish "their own" homemade right-eousness as a substitute for the righteousness that comes from God.

The righteousness that God sponsored was that which Moses described in Leviticus 18:5 *and* Deuteronomy 30:12–13. The Greek expression *kai . . . de* links and approves, rather than contrasts, the two Mosaic citations as being in support of the contention that God's righteousness has remained the same all along while the Jews have gone about seeking their own version of the same.

Our generation needs to hear the shout from Paul in Romans 3:31 all over again: "Do we, then, nullify the law by this faith? Not at all! Rather, we uphold the law." Therefore, it never was, and still is not, a matter of trying to attain to the righteousness of God by means of the law. No one ever attracted God's righteousness on that basis—not even hypothetically. As Paul cried out, "Is the law, therefore, opposed to the promises of God? Absolutely not! For if a law had been given that could impart life, then righteousness would certainly have come by the law" (Gal. 3:21). But Paul knows of no such plan, not even hypothetically.

Another passage appearing several times in these chapters is 2 Corinthians 3. Here again, it is clear that modified dispensationalism has not gone beyond *Dispensationalism Today*, for this text does not demonstrate the inferiority of the old covenant in contrast to the new covenant. Paul repeatedly and most carefully insisted that he was contrasting only the ministries under the two covenants, not the two covenants themselves (as the New English Bible translated it, even though it had to violate the rules of agreement of the antecedent in order to do so). "What was fading away" was not the old covenant but the ministry that Moses had in comparison with the fantastic ministry that the ministers of the new covenant now own.[8]

Whatever major problems still remain, even for a modified dispensationalism, must surely revolve around straightening out the relationship of law to grace and obedience to promise. Leviticus 18:5 did not urge Old Testament believers to "do" in order to "live." The whole of Leviticus 18 is framed at the beginning and the end by the statement "I am the LORD your God." Only those who had the Lord as their God were called to obey. Only in so obeying would they taste what living, and living more abundantly, is all about.[9]

The Mystery of God: Absolute or Comparative?

Surely there is progress on this classical standoff when Robert Saucy acknowledges that the "gospel of God" for which Paul was set apart was "promised beforehand through his prophets in the Holy Scriptures"

---

[8]See Walter C. Kaiser, Jr., "The Weightier and Lighter Matters of the Law: Moses, Jesus, and Paul," in *Current Issues in Biblical and Patristic Interpretation: Studies in Honor of Merrill C. Tenney Presented by His Former Students,* ed. Gerald F. Hawthorne (Grand Rapids: Eerdmans, 1975), 176–92, esp. 185–91.

[9]For a fuller statement on this topic, see Walter C. Kaiser, Jr., "Leviticus 18:5 and Paul: 'Do This and You Shall Live' (Eternally?)," *JETS* 14 (1971): 19–28; also idem, *Toward an Old Testament Theology* (Grand Rapids: Zondervan, 1978), 110–13; idem, "God's Promise Plan and His Gracious Law," *JETS* 33 (1990): 189–302.

(Rom. 1:1–2) and is certainly the same message that Paul later called "the mystery of the gospel" in Ephesians 6:19. What a wonderful breakthrough! No wonder Paul explained to Festus and Agrippa that he was "saying nothing beyond what the prophets and Moses [!] said would happen—that Christ would suffer and, as the first to rise from the dead, would proclaim light to his own people and to the Gentiles" (Acts 26:22–23).

Saucy sets the problem up most wonderfully when he next asks, "If the mystery of Christ and that of the divine plan of salvation has already been the subject of Old Testament prophecy, then in what sense can it be said to have been hidden and only now revealed by the New Testament apostles and prophets?"[10]

Disappointingly, Saucy concludes that the mystery in Ephesians 3:5 must be contrastive, rather than comparative in nature—the mystery "was not made known to men in other generations as it has now been revealed." Saucy cannot accept the fact that it simply was better known now than it had ever been revealed in the past; no, it was never revealed before: it was just now being revealed. Yet, in the same breath, Saucy is willing to grant that there must be some connection between the Old Testament prophecies anticipating God's salvation that would come to all the nations and the mystery of the union of Jews and Gentiles in Ephesians 3. He almost seems to be saying both yes and no at the same time: yes, the mystery of Ephesians does relate to the union of Jews and Gentiles as predicted in the Old Testament prophecy; no, the mystery is not one of degree or a comparison of the amount of revelation or degree of realization with the Old Testament, it is totally new and absolutely different from anything ever said on any topic that is similar to this one.

I am pleased at the large amount of agreement I find between Robert Saucy and myself on the content of the mystery. He clearly affirms that the unity of Jews and Gentiles in the church is a partial fulfillment of the Old Testament promises. This represents a terrific amount of progress. Yes, there may be *functional* distinctions between Israel and the Gentile believers in the future, but that does not impair their spiritual equality.

CHALLENGES TO *DISPENSATIONALISM TOMORROW*

Dispensationalism Today needs to have a sequel written in the next two to three years: perhaps it could be titled *Dispensationalism Tomorrow*. In that volume I would urge that primary consideration be given to each of the issues that still remain for this system of organizing

---

[10]In chap. 4 above, in the subsection "The Hiddenness and Revelation of the Mystery."

theology that has so many positive aspects about it and for which I feel such a strong affinity.

The Need to Disavow Completely the Postponed Kingdom Theory

One of the pleasant surprises that has emerged from contemporary defenses of dispensationalism, as illustrated in this book, is that few, if any dispensationalists, feel compelled to raise the topic once dear to this system: the postponed kingdom theory.

The postponed kingdom theory has raised more problems than it has solved. It plays havoc with the eternal plan of God to send his Son to die on the cross (Rev 13:8), in that it provides for a hypothetical possibility that the cross would not have been necessary had the Jews accepted Christ's offer to set up the kingdom immediately. Furthermore, if our Lord had wanted the Jewish people to acknowledge him as King, why did he refuse their desires to do just that after the crowd saw how he could miraculously multiply bread (John 6:14–15)?

The Need to Develop a Theology of the Law

It is clear from our arguments about the meaning of Romans 9:30–10:13 that our Lord never found fault with the law itself, but always with those who thought they could develop their own homemade brand of righteousness that would, in turn, earn them salvation. Repeatedly, our Lord found fault with the people ("because they broke my covenant," Jer. 31:32; and "but God found fault with the people," Heb. 8:8).

Dispensationalism has rightly stressed God's grace, and for this it must be praised as highly as we appreciate its strength in retaining a central place in its theology for physical Israel. But it is at its weakest point when it goes to integrate the themes of law and obedience into those strengths.

To teach that Christians are obligated only to those aspects of the moral law that we find repeated in the New Testament is to set the church up for another fiasco such as evangelical Christianity experienced after the 1973 *Roe v. Wade* Supreme Court decision on abortion. I well remember trying to answer questions from evangelicals in the late sixties and early seventies on whether abortion was allowable; after all, the New Testament did not comment on the issue, therefore whatever each person decided must be acceptable to God! But now, some twenty-seven million deaths later, there is suddenly some sense that somehow we shortchanged ourselves in the interpretation of Scripture. Maybe we should have listened to the Old Testament—even if we had taught that nothing on this subject was repeated in the New Testament. A theology of the law is desperately needed. If nothing else convinces us, then note how many tens of thousands have been pressing into seminars in almost every major city in the land to find out how we should resolve basic youth conflicts by using the principles from the law as repeated in the book of Proverbs! The church was hungry for teaching in this neglected area.

The Need to Integrate Old Testament Theology into New Testament Systems

Much work needs to be done in all of evangelical theology about how we can properly handle the types of continuities and the types of discontinuities between the Testaments. Among the topics needing immediate attention are these: What was the object of faith for those who believed during the days of the Old Testament? In what sense was the Holy Spirit responsible for regenerating grace, indwelling guidance, and the various gifts of the Spirit in that olden age? What was the expectation of the Old Testament saint about life after death? If premillennialism represents a distinctive philosophy of history wherein God completes in our kind of space and time what he promised he would do—namely, restore Israel to its land and set up his kingdom on earth with himself as ruler—why has dispensationalism not developed a corresponding view of Christ and culture based on Old Testament biblical theology, but has left this aspect to be developed by covenant theology instead? There are more areas, but this is a representative list that indicates where further development would help round out the case.

The Need to Avoid Certain Current Hermeneutical Trends While Restating a Distinctive Position

In his introductory essay, Craig Blaising deftly analyzes the hermeneutical quandary that is not unique to dispensationalism but is one in which most evangelicals find themselves. It is a matter of great satisfaction to observe how younger scholars in this movement (as in all of evangelicalism) have moved away from what Blaising called Baconian perceptions, wherein a kind of concordance of biblical passages was collected under each topic, to a dependence on exegesis of large teaching blocks of biblical text with a strong preference for biblical theology over philosophical categories and systemic organizations.

But another liability has reared its ugly head: the possibility that some of the spirit of modernity might snatch away these gains when midrashic techniques and legitimate forms of escalation in typologies are used as the bases for denying (or seriously diminishing the point) that the Old Testament text predicted or supported what was being claimed by the New Testament writers. That is a very expensive price to pay for

375

progress, especially when our Lord so soundly rebuked the two disciples on the road to Emmaus in Luke 24 for failing to have understood that his life, death, and resurrection had been forecast in the Old Testament Scriptures. We too will stumble over the very Stone that many, but thankfully not all (Luke 1:25, 38), of the Jews of Jesus' day did.

The grammatical-historical method of exegesis has served us all very well. But in recent decades, the hue and cry has gone up from scholarship at large to allow the reader and the modern situation to have as much (or in some cases, more) to say about what a text means as has traditionally been given to the original speaker of the text. Nowhere will the implications of such views impact our theologizing more significantly than in the way we claim New Testament writers used Old Testament texts—especially when they cited them to substantiate doctrine or to vindicate the Christological and messianic point they were advocating before a Jewish audience.

The time has come for a brand new statement as to how dispensationalism (and evangelicalism at large) will handle such problems. Can we profit from the insights of modernity without being sucked into its vortext? This will be the question of the next years.

CONCLUSION

Dispensationalism, Israel and the Church is a bold but responsible attempt to genuinely reaffirm for our generation how dispensationalists respond to some of the difficult problems of theology and exegesis in our day. I applaud both its spirit and its methodology—along with many of its conclusions. In generations to come, many will no doubt look back to these chapters and thank God for the labor of love that was invested here. Not too many years ago, such a volume could not even have been imagined, or perhaps not even permitted, by many within our movements. But these are new days for manifesting the grace of God.

May the conversation begun here continue. And may we who have contributed continue to grow in the grace and knowledge of our Lord Jesus Christ, so that when we appear before him, we may have less to blush about in our theologies as we all give an account of the deeds done in the body (2 Cor. 5:10), not for salvation or entrance into heaven, but by way of our Lord's inspection of the fruit we bring to him.

Dispensationalism, Israel and the Church: Assessment and Dialogue

Craig A. Blaising and Darrell L. Bock

We now come to the point where we need to step out of the trees and view the forest as a whole. What has been accomplished in the preceding biblical studies and responses, and what are the implications?

The introduction drew attention to the fact that dispensationalists are reexamining the meaning of dispensationalism. This reexamination has focused on a proposal made more than twenty-five years ago concerning the essence, or sine qua non, of dispensationalism. Subsequent discussion has come to focus on what was thought to be the central feature of that essence, "the distinction between Israel and the church." Over the past several years, however, a number of dispensationalists have questioned (1) whether the way in which this distinction has been stated accurately reflects the relationship between Israel and the church in biblical theology, and (2) whether this distinction properly defines dispensationalism.

The authors in this book have conducted an extensive reinvestigation of the relationship between Israel and the church in New Testament theology. Although other aspects of their relationship and other biblical texts could yet be examined, enough has surfaced in these studies to indicate a revision in the dispensational view. There are important distinctions between Israel and the church in biblical theology, but there are also real theological connections that link them together in ways not expressed previously in dispensational thought. What is striking is the extent of these unseen connections demonstrated throughout the essays of this book.

Someone might say that since "the distinction between Israel and the church" is the essence of dispensationalism, then any change or modification of that view is departure. The problem with this is that it ignores the fact that *essentialist* dispensationalism (that which found its dispensational identity in the sine qua non) was only one form of a tradition in which other forms preceded it. This in itself raises the possibility that other forms may also follow. The situation calls for an investigation of the history of dispensational self-perception and self-definition, which is part and parcel of the history of the tradition. That was the burden of the introduction. It leads us to search for a new definition of dispensationalism, one that embraces the various historical manifestations of the tradition and that places the emergence of this postessentialist form of dispensationalism in perspective.

Another answer to the question whether the essays of this book reflect dispensationalism comes from considering how the reexamination of essentialist dispensationalism emerged. Structured into the "essence of dispensationalism" along with "the distinction between Israel and the church" was a commitment to "the literal interpretation of Scripture." But this statement on hermeneutics derives its applicational force from a commitment to biblical authority. In other words, one should see the hermeneutical principle undergirded and supported by the Scripture principle. Although hermeneutical methodology has been rethought and is no longer perceived as an exclusively dispensational hermeneutic (again see the Introduction above), the commitment to understand and incorporate biblical teaching into dispensational theology remains. The present phenomena of dispensationalists biblically revising what they think about Israel and the church in order to reflect more accurately their relationship in Scripture is precisely a crisis between the Scripture principle and the dispensations principle within the supposed sine qua non. Such a crisis is not external but internal— that is, within the principles of the tradition, within what had been thought to be the definition of dispensationalism. When these things are considered along with a historical understanding of the dispensational tradition, it is evident that what is now taking place is the emergence of a new phase in the history of American dispensationalism. The complexity of the situation is such that a new biblical understanding of Israel and the church, a change in the method of defining dispensationalism, and the emergence of a new dispensationalism are all interrelated features of the same phenomena.

In the remainder of this conclusion, we would like to (1) offer a definition of the dispensational tradition, (2) survey what appear to be the characteristics of the new dispensationalism, and (3) comment on matters for dialogue that surface through the remarks of our responders.

A DEFINITION OF AMERICAN DISPENSATIONALISM

In proposing a definition for dispensationalism, we look for the historical emphases that as a pattern have demonstrated, shaped, and guided the tradition through its various manifestations. We focus on American dispensationalism and leave aside the tradition of Brethren and Darbyite dispensationalism as it developed outside of this context. We also realize that much of this tradition has taken shape as a North American theology, but one whose features have been carried south, east, and west in missionary ministries. Only recently have second- and third-world dispensational theologians begun to rethink the first-world theological tradition contextually.[1] We look forward to their contributions.

With these factors in mind, we speak of dispensationalism as a tradition within American Evangelicalism, sharing common features of evangelical orthodoxy. It is a tradition that has emphasized the universal church as the framework for Christian unity and spirituality, seeking its practical manifestation in ways that do not conflict with the concept of the local church. It has advocated the authority of Scripture and has emphasized the theological relevance of biblical apocalyptic and prophecy. It is a futurist premillennialism that has strongly maintained the imminent return of Christ and a national and political future for Israel in the divine plan for history. It is characterized by a canonical approach to Scripture that interprets discontinuities of the Old and New Testaments as historical changes in divine-human dispensations reflecting different purposes in the divine plan. As an element of dispensational change, it has emphasized unique features in grace for the present dispensation of the church.

Four discernible phases of the dispensational tradition can be identified, each one accenting certain features of this pattern and adding its own characteristic emphases: (1) Niagara premillennialism (pre-Scofieldian dispensationalism), (2) Scofieldism, (3) essentialist dispensationalism, and (4) postessentialist, or progressive, dispensationalism. Further historical study is needed, which may lead to some modification of this classification scheme. It might be necessary to see Lindseyism (the popular apocalypticism of Hal Lindsey and those who follow his example) as a separate historical phenomena in the movement, although there are compelling reasons for classifying it as a variant of essentialist dispensationalism. There is also the matter of Pentecostal and charismatic dispensationalism, whose history needs further study.[2]

---

[1]See, for example, Emilio A. Núñez and William D. Taylor, *Crisis in Latin America: An Evangelical Perspective* (Chicago: Moody Press, 1989).

[2]See, for example, G. Sheppard, "Pentecostals and the Hermeneutics of Dispensationalism: The Anatomy of an Uneasy Relationship," *Pneuma* 6 (1984): 5–33; and D. Oss, "The Hermeneutics of Dispensationalism Within the Pentecostal Tradition" (paper presented to the annual meeting of The Dispensational Study Group, Kansas City, Mo., Nov. 21, 1991; publication forthcoming in *GTJ*).

Craig A. Blaising and Darrell L. Bock

PROGRESSIVE DISPENSATIONALISM

What are the features of the present, postessentialist dispensationalism? Certainly, it shares the common characteristics of the dispensational tradition and in fact traces its theological heritage through this tradition. For example, it strongly affirms the authority of Scripture. Like previous forms of dispensationalism, it demonstrates a proclivity for testing and altering traditional forms of theology for a more accurate conformity with Scripture (primarily in areas of dispensations and eschatology). In this case the tradition being tested and altered is the previous form of dispensationalism.[3]

The approach to Scripture is by means of historical, literary hermeneutics, which includes concerns not only for grammar and lexicography but also for structural and compositional matters, genre, and intertextual features such as typology. This approach (also simply called historical-grammatical hermeneutics) is shared broadly in evangelicalism, so consequently present-day dispensationalists do not think of themselves as having an exclusive hermeneutic. Another feature of the present approach to Scripture is the recognition of the role of biblical theology as manifested in the progress of revelation as it impacts the interpretation of any individual passage. Such a thematic approach also includes the study of related concepts, not just individual terms. In addition, present-day dispensationalists have a conscious awareness of the role of tradition in interpretation and are cognizant of the interplay of preunderstanding, text, and community in the hermeneutical process. These additional features distinguish different interpreters along with individual levels of skill in the previously mentioned matters of exegesis and biblical theology.

The label *progressive dispensationalism* is being suggested because of the way in which this dispensationalism views the interrelationship of divine dispensations in history, their overall orientation to the eternal kingdom of God (which is the final, eternal dispensation embracing God and humanity), and the reflection of these historical and eschatological relations in the literary features of Scripture.

The Progressive Relationship of Past and Present Dispensations

Consistent with earlier dispensational views, the contributors to this book see a change in the relationship between God and humanity in the new dispensation that emerged through the Christ event. Ware, Bock,

---

[3]On the history of changes between previous forms of dispensationalism, see the Introduction above.

Hoch, Saucy, and Burns all speak of the *new* state of things in which Gentiles are included with equal standing alongside the remnant of Israel. Both receive blessings from the inaugurated new covenant, blessings that are emphasized as *new* in biblical theology, being differentiated as an advance over the old covenant. Yet, as Hoch, Saucy, Glenny, Barker, and Ware point out, these blessings are coming in fulfillment of promises about Israel and Gentiles made during the previous dispensation, the dispensation of the Mosaic covenant. Consequently, there is continuity from promises about Israel and Gentiles under the old covenant to the fulfillment of those promises upon Israel and Gentiles under the new covenant. It is continuity through *progress:* the progress of promissory fulfillment. But it is also the progress of the *novum,* the new. As Saucy carefully points out, there is continuity and advance, in the notion of mystery used by Paul to describe the new dispensation, the church. The element of newness can be expressed radically by Paul as an end of the law, as Lowery has said. And yet the moral and ethical teaching of the law is carried forward, as Martin and Barker have noted. Continuity and discontinuity manifest themselves in the progress of dispensational change.[4]

The Progressive Relationship of Present and Future Dispensations

As all the contributors have stated, the New Testament does not describe the present dispensation as the final redemption. There is the expectation of a future dispensation. But how are the present and the future dispensations related? These studies uniformly assert that the New Testament teaches a strong continuity between the present dispensation of the church and the future dispensation in which all things in heaven and earth will be united in Christ (see Saucy on the futurity of the dispensation in Eph. 1:10). This continuity is variously expressed in terms of one (new) covenant that unifies both dispensations (as noted by Ware and also by Barker, Bock, and Burns). Both dispensations are also united as aspects of the messianic reign of Christ, as Bock, Barker, and Saucy have noted. Bock especially has underscored how *both* dispensations are seen in the New Testament as fulfillments of the Davidic covenant. When this is added to new-covenant unity and to fulfillment of the Mosaic (Lowery and Martin) and Abrahamic (Hoch and Bock) covenants, we can see in this dispensation the basis for the integration of all the covenants in the redemption

---

[4]For this reason many of the chapters stress the both-and character of eschatological fulfillment.

(Hoch) inaugurated (Bock and Barker) in this dispensation and fulfilled in the future.

The Future of Israel and the Nations

Both the present and future dispensations are united as fulfillments of promises made under the old dispensation. Yet there is progress and change from the present to the future. The present and future dispensations fit the already—not yet scheme of New Testament theology, as the various chapters point out. Bock notes how the expectation of the national promises to Israel are structured in Lukan theology in anticipation of a future dispensation. Burns, Hoch, and Saucy note the same in Pauline theology, as do other contributors as well. This *progress*, from already-inaugurated blessings to the not-yet-realized fullness of those blessings as well as to other features not yet experienced at the present time, indicates that this dispensationalism has a broader concept of redemption than may have been expressed by other traditions in evangelicalism, namely, that redemption is holistic: it includes the salvation not only of individual souls but of a humanity in its wholeness, as composed of its corporate and social dimensions. The promise of the salvation of *nations* and the dispensational expectation of blessings, not just upon the nation of Israel, but also upon Gentile nations, is the extension of salvation into political and national dimensions. Burns has noted the temptation of anti-Semitism in the tendency to collapse these features into a homogenous concept of individual salvation. He has also pointed out the continuities drawn in Romans 11 from the Old Testament expectation of the remnant of Israel to the presence of Jews with Gentiles in the church today and then to the expectation of national salvation in the future dispensation. Since redemption will be extended in national and political dimensions in the future, and since progressive dispensationalism does not see the church as a parenthesis, unrelated to what came before and to what comes after, the question is raised about the *present* role of the church as a witness to and advocate for social and political righteousness. The present form of the kingdom as a "sneak preview" (Bock) of the future kingdom requires this progressive dispensationalism to develop a clear theology of social and political concern.

Christocentricity

Just as Barker sees the theme *kingdom* as integrating Old and New Testament theology, so also in the other essays *Christ the King* is seen as the agent, director, and fulfillment of dispensational change. He fulfills the promises of the old dispensation. He inaugurates the present dispensation, that of the eschatological Spirit, through his atonement, resurrection, and enthronement. He is the one who will come to complete the restoration of all things. The dispensationalism of this book distinguishes itself from the immediately preceding dispensationalism and Scofieldism by the fact that instead of being anthropologically centered on two peoples, it is Christologically centered. The movement from the past to the present and then to future dispensations is not due to a plan for two different kinds of people but rather is due to the history of Christ's fulfilling the plan of holistic redemption in progressive phases (dispensations). The previous dispensation anticipated and then witnessed him. After his ascension to the Father's right hand, Christ inaugurated the present dispensation of his earnest, the gift of the Holy Spirit. The future dispensation is the dispensation of his return and consummative rule.

The Millennium and the Final State

To this point, nothing has been said explicitly about the Millennium. However, these dispensationalists are premillennialists, as have been dispensationalists throughout the history of their tradition. But this new dispensationalism sees a greater continuity between the Millennium and the eternal kingdom than was the case in some forms of essentialist dispensationalism. Turner notes that the difference between the Millennium and the new earth is one of degree, not kind. The transition from the former to the latter is not the change from the material to the spiritual, the substantial to the ethereal, but the completion of the redemption (not annihilation) of the whole created order. The continuity is such that Barker, for example, sees them together as one dispensation.

Israel and the Church

But now the question returns to Israel and the church. What is the relation of these groupings, these classifications, to the redeemed humanity of the future kingdom dispensation? These essays indicate a dispensationalism that rejects the notion of two peoples in the sense of two different humanities with parallel destinies. The Israel-church distinction is a distinction primarily of two dispensational groupings of humanity: (1) the grouping in the former dispensation, in which divine blessings were poured out upon Israel while Gentiles were alienated or subordinated, and (2) the grouping of the present dispensation, in which divine blessings of the Spirit are going to Jews and Gentiles equally while national blessings are in abeyance. The *progressive* relationship of both of these dispensations to the future dispensation of kingdom fulfillment suggests that the equality of Jew and Gentile in the regenerating, renewing, Christ-uniting ministry of the Holy Spirit will both be carried forward and enhanced (glorification), for this is a blessing of the one new covenant that unites both dispensations. This continues even while redemption is expressed on a national, political scale with all nations at peace, oriented to Zion, the new Jerusalem from which the Son of David, the Christ of Israel and the nations, rules. Israel and the nations on the one hand and the church on the other are neither replacement peoples nor parallel, dual-track peoples but different redemptive dimensions of the same humanity.

The category *church* refers to union by the Holy Spirit to Christ through which his fullness of life and righteousness manifests itself in the new humanity. Israel and the Gentiles speak of the anthropological plurality, the ethnic, political, and cultural groupings of redeemed humanity, since humanity is not simply a homogenous collection of individuals. To see it as the mere association of individuals is not only anthropologically deficient but renders one conceptually unable to understand the future fulfillment of national promises not just to Israel but to all nations. It is a subtle form of racism manifested as the denial of racial difference. It has been manifested in the history of Christianity as anti-Semitism in the view that the church has replaced Israel so that there is nothing nationally, politically, or ethnically remaining in divine redemption. But this can also manifest itself toward other people groups as well in the form of cultural repression in the process of Christianization. A progressive dispensational theology needs to promote proper contextualization from an eschatological perspective.

In the dispensational theology of the Ephesian letter, the final dispensation is one in which all things will be united in Christ. This is not a unity that obliterates all possible distinctions but one that harmonizes them in a way never before seen. The model as well as the principle of unity is Christ, in whom humanity and deity have not been rendered indistinct but have been harmonized in the oneness of his person in a way that challenges the limits of human language.

Inclusive Theological Reflection

Knowledge about Christ and the dispensations of his blessings are the property of the church universal (Eph. 4:11–16 in the context of 1:10, 15–23 and 3:9). This means that dispensational theology should be a dialogic phenomena inclusive to the extent of all who are in Christ. It is aided by an inclusive hermeneutic that is reflected upon for improvement in its deployment. It is in fact a hermeneutic that is aware of the communal and dialogic nature of understanding. It is carried forward by the practical steps of offering our proposals and studied conclusions to others in Christ for critical evaluation and then reversing the procedure as we hear back from them. The key point is *listening, hearing:* hearing the Scripture, hearing each other, and then listening to the Scripture, listening to each other, and hearing the Scripture again. It is a process that is neither embarrassed by nor impatient with disagreement, diversity, or pluralism but rather expects such and puts it to work for the mutual benefit of the body of Christ.

This book represents a community of scholars from the dispensational tradition who are in the process of reengaging that tradition with the Scripture. The responders have brought their own traditional concerns into a dialogue with that process. The limitations of the book are evident throughout. Not every relevant portion of Scripture has been examined, not every possible participant could be included, not every theological tradition has been engaged. But this work can function as a catalyst to a greater, more inclusive theological dialogue on the history of redemption. The responders have raised issues that should be responded to in turn. Lack of space prohibits extensive rejoinders in this volume. But we can use the occasion to *hear carefully* what is said, while thanking our responders for their contribution to the discussion. Future publications need to carry the dialogue forward.

We believe there is a dispensational theology in the Scripture. The tradition called "dispensationalism" seeks (and has always sought) to understand it. Covenantalism, with its interest in the progess of redemption, is seeking (and has sought) to understand this theological phenomena as well. Others also have important contributions to make. We must all work together for the glory of God and the benefit of the faith, hope, and love of the church.

ISSUES OF MUTUAL AFFIRMATION
WITH OUR RESPONDERS

In a debate with as long and polemical a history as the evangelical, eschatological debate, it is easy to forget how much evangelicals share among themselves as they discuss the future of God's plan. Often in looking to the future, which we see only dimly (1 Cor. 13:12), we can forget the past, about which Scripture speaks so clearly, namely, the fact that we all are members of Christ's body (Eph. 4:1–6). We share all the elements Paul names: one body, one Spirit, one hope of our calling, one Lord, one faith, one baptism, and one God and Father over all. This early statement predates all extracanonical creeds and sets the basic parameters for our moral obligation to one another as fellow members of the body of Christ.

One of the tragedies of the current Christian evangelical scene is the divisive tendencies present in many strands of the community. When the subtradition is more crucial than the Christian tradition, we fragment the unity to which God has called us and for which the Lord intercedes (John 17). We disobey his commandment to love one another as he loved us, and we lose our testimony to the larger world (John 13:34–35). Polemical divisions and backbiting contradict our proclamation of reconciliation with God and others in Christ. When we cannot function well in the midst of our own disagreements, how can we expect the world to believe our message of reconciliation? We commit Christian genocide, an expression that should be an oxymoron but that often is too real, and we all lose credibility in the process. All traditions are at fault here, and God is not honored in the process.

In our zeal for creedal commitment, we can draw lines to identify our subtradition and forget that we share a larger, more fundamental identity. This is not to deny the value of subtraditions or their contribution to the whole body of Christ, but it is to say that the task before the Christian community to reflect the love of Christ and evangelize the world is so vast that no subtradition can do it all by itself. It is also to say that the basic commitments and obligations to which God calls us commit us to the whole of his body, not just the part of it in which we function most easily. What we share with our responders in this book is an honest desire for dialogue and a pursuit of the truth, but not at the expense of a fundamental unity that we know that God has given to us.

The reason for this shared commitment is that we believe many things in common. Willem VanGemeren's response mentions a commitment to *Scripture,* to the *Trinity,* and to the *Savior.* It is but the starting point. There are many points of agreement, even beyond the basic things mentioned in Ephesians 4. Some of them actually reach into the topic under discussion. Here is that larger list.

We share a commitment to *salvation by grace.* In this, all acknowledge that if salvation is to come to any person, it is always by grace, is based on Christ's work, and comes through faith. We can still debate the relationship of Old Testament law and grace (as Kaiser does with Lowery), but we all acknowledge that this dispensation or era is directed by the law of the Spirit, who as covenant fulfillment and pledge is given to the believer to transform his or her life into one that pleases God (Rom. 8:1–39; Eph. 1:14; 2 Cor. 3:7–18). VanGemeren's era of the "Spirit of restoration" where Jew and Gentile are unified in the church is a description we can share for the present age.

In topics that reflect more directly the concern of the biblical studies in this volume, we all share a view that expresses *the importance of the church in God's plan.* It is no afterthought or aside. To assert the church's centrality is not to deny the importance of a locale or a building or a given group, but it is to affirm one people, who are sent into the world to impact it through life and testimony with a demonstration of God's love and the proclamation of his truth, particularly those central matters that Paul highlights in Ephesians 4. There is no call to a pessimistic withdrawal in order to wait for the Lord's return. Rather, we as light are to engage darkness and point the way to him, both by how we live within the community and through relationships that serve our neighbors outside of it.

We share a view of *the union of redemption and of the people of God.* On this point, the responders may see more difference with us than we sense we have with them. The fact that God works through distinct institutions in distinct time frames need not mean that God's people are kept distinct. This confuses who with how. Ephesians 2 is clear that the barrier between Jew and Gentile is removed for all time. This is one of the transdispensational features of Christ's work. Millennial saints will be Christians, and their identity in Christ will transcend their racial distinctions, just as it should be in the current era of the church. Nonetheless, just as one can see that the church today is basically Gentile, the community of the future will see the renewal of Jewish inclusion. Again VanGemeren's openness to ethnic Israel's future in that he is "not opposed to a millennial kingdom" shows that our dialogue has potential in lessening a major rift in the evangelical community. He is right to say that the Millennium has been the focus of dispensationalism. As one of the major points of difference, it needs discussion. Some of Kaiser's concerns about not minimizing the role of Old Testament hope also belong here, and we share his concern that the Old Testament expression of hope be preserved. Nevertheless, as Turner shows, the Millennium is not the end of God's history, another point of mutual affirmation.

We have *a hope that is both heavenly and earthly.* Again developments among covenantal scholars have proved helpful here. Hoekema affirms (as noted by Waltke) that the fulfillment of Old Testament promises must include the earth as well as heaven, a point that has not always been appreciated in covenantalism. God's plan will reunify the creation. Waltke's statement that if there were one land promise in the New Testament, he would join us, shows how thin the line is in his thinking, even in the midst of vigorous disagreement. No longer is either tradition locked exclusively into a dualism that keeps heaven and earth apart. Groups in both camps are taking a fresh look at these matters and seem to be traveling along similar lines.

Finally, we share *the hope of eternity with God in a new heaven and a new earth.* In short, our end point is the same, though the traditions see the plan taking different routes in getting there. Our covenant brothers see a two-stage plan (church, new heavens and new earth), we see three (church, Millennium, new heavens and new earth), but home is the same "golden" community when history reaches its eternal goal.[5]

This long list constitutes significant agreement. That must never be forgotten. Nonetheless, one cannot ignore the fact that differences remain. The chapters and the responses make this clear. Some differences are significant in that they impact how one sees the emphases of Scripture and may affect how one pursues priorities in ministry. Commitment to unity does not mean that the church is absolved of its responsibility to pursue and believe the truth. But dialogue on disagreements should be pursued with a sense of humility, recognizing that none of us and none of our traditions is infallible. Dialogue must move across traditions, not just within them, lest we deny by our practice the unity into which God has placed us in Christ. In addition, that dialogue is best attained when we seriously attempt to hear each other's concerns in the midst of the debate, not just dig into a defensive mode. Such listening is not compromise; it is respect for the Spirit's presence in the whole of the community. It involves the recognition that each theologian's portrait represents a high level of judgment, picturing many details of a complex subject. Sometimes looking at a picture from different angles helps to raise new and beneficial perspectives on the subject. So we turn to issues on the table, knowing that there are future days for fruitful and reflective dialogue.

ISSUES ON THE TABLE

Five issues surface through the responses given in this book. The first is not as significant as it initially appears. Three issues reflect different synthetic judgments about the Israel-church relationship. The final matter concerns the hermeneutics of progressive revelation, which in turn affect the other issues on the table.

VanGemeren raises a question about *the extent of Christ's current reign.* Actually there is much agreement here. VanGemeren, however, suggests that Bock's essay limits Jesus' realm to the church. But this is an overstatement. Bock argued that the *focus* of the realm is in the church. But he went on to say that there is an aspect of realm that covers every person, since Jesus sits at the Father's right hand as Judge and consequently has the authority now to challenge people to respond to him. His authority over salvation means that his authority extends over

---

[5]We play with VanGemeren's bronze, silver, and gold image here. The differences seem to boil down to a slight difference on the nature of the "bronze" era, no silver era for VanGemeren, and a similar gold era for all. But note the comments on Christ's reign in the next section, a point that may suggest that the differences in the bronze era are not that great either.

all, both saved and unsaved. From his ruling position at the right hand of the Father, Christ has sent the Holy Spirit to convict the world of sin, righteousness, and judgment (John 16). This conviction is an extension of his worldwide reign. All will recognize him as Lord. Those who are saved acknowledge him as Lord of salvation now. The unsaved will confess him as Lord in the Judgment. Those who are saved are brought into a new institution, the church, which itself transcends other human institutions in manifesting the activity of God. Although God's activity is most prevalent here, this is not to say that he is absent elsewhere.

The first point of genuine discussion is *law and Spirit.* This is a complex topic. Two chapters addressed the issue, while two others touched on it (Lowery, Martin, Ware, and Barker). VanGemeren sees too much disjunction between law and Spirit in Lowery's essay. VanGemeren himself argues for a more unified view of the law in which it continues to function in a positive sense today. He also speaks of the internalization of the law by the Spirit in the Old Testament. He sees the difference between the Testaments as one of degree rather than contrast. Kaiser's concerns are similar. He wishes to maintain a role for the law today, especially in moral matters, where it functions as a guide. On this basis, issues like abortion can be more directly addressed by the church today. For him, these moral matters have abiding significance and do not need reaffirmation to be applicable. But how does one determine which aspects of the law are "moral" and "abiding?"

Other questions abound. Is not Lowery's article reflective of the discontinuity of Paul's own language in a text like 2 Corinthians 3? Was not the old administration under Moses so inadequate that a new (not renewed) covenant and a new means to administer it had to be promised? Does not Paul suggest that the law was brought in alongside *for a time* (Gal. 3:19–26)? Did not the disciples, whatever experience of the Spirit they had during Jesus' earthly ministry, need to wait for "the Father's promise" in order to receive enablement for their ministry (Luke 24:49; Acts 2:30–36)? Does this not indicate that something very significant and eschatological was lacking in the previous era? Were not many elements of the old regime suspended, as Hebrews makes clear, so much so that the old era is passed?

The responders are all aware of these questions, but their answers take different tacks. Their solutions evidence significant diversity within their traditions. VanGemeren, following the lead of John Murray, emphasizes a comprehensive covenant of grace, so that the administrative shifts in God's plan are a matter of degree, as opposed to representing a fresh, new work. Waltke sees movement and progress in revelation, so that promises are resignified as what he calls the unconscious symbol is filled out with its conscious referent in the New

Testament. Such resignification means that new steps are taken in God's plan, steps that clarify the original revelation. There is more discontinuity in Waltke than in VanGemeren's approach. This difference in the Reformed tradition is seen in other works as well. Palmer Robertson also argues for more discontinuity than VanGemeren. Waltke is in fact closer to Kline and Robertson on such issues.[6]

The differences are significant and reflect the same tensions of continuity and discontinuity that concern dispensationalists. Neither tradition is monolithic. While VanGemeren sees advance in degrees, Waltke emphasizes discontinuity between the original Old Testament expression and its New Testament referent (this is what he calls unconscious symbolism, a point to which we shall return later). Kaiser also wrestles with the relationship of continuity and discontinuity here, but he takes a different approach, looking for a "both-and" solution. The diversity reflects just how knotty this problem is.

Another area of disagreement is *the future of Israel as a nation*. Kaiser sides solidly with the dispensationalists here. Both affirm that Israel has a future. VanGemeren seems more open to a possible future for Israel and even the possibility of a millennium. For Waltke, the issue centers on the land. But is his criterion for "proof" too narrow, demanding as he does an explicit New Testament affirmation of Israel's inheritance in the land in order for Old Testament promises to be taken in their historical sense? Is *land* the central issue Waltke makes it? If Christ reigns from *Israel* and has authority over the whole earth, does this not solve the question about the land promises to Israel? What does Jesus mean when he promises the disciples will rule over the twelve tribes of Israel in the regeneration (Matt. 19:28)? If Israel as a nation were not a significant part of the issue, it would have been much easier to speak simply of reigning over humanity or over the earth. It is not Israel by itself, but the universal and eternal kingdom of God that is the goal of history. But to say that Israel is not the goal does not exclude its national role in that history. Waltke criticizes Burns for not producing a New Testament text that speaks of promising the land to Israel. But why should one expect such a promise when at the time Romans was written Israel was still in the land? In addition, Zechariah, as he articulates messianic hope through the Spirit, names the removal of all enemies in his praise of John's birth (Luke 1:69–74). He is in the Land of Promise as he utters this hope.

An associated issue is what the abolition of sacrifices in Hebrews means transdispensationally for God's plan. Waltke seems to suggest

---

[6]O. Palmer Robertson, *The Christ and the Covenants* (Phillipsburg, NJ: Presbyterian and Reformed, 1981), 123.

that any retention of sacrifices is a return to "'weak and beggarly' shadows of the Old Testament." But the only sacrifices that Hebrews prohibits are those related to sin. This point does not guarantee that sacrifices are reinstituted, but neither is the possibility of national cultic activities automatically excluded. The issue needs to be decided on the basis of other texts. It is possible, for example, that some of these features are included in "the restoration of all things" (Acts 3:21).

Obviously a third area of difference is *the significance of a millennium and its role in the divine plan.* Nothing Waltke says about fulfillment in a new heaven and a new earth excludes a millennium. The Millennium as perceived in progressive dispensationalism is not a mere reinstitution of Old Testament forms and realities. Neither is it the center of God's plan. But it does not fall out either. Revelation 20:1–6, though not directly treated in any of the chapters, introduces the term and emphasizes it, while distinguishing it from the final phase of redemption. The Millennium is a goal in history, although not the final goal. To include a new heaven and a new earth does not in itself logically entail an exclusion of a millennium. Waltke rejects a millennium understood in the form and limits of Old Testament language. But is that the only form of millennium possible? Does not New Testament revelation enhance and clarify its makeup? Progressive dispensationalists argue for the latter and see it in harmony with Old Testament expectation and hope.[7] This point is made eloquently by Kaiser.

Waltke also wonders about the value of the term *dispensationalism.* In his view Israel either is reduced to the status of a remnant in the one people of God with no distinct national and political identity or is a

---

[7]J. Feinberg, "Systems of Discontinuity," in *Continuity and Discontinuity: Perspectives on the Relationship Between the Old and New Testaments: Essays in Honor of S. Lewis Johnson, Jr.,* ed. John S. Feinberg [Westchester, Ill.: Crossway, 1988], 76–79. According to Feinberg, "The unconditionality of the promises to Israel guarantees that the New Testament does not even implicitly remove the promises from Israel." Or again, "Unconditional promises are not shadows." This means that we cannot pit Old Testament revelation against New Testament revelation in such a way that the original author's meaning is totally redefined, even if the claim is that the redefinition is a heightening. Waltke's $5 to $5,000 metaphor has crucial problems. There is an important equivocation regarding the recipient of the award ("fathers" in his illustration). There is another equivocation in the award itself (the $). The first does not take account of the complex nature of humanity, involving as it does both individual and corporate aspects. The corporality includes political, social, and ethnic concerns. Waltke does not observe how the shift of referent from the Old Testament to the New involves a dimensional change, so that the former includes the national aspect, while the latter holds it in hope. In the equivocation on the award, he does not see these social and communal aspects in divine redemption. Israel in the eschaton is not merely a collection of Jews individually regenerated but a social, national, and political community of regenerated people. The question is not just that of receiving a gift, but of receiving what was expected, however many other blessings are given as well. The question is whether Israel is given a stone in place of the expected bread, however beautiful or precious the stone may be.

different people from the church, distinguished by their inheritance of the Land of Promise. If dispensationalists no longer accept the notion of two distinct peoples of God, which the biblical studies in this book do not, then he feels that they must see Israel in terms of his former option. But if that is so, then he believes that the future does not augur well for dispensationalism as a system.

We do not believe these are the only options. Israel and the church should be seen as different dimensions of redeemed humanity. Israel and the Gentiles refer to the national and ethnic dimensions of humanity. Consequently there is no contradiction between the idea of a redeemed remnant and the inheritance of a nation in its Land of Promise. It is crucial to understand that promises made to Israel are to be fulfilled by Israel and not in something reconstituted to take its place. To include others in the promise of redemption does not mean that the national promises of Israel have been excluded, as Kaiser also notes. So when Peter in Acts 3 speaks of all that the Old Testament promised, he includes the promises made to Israel, while adding other elements as well. One wonders if many of these questions have as much of an either-or quality as some on both sides tend to frame them?

The final issue on the table is hermeneutical. The issue is not a distinct hermeneutic but debate about *how to apply the hermeneutic that we share.* The question most simply put is, How does "new" revelation impact "old" revelation and expression? There are three approaches to this question.

First, does new revelation *repeat* old revelation or add to it in such a way that the original revelation is not affected at all? This appears to be the answer of older dispensationalism with its parenthesis concept of the church. One defines Old Testament terms that reappear in the New Testament simply by going back to the Old Testament and looking for the "literal" meaning.

Second, does the New Testament *unveil "unconscious symbolism"?* Waltke believes that Old Testament revelation is resignified by New Testament revelation, and the effect is a change in its interpretation. (VanGemeren, in contrast, believes that such resignification results in progress and continuity.) Rather than talking about an earthly, carnal kingdom, as the original language of the human prophet suggests, the "unconscious symbol" is the new heavens and new earth as the New Testament indicates by its emphasis on this theme and its exclusion of discussion about the land. One can raise the question that if language says one thing in terms of intention but really means something else, then is this not still a type of allegory?

Third, does the New Testament *complement* Old Testament revelation? According to this approach, the New Testament does introduce change and advance; it does not merely repeat Old Testament revelation. In making complementary additions, however, it does not jettison old promises. The enhancement is not at the expense of the original promise.

Here are three approaches to the Old Testament in the New. The last two approaches share a recognition that revelation does not stop at Malachi and that Jesus and the apostles elaborate on the promises of the Old Testament, adding new revelation while maintaining ties to the old Scripture (as seen in the New Testament treatment of themes like mystery; see Luke 24:43–47; cf. Eph. 3:4–6; Col. 1:25–29; and esp. Rom. 16:25–26).[8] For the progressive dispensationalist there is continuity, yet complementary New Testament features suggest discontinuity as well. The differences that VanGemeren and Waltke have with progressive dispensationalists (not to mention their differences with each other) are influenced by a preunderstanding of this revelatory question. But this preunderstanding is also shaped by the influence of respective theological traditions (as both VanGemeren and Waltke have noted). Is it possible that covenantalist approaches to the question of the relationship of Old Testament and New Testament hope are already determined by a traditional structure framed within the linguistic dimensions of the New Testament before the biblical theology of the Old Testament has been properly understood in its historical setting? Does not the historical interpretation of the Old Testament offer important alternatives for understanding the New Testament use of the Old? These studies argue that such historical interpretation is complementary with New Testament language and hope.

The issues on the table need further treatment and development. It is to be hoped that this can occur within a new, more calm environment of frank dialogue in the midst of asserting and reaffirming our larger unity in Christ.

CONCLUSION

Dispensationalism has a rich history. Some of it is steeped in controversy, while other elements of it reflect abiding contributions to the larger body of Christ. The movement seems to surface a wide array of emotions in people of various persuasions. Some love it; others hate it; others grapple to understand it. But one wonders if the issues of

---

[8]In referring to *mystery*, the term does not mean new revelation but is drawn from imagery like Daniel, where the רָז is explained. What emerges is that some features are new, while others develop Old Testament themes. Contrast the idea of something being hidden from the ages or from men in Eph. 3:4–6 and Col. 1:26–28, with the tie to the Old Testament Scriptures in Rom. 16:25–26.

Israel, the kingdom, and of apocalyptic hope would have received near the attention they do today in evangelical circles had it not been for the dispensationalists' emphasis on such questions. In fact, the questions of hermeneutics, the covenants, and God's plan have received stimulus from the tradition, even in those points where its own development suggests that older formulations of the issue were not necessarily or entirely on target. But this is the nature of theological dialogue in the context of community.

This work indicates where many dispensationalists are today, while recognizing that it is part of a larger theological community that is the body of Christ. Our discussion should continue, but not at the expense of our unity. We share many things in common and disagree on a few matters. We share a big task for which God holds all of us in his church responsible. So we must continue to talk to one another, both inside and across subtraditions. Such diversity in the midst of our unity need not be a cause for alarm, if we can learn how to stimulate one another to love and good deeds. Perhaps in learning from one another and our varying emphases, rather than seeing each other as the enemy, we can come to appreciate why God has allowed such diversity to exist in the midst of his one people.

Select Name and Subject Index

This index highlights only major discussions of topics and authors who are either cited extensively in quotation or whose position on a given point is of special significance. A priority has been given to subjects.

395

Scripture Index